The Cambridge Companion to the Bible is unique in that it provides, in a single volume, in-depth information about the changing historical, social, and cultural contexts in which the biblical writers and their original readers thought and lived. The authors of the *Companion* were chosen for their internationally recognized expertise in their respective fields: the history and literature of Israel; postbiblical Judaism; biblical archaeology; and the origins and early literature of Christianity. The *Companion* deals not only with the canonical writings, but also with the apocryphal works produced by Jewish and Christian writers. The setting for the entire range of these biblical writings is depicted and analyzed, with abundant illustrations and maps to assist the reader in visualizing the world of the Bible.

THE CAMBRIDGE
COMPANION TO
THE BIBLE

THE CAMBRIDGE
COMPANION TO
THE BIBLE

HOWARD CLARK KEE

Boston University, emeritus

JOHN ROGERSON

University of Sheffield

ERIC M. MEYERS

Duke University

ANTHONY J. SALDARINI

Boston College

CAMBRIDGE
UNIVERSITY PRESS

PUBLISHED BY THE PRESS SYNDICATE OF THE UNIVERSITY OF CAMBRIDGE
The Pitt Building, Trumpington Street, Cambridge CB2 1RP, United Kingdom

CAMBRIDGE UNIVERSITY PRESS
The Edinburgh Building, Cambridge CB2 2RU, United Kingdom
40 West 20th Street, New York, NY 10011-4211, USA
10 Stamford Road, Oakleigh, Melbourne 3166, Australia

First published 1997
Reprinted 1997, 1998

Printed in the United States of America

Typeset in Palatino

A catalogue record for this book is available from the British Library

Library of Congress Cataloguing-in-Publication Data
The Cambridge companion to the Bible / Howard Clark Kee …[et al.].
p. cm.
Includes bibliographical references and index.
ISBN 0-521-34369-0
1. Bible – Introductions. 2. Bible – History of contemporary events.
3. Bible – History of Biblical events. I. Kee, Howard Clark.
BS475.2.C26 1997
220.9 – dc20   96-43914

ISBN 0-521-34369-0 hardback

CONTENTS

PART THREE: THE FORMATION OF THE
CHRISTIAN COMMUNITY

INTRODUCTION

Howard Clark Kee

I. WHY THE BIBLE IS IMPORTANT

Nearly everyone who has ever heard of the Bible knows that it contains the sacred writings that are basic for Jews and Christians. For Jews, the Bible is the group of writings that tell the story of those who claim to be God's people, from the creation of the world down through various historical events which come to a climax in the return of the people Israel to the land of Palestine after a period of forced migration. In addition to the historical narratives and the comments of the prophets (who speak on God's behalf about the divine purpose for the people of God and about their failures to fulfill God's will), there are documents that present aspects of their common life, in prose and poetry, such as worship (as in Psalms) and perennial wisdom (as in Proverbs).

Christians recognize as "the Bible" not only these writings, which originated within Jewish life and thought, but also documents that describe or that derive from those persons and events that gave rise to Christianity. Christians designate this second group as "the New Testament" and refer to the sacred Jewish writings as "the Old Testament." "Testament" is an older English translation of the Hebrew word meaning "covenant" or "agreement."

In addition to the writings included in the Jewish and Christian *official* versions of the Bible, however, there are a number of writings that some Jewish or Christian groups in the past and present have regarded as of equal value or as essential supplements to the biblical sources themselves. Included in some Christian Bibles, for example, are the Wisdom of Solomon and 1 and 2 Maccabees. In the early church, some groups used Gospels other than the four now found in the New Testament. In this *Companion to the Bible* we shall examine all those writings widely considered to be authoritative, but we shall also look at a number of the writings that were given official status only by some groups within Judaism and Christianity. Accordingly, we shall refer to all documents that fit into this broad definition as "biblical"

COVENANT/TESTAMENT

THE HEBREW WORD *BERIT* is used for formal agreements reached between two parties, each of whom assumes certain obligations. In the Jewish scriptures and in documents from the ancient Near East, such contracts are evident between nations, between rulers and their subjects, and between individuals (e.g., Gen. 31:43–54, 2 Sam. 5:3, 1 Kings 5:26). But especially significant are the agreements made by the God of Israel with his people. Antecedents for the covenant between Yahweh and the twelve tribes at Mount Sinai (Exod. 19–24) include God's covenant with Abraham, in which God promises Abraham many descendants and vast territory (Gen. 15). Initially, God puts no conditions on Abraham, and the same is true of God's covenant with David, which promises him an unending line of successors to the throne of Israel (2 Sam. 7). When divine judgment on God's people drives them from the Promised Land and places them under foreign rule, the prophet Jeremiah voices the assurance of a "new covenant" (Jer. 31:31–4) by which the people of Israel will be inwardly transformed and their knowledge of God will become personal and direct. It is this expectation that is taken up in the early Christian tradition and is seen as in the process of fulfillment through Jesus (1 Cor. 11:23–5; also in some manuscripts and ancient versions of Mark 14:24).

The Greek word *diatheke*, which means "contract, compact" and thus matches the Hebrew term well, was also widely used for "last will and testament." Hence it came to be translated in the early Latin versions of the New Testament as *testamentum*. When the phrase "New Covenant" was used as the title of the whole collection of early Christian writings, with the implicit claim that Jesus had fulfilled the prophecy of Jeremiah, it too was translated into Latin as "Novum Testamentum" and thus into English as "New Testament."

while noting those that were granted official status only by one group or another. We shall date these writings and the events they report as B.C.E. or C.E., using the probable year of the date of the birth of Jesus – the Jewish teacher whom the Christians acclaim as Messiah – as the turning point in our chronology. The abbreviations designate the epochs "before the common era" and "in the common era."

The importance of the Bible is not merely religious, however, since its literature has had a profound impact on other literatures, on views of human history and society, and on personal and social ethical norms, especially in Western culture. Accordingly, the study of the Bible must involve the work of historians, archeologists, and philologists on cultural and linguistic aspects of human life, and the work of theologians and ethicists, who seek to discern and describe the religious aspects of the biblical accounts. Since the biblical writings were written in several different languages (Hebrew, Aramaic, and Greek) and in a wide range of cultural and historical periods, it is essential to approach the Bible in a way that takes into account a range of scholarly perspectives: literary, social, cultural, historical, and theological.

II. HOW TO USE THIS BOOK

A basic assumption underlying this volume is that to read and study the Bible with understanding one must have as a constant guide information on the changing circumstances in which the biblical writers and their original readers lived. Hence this work is entitled *Companion to the Bible*. It seeks to provide for the reader basic knowledge of the cultural contexts in which the biblical books were produced, including the history, languages, and religious beliefs and philosophical insights of both the writers and the people they wrote about. The *Companion* is largely chronological in its organization, moving from the earliest historical and cultural circumstances depicted in the biblical accounts, through the changing conditions of the history of Israel, down to the end of what is regarded by Jews as the biblical period at the beginning of the common era, and to the emergence of Christianity out of the Jewish matrix and its development down into the second century C.E. The biblical writings, broadly defined, are examined in their respective contexts. Descriptions of the various lands and peoples of the Bible are offered at the conclusion of this introductory chapter. Maps are supplied to help the reader understand the geographical context. The illustrations specify features of the cultural context. In boxes throughout are definitions of terms and descriptions of individuals, movements, and practices of basic importance to the biblical writers. Indexes of subjects and of references to the biblical and related writings will enable the reader to trace themes, to locate passages relevant to particular lines of inquiry, and to correlate features of the biblical writings with their specific contexts.

The book is written mostly in the form of continuous narratives, in which the successive stages of the biblical writings and their context are described. Readers seeking information about a particular book, concept, or event should consult the indexes.

In the analysis of the biblical texts, which constitutes the major portion of this book, we move through the literature by two coordinated modes of organization: (1) chronological sequence and (2) type of literature. Within each of the parts there is a balance between descriptions of the successive epochs in which these documents were produced and the various aims and literary styles of the documents. The documents analyzed include not only those writings recognized today as authoritative by various religious traditions but also associated works that have been regarded as "biblical" by some religious groups. The examination of these documents of disputed authority enables us to see concretely the diversity of the biblical traditions and the special interests that led certain groups to include these works on their authoritative lists.

III. THE IDENTITY AND DESTINY OF GOD'S PEOPLE

A. WHO ARE GOD'S PEOPLE? HOW DOES GOD SPEAK TO THEM?

The biblical writers are distinctive among the authors of the great religious documents of the world in that they shared two convictions: that God speaks to his people in the concrete circumstances of human history, and that the divine message, though spoken through individuals, is concerned for the personal identity and welfare of the members of the religious community. Often in the

Ram caught in a thicket. Found in a cemetery at Ur, on the Euphrates midway between Baghdad and the Persian Gulf, and dating to 2500 B.C.E., this image of a ram eating leaves recalls the story of Abraham finding a ram caught in a thicket by its horns (Gen. 22:13).

University Museum, University of Pennsylvania

Mount Gerizim and the Shechem Valley. Mounts Gerizim and Ebal are on opposite sides of the valley where Shechem and Jacob's well were located in what came to be known as the district of Samaria. When the northern tribes broke with the southern, Judean tribes, they not only formed a separate monarchy but also, after the Samaritans were allowed to return from exile in Babylon in the sixth century B.C.E., appear to have built a temple on Mount Gerizim to match the temple in Jerusalem, although only vestiges of it remain.

Joint Shechem Expedition

biblical writings, reports are given of some private disclosure by God to an individual, but the communication is not intended for that person alone. Rather, it is addressed to the group of which this single intermediary between God and his people is a representative. This perspective characterizing biblical religion contrasts with that of many religions in which the divine message is otherworldly or mystical or both. Those other religious outlooks often offer ways to escape from the evils of the present, physical universe or to turn inward and find fulfillment in one's own inner experience of the divine.

The conviction that God addresses his people in the circumstances of their common history is represented throughout biblical tradition as a whole and requires the reader of the Bible to give careful attention to the concrete circumstances of social, cultural, and historical existence in which it is claimed that the word of God has been heard by his people. Throughout the whole range of the biblical writings, however, those who see themselves as God's people live in circumstances that are changing. The changes occur with regard to both the inner structures of the group (the values and goals which it adopts) and the social and cultural conditions in which it lives. It may be useful for us to sketch in a preliminary way some of the ways in which these conditions changed.

The early traditions of the origins of the people Israel portray them as a loose confederation of tribes based on common ancestry and a sense of identification with the religious experience of their ancestor Abraham. The migration to Egypt in a time of threatening famine led to their enslavement by the pharaoh. They discerned direct divine intervention in their successful flight from Egypt and in their being led through the desert of Sinai to the borders of Canaan, the Promised Land. On arrival they were once more a tribal confederacy, sharing (in

addition to their common ancestry) the belief that their God was in their midst, present in the portable shrine (the ark of the covenant) that they brought with them out of Egypt. The founding principles of their group identity were given to them by revelation through Moses, their leader, at Mount Sinai. To this code they jointly committed themselves. To fulfill the ritual obligations of the code, they subjected themselves to the regulations prescribed by the priests.

In the land of promise they lived more or less separate – and sometimes competing – tribal existences, bound by their common history and their devotion to the God who dwelt in their midst in the shrine, which on occasion was moved from place to place. Their leaders arose in times of crisis to settle internal disputes or to defend them from external enemies. The decision to erect the temple in Jerusalem as a permanent house for Yahweh, their God, coincided with the designation of a national leader, a king chosen from one of the twelve tribes. The monarchy lasted only a few generations and ended with two shrines competing for the claim to be Yahweh's residence among his people: in Jerusalem and on Mount Gerizim in Samaria. First the northern and then the southern group of tribes were taken off into captivity in Mesopotamia, and the shrines lay in ruins until the decision by Cyrus, the Persian ruler of the Middle East, to allow the tribes of Judah to return to the land of Palestine. From the rise of the monarchy down through the period of the exile in Babylon and the return, certain figures arose in Israel to utter predictions and protests and to call the ruler and the people to account before God. These were the prophets of Israel. After the monarchy was gone, leadership and identity for the Jews were provided through the priests. Traditional aids for individual and group worship were brought together to form the Book of Psalms. The wisdom traditions were edited in such books as Proverbs and Ecclesiastes.

With the takeover of the land by Alexander the Great and his hellenistic successors, the Jews were subjected to enormous pressure to conform to Greek-style culture. Their resistance was led by a priestly family, the Maccabees (or Hasmoneans), and resulted in the establishment of a dynasty that became increasingly objectionable to many Jews because its kings were from the priestly line and thus were not descended from David, the model king. Further, the Hasmonean rulers became increasingly secular and harsh. As a result, various groups arose among the Jews whose members sought to find fulfillment of their sense of special relationship with God outside the frameworks provided by either the temple priesthood or the political establishment. It was in this context that movements arose from within Judaism which were to have such profound importance for the subsequent history of biblical religion: the Pharisees, the Essenes (or Dead Sea community), and the Christians. In all these changing circumstances the twin convictions remained that God addressed his people through chosen instruments and that it was obligatory for his people to confirm their special relationship to God.

Closely linked with the changing context of revelation was the constant modification of what these historical communities

HELLENISTIC

FROM THE GREEK WORD meaning "Greek" – Hellene – came the verb "to hellenize," or to convert to Greek culture and style of life. Alexander the Great and his successors as rulers of the Middle East – especially the Ptolemaic monarchs in Egypt and the Seleucid rulers in Syria – saw this process of "Greek-izing" as a central goal of their rule over these non-Greek territories. They thought of themselves as bringing true culture to these benighted peoples. In addition to rebuilding the cities in the Greek style, they promoted Greek education and culture and devotion to the Greek gods among their subjects. The term "hellenistic" has been applied by historians to the period lasting from the rise of Alexander in the late fourth century B.C.E. to the time of the coming of the Romans to the eastern Mediterranean in the mid–first century B.C.E.

Relief from sarcophagus of Alexander the Great. Pictured here is Alexander's most important battle, when his defeat of the Persian army at Issus, in a narrow stretch of land in southern Turkey, gave him access to all the lands to the east, including Syria, Mesopotamia, and as far as India.

Department of Archaeology, Bryn Mawr College

understood to be the nature of their relationship to the God who spoke to them about his purpose and their destiny. At the same time, the perception of who the human instrument was through whom God had addressed them – a king, a tribal leader, a prophet, a priest, someone especially gifted to interpret the tradition – varied significantly from time to time and place to place. There is no set pattern of divine communication in the biblical writings, nor is there a single view of how one was to define the people of God addressed by him. The two persistent themes running throughout the biblical writings are that (1)

THE DEAD SEA SCROLLS AND THE QUMRAN COMMUNITY

KHIRBET QUMRAN IS THE modern name for the ruins at the site of the Jewish monastic community that withdrew in the first century B.C.E. from life in Jerusalem and the mainstream of Jewish society to live together what their founder and his followers were convinced was the pure life of devotion to God, until – as they were convinced – he would intervene in their behalf and grant them the priestly role in a renewed temple in Jerusalem.

The community was located on a bluff overlooking the north-western end of the Dead Sea. The Wadi Qumran (a wadi is the rocky bed of a seasonal stream), just below their sacred site, provides a runoff for water from the temple site in Jerusalem. According to Ezekiel 47, through this channel a mighty stream would flow from the renewed temple and would transform the salty Dead Sea into a freshwater lake. The community had a central building where they gathered to study, to prepare copies of their writings, and to eat common meals. There are also ruins of other structures, including pools (possibly for baptisms), caves where some members appear to have lived, and tombs for their

deceased. The Dead Sea community lived on this site awaiting the divine renewal of God's people, of Jerusalem and the temple (with themselves in charge), and of the land of Israel.

The documents found there include the oldest surviving copies of the Jewish scriptures, in addition to commentaries on the prophets of Israel, predicting the imminent fulfillment of the prophecies for and through this community. Basic writings describing the origins, organization, rules, and destiny of the community were also found, of which the most revealing is the Scroll of the Rule.

Qumran caves. After local Bedouin in 1947 discovered the first of the scrolls in a cave overlooking the Dead Sea, other caves and other manuscripts were found, and the ruins of the community center were explored by archeologists in subsequent years. The oldest extant copies of Old Testament books and previously unknown texts produced by the Jewish monastic community based at the site have been found preserved in the caves.

H. C. Kee

there is a people of God, and (2) they have been spoken to by God. The content of the message and the community context in which it was heard changed throughout the centuries of the biblical period. But in every case, the authority of what was uttered is traced to God. The responsibility for and the consequences of the response rested with those who, by various criteria, saw themselves as God's people.

B. THE BIBLICAL WRITINGS AND THE CULTURAL SETTING

As the social and political setting of the covenant people changed over the centuries, so did both their linguistic and their literary styles. The oldest Hebrew literary traditions included in the Bible, which consist of epic accounts of the origins of the people Israel, seem to have originated about the year 1200 B.C.E. During or after the exile, they were incorporated with later traditions into what we know as the Pentateuch. The oldest surviving inscriptions and documents in Hebrew – which is akin to Akkadian (the language spoken in ancient Babylonia) but is even more closely related to the Semitic languages spoken in Palestine (Canaanite and Phoenician) – date from about the tenth century B.C.E. By the eighth century, however, Aramaic (which was spoken by a Semitic group that invaded Palestine and Syria from Mesopotamia) had become the major language of the Middle East. In the sixth century the Persians made Aramaic the official language of their empire, which included the land of Israel. Hebrew continued as the traditional religious language of Israel, but increasingly Aramaic was used for oral and written communication by the Israelites. Parts of Ezra and Daniel are in Aramaic, and it later became necessary to provide translations and paraphrases of the Jewish scriptures in Aramaic in order for the readers and worshipers to understand them. By the fifth century C.E., the Aramaic versions were officially

PENTATEUCH

TAKEN LITERALLY, THE term indicates a book in five parts. It is widely used in biblical scholarship to refer to the first five books of the Bible: Genesis, Exodus, Leviticus, Numbers, Deuteronomy. These books have been traditionally attributed to Moses. In Jewish usage, these writings are often referred to as Torah ("instruction") or the law of Moses. It seems likely that the Pentateuch is the end product of a period of development and modification that extended from the second millennium B.C.E. down to perhaps as late as the fifth century B.C.E. Details of this development and analyses of the contents of the Pentateuch are presented throughout Part I.

Isis and Horus. Isis, the Egyptian goddess of fertility, is often portrayed with her son, Horus, who earlier was worshiped as the god of the sun and the moon. Later, when Isis is depicted as the sister–wife of Osiris, she gives birth to Horus.

H. C. Kee

recognized by the rabbinic leaders as suitable for religious and devotional reading of the scriptures. Meanwhile, an artificial form of Hebrew was revived to serve as the official medium of interpretation of the Bible among the rabbis in the works known as Mishnah and Talmud, which were written in the period from the second to the sixth centuries C.E.

From the late fourth century B.C.E. on, however, more and more Jews were reared in a Greek-speaking environment. By the third century B.C.E. thousands of Jews were living in Egypt, where they were powerfully influenced by hellenistic culture and learning. Their basic language was Greek, and they were schooled in Greek literature and philosophy. Since they were unable to read the Bible in the original Hebrew and Aramaic, the pagan ruler of Egypt reportedly collaborated with the Jewish leadership in Jerusalem to have a Greek translation made of the Pentateuch, which in subsequent centuries was followed by translations of the other books of the Bible. A legend arose about the miraculous agreement among the seventy independently working translators, and the translation in its final form came to be known as the Septuagint, from the Greek word for "seventy." It was widely used throughout the Greco-Roman world, by Jews and later by Christians as well.

Books such as 4 Maccabees not only were first written in Greek but retell the story of Judas Maccabaeus's triumph over the hellenistic rulers in terms that show the direct influence of Greek philosophy, such as the Stoic philosophical notion of virtue triumphing over adversity. The book variously known as the Wisdom of Ben Sira, Sirach, and Ecclesiasticus shows another kind of influence of hellenistic culture, in that it counters the older biblical writings' uniform denunciation of physicians as magicians and agents of evil powers. Instead, Ben Sira honors them as instruments of God and does so at precisely the historical moment when Greek medicine under Hippocrates was coming into prominence and enjoying increasing respect. Ideas that derived from older biblical tradition from this time on are stated in terms taken over from Greek culture, in order to make the tradition relevant to the changing times of the later writers.

Similarly, the biblical writers used as media for communicating to their contemporaries the literary styles and forms that were employed in their own era. In many cases, these literary patterns were adapted or modified, but the underlying structures and strategies used by other religions and cultures of their time are readily recognizable. Epic narratives, to which we have already made reference, were an important feature of the literatures of various ethnic and cultural groups in the ancient Middle East. The biblical writers used this genre for their own purposes, both in the Pentateuch (especially in Genesis) and in the historical writings. The forms of poetry, and especially of hymns and liturgical passages, are also similar to those found in other ancient Semitic literatures of the same period. The biblical legal codes have their counterpart in contemporary legal traditions of other societies. In various ways, the wisdom traditions of Israel resemble the proverbs and oracles of contemporary cultures. Similarly, the prophetic oracles have their rough equivalents in other Semitic cultures.

As one moves down into the hellenistic period, other features of biblical tradition may be seen to be similar in form and analogous in meaning to aspects of non-Israelite culture. For example, just as in Egyptian mythology the goddess of knowledge, Ma'at, came to be seen as the instrument through whom the world was created, as well as the agent for conveying divine knowledge to the true seekers, so in Israel Wisdom is personified as the divine consort and aide in creation and the one through whom the knowledge of Yahweh is conveyed to his people. In Egypt during the hellenistic period, the creative and revelatory role of Ma'at was transferred to Isis, who was portrayed in the mythology of the period as personally concerned for her worshipers and as revealing herself to them in mystical communion. The functions of Isis as intermediary between God and humans are paralleled in other writings of the hellenistic period. It is this model of divine communication and relationship which has been taken up and transformed by the author of the Gospel of John. Further, he assigns them to a male figure, the Logos (or Word), which he identified with Jesus. During the hellenistic and Roman periods, the styles for composing letters, for making speeches, for telling popular stories about religious persons and their experiences with the gods, and for writing history strongly influenced the biblical writers as well.

It is important to note not only the similarities between these religious and literary features of the world contemporary with the biblical writers and the style and content of their own work but also the differences. In each case, certain aspects of the convictions of the biblical communities required them to adapt the concepts and literary modes of their time for their own particular purposes.

In at least one case – that of the gospels – the biblical writers seem to have created a new literary type. Features of the Gospels resemble contemporary literary forms, including the biography and what anthropologists call a "foundation document," that is, a writing which presents an account of the circumstances under which a religious movement was founded and indicates the basic pattern of life and thought that the followers of that leader are to observe. As we shall see, not all our gospels possess both these features. And the specific form in which these elements are combined in the Gospels seems to have been a unique contribution to world literature.

C.   THE LITERARY EVOLUTION OF THE BIBLICAL WRITINGS

One important dimension of the development of the biblical writings is that they evolved in each case from oral to written forms. Individual epics, for example, were woven into a sequential narrative. The hymns of praise and petition were over a period of time incorporated into other documents, legal or historical, or arranged into a body of liturgical material, such as the Book of Psalms. The legal material grew from simpler to more complex forms as the

STOICISM

STOICISM IS THE PHILOSOPHical school of thought that grew out of the work of Zeno (ca. 320–250 B.C.E.), who taught publicly in the porticoes – or Stoa – of the marketplace in Athens. His teaching emphasized reason as the pervasive force that sustained the universe. He insisted on the material nature of the universe, as contrasted with the ideal realm of reality in the philosophy of Plato. Cleanthes, who developed Zeno's ideas further, pictured God as the unseen force which gave life and purpose to the universe. The life of virtue for human beings was to live according to that law of nature. If the universal law were perceived and obeyed, human society could achieve peace and prosperity. The Stoic movement went through three phases: Old, Middle, and Later Stoicism. In the Middle period, history, philosophy, and the natural sciences were studied with the aim of discerning the penetration of logic and natural law. The divine presence is described as pneuma, which means spirit. Later Stoicism is represented by the Roman philosopher Seneca (4 b.c.e.–65 c.e.). He discussed human suffering, which was a problem for those who stressed the divine presence and action. He depicted it as the divinely intended process by which humans were tested and purified. Epictetus (50–120 c.e.) emphasized that it was the human capacity for understanding and responding to the divine purpose – that is, conscience – which made possible human conformity to the law of nature.

GOSPEL AND SYNOPTIC GOSPELS

THE WORD "GOSPEL" IS A translation of the Greek noun *euangelion*, which means "good news." Most frequently used in the Christian scriptures with reference to the message about Jesus as God's agent to renew his people and establish his rule on earth, it appears commonly in Paul's letters. The Hebrew word *basar* has connotations similar to the Christian term "gospel." It is used in the Jewish scriptures to announce the new things that God is about to do in behalf of his people and of the created order (Isa. 40:9, 41:27, 52:7, 61:1). It is not surprising that (1) the early Christians claimed that this hope was being fulfilled through Jesus (Luke 4:16–21), and (2) the equivalent noun, *euangelion*, was applied to the basic documents in which the message and activities of Jesus were reported.

Perhaps because the word appears in the opening phrase of Mark, it came to be used for the first four documents to be included in the Christian scriptures. The first three of these documents have a roughly similar format and have long been designated as the synoptic Gospels (or the Synoptics), because they have the same basic literary approach to the story of Jesus. John's gospel is quite different from the others in form and content.

circumstances of Israel's historical existence changed and its needs varied with the cultural conditions. The same is true of prophetic oracles, which were supplemented by later material and organized into the collections in which we now find them. Similarly, the wisdom tradition was expanded from its older forms as speculation grew about the role of Wisdom in the creation of the world and as efforts were made to correlate what pagans claimed about wisdom (philosophy) with the wisdom the biblical tradition asserted had been revealed by God to his people. The oral components of the Gospels may also be identified through careful analysis, even though the overall use made of them by the Gospel writers is unique, as noted.

The change from oral to written forms involved extensive editing of older material, as well as arranging it in the present patterns in which it is preserved in our biblical books. In addition to the weaving of narratives into a consecutive epic form, the present form of the first five books of the Bible shows clearly that the material has been compiled and expanded over a period of centuries and in a variety of circumstances. Central in this complex is the law given in expanded and repeated form, together with narratives and genealogical lists tracing Israel's origins back to the founding fathers. The heavy underscoring of the ritual aspects of the law in the period covered by the Pentateuch is a sure sign that in its final editing, the hand of the priestly leaders of Israel was at work reshaping the tradition.

This fact suggests at least two of the major motivations that were at work in this recasting of older biblical tradition: (1) to bring the tradition up to date, so that its relevance for the present situation in the life of Israel is immediately apparent; (2) to harmonize or blend diverse traditions to provide an overall unity to the tradition as finally recorded. This process is also evident in the historical and prophetic materials. The Books of Chronicles, for example, when compared with the accounts of the same events in the Books of Kings, show that the values and the point of view of the priests in the period after Israel's return from exile in Babylon have had a shaping effect on the Chronicler's version of Israel's history. Also, in the period after the exile, traces of Persian ideas appear in the biblical writings, such as the notion of Satan as God's adversary. In the case of the prophets of Israel, earlier predictions that did not take place as expected are balanced in the present versions of the writings of the prophets by the addition of later material. For example, the prophecies of the eighth-century B.C.E. prophet Isaiah that predict God's punishment of his disobedient people are supplemented by predictions about the end of the age (Isa. 24–7) and then by later reports and celebrations of Israel's return to the land (Isa. 36–9) and hopes for the future fulfillment of God's purposes for his renewed people (Isa. 40–66). Less obviously, but just as significantly, other prophetic writings received later supplements, as is the case with Amos, Zechariah, and Malachi.

D. THE AUTHORITY OF THE BIBLICAL WRITINGS

Equally as significant as the editing of and additions to the scriptural writings is the fact that, in both Judaism and Christianity, documents addressing the issues of the identity and destiny of the people of God continued to be produced long after the documents that are included in the Bible had achieved the form in which we know them. The problem arose for both Jews and Christians, therefore, to draw up an official list of those writings that were to be considered authoritative for their respective constituencies. Called "canons," from the Greek word meaning "norm" or "standard," these lists were not uniform among either Jews or Christians. Many Jews, for example, recognized as authoritative all the writings included in the Septuagint, whereas others around the end of the first century C.E. adopted a list of books that had been originally written in Hebrew or Aramaic, not in Greek. When in Part III of this book we discuss the canons of scripture, we shall see that the Christians did not and do not agree among themselves as to which books compose their canon.

Many of the books that Jewish or Christian groups tried to get accepted as authoritative were modeled after those that did find a place on the official lists. Other writings purported to be essential supplements to the canonical books. The supplemental books for the Jewish scriptures included writings claiming to be the "last will and testament" of one or other of the figures of ancient Israel, such as Abraham or the sons of Jacob. Other writings not generally recognized by Jews as official include collections of psalms or odes attributed to Solomon and prophetic oracles in the style of the later prophets and such priestly leaders as Ezra. Although a modern sense of historical authenticity and trustworthiness might deplore such spurious claims of authorship, one must remember that part of the aim of these writings was to show how these ancient figures and their insights into the ways of God were relevant for the present situations of the later writers. Certain small groups that broke away from the mainstream of their tradition, whether Jewish or Christian, also offered writings that supplemented or gave a distinctive interpretation to the older scriptural writings. In Judaism of the late first century B.C.E., for example, the Dead Sea community had its own explanations of the scriptures and its own guidebooks on the origins, aims, and destiny of the group. Beginning in the second century C.E., groups known as Gnostics (which means, roughly, "those who are in the know") had their own versions of the gospel tradition and their own additions to what Jesus was supposed to have taught his inner circle of followers.

Parallel with the development of the official lists of the scriptures was the appearance in both Judaism and Christianity of writings that claimed to offer the true and proper interpretation of the canonical writings. At the site of the Dead Sea sect in Qumran, for example, extensive commentaries on books of the Bible, such as Isaiah, were found. Their characteristic style is to show in detail how what the sacred writer wrote has relevance to, and fulfillment in, the present experience of this group. Beginning informally in the first century

Qumran manuscript. The relative stability of temperature and humidity at this site almost thirteen hundred feet below sea level was the major factor in the survival of the Dead Sea manuscripts. They provide direct knowledge about the Jewish group based at Qumran, which was critical of the priestly establishment and which looked forward to divine vindication of the group and its elevation to power in a renewed Jerusalem.

H. C. Kee

ALEXANDRIA

IN 332 B.C.E, ON AN ANCIENT site in the delta of the Nile, on the shore of the Mediterranean, Alexander the Great began to plan for a city that would serve three objectives: a naval base for his fleet, a commercial base for exchange between his native Macedonia and the wealth of the Nile Valley, and a center for implanting hellenistic culture in this conquered land. He died before his plans were complete, but his successors followed through on the project and created one of the great cities of the hellenistic era, in which study was carried out and an incomparable library assembled, covering the fields of philosophy, natural science, history, and medicine. Down into the early centuries of the Christian church, Alexandria was a major center of cultural and intellectual life.

B.C.E., and taking distinctive shape in the period from the second to the sixth centuries C.E., the rabbinic method of offering interpretations of scripture relevant for the present covenant community produced documents known as Mishnah and Talmud. This movement developed its own style and process of training leaders for this interpretive task. Prior to this development, in Alexandria at the turn of the eras there had appeared the towering figure of Philo, the Jew whose many writings interpret the Jewish law allegorically, seeking to demonstrate the basic kinship between the inner meaning of scripture and the philosophical insights of Plato and the Stoics. That same approach was adopted by those who established the Christian catechetical school in Alexandria. In the third century C.E. this school was headed by Origen, whose interpretation of the Gospel of John follows a method similar to that of Philo. This technique was not regarded as distortion but as a means of demonstrating the relevance of the sacred writings to the interpreter's own day.

E.   THE HISTORICAL VALUE OF THE WRITINGS

With the development of the Christian creeds in the third century C.E. and subsequently, scripture was turned to as an authoritative base for documenting and confirming the credal affirmations. In the Protestant Reformation of the sixteenth century, Scripture was understood to be a mode of direct address by God to his people, and in many quarters, texts of scripture were appealed to as proof of what the theologians were affirming in their doctrinal systems. Those strategies were sharply challenged, however, beginning in the seventeenth century, when ancient documents, including the Bible, began to be studied by academics with two scholarly objectives in mind: (1) to determine what the original wording of the ancient texts had been, and (2) to reconstruct the historical origins of these writings.

The first undertaking was to examine and compare the earliest copies of the various parts of the Bible in order to reconstruct, as nearly as possible, its original text. At that time, the oldest copies of the books of the Jewish Bible were relatively modern: from the tenth century C.E. In the middle of the present century, however, copies of parts of the Bible going back to the turn of the eras were discovered among the Dead Sea Scrolls, including the complete text of Isaiah. The tenth-century standardized text of the Hebrew Bible matched remarkably well, however, with the text used by ancient Christian biblical scholars,

PLATO

DURING HIS LONG LIFE (427–348 B.C.E.), Plato founded and lectured at the Academy, a school in Athens, and wrote dozens of works in various forms: laws, letters, dialogues. His work concerned the whole range of human action: political, ethical, psychological, logical, physical, metaphysical, and religious. The basic concepts in his mature work are that there is an eternal, divine mind whose purpose and power shape the structure of the universe and the destiny of its

inhabitants; that all phenomena whether tangible objects or abstract ideas and principles, are only imperfect copies of the heavenly paradigms or ideal forms of reality; these ideas exist eternally, whereas all the earthly copies are subject to decay; in all creation, only human beings possess the capacity to discern this ultimate reality of the universe and come to understand it through reason. To live the good life is to sharpen this grasp of reality and to guide one's personal and social existence by means of these eternal principles.

such as Origen (185–254) and Jerome (347–420). Further attestation of the text of the Hebrew Bible comes from other ancient sources. After the split in ancient Israel between the northern and southern tribes in the ninth century B.C.E., what is known as the Samaritan version of the Pentateuch developed. The oldest copies of this antedate those of the standard Hebrew Bible of late antiquity, but its text resembles that of the Septuagint, and both these forms of the Jewish Bible are remarkably close to the traditional Hebrew text.

The oldest copies of the complete New Testament go back to the fourth century C.E., but the majority of the surviving manuscripts of the New Testament represent a fairly late standardized version of the Greek text, which includes additions and which adjusts differences between the Gospel accounts of Jesus. Extant fragments of the gospels, however, go back to the third and even the second century. These manuscripts bring the scholar within a few decades of the time when these early Christian books were originally composed. On the basis of details of their contents, the ancient copies of the Christian biblical writings have been classified into the Common Text (which is found in the majority of the Greek manuscripts, most of them late); the Neutral Text (which survives in only a few copies, but which may be closest to the original); and a group usually known as the Western Text, which seems to lie behind the Latin version in use in western Europe from early medieval times onward. Complete copies of the Neutral Text include a manuscript found at Saint Catherine's Monastery on Mount Sinai (Colorplate 1) in the last century and one at the Vatican library. Each of these manuscript traditions also shows some affinity with copies of ancient translations of the Christian Bible into such languages as Coptic (in Egypt), Syriac, and Armenian.

The second scholarly task was the effort to recover the historical origins of the biblical writings, as contrasted with the time and circumstances which they claim to be reporting. As early as the third century, the pagan philosopher Porphyry (233–304) had shown that the Book of Daniel did not date from the time of Jewish exile in Babylonia (sixth century B.C.E.), as its narrative suggests, but from the reign of Antiochus IV Epiphanes (early second century B.C.E.), in the hellenistic era. By the seventeenth century, Thomas Hobbes, in his *Leviathan* (1651), was trying to prove that the Pentateuch had been written after the time of Moses. In 1753, the French Catholic physician and scholar Jean Astruc advanced the theory that there were multiple sources behind the books of Genesis and Exodus, and that they could be distinguished by whether they referred to God as Yahweh (God's special name, revealed only to Israel) or simply as God (for which the Hebrew word is *elohim*). This proposal was expanded and refined in the nineteenth century by K. H. Graf (1865) and J. Wellhausen (1878), so that there emerged a widely held theory that there are four literary strands behind the Pentateuch in its present form: J (Yahwist; abbreviated as J, rather than Y, following the German *Jahwist*), E (Elohist), P (Priestly), and D (Deuteronomist). The last two strands represent respectively the priestly and the legal revisionist reworking of the Pentateuchal traditions in the period during or just after the

ORIGEN OF ALEXANDRIA

BORN IN THE LATTER PART of the second century, Origen's intellectual brilliance and discipline were such that at age eighteen he was appointed by the bishop of Alexandria as head of the Christian catechetical school there. His eloquence and his mastery of classical Greek and hellenistic philosophical literature were such that heathen scholars came to hear his lectures and to engage him in learned conversation. His extensive writings (many of which have not survived to the present) included debates with the critics of Christianity (especially in his late work, Against Celsus), detailed studies of Old and New Testament texts (for which he used allegorical methods like those of the earlier Jewish scholar Philo of Alexandria), and detailed comparative analysis of various copies and versions of the Jewish scriptures (the Hexapla). Opposition to him from certain Christians and the threat of persecution by the Roman authorities led him to move to Caesarea in Palestine, where his skills as a writer and his popularity as a lecturer continued to attract many believers as well as pagan intellectuals.

exile in Babylon. The first two strands, J and E, are the oldest strata of the tradition. Also in the nineteenth century, scholars sought to show that the earlier prophetic utterances had been worked over, expanded, supplemented, and otherwise edited at the end of, or after, Israel's return from exile, and only then achieved the form that we now possess.

In studies of the historical and literary origins of the Christian biblical writings, the most significant challenge to the traditional views came from John Locke (1632–1704). He portrayed Jesus as the spokesman for natural law and rational religion. Both the supernatural claims made by the New Testament writers in his behalf and the notion that his wisdom was available only to the inner circle of his followers Locke saw as a perversion of the real aims and methods of Jesus. Matthew Tindal (1657–1733) took this approach a major step further in his work, *Christianity as Old as Creation; or, The Gospel a Republication of the Religion of Nature.* In this essay he raised serious questions about the integrity of the disciples and implied that they had misunderstood and distorted Jesus' intentions. H. S. Reimarus (1694–1768) followed up on this interpretation of the Gospel evidence and claimed that Jesus had actually preached nationalistic hopes of an uprising against Rome but that his disciples had pictured him as a universal savior whose realm was solely within the life of the human spirit.

By the middle of the nineteenth century, efforts were made to show that the supernatural aura surrounding the figure of Jesus was the construct of pious imagination or the result of mythical interpretation of Jesus and his activities (in the *Life of Jesus* by David Friedrich Strauss, 1808–74). Attempts to strip away the mythical and to disclose the true historical Jesus were strongly influenced by early-nineteenth-century philosophical ideas, such as those of Immanuel Kant (1724–1804) and G. W. F. Hegel (1770–1831). In this perspective, Jesus was represented as the embodiment of the highest moral ideas, and the stories of his exorcisms and miracles, as well as his predictions of the end of the age, were dismissed as regrettable later additions. His announcement of the coming of God's rule was seen by some interpreters, however, as a timeless invitation to attain to spiritual obedience within the self.

F.   THE AIMS OF THE BIBLICAL WRITERS

Throughout the nineteenth century, concurrent with the attempt to separate out the literary sources behind the Pentateuch, scholars were seeking to discover what the special aims and interests were of those who edited the biblical material into the form in which it has come down to us. The same sort of inquiry was under way for the prophetic, wisdom, and poetic writings. The question was not simply, What do the documents tell us? but, For what purposes and with what assumptions were they written? Meanwhile, beginning in the eighteenth century scholars had been giving attention to questions about sources for the gospels and about literary relationships among such groups of early Christian writings as those attributed to Paul, John, and Peter. Questions were raised about authenticity as well as about authorship. In the first quarter of the present century, scholars sought to discover not merely the possible literary sources behind the Gospels as we have them but the oral forms in which the tradition had been passed on before the Gospels were written. The "form critics," as they came to be called, were interested in determining both the original forms of these traditions and what function they served in the life of the early Christian communities which preserved them. These functions included preaching, instruction, and worship. Similar questions about the forms of the oral tradition were raised by those studying the Jewish scriptures as well.

In recent decades, interest has shifted from what the oral or literary components of the biblical writings were to what the final writer or editor has done with this material. This mode of analysis has been used with the legal, prophetic, poetic, wisdom, gospel, and rhetorical traditions of the Bible. The questions are: What purposes are served by the biblical material as we have it? How did the editor see his role in relation to the community for which he prepared the material, and what role did he foresee for the community in the overall purpose of God? From the way in which the tradition has been modified, what can one infer about the social and cultural context of the community to whom it was addressed in the form in which we now have it? What are the values and ethical norms explicit or implicit in these writings? What did the community for whom the writing was prepared fear, and what did it hope for? Who were its leaders, and what was the ground of their authority? It is with these sorts of questions in mind that we must undertake our analyses of the biblical writings.

G. THE LANDS OF THE BIBLE

Before beginning our study of the context, contents, and intent of the biblical material, we must consider carefully the lands in which these insights arose and these events occurred. The physical context is as important as the cultural context for understanding how the history of the biblical period developed. The initial focus is on the lands stretching from the valley of the Nile in Egypt, across Palestine and Syria to the Land between the Rivers – known variously as Mesopotamia or Babylon or, in modern times, Iraq – and to Persia beyond the rivers. Also important in the later biblical records are those centers of civilization that extend westward from the upper end of the Persian Gulf across the mountain ranges and plateaus south of the Caspian Sea to the Mediterranean Sea. From the sixth century before our era onward, we shall also be concerned with the mainland of Europe, from the north of the Greek peninsula across the Adriatic Sea to Rome.

The peoples who inhabited these lands have been classified on the basis of the languages they used, although several of their languages do not fit the traditional classifications. In Genesis 10, the nations of the Middle East are grouped on the basis of their traditional

---

FORM CRITICISM

BASED ON ANALYSIS OF other literatures that moved from oral to written stages, New Testament scholars earlier in this century developed terminology for classifying the material included in the Gospels (especially the first three). The aim was to discern how the tradition was transmitted and, if possible, what functions the tradition was intended to serve within the early Christian communities. One scheme for formal classification of the Gospel material is the following

  A. Saying tradition
    1. Aphorisms
    2. Parables
    3. Sayings clusters (formal and topical groupings)
  B. Narrative tradition
    1. Anecdotes
    2. Aphoristic narratives
    3. Wonder stories
    4. Legends:
      a. Biographical legends
      b. Cult legends
    5. Passion narrative

Stela of Ur Nammu. The fragments of this pillar have been reconstructed in various ways. The stela measures 5 × 10 feet and depicts the building of a sacred pyramid (ziggurat) about 2000 B.C.E. Also portrayed are King Ur Nammu in prayer, with angels descending; the god (Nanna) and goddess (Ningal) present as the work begins; and the king with the tools of architect and builder.

University Museum, University of Pennsylvania

relationship to the sons of Noah. The sons of Ham were the Egyptians, Cushites (Ethiopians), and Libyans. The sons of Shem were the Assyrians, Babylonians (Akkadians), Canaanites, Phoenicians, Arameans, Amorites, Moabites, Edomites, and Hebrews. Not included in the biblical list, but figuring importantly in the biblical story, are the linguistic groups known as the Indo-Europeans: Greeks, Romans, Lydians, Medes, Persians, Scythians, Hittites, and Philistines.

1. Egypt

The Nile Valley (Colorplate 2) is not only the central physical feature of Egypt but represents the less than 4 percent of the land that was and is habitable. The rest is mostly desert, except for some areas along the seacoast. The water of the Nile comes from the high country of east-central Africa; rainfall in Egypt outside the Nile Valley is negligible. After passing over a series of cataracts, the last of which is at modern Aswan, some 400 miles from the Mediterranean, the river winds gently between limestone cliffs that rise mostly well back from the river channel itself. Its tributaries arise 350 miles south of Aswan. Near the sea, its silt has formed an enormous delta (about 100 by 150 miles), which is fertile and has been highly cultivated since antiquity. From there it used to flow out into the Mediterranean through a series of mouths, but in modern times these have been reduced to two.

The Western Desert is a limestone plateau, broken by some sub-sea-level depressions. The best known of these is Lake Moeris, which was apparently watered by a natural runoff from the Nile perhaps dating back to about 2000 B.C.E. The lake is mentioned by this name in a Greek writing of the fifth century B.C.E. The Eastern Desert (Arabian Desert), on the other hand, includes a series of mountains that reach to heights of 7,000 feet. There are some springs and some scanty vegetation in this region, which extends to the Gulf of Suez and the Persian Gulf.

Upstream from Egypt proper lie the districts known as Cush (Ethiopia) and Nubia, both of which figure in the ancient literature. Ethiopians were among the early converts to Christianity, and the early Christian scriptures seem to have been translated rapidly into Ethiopian, which is akin to ancient Egyptian. The seasonal rains in the upper (Southern) Nile Valley caused flooding in Egypt, which resulted in the annual cycles of crops in that country. The worship of Osiris, the god of the Nile, was directly linked with this pattern of fertility in this river valley.

The two major centers of Egyptian civilization were Thebes, which is downstream from the first cataract, and Memphis, which is upstream from the delta. After the fourth century B.C.E., the dominant political and cultural center in Egypt was in the Nile Delta, where Alexander founded a great city to promote Greek culture and named it for himself: Alexandria. In the vicinity of Thebes are the ruins of some of the great temples of ancient Egypt, whereas at Giza (on the site of Memphis, near modern Cairo) are the great pyramids (Colorplate 3).

Historians have traced the course of twenty-six Egyptian dynasties, dating from about 3000 B.C.E. to the seventh century B.C.E., when Egypt was conquered by the Persians. In the period known as the New Kingdom (1570–1090), the Egyptians controlled the territory from some distance south of the cataracts of the Nile across Palestine to Syria and parts of Mesopotamia. In diplomatic correspondence from the reign of Akh-en-Aton (1369–1353) there appear references to a people called Hapiru (or Habiru), who were causing difficulties for tribal rulers in Syria–Palestine, who were subject to Egypt. Some scholars have sought to link these people with the tribes of Israel. From the Nineteenth Dynasty (1303–1202) have survived records of Egyptian military victories in Palestine and Syria, including the section known as Canaan. Rameses II (1290–1224) is reported to have used Israelite slaves in the construction of cities in Lower Egypt (Exod. 1:11). From the story of Abraham's stay in Egypt (Gen. 12:10) through the account of the Exodus (told in Genesis and Exodus) to the report of Jesus being taken to Egypt by his family (Matt. 2:14–15), this land figures importantly in the biblical narratives.

2.　　Sinai

This triangular land bridge joins Africa and Asia. Its northern limits front on the Mediterranean, where a sea-level land route was a major commercial link in this part of the world. The east and west sides of the peninsula abut on what in modern times are known respectively as the Gulf of Aqaba and the Gulf of Suez. The latter now gives access to the Suez Canal. From the sandy shores and inlets of the Mediterranean coast, Sinai slopes upward in elevation toward the south. The northern plateau is a plain of flint, limestone, and sand dunes. The southern half, however, rises steadily and is crossed by many wadies (seasonal watercourses, which drain the land in the infrequent event of rain) and culminates in mountain peaks. The highest of these is Gebel Musa (Mountain of Moses; also known as Mount Sinai and Mount of Saint Katherine), the mountain where tradition says God gave the law to the people Israel through Moses. Abundant evidence of commercial and military passage through the Sinai exists, but there seems to have been chiefly nomadic population there throughout the millennia.

3.　　Negev and the Lands West and East of the Jordan

Beginning to the north of the Sinai peninsula and extending north as far as Syria, the land is divided roughly into a series of north–south strips. The coastal plain varies in width and is broken only by the mountain ridge of Carmel, which juts out into the sea and forces the trade routes inland to find passes over the mountains. To the east of the sea plain is a range of low hills, reasonably well watered during the annual rainy season and suitable for cultivation. Farther east is the main ridge of the mountains, reaching elevations of more than two thousand feet above the Mediterranean. Valleys among these hills make north–south travel possible and also from the Jordan Valley up into the hills. The eastern slopes of these hills are desolate, and drop off rapidly into the Jordan Valley (Colorplate 5), which at its southern end goes down to more than 1,200 feet below sea level. The Jordan itself rises in the mountains north of the Sea of Galilee and then descends gently to the south. This valley has been paralleled from most ancient times by major travel routes. The area east of the Jordan is agriculturally marginal, but from Greek times onward was able to support substantial Greek-style cities, for which water was provided by aqueducts from the eastern mountains. The rain-laden clouds coming in off the Mediterranean provide seasonal rains for the western slopes of the mountains on both the east and west banks of the Jordan. Beyond these mountains, and in other areas where rainfall is minimal, the land is barren and suitable only for nomadic life.

Among the various peoples mentioned in the Bible as living in the land between the Mediterranean and the Arabian Desert on both sides of the Jordan Valley are some linked in the biblical accounts (Gen. 25) with place-names in Arabia or with persons who figure in the biblical narratives: Midianites and, in the area south and east of the Dead Sea, Moabites, Edomites, and Ammonites. These all seem to have been Semitic-speaking peoples who lived seminomadic lives or were settled in small city-states. A later group of this type, the Nabateans, provided the Romans with puppet rulers, such as Aretas, who is mentioned in 2 Cor. 11:32 as ruler of Damascus while Paul was being persecuted there. The spectacular remains of their capital city, Petra, are still visible in southern Jordan. It was through this region that the Israelites passed on their way into the land of Canaan, following the Exodus from Egypt. Another group, the Edomites (or Idumeans), seem to have been crowded out of their copper-mining territory on the southeast side of the Dead Sea and to have moved to the southwest side in Roman times. It was from the Idumeans that the Romans chose Antipas, the father of Herod the Great, as their regional administrator.

To achieve their objective of conforming the local populace in the territory east of the Jordan to hellenistic culture, an elaborate effort was made to build or rebuild cities in the area after the pattern of hellenistic cities. This meant constructing pagan temples, theaters, hippodromes, gymnasia, baths, and other features of hellenistic cities of Greece and Asia Minor. In the first half of the first century B.C.E., ten of these cities formed a loose union, called the Decapolis (meaning "ten cities"). Of these cities, one lay west of the Jordan (Scythopolis, known in earlier times as Bet She'an), and one was in Syria (Damascus). Of the others, the following appear in early Christian literature: Gerasa, Gadara, Pella (named for the city of the father of Alexander the Great), and Ammon, east of the Jordan, which became Philadelphia. These places show dramatically the extent of exposure of the people of the biblical lands to hellenistic culture. In the region surrounding the Sea of Galilee there were pockets of resistance to hellenization, but other cities, such as Sepphoris – a few miles from the village of Nazareth – had all the features of hellenistic centers of culture.

Neolithic tower at Jericho. Excavations at Jericho uncovered the remains of a tower from Neolithic times predating the oldest Palestinian pottery. It may date to as early as 7000 B.C.E., nearly six thousand years before the Israelites entered the land under Joshua, about 1200 B.C.E.

American Schools of Oriental Research

Farther east are the regions identified simply as "Arabia," from which tribute was paid to Solomon (1 Kings 10:25) and where Paul fled following his vision of the risen Christ (Gal. 1:17, 4:25). One of the oracles in Isaiah (Isa. 21:3–17) is against Arabia.

4. Canaan

The land of Canaan, as it is often referred to in the scriptures of Israel, is a narrow strip of land between the mountains east of the Jordan Valley and the sea. Because of the dominant role played in this part of the world by the Philistines, who entered this region about 1200 B.C.E. and who figure importantly in ancient accounts of wars and diplomatic dealings, the region is often referred to as Palestine. From the southern end of the Dead Sea to the Mediterranean coast is about 75 miles. From the sources of the Jordan in the north to the Mediterranean is about half that distance. The Jordan flows from sources on the slopes of Mount Hermon (which reaches an elevation of 9,100 feet) down to the Sea of Galilee, which lies 695 feet below sea level, and then on down the valley to the Dead Sea, which is 1,290 feet lower than the Mediterranean. The Jordan rift extends to the south of the Dead Sea in the form of an arid valley known as the Araba. Throughout the valley of the Jordan, and especially in the section adjacent to the Sea of Galilee, there are agriculturally productive lands. Jericho, near the southern end of the valley, has springs which have been used from prehistoric times to water crops, which produce in that warm and sheltered place throughout the year. Some archeologists surmise that it is the oldest continually inhabited place on the face of the earth.

The mountains and rolling hills that form the western slope of the Jordan rift range in height from a 4,000-foot peak in the Galilee region to the 3,000-foot peaks of Mounts Ebal and Gerizim (in the region that came to be known as Samaria) to 2,500 feet at Jerusalem. These mountains are barren on the east, since the winter rains that come in off the Mediterranean fall on the western slopes. Most of the towns and villages of the land were on the western slopes, including the ridges which reach south and north from Jerusalem and which mark off Samaria and Galilee, and in the upland valleys and plains that extend westward toward the sea. The coastal region is relatively narrow, and except for the region around Acco and Mount Carmel, lacks natural harbors. In Greek and Roman times, harbors were constructed along the coast, and cities in the Greco-Roman style flourished there, including Ashkelon, Ashdod, and Caesarea. Ptolemais (formerly Acco) and, north of Palestine, Tyre, Sidon, and Antioch became model centers of hellenistic culture in social, cultural, and architectural style. The Phoenicians, whose economic and military skills enabled them to control territories in other parts of the Mediterranean, dominated these northern coastal cities. In the days of the patriarchs, however, the culture was predominantly Semitic.

Archeological excavations in Palestine and Syria have provided extensive knowledge of the Semitic groups that settled in this area, or

THE CLIMATE OF PALESTINE

THE DIVERSITY OF THE weather patterns in Palestine is the result of the convergence of three factors: (1) the latitude of the location; (2) the different kinds of air masses that cross the region during the year; and (3) the variations in terrain and elevation.

The latitude of Palestine (between 31° 15' and 33° 15' N) places it on the northern edge of the Subtropical Zone, but the intrusions of air masses from the Temperate Zone to the north result in a considerable range of heat, humidity, and precipitation. The summers are warm with little rain, but the winters are cool and often stormy. The transitional periods between the seasons bring rains and sometimes extremely hot, dry, dusty periods caused by air masses from the desert (called *khamsin*).

The dominant forces in the summer are the warm, calm air masses over the eastern Mediterranean, but in the winter cold air from the Atlantic and northern Europe, or even from Central Asia, clashes with warm tropical systems arising in Africa, and the result is severe storms of wind and rain. The rains come in mostly from the sea and fall chiefly on the coastland and the western faces of the main north –south ridges and mountains in the interior, while decreasing sharply in the desert areas of the south and east. Along the coastal plain there is also heavy dew, summer and winter.

The major topographical features in Palestine are (*a*) the coastal plain; (*b*) the ridges and mountains west of the Jordan River; (*c*) the Great Valley, in which are the Jordan River, the Sea of Galilee, and the Dead Sea; (*d*) the desert areas; and (*e*) the east Jordan Plateau. Humidity, precipitation, and heat level vary widely in these different regions. Humidity and rainfall are high along the Mediterranean coast, and even higher in the hilly districts of the interior. Along the coast, summer temperatures range from a summer maximum of about 100°F to winter lows in the upper forties. The ridges and hills are cooler in the summer, but in the winter the temperature frequently hovers in the fifties and forties, and occasionally there are days of frost, especially in January. Much colder temperatures occur in the higher elevations in the north, but are milder in the Great Valley from Galilee south to the lower Jordan and Dead Sea, where there is little rainfall and the temperatures are predominantly warm. East of the Jordan the land is higher, and mountains there attract rainfall from the clouds that drift in from the Mediterranean, although the fertile land there is a relatively narrow strip, giving way to true desert in the east. The seasons do not change abruptly, and even in the winter, periods of rain alternate with clear stretches, although there are occasional snows. Early rain in the spring softens the soil for planting, and late rains in the early fall improve the harvests. But in some years there is a severe decline in precipitation, which may extend over several years, so that the resultant drought brings on a famine in the land, as was the case when Jacob and his family had to move to Egypt (Gen. 41:53–7). There the abundant water flow was dependent on conditions in central Africa at the sources of the Nile and not on the variable factors of the eastern Mediterranean region.

that moved through in their nomadic wanderings. These include the Amorites, who seem to have alternated between settling in certain sites, where they seized power (in places ranging from Babylon to Aleppo in north Syria), and nomadic existence. The latter is apparent in Jericho, where during their period of occupation of the city they seem not to have built houses or city walls but to have lived in tents.

The Canaanites were in Jericho during the Neolithic period, dating back to the eighth millennium B.C.E. They continued to occupy various sections of Palestine in subsequent centuries. They seem to have engaged in considerable merchant activity and to have attained a high level of cultural achievement. Included among the subgroups of the Canaanites mentioned in the Bible are the Kenites, Perizzites, Kadmonites, Jebusites (who occupied the city that was later to be known as Jerusalem), and the Hivites.

Mount Gerizim. In the central hill country of Palestine, a pass exists that is overlooked by a mountain on each side: Ebal to the north, and Gerizim to the south. Just to the east is Shechem, where Jacob bought a plot of land (Gen. 13:18–20) and where the well associated with him is located. Major routes lead from this pass north toward Galilee, south toward Judea, and east to the Jordan Valley.

Gordon Converse

Other important residents, especially north and west of Palestine, were the Phoenicians, or Sidonians as they later were called. They were sea traders, with commercial connections around the Mediterranean. Their exports included cedar from the mountains in Lebanon and purple dye, which they extracted from sea snails. Their cosmopolitan style is evident from their cities which have been excavated, including Tyre, Sidon, Ugarit, Gebal, and certain levels at Ashdod. They provided essential aid to Solomon in the building of the temple of Yahweh in Jerusalem. In time their territory was taken over by the Persians, and later by Alexander the Great. In hellenistic times, shrines, theaters, baths, and other manifestations of Greek culture were erected in cities along the coast and in Galilee but also in such traditional centers as Samaria, Jericho, and Jerusalem.

5. Syria

Instead of modest hills and low mountains, as in Palestine, southern Syria is divided by a twin range of very high mountains, known in modern times as Lebanon and Anti-Lebanon, that reach elevations of more than 9,000 feet. Between these formidable ranges lies the Beqaa, a lofty valley where shrines to various deities have been erected from early times. The Beqaa rises in the north to a plateau 8,100 feet above sea level. The road linking Damascus and Beirut crosses the Beqaa farther south at an elevation of more than 5,000 feet. These ranges are the source of the water that forms the Litani River to the south and feeds the Orontes to the north. The Litani Valley is fertile, whereas the Orontes flows through more barren territory, reaching the sea at the point where the hellenistic rulers of Syria in the third century B.C.E. built the city of Antioch. Damascus is on the eastern side of the Lebanon range and was a major center of hellenistic culture in the same period that Antioch was the capital of Syria.

The coast of Syria varies from the sandy beaches around Tyre in the south to the more rugged coast between Beirut and Tripoli to the rocky cliffs and headlands north of Latakia. The northeastern limits of Syria are formed by the Taurus Mountains, which extend eastward from Turkey. A narrow coastal strip at Issus alone provides access from the east to Tarsus and the upland country of Asia Minor. The northwestern sections of Syria are part of the broad valley of the Euphrates, which rises in the mountains north of Syria to begin its long, slow flow into the Persian Gulf. A triangular section historically linked with Syria reaches across the Euphrates to its twin stream, the Tigris, farther to the north and east. On the eastern border, which is marked by lower mountain ranges stretching north and east from beyond Damascus, one of the chief cities is Palmyra. South and east of Damascus is the rocky, volcanic region known as the Hauran, which reaches its highest point in the mountain known since Islamic times as Jebel Druse (5,900 feet). Eastward from this section is the Arabian Desert. The major trade routes from the east followed the course of the twin rivers from Mesopotamia, passing through the valleys of Syria on the way to Palestine and Egypt.

Baalbek. Located in a valley in what is now eastern Lebanon, Baalbek was a center for the worship of the Near Eastern fertility god Baal. In Hellenistic times the deity honored there was Helios, the god of the sun, and the city became known as Heliopolis. The Romans under Augustus established a Roman colony and garrison there, and Antoninus Pius (reigned 138–61 C.E.) launched the construction of a great temple to Jupiter Heliopolitanus, which was not completed until the reign of Caracalla (211–17). Some of the enormous stones in the surrounding wall measure more than 60 × 14 × 11 feet. In the sixth century the great court of the temple was converted into a church.

H. C. Kee

Ziggurat at Ur. Given the lack of mountains in the Tigris–Euphrates Valley, this mass of clay was erected to serve as a high place where the god could be worshiped appropriately. The pottery jars were embedded in the sides of the structure for purposes of decoration but also to offset erosion. The shrine proper was located at the top of the edifice, which dates from the fourth millennium B.C.E.

University Museum, University of Pennsylvania

6. Mesopotamia

This term refers to the land that lies between the Tigris and Euphrates Rivers in the central part of modern Iraq. This region can be divided into three distinct sections: (1) the desert area south and west of the line at which the desert plain drops off to form the valley of the Euphrates; (2) the central lowland, which includes the area between the rivers and the delta at the point where the rivers join, from which the combined stream flows into the Persian Gulf; (3) the land north and east of the Tigris that extends up to the mountain ranges of Turkey in the north and Persia in the south.

The central lowland itself is divided into three different segments: (1) the northern part, south of the Turkish mountains and largely desert; (2) the plain along the northern Tigris (which extends to the foot of the Persian mountains), where Assyria rose to a place of dominance in the Middle East; (3) the well-watered section of the valley, beginning north of Baghdad and reaching down toward the gulf. In the biblical period, the center of power shifted back and forth from the cities of the lower valley (Ur, Nippur, Babylon) to those in the Assyrian plain (Asshur and Nineveh). This region of the ancient world formed the natural link, culturally and economically, between the civilizations of the Mediterranean region and those to the south and east along the Indian Ocean. The history of Israel is involved with this part of the world from the times of the patriarchs, when Abraham came from Ur, through the experience of the Babylonian exile, to the development of the Babylonian Talmud in the second to sixth centuries of our era.

7. Persia

The area known in modern times as Iran, and in earlier days as Persia, includes four topographical regions: (1) The so-called Zagros fold consists of a series of mountain ranges reaching from the area west of the lower end of the Caspian Sea, southward and eastward above the valley of the Tigris, along a series of lower mountains extending eastward along the Arabian Sea to the borders of India. (2) The northern highlands overlook the Caspian Sea from the south; between these peaks (which reach elevations of 18,000 feet) and the sea is a plain varying in width from 70 to 10 miles. It is the best-watered part of Iran and is now the most densely populated. (3) The eastern mountains are barren and subject to violent wind- and sandstorms. They form part of the range which includes the Himalayas to the east. (4) The central plateau includes some high mountains and many lakes, some of which have dried up. Across it are strings of oases, so that travel in this region was relatively simple even in antiquity. It was in the area where this plateau adjoins the southern stretch of the mountains that Darius built his capital city, known as Persepolis, in 515 B.C.E. The tribes that lived in these regions were numerous and competitive. Among those which rose to the dominant position in the biblical period were the Persians, the Medes, and the Parthians. Their rise and fall and those of the Mesopotamian powers – and later of the Greek and Roman powers – were interconnected. Probably certain features of Persian religion influenced biblical religion as well.

8.   Asia Minor (Anatolia)

Asia Minor, or Anatolia, is a huge peninsula more or less rectangular in shape, extending about 900 miles east and west and 300 miles north and south. It covers roughly the same territory as modern Turkey. It is bounded on the north by the Black Sea, on the south by the eastern Mediterranean, and on the west by the Aegean Sea, which separates it from the mainland of Greece. The central part of the land consists of a plateau, which averages 3,000 feet above sea level and is surrounded on each side by mountains, which slope sharply down to the sea on the west and south. On the east, they form a great natural barrier extending from the southern border with Syria up to the area between the Black and Caspian Seas.

The Black Sea coast is about 750 miles long, most of which consists of a narrow strip of irregular width between the sea and the mountains. In some areas, however, there are fertile valleys and forests. Here were located a number of provinces that figure in the literature of the Roman Empire and of early Christianity, including Bithynia, Pontus, and Paphlagonia. Western Anatolia is an area that slopes upward from the sea to the central plateau. In the western part of the central plateau was the province of Galatia, named for the Celtic people who had migrated there from western Europe. Along the western coast of Anatolia there are deep indentations, where many natural harbors were developed into important commercial centers. Parts of the west coast consist of fertile valleys and plains, with the result that many of the important cities of Asia Minor arose in this part of the land. The mountain peaks range in height from 5,000 to 8,000 feet. One of the most fertile sections is near Pergamum, which was an important center politically. It was also significant religiously, in that it was one of the centers for honoring the healing god Asklepios, as well as a major location for divine honors to the Roman emperor.

Cilician Gates. Cilicia is a district in southeastern Asia Minor that includes the southern section of the Taurus Mountains and the hills and plain reaching down to the Mediterranean coast. The great highway that led from the western part of Asia Minor and the central Anatolian plateau to Syria passed through the rock-lined Cydnus River valley, which was known as the Cilician Gates. Nearby on the Cilician Plain was the city of Tarsus, important for commercial and military (especially naval) activities and a major intellectual center for Stoic philosophy. Acts 9:11, 21:39, and 22:3 identify Paul as a citizen of Tarsus.

H. C. Kee

The steep Taurus Mountains to the east of Anatolia extend northeast from the seacoast and form the natural boundaries with Syria, Mesopotamia, and Iran. The rugged ranges, cut by steep valleys and winding rivers, rise to peaks of around 13,000 feet. From the Anatolian plateau, an ancient route leads southward to the sea, through a valley long known as the Cilician Gates. To the south lies a coastal plain, on which was located the city of Tarsus, which served as a major center for Greek philosophical study in the Greco-Roman period. Just to the east is the narrow coastal plain of Issus, where Alexander defeated the Persians and began his conquest of the lands from Egypt to India.

Links with Europe were made easy by the narrow stretches of water which pass through the Bosporus and the Dardanelles, where the Black Sea empties into the Mediterranean. To the southeast of this isthmus lay the cities of Troy and Ephesus. To the west was to rise Constantinople, from which in the fourth century Constantine tried in vain to join the eastern and western segments of the former Roman Empire.

9.   Greek Lands

Of the various ethnic and cultural regions into which Greece was divided in antiquity, the following are significant for our purposes: Thrace, Macedonia, Illyrica, and Achaia.

Thrace, which included the area west of the Dardanelles and the Black Sea that now comprises northeastern Greece and parts of western Turkey, Bulgaria, and Romania, was separated from the rest of Greece by a range of mountains, which established its southern limits. The southern sections of Greece seem to have regarded the Thracians as little more civilized than barbarians, as contrasted with the sophisticated culture of Athens and its surrounding region.

Macedonia included parts of northern Greece bordering Thrace, but

Oracle at Delphi. A famous temple and oracle of Apollo were located in Delphi, six miles north of the Gulf of Corinth. According to legend, Apollo slew Pytho, a female snake who was probably the earth goddess, at Delphi. From all over the world came seekers, whose questions to the god had to be submitted in writing. The messages from the god were given by priestesses (called Pythians) who, after having chewed sacred leaves and drunk from the spring that was channeled into the temple, sat on the sacred tripod. When the priestess had uttered the god's response, it was edited and put in verse form by the resident prophets and holy men affiliated with the oracle.
H. C. Kee

it extended to the Adriatic Sea in the west. Its terrain consisted of mountain ranges, valleys, and plateaus, with the Via Egnatia crossing through it to the Adriatic. This highway was of major importance militarily and commercially in the Roman period. Macedonia was the home of Philip, the monarch who took over Greece and the Greek cities of Anatolia in the fourth century B.C.E., and of his even more famous son, Alexander. Plains line the rivers that flow in Macedonia, so the region was well suited for agriculture. Its cities included Thessalonica, Neapolis (modern Cavalla), and (in ancient times) Philippi, named for the local monarch.

The center for the Eleusinian Mysteries, reconstruction. Located about 14 miles west of Athens overlooking the bay, Eleusis was famed as the locus of the enactment of mysteries in the Hall of Initiation (Telesterion). The myth on which these ceremonies were based told how Hades, the god of the underworld, had taken to that region Kore, the daughter of Demeter, the goddess of grain. During her sorrowing search for her daughter, the fertility of the earth languished. On finding her, Demeter learned that her daughter had eaten some seeds in the underworld and therefore could never be wholly free from that place. The compromise was that she would spend half of each year with her mother and half with her captor. The enactment of the myth in dance and drama was understood as ensuring the fertility of the crops but also as providing the initiates assurance of participation in the life of the world to come.

Department of Archaeology, Bryn Mawr College

West of Macedonia lay Illyrica (or Illyricum), which included part of what is now known as northwestern Greece, Albania, and southwestern Yugoslavia. The western terminus of the Via Egnatia was located in Illyrica. Excavations in this region show the extent and high level of Greek civilization there.

The main part of modern Greece, including the Peloponnesus, was known in Roman times as Achaia. Its upper limits began south of Thessalonica and Epirus. It included two major cities: Athens and Corinth. Athens was of major cultural importance, as represented by the philosophical schools of Plato and Aristotle which arose there. But it was also significant religiously, since it was the seat of Athena, and within the province were the centers of devotion to Apollo (at Delphi), to Dionysus (at Eleusis, just west of Athens), and to Asklepios, whose healing shrine was at Epidauros not far from Corinth. Corinth was of major economic importance, since it sat astride the narrow neck of land that connects the mainland of Greece with the Peloponnesus and thus was the channel through which much of the east–west trade passed in the Mediterranean. It was famous in classical times for the shrine of the fertility goddess Aphrodite, which was located on a mountain just outside the city.

10. Major Mediterranean Islands

The following islands are mentioned in the biblical narratives: from east to west, Cyprus, Crete, Malta, and Sicily. Cyprus lies south of Anatolia and west of Syria. It is 140 miles long and 60 miles at the widest point. Two prongs project eastward from the main part of the island; between these lies Salamis, the principal city of the island in ancient times. The terrain ranges from the sandy beaches to the southwestern mountains, which reach a height of 6,500 feet. The forests which covered the island in ancient times have now largely disappeared. Paul and other apostles and apostolic associates paid visits to the island or had connections there.

Crete lies off mainland Greece and is 160 miles long and ranges from 7 to 36 miles in width. The northern coast is indented with what form natural harbors, whereas the southern coast has none. Near the southernmost point of the island is a small harbor, known as Fair Havens, where Paul's ship is reported to have stopped briefly on his journey to Rome (Acts 27:8).

Malta is a group of small islands, the chief of which measures 17 by 9 miles. Most of the coast of this island is lined with steep cliffs, but there are some bays to the east, one of which is traditionally linked with Paul. The hills are no more than 750 feet high, and there are no rivers or lakes on the island.

Just off the southern tip of Italy lies Sicily. The strait between them is only two miles wide. Much of the main island consists of a plateau about 900 feet above the sea. But Mount Etna, an active volcano, rises to more than 10,000 feet. Sections of the island are well watered by springs and streams. The island early became a center of Greek culture and continued to participate in this culture, even though in the fifth century B.C.E. it was taken over by the Carthaginians, who originated on the coast of North Africa. By the late third century, Sicily was under Roman control.

11.   Italy

The great peninsula of Italy extends from the Alps southward more than 700 miles into the Mediterranean. The central part of the peninsula is dominated by the Apennine Mountains, of which the watershed is closer to the Adriatic on the east than to the sea on the west. The peaks range from 4,000 to 9,500 feet in height. Among the rivers flowing to the west from this ridge, the best known is the Tiber, on which Rome is located, and which flows into the sea at the port of Ostia, about 15 miles southwest of Rome.

The Tiber in Rome. Rising in the Apennines at an elevation of more than 4,000 feet above sea level, the Tiber flows about 250 miles through ravines and valleys until it crosses the plain where Rome is situated on its way to the sea. From prehistoric times, silt has extended the land at its mouth to form the coastal plain. Emperor Claudius opened another mouth for the river by building a canal at Fiumicino.

H. C. Kee

More than one hundred miles south of Rome two mountain ranges branch out from the main ridge and extend to the sea, forming the Bay of Naples and the Bay of Salerno. Overlooking the Bay of Naples is Mount Vesuvius, and near the base of the mountain are the ruins of Pompei and Herculaneum, both destroyed when the volcano erupted in the late first century C.E. The peninsula branches into two smaller parts, representing what are commonly known as the heel and toe of the boot of Italy. On the heel lies Brundisium (Brindisi), which was a major port for trade to and from the eastern Mediterranean and was the southern terminus of the Appian Way, the major north–south highway in Italy.

BIBLIOGRAPHICAL ESSAY

In the two centuries before and the two after the turn of the eras, the literature now known as the Bible was brought together – some of it to constitute the Jewish scriptures and the rest to form what came to be known as the New Testament. To understand these writings it is essential to be informed about the historical developments, the geographical and ethnic settings, and the changing cultural features of the contexts in which these documents – and others akin to them – were produced.

Excellent surveys of the lands of the Bible in terms of historical developments there are Yohanan Aharoni, *The Land of the Bible: A Historical Geography,* rev. and enl. ed. (Philadelphia: Westminster, 1979); and John Rogerson, *Atlas of the Bible* (Oxford: Equinox, 1985; repr., 1987). For a fine summary of archeological finds illuminating biblical history, see Jerome Murphy-O'Connor, *The Holy Land: An Archaeological Guide from Earliest Times to 1700* (Oxford and New York: Oxford University Press, 1992). Useful studies of the history of Israel include John Bright, *A History of Israel* (Philadelphia: Westminster, 1981); J. Alberto Soggin, *A History of Ancient Israel: From the Beginnings to the Bar Kochba Revolt, A.D. 135* (Philadelphia: Westminster, 1985); and the comprehensive, multivolume work *The Cambridge Ancient History,* vol. 1, pts. 1 and 2, *Early History of the Middle East* (Cambridge: Cambridge University Press, 1980); vol. 2, pt. 1, *The Middle East and the Aegean Region, 1800–1350 B.C.* (1973); vol. 2, pt. 2, *The Middle East, 1350–1000 B.C.* (1975); vol. 3, pt. 2, *The Assyrian and Babylonian Empires, 8th to 6th Centuries* (1991); vol. 4, *Persia, Greece, and the Western Mediterranean* (1988).

Broad studies of ancient religions, including those of the ancient Near East, are Mircea Eliade, *The Sacred and the Profane: The Nature of Religion* (New York: Harper Torchbook, 1961); Rudolf Otto, *The Idea of the Holy,* 2d ed., trans. J. W. Harvey (London: Oxford University Press, 1950); and Helmer Ringgren, *Religions of the Ancient Near East,* trans. J. Sturdy (Philadelphia: Westminster, 1973).

The finest available set of translations of texts from the ancient Near East is that of James B. Pritchard, *Ancient Near Eastern Texts Relating to the Old Testament,* 3d ed. (Princeton: Princeton University Press, 1978), to which was added a volume of pictures, *Ancient Near East in Pictures with Supplement* (Princeton: Princeton University Press, 1969). Abbreviated editions were published by Princeton University Press in paperback in 1975.

A comprehensive study of the Jewish scriptures, including extensive bibliography, is Berhard W. Anderson, *Understanding the Old Testament* (Englewood Cliffs, N.J.: Prentice-Hall, 1986); the British edition is *The Living World of the Old Testament* (Essex, U.K.: Longman Group, 1988). Two very different approaches to this literature are those of Brevard S. Childs, *Introduction to the Old Testament as Scripture* (Minneapolis: Augsburg-Fortress, 1979), and Norman K. Gottwald, *The Hebrew Bible: A Socio-literary Introduction* (Philadelphia: Fortress Press, 1985). For a fine survey of critical scholarly methods for the study of the Hebrew scriptures, see Douglas A. Knight and Gene M. Tucker, eds., *The Hebrew Bible and Its Modern Interpreters* (Philadelphia: Fortress Press, 1985).

In the period following the return of the Jews from exile in Babylon, the dominant cultural and political impact on them was from the Persian and then the hellenistic and Roman rulers who controlled Palestine: first the Ptolemies of Egypt, then the Seleucids of Syria, and finally the Romans. The period from the exile to the first Jewish revolt against the Romans is surveyed in the essays found in John H. Hayes and J. Maxwell Miller, eds., *Israelite and Judaean History* (Philadelphia: Westminster; London: SCM Press, 1977). Details of developments within Judaism in the latter period are offered in E. Schürer, *The History of the Jewish People in the Age of Jesus Christ (175 B.C.–A.D. 135,* 3 vols. (Edinburgh: T. & T. Clark, 1973–87).

Introductions to the Jewish literature produced in the postexilic period are offered in George Nickelsburg and Robert A. Kraft, eds., *Jewish Literature between the Bible and the Mishnah* (Philadelphia: Fortress Press, 1981; London: SCM Press, 1981). A survey of scholarly assessment of that literature and of historical reconstructions of the period is available in G. W. Nickelsburg and R. A. Kraft, eds., *Early Judaism and Its Modern Interpreters* (Atlanta: Scholars Press, 1985). A perceptive study of the origins of apocalyptic – the Jewish phenomenon that was to have a significant impact on the origins of Christianity – is Paul D. Hanson, *The Dawn of Apocalyptic* (Philadelphia: Fortress Press, 1975). A fine translation of the Dead Sea Scrolls is Geza Vermes, *The Dead Sea Scrolls in English,* 3d ed. (London: Penguin, 1987). Jacob Neusner has produced scores of writings on the origins and development of rabbinic Judaism, but his early study of the origins of the Pharisees offered a major insight concerning the context of early Christianity and has had an enduring and widespread impact: *From Politics to Piety: The Emergence of Pharisaic Judaism* (Englewood Cliffs, N.J.: Prentice-Hall, 1973). Translations and analyses of noncanonical Jewish writings from the period before and after the turn of the eras are offered in my introductions and annotations in H. C. Kee, ed., *Cambridge Annotated Study Apocrypha* (Cambridge: Cambridge University Press, 1994), and in J. H. Charlesworth, ed., *The Old Testament Pseudepigrapha,* 2 vols. (New York: Doubleday, 1983–5).

PART ONE

THE OLD TESTAMENT WORLD

Eric M. Meyers and John W. Rogerson

I. THE WORLD OF THE ANCESTORS (GENESIS THROUGH DEUTERONOMY)

A. THE WORLD OF THE WRITERS, THE WORLD OF THE WRITING, AND THE WORLD OF THE MODERN INTERPRETER: THE ORAL TRADITION AND THE DOCUMENTARY HYPOTHESIS

The first five books of the Bible describe the creation of the world (Gen. 1–2) and the history of earliest mankind, including the destruction of the world by a flood, before beginning the story of Israel's ancestors with the call of Abraham to come to the land of Canaan (Gen. 12). The story continues with the lives of Isaac and Jacob and how the latter's twelve sons went to Egypt and, after their descendants had become a sizable people, how they were forced into slavery by a pharaoh. Moses, a Hebrew brought up at the Egyptian court, leads the Hebrews out of slavery and through the wilderness of Sinai to the threshold of Canaan. On the way he gives to the people a set of civil, religious, and ceremonial laws that identify the Hebrews as the people of Yahweh, the God who first called Abraham and who delivered the Hebrews from slavery. Deuteronomy is the address of Moses to the people as they stand poised to cross the river Jordan and take possession of Canaan, the land promised to Abraham and his descendants.

Until two hundred years ago scholars believed that the history contained in these books was accurate, and that its science (the accounts of the creation of the world) could be shown to be in harmony with the findings of modern science. Its geography, as implied in the description of the peoples of the world (Gen. 10), had been shown to be inadequate by the voyages of discovery from the fifteenth and sixteenth centuries onward, and such a shrewd interpreter as Calvin had argued that Genesis 1 did not teach modern physics and astronomy but described the creation of the earth for the benefit of ancient Hebrew observers, who knew nothing about modern science. In spite of this, arguments about the accuracy of the Genesis cosmology raged among theologians for much of the nineteenth century.

In Old Testament scholarship, two discussions in particular that began in the late eighteenth century set the agenda for interpreting the Books of Genesis through Deuteronomy today: when and how were these books written, and how do they relate to stories about the creation and Flood similar to those in Genesis that are known to us from Israel's neighbors in the ancient world? The question about ancient Near Eastern stories similar to those in Genesis will be discussed in section B. The remainder of this section will deal with when and how the Books of Genesis through Deuteronomy were written.

Given that writing, albeit in very rudimentary form, was invented in the fourth millennium B.C.E., and that by 2500 B.C.E. writing systems were sophisticated enough to record laws and narratives, it would have been possible in theory for the stories of the Hebrews, from Abraham onward, to have been written down at the time. Abraham lived, in a conservative critical view, about 1750 B.C.E. However, the fact that writing existed did not mean that it was widely used. In particular, until the invention of the alphabet, literacy involved the ability to write and read hundreds of different signs, and it was a skill confined to a small profession in the service of rulers and temples.

The invention of the alphabet around 1500 B.C.E. reduced the number of signs needed for writing from hundreds to around thirty; and as the alphabet used for writing Hebrew developed, it made do with twenty-two signs. This obviously meant that literacy could be acquired very much more easily than before, and that it need not be confined to a small professional class. However, the simplification of writing resulting from the invention of the alphabet did not bring an increase in literacy, for the reason that ordinary people only

Egyptian scribes at work, from the tomb of Mereruka at Saqqara. Village headmen are depicted being brought before local tax officials and flogged at a whipping post for nonpayment of taxes. The scribes record the evidence.

ON THE ORIGIN OF WRITING

WRITING PROBABLY BEGAN as a way of recording economic activity or establishing ownership. The earliest attempts, appearing around the middle of the fourth millennium B.C.E., were pictographic. As scripts developed, they became ideographic; that is, a word-sign came to represent a whole range of ideas.

Sumerian is the oldest language important for Old Testament study. The Sumerians invented a pictographic cuneiform script sometime before 3000 B.C.E. Cuneiform (meaning "wedge shaped," from the shapes created on wet clay with a stylus) evolved from a pictographic script into a system of about one thousand ideographic and syllabic phonetic signs and became the principal writing system of the ancient Near East. It was adopted by the Akkadians, another Mesopotamian people, in the third millennium B.C.E. By the fourteenth century B.C.E., their language, Akkadian, had become the lingua franca of the ancient Near Eastern world and was used, along with their cuneiform script, by such diverse peoples as Elamites, Hittites, Hurrians, and Urartians. Ugaritic, a very early dialect of the Northwest Semitic family of languages (to which Hebrew belongs), was also written with cuneiform signs, but it was an alphabetic, rather than a syllabic script and was written with, originally, about twenty-nine signs.

Cuneiform was particularly suited to the Mesopotamian area because its characters were easily inscribed on tablets and cylinders made from the region's abundant clay. After being inscribed, the moist clay was sun- or oven-dried to harden and preserve it. Stone was in short supply, however, so only important records merited inscription on commemorative monuments (known as stelae). Many letters, business documents, and literary texts relevant to Old Testament study exist in cuneiform.

Ancient Egypt used hieroglyphics rather than cuneiform as its writing system. Hieroglyphs were essentially pictographic. There were about 700 Egyptian hieroglyphs, although they were not all in simultaneous use. These characters were inscribed in stone on numerous pyramids, tombs, obelisks, and temples from as early as 3000 B.C.E. The papyrus plant, which grew freely in the Nile Valley, was easily prepared for writing, and texts written on this medium were well preserved by Egypt's arid climate. Egyptian hieroglyphics had a seminal influence on the development of the Semitic alphabet (see sidebar on facing page).

Both the Egyptian and Mesopotamian writing systems eventually utilized the principle of phonetization. Pictures or wedge shapes came to represent phonetic syllables (consonant + vowel or vice versa). From there developed alphabetic writing systems, in which one symbol stood for one consonant or vowel.

(facing page, bottom) Origins of the Hebrew script and language.

Courtesy of E. Isaac, Institute of Semitic Studies, Princeton, N.J.

rarely needed to write things down and could employ professional scribes when they had such needs. Written documents recorded such things as the ownership and sale of land and adoptions of children, that is, legal matters. There was no writing for popular consumption and entertainment. The main use of writing still lay with rulers and temples, and written records were reserved for treaties and correspondence between rulers, laws, accounts and inventories, reigns and notable deeds of rulers, and sacred texts. The needs of ordinary people for entertainment were met by storytellers, who preserved oral accounts of heroes of the past and who recounted them vividly for their audiences. Oral tradition will be discussed later in this section. For the moment the important question is when the stories about Abraham and his descendants began to be written down. This question has two parts: when were conditions in Israel favorable for the writing down of traditions, and what can be deduced from Genesis–Deuteronomy about their time and mode of writing?

FIRST ALPHABET, FIRST SCRIPTS

THE FIRST ALPHABETIC script appeared in Syria–Palestine around the middle of the second millennium B.C.E. The earliest known alphabetic inscriptions were found in the ancient Egyptian turquoise-mining town of Serabit el Khadim in the Sinai peninsula. In these so-called proto-Sinaitic inscriptions, each pictographic sign represented the consonant with which the object it symbolized began. This ingenious development doomed the elaborate writing systems of Egypt and Mesopotamia to obscurity, for a system of thirty or fewer signs ultimately made writing accessible to ordinary men and women. The art of writing was no longer necessarily confined to professional scribes with extensive training.

These very early symbols evolved into the proto-Canaanite (or Old Canaanite) script. By 1200 B.C.E. the letters had been simplified and were more abstract than pictorial. Their names and order had been established by the fourteenth century B.C.E. By the mid-eleventh century the twenty-two letters, their individual forms, and the direction in which they were written had also been stabilized. This proto-Canaanite script received its classic expression in the Phoenician alphabet of the Early Iron Age (ca. 1000 B.C.E.).

From either this Phoenician script or its proto-Canaanite precursor were developed the great national scripts of Hebrew, used by the Israelites who occupied Palestine, and Aramaic, the national language of the Assyrian kingdoms. The national scripts of Moab, Ammon, and Edom are closely related to the Hebrew of this early period, although they were influenced heavily by Aramaic in later centuries. The Greeks also borrowed the Phoenician alphabet, which they had fully adapted to the needs of their own language by the ninth century B.C.E.

By the ninth century B.C.E., Aramaic, Hebrew's linguistic cousin, had become the diplomatic and commercial language of Syria–Palestine. After the termination of ancient Israel's political existence in 587 B.C.E., Hebrew gradually came to be used only as a language of scholarship and liturgy. The archaic Hebrew characters in which much of the Old Testament was probably first written also fell gradually under the influence of Aramaic script.

The Semitic Background of Our Alphabet

LATIN (ENGLISH)	ORIGINAL NAME	GRAPHIC PICTURE	EARLIEST KNOWN FORMS	SOUTH SEMITIC (SABAEAN)	MODERN ETHIOPIC	N. WEST SEMITIC (EARLY HEBREW)	PHOENICIAN	MID-EARLY GREEK	ARAMAIC (MODERN HEBREW)	ARABIC
A	'alf	ox-head								
B	bēt	house								
C, G	gaml	throw-stick								
D	dāg	fish								
E	hē	man calling								
U, V, W	waw	mace								
Z	zēn	?								
H	ḥēt	fence								
I, J, Y	yad	hand w/closed fist								
K	kapp	palm								
L	lamd	ox-goad (whip)								
M	maym	water (waves)								
N	naḥāš	snake								
O	'ayin	eye								
F, P	pēh	mouth/corner								
Q	qu (p-)	?								
R	ra's	head								
S, X	tann	composite bow								
T	taw	cross-marker								

The early Israelites adopted the Canaanite alphabetic script, shown here on a schoolboy's calendar incised on a tablet found at Gezer. This is the earliest Hebrew text of significant length and records the seasons of the year and the agricultural activities associated with them.

Biblical Archaeology Slides, no. 113

1.   The Documentary Hypothesis

By the end of the eighteenth century, the theory had emerged that the opening books of the Bible were based upon two sources: an earlier source that used the divine name 'elohim (God) and a later source that used the name Yahweh. A major breakthrough occurred early in the nineteenth century when W. M. L. de Wette argued that Deuteronomy was not only the lawbook discovered in the temple in 622 B.C.E. (see 2 Kings 22:8–10), but that it could have been written only in the seventh century B.C.E. The identification of Deuteronomy as the discovered lawbook was not new. What was new was the seventh-century dating and the argument on which it rested. De Wette pointed out that whereas Deuteronomy commands that sacrifice to God must be offered only at a single sanctuary (see Deut. 12:4–14), Israelite leaders such as Samuel (ca. 1030 B.C.E.) used a number of sanctuaries. He concluded that the single-sanctuary command in Deuteronomy was an innovation in the time of Josiah (622 B.C.E.) and that prior to the seventh century there had been no restrictions on where sacrifice could be offered.

If Deuteronomy, which commanded a single sanctuary, was composed in the seventh century, it followed that the stories that described Abraham and Jacob building altars at sanctuaries such as Shechem, Bethel, and Mamre were written before the seventh century. A relative dating of the sources began to be established. In the second half of the nineteenth century attention was focused on what was believed to be the oldest document, that which used the divine name 'elohim and contained much of the priestly legislation. Scholars such as the missionary bishop J. W. Colenso (1814–83) and the Dutch professor Abraham Kuenen (1828–91) carried out the fundamental researches that enabled the German scholar Julius Wellhausen (1844–1918) to demonstrate the comparative lateness of the priestly material and to set this in the context of a view of the history of Israelite religion that owed much to de Wette and Kuenen.

According to Wellhausen's synthesis, first proposed in 1878, the Books of Genesis through Deuteronomy are based upon four documents. Documents J (which uses the divine name Yahweh) and E (which uses 'elohim) were written during the monarchy (tenth to eighth centuries B.C.E.) when Israelites sacrificed at local sanctuaries. This type of religion is implied in these documents and in the Books of Samuel. Deuteronomy (D) is associated with Josiah's reformation in the late seventh century. The reform closed all the sanctuaries save for that in Jerusalem and reformulated some of the laws in J and E in the light of the centralization of sacrifice and worship in Jerusalem. The document containing the priestly traditions (P) was written during and after the exile in the sixth to fifth centuries B.C.E. Its stress on the details of ritual and sacrifice developed what had begun with Deuteronomy, when the first attempts were made to regulate the free and spontaneous worship implied in J and E. Wellhausen's synthesis, called the documentary hypothesis, begged many questions; for example, it assumed that spontaneous worship was earlier than

IBN EZRA, EARLY CRITIC OF THE PENTATEUCH

BEFORE THE ADVENT OF historical-critical study of the Bible in the late eighteenth century, the dominant belief in both synagogue and church was that Moses had been the author of the entire Pentateuch. This belief is first reflected in the New Testament (Matt. 19:7, Mark 12:26, Acts 15:21, Rom. 10:5). The tradition of Mosaic authorship, however, has its roots in the Hebrew Bible itself, where Moses is often credited with having written down the divine revelation in order to explain it before the people (Exod. 24:4; Num. 33:2; Deut. 31:9, 24). In later Old Testament works Moses is also considered an important figure in the transmission of Israel's law (Mal. 3:22, 2 Chron. 25:4, Ezra 3:2).

The first real criticism of the notion of Mosaic authorship came in a veiled remark in a commentary on Deuteronomy by the eleventh-century Spanish rabbi Abraham Ibn Ezra. Ibn Ezra pointed to five instances in the Torah (the Pentateuch) that clearly seemed to be post-Mosaic additions or expansions – the account of Moses' own death and burial in Deuteronomy 34 being the most obvious instance. He also correctly noted that the mention of the "mount of Yahweh" (i.e., the temple mount in Jerusalem) in the story of Isaac's binding (Gen. 22:14) is anachronistic because the temple did not exist before King Solomon's time.

The task of exploring the full ramifications of Ibn Ezra's critical observations fell to subsequent generations. No one ventured along the challenging path he charted until scholars began employing the new critical skills forged in the Enlightenment. His work is, however, evidence of the close, careful study of Scripture in the Jewish–Christian tradition, which seeks to understand the complicated process by which the Bible came into being. Nineteenth-century scholars took Ibn Ezra's lead and continued to note anachronisms, repetitions, discrepancies, and different styles and linguistic usages in the Pentateuch. From their observations emerged modern theories about the formation of the Pentateuch, especially the widely held documentary hypothesis in both its general and its more nuanced expressions.

THE DOCUMENTARY HYPOTHESIS

FROM THE LATE NINETEENTH century until today, a broad consensus has existed among students of the Old Testament concerning the compositional history of the Pentateuch. Based on careful analysis of the text, scholars believe the Five Books of Moses to be an editorial compilation of four distinct sources, usually labeled in their chronological order as J, E, D, and P.

The abbreviation J denotes the so-called Yahwistic source (after the German spelling *Jahveh*), which has its basis in the traditions of the southern kingdom of Judah and dates from about 950 B.C.E. The Elohistic source (E) is closely interwoven with J, though it betrays special concerns of its own. The E source is particularly aligned with concerns of the northern kingdom of Israel, and scholars assign it a date of ca. 750 B.C.E. The letter D stands for Deuteronomy. The Deuteronomistic source is limited in the Pentateuch to the book from which its name is derived. It is associated (at least in part) with the work found in the temple at Jerusalem during the last quarter of the seventh century B.C.E., which served as the basis of the reforms of King Josiah (2 Kings 22). The Pentateuch's priestly source is designated P and makes up the largest portion of the Pentateuch. It dates in its present form to around 550 B.C.E. and is concerned with traditions of Israel's cultic worship.

These Pentateuchal strands are no longer thought to represent discrete, unified documents as they were when this theory was first formulated. The history of any one of these four major streams of tradition may well be as complicated as the history of the Pentateuch as a whole. Scholars disagree about the exact extent and influence of each source. However, the "JEDP" hypothesis provides a conceptual framework that accounts for the broad patterns and developmental history of the complicated literature in the Pentateuch.

worship whose ritual was carefully prescribed. These questions are not our concern at present, however. What is important is that Wellhausen established a framework for the identification and dating of the sources of Genesis–Deuteronomy which, in spite of much criticism and modification, is still massively influential. It entails that the stories about Abraham, Isaac, and Jacob, the Exodus from Egypt, and the journey of the Hebrews to Canaan were first put into something like the written form we know no earlier than the tenth to ninth centuries B.C.E., that most of Deuteronomy was written in the seventh century, and that the final form of the whole as we know it was not completed until the sixth to fifth centuries.

2. The Sociology of the Composition of Genesis–Deuteronomy

The Wellhausen synthesis assumes that the first writing down of parts of Genesis–Deuteronomy was done in the tenth to ninth centuries B.C.E. A widely held view is that, from the time of David and Solomon (tenth century), the conditions existed in Jerusalem to make the writing down of traditions possible and likely. As rulers of a small empire, David and Solomon needed a group of literate administrators. These were most likely recruited from Egypt initially, but probably one of their duties was to establish a school for training Israelite scribes.

This view has recently been challenged by scholars who hold that there is no archeological evidence for a small Davidic–Solomonic empire, and that there was thus no need for a scribal school. An excellent statement of this opinion is that of P. R. Davies, who argues that the sociological conditions for the growth of Hebrew literature did not exist until after the exile (i.e., after 587/6 B.C.E.). He dates many of the stories with which we are concerned in this section to the Persian period (sixth to fourth centuries B.C.E.).

The most important recent work in this area is that of D. W. Jamieson-Drake (1991). He has produced computer-generated models for a number of important indices which show the extent to which Judah was a centralized state during the monarchy and thus needed a scribal-based administration. The indices include location of settlements and land use, the number of public works, the extent of literacy, and the distribution of luxury items. In each case, Jamieson-Drake's bar charts show a dramatic increase in these indices in the eighth century compared with previous centuries, an increase sustained or exceeded in the seventh century and followed by a dramatic decline in the sixth century.

A minimal conclusion from these findings is that all the conditions for scribal schools and literacy existed in eighth-century Judah, and that the time of Hezekiah (ca. 727–698 B.C.E.) is a likely one for such activities. Can we push back to the time of Solomon? We can if we assume the correctness of the biblical tradition that Solomon built a temple and palace in Jerusalem (not to mention other fortifications in the land) using foreign and forced labor. Accounts would have had to be kept and labor organized. Even if he did not preside over a small empire, Solomon would have needed an in-house group of literate administrators, and thus the conditions for the beginnings of Israelite literature would have existed even if they made only a small impact upon the indices used in Jamieson-Drake's study.

This brings us back to the tenth century as a possible time when traditions about Israel's ancestors were first written down. Even so, the gap between the tenth century and the time when the first ancestors may be presumed to have lived is enormous.

On the Bible's own chronology (1 Kings 6:1, Exod. 12:40–1), Abraham lived around 1950 B.C.E. Conservative critical estimates have suggested 1750–1450 B.C.E. Even if we take the lowest figure, 1450, we still have a gap of over 450 years between the time of Abraham and the writing down of stories about him. We need to ask ourselves how much we know about what was happening in our own countries 450 years ago, when we have the advantage of written records and history books about the time. On the other hand, many readers of this book have no experience of living in a culture where oral tradition is important.

3.   Oral Tradition

Old Testament scholars first became interested in oral tradition at the end of the eighteenth century; but it was in the first part of the nineteenth century that there was a breakthrough in this area. Classical scholars such as B. G. Niebuhr and K. O. Müller began to use the legends and myths of ancient Greece and Rome to assist in the writing of histories, and the brothers Jacob and Wilhelm Grimm began their collections of German myths and folktales. The first scholarly history of Israel, which began to appear in 1843, was by Heinrich Ewald, who had been a colleague of Müller and the Grimm brothers and devoted much attention to the part played by oral tradition in preserving information about Israel's ancestors. Ewald held that the stories of the ancestors preserved memories of the interactions of groups of people, and that characters such as Abraham and Jacob had become stereotypes embodying much admired virtues. He also suggested that the less anything is known about a character (e.g., Isaac as opposed to Abraham and Jacob), the more remote that character is in history. Ewald appreciated, then, that although oral tradition can preserve memories of actual events, it has a tendency to shape and idealize the characters whom it portrays.

There was little advance on Ewald's work until Hermann Gunkel, at the end of the nineteenth century, applied the study of oral traditions to his commentary on Genesis, the three editions of which (1901, 1902, 1910) differed considerably from each other. Gunkel became convinced that the folktale was the earliest of the genres folktale, myth, and legend and that examples of folktale motifs in Old Testament literature were evidence that ancient Israel had a living folktale tradition. Gunkel's research did not answer the question of the historical value of oral traditions. It did, however, serve as a reminder that oral tradition was a vital part of ancient Israelite life; we can also make the further point that this tradition did not cease when literacy began to spread in Israel and Judah. In all probability written and oral versions of stories of the ancestors existed side by side and exerted mutual influence. The written versions were most likely intended to serve religious and political ends by claiming that God had guided and inspired the ancestors so that the people as a whole were the people of God.

It is probable that the oral traditions have preserved genuine memories, such as that the original homeland of the ancestors was not Canaan but northern Mesopotamia, and that the ancestors were originally city dwellers who became pastoralists with no fixed abode. The Exodus story preserves memories of slavery in Egypt and an escape attributed to divine intervention. The wilderness stories preserve memories of groups living in or traveling through the Sinai desert.

Why were these stories preserved, told, or retold? In many cases it was for entertainment. Typical folklore motifs, such as that of the

---

GUNKEL AND FOLKLORE RESEARCH

Early in the twentieth century many scholars began to apply to the Bible new canons of criticism that they had learned from the growing field of folklore studies. A leader in the field was the German professor Hermann Gunkel, whose book *Das Märchen im Alten Testament* (The folktale in the Old Testament, published in 1917) examined the role folklore played in the formation of the Hebrew Bible.

Folklore researchers identified certain basic forms, conventions, and themes used by a variety of cultures to transmit their collective stories orally, from one generation to the next. Gunkel argued that folktales were in fact the most primitive expressions of a people's unique history. He studied the motifs that folktales employed and the conventional beliefs associated with them, and he used this knowledge to analyze and classify Old Testament narratives.

Gunkel believed, with much justification, that many biblical stories had undergone a long process of oral transmission and shaping before they were committed to their present written form, and that in that process, Old Testament narratives had been influenced by folktale motifs. An essential characteristic of folktales is that they ascribe human personality to the forces of nature. Ghosts and magic also play an important role. Gunkel found the residue of these characteristics and beliefs in many parts of the Old Testament. There are stories about haughty brambles (1 Kings 14:9), clever snakes (Gen. 3), and sassy donkeys (Num. 28). Giants stalk the land (Gen. 6:4); strange men appear at tents (Gen. 18); cloaks mysteriously part the water (2 Kings 2:13); staves turn into serpents and back again (Exod. 4:3); men speak from beyond the grave (1 Sam. 28). Gunkel also noted that the Old Testament utilized storytelling motifs that were common among many cultures, including traditions about exposing children to die (Exod. 2, the story of Moses in the bulrushes) and the recurring theme of the poor lad who becomes king (cf. the central biblical characters of Joseph, Saul, and David).

Gunkel envisioned ultimately using his knowledge of folklore to assess the historical reliability of biblical narratives. He tended to assume that any story which employed folktale conventions was necessarily unhistorical. Further research has, however, shown that many folktales contain kernels of historical reality and that folklore studies cannot be used to assess uncritically the historical value of oral traditions as Gunkel thought.

The real value of Gunkel's work is in its contribution to our understanding of how the narratives of the Old Testament were shaped and passed down before they reached their final written form. Gunkel spelled out the interplay between historical events, folktale motifs, and oral transmission and reaffirmed the principle that accurate historical records are only one way of revealing truth.

**CHART OF HISTORY
AND LITERATURE WITH
BIBLICAL CHRONOLOGY
(* = approximate dates)**

1. PATRIARCHAL AGE
   (2000*–1300*)
2. AGES OF MOSES, JOSHUA,
   JUDGES: Tribal period
   (1300*–1000*)
3. UNITED MONARCHY: Saul,
   David, Solomon (1020–931)

4. DIVIDED MONARCHY
   (931–587/6)
   Tenth–ninth century

   Eighth century
   (Fall of N. Kingdom,
   722/1)

   Seventh century
   (Josiah: 640–609)

5. EXILIC PERIOD
   (587–538)

6. POST-EXILIC PERIOD
   (538–70 C.E.)
   Return from exile, 538–516
   (Restoration)
   (beginning of Persian
   Period)
7. Persian Period (516–332)

early (oral?) revisions of
patriarchal stories, etc.
some early poems (e.g. Exod. 15,
Judg. 5, Ps. 29, Deut. 33, Gen. 49)

more early poems in I—II Sam.;
some Davidic psalms; early
versions of court history

oldest prose of Pentateuch: ''J''
(950*), ''E'' (850*)
Amos (760–750*); Hosea (745–701*)
early prose parts of Former
Prophets (800*–700*)
First Isaiah (740–701*)
Micah (725–690*)
more psalms (dates uncertain)
Zephaniah (630–625*)
Habakkuk (625–600*)
1st edition of ''D'' (Deut.–Kgs.)
and Deuteronomy
Nahum (ca. 612–610)
most of Jeremiah (626–586)
parts of Jeremiah
final edition of ''D'' (by 586)
Ezekiel (593–560*)
compilation of Pentateuchal
materials, including ''P'' (by
560)

Second Isaiah (538–520*)
Haggai (520)
First Zechariah (520–518)

Job (ca. 500)
collecting more psalms; final
compilation of Psalter (by 250)
Third Isaiah (500–450*?)
Malachi, Joel, Obadiah (490–450*)
Compilations of Proverbs (ca. 400)
Second Zechariah (fifth–fourth
century?)
Jonah, Ruth, Song of Songs (ca.
400)
Ezra/Nehemiah/Chronicles (450–
350*)

(continued on next page)

| (*continued*) | 8. Greek (Hellenistic) Period (332–163) | Former & Latter Prophets collected together
Ecclesiastes (ca. 300)
Esther (?)
Canonization (?) of Peutateuch (by 300*)
Translation of Pentateuch to Greek (beginning ca. 250)
Daniel (166/5)
Canonization of Prophets, Psalms (second century)
Canonization of Writings (and |
| | 9. Roman Period (163– continues into fourth century C.E.) | therefore close of canon of Hebrew Bible), at Jamnia, 90 C.E. |

younger brother (Jacob) getting the better of his elder brother (Esau), suggest this. But the stories also contain material that makes important claims. The story of Abraham's purchase of a burial ground near Hebron preserves a claim to land. Perhaps the persistent reference to the origins of the ancestors in Haran in northern Mesopotamia does the same. Also, the stories help the listeners to identify themselves as members of clans or maximal lineages named after heroes such as Abraham and Jacob and the latter's sons. In other cases, such as the Exodus story, the traditions were preserved and shaped as the deliverance from slavery was regularly celebrated.

It has to be acknowledged that, in the written form in which we have them, the stories of the ancestors have been idealized, shaped, telescoped, and stereotyped, so that although they are not the *creations* of the time at which they were written down, they reflect to some extent the political and religious *imperatives* of the time that they were first written down, that is, of the early monarchy (tenth to ninth centuries B.C.E.), through to the time when they received their final form (sixth to fifth centuries B.C.E.). Yet they also distinguish carefully in some respects between their historical setting within the biblical literature and the later periods in which they must have been written down. For example, there is no mention of priests in the stories of the ancestors. They offer sacrifices themselves, whereas the services of priests were necessary at the time when the stories received their final form.

In reading the Old Testament, we must be aware that these stories originated, were shaped, and functioned in a different world from our own. Their purpose was not to preserve or describe history according to modern standards. It was to inform, entertain, express identity, and interpret present situations; and it was also to articulate and celebrate belief in the promises of God and the destiny of mankind.

B. THE WORLD AND ITS INHABITANTS (GENESIS 1–11)

1. The Nature and Functions of Myth

The title of this section implies that Genesis 1–11 is in some sense mythical or that these chapters contain myths. This being so, it must be stressed immediately that the words "myths" and "mythical" are being used in a technical sense and not according to their popular meaning of something that is not true. The reason for using the word "myth" in connection with Genesis 1–11 is that these chapters are in some ways similar to the traditions about the origins of the world and humanity found among Israel's neighbors; and in all cases the traditions in the Bible were written down later than similar writings in neighboring countries. In other words, it has become clear that Genesis 1–11 contains material that is attested elsewhere in the ancient Near East. The study of this nonbiblical material is therefore an aid to the better understanding of the origin and function of traditions in Genesis 1–11.

The origin stories of the ancient Near East helped societies of those times to cope with the difficult and puzzling world in which they had to live. This was a world with a harsh physical environment where water, vital for food production, came sometimes in the sudden destructive abundance of floods and at other times was absent,

---

WATER, LAND, AND LIFE IN THE ANCIENT NEAR EAST: EGYPT AND MESOPOTAMIA

THE CIVILIZATIONS THAT flourished in the essentially dry climate of the ancient Near East were strongly influenced by the role of water in their environment. From June to September of every year, the Nile in Egypt swelled beyond its banks and brought an inundation of fresh, fertile silt to that parched and barren land. Though some human effort was required to utilize the Nile's floodwaters, and the amount of the annual flow was subject to some fluctuation, the Nile's regularity inspired in the ancient Egyptians a sense of confidence in the cosmos and an assurance of order and stability in the world. Life was comfortably reliable. Life was also seen as renewable, even to the extent that the Egyptians believed that their good existence would not end with death. Just as the Nile brought life-giving water in the new spring, so would humankind awaken to new life in the world to come.

Mesopotamian civilization also grew up around an important watershed area, the floodplains of the Tigris–Euphrates river valley. In general, however, the environment there was less friendly. Nature contained an element of force and violence in Mesopotamia that was missing in Egypt. The Tigris and Euphrates Rivers, unlike the Nile, rose unpredictably. They were prone to change their course and turn villages into swamps.

Mesopotamians endured an irregular climate, too. Seasons of torrential rains swept away in destructive floods hard-earned human accomplishments in agriculture and irrigation; devastating droughts smothered crops with dust. Faced with such an environment, Mesopotamian civilization developed a distrust for the power and ultimate significance of human beings. The tragic potential of life was clear when human beings found themselves caught in an interplay of giant forces against which they had no power. The Mesopotamian cosmos was ordered, too, but it was not the safe and reassuring order of Egypt. Nature showed the world to be a seething cauldron of powerful, conflicting wills. Thus order was achieved, not given. Immortality remained the prerogative of the gods.

---

causing the prolonged agony of drought. It was a world of violence between neighboring peoples and of violence even within close-knit social groups. It was a world in which sickness and death were everyday mysteries and the preservation of the species through the bearing of children was both uncertain and dangerous for mothers.

Ancient Near Eastern myths, that is, stories mostly about gods and goddesses or heroes and heroines set in the beginning of time, sought to explain and reflect on the dangers and mysteries of everyday life. Some proposed that the lot of humanity was hard because the gods had created humans to do tasks that the gods wished to avoid. In other cases humanity suffered by being the innocent victims of quarrels and fights between gods, especially those personifying water and drought. Another theme was the fruitless quest of humanity to gain the secret of immortality, so that humans would, like the gods, be freed from the fear of death. The prevalence of flood stories is evidence for the importance of water in the everyday lives of people, as well as an expression of anxiety about the power of water to destroy human attempts to tame the forces of nature.

Flood stories are linked with creation stories in more than one society, and narratives that juxtapose order (creation) and chaos (floods) express the paradox of life for ancient societies. Life was a constant struggle to impose order upon human activities, because that order assisted survival. At the same time, attempts to order life and to understand the world as ordered were threatened by disruptive forces. The myths articulated a view of life in which order and security were longed for but rarely enjoyed. It has been noted that motifs from the myths of the ancient Near East are used in varying ways in the literature of the region; these motifs served as building blocks with which differing attempts to explain the origin and significance of life could be constructed. This brings us to Genesis 1–11 and explains why these chapters both have much in common with other ancient Near Eastern traditions and yet present a unique reflection upon the origins and purpose of the world.

One feature of Genesis 1–11 that indicates the mythical function of the material is that the chapters are set in a time different from that of the readers. The following phrases act as markers, dividing the time of the narratives from that of the readers:

1:1   When God began to create [note: in modern translations, this rendering is in the main text or in a footnote] . . .

2:4b   In the day that the LORD made the earth and the heavens . . .

2:25   And the man and his wife were both naked and were not ashamed.

3:1   Now the serpent was more subtle . . .

6:1   When the people began to multiply on the face of the ground . . .

6:4   Nephilim [giants] were on the earth in those days . . .

11:1   Now the whole earth had one language and few words . . .

These markers not only divided the time of the narratives from that of the readers but indicated how the narratives were to be read and to be related to the world of the readers. Thus, although Israelite readers accepted the stories of Genesis 1–11 as literally true, they did not expect in their everyday lives to meet serpents that would converse with them, fruit trees that would confer immortality, or men (and, presumably, women) who lived to be hundreds of years old. Also, although they accepted that a flood had once covered the earth, they did not expect that to happen to them now, even if local floods could be destructive.

But if the narratives spoke of a time different from that of the readers, it was a time in which things familiar to readers had come into being. These included the Sabbath (Gen. 2:2–3), marriage (2:24), clothes (3:7), the pain of childbirth (3:16), death (3:22–4), murder (4:8), sacrifice (8:20), different languages (11:7), and peoples well known to the Israelites, such as the Egyptians, the Philistines, the Canaanites, and the inhabitants of Assyria and Babylon (Gen. 10). Thus the world familiar to the Israelites was grounded in a world and time different from that of their everyday experience. The stories about this earlier, different time helped Israelites to understand and cope with their everyday world. In this sense they functioned as myths and served the same purpose as the myths of surrounding peoples, even if in their final form they expressed the religious beliefs unique to ancient Israel.

2. Ancient Near Eastern Cosmologies

In this section, material from the ancient Near East will be compared with that in Genesis 1–11 in order to indicate the similarities and differences between the two.

Genesis 1:1–2:4a

Ever since its discovery in 1875, the Babylonian creation story (written ca. 1120 B.C.E.), called by its opening words, Enuma Elish, has been compared with Genesis 1. The following table indicates the similarities:

Enuma Elish	Genesis 1:1–2:4a
Divine spirit and cosmic matter are coexistent and coeternal	Divine spirit creates cosmic matter and exists independently of it
Primeval chaos: Tiamat (a goddess of watery chaos) enveloped in darkness	The earth is a desolate waste, with darkness covering the deep (*tehom*)
Light emanates from the gods	Light created
Creation of the firmament	Creation of the firmament
Creation of dry land	Creation of dry land
Creation of the luminaries	Creation of the luminaries
Creation of humanity	Creation of human *males*
Gods rest and celebrate	God rests and sanctifies the seventh day

However, this table needs to be amplified by pointing out that Enuma Elish is a narrative about a struggle between the gods in which the god Marduk becomes their champion against the goddess Tiamat, defeats her, and creates the world out of her dismembered carcass (*ANET* [see Bibliography], pp. 60–72). It no doubt articulates the wish for order to prevail over chaos (quite apart from its political function to exalt Marduk, the god of Babylon). But even if the above table exaggerates the similarities with Genesis 1, it shows that creation as the establishment and maintenance of order was a fundamental idea in the ancient Near East, and one basic to Genesis 1. One of the greatest differences between the texts is that there is no struggle between the gods prior to creation in Genesis 1. Israelite belief in the supremacy of the God of Israel rules this out, although some scholars have seen allusions to the motif of the divine struggle in passages such as Ps. 89:9–12:

> You rule the raging of the sea;
> > when its waves rise, you still them.
> You crushed Rahab like a carcass,
> > you scattered your enemies with your mighty arm.
> The heavens are yours, the earth also is yours;
> > the world and all that is in it – you have founded them.

Genesis 2:4b–25

This passage concerns mainly the creation of men and women and their lot in the world. The Old Testament passage is positive and friendly. The man is created to tend a garden that is abundantly watered and lacks thorns and thistles. The animals appear to be benign; the woman is created to be a partner. This contrasts sharply with other ancient Near Eastern texts. Both Sumerian and Akkadian texts assert that humans were created so that they could perform manual labor for the gods such as building canals and cities. In Enuma Elish humanity is created from the blood of an executed traitor god:

> "Kingu it was who created the strife,
> And caused Tiamat to revolt and prepare for battle."
> They bound him and held him before Ea;
> Punishment they inflicted upon him by cutting (the arteries of) his
> > blood.
> With his blood they created mankind.
> > (Heidel, *The Babylonian Genesis,* p. 47)

It is tempting to see in this passage an explanation for the willful and destructive tendency in human beings; they are made from the blood of a god who instigated rebellion against order and who was executed for treachery.

A closer parallel to Genesis 2 comes from the Epic of Gilgamesh (possibly written ca. 1600 B.C.E.), where the uncivilized man Enkidu is created as follows:

> [A]ruru washed her hands, pinched off clay, (and) threw (it) on the
> > steppe:
> [   ] valiant Enkidu she created, she offspring . . . of Ninurta.
> > (Heidel, *The Gilgamesh Epic and Old Testament Parallels,* p. 19)

Genesis 2 is somewhere in between these two conceptions. Man has an earthly part and a divine part, but the divine part is indirect: the breath (Hebrew *neshamah*) that God breathed into him is a gift, and not an inherent part of [man] humans.

Genesis 3

Texts about the loss of a state of paradise and the loss of immortality have been found in the ancient Near East. The Sumerian Enki and Ninhursag (probably first half of the second millennium B.C.E.; see *ANET,* pp. 37–41) speaks of the land of Dilmun, which is "pure, clean and bright" and where

> The lion kills not.
> The wolf snatches not the lamb,
> Unknown is the kid-devouring *wild dog,*
> . . . its old woman [says] not "I am an old woman";
> Its old man [says] not "I am an old man."

This state of affairs, similar to that in Genesis 2 and found again in the Old Testament at Isa. 11:6–9 and 65:20–5, is disturbed when the divine ruler of Dilmun, Enki, cuts down and eats eight plants created by the goddess Ninhursag. She curses Enki, he apparently begins to experience pain, and Ninhursag creates eight deities from the parts of Enki's body where he experiences pain. Thus sickness and possibly death come into a world that previously did not know them, as the result of cutting down and eating some plants.

The search for immortality is a main theme of the Epic of Gilgamesh. In the earlier Sumerian story The Death of Gilgamesh (first half of the second millennium; *ANET,* pp. 50–1), Gilgamesh has to be content with the fact that he had been a great king and that he will live on in his reputation. The Akkadian Epic of Gilgamesh is much more pessimistic. The death of his friend Enkidu plunges Gilgamesh into despair and into a quest for immortality in which his failure is the more tragic because he comes so near to success. It is a serpent that frustrates the hero. Gilgamesh journeyed far to visit Utnapishtim, who survived the Flood by building a ship and who was granted immortality. From him, Gilgamesh learns of a plant at the bottom of the sea that restores people's youth. Gilgamesh obtains the plant but, on his return journey, loses it to a serpent while bathing in a pool.

Another text that connects the loss of a happy world with human rebellion is the Egyptian myth of the heavenly cow. A time when there was harmony between the gods and humanity is disrupted when the humans rebel. This ideal world was subject to decay followed by regeneration, a process that affected Re, the creator god. Humanity was punished by the destruction of the world by fire; but the creator god rescued some humans and established a new, but inferior world. Access to the former world was now by death.

Genesis 6–8

There are several versions of Flood stories from the ancient Near East, in which various heroes survive. In a Sumerian version the

This tablet of cuneiform was found at Late Bronze Age Megiddo (fifteenth or fourteenth century B.C.E.) and contains a portion of the Mesopotamia Flood story from the Epic of Gilgamesh. Discovery of this tablet in ancient Palestine is a reminder that the Bronze Age inhabitants of the land had copies of the literary masterpieces of Mesopotamia. Formal literary texts like this were written on both sides of the tablet.

Biblical Archaeology Slides, no. 112.

hero is Ziasudra, and he survives a seven-day flood by building a boat. An Akkadian hero is Atrahasis, and the flood that he is warned by a god to prepare for is sent by the gods because the human race had become too numerous and too noisy! Atrahasis is instructed to take into his ship not only his family and relations but animals also. In the Flood story that appears in the Epic of Gilgamesh the hero, Utnapishtim, is warned by a god to make preparations, and he takes craftsmen on board his ship as well as his family and animals. This version contains themes familiar from the Genesis stories. As the flood subsides, Utnapishtim sends out a dove and a swallow, both of which return. A raven does not return, from which it is concluded that the earth is fruitful once again. On leaving the ship, the party offers sacrifices to the gods, who gather like flies at the smell.

The Worldview Implicit in Genesis 1

The above examples have shown the variety of attempts in the ancient Near East to explain the origin of the world, of humanity, and of things harmful to humanity such as death, sickness, hard labor, and floods. Genesis 1–11 not only fits into this milieu but shares the view of the composition of the physical world implicit in them. As set out in Genesis 1, the basic element on which everything else rests is water. Even the dry land rests on water, so that when the Flood is let loose in Genesis 6, this is done partly by allowing the subterranean waters to burst up through the earth (Gen. 7:11). Over the earth and waters, like a turned-over bowl, is the firmament. This dome contains the area of the sky, but above it are other waters (Gen. 1:7), which also contribute to the Flood when the windows of the heavens are opened (Gen. 7:11). What is striking about this cosmogony is the prevalence of water. The land of Israel was not greatly blessed with reliable rainfall, and readers should note how often the word "famine" occurs in the Old Testament. From an Old Testament standpoint, this commodity that was vital to life was an abundant part of the world's makeup. Its unreliable availability was not due to chance or the whim of God but to Israel's unwillingness to obey God's laws.

3. The Nature of the World and Its Inhabitants

We have seen above that the motifs found in ancient Near Eastern myths were employed in a variety of ways to produce differing accounts of the world's origins and that this is what we find also in Genesis 1–11. In the fifth to fourth centuries B.C.E., priestly writers put the stories in Genesis 1–11 into a framework that served to express the distinctive religious beliefs of ancient Israel.

The clue to reading Genesis 1–11 is the contrast between 1:26–30 and 9:1–7. In the former passage mankind (male and female) is created in God's image and given a shepherding role in relation to the rest of the creation. It is noteworthy that this is a vegetarian creation (including for the animals), which indicates that animals will not be violent to each other and that humans will not exploit them. In Gen. 9:1–7, when the mandate to the human race is renewed after the Flood, things are

BABYLONIAN FLOOD STORIES

THE BIBLICAL FLOOD stories belong to a popular kind of narrative in the ancient world. They bear their closest resemblance to the literature of Mesopotamia. The Mesopotamian Flood stories date from at least the time of ancient Sumer (ca. 2500 B.C.E.), though they exist now only in copies from the seventeenth century B.C.E. and later. They were widely disseminated in the ancient Near East.

The Atrahasis Epic tells of the creation of humankind from clay composed of divine blood mixed with dust. As in the creation myth Enuma Elish, human creatures were created to relieve the gods of their mundane duties. The human population swelled beyond control, however, and their noise was bothersome to the gods. A coalition of gods threatened the offending creatures with a number of thwarted punishments, culminating with a plot to drown all of them. But a friendly god warned the hero Atrahasis in a dream that he should build a boat to escape the coming flood, which he does.

The most famous and most complete of the Mesopotamian Flood stories is a later addition to the famous Epic of Gilgamesh. The original story concerns the adventures of Gilgamesh, the king of Uruk, and his companion Enkidu. The two friends set out to gain immortality through their memorable deeds, one of which drew the fatal wrath of the gods on Enkidu. A bereaved Gilgamesh then goes in search of *real* immortality from his ancestor Utnapishtim, who once learned the secret of eternal life. After a series of fiery trials, Gilgamesh arrives at his destination only to be disappointed. Utnapishtim, it seems, had become immortal by virtue of an unrepeatable circumstance: he and his wife had survived a great flood and by a special dispensation had been granted the divine prerogative of life eternal.

A number of interesting similarities exist between the Genesis acount of Noah and the Flood story as narrated by Utnapishtim in the Epic of Gilgamesh. In both, the deluge comes by divine decree and one individual is chosen to be warned of the impending disaster and told to build a boat according to exact specifications. Both traditions include instructions about what is to be taken aboard the vessel, and in both the flood destroys both the people and the beasts that are left behind. Both Noah's ark and Utnapishtim's boat come to rest on high mountains, and both characters send birds out to determine if the land has again become livable. In a final striking parallel, both heroes build altars and sacrifice to their gods.

Such parallels do not imply that the collector of the Genesis traditions simply borrowed a Mesopotamian story to frame his own narrative. The Hebrew and Babylonian texts are each consonant with their culture's worldview, and the biblical version is clearly written from the perspective of ethical monotheism. The biblical authors thoroughly revised the Mesopotamian traditions to create their own highly distinctive version.

different. The creation is no longer vegetarian. Meat is allowed to humans so long as it is not eaten with its blood still in it, and it is implied that animals can now prey upon other animals. Accordingly, the role of humanity in regard to the animals is strengthened. Animals will fear humans, which presumably implies that humans will have more of a policing role than a shepherding one in a world in which violence will be endemic.

Why has the world changed, necessitating the revised mandate which indicates the loss of a better world? The answer is given in Genesis 3–8 and develops a theme deeply embedded in ancient Near Eastern mythology, namely, that creation is order and that human attempts to disrupt order undermine the creation. Genesis 1 is all about order, as the world is divided into water, earth, and sky, and plants, animals, sea creatures, and even stars are assigned to their proper places. Genesis 2 continues this theme. By naming the animals the man orders and classifies them; and his partner comes not from the animals but from his own substance. The command not to eat the fruit of a certain tree introduces a moral boundary. It is not only objects and animals that belong to a particular place in the order of things; actions, too, have places within their proper spheres.

From Genesis 3 onward there are repeated violations of the boundaries that maintain the order of creation. The serpent encourages Eve to disobey God's command so that she and her husband will become like God (or the gods), knowing good and evil. This is an incitement to cross the boundary that divides the human from the divine. In Genesis 4 Cain transgresses the bonds of family obligations by murdering his brother, Abel; and one of the results is that the ground loses its fertility (4:12). Both Genesis 3 and Genesis 4 indicate that breaking moral laws undermines the natural order of creation. At the beginning of Genesis 6, a difficult passage about the "sons of god" marrying the daughters of men suggests another violation of the boundary between the human and the divine. When the Flood narrative begins, one reason for the divine decision to send the deluge is that "all flesh had corrupted their way upon the earth" (6:12). Put in other words, humans and animals had destroyed the integrity of creation by violating the moral boundaries that were part of its order.

Because the inhabitants of earth have undermined the created order, it is necessary for the world to be destroyed and for an order appropriate to the destructive tendencies to be established. The Flood does not destroy the earth completely, but it allows a new start to be made, with a revised mandate that recognizes that the creation cannot be vegetarian and at peace with itself. Further, humanity is given a warning, in the form of the rainbow that appears from time to time. We, today, think of the rainbow as a symbol of peace, and we use it in that way. But the content of the Old Testament, reinforced by the extensive iconographic studies of Othmar Keel, makes it clear that the bow is a symbol of war, and the broken bow a symbol of peace (Ps. 46:9). The bow mentioned in Genesis 9:12–16 is the sign of a promise that the earth will not again be destroyed by a flood; but it is also a warning to the human race, whose misconduct was one of the causes of the flood, that God will defend his created order against the attempts of humanity to undermine it.

The narratives of Genesis 1–11 show, as they continue beyond 9:1–7, that humanity remains rebellious and destructive in the world as it has come to be after the Flood. One of Noah's sons fails to observe the conventions of decency and respect for his father, and his descendants are cursed by Noah. In Genesis 11 the human race seeks to invade the divine sphere by building a tower that will reach to the heavens. They do not want to be human in God's world, accepting their allotted place; they wish to base their position upon their own achievements without God. Their scattering abroad as peoples separated by the barrier of language is the prelude to the next part of the story, the call of Abraham in Genesis 12.

In their present form Genesis 1–11 cannot be separated from what follows; for these chapters are not simply an open-ended reflection upon the inscrutable lot of humanity, similar to the advice in the

Sumerian story of Gilgamesh that he must simply learn to accept his fate. Chapters 1–11 are part of a larger story in which God takes the initiative with a view to producing a humanity that will gladly accept its divinely appointed place in the world. This story has been described as an education of voluntary creatures to make them free. And with the hope that a humanity worthy of the world may emerge, there comes the hope in the Old Testament that the original creation will be restored. The vegetarian and peaceful creation is envisioned in passages such as Isa. 65:17–25, which concludes with the words

The wolf and the lamb shall feed together,
the lion shall eat straw like the ox;
but the serpent – its food shall be dust!
They shall not hurt or destroy in all my holy mountain,
says the LORD.

These words, reminding us of the Sumerian myth Enki and Ninhursag (see above, p. 000), bring us full circle. The material in Genesis 1–11 is deeply rooted in the myths of the ancient Near East, that is, in those stories about gods, goddesses, and heroes that attempt to explain and come to terms with the paradoxes of human existence. In the Old Testament, however, these myths have been pressed into service to help express Israel's faith in a God who is not withdrawn from creation but who is constantly involved in it, a God who has chosen to work through a special people in order to bring to the whole human race that perfect freedom which comes from joyful recognition of his sovereignty.

C. THE ANCESTORS OF ISRAEL (GENESIS 12–50)

1. Archeological and Sociological Reconstruction of the Period

Into which archeological period can the stories of the ancestors (Abraham, Isaac, and Jacob) best be placed? An answer that held the field for several decades was that the Middle Bronze (MB) IIB–C periods (ca. 1800–1550 B.C.E.) provided a fitting context. Recently, there has been growing support for a setting in the Late Bronze (LB) Age (ca. 1550–1200).

MB IIB–C was favored for several reasons. First, it was suggested by the chronology of the Old Testament. In 1 Kings 6:1 it is stated that the Exodus from Egypt occurred 480 years before the beginning of the building of Solomon's temple, and Exod. 12:40 gives a figure of 430 years for the duration of the sojourn in Egypt. If the temple building began in 957 B.C.E., the addition of 910 years brings us to 1867 B.C.E. for the latter part of Jacob's life, when he went to Egypt in his old age (Gen. 47:27–8). Second, the stories of the ancestors refer to customs that have parallels in texts of neighboring peoples in the Middle Bronze Age. An example was the desire of Abraham to adopt a son because he had no heir (Gen. 15:2). Although the Old Testament is otherwise silent about adoption as a feature of ancient Israelite life, tablets from Nuzi

MARI

THE MIDDLE BRONZE AGE (ca. 2200–1550 B.C.E.) ushered in a period of major social and political changes in the ancient Near East. During that period a number of Mesopotamian city-states were overrun by a Semitic people known to the native inhabitants as Amurru, or Amorites (from the Akkadian word meaning "westerner"). These seminomadic "foreigners" were the dominant power in northern Mesopotamia in the latter half of the eighteenth century B.C.E., ruling from the impressive city-state of Mari.

Mari was situated along the southern bank of the middle Euphrates in what is modern-day Syria. A river port located along two major caravan routes, Mari grew to be a city of considerable importance. Excavations at the ancient city have revealed a rich Amorite culture. Researchers uncovered a temple to the goddess Ishtar, a ziggurat (temple tower), and an eight-acre palace containing almost three hundred rooms. In the palace were found some 25,000 cuneiform tablets dating from the nineteenth to the eighteenth century B.C.E. They included economic, administrative, and legal texts as well as the royal correspondence of Mari's last king, Zimri-Lim. The Mari texts bear witness to a civilization that practiced extensive irrigation agriculture and long-distance trade. Busy commercial traffic made the city extraordinarily rich. Mari flourished until it fell to the Babylonians at the hands of the great Hammurabi in the eighteenth century.

Texts from Mari are important for establishing the history and geography of northern Mesopotamia, but they also make reference to several well-known locations in Syria–Palestine. In addition, scholars have used the Mari texts to learn more about the prehistory of Northwest Semitic languages, the linguistic family to which biblical Hebrew belongs. Some visionary–cultic figures referred to on artifacts from Mari may also be helpful in identifying an early form of prophetic activity.

The Mari documents have been used to argue for a scenario in which the patriarchs of Genesis are dated to the same general chronological period as the Mari texts. Some scholars have linked the migration of the patriarchs to the great Amorite movements, roughly contemporary with the golden age of Mari (eighteenth century). They have bolstered their case by noting personal names in the Mari texts parallel to the biblical Abraham, Laban, and Jacob. Some have also drawn parallels between the sociological world of the patriarchs and the way of life in ancient Mari. But neither names nor social conditions are exclusive to any particular era, so the importance of the Mari texts for dating the patriarchs must not be exaggerated. The Mari documents most certainly help fill out the history and early customs of the Amorites, cousins of the Hebrew people, who later spread throughout Syria–Palestine.

The most valuable aspect of the Mari archives in terms of biblical studies is the information they provide about upper Mesopotamia, the region traditionally associated with the biblical patriarchs. The city of Haran, to which Abraham migrated from his home in Ur of the Chaldees (Gen. 11), was an important trading center in the cultural orbit of Mari and also played a significant role in its politics. The archives also have illuminated the movements of various ethnic groups around the beginning of the second millennium. Perhaps most important, they shed light on a type of society where city dwellers coexisted with partially settled pastoralists – an arrangement likely to have been practiced as well in early Israel several centuries later.

in northern Mesopotamia indicate that adoption was practiced there; and we must remember the claim of the Genesis stories that Abraham's family came from northern Mesopotamia (Gen. 11:31–2). Third, names similar to those of the ancestors are attested in northern Mesopotamia. Striking examples are Abam-ram and Jacob-el, and these are Amorites, that is, Semitic immigrants into northern Syria and Mesopotamia around 2000 B.C.E.

A recent defender of the setting of the ancestors in MB IIB–C is Amihai Mazar, who argues, in addition to the point about customs mentioned above, that most of the cities named in the Genesis narratives were occupied and fortified during MB IIB–C.

The last twenty years have seen fierce arguments about the points in favor of the MB IIB–C setting. The figures given in 1 Kings 6:1 make the Exodus too early (i.e., fifteenth century B.C.E.), whereas the genealogy of Moses (Exod. 6:16–20) indicates that there were only four generations from Jacob to Moses, which is impossible to square with the 430 years of sojourn given in Exod. 12:40. It has been pointed out that the occurrence of names and customs in MB IIB–C texts does not prove anything about the date of the stories in Genesis since such names and customs could have persisted long after the MB II period.

Perhaps the strongest argument against setting the ancestors in MB IIB–C Canaan is the fact that the land was replete with cities and settlements at that time, whereas in the Late Bronze Age there was a dramatic decline in the number of settlements. Also, we have evidence for the existence of so-called nomadic peoples in Canaan in the LB period. Israel Finkelstein has summarized the situation in Canaan in MB II, a noteworthy feature of which was the unprecedented number of settlements in the central hill country in addition to the cities in the usual places of occupation – the fertile parts of the coastal plain, the Shephelah, and the northern valleys. Around 200 sites of the MB IIB–C period have been reportedly found in the central hill country, with more discoveries expected as surveying continues.

The implication of this situation as a setting for the traditions about the ancestors is that the stories themselves give the impression of a largely uninhabited land. When the flocks and herds of Abraham and his nephew, Lot, become so numerous that the land cannot support both of them, they agree to divide the land, with Abraham choosing the land of Canaan and Lot going to the Jordan Valley (Gen. 13:5–12). Of course, these biblical narratives may not contain any accurate material about the nature of the land at the time when Abraham and Lot were there; but if we want to guess at a plausible setting for the

NUZI

DURING THE SEVENTEENTH century B.C.E. Indo-European people called Hurrians began pushing into Mesopotamia from the north. They settled eventually in every part of Asia Minor (and also in Palestine, where they are known in the Old Testament as Horites or Hivites). Their greatest concentration was in northern Mesopotamia, where they established the kingdom of Mitanni (ca. 1500–1370). In this solidly Hurrian area lay the city of Nuzi.

Nuzi is best known for the collection of some five thousand private and public legal cuneiform texts uncovered there. Situated far to the northeast of Syria–Palestine in modern-day Iraq, Nuzi's remoteness belies its ancient standing as a major center linking east and west. The region of Haran, where the patriarchs lived before arriving in Palestine, was controlled by Hurrians; and although little is known directly about that region, scholars have been able to reconstruct a great deal about its social and political customs from the records of the Hurrian community at Nuzi. Many enigmatic biblical concepts and practices have been traced back to Hurrian society

through the documents at Nuzi. For example, some compare the Hurrian practice of establishing birthright by parental decree (rather than chronological priority of birth) to the biblical patriarchs' freedom from the rules of inheritance (Gen. 27, 49). Others note similarities of Nuzi marriage contracts and adoption procedures to events in the patriarchal narratives.

For some historians these parallels are indicative of the accuracy with which Israel remembered the culture of its founders. Even those who infer a direct relationship between Nuzi and the biblical patriarchs are forced to note significant disparities between the two materials, however. In recent years scholars have begun to question whether such a relationship exists at all. The Nuzi documents are still valuable for comparing Hebrew and Hurrian social practice and family life. Yet many of the explanations of patriarchal customs derived from these materials are no longer accepted. In some cases it is not even clear whether the texts reflect a unique Hurrian culture or simply testify to common Mesopotamian practice. Thus the Nuzi documents may be of less value in resolving problems in patriarchal chronology than scholars had hoped.

Since they must move with their flocks according to the seasons, the Bedouin have always been tent dwellers. This pastoral way of life is evident in accounts of the biblical patriarchs (see Gen. 12:8; 13:1–5, 12).

Biblical Archaeology Slides, no. 28

stories taking into account what they say about their own times, we have to conclude that they do not fit well into the flourishing and well-settled Canaan of MB IIB–C.

On the other hand, the Late Bronze Age is much more promising as a context. In the central hill country, where a number of the stories are set, there was a drastic reduction of settlements. As opposed to 116 MB II sites in the tribal area of Manasseh, there were at most 31 LB sites (Finkelstein 1988, pp. 339–40). Ephraim, Benjamin, and Judah were similarly sparsely occupied from the point of view of permanent settlements in the LB period. This picture is much more in tune with the content of the stories of the ancestors, where the heroes only occasionally come into contact with other peoples and otherwise live in a land that seems to be little occupied.

The drastic decline in the number of settlements does not necessarily entail, of course, a similar decline in population. It is likely that, for reasons we can only guess at, some of the people who abandoned their permanent settlements became pastoralists, moving from place to place. The presence of a significant "nomadic" element in a Canaan with a few main cities certainly corresponds to the picture implied in the stories of the ancestors. It is also attested by references in Egyptian texts to the nomadic *shasu*.

The *shasu* are mentioned in Egyptian texts from the time of Thutmosis II (1482–1479 B.C.E.) to that of Rameses II (1184–1153). They occupied parts of Canaan, Transjordan, and the northern Negev south of Judah – the setting of the stories of Isaac, Jacob, and Esau. They were tent dwellers and pastoralists and organized into lineages presided over by leaders. To the Egyptians they posed the usual threats that "civilized" people perceive when encountering "nomads": they seemed to be anarchistic, violent, and dangerous. Some of the *shasu* who were subdued by the Egyptians became slaves; others became soldiers.

What was the relationship, if any, between the *shasu* and Israel's ancestors? Although there is room for argument, it is a reasonable assumption that the Israel we encounter in the twelfth century B.C.E. has its roots in the *shasu* tribes. If we can reasonably say that Israel's ancestors were part of the *shasu* peoples documented by the Egyptians, we have the very good fortune to possess Egyptian iconographic material about their appearance. They wore short beards and had a distinctive hairstyle, with the hair combed up and back and held in place with a headband. They wore a knee-length tasseled garment, which brings to mind the command in Num. 15:38–9 that the Israelites must wear tassels on the corners of their garments.

It is now time to deal with the way of life of the ancestors, assuming that they were pastoralists moving from place to place. The description "nomad" or "seminomad" is often used of such people; but these terms are notoriously imprecise and bring together two quite different activities: herding and movement. Depending on the type of herding, the "nomadism" will vary according to the amount of pasturage needed by different kinds of animals.

Although camels are mentioned among the animals possessed by the ancestors (e.g., Gen. 12:16), this cannot be correct. The issue is not that of the date of the domestication of the camel but of the use of the camel in and around Canaan; and the evidence of iconography is against the use of camels in Canaan in the Late Bronze Age. The ancestors must have had flocks primarily of sheep and goats, and there is a good description of their typical way of life in the Joseph stories (Gen. 37). Although we are not told in the story exactly where Jacob was living, a reference to the valley of Hebron (Gen. 37:14) indicates the Hebron area. From here, Joseph is sent by his father to seek out his brothers, who are pasturing the flocks near Shechem, sixty miles to the north as the crow flies. On arriving in Shechem, Joseph finds that his brothers have moved nearly twenty miles further to the north, to Dothan. There are, of course, difficulties about accepting the Joseph

Asiatics bringing eye-paint to Egypt; wall painting in the tomb of Khnumhotep III (Eighteenth Dynasty) at Beni Hasan. These bearded figures are usually associated with the Hebrews or, more generally, with people of Semitic background.

stories at face value as authentic history; but there can be no doubt that the geographical conventions implied in the story reflect accurately the conditions of pastoralists in ancient Canaan. Shechem is situated at a point in the central hill country where small fertile valleys begin to merge with larger ones, until the broad plain of Dothan is reached, with the great triangular Jezreel Valley only a little further to the north. The further north one goes, the greater is the annual rainfall. The picture that is given, then, is one of pastoralists traveling many miles from their home base to find grazing and ending up in the fertile and wetter valleys of the northern hill country. Other features of the story are also illuminating. Joseph's dream in which he and his family were binding sheaves in the field (Gen. 37:5–8) indicates that Jacob's group not only was pastoralist but also had an agricultural base. Yet this was not a permanent base. When famine becomes severe, Jacob and his family leave the Hebron area and travel to Egypt. The Joseph stories thus present a vivid and realistic picture of a group practicing mixed agriculture and pastoralism, ranging a hundred miles from their base in search of pasturage, and being forced to abandon their base when the ecological balance tips against them and famine ensues.

All this seems to indicate a peaceful world. In reality, the Late Bronze Age in Canaan was a turbulent period. For much of the time Canaan was subject to Egypt, to whom the rulers of the city-states looked for protection. The iconographic evidence surveyed by Othmar Keel shows that the art of the period featured warlike and political gods, and portrayals of humans emphasized battle, domination, loyalty, and legitimation. This evidence comes, of course, from the cities, whereas the "nomadic" peoples have left no such remains. One reason why settlements were abandoned may have been that their inhabitants preferred the freedom of nomadism to the pressure of conflicting demands for loyalty imposed upon villages.

One group responsible for contributing to the violence and tension of the period were the Habiru, and the El-Amarna letters, written in the fourteenth century from Canaanite city rulers to Pharaoh Amenophis IV, contain pleas for help against this group. The Habiru were probably more of a social class than an ethnic group. Whether the names Habiru and Hebrew are etymologically connected and whether the ancestors of Israel were part of the Habiru are topics that have generated much heated debate. Although the etymological similarity has never been convincingly demonstrated, the Habiru question arguably illuminates one otherwise puzzling chapter in the stories of the ancestors, Genesis 14. The problems presented by the names of the kings who, according to Genesis 14, invaded the Jordan Valley, the Dead Sea region, and parts of Transjordan and the Negev are too complex to be discussed here. But if it seems out of character for Abraham to fight against these kings and to pursue them as far as to the north of Damascus (Gen. 14:15), the references to the Habiru remind us that there were in Late Bronze Age Canaan landless groups with fighting potential who could disrupt the affairs of powerful city-states. It has been suggested that Genesis 14 portrays Abraham rather like one of the Habiru (note Gen. 14:13: "one who had escaped came, and told Abram the Hebrew. . . . "). Although this is interesting, it is probably safer to locate Abraham and the other ancestors among the *shasu*, remembering that, according to the Egyptian iconography and texts, these so-called nomads could also be warlike.

What can we conclude about the religion of the ancestors, assuming them to have lived in Late Bronze Age Canaan? It has been suggested that the Late Bronze Age in Egypt, Canaan, and Mesopotamia was a time in which personal religion flourished and that this accords well with what we find in Genesis 12–50. In these narratives God has a closeness to the ancestors not paralleled elsewhere in the Old Testament. For example, God appears to Abraham in the form of or as one of three men in Genesis 18, and in Genesis 32:22–32 Jacob wrestles with an angel who seems to be a manifestation of God. The religion of the ancestors is presented as the God of the father or fathers (e.g., Gen. 31:52–3), a religion in which a supreme God who is not identified with a particular sanctuary initiates a personal relationship with a leader or ancestor, and who is worshiped by his descendants as the God of that

THE HABIRU PROBLEM

THE PEOPLE KNOWN AS Habiru have featured prominently in scholarly discussions about the origins of the Hebrew people. The term "Habiru" (more properly 'Apiru or its cuneiform ideogram equivalent (SA.GAZ) occurs in over 200 texts that date to the second millennium B.C.E. and that come from every part of the ancient Near East. The term appears to refer not to a specific national or ethnic group but rather to a class of individuals. In some texts 'Apiru appear as vagrants who raid and otherwise generally harass resident populations; in other records they are mercenaries whose services are available to the highest bidder. Some 'Apiru seem to have been more like migrant workers who occasionally entered into voluntary servitude. Wherever the 'Apiru appear, they are foreigners or resident aliens, a kind of rootless outsider class relegated to an inferior social status.

Defining the term "'Apiru" etymologically is difficult. It has been related to Semitic linguistic roots meaning "to provide," in the sense that the 'Apiru were ones who depended on the rations provided by their patrons to survive; or "dust," in the sense that they were dusty people, bedouins from the desert sands; or "earth," in the sense that the 'Apiru dwelled in a political "no-man's-land" away from urban population centers. The cuneiform designation means either "aggressor" or "bandit," and it may well be applied simply to any rebellious and marauding people. The resemblance between the words "'Apiru" and "Hebrew" has been noted by Old Testament scholars; some have even suggested that the patriarchs belonged to that ethnic group.

Recent theories about the Israelite conquest of Canaan have identified the 'Apiru with socially disaffected inhabitants of Palestine who took part in a broad egalitarian revolution from which the nation of Israel was formed. These revolutionary groups are conceived as being composed of anyone occupying the lower levels of Canaanite society who threatened the established order. This ready identification of the 'Apiru with the founders of Israel has also been criticized as an oversimplification.

The words "'Apiru" and "Hebrew" cannot be equated linguistically unproblematically. Moreover, the term "Hebrew" is always used in the Old Testament to designate the Israelites as opposed to another ethnic group, and the term 'Apiru appears to be more of a social category than an ethnic designation. Thus, a direct relationship between the 'Apiru and the ancestors of Israel is not likely. Still, the patriarchs belong to the same historical era and seem to have shared a similar lifestyle with the 'Apiru, and they perhaps belonged to the same broad social stratum of the ancient Near East. The terms may be connected only insofar as the biblical Hebrews could also be seen as an element marginal to society, that is, as one example of a people who could be called 'Apiru.

person. Although we need to be cautious about how we use the narratives of Genesis 12–50 for information about the historical Abraham, Isaac, and Jacob, it can be affirmed that their picture of ancestral religion as one of personal piety fits well into what is known of the religion of Late Bronze Age Canaan.

2.   Stories of the Ancestors

Genesis 12–50 can be divided roughly into three blocks: the Abraham–Lot cycle (12–25:11), the Jacob cycle (25:12–36:43), and the Joseph stories (37–50). Until recently it was widely held that the first two cycles were based upon oral traditions that were collected in the early monarchy in both the southern kingdom, Judah (J source), and the northern kingdom, Israel (E source), and that these sources were later combined by a redactor. Attempts to divide the Joseph stories into J and E (the first such attempt was that of K. D. Ilgen in 1798) commanded less agreement. More recent studies have concentrated upon the internal literary links to be found in the three blocks. These are more obvious in the Joseph cycle, which is one of the two most polished pieces of narrative in the whole Old Testament (the second comprises the latter part of 1 Samuel and 2 Samuel 1–20). But if the Abraham and Jacob cycles are less obviously literary wholes than the Joseph stories, this does not mean that they lack literary unity and artistry. A shift away from seeing Genesis 12–50 as compilations from oral tradition to seeing them as literary compositions has occasioned some unnecessarily negative conclusions about the possibility that they are based upon oral reminiscences of the premonarchic period. But this approach has also shed valuable light upon the composition history of the chapters.

In the first place it explains a puzzle: why, if Jacob is the father of the twelve tribes of Israel and the ancestor whose name is changed to Israel (Gen. 32:28), does the story of the Hebrew people begin with Abraham? The answer probably is that the traditions about Jacob grew toward their present form in the northern kingdom of Israel, while those about Abraham had a separate genesis in the southern kingdom of Judah. The dominant position of Abraham reflects the political realities of the period when the cycles were joined together. This was probably after the fall of the northern kingdom in 721 B.C.E., when Judah alone remained and was able to lay claim to represent the whole of the territory of Israel. The Judahite Abraham was thus pictured as prior to, and more prominent than, the Israelite Jacob. It is also to be noted that the Abraham traditions center primarily upon the Judahite capital Hebron, whereas those concerning Jacob feature the Israelite cities of Bethel and Shechem. Although in their present form these stories date from the sixth to the fifth centuries B.C.E. and reflect many of the realities of the period of the monarchy, it is likely that Abraham and Judah were ancestors of the groups of Israelites that later constituted the kingdoms of Judah and Israel, and that traditions about them were preserved among their descendants as claims upon land and as ways of knowing genealogically who was related to whom. This latter point was important when it came to settling disputes and to joining together for mutual defense against those who were regarded as enemies. The stories of Joseph were also most likely composed in the northern kingdom of Israel, given that their hero, Joseph, is the father of the tribes of Ephraim and Manasseh, the two tribes that occupied most of the central hill country and were the backbone of the kingdom of Israel. The Joseph stories were probably added to the Jacob cycle in the north so as to complete the story of Jacob from birth (Gen. 25:21 ff.) to death (Gen. 49:33).

For all that Genesis 12–50 reached their final form in the sixth to fifth centuries, it is to be noted that their authors went out of their way to present the era of the ancestors as a period different from that of the tenth to fifth centuries. We have already noted customs such as adoption that do not appear to have been common in the Israel of the time of the literary growth of the stories. Also, the practice of Abraham begetting a son by his wife's servant, and of Jacob begetting sons by the maids of his two wives, has no parallel in Israel's later customs.

In matters of religion the period of the ancestors is also presented as different from that of later Israel. There is no priesthood, and Abraham builds altars at Bethel (Gen. 12:8) and Hebron (13:18), Isaac builds an altar at Beersheba (26:25), and Jacob not only builds altars at Shechem (33:19–20) and Bethel (35:3–7) but is said to have offered sacrifice on the mountain where he made a pact with Laban (31:54) and at Beersheba (46:1). The religion of the ancestors as portrayed in Genesis 12–50 is thus one in which God can be approached by the head of the family, who can build altars and offer sacrifice without the need for priestly mediation.

Yet for all that these stories maintain a distance between their world and that of their time of literary growth and composition, they reflect the political realities of the later periods. Many of the narratives deal with relationships between the ancestors and peoples who were part of Israel's political world at the time the stories began to be written down (eighth century B.C.E.). Lot is the ancestor of the Transjordanian peoples of Ammon and Moab, and Ishmael personifies the nomadic peoples known to have inhabited north Arabia, although located in the Old Testament in the Negev. Esau personifies Edom (36:1), and Laban represents the Aramean states to Israel's north. A persistent theme is that of the difference between the ancestors and the indigenous Canaanites. This comes out strongly in the story of Abraham sending his servant to Haran in northeast Mesopotamia to seek out a wife for Isaac from among his own kinsfolk, whereas Esau is implicitly condemned for marrying Canaanite women (26:34–5, 36:2–3). There is no reason to doubt the tradition that the roots of the ancestors were in northern Mesopotamia, and it is likely that the narratives function to define Judah and Israel as separate from the peoples of Canaan, among whom they had lived so long.

In fact, the theme of the differences between Judah and Israel, as personified by the ancestors, and the neighboring peoples of the time of the monarchy is pressed effectively into theological service to articulate the choosing by God of Judah and Israel to bring blessing to all peoples. Ammon, Moab, the nomadic peoples, Edom, and the Aramean states are presented as being related to Judah and Israel; yet they are not chosen by God. Ammon and Moab come into being through Lot's incest with his daughters (19:30–8), and Edom through Esau's marriage to Canaanite women. Jacob (Israel) outwits Laban (the Aramean states) after having served him. Ishmael (the nomadic peoples) is expelled by Abraham but is treated favorably by God. The narratives thus show how God is at work among a group of peoples, testing and refining them, and choosing to work through the ancestors in particular. Nowhere is this theme more strongly stressed than in the Joseph stories: at the climax, when Joseph reveals himself to his brothers, he says that it was God who sent him to Egypt, even though his brothers were the instrument through whom God worked (Gen. 45:4–8).

However, if the narratives portray God as the one who is leading and guiding the ancestors so as to achieve his purposes, they also inject a strong sense of danger and of human reluctance to cooperate with or to trust in God. In Genesis 12 Abraham, having been promised the land of Canaan and that his descendants will be a great nation, goes to Egypt because of famine and is not prepared to admit that Sarah is his wife. In Genesis 26, a similar story, Isaac does not go down to Egypt, thus obeying God's command; but he still tries to pass Rebekah off as his sister and not his wife. Abraham, having been promised that he will sire a great nation, tries to bring this about by his own initiative, first by adopting Eliezar (Gen. 15:1–6) and then by having a son by his wife's Egyptian maid, Hagar.

The theme of danger from God himself is exemplified in the strange and profound stories of the binding of Isaac (Gen. 22) and of Jacob's wrestling with the angel (32:22–32). In the first story God appears to command Abraham to destroy the divine plan – because Isaac, who is to be sacrificed, is the child promised by God to Abraham to realize the divine purposes. In the story of the wrestling, we are not told that the assailant tried to kill Jacob; but he did disable him and had Jacob been completely defeated, this would presumably have prevented his reconciliation with Esau, with other consequences we can only guess at. Such stories express, either intentionally or at a less conscious level, the fact that the divine plan to bless the nations through God's choosing of the ancestors and the peoples they personify will have a rough and ambiguous passage in the world described in Genesis 1–11.

Thus the stories of the ancestors can be read at many levels: as a claim to the land of Canaan, as reflecting the political realities of the monarchy so far as relations with neighboring peoples are concerned, and as embodying and developing popular stories about actual ancestors. Theologically, they express the lessons learned through Israel's painful history: that the work of blessing the nations does not proceed smoothly.

D. FROM EGYPT TO CANAAN

1. The Exodus in History and in Tradition
Historical Data on the Exodus and Wilderness Periods

The narrative of Genesis 46–Exodus 15 describes how the whole of the Israelite people left Canaan to sojourn in Egypt as a result of famine and how Joseph became, in effect, the ruler of the land. It relates that the families of Jacob and of his twelve sons became so numerous in the course of time that after an abortive attempt to restrict their numbers, the pharaoh organized them into slave labor groups, from which they were delivered only when Moses led them from Egypt and then on through the wilderness to the threshold of the land of Canaan. There are many reasons why modern scholarship cannot accept this account at face value.

First, as we shall see when dealing with the conquest of Canaan by the twelve tribes, the fact of such a conquest is very problematic. The occupation of the land was much more likely to have been a process in which wandering pastoralist groups established settlements. Second, those settlements were almost entirely in the northern hill country, with little penetration into Judah. Indeed, Judah plays no part in the history of Israel as reconstructed by modern scholarship until the late eleventh century. Third, the narratives themselves contain difficulties that indicate that they are idealizations written hundreds of years after the events.

A difficulty first identified in the eighteenth century is the figure of 600,000 men on foot, apart from women, children, and their flocks, who left Egypt at the time of the Exodus (Exod. 12:37). The German orientalist H. S. Reimarus, whose work was published in 1777, after his death, estimated that the total number of Israelites leaving Egypt would have been over 3 million, needing six thousand carts, one hundred thousand horses, three hundred thousand oxen, and six hundred thousand sheep. An estimate of the length of the column crossing the Red Sea put it at over eight hundred miles! The view that 600,000 is a scribal error cannot be sustained, since this figure is implied in other passages, such as Exod. 38:26 and Num. 1:46.

Another difficulty arises from the Passover ceremony, which the Israelites observed when they left Egypt. The Old Testament narratives are singularly silent about the Passover until the reign of Hezekiah of Judah (ca. 727–698 B.C.E.; see 2 Chron. 30), and the instructions about observing the Passover in Deut. 16:1–8 imply that Israel is settled in its own land and is worshiping at a single sanctuary. Whereas Exodus 12 tells the Israelites to kill the Passover lamb family by family, presumably wherever they are, Deut. 16:1–8 prescribes that the lamb must be killed and eaten at the central sanctuary.

There are many considerations that make modern scholarship conclude that the picture of all Israel going to Egypt and experiencing the Exodus, Passover, and wilderness wanderings is an idealization from much later times. However, it does not follow from this that no group that later became part of Israel experienced what they believed to be a miraculous deliverance from Egypt. The figure of Moses in the tradition is too dominant to be a fabrication, but the tradition that Moses was, if not an Egyptian, at least a Hebrew who grew up at the Egyptian court is unexpected to say the least. If, as has been suggested above, the Israelites were part of the pastoralist *shasu* peoples, some of them almost certainly became slaves in Egypt and escaped to freedom. In the process they had what they believed to be an encounter with God which became the basis of a powerful theology.

When did these proto-Israelites enter Egypt, how long did they stay, and under what conditions? If we assume that the ancestors lived in the Middle Bronze Age, it is tempting to put the entry into Egypt during the period when the Hyksos ruled Egypt (ca. 1730–1552 B.C.E.). These were Semitic invaders, and it has been suggested that the story of Joseph's rise to power would be credible during the period when Semitic kings ruled Egypt. However, this hypothesis probably does not allow sufficiently for the fact that the biblical stories of the ancestors are literary creations of the ninth to fifth centuries in Israel. Further, it has been argued in section C that the Late Bronze Age provides a more plausible setting for the ancestors, and if we connect them with the *shasu* "nomads," we have plenty of evidence for such groups entering Egypt and staying there. A famous reference occurs in Papyrus Anastasi VI of the end of the thirteenth century B.C.E.. It is the report of a frontier official that

> we have finished letting the Bedouin (Egyptian: *shasu*) tribes of Edom pass the Fortress of Mer-ne-ptah. . . . which is (in) Tjeku, to the pools of Per-Atum. . . . to keep them alive and to keep their cattle alive. . . . (*ANET*, p. 259)

The region to which these *shasu* were being admitted is the region in which the Israelites of the sojourn in Egypt are located in Exodus 1–15, to the east of the Nile Delta.

If we assume that some proto-Israelite *shasu* entered Egypt, say, in the thirteenth century at a time of famine elsewhere, what sort of country did they enter? It was one that stretched along the course of the Nile, with the southern extent of Egyptian domination varying. The Nile made Egypt a fertile and prosperous country able to control other areas as far as northern Mesopotamia. In the fourteenth century B.C.E. Pharaoh Amenophis IV (ca. 1358–1340) tried to introduce a radical religious reform which abolished the worship of all gods save one, the god Aten. Aten was the manifestation of the sun in rays of sunlight; thus he could not be represented in human or animal form. He was praised in hymns as the creator of the earth and its inhabitants and as the lord of foreign lands. The lofty monotheism of hymns praising him has been likened to that in Psalm 104. This religious reform failed, partly because the new religion was abstract and remote from ordinary people. In its place there emerged the religion of Amun-Re, a god who combined something of the universal power of Aten with an approachability for ordinary worshipers. At the same time, the iconographic evidence collected by Othmar Keel indicates that Amun-Re was regarded as a hidden god in spite of being accessible (Keel et

THE HYKSOS

THE WORD "HYKSOS," A contracted form of the Egyptian words meaning "rulers of foreign peoples," refers to the ethnically composite group that dominated Syria–Palestine and Egypt during parts of the Middle Bronze Age (1800–1500 B.C.E.). During the Second Intermediate Period of Egyptian history, the Hyksos dynasties controlled much of northern Egypt. This period of non-native rule encompassed the reign of six kings, spanning some 108 years.

The origins of the mysterious Hyksos are widely debated, though most scholars agree they were a mixture of Asiatic peoples among whom Semites predominated. The Hyksos first infiltrated the Nile Delta region from the northeast during the politically unsettled period at the close of Egypt's Twelfth Dynasty (ca. 1792 B.C.E.). Their advance is often understood as a part of the great Amorite migrations of the Middle Bronze Age. The Hyksos began assuming power in Egypt by 1730, founding their first dynasty at the capital city of Avaris in 1670. They extended their dominion throughout Lower Egypt, as far south as the ancient capital of Memphis. Their rulers adopted the traditional style and bureaucratic organization of the indigenous pharaohs, and Semitic people gradually replaced native Egyptians in official positions. Joseph's rise to power (Gen. 40–41) and his kinsmen's migration to Egypt may be associated with this historical period.

Deepening dissatisfaction with these foreign rulers spawned a burst of nationalism that culminated in the formation of Egypt's New Kingdom in 1552 B.C.E. Kamose began expelling the Hyksos from Egypt around that time, but he did not capture their capital. That task fell to his brother, Amose, who took Avaris after a ten-year struggle. He pursued the remaining Hyksos into Palestine, where they sought refuge. After a siege of three years, their fortress city of Sharuhen also fell to the Egyptians. The fall of the Hyksos from power may be reflected in the biblical text as well. When Exod. 1:5 speaks of "the new king over Egypt who knew not Joseph," it is perhaps commenting on the return to power of native Egyptians, who held the Semitic Hyksos in contempt. If so, the changing fortunes in Egypt of the Hebrews, another Semitic people, may well be directly related to the departure of the Hyksos. The early New Kingdom was also marked by an exclusivistic, militant spirit that would form the proper context for many of the events in the Old Testament's portrayal of the Israelites and their escape from Egypt.

Later Egyptian tradition portrayed the Hyksos as barbarians and destroyers of culture. A century after they had expelled the Hyksos, Egyptians were still bemoaning the ruin brought by those "foreigners." Even in the fourth century B.C.E., an Egyptian historian described the Hyksos as a "smiting blast of God." Although the Hyksos certainly damaged Egypt's pride and sense of national security, they were hardly the brigands later generations made them out to be. From architectural remains in Syria–Palestine and the Egyptian Delta we know them to be representatives of the highly urbanized Phoenecian–Palestinian cultures of the Middle Bronze Age. They seem to have adapted quite well to the Egyptian world. Their skill in metallurgy and crafting jewelry shows they did not lack advanced cultural skills.

The Hyksos were also mighty warriors, credited with introducing the horse-drawn chariot to the ancient world's armory. Some historians also date the introduction of the composite bow to their era. The importance of military power to Hyksos culture is reflected both in their massive urban fortifications and in their characteristic burials, in which the warrior and his horse were interred together in the same grave.

al. 1992, pp. 124 ff.). The Egyptian religion of the thirteenth to twelfth centuries provides a plausible context for the emergence of Israelite belief in a God of universal power that was not amenable to artistic representation by humans but was active on behalf of his chosen people.

In the thirteenth century Pharaoh Rameses II began to build a new city, called Pi-Rameses, in the northeastern part of the Nile Delta near the modern city of Qantir. This was a large site, and there were a number of other building projects in the vicinity. Exod. 1:11 records that the Israelites in Egypt were forced to build the cities of Pithom and Raamses, and although the identifications of these sites is not entirely unproblematic, they have been located at Tell el-Maskuta and Tell el-Daba, respectively, in the northeastern part of the Nile Delta. The building projects of Rameses II are the likely historical occasion of the enslavement of a group of proto-Israelites and of their escape to freedom. Can we go further?

Johannes De Moor has suggested that it is possible to identify Moses with a Canaanite who rose to a position of great power in Egypt at the beginning of the twelfth century. His Egyptian name was Rameses-Is-the-Manifestation-of-the-Gods, the first part of which contains the "Moses" element. His Semitic name was Beya, and De Moor argues that he was a trained scribe who had scant regard for the gods of Egypt. On the death of Seti II in 1197, Beya became, in effect, the ruler of Egypt, since Pharaoh Siptah was a boy. In his third year of rule, Siptah gave permission to Beya to build a tomb in the Valley of the Kings – a signal honor. When civil war followed the death of Siptah in 1192, Queen Mother Tausret, Beya, and their supporters fled from Egypt. De Moor points out that the building of the stone city of Raamses continued after the death of Rameses II in 1212 and suggests that, in this case, the slavery and Exodus might be brought down to the time of Beya, thus making possible his identification with Moses.

It has been pointed out that the biblical account differs significantly from the story of Beya. Moses is never portrayed as a ruler of Egypt, and he flees from the Egyptian court after killing an Egyptian who was ill-treating a Hebrew. He returns from his Midianite place of exile when God commissions him to lead the Hebrews to freedom. It also has to be said that the attempt to identify Moses with a historical figure who was a literate Canaanite prominent in the Egyptian court goes against much modern scholarship, which has been dubious about finding a historical figure behind the legendary material of Exodus 1–15. It may be, however, that such scholarship has been too cautious. It is probably best to keep an open mind about whether the historical Beya is the reality behind the stories of Moses. What does seem to be secure is the assumption that sometime in the thirteenth century B.C.E. and most likely during the reign of Rameses II, a group of proto-Israelite *shasu* escaped from slavery, linked up with other pastoralists, and formed what was later to be Israel.

Faith, History, and the Uses of Narrative

God's freeing of Israel from slavery was a powerful theological conviction that shaped Old Testament law, prophecy, and worship. In the Deuteronomy version of the Ten Commandments (Deut. 5:6–21) the reason for keeping the Sabbath is given as

that your male and female slave may rest as well as you.

The text continues

Remember that you were a servant in the land of Egypt, and the LORD your God brought you out from there with a mighty hand and an outstretched

A monumental seated statue of Rameses II of Egypt in the first court of the Luxor temple and colonnade decorated by Tutankhamon. Rameses, identified by some scholars as the pharaoh of the Israelite oppression, was a great builder of palaces, temples, and colossal statuary.

Courtesy of The American Schools of Oriental Research

arm; therefore the LORD your God commanded you to keep the Sabbath day.

Appeal to the Exodus deliverance as the motive for keeping God's commandments is found many times in Exodus and Deuteronomy. In prophetic texts a famous passage is that in Hos. 11:1:

When Israel was a child, I loved him,
    and out of Egypt I called my son.

In Isaiah 40–55 imagery from the Exodus and wilderness wanderings is used to describe how God will bring back his people from exile in Babylon (e.g., Isa. 43:15–21, 51:9–11). Among the Psalms, 105 and 106 recall the deliverance from Egypt and the wilderness wanderings (see also Pss. 135 and 136).

The powerful influence of the Exodus story contrasts strikingly with the little that can be said about what actually happened. As noted above, the nearest that we can get to the actual event may be to assume that some proto-Israelites among the *shasu* were forced into the building gangs of Rameses II, from which they escaped with (as they believed) divine help. To this gap between literary and historical events, we have to add the difficulty that the narratives undoubtedly contain material that cannot be accurate. It has already been noted that it is impossible that all the tribes of Israel took part in the Exodus and that this matter will be raised again when the occupation of Canaan and the formation of Israel are discussed. Another possible difficulty concerns the Passover. Many scholars hold that the ceremony of killing a lamb and of daubing its blood on the door of the tent is something done by nomads when they move from their winter (desert) pasture closer to populated areas. The blood is to ward off the evil and danger believed to be associated with more populated land. In this view (which is not free of difficulties), the Passover was not observed at the time of the Exodus. It is a ceremony observed annually by nomads that was gradually historicized and that thus became part of the Exodus story. Even if we think that this is a cavalier way of treating the Bible, we have to admit that there is at least one puzzle in the Passover story. Why did the angel who killed the firstborn need to see the blood on the door in order to know whom not to destroy? In the stories of the plagues, God afflicted the Egyptians while sparing the Israelites (e.g., Exod. 9:7, 22–6). Why was an extra sign needed at the Passover?

The purpose of the last two paragraphs is to introduce the problem of faith and history. If the Israelites believed that God had done things at the Exodus whereas modern scholarship with all due humility finds difficulties in the narratives in which this belief is expressed, does this mean that the faith of Israel was based upon lies? To answer this question we have to discuss the relation between history and narrative, and the function of narrative.

Our access to the past is mainly by way of narrative. If we are asked to give evidence to the police about a motor accident that we observed, we have to tell a story – and tell that story from the point of view of where we were standing and how the events affected us. There will be many things that we do not know, facts that will only become apparent when a doctor has examined the driver, a mechanic has examined the automobile, and the police have measured skid marks on the road. A final report – which will be in the form of a written narrative – may well describe the accident in a way very different from our own account and observations; yet it will not be suggested that we did not see the accident or draw the conclusion that we did on the basis of what we saw.

If we had been present when a group of *shasu* people escaped from slavery and were pursued by soldiers, from whom they escaped by successfully crossing a stretch of water, we would not have observed anything that seemed divine or miraculous. To the escapees themselves, or to their leader(s), however, things may have looked quite different. Their religious beliefs may have made them certain that their escape, against all the odds, was not something that they could have achieved on their own; and what others might have seen as fortunate coincidences in their favor, they saw as the work of their God on their behalf. The remarkable thing is perhaps not so much how they understood the events at the time but how their story about the meaning of these events began to shape their understanding of who they were and what their obligations were to God and to each other. For this story was not just a remembrance of the past: it defined who the subjects of the story were in the present. It did not articulate simply what God had done in the past; it made possible their faith in God in the present, a faith that had far-reaching moral obligations.

As this story was told and retold and was celebrated in worship, two things happened. The first was that people who had not experienced the escape accepted the story as their story too, so that it became a way in which they could believe and trust in the God who had set the captives free. To put it another way, the story articulated the character and nature of God in a way that helped people to have faith. The second thing was that the story was embellished in order to leave hearers in no doubt that God had acted "with a mighty hand and an outstretched arm." The miraculous element in the stories of the plagues and the crossing of the Red Sea was heightened, while in the ceremony of the Passover, whatever its origins, a means was provided whereby the deliverance could be celebrated regularly. No doubt in this process many features of the story were elaborated in ways which are not historically true. Yet this was not an exercise in falsification; it was part of a process in which the story grew as it expressed the faith in God of generation after generation. Ultimately, the truth of the story of the Exodus is not to be assessed according to its approximation to modern scholarly reconstructions of history. Its truth is to be seen more in moral terms. As we shall see, the Exodus story constantly challenged the Israelites to self-criticism. It condemned slavery within Israel and enjoined the gracious treatment not only of the poor, the weak, and the oppressed but also of domestic animals, fields, and vineyards. In its fullest sense, then, the story of the Exodus was not just a story about a past event. It was a narrative that helped God and Israel interact for generation after generation, making known the divine character and how the redeemed people were to live responsibly in the divine presence. None of this helps us to know whether the story is true in the sense that there really is a God who helped some slaves escape from slavery in Egypt. This is a matter that can only be decided by readers as they follow through the story for themselves and see how it affects them. There is one certain datum, however. Israel had this faith, and its influence upon their literature was far-reaching. How it entered into Israelite history and society will be considered in later sections.

2. The Story of the Exodus

This section deals with the Exodus story as contained in Exodus 1–15. But this is not the only place in the Old Testament where the

Exodus is recalled; it is also recounted in Psalms 105 and 106. The concentration will be upon the material in Exodus, however, with special reference to its literary and theological themes.

The narrative begins with the names of the sons of Jacob who had entered Egypt. The eleven sons personify eleven tribes, the picture being completed by reference to the death of Joseph (1:6). Thus the story is about all Israel, and the introduction helps later Israelite readers to see the story as their story. The two following sections (1:8–13, 15–22) are, at the level of fact, contradictory. A ruler who needs slaves to work on building projects is unlikely to want to restrict their numbers. Or if he does wish to keep their numbers down, it seems more logical to kill at birth baby girls rather than baby boys. But having mentioned the use of Hebrews to build the pharaoh's cities in verses 8–13, the narrative shifts to a new goal: that of the birth and Egyptian upbringing of the future deliverer.

The incident of the two midwives (vv. 15–22) is a valuable clue to the type of literature we are dealing with. In the story they hold conversations directly with the pharaoh, though in an absolute monarchy, this would be complete nonsense. The godlike Egyptian ruler was shielded from his people by an impenetrable bureaucracy. But this is popular literature, and in this literature midwives can converse with and defy the highest earthly rulers. Also, only two of them are needed to service the entire Israelite people! Whether the midwives were Hebrew women or Egyptians acting as midwives to the Hebrews can be argued. The fact that they have Hebrew names is irrelevant in a type of literature that accommodates the story to the needs of ordinary hearers or readers. If they *were* Egyptians, then there is a contrast between a ruler doing wrong and two of his subjects defying him because they fear God and intend to do what is right.

The next section (chaps. 2–4) concentrates upon Moses' birth, his Egyptian upbringing, his solidarity with his people, and his flight to Midian after he has killed an Egyptian who was beating a Hebrew. Two important themes emerge in chapter 2. The first is that of the rejection of Moses by his own people. It might have been expected that Moses' killing of the Egyptian who was beating a Hebrew would have earned him gratitude; but only the next day a Hebrew reminding Moses of the killing makes it clear that Moses is to have no authority over the Hebrews. Moses' ambiguous identity is also indicated when, having arrived in Midian and having helped the daughters of a Midianite priest, Moses is described by the maidens to their father as an Egyptian. The second, and related theme, arises from the name of Moses' son, Gershom, borne by one of the maidens. This is explained as meaning "I have been a sojourner [Hebrew *ger*] in a foreign land" (2:22). The question is, which land? Of the two possibilities, Midian and Egypt, the latter would indicate that although Moses is seen by others as an Egyptian, in his heart he feels to be an exile in Egypt.

Chapters 3–4, the call of Moses, have features in common with the accounts of the calls of prophets (cf. Isa. 6:1–10, Jer. 1:4–10, Ezek. 2:1–10; cf. Amos 7:14–15). The parallels with Isaiah's call are clearest, with common themes being the manifestation of God's presence, the feeling of inadequacy to carry out the task, and the ambiguity about whether the people of Israel will hearken to the message. In the case of Moses, obstacle after obstacle is placed in the way of the divine commission. He is not important enough to speak to the pharaoh (3:11) – but the midwives spoke to the pharaoh and they did not grow up in the Egyptian court! He does not know God's name (3:13), and the people will not believe that God appeared to him (4:1). Even after God has given Moses power to perform signs to convince the people of his commission (4:2–9), Moses argues that he lacks the necessary eloquence to be a spokesman for his people. The narrative is undoubtedly expressing here the harsh lessons learned by prophets and others about the suffering involved in mediating between the initiative of a gracious God and the indifference or hostility of the beneficiary people. Initially, Moses need not have worried. The people accept the news of God's intention to set them free without demur (4:31). Later, it will be different.

A strange and difficult passage at 4:24–6 needs a brief comment. It relates that the Lord met and sought to kill Moses on his way back to Egypt. His Midianite wife, Zipporah, saved Moses by touching Moses' feet (genitals?) with their son's foreskin. This passage has provoked many differing interpretations, out of which two observations are presented here. The first is that God's anger is directed against the halfhearted way that Moses has accepted his task. It is a foreign woman, Moses' Midianite wife, who has the faith that Moses will win through and the foresight to act to defend Moses. The second point is that Moses' symbolic circumcision resolved the ambiguity of his identity. He is now a circumcised Hebrew, not an Egyptian liable to be killed in the future as a firstborn son (cf. 4:23).

Chapters 5–11 contain a series of episodes of meetings between Moses and Aaron and the pharaoh in which the petitions of the Hebrews escalate from a request to go into the wilderness to sacrifice (5:3) to a demand that they be released from the pharaoh's service altogether (9:1). The demands are reinforced by plagues, and the interviews are characterized by alternating agreement and refusal on pharaoh's part. The narrative ascribes this vacillation to both pharaoh's own obstinacy (e.g., 8:15) and to God's hardening of pharaoh's heart (e.g., 9:12).

In their final form these chapters are a literary masterpiece in the way they maintain the expectations of the reader and bring the narrative to the climax of the tenth plague, that of the death of the firstborn. It has long been recognized that this masterpiece has been put together from different sources. Attempts to divide the plague stories into the three sources J, E, and P on the basis of who initiates the plague (Moses, God directly, or Aaron on Moses' instructions) are not wholly convincing. However, a priestly tradition with distinctive vocabulary, in which Aaron acts on Moses' instructions, can be identified, and it is instructive to separate out this material and to compare it with the nonpriestly traditions and those in Psalm 105.

	Plagues 1–9	
Priestly	**Nonpriestly**	**Psalm 105**
water into blood (7:19–24)	water into blood (7:14–18)	darkness (v. 28) water into blood (v. 29)
frogs (8:5–15)	frogs (8:1–4)	
gnats (8:16–19)		frogs (v. 30)
	flies (8:20–4)	
	cattle plague (9:1–7)	flies and gnats (v. 31)
boils (9:8–12)		
	hail and thunder (9:22–6)	
	locusts (10:12–15)	hail + lightning (vv. 32–3)
	darkness (10:21-23)	locusts (vv. 34–5)

The analysis suggests that there were varying traditions about the plagues, and that the total of ten plagues is the result of the final composition of the narrative.

The chapters dealing with the plagues lead into the account of the institution of the Passover (chap. 12), into which the tenth plague is dovetailed. In its present form chapter 12 envisages the celebration of the Passover in Israel, for verses 14–20 add details about the Feast of Unleavened Bread, a festival which lasts seven days and which was almost certainly originally an agricultural festival associated with the barley harvest (March/April) in Israel. The number of those leaving Egypt after God had destroyed the firstborn of Egyptian children and animals (600,000; see 12:37) has already been discussed. Within this type of literature, the historical problems created by such numbers are irrelevant (note the absurdly small number – two! – of active midwives among the Hebrews).

The Israelites' leaving of Egypt brings one last change of mind by pharaoh, which leads to his downfall at the Red Sea. With his army he chases the departing Israelites, but whereas the Israelites get across the sea, pharaoh and his army are overwhelmed by it. There has been much discussion about how to translate the Hebrew words normally rendered "Red Sea" as well as about the location of the sea. The translation "Red Sea" goes back to the Greek translators of the Hebrew Bible, who understood by the designation what we call today the Gulfs of Suez and Aqaba. A suggestion that has found much favor is that the Hebrew *suph* is the equivalent of the Egyptian *twf(y)* (papyrus) and that the correct translation is "Sea of Reeds." This opens up the possibility of locating the deliverance at the sea either at one of the lakes along the line of what is now the Suez Canal or at the lagoon on the Mediterranean, Lake Sirbonis. The most important question to ask is what the author and the implied readers understood by the Hebrew words. Although the word *suph* is used at Exod. 2:3, 5, to mean the rushes in the Nile, the accounts of the deliverance in chapters 14 and 15 do not give the impression that the author (or authors) has in mind a lake of reeds or rushes. At 1 Kings 9:26 the Hebrew refers to the Gulf of Aqaba; and it is probably safest to assume that the author of Exodus had in mind a large, uncrossable sea such as the Gulf of Aqaba, and that neither the author nor the implied readers had sufficient knowledge of the geography of Egypt to know precisely where the crossing had taken place. This does not rule out a small lake to the east of the Qantir region or Lake Sirbonis as possible stretches of water crossed by escaping proto-Israelites. The question is what the narrator had in mind, and the answer seems to be that there was a miracle on a large scale.

This warns us against trying to rationalize the account by attributing the Israelites' deliverance to a change in the tide, for example. The narrative as we have it cannot be rationalized. God is miraculously present as a pillar of cloud by day and a pillar of fire by night (13:21–2), and the sea is divided by a wind that is strong enough to separate the sea and to dry a path, without at the same time harming the Israelites. Modern readers who have seen and felt gale-force winds will readily appreciate this point. The deliverance is, in effect, the eleventh plague, with engulfing waters brought upon the pharaoh and his army in the same way that many plagues are initiated – by Moses stretching out his hand at God's command. The importance of chapter 14 lies not so much in how the miracle is presented as in the introduction of two themes, one of which will become a common feature of the wilderness narratives. The first is that of the people's regret that they have been delivered from slavery (14:11–12). The second is the emphasis on the salvation that God alone can give (14:13–14) and that his people must accept in faith.

The Exodus story is rounded off by the poetic hymn of 15:1–19, a piece about whose date and original setting there is little scholarly agreement. Feminist interpreters have suggested that the song was originally composed and sung by Miriam (see v. 21) and that male editing has ascribed the song to Moses and made it seem as though Miriam and the women simply imitated the men.

3.   Israel in the Wilderness

Exodus 15:22–19:25 bring the Israelites from the Red Sea to Mount Sinai. About half the material deals with the discontent of the people at conditions in the wilderness and their continued regret at having left their slavery in Egypt. It is clear that, in their present form, these chapters (15:22–17:7) contain stories that were used to instruct Israelites about the proper observance of God's laws. A conspicuous example is 16:13–30. This records the gift of the manna, of which the Israelites are to gather each day sufficient just for that day. If kept longer, it goes bad, except on the sixth day, when a double amount is gathered to suffice for the sixth day and the Sabbath. This is, of course, an anachronism, since the Israelites have yet to be commanded to observe the Sabbath (Exod 20:8–11). But such things do not matter in this type of literature, and the story is an excellent object lesson about observing the Sabbath. The miracles of the quails and the manna can be rationalized. Quails (*Coturnix coturnix*) cross the northern part of

SINAI

THE SINAI PENINSULA IS A large, wedge-shaped block of land that forms a major land bridge between Africa and Asia. With a total area of some 24,000 square miles, Sinai's borders are clearly defined by the Mediterranean Sea in the north, the Red Sea in the south, the Gulf of Suez in the east, and the Gulf of Aqaba in the west. Sinai is actually a part of the Saharo-Arabian Desert, so its climate is quite arid. Annual rainfall averages from 2.5 inches in the north to less than 1 inch in the south. Geographically, Sinai is divisible into three regions: the north, a low, sandy plateau marked by expansive sand dunes dotted with oases; the central region, a high limestone plateau with little rainfall and sparse vegetation; and the south, covered by rough granite mountains whose highest peak reaches an elevation of 8,660 feet.

Sinai's climate is hostile, but the area is not uninhabitable. Archeological evidence suggests the peninsula has been intermittently occupied for over 30,000 years. Egypt began exploiting the southern region's lode of turquoise no later than 2650 B.C.E., and copper mining was common throughout the second millennium B.C.E. The coastal zone especially has served through the ages as an important military thoroughfare.

The Old Testament references to Sinai are to distinct tracts of territory within the larger Sinai peninsula. The wildernesses of Shur, Sin, Paran, and Zin are the biblical designations for desert regions of the peninsula. The wilderness of Sinai is traditionally located in the south-central part of the peninsula. In this region Moses is said to have seen the burning bush; there the Israelites were encamped when they received the law. Often the Old Testament uses the word "Sinai" to designate a range of mountains (Deut. 33:2) or, still more specifically, to indicate the single mountain peak on which Moses received the law.

This "Mount Sinai" is known to biblical writers by several names ("the mountain," Exod. 19:2; "mountain of God," Exod. 3:1; "Mount Horeb," 1 Kings 19:8), but its exact location is still a mystery. As many as a dozen mountains in Sinai and western Arabia have been designated as the sacred place, and scholars still debate the location of Mount Sinai in relation to the continuing controversy over the route of Israel's Exodus from Egypt. Some suggest a location near Kadesh-barnea in the north, based on other areas sometimes mentioned in close proximity to Mount Sinai. A majority prefer a candidate far-

ther south. Since the fourth century, Christian tradition has held Mount Sinai to be modern-day Gebel Musa ("Mountain of Moses"), a 7,363-foot peak situated in the mountain ranges of the Sinai peninsula's southern tip.

Communities of Christian monks have lived at the foot of Gebel Musa since at least 373 C.E. Early in the fourth century Emperor Constantine's mother, Helena, built a small church on its northwestern slope. The Byzantine emperor Justinian founded the present Monastery of Saint Catherine at its base in 527. Gebel Musa received new attention in 1859 when Constantine Tischendorf found in the monastery a fourth-century C.E. Greek manuscript of the Old and New Testaments, one of the earliest in existence.

Whatever its precise location, Mount Sinai became a significant focus and symbol of divine revelation (Exod. 43:16, Deut. 33:2). The memory of Mount Sinai was inextricably linked with the history of the covenant made there between Yahweh and the people of Israel (Neh. 9:13) and the commandments associated with it (Mal. 4:4). The Lord's presence on this peak came to stand for the reality of divine protection (Judg. 5:4–5, Ps. 68:8). Thus the prophet Elijah sought Mount Sinai in a time of distress, hoping for a fresh revelation from God there.

the Sinai desert on their way to the Sudan in August–September and then again in March on their way back north. Manna is a substance secreted by the tree or shrub *Tamarix mannifera,* that falls to the ground forming a small disk. Thus both sources of food can be found in the Sinai desert naturally. But it must be emphasized that in Exodus 16 the provision is presented as miraculous, and in the case of the manna becomes an object lesson about observing the Sabbath.

4. Israel at Sinai

Covenant in the Ancient Near East and in Israel

Once they have arrived at Mount Sinai, God promises the Israelites that if they keep his covenant, they will be his own possession among all peoples (19:5). After the giving of the Ten Commandments (20:1–17) and the "ordinances" (21:1–23:19), there is a ceremony in which the Israelites agree to obey what is contained in the "Book of the Covenant" (24:7), after which the people are consecrated by the blood of the covenant (24:8).

This is not the first time that the word "covenant" (Hebrew *berit*) has occurred in the Old Testament. After the Flood, God makes a covenant with Noah (Gen. 9:8–17), and after the call of Abraham, God makes covenants with him and with Isaac and Jacob (Gen. 15:18, 17:2–21; Exod. 2:24). There are also various covenants between the ancestors and local peoples (Gen. 14:13: "these [the Amorites] were allies of [lit., possessors of a covenant with] Abram"). As will be shown, the history of the notion of covenant in the Old Testament is complex. The present section draws attention to a discussion that became prominent in the 1960s and that was based on comparisons between Hittite suzerainty treaties of the fourteenth to thirteenth centuries B.C.E. and material in the Old Testament such as the Ten Commandments, the Sinai narrative, and the Book of Deuteronomy.

The Hittite treaties were published in the early part of the twentieth century, and a selection can be found in *ANET*, pp. 201–6. Although there are some variations, the following basic structure of the treaties is apparent:

1. Preamble
2. Historical prologue
3. Stipulations
4. Provisions about the text being deposited and read publicly
5. List of divine witnesses to the treaty
6. Blessings and curses

Several of these items can be illustrated from the treaty between Mursilis and Duppi-Tessub

---

ANCIENT NEAR EASTERN COVENANTS

COVENANTS ARE PROMISES made between two parties, bound by formal oaths, concerning future actions and relations. In the ancient world, covenants were made within recognized legal communities and between different sociopolitical groups and actually represented international treaties.

The earliest covenant–treaties, although fragmentary, date from at least the middle of the third millennium B.C.E. in ancient Sumer. Covenants are also mentioned in the Mari archives (nineteenth to eighteenth centuries B.C.E.), but with insufficient detail of content or procedure to be studied effectively. By far the most useful and extensive documentation of ancient covenant forms comes from the Hittite Empire of the Late Bronze Age (ca. 1450–1200 B.C.E.).

Scholars have taken the Hittite treaties to be illustrative of a highly developed form available to many societies of the ancient Near East. There are two types of Hittite covenants: suzerainty treaties and parity treaties. Suzerainty treaties establish a firm relationship of support between two parties of unequal status: the sovereign and his vassal. The vassal is obligated by the treaty to abide by the stipulations of his overlord (in this case, the Hittite king). In parity (bilateral) treaties, two parties of equal status are bound to obey identical stipulations.

Certain broad similarities exist between the written Hittite treaties and the major covenant traditions of the Old Testament. Since such treaties come from the time frame normally assigned to Moses, some scholars have attempted to use them as evidence for the Mosaic origin of Israel's legal traditions. However, the differences between the two are great enough that any direct influence seems to have been unlikely. The Hittite covenants nevertheless add to our understanding of an important social convention of the ancient Near East that played a key role in the origin and formation of biblical tradition.

(*ANET,* pp. 203–5). In the preamble Mursilis establishes his identity as the major party:

> These are the words of the Sun Mursilis, the great king . . .

The historical prologue recalls that

> Aziras was the grandfather of you, Duppi-Tessub. He rebelled against my father, but submitted again to my father. . . . [and much more].

Then come clauses about future relations between the two countries in which Mursilis demands the exclusive loyalty of Duppi-Tessub, military clauses which also emphasize Duppi-Tessub's need to be absolutely loyal, and clauses about dealings with foreigners and others, in a similar vein. Dozens of gods are named as witnesses to the treaty, and the text ends with blessings and curses:

> . . . should Duppi-Tessub not honour these words of the treaty and the oath, may these gods of the oath destroy Duppi-Tessub. . . . But if Duppi-Tessub honours these words of the treaty. . . . may these gods of the oath protect him. . . .

A stipulation about depositing and reading the treaty is not extant.

At first sight the above does not appear to be similar to anything in the Sinai story; but as certain observations are made, the parallels begin to emerge. The Ten Commandments begin with words identifying the major party, "I am Yahweh your God," and continue with the historical reference "who brought you out of the land of Egypt." In the commandments that follow, the need for Israel's exclusive loyalty to Yahweh is stressed.

The Ten Commandments do not contain provisions for depositing and reading, invocations of gods, or blessings and curses. Yet in Exod. 24:7 the Book of the Covenant (see the section on Israel's law) is read to the people, and Exod. 25:21–2 mentions the ark as a box that will contain the testimony that God will give the people. In Exod. 23:22–33 there are blessings in the sense that if Israel serves God unswervingly, then he will drive out the Canaanites and other peoples from the land of Canaan and make Israel a great nation there. Curses can be inferred from these blessings. If Deuteronomy is considered in this connection, the following sections can be identified:

> Historical prologue (chaps. 1–4)
> Stipulations of the covenant (chaps. 5–26)
> Command to write the words of the law (27:8)
> Blessings and curses (chaps. 28–9)
> Heaven and earth called as witnesses (30:15–20)

In the early phase of the discussion, these apparent similarities led some scholars to conclude that in the period before the monarchy, Israel took and used the model of a treaty between two nations to express its covenant relationship with Yahweh. Thus the covenant idea was seen to be an early feature of Israel's religion, and the argument was buttressed by the belief that only the second-millennium treaty forms provided parallels to the Old Testament texts. Later forms did not. Two factors have largely disposed of this position. The first is the discovery that Assyrian treaties of the seventh century display the same structure as the Hittite treaties. The second is that the literary growth of the Exodus and Deuteronomy material is known to be so complex that the significance of such parallels cannot be determined so straightforwardly.

The passage that most likely contains the earliest material about the covenant is Exod. 34:10–26. Its core (vv. 17–26) contains some features which indicate that the material may be old. It begins with the command

> You shall not make cast idols

followed by instructions about observing the Feast of Unleavened Bread in the month of Abib, the month of the Exodus. There is no reference at this point to the Passover. Next there are instructions about dedicating to God all firstborn sons, cattle, and other domestic animals. A Sabbath command appears in the following form:

> Six days you shall work, but on the seventh day you shall rest; even in plowing time and in harvest time you shall rest.

Then the observance of two other agricultural festivals is enjoined: the Feast of Weeks (the wheat harvest) and the Feast of Ingathering (fruit harvest in the autumn; also called the Feast of Booths). The final instructions are that leaven must not be added to sacrifices, that first fruits must be brought to the sanctuary, and that the Israelites must not

THE DIVINE NAME

THE TETRAGRAMMATON (four-letter word), YHWH, occurs about 6,800 times in the Old Testament. It is written without vowels, though scholars believe the correct pronunciation to be something like "Yahweh." According to tradition, this personal covenant name of Israel's God was revealed to Moses at the time of the Exodus (Exod. 3). However, some strands of the Pentateuchal traditions trace the use of this name back far beyond Moses to the time of Enosh, the grandson of Adam (Gen. 4:26). *Enosh* means "man" in Hebrew, and the use of the name from the creation story onward in the J source is a later attempt to view all of human history in light of

the historic events of the Exodus. A theological point is being made: YHWH is the God not only of Israel but of all humanity.

Etymologically, the name YHWH is masked in obscurity. The several abbreviated forms in the biblical narrative may be evidence that the longer form is older. The shortened form "Yah" occurs about twenty-five times in the Old Testament (e.g., in the cultic cry "*hallelu-yah,*" "praise Yah!"), and theophoric names often use a short form (e.g., "Joel," "Yo is God"; "Isaiah," "Yahu is salvation"). The name's complete form is attested in early biblical narratives and in extrabiblical documents from the sixth century B.C.E., a good indication that the four-letter YHWH is original. As for its meaning, linguists have sug-

gested that YHWH might be derived from words meaning "to act passionately," thus emphasizing the divinity's loving concern; or "to speak," stressing god's revelatory function; or "to blow" or "to cause to fall," indicating that YHWH was originally a storm god. More likely, YHWH is to be linked with the verb *hyh,* "to be." Scholars have attempted to trace the use of this divine name to either Mesopotamia or Syria, though its origin lies most likely in the Sinai peninsula. It was there that Moses came in contact with Jethro (Hobab/Rhuel), the high priest of Midian. Moses married Jethro's daughter Zipporah and perhaps became aware for the first time of the name of Jethro's god, YHWH.

boil a kid in its mother's milk. A reference to Passover in verse 25 is clearly a later gloss.

It is tempting to see here early raw material that was later developed into material more familiar to us. The dedicating of firstborn sons and animals after the mention of Egypt is reminiscent of the tenth plague, whereas the commandments about making no cast gods and about resting on the seventh day suggest an embryo form of the Ten Commandments. Most striking is the agricultural content of the commandments, with stress upon practices that will apparently distinguish the Israelites from their Canaanite neighbors, such as not working on the seventh day, not adding leaven to sacrifices, and not boiling kids in their mother's milk. If these surmises are correct, we have a rudimentary covenant which binds to God a group of people who had been delivered from Egypt and who are living among Canaanites in the land of Israel. Their identity as a separate people bound to their God is articulated negatively and positively: negatively by avoiding certain Canaanite practices and positively by treating the principal agricultural festivals as occasions for acknowledging dependence upon God. This is probably the closest we can get to an early covenant idea in ancient Israel, although it is far from easy to suggest a date. Anywhere between the eleventh and ninth centuries B.C.E. is possible.

The next stage in the development of the covenant idea was probably during the reign of Josiah (640–609 B.C.E.). After a long period of subjugation of Judah to Assyria (probably from around 700 to 627), Josiah was able to gain Judah's independence. In opposition to the vassal treaties that had probably been imposed upon Judah by successive Assyrian kings, independence was expressed in terms of Judah (representing all Israel) being the vassal of Yahweh and bound to him by a covenant which he had sworn to the ancestors. This view of Judah's relationship to Yahweh was incorporated into the Book of Deuteronomy, with its insistence that the people should be absolutely loyal to Yahweh and worship him at one sanctuary only. The covenant as formulated in Deuteronomy contains warnings about the curses that will fall upon Israel if God's commandments are ignored.

When Jerusalem fell in the early sixth century B.C.E. and the people were exiled to Babylon, it appeared that the curses threatened in the Deuteronomic covenant had been activated. But the view that the exile was the occasion to discharge these curses helped Judah to survive the catastrophe. New responses that were called forth included the promise in a later addition to Jeremiah (31:31–4) that God would make a new covenant with his people, not like the old one at the time of the Exodus, which the people broke. The priestly historical work, written in the fifth century and found in parts of Genesis, Exodus, and Numbers, expresses the view that God's covenant cannot be broken, in spite of Israel's disobedience. The covenant is now taken back to the time of Noah – a covenant with the whole human race – and to Abraham (Gen. 17:1–7).

Law in the Ancient Near East and in Israel

Written laws in the ancient Near East antedate those in the Old Testament by over a thousand years (see the useful collection in *ANET*, pp. 160–98 and 523–8). The earliest extant Sumerian laws date from around 2100 B.C.E. Written laws presuppose a society that is centrally governed and that has become sufficiently diverse for the need to arise to regulate activities such as commerce, the family, property, slavery, prices, and wages. Thus, for example, the rulers of the empire of the Third Dynasty of Ur in southern Mesopotamia (ca. 2100–2000 B.C.E.) presided over twenty-three city-states, each with its civil and military rulers and paying monthly taxes to the king. The administration of such an empire required scribes and scribal schools, which in turn meant that laws were written, and records of court proceedings were kept. Yet it is generally agreed that the collections of laws that kings caused to be written were not complete or comprehensive, and that

ISRAELITE LAW IN ITS ANCIENT NEAR EASTERN CONTEXT

IT IS LIKELY THAT THE ANCEStors of Israel brought with them a stock of legal traditions from Mesopotamia, which found their way centuries later into the law codes of the Hebrew Bible. Several collections of Mesopotamian laws have survived, the oldest of which date from the end of the third millennium B.C.E. (e.g., the collections of Ur-Nammu of Ur, ca. 2050, and of Lipit-Istar of Isin and Bilalama of Eshunna, ca. 2000). The most famous and best-preserved collection was promulgated by Hammurabi, king of Babylon in the first half of the eighteenth century B.C.E.

The code of Hammurabi, like much of the legal material in the Old Testament, does not claim to encompass the full range of regulations and procedures that governed ancient societies. It is rather a collection of selected legal guidelines valid in certain carefully prescribed circumstances. In most cases the laws are cast in a casuistic form; that is, they describe specific prohibitions and penalties. The standard formulation is "If a person commits this crime, then this will be the punishment." A number of intermediate clauses often make exceptions for extenuating or exacerbating circumstances.

Particularly interesting are parallels between ancient Near Eastern law and the collection of laws in Exodus 20–3, known as the Book of the Covenant. Most scholars date the Book of the Covenant well after Israel's entrance into Canaan since it presupposes a settled people, living in an agricultural society in close relation to foreigners. Yet this collection no doubt reflects earlier material. It is structured in the traditional form of ancient Near Eastern law codes; prologue (20:22), laws (20:23–23:19), epilogue (23:20–3). Most of its laws are cast in the casuistic form, which was dominant in the ancient Near East. Many laws in the Book of the Covenant share identical or near-identical formulations with those found in Mesopotamian law codes.

Yet there are also significant differences between Israelite and Mesopotamian law. Ancient Israel normally modified the traditions it received in light of its religious sensitivities. In some cases biblical materials address the same problem as the Mesopotamian laws (an indication of their shared cultural background) but offer a different legal treatment. As a whole, Israelite law was more concerned with personal, rather than property rights, and it ventured beyond Mesopotamian law to give religious and cultic instruction as well. Penalties in Israelite law were generally more humane than their ancient Near Eastern counterparts. Finally, Israel gave prominence to legal traditions whose form stressed categorical imperatives and prohibitions (e.g., "Thou shalt not . . .") rather than conditional statements. Although it was not unique to Israel, this apodictic form (Greek "pointing out [a command]") commended itself to Israel because of its ability to convey the absolute character of Yahweh's covenant demands upon his people.

they were chiefly attempts to convince the gods and posterity that the king had fulfilled his role as the upholder of justice.

We find the same incompleteness in the Old Testament laws. Whereas the laws of Hammurabi (1792–1750), themselves regarded as not comprehensive, deal with marriage, divorce, adoption, the rights of prisoners-of-war, redress against a physician for injuries received during medical treatment, and redress against the builder of a faulty house, in the older Israelite legal material these matters are either completely ignored or only barely alluded to. Further, especially in Deuteronomy, laws are set forth that do not specify details but appeal simply to a person's generosity. A good example is the release of slaves in Deut. 15:12–18. Instead of prescribing that a released slave should be given so many sheep and so much wheat, the injunction is "Provide

DIVINATION

DIVINATION, THE PRACTICE of seeking information from superhuman powers by physical means, was a common feature of life in the ancient Near East. Both natural and human phenomena were employed. Diviners examined the progression of heavenly bodies or meteorological events. Deliberate actions like shooting arrows, casting lots, and seeking communication with the dead (necromancy) were also employed.

Ancient Babylon developed the art of soothsaying into a widespread, socially important, and semi-scientific discipline. In classical antiquity, the name "Chaldean" (an ethnic designation for citizens of the Neo-Babylonian Empire) became synonymous with "magician" (see Dan. 1:4; 5:11). The Babylonian diviners excelled mainly in the field of hepatoscopy, that is, the examination of livers from sacrificial animals. In Mesopotamian thought, the liver was the seat of life, and it was thought to be a proper vehicle for discerning the gods' will and intentions. Large collections of model livers from

every time and place in which Babylon and Assyria held sway in the ancient world testify to the extent and importance of this branch of divination. Hepatoscopy was also a common practice in ancient Mari, in both state and private affairs.

As was the case with all magical practices, divination came to be forbidden to the Israelites (Lev. 19:26, Deut. 18:11). Israel's abstinence from magic and divination became an important mark of its unique status and belief among the other peoples of Palestine (Canaanites, Philistines) and the great nations of the ancient Near East (Egypt, Babylon, Assyria). The Israelites believed that Yahweh communicated his will to them, but only through carefully proscribed channels. Israel's developing theology came to draw a sharp contrast between any attempt at foretelling the future by artificial means and legitimate, divinely inspired prophecy (Deut. 18:14–15). Not surprisingly, the prophets become the chief opponents of divination. They were tireless in their battle against magical practices, which were often widespread in the land of Israel

(Mic. 3:7, Isa. 44:25, Ezek. 12:24).

However, an earlier time in Israel's history when divination was freely practiced has left its mark on the Hebrew Bible. Shaking and dropping or shooting arrows as a means of discerning God's will appears to be the background for incidents in the lives of David and Jonathan (1 Sam. 20) and of Joash (2 Kings 13). Certain places were associated with the practice of divination, especially sacred trees (e.g., the diviners' oak, Judg. 9:37; perhaps associated with Abraham's oaks of Mamre, Gen. 12:6). Isa. 57:3 suggests that eventually Israel's soothsayers were organized as professional groups. No less a personage than King Saul resorted to the medium at Endor to summon the dead prophet Samuel when there had been no answer from the Lord.

Israel's cult also allowed direct communication from God by means of the obscure Urim and Thummim, a kind of divination by lots with wide precedent throughout human history. The ephod and teraphim, whose exact identification is also unclear, were also used to obtain information from God (Zech. 10:2, Hos. 3:4).

him liberally out of your flock," followed by the imperative "thus giving to him some of the bounty with which the LORD your God had blessed you" – surely a miser's charter! Old Testament collections of laws, therefore, are only a selection of the laws that must have existed to enable life in the states of Judah and Israel to be properly regulated; and their presence is as much an indication of Old Testament ethics and theology as of legal practice. In some cases (and this may be true also of ancient Near Eastern laws) they may be the result of professional scribal activity divorced from the actual practice of law.

The written laws in the Old Testament presuppose the sociological conditions in which laws are promulgated by central authority and enforced by courts. But these conditions probably did not exist until the ninth or eighth century B.C.E. in Judah and Israel. There are indications from the Old Testament itself of more informal legal arrangements before and alongside the establishment of courts. Four stages of legal process have been suggested by Michael Fishbane: (1) direct appeal to God or use of an oracle or ordeal, (2) making an ad hoc decision, possibly with the help of an arbitrator, (3) laws collected, systematized, and administered by established legal authorities, and (4) law making and drafting by professional lawyers or scribes.

The first category is found when there are no witnesses or adversarial or investigative procedures. In the longer text of 1 Sam. 14:40–2 and in Josh. 7:16–19, the divine lot is used to identify Jonathan and Achan as culprits. At Exod. 22:7 and 10, where property entrusted to someone to look after has been lost or stolen, that person can take an oath that he has not misappropriated the property. The assumption is that if he is guilty, he will not dare to take an oath that will include some such formula as "May God do to me and more also if I have stolen this property." In the second category we find characters such as Deborah, Samuel, David, and Solomon dispensing justice in an ad hoc manner. Indeed, one reason why Absalom was able to stir up a revolt against David was that David was not hearing cases brought to him for arbitration, nor appointing a deputy (2 Sam. 15:2–4). In the previous chapter (2 Sam. 14) a woman is procured to bring a bogus case for David's decision as a means of getting him to recall Absalom to court. We also read of cases being decided on an ad hoc basis by the elders of villages meeting "in the gate." There are also self-help methods of crime prevention and law enforcement, such as the right of a relative of a murdered person to seek out and kill the murderer (Num. 35:9–34). These two categories are more concerned with how to administer justice rather than with what laws to administer; but this is necessarily so where ad hoc local decisions are made. Much more centralized power is needed if courts are to administer centrally enacted laws.

According to 2 Chron. 19:4–11, it was Jehoshaphat, king of Judah (ca. 871–848), who placed judges in the fortified cities of Judah and charged them to administer justice impartially. Such courts, whenever they were established, would have administered laws that existed as local oral traditions, as well as formulating their own decisions. The existence of written collections made possible the interpretation and extension of the scope of existing laws. Examples are Exod. 23:11b, where the words "you shall do the same with" extend the law about leaving fields fallow to include vineyards and olive orchards; and at Exod. 22:9, the words "or any other loss" extend the scope of a law about entrusting animals to another's care. As scribal administrative activity increased in Judah and Israel, occasion was provided for the drafting of laws as an end in itself divorced from legal practice. Moshe Weinfeld has argued that, in their final form, the collections of laws in Deuteronomy come from a wisdom school of scribes who were attempting to articulate a particular ideology rather than being engaged in legal practice.

Israel's Law: The Ten Commandments, the Book of the Covenant, and the Holiness Code

The Ten Commandments exist in the Old Testament in two versions: at Exod. 20:1–17 and Deut. 5:6–21. The two versions are not identical. This can be seen most clearly if Exod. 20:10–11 is compared with Deut. 5:13–15. The two passages give the reason why Israelites should observe the Sabbath (seventh day). In Exodus the reason given is that God rested on the seventh day after creating the world. The Deuteronomy passage is quite different and says that because God freed the Israelites from slavery in Egypt, Israelites must treat their own servants humanely by allowing them to rest on the Sabbath. These are the obvious differences; but there are many small differences, and readers interested in them should copy out the two texts side by side.

There is also disagreement about how the commandments should be numbered. Orthodox Jews take the first commandment to be Exod. 20:2: "I am the LORD your God"; and the second to be 20:3: "you shall have no other gods before me." Christians take 20:3 as the first commandment but disagree about whether verses 4–6 continue the first commandment (the Catholic and Lutheran traditions) or whether verses 4–6 are the second commandment (the Reformed Protestant tradition). The basic issue is whether the word "them" in verse 5 ("you shall not bow down to them") refers back to the idols of verse 4 or to the other gods of verse 3. Although the differences between the two versions and the disagreements about how to number the commandments do not prove that they have had a long history before reaching their present form, this is the most likely explanation.

In their present form the Ten Commandments fall into two groups. Those in Exod. 20:2–11 (Deut. 5:6–15) deal with Israel's duty to God: his exclusive claim upon them, the prohibition of idolatry and of making wrong use of God's name, and the commandment to observe the Sabbath. The remaining commandments concern interhuman relationships and forbid murder, adultery, theft, giving false evidence, and coveting, and they enjoin the honoring of one's parents.

There is no scholarly agreement about the origin and date of the Ten Commandments, except that they probably took a long time to reach their present form. The reason for the lack of agreement is that the commandments touch on issues about which we have little information, or which can be interpreted in several ways. For example, although we know that the Sabbath was observed after the exile (sixth century B.C.E.), we do not know to what extent it was kept or how it was viewed before the exile. Does this mean that there was no Sabbath commandment until the sixth century? As another example, Exod. 20:4 forbids the making of idols. But idols have been found in ancient Israel from the ninth century onward. Does this mean that the commandment did not exist or was not known or was known and ignored; or were the idols used by non-Israelites, or did official religion differ from popular religion?

All that we can say for certain is that the main thrust of the commandments was appropriate to the Israelites in many situations. They remind the Israelites of delivery from foreign bondage, enjoin them to be loyal to Yahweh, and lay down basic rules for maintaining religious and social life. The commandments are thus appropriate to the time of Moses (although they presuppose settled agricultural life and the possession of servants) and also to the time of the independence of Judah from Assyria in the reign of Josiah (640–609) and the return from exile (ca. 520 B.C.E.).

The so-called Book of the Covenant (Exod. 21:1–23:19; for the name see Exod. 24:7) is generally regarded as the oldest collection of laws in the Old Testament, and it is divided into two main parts: (1) 21:1–22:20 (Hebrew Bible: 22:19) (2) 22:21 (Hebrew Bible: 22:20)–23:19. The first part deals with three main subjects: slavery (21:2–6 and 7–11), injuries to persons (21:12–17 and 18–32), and injuries to property (21:33–22:15 [Hebrew Bible: 22:14] and 22:16–20 [Hebrew Bible: 22:15–19]). The second part is more difficult to characterize, except to say that it consists mostly of categorical commandments, that is, commandments that apply to all persons and situations regardless of circumstances. This is in contrast to the first part, in which the commandments are mostly casuistic, that is, carefully defining the circumstances in which the laws apply. An example of a categorical law from the second part of the Book of the Covenant is Exod. 22:28 (Hebrew Bible: 22:27):

> You shall not revile God, nor curse a leader of your people.

A typical casuistic law from the first part of the Book of the Covenant is Exod. 21:33–4:

> If someone leaves a pit open, or digs a pit and does not cover it, and an ox or a donkey falls into it, the owner of the pit shall make restitution.

Whereas the first part of the Book of the Covenant is almost entirely secular, the second part introduces cultic regulations, mixing them with injunctions that are designed to protect the weak. A good example, as well as a striking version of the command to rest on the seventh day, is at Exod. 23:12:

> Six days you shall do your work, but on the seventh day you shall rest; that your ox and your donkey may have relief, and your homeborn slave and the resident may be refreshed.

Within the first part of the Book of the Covenant, there is evidence of editorial activity. Thus Exod. 21:22, prescribing the penalty for a man who accidentally injures a pregnant woman, allows that he be fined "what the woman's husband demands." An addition brings the penalty under the scope of the court: "paying as much as the judges determine." Three verses, Exod. 21:15–17, stand out in the first part, because they are categorical laws surrounded by casuistic laws:

> Whoever strikes father or mother shall be put to death.
> Whoever kidnaps a person. . . . shall be put to death.
> Whoever curses father or mother shall be put to death.

The most likely explanation is that they are an independent group of categorical laws inserted into a context dealing with injuries against persons.

The two parts of the Book of the Covenant, with their quite different emphases, must have been separate collections. The first part, which has parallels with the laws of Hammurabi (*ANET*, p. 176, laws 245–53 for laws on goring oxen, damage to property, and property entrusted to another's care), contains examples of Israel's secular law, part of Israel's share in a legal tradition common in the ancient Near East. The second part (and cf. Exod. 34:17–26) defines the life of a group of people in relation to belief in a God who freed his people from slavery. They are not to follow the religious practices of their neighbors, and their common life is to be characterized by compassion for anyone or anything that can be exploited (including domestic animals, wild beasts, fields, vineyards, and olive orchards). This compassion will imitate the compassion shown by God in freeing them from slavery.

Although the two parts were probably not combined and incorporated into the Sinai narrative until the seventh century, they are certainly older than that. Hints at self-help rather than court-administered justice (e.g., Exod. 21:22) may suggest the period of the early monarchy for the first part, whereas the second part could be even earlier. In their present context, however, they are not meant to be a comprehensive version of Israel's laws. They are illustrative; and even the secular first part is begun with laws about slavery in order to make the point that Israel is to be a free people, and that when slavery occurs (usually because of debt), its effects must be limited.

In Leviticus 17–26 there is another collection of laws usually called the Holiness Code, the scholarly designation "code" giving the wrong impression that it was an official law code that was centrally enforced. It was probably composed in the fifth century B.C.E. and betrays a priestly origin, whereas the Book of the Covenant never mentions priests. In Leviticus 17–26 several sections deal with priests and the special regulations that govern their lives (e.g., 21:1–22:9). The two collections overlap where they deal with respect for parents, the treatment of slaves, and the observance of festivals. However, the emphasis of Leviticus 17–26 differs from that of the Book of the Covenant (Exod. 21–23). In Leviticus, the purpose of regulated order is so that God's blessing can be upon the land. For example, in Leviticus, God's holiness requires a strict separation between priests and the people, and between Israel and other peoples. Exod. 22:31 (Hebrew Bible

22:30) says that the flesh of an animal corpse found in open country may not be eaten by humans, whereas Lev. 17:14–16 prescribes a ritual for anyone who eats the flesh of an animal that died naturally or was killed by other animals.

Chapters 19 and 25 deal with "secular" matters. The core of chapter 19 is verses 11–18 and 26–36, and in them we find the concern about protecting those who are vulnerable that has been noted in the Book of the Covenant. One of the two great commandments in the New Testament – "you shall love your neighbor as yourself" – is found at verse 18. We may have in these verses another older collection whose purpose was to order the life of a group as the people of Yahweh.

Leviticus 25 begins with the charge to let the land lie fallow in the seventh year – a theological ideal rather than an agricultural necessity, for fallowing needed to take place much more frequently than once in seven years. Regulations about the seventh year then lead to laws about the fiftieth year, the Jubilee, the year in which all property reverted to the original owners, and all slaves were released. There are also regulations designed to ease the hardship of those obliged to raise loans (no interest is to be charged) or who have to become hired servants. Whether or not the Jubilee was ever observed, its importance is as a theological statement. The chapter recognizes that, with time, inequalities caused by such things as variations in climate or illness or pests cause some people to become dependent on others, possibly losing their land and then their freedom in the process. The Jubilee is there to counteract these inequalities that arise. The loss of freedom that they bring is not tolerable in a society which was once enslaved and then delivered by God. Once again, we see that the purpose of laws is as much to make a statement about the kind of common life that God requires as to regulate legal practice.

5.   From Sinai to the Land

In Num. 10:11–33:48 the journey from Mount Sinai to the plains of Moab (where Moses, according to the narrative, speaks to the Israelites the words known to us as the Book of Deuteronomy) is described. From Exod. 25:1 to Num. 10:10, the people are still encamped at Mount Sinai, and their presence there is the occasion for the giving of the priestly legislation (principally, though not entirely, Leviticus), as well as instructions about making a portable sanctuary (Exod. 25–7, 35–40), the organization of the "tribes" into parties for the journey, and the organization of the Levites (Num. 1–4). The material from Exodus 25 to the end of Numbers has a complex literary history and reached its final form during and after the exile (sixth to fifth centuries B.C.E.). The process is too complex to be traced here. What is clear, however, is that the material makes important theological statements, and to illustrate this the following incidents will be discussed: the golden calf (Exod. 32, 34), the mission of the spies (Num. 13–15), the rejection of Moses (various passages), the brazen serpent (Num. 21:4–9), and the Balaam–Balak encounter (Num. 22–4).

In the story of the golden calf, the tarrying of Moses on Mount Sinai

THE TENT AND THE TABERNACLE

THE "TENT OF MEETING" IS mentioned some 130 times in the Old Testament. Known also as the "Tent of the Testimony," the "Tent of Yahweh," or simply as "the Tent," it is the place where Yahweh comes to meet Moses and Israel in the desert after the revelation on Mount Sinai. In some accounts this portable tent-sanctuary is called the tabernacle (from the Hebrew verb meaning "to dwell"), since it was the structure in which Yahweh was said to be dwelling among his people.

Exodus 25–31 contains an elaborate description of the desert tabernacle, specifying pattern, place, mode, and timetable for erecting the portable sanctuary, and Exodus 35–40 reports the successful completion of these instructions (although there are some differences here in the order of assembly and the contents). These chapters in Exodus portray the tabernacle as an ornate portable temple whose overall dimensions were 45 × 15 × 15 feet. The tabernacle was a tent consisting of ten embroidered linen curtains, covered by layers of dyed animal skins and supported by a series of forty-eight frames made of acacia wood. The final covering was dyed an unusual red. Inside, the tabernacle was partitioned into two rooms: an outer and an inner chamber. The latter was known as the "holy of holies" and was separated from the outer chamber by a thick veil. In the outer chamber stood the table of presence (King James Version "shewbread") and the golden lampstand with seven branches (and perhaps an altar of incense). The inner sanctuary held the ark of the covenant, covered by the mercy seat and guarded by two cherubim with outstretched wings.

The biblical text makes no mention of the tabernacle between the time when Israel entered the land and when David brought the ark to Jerusalem. The ark of the covenant apparently came to rest temporarily at Shechem (Josh. 8:30 ff., 24) and later in a more permanent structure at Shiloh (Ps. 78:60; Josh. 18:1, 19:51), though God speaks of moving around "from tent to tent" (1 Chron. 17:5; cf. 2 Sam. 7:6). The priestly tabernacle in Exodus 25–31, then, may well represent a projection into the past of the details of the tent David built to house the ark of the covenant in his new capital. That tent perhaps symbolizes David's attempt to integrate Mosaic traditions with elements from the culture of Syria–Palestine. David's tent, like the tabernacle described in Exodus 25–31 and 35–40, was a transitional structure, somewhat between the simple, portable container that held Israel's most sacred artifacts and Solomon's more permanent and elaborate temple.

causes the people to ask Aaron to make gods "who shall go before us." Aaron tells the people to give him their golden jewelry, and from this he makes a molten image of a calf. The people cry out:

> These are your gods, O Israel, who brought you up out of the land of Egypt. (32:4)

Aaron builds an altar and proclaims a feast to Yahweh (32:5). The story raises many questions. How does it relate to the setting up of golden calves at Bethel and Dan by Jeroboam (931–910 B.C.E.), together with the proclamation that these were the gods that delivered Israel from Egypt (1 Kings 12:28)? Does the proclamation of a feast for Yahweh reflect a time in Israel when Yahweh was believed to be enthroned on a bull? Is there an implicit criticism of priesthood, given the prominent role of Aaron in the apostasy? Tentative answers to the first two questions may be provided by the iconographic evidence assembled by Keel and Uehlinger. They hold that there is a marked falloff in the representation of calves in Iron Age II (ninth century B.C.E.) compared with the Late Bronze Age and Iron Age I (1350–900). This suggests that Jeroboam, in the tenth century, was appealing to traditional religion rather than introducing something new to Israel. The Exodus material is most likely dependent upon that in 1 Kings 12:28 and is a criticism of the northern kingdom and of the calf symbolism with its pagan connections. However, in context, the golden calf story makes several theological points.

The first of these is that the people of Israel are basically unreliable as the recipients of God's redemption. The apostasy is not a turning away from God on the part of the children or grandchildren of those delivered from slavery. It is an apostasy of the slaves who are now free, who had said, in Exod. 24:7:

> All that the LORD has spoken we will do, and we will be obedient.

Thus the incident reflects the experience of the leaders of the Israelites in the Old Testament that the people's loyalty to God is very fragile. Second, the fact that the covenant is renewed in spite of having been broken so quickly is a matter of hope for later readers faced with crises such as the exile (the story may be a response to the exile). Exodus 34 appears to renew the Ten Commandments as the basis for the covenant, although whether other commandments are added (e.g., Exod. 34:17–28) is disputed by commentators. Either way, the covenant is renewed, but not before the people have been punished (Exod. 32:25–35).

The mission of the spies (Num. 13–15) continues to explore the theme of the fragile loyalty of the freed Israelites. The spies, one from each tribe, visit the land of Canaan. They bring back a gloomy report:

> The land that we have gone through as spies is a land that devours its inhabitants; and all the people that we saw in it are of great size . . . and to ourselves we seemed like grasshoppers, and so we seemed to them. (Num. 13:32–3)

The result of this gloom is a renewed outcry from the people that expresses their regret that they left Egypt. They plan to choose someone who will lead them back to Egypt (Num. 14:4). The intercession of Moses is needed to persuade God not to disinherit the people; but God resolves that none of the generation that left Egypt will enter Canaan except for Joshua and Caleb, the two spies who brought back good reports. Again, then, we have a narrative that can bring hope to readers in situations where the obstinacy of the people seems to annul the purposes of God. Yet the section ends with a sting in its tail. The people suddenly decide that they will, after all, try to occupy Canaan. But they try without God's help and against Moses' advice (Num. 14:35–44). Their subsequent defeat ironically bears out what the gloomy report of the spies had warned.

Among those condemned not to enter the Promised Land because of the people's turning from God is Moses himself. He thus suffers a kind of double rejection: from the people and from God. The first rejection was as early as Exodus 2, when a Hebrew reminded Moses that he had killed an Egyptian. The rejections continue through the plague stories (e.g., Exod. 5:20–1) and the journey to Sinai. The making of the golden calf is another rejection, while at Numbers 12 Aaron and his sister Miriam reprove Moses, and in Numbers 16 there is a rebellion against Moses by Korah, Dathan, and Abiram. The theme of the rejection of the servant of God is found also in prophetic literature, especially in Jeremiah and in the song about the servant of God in Isa. 52:13–53:12. It no doubt reflects the experience of those who tried to be faithful to God, and the fact that Moses also suffered in this way is meant to give hope to such readers. Further, the picture of religious experience that is set out here is enhanced by showing that such sufferers seem to undergo the divine judgment against the unfaithful people. Not only is Moses denied entry to Canaan, but he wishes he could die (Num. 11:15); and the prayers that he prays are full of urgency and pathos (Num. 11:11–15, 14:13–19).

The story of the brazen serpent (Num. 21:4–9) begins as a complaint story on the part of the Israelites, who once again regret that they left Egypt. The setting is a new phase of the journey, designed to take the people to the east of the territory of Edom, the king of Edom having denied passage through his territory (Num. 20:14–21). In response to the people's complaint God sends fiery serpents (Hebrew *nehashim seraphim*) among them which administer fatal bites. The people repent and ask for help. God commands Moses to make a fiery serpent and put it on a pole. When the bronze serpent has been made, it brings healing to any person who has been bitten and who looks at it.

The passage has links with 2 Kings 18:4, where it is recorded that Hezekiah destroyed the bronze serpent that Moses had made because the people burned incense to it. Its imagery also appears in Isa. 6:1–3, where the heavenly attendants of God are described as winged *seraphim* (serpents). Keel's iconographic researches show that winged serpents are found on seals in both Judah and Israel from the eighth century B.C.E., and that from the end of that century this Egyptian symbol of protection was accepted in the land. Although this is most helpful, it leaves us having to make guesses about the stories in Numbers 21 and 2 Kings 18. The view taken here is that there was a bronze serpent venerated in Jerusalem that was pagan in origin. Hezekiah destroyed it during his reform at the end of the eighth century. The Numbers 21 story, dating from before the reform, was probably an Israelite justification for worshiping an object that was probably originally a Canaanite cultic figure. Hezekiah's action was designed to remove from the cult an image that people were worshiping. This did not prevent, however, the representation of this protective symbol on personal seals.

Within the context of Numbers 21:4–10, the narrative makes several points. First, the punishment of the people is reminiscent of the plagues in Egypt that were occasioned by pharaoh's obstinacy. The deliverance, when it is granted, is not a blanket one. Presumably the story implies that there were Israelites who did not look at the brazen serpent and who died as a consequence. Thus the people who lived were those who trusted in God's commandment and obeyed it.

The Balaam stories cover Numbers 22–4. Their setting is the plains of Moab on the east side of the Jordan opposite Jericho, where the presence of the Israelites puts fear into the Moabites and causes their king, Balak, to send for Balaam to come and curse the Israelites. The implication is that Balaam is a powerful seer whose oracles can have visible results. His location "near the River" (i.e., the Euphrates) some 400 miles away shows what enormous trouble Balak takes in order to get Balaam's services. Balaam will not make the journey until he is sure that it is God's will. On arrival he delivers four oracles, three of which bless Israel instead of cursing it, and the fourth of which curses the enemies of Israel, including Moab. The most interesting of the four oracles of Balaam are the last two, because they refer to Israel's neighbors and raise the question of the oracles' date. The fourth oracle (24:15–24) mentions Moab, Edom, Amalek, and the Kenites. It also mentions an Assyrian captivity for Kain as well as ships from Kittim afflicting Asshur and Eber. Proposed dates for this speech range from the twelfth century (De Moor sees a reference to the invasion of the Sea Peoples) to the post-exilic period (sixth to fifth centuries B.C.E.).

KUNTILLET 'AJRUD

ARCHEOLOGICAL EXCAVAtion of a small site in the Negev near what would have been the southern border of the Judean kingdom uncovered a building complex that was occupied for a short time during the mid–ninth century B.C.E. The reason for the location of this installation at Kuntillet 'Ajrud is indicated by the nearby roads connecting Kadesh-barnea in southern Judah with Elat and the lower Sinai. Some finds underline the connection: shells from the Red Sea and the Mediterranean, branches of cedar and sycamore wood, and the wood of pistachios, which grow only in southern Sinai. Unlike any other known Negev fortress of the Israelite period, Kuntillet 'Ajrud ("the solitary hill of the water wells") does not seem to have served a military purpose. The site appears to have been a religious center that perhaps had some connection with journeys of the Judean kings to Ezion-geber, the Israelite port on the Red Sea. The center may have been identified with one of the Israelite traditions concerning Sinai. Travelers could pray at the holy place, each to his own god, asking a divine blessing for his journey.

Material unearthed at Kuntillet 'Ajrud bears witness to the close association of Israelite religion with cultic beliefs, practices, and artistic representations of the larger Syro-Palestinian environment. The site contains the remains of two structures. The more important building measures approximately 25 × 15 meters. Its walls were apparently painted with colorful floral motifs. An entryway led from a small court into a long room that provided the site's most important finds. The room had benches along the walls which took up most of the floor space, indicating that they represented the room's main function. At each end the "bench room" was connected by a small passageway to compartments that served as *favissae*, depositories for the sacred offering vessels that had initially been placed on the benches and that had then been removed and replaced by new gifts.

The finds at Kuntillet 'Ajrud are especially important because they included a large number of inscriptions from the biblical period – a time frame from which the remains of written records are scanty. The few writings that survive elsewhere in Palestine from the time of the first temple deal with political and administrative matters. The inscriptions from Kuntillet 'Ajrud include dedications, prayers, and blessings that were incised on pottery and stone or written with ink on plaster. Among the inscriptions is a rather enigmatic reference to Yahweh and his consort ("Asherah").

Several large storage jars carried a variety of drawings and designs. Figures of gods, people, and animals appear. Among the crudely drawn pictures were representations of male and female deities, a cultic procession, a tree of life flanked by two ibexes, and a cow licking the tail of a suckling calf. The designs are common to the world of art in Syria–Palestine. They suggest a large degree of integration between the traditions of Israel and the wider arena of culture in Syria–Palestine during the Iron Age.

About a hundred cloth fragments (mostly linen, with some wool) were also found at Kuntillet 'Ajrud, the only regional remains of textiles from the monarchic period available to date.

Possible light on the material has been shed by the discovery of an inscription at Tell Deir Alla (biblical Succoth in Transjordan). It is dated around 700 B.C.E., and although its fragmentary nature and its language make its interpretation very difficult, it clearly mentions Balaam the son of Beor (cf. Num. 22:5). As translated by Hans-Peter Müller, its opening lines read:

> This is the inscription of [Balaam the son of Beor], the man who sees the gods. See (?), the gods came to him by night [. . .] and they spoke to Balaam the son of Beor as follows.

The remainder of the inscription (another twenty-three lines) tells of the gathering of an assembly, whose purpose, however, is not clear. The opening has similarities with Num. 22:20 ("That night God came to Balaam") and perhaps explains the problematic Hebrew phrase at 24:3, "the man whose eye is clear." A phrase toward the end of the inscription which speaks of a shoot coming to a place (whose name is lost) is reminiscent of the enigmatic words of Num. 24:17: "a star shall come out of Jacob." A reasonable assumption is that the Balaam stories are based on traditions about a non-Israelite prophet, an example of which has come to light in the Deir Alla finds.

In context, the Balaam oracles show how even a non-Israelite prophet is sensitive to the word of the God of Israel, and how his words assure future blessing for Israel on their way to the Promised Land. Numbers 32 then tells of the conquering of those parts of Transjordan that were to be occupied by the tribes of Reuben and Gad.

6.   The Deuteronomic Law

The Social and Religious World of the Deuteronomists and the History of the Deuteronomistic Movement and Its Literature

The identity, origin, and history of the Deuteronomistic movement (if "movement" is the correct word) is probably the most complex and keenly argued subject in current Old Testament scholarship. If affects not only the Book of Deuteronomy but also the so-called Deuteronomistic History (in English Bibles the Books of Joshua to 2 Kings minus Ruth, so called because of vocabulary and ideas distinctive to the Book of Deuteronomy that occur throughout Joshua–2 Kings) and involves the following questions: How did the Deuteronomistic History reach its present form? Was it composed by a single author in the exilic period (sixth century), or did a substantial first draft exist by the time of Hezekiah (late eighth century) or Josiah (late seventh century)? How did the Book of Deuteronomy reach its present form, and how and when was it linked to the Deuteronomistic History? Did the Deuteronomistic History receive the attention of several editors in the postexilic period (sixth to fifth centuries B.C.E.)? The sketch that follows draws on the views of scholars of differing opinions.

In what follows the word "Deuteronomists" will be used to describe successive generations of Israelites whose literature and outlook received classical expression in the Book of Deuteronomy and the final form of the Deuteronomistic History. It is probably correct to look for their origins in the northern kingdom of Israel. Deuteronomy itself envisages a ceremony of blessing and cursing on Mounts Ebal and Gerizim (Deut. 27) and although the relation of this material to the rest of the book is a matter of debate, the intention of the text is clear: on entering the land of Canaan the people are to assemble at or near Shechem, in the heartland of what became the northern kingdom. Other indications of northern origins are found in the Deuteronomistic History. The Book of Judges makes virtually no mention of Judah and concentrates mostly upon northern leaders. In the Books of Kings, stories about the northern bands of prophets led by Elijah and Elisha dominate the text from 1 Kings 17 to 2 Kings 10. This does not amount to proof of the northern origins of the Deuteronomists; but it poses the question of how, if the Deuteronomists were Judahites, they had access to so many northern traditions. However, assuming a northern origin for the Deuteronomists also creates a problem. To what social group did they belong? Were they groups of prophets, in which case were they in a position to produce literature or record traditions? Were they Levites, in which case where did they fit into the religious setup in Israel? Were they prominent members of the Israelite administration such as Obadiah, who, according to 1 Kings 18:3–16, sided with the prophets against Ahab and Jezebel?

The last suggestion would explain why there were written traditions about leaders and prophets in the northern kingdom, but would leave unexplained how such administrators or their supporters were able to come to Judah, as we must suppose they did, after the destruction of the northern kingdom by the Assyrians in 721 B.C.E. We can do no more than make informed guesses. That there was a large increase in population in Jerusalem at the end of the eighth century is attested archeologically, and if we suppose that this was due to people moving down to Judah from the former northern kingdom, we can surmise that the guardians of the northern traditions were among them. If we suppose, further, that they were connected with the scribal, administrative class from the northern kingdom, we can conclude that they linked up with the Jerusalem scribal elite, and that there began a literary enterprise whose aim was to describe the history of Israel from presettlement times to the time of Hezekiah. One purpose of this history was to show that Judah now represented Israel as a whole and to press the claims of Jerusalem to be the capital of Israel and the Davidic king to be the king of Israel. The facts were that Judah had been insignificant in the story of Israel (on the period of David and Solomon, see below, pp. 119–124) and for most of the ninth and part of the eighth centuries had been a vassal state of Israel ruled from Samaria.

Hezekiah's rule (ca. 727-698) was a time of asserting the independence of Judah as opposed to dependence upon Assyria, which had been his father's (Ahaz) policy. The arrival of the Deuteronomists with their strong loyalty to Yahweh encouraged a religious reform as well as the articulation in literature and storytelling of Judah's identity as the true heir of all Israel. However, at the close of his reign, Hezekiah was defeated by the Assyrians, and although Jerusalem remained uncaptured, Judahite independence was lost for much of the seventh century (from ca. 700 to 627). During this period, Assyrian influence upon Judahite iconography is demonstrable, and in the sphere of religious iconography there is a noticeable increase in astral symbolism. The divine powers were represented by symbols taken from the interpretation of the night sky. Also, there was a tendency to represent gods in human form, and Asherah, in the previous period a life-giving object in the form of a tree, took on human characteristics. We must suppose that during this period the Deuteronomists kept a low profile, waiting for the time when they could reimpose their particular type of faith in Yahweh upon the whole nation.

This opportunity came after the death of Manasseh (642 B.C.E., the accession of his grandson Josiah (640), and the waning of Assyrian power. According to 2 Kings 22:8, "the book of the law" was discovered in the temple while the temple was being repaired in 622 B.C.E. As a result of the discovery the king gathered the representatives of the nation, and a covenant between the people and Yahweh was made (2 Kings 23:1–3). There then followed a reform in which the temple was cleansed of vessels made for Baal and Asherah and other gods, places of worship other than Jerusalem were destroyed, and the Passover was celebrated as a national festival. It has long been held that the book of the law found in the temple was Deuteronomy or part of it; but the "discovery" and its implications need to be discussed further.

Because of the correspondence between Deuteronomy's demand for the centralization of worship, which included the destruction of other gods, and the actions carried out as Josiah's reform, it is too simplistic to assume that 2 Kings 22:3–10 is an "independent" account of the discovery of a lawbook that can be identified as part of Deuteronomy. The fact is that 2 Kings 22:3–10 is part of the Deuteronomistic History and thus a facet of the complex interrelationships between the Deuteronomists, the Deuteronomistic History, and the Book of Deuteronomy as we have it. There is no reason to doubt that a lawbook was discovered, but we can be confident that the discovery was not fortuitous. It is hard to believe that the lawbook was hidden by people who had no idea whether or when it would be found, or that, only because it was fortuitously found, a religious reformation ensued inspired by its content. Although we can only guess, a good case can be made for the following scenario. As Assyrian power weakened during the early part of Josiah's reign, the Deuteronomists began to prepare for independence. By 622 B.C.E. conditions were suitable for reform, including the repair and purging of the temple, all of which were part of a new phase in the life of the nation in which subservience to Assyria was repudiated and a covenant with Yahweh was made, a covenant which took the form of a loyalty oath as known from international agreements of the time. As part of this process, the book of the law was produced from the temple. What it contained will be discussed shortly; but the correspondence between what was done in the reform and what we find in Deuteronomy does not prove that the reform was based upon Deuteronomy as we know it. Deuteronomy may just as much be based upon the reform as being the pattern for it.

Of what, then, did the book of the law consist? One suggestion is that it contained part of Deuteronomy 12–16 and 26. A new section begins in 12:1 with "These are the statutes and ordinances." Chapter 16 contains regulations about celebrating the Passover at the central sanctuary and ends with material not unlike Exod. 34:10–27. It is noteworthy that Deut. 16:21 forbids the planting of "any tree as a sacred pole [Asherah] beside the altar that you make for the LORD your God." Keel's evidence suggests that the Asherah as a tree symbol was an eighth-century feature, whereas in the seventh century Asherah was more often represented in human form. Deut. 16:21 could therefore be an eighth-century composition and thus part of the book found in the seventh century in the temple.

If part of Deuteronomy was produced from the temple, how did the book reach its final form? There were probably several stages. First, chapters 12–26 were cast into the form of a lawbook, broadly following the sequence of the Ten Commandments and perhaps intended as a commentary thereon. Second, the material was given the form of a loyalty oath agreement by the addition of the historical prologue (chaps. 5–11) and the material about making the covenant (chaps. 27–8). This version of the book may have been the basis of the covenant between the nation and Yahweh at the time of Josiah. We must not necessarily suppose that the covenant ceremony described in 2 Kings 23:1–3 happened immediately after the discovery of the lawbook. This book could have been expanded and then been used as the basis for the covenant. The final stages of Deuteronomy's growth were a response to the crisis of the falls of Jerusalem in 597 and 587/6 and their aftermath; the book continued to be written and edited during the exile (sixth century).

In their present form both Deuteronomy and the Deuteronomistic History presuppose the fall of Jerusalem and the exile. Deuteronomy is presented as a speech by Moses to the Israelites on the eve of entering the land of Canaan; but it is clear from passages such as Deut. 30:1–4 that the exile has occurred:

> When these things have happened to you . . . if you call them to mind among all the nations where the LORD your God has driven you, and return to the LORD your God . . . then the LORD your God will restore your fortunes . . . and gather you again from all the peoples among whom the LORD your God has scattered you. . . . and the LORD your God will bring you into the land that your ancestors possessed, and you will possess it.

The Israelites are now either poised to return to the land of Israel or have returned; and Deuteronomy sets forth the new covenant by which they are to live (the covenant of the plains of Moab), and the Deuteronomistic History is an account of and explanation for the faithlessness that led to the fall of Jerusalem. It was as a result of the exile, then, that Deuteronomy received its framework of chapters 1–4 and 30–4, that the Deuteronomistic History reached its final form, and that Deuteronomy was linked to the Deuteronomistic History, for example, by showing how Joshua (Josh. 8:30–5) fulfilled the instructions of Deut. 27:1–8.

It is also the case that the Book of Jeremiah received its final form at the hands of the Deuteronomists; and this fact, together with recent discoveries, sheds new light on the Deuteronomists. On being discovered in the temple, the book of the law was given to Shaphan the secretary for transmission to the king. The family of Shaphan was involved in supporting Jeremiah. The prophet's letter to the exiles in Babylon was delivered by Shaphan's son Elasah (Jer. 29:3), and when the scroll that Jeremiah had dictated to Baruch was read to the state officials, it was read in the chamber of another son of Shaphan, Gemariah. Yet another son of Shaphan, Ahikam, protected Jeremiah when he was accused of treason (Jer. 26:24), and it was Ahikam's son Gedaliah who was appointed governor of Judah by the Babylonians after 586 and to whom Jeremiah was entrusted. The family of Shaphan, then, was an elite group within Judah's administration and in sympathy with Jeremiah.

That this family was numbered among or was the mainstay of the seventh- and sixth-century Deuteronomists is suggested by the bullae published by Yigal Shiloh and Nahman Avigad in 1986. One, from Shiloh's excavations at the City of David and dating from the seventh–sixth centuries B.C.E., gives the name Gemariah son of Shaphan, and another, from the "burnt archive" (possibly from the Tell Bet Mirsim area), is of Berakiah son of Neriah the scribe. Keel points out that, of the 55 bullae from Shiloh's collection, only 4 have artistic figures, and the remainder either have no decoration apart from the name or a bare minimum of artistic elaboration. The same tendency is observed in the 255 bullae of Avigad's collection. Keel sees in this preference for bullae without artistic embellishments a sign of adherence to the Deuteronomistic reform, with its command to destroy all images (Deut. 12:3). Thus it is reasonable to conclude that the Deuteronomists included elite administrative groups in Judah of the seventh to sixth centuries, people who were connected with the "discovery" of the law-book in 622, who supported Jeremiah, and who were not necessarily deported to Babylon after 586. This would explain, among other things, the elevated, "courtly" style of Deuteronomy and the apparent knowledge and use of international forms of agreement such as the oath of loyalty. The importance of the Deuteronomists for the faith and literature of the Old Testament cannot be overestimated.

The Structure and Theology of Deuteronomy

Deuteronomy can be divided into the following sections:

Deuteronomy 1:1–4:43 This section is the introductory address of Moses to the Israelites, who are assembled in the plains of Moab. It rehearses the journey of the people from Mount Horeb (Sinai) to the threshold of the Promised Land. It is based upon material from Exodus and Numbers and emphasizes the lack of faith of the people in spite of God's provision for them. A key verse is 1:27:

You murmured in your tents, and said, "Because the LORD hated us he has brought us forth out of the land of Egypt, to give us into the hand of the Amorites, to destroy us."

Deuteronomy 4:44–11:32 This section is difficult to characterize. It places the Ten Commandments in a prominent position (5:1–22) and then combines other injunctions with incidents from the period of the wilderness wanderings to serve as object lessons. Among the incidents related are the worship of the golden calf (9:6–21), the miracle at the Red Sea (11:2–4), and the rebellion of Dathan and Abiram (11:6).

Within this section a theology of grace has been discerned. It emphasizes that God did not choose Israel and deliver the people from bondage because they were deserving, but rather, God saved them because of his love for them and because of his oath to their fathers (7:6–10). Elsewhere, it is pointed out that God did not enable Israel to enter Canaan because of Israel's righteousness but because he was punishing the wickedness of the nations already there in so doing (9:4–5). This point is underlined in the following verse:

Know, therefore, that the LORD your God is not giving you this good land to possess because of your righteousness, for you are a stubborn people.

At the same time, this rebellious people whose standing before God is dependent on his grace is called upon to love him in response and unconditionally. The opening words of the Jewish prayer, the Shema, (*shema* means "hear!") are taken from Deut. 6:4–9:

Hear, O Israel: The LORD our God, the LORD is one; and you shall love the LORD God with all your heart, and with all your soul, and with all your might.

Nevertheless, this section is permeated with warnings about the curses that will come upon the people if they forsake him.

Deuteronomy 12:1–26:19 This section is the heart of the book as a collection of laws. To some extent it is based upon laws from the Book of the Covenant (Exod. 21–3), or upon a similar collection; but its outlook is very different from that of the Exodus material. First, the theme of exclusive loyalty to God is prominent. The images and altars of the gods of the "nations" in the land of Israel are to be destroyed (12:1–3) and sacrifices are to be offered only at the place which God chooses (12:4–14). Any prophet, kinsperson, or "base fellow" who incites the people to follow others gods is to be put to death, and any city that serves other gods is to be destroyed (13:1–18). Second, the laws are directed to a nation. This is why apostate cities must be destroyed, why the Passover is to be celebrated at the central sanctuary (16:1–8), why judges must be appointed in every town (16:18–20), why the king must write out and learn the laws (17:18–20), why there are rules about the nation going to war (20:1–20), why there is a ceremony for cleansing the land from bloodguilt when there is an unsolved murder (21:1–9), and why foreigners are excluded from the "assembly of the LORD" (23:2–8).

Phylacteries from Qumran. These containers are worn by pious Jews in daily worship and have inscribed scrolls inside them with passages from the Bible (e.g., Deut. 5:1–21, 22–3; 6:1–9; 6:4–9).

A third theme is provision for the poor and defenseless. Indeed, 15:4 declares that "there will be no poor among you." Released slaves must be generously endowed with provisions (15:12–18), the sojourner, the fatherless, and widows must be provided for at the great festivals and at harvest times (16:11, 14; 24:19–22), female prisoners-of-war are to be protected (21:10–14), runaway slaves must not be given back to their masters (23:15–16), and the poor and needy who have become day laborers must be protected (24:14–15, 17–18). Whereas Exodus 21:7–11 envisages freedom for female slaves only if they marry the master or his son, Deut. 15:12 extends to female slaves the same right of release, after six years of service, as male slaves.

One of the paradoxes of the laws in Deuteronomy is that they combine laws about religious observances with an attitude that is more secular than priestly. Chapter 12 concerns the location of the central place of worship and how to deal with the killing of meat. Chapter 14 regulates clean and unclean food; chapter 16 prescribes how the Passover is to be celebrated; chapter 18 deals with the Levites; and chapter 21 has a ceremony for atoning for an unsolved murder. Yet, as Moshe Weinfeld has pointed out, the purpose of Deuteronomy is not to advance the cult but to curtail it. It is noteworthy that, in the ceremony in Deut. 21:1–9, in which a heifer's neck is broken as an atone-

THE SHEMA

DEUT. 6:4 HOLDS A PROMInent place in the liturgy, literature, theology, and practice of Judaism. From ancient times this verse apparently formed an important part of the regular service of sacrifice at the temple. The Shema (from the first word of Deut. 6:4 in Hebrew, the imperative "Hear!") is a section of biblical text used in the daily liturgy, although in classical times the sections included were not fixed. In its definitive form today the Shema consists of Deut. 6:4–9, Deut. 11:13–21, Num. 15:37–41, and appropriate benedictions. The faithful are enjoined to recite the text twice each day, upon rising in the morning and before falling asleep at night (Deut. 6:7).

The three biblical passages of the Shema, and the Ten Commandments (Exod. 20:2–17)

were written on parchment, and the rolled-up parchment slips were put inside phylacteries, or prayer capsules (Hebrew *tefillin*). Pious Jews bound phylacteries on their left arms and foreheads when they prayed. The custom of praying daily with phylacteries has its scriptural basis in Deut. 6:8, 11:8, and Exod. 13:9, 16. Archeological evidence suggests that *tefillin* were already used during the time of the second temple (525 B.C.E.–70 C.E.).

Deut. 6:4–9 is also one of the two passages written on the mezuzah, a tiny parchment scroll inserted into a case and affixed to the door of a Jewish home. The practice is enjoined in Deut. 6:9 and 11:20. The earliest evidence for the fulfillment of the commandment to place such a scroll on the doorpost also comes from the second temple period.

In addition to its devotional

importance, the Shema has in modern times come to be regarded as "the Jewish confession of faith par excellence," or "the fundamental doctrine of Judaism." These interpretations are associated with classic rabbinic expressions of the Shema's meaning, which can be summarized in two phrases: accepting the yoke of the kingdom of heaven and proclaiming the unification of God's name. The former, a more ancient interpretation, confesses God's preeminent sovereignty, unrivaled power, and providence. Moreover, it calls for the citizens of God's kingdom to be bound together in their own corporate identity, free from the lesser, political kingdoms of the world. The second phrase represents a response largely to Christian theology and to persecution, articulating the immutable oneness of the single divine being, Yahweh.

ment for an unsolved murder, it is the elders who carry out the killing even though Levitical priests are present. The Israelite who brings his offerings of first fruits to the sanctuary is the central figure in the ceremony and liturgy of the offering (26:3–11). The priest plays a largely passive role. The section about sacrifice and about the slaughter of meat not intended for sacrifice (12:15–28) works out the logic of the centralization of the cult. Although we do not know whether, in practice, all slaughter of animals, apart from game, for whatever reason was at one stage considered to be a sacrifice that needed to be carried out by a priest at a local sanctuary (cf. Lev. 17:1–7), Deuteronomy certainly labors the point that a single sanctuary will entail that the killing of animals in the land will largely have to dispense with the need for a priest to do the killing. It will be done by individual Israelites, who must, however, dispose of the blood correctly. Thus we have the paradox that a collection of laws closely connected with a religious reform has a secularizing tendency, or if not that, a movement from an institutional to a more personal form of religion in which social concern is urged upon individuals as they reflect on the deliverance from slavery that God achieved for the people.

There is another paradox to be noted. The laws combine a heightened concern for the poor and needy with a heightened stress on intolerance. The images of other gods must be utterly destroyed (12:1–3), as must apostate cities (13:12–18), the cities of the "nations" in the land of Israel (20:16–18), and all the males in cities outside the land that are defeated by the Israelites (20:10–13). Such sentiments are a way of expressing the need for Israel to show exclusive loyalty to Yahweh.

Deuteronomy 27 This chapter contains the so-called Shechemite Dodecalogue (Twelve Commandments), which may reflect a very old tradition. It extends the legal section to the important chapter 28, which states the blessings and curses connected with the covenant, and which presumably concluded the book at one stage in its composition.

Deuteronomy 29–30 These chapters contain a farewell speech by Moses, similar to farewell speeches in the Deuteronomistic History such as those of Joshua (Josh. 23) and Samuel (1 Sam. 12), in which brief summaries of Israel's history are set forth. This speech addresses Israel's exilic or postexilic situation.

Deuteronomy 31–4 These chapters link Deuteronomy with the Book of Joshua (especially the account of Moses' death in chap. 34) and include two poems: the Song of Moses (chap. 32) and the Blessing of Moses (chap. 33). These may well be ancient poems in origin, and it is noteworthy that, in the blessings of the tribes (chap. 33), Judah receives only one verse whereas the Joseph tribes of Israel's northern heartland receive five verses. A northern origin is suggested by this fact.

II. THE WORLD OF ISRAEL'S HISTORIANS (JOSHUA, JUDGES, SAMUEL, KINGS, CHRONICLES, EZRA, NEHEMIAH)

Is it correct to speak about "Israel's historians"? The answer is yes and no, and we begin with the negative. The so-called historical books belong, in the Jewish division of the Bible, to the Former Prophets (Joshua to 2 Kings, except Ruth) and the Writings (Chronicles to Song of Solomon and Ruth, Lamentations, and Daniel). The Jewish tradition, therefore, does not strictly have a category of historical books. From a modern humanistic standpoint, it has been denied that the authors of the Old Testament were historians on the grounds that historians can only write about the past from a humanistic perspective, a perspective that has no place for God or gods in the process of history.

It is true that when we write history today, even biblical or religious history, we try to explain what happened in human terms, from social, economic, or political standpoints. Even historians who believe in God leave the divine out of attempts to understand the past, for the simple reason that it is impossible to know the mind or the workings of God. The Old Testament writers did not have this difficulty. They believed that God had communicated his laws to Israel and that he had informed inspired men and women, especially prophets, about what he had done and what he intended to do. In this sense it is entirely appropriate that most of the "historical books" should have been classified as the Former Prophets.

But it is possible to exaggerate the difference between the biblical authors and modern historians. Although the former lacked the resources of modern historians such as reference libraries (although there were libraries in the ancient world, for example, that of the Assyrian king Ashurbanipal in Nineveh), they certainly kept records of major events, and later historians drew on these when writing their accounts of Israel's past history. Where there were gaps in their knowledge they made informed guesses, just as modern historians do; and if they had their biases and interests, in this they were also no different from modern historians. We must, therefore, avoid two extremes. We must not suppose that biblical writers wrote history with the resources and therefore the accuracy of modern historians and that their efforts must remain above criticism or improvement. On the other hand, we must not automatically dismiss their achievements. They displayed genuine historical instincts within their limited resources, and if their results seem more storylike than historylike, we must remember that all history writing is narrative and, to some extent, story.

A. THE DEUTERONOMISTS' HISTORY

The terms "Deuteronomist" and "Deuteronomistic History" were explained above (pp. 88–95). Although the Deuteronomistic History work did not reach its final form until after the exile (sixth century B.C.E.), substantial parts had certainly been completed by the end of the reign of Josiah (609 B.C.E.). The history tells the story of Israel and Judah from the entry to the land of Israel to the destruction of the temple in Jerusalem in 587/6 and the early days of the subsequent exile. In what follows, we will examine each biblical book from the point of view of its literary history and of what we know about the history and sociology of the period described by each book.

1. Joshua

Archeological and Sociological Data on the Conquest

As described in Joshua, the conquest of Canaan was the action of the twelve tribes under the leadership of Joshua. After they crossed the Jordan, the Israelites established their camp at Gilgal (Josh. 5:2–12), at a site usually considered to be to the north of Jericho in the Jordan Valley. After destroying Jericho, the Israelites pushed up on to the Bethel hill country, eventually capturing Ai and moving to the west where a coalition of kings of cities in the Jerusalem saddle and the Shephelah was defeated in the valley of Aijalon. This was followed by a campaign against the city of Hazor in lower Galilee. Josh. 12:7–24 presents a list of kings who were defeated by Joshua and the Israelites. These include kings mentioned in previous chapters as well as kings of cities whose defeat is not otherwise described. Joshua 13 outlines

The Valley of Liban runs along the natural north–south route of the mountains between the Galilee and Jerusalem. Villages are characteristically located on the lower hill slopes, and the higher slopes provide some lean forage for flocks.

Biblical Archaeology Slides, no. 8

THE CENTRAL HILL COUNTRY

DEUTERONOMY SUGGESTS that when the Israelites began to settle in Canaan, they were taking possession of an extensive open countryside that was fruitful and productive – a land "flowing with milk and honey" (Deut. 7:7–8). Archeological evidence and other biblical narratives show that claim to be a somewhat deceptive ideal. The original area in which the Israelite tribes settled seems to have been limited both in its size and in its agricultural potential.

Apparently the earliest Israelite settlements in Palestine were made in the "hill country" of Judea, Samaria, and the Galilee. The region is a strip of rugged, mountainous land located generally between the Jordan Rift Valley and the coastal plain. Sparsely populated before the Israelite occupation, the area consists of an irregular configuration of rocky hills and valleys that were heavily forested in the Early Iron Age (see Josh. 17:18). Evergreen oaks (*Quercus calliprinos*, Hebrew *'elon*) and deciduous terebinths (*Pistacia palaestina*, Hebrew *'elah*) were scattered among dense thickets of tall shrubs known as maquis. Isolated from each other and the urban life of nearby Canaanite city-states, the central hill country settlements were generally inaccessible. Often they were built on high crags that improved their defensibility but further increased their isolation. These settlements were far enough away from the established routes of intercontinental commercial and military traffic so as to be essentially unnoticed.

With their chariot armies and superior military technology, Canaanites held the fertile plains and valleys of Palestine during the Late Bronze Age and Early Iron Age. Hill country settlements were made in generally unwanted land that was only marginally productive. Soils in the region were poor, rocky, and easily eroded. Fields for orchards and crops had to be artificially constructed. This mountainous area also provided few perennial sources of water. Great seasonal and annual variations in rainfall made a constant water supply even more difficult to maintain. Intense rainfall in the winter months led to high rates of runoff, and that water was consequently lost for agricultural purposes. Groundwater evaporated quickly during the hot, dry summer.

Still, the picture was not so bleak in every part of the hill country. Its ecosystems are marked above all by diversity. Topographers today divide this small area into no fewer than seventeen subregions. Some sites enjoyed far better agricultural circumstances. Places like Hazor and Shiloh were proximate to continuous springs and situated on hills astride fairly level, small plateaus. But in the Early Iron Age the Palestinian highlands were still frontier territory. In this complex and often inhospitable environment Israel made its first home.

the division of the land among the tribes, and the book ends with Joshua gathering the tribes together at Shechem, where they make a covenant together expressing their allegiance to Yahweh.

What is striking about the account of the conquest is that it covers so little of the land. It is true that there are summary passages such as Josh. 10:40–2 that tell us that Joshua smote the whole land and left no one alive in it; but these passages belong to the latest parts of the book and are contradicted by passages such as Josh. 16:10 and 17:12–13 that state that certain tribes were unable to conquer some of the cities within the areas that were allocated to them.

With the rise of Palestinian archeology in the present century there was an initial belief that excavations at cities such as Jericho confirmed the accuracy of the account of the conquest in Joshua. As more sites were excavated, however, and as earlier excavations were reassessed, the picture became ambiguous. On the credit side there seemed to be archeological evidence to support the claim in Joshua that the Israelites destroyed Lachish, Hazor, and Debir (if Debir is to be located at Tell Bet Mirsim, a debated issue). On the debit side, no evidence could be found that Jericho and Ai were inhabited at the time of the Israelite set-

JERICHO

ACCORDING TO THE BIBLIcal account, the Israelites' first contact with the people inhabiting the land of Canaan took place at Jericho. The story from Joshua 6 is familiar. Joshua sent two spies, who reconnoitered the city with the help of Rahab the harlot. Based on their intelligence, the Israelite tribes prepared an army of forty thousand soldiers for the attack. But the city was shut tight against the campaigning Israelites; they were unable to breach its defenses. Then the children of Israel marched around the city once a day for six days. On the seventh came the famous trumpet blast, and "the walls came tumbling down." The city was stormed and put to the torch. Only Rahab was saved. Joshua placed a curse on any who undertook to rebuild the troublesome city.

From the earliest days of Syro-Palestinian archeology researchers have attempted to find the walls of Jericho that crumbled during the Israelite conquest of Canaan. An 1868 investigation at Tell es-Sultan, the site of Old Testament Jericho, was uneventful. But in the 1930s archeologist John Garstang found a Canaanite city on that mound that had been destroyed by earthquake and fire. He proclaimed that city as the Jericho conquered by Joshua, and many were pleased that the new

"science of archeology" had validated the historicity of the biblical narrative. But in 1950 a series of innovative excavations by Dame Kathleen Kenyon showed Garstang to have been mistaken.

Kenyon's excavations unearthed over six millennia of occupation at Tell es-Sultan, stretching back to an eighth-millennium B.C.E. layer that may well have been the first city in the world. That city, with its massive fortifications, impressive public works, and extensive irrigation system, was destroyed around 6800 B.C.E. During the Early Bronze Age (3300–2300) the city was rebuilt no fewer than fourteen times. Kenyon showed that the tumbled walls that Garstang had attributed to biblical Jericho had actually belonged to the final phase of Early Bronze Age Jericho, destroyed about 2300 (a full one thousand years before the era in which Israel was settling in Canaan). A third major period of occupation ended when a city that had flourished in the Middle Bronze Age (1900–1500, the Hyksos period) was destroyed in a great conflagration around 1500. Garstang's ashes proved to have been from this destruction, still several centuries before Israel began to occupy the highlands of Canaan. At the time when Joshua should have been campaigning through the Promised Land, Kenyon found that the site of ancient Jericho had been unforti-

fied. There was only meager evidence of any occupation at all.

Various suggestions have been made to explain this apparent discrepancy between the biblical narrative and the archeological evidence concerning Jericho. The upper strata of Tell es-Sultan were badly eroded, and some scholars insist the structures that could corroborate Joshua's account of the fall of Jericho have long vanished as rain-washed debris. Still others understand Joshua 6 as an imaginative way of explaining the ruins of Tell es-Sultan that could have been lying about as the Israelites began to settle in Palestine. Perhaps the biblical story is simply a logically necessary chapter in Israel's national history of its "conquest," since Jericho is the most likely geographical location from which to begin an invasion of Palestine from the east.

All of these suggestions are speculative, however, since the vital evidence from 1400–1250 B.C.E. (the period scholars think most likely for the beginning of Israel's occupation of Canaan) is incomplete at Jericho. Still, scholars generally view Jericho as evidence against a conquest model of Israel's settlement in Palestine – an example of how the traditions of the Israelite tribes were inflated, transposed, and compressed in the slow process of constructing a cohesive history of the unified nation of Israel.

tlement (late thirteenth century). The debate between those who held that archeology supported an Israelite conquest and those who ascribed the destruction of towns such as Lachish and Tell Bet Mirsim to the Philistines or to inter-Canaanite feuding was inconclusive. Those denying the conquest theory argued that the so-called Israelite conquest entailed the peaceful settling of seminomadic peoples.

These views, as well as an alternative first suggested by George E. Mendenhall, who proposed that the conquest was an internal revolt of

AI

THE SECOND STOP OF Joshua's campaign against the cities of Canaan, as transmitted in the Bible, was Ai. As he had done at Jericho, the Israelite military leader sent men to spy out his objective. The spies reported that a force of only two or three thousand could take the city. Yet when Israel attacked, their forces were routed. This unexpected defeat was laid at the hands of Achan, a tribesman of Judah who had violated the ban on taking booty from the captured city of Jericho. Achan's evildoing having been extirpated by his execution, the Lord planned a second attack on Ai. The battle plan of deception and ambush is recorded with realistic detail in Joshua 7–8. Ai's army was wiped out, its inhabitants were killed, its buildings were burned, and its king was executed – buried under a mound of rocks.

At Khirbet et-Tell (the site of ancient Ai), however, there is no evidence of human occupation during the period when the Israelites were most likely to have been settling in Canaan. Extensive excavation from the mid-1960s through the early 1970s uncovered a settlement dating from the Early Bronze Age (ca. 3100) that had grown to a major walled city of almost thirty acres by the early third millennium. That city was destroyed around 2000. The site was then unoccupied for 1,100 years, including the Late Bronze Age (1400–1250), during which most scholars conjecture the Israelite tribes began to occupy the Palestinian highlands.

Excavators did uncover an Early Iron Age settlement (1250–1000) at Khirbet et-Tell that many adduce as among the first indications of Israelite occupation in Palestine. This small, unwalled Iron Age village was the setting for a new culture of farmers and shepherds who built cisterns and used characteristic pillars to support the roofs of their usually four-room houses. Many similar installations appeared throughout Palestine about the same time, some at new sites and others at sites like Ai that had been occupied before. It is difficult, however, to identify this culture as distinctively Israelite; it shares the milieu common to many Iron Age settlements in the larger region of Syria–Palestine.

Even if the Iron Age settlers at Ai can be identified as Israelites, they did not establish their new dwelling by military conquest. They occupied a site that had been abandoned for fifty generations. Then what of the biblical story of Ai? Does it have any historical basis that can be verified archeologically?

A few scholars insist that et-Tell is not the site of Old Testament Ai and that the real location of Joshua's victory has yet to be unearthed. Most, however, agree that et-Tell has been correctly identified. Others have proposed that Iron Age Ai had two building phases: Canaanite and Israelite. They suggest that a minor remodeling of the first phase represents the Israelite takeover, a minor raid that became the Bible's exciting story through years of retelling. Unfortunately, ceramic and structural evidence do not really support such an interpretation. The distinguished biblical scholar and prominent archeologist William F. Albright suggested that the biblical story of Ai was really the report of a battle at nearby Bethel (modern-day Beitin) – a site that does have evidence of complete destruction in the Late Bronze Age. He proposed that somewhere in its transmission across the generations confusion arose about the story's setting. Some propose that Joshua's story is a kind of historical speculation, an etiological narrative that gives a colorful explanation for the rock-heaped ruin of Ai that the Israelites encountered when they settled in Palestine. Finally, some understand Joshua 7–8 as a tale created to make a theological – not a historical – point.

In general, archeology has eliminated the historical underpinning of the biblical account of Ai's destruction by an army of conquering Israelites. How the remains at Ai are interpreted beyond that consensus depends as much on the excavator's model of Israel's settlement in Canaan as it does on the material evidence. Careful investigation at Ai and other sites like it has served the important purpose of challenging long-standing assumptions about the history of Israel, and it has forced scholars to look for other perspectives from which to understand Joshua and the conquest of Canaan.

peasants against their Canaanite overlords, seem to have been overtaken by the evidence of the dramatic increase in settlements in Israel in the Iron Age. Toward the end of the Late Bronze Age only 25–30 cities were occupied in the area from the Beersheba Valley in the south to the Jezreel Valley in the north, and only 7–8 sites were occupied in upper and lower Galilee. In the early Iron Age the situation changed dramatically. The number of sites between the Beersheba and Jezreel Valleys increased to 240, and there were 68 in Galilee. These figures refer, of course, to sites that have been discovered and they cannot be regarded as definitive totals. However, even allowing for their incompleteness, they can be taken as proof of a spectacular change in settlement pattern in Israel from the thirteenth century onward.

At first sight, the new evidence might seem to be a confirmation that an Israelite invasion took place; but it would be too hasty a conclusion. The remarkable thing about the new evidence is that it indicates that most of the Iron Age settlements were in precisely those areas of Israel, namely, the central hill country later known as the territory of Ephraim and Manasseh, about which the Book of Joshua says almost nothing. It has long been recognized that an odd feature of the Book of Joshua is that although Joshua assembles the tribes at Shechem, located in the Bethel and Samaria hill country, the book lacks an account of the conquest of that area. The new evidence about the settlement patterns only serves to make this problem more acute.

Israel Finkelstein describes a gradual process of settlement over some two hundred years by people who were initially pastoralists (i.e., dependent mainly on sheep and goats). At first, they settled in areas most suited to a combination of pastoralism and cereal growing, that is, the desert fringes to the east of the Bethel and Samaria hills. From here they spread to the west and the south, at first occupying the valleys, which had long since been cleared of trees, and then settling in and beginning to clear the wooded parts of the central hill country. An important fact is that settlement in Judah was small compared with that in the Bethel and Samaria hills.

But were these settlers Israelites? The answer given to this question will depend upon a person's view of the nature and development of Israelite religion. Those who hold that Israel's religion was primarily the creation of prophetic groups from the ninth century onward may well maintain that the settlers of the thirteenth century were "Canaanites," from among whom "Israel" gradually developed a separate identity. Those who hold that faith in Yahweh bound together social groups that had common ancestors, and that these groups believed that Yahweh had delivered at least some of them from slavery in Egypt, may well argue that the settlers were indeed Israelites. Whatever the answer, the question is important for several reasons. It reminds us that we cannot accept uncritically the picture presented in Joshua of Israelites invading a land already occupied by Canaanites. Finkelstein's evidence seems to indicate large-scale occupation of a land *devoid* of settlements; in which case we have to ask where the Canaanites came from! At the same time we must be aware that archeological and sociological explanations have their limitations. If they cannot prove that the settlers were Israelites, neither can they disprove that they were. A mediating position would be that the settlers included Israelites in sufficient numbers for the reference to Israel in the victory stela set up by the Egyptian pharaoh Merneptah in 1207 B.C.E. (see *ANET*, pp. 376–8) after invading Canaan to be understood in its commonly accepted sense – that Merneptah was referring to a people called Israel, probably in the Bethel and Samaria hill country.

Where had the settlers come from? Although we must not dismiss the likelihood that some had escaped from slavery in Egypt and had linked up with relatives on the fringes of Israel and Transjordan, the majority of settlers were pastoral seminomads descended from people who had lived in Canaan in the Late Bronze Age and whose adoption

HAZOR

JOSHUA 11:10–13 RECORDS the Israelite defeat of the city of Hazor. Located in the northern Galilee, Hazor was the premier settlement in Palestine during the Middle and Late Bronze Ages (2300–1200 B.C.E.). This grand city of perhaps 40,000 people occupied about 200 acres in two major fortified areas. Unlike Jericho, which is not mentioned in any extrabiblical document, Hazor is known to us from Egyptian Execration Texts (a collection of texts listing places to be cursed and dating to ca. 2000 B.C.E.), the Mari archives (ca. 1900 B.C.E.), and the Amarna letters (ca. 1400 B.C.E.). It was an important center of commerce. Tell el-Qedah, the mound on which the ancient upper city of Hazor was located, was a key control point for the major military and commercial routes that passed nearby. The Bronze Age city was a center for Canaanite culture as well. Its temples and palaces played a central role in the cultural prehistory of ancient Israel's religious and political institutions.

All the glory that was Hazor came to an abrupt and violent end late in the thirteenth century B.C.E. Sacked and burned to the ground, the city was resettled shortly thereafter by a small group of less culturally advanced, seminomadic people. These new settlers lived much more modestly, with a much simpler lifestyle. Dwelling in an unfortified area, they made their homes in tents and huts, each with its own storage pits and cooking installation.

This archeological reconstruction meshes well with the biblical account of Hazor's destruction by the Israelites: violent destruction of the impressive Canaanite city comes before the settlement of new people. (A second report, in Judges 4, where the defeat of "Jabin, king of Hazor," comes *after* the Israelite settlement in the land, still remains unexplained in that case.) Along with cities in the Judean highlands like Lachish, Eglon, and Kiriath Sepher, Hazor has been cited as corroborating the essential historicity of the Bible's account of how Israel took possession of the land of Canaan by force. According to such a view, the takeover seems to have been by means of systematic, or at least generally organized, military conquest. Evidence from the Iron Age resettlement of Hazor has also been added to the catalogue of remains said to represent a uniquely Israelite material culture in eleventh-century B.C.E. Palestine.

Nonetheless, the data from Hazor are far from undisputed. There is no way to know if the destruction of Hazor can be unequivocally attributed to one or more of the Israelite tribes. Political ambitions in Egypt's Nineteenth Dynasty and general unrest in the Canaanite city-states of the Late Bronze Age make it equally possible that Egyptians or rival Canaanites destroyed Hazor. And Hazor's destruction may not necessarily have resulted from military attack; perhaps a natural disaster or peacetime human agency is to blame. Some scholars even doubt the existence of a distinctive Israelite material culture. Indeed, there is no definitive evidence that requires Hazor's Iron Age inhabitants to be identified as Israelites.

However scholars may interpret the destruction of Canaanite Hazor, its Iron Age resettlement contributes to a larger picture that shows an era of great change and unrest in Palestine during the twelfth to eleventh centuries B.C.E. New players enter the stage of history, probably at Hazor, and many identify the new settlers as among those who would later join together to form the nation of Israel.

of a seminomadic way of life had been responsible for the dramatic decline in the number of settlements in the Late Bronze Age. In other words, if we take a period of 400 years from 1600 to 1200, we can suppose that, for reasons unknown to us, a majority of people in Canaan adopted a lifestyle in which they abandoned their settlements and depended mainly on sheep and goats, living on the fringes of the areas still occupied by prosperous city-states. During the thirteenth century the trend began to reverse, and the land began to be settled once more.

We can only guess at the reasons for these reversals. They may have been caused by the attacks of the Habiru upon cities in the fourteenth century or they may have been caused by pressure from Egypt. Another possible explanation – for which evidence is not available – is that changes in climate such as prolonged droughts forced settled communities to become seminomadic. The reversal toward renewed settlement may have depended upon changed political circumstances, such as the inability of city-states to provide the seminomads with grain in return for animal products. In this case, the seminomads would be forced to become their own grain producers, and this would require them to establish permanent settlements.

Two new factors significantly affected the lives of those who resettled in the land. First was the arrival of the Philistines as part of the migrations of the Sea Peoples in the twelfth century. They would later try to conquer Israel. Second, however it had come about, some of the settlers in the Bethel and Samaria hills were bound together by faith in Yahweh, who had liberated his people from slavery in Egypt. These two new factors would be decisive for the subsequent history of Israel and Judah.

The Iron Age settlements in the Bethel and Samaria hills varied in population size from 100 to 1,000 inhabitants. Many took the form of an elliptical circle of broad-roomed houses, each house enclosing a central courtyard. In areas where the growing of cereals predominated, many small silos for storing grain were found within the courtyards; in olive-growing areas the produce was stored in collared-rim jars. It is generally accepted that the shape of the settlements imitated the shape of settlements of tent dwellers and thus is evidence that the settlers in Iron Age Israel were making the transition from seminomadic to permanent settlement. The broad-roomed houses probably developed into the so-called four-roomed houses which are such a feature of Iron Age architecture in Israel and elsewhere in the region. The average size of a household was five, fam-

This distinctive pottery, found at sites along the southern coast of Palestine from the twelfth and eleventh centuries B.C.E., was produced by the Philistines. These examples from twelfth-century Tell Ashdod show the influence of the Mycenean painted pottery traditions, which the Philistines encountered on the way to their new homeland in Canaan.

Biblical Archaeology Slides, no. 128

ISRAELITE FARMING AND TECHNOLOGY

EARLY ISRAEL'S ECONOMY was based on agriculture, supplemented by animal husbandry. Families were generally self-sufficient, passing along skilled craftsmanship in ceramics, textiles, and metallurgy from generation to generation. The people who farmed the Palestinian highlands during the Early Iron Age were faced with formidable challenges. In addition to the day-to-day activities necessary for survival in a preindustrial society, the Israelite settlers had to perform a range of pioneer tasks specific to their hill country environment. Before crops could be planted, land had to be cleared of its dense overcoat of trees and shrubs. In many places numerous rocks that cluttered cultivatable land also had to be removed. In other places artificial fields had to be constructed by building terraces along steep, otherwise agriculturally useless slopes.

More than any other Iron Age technology, agricultural terracing opened up the Palestinian highlands to productive farming. Terraces transformed generally useless natural slopes into a series of level fields suitable for crop production. The artificially flattened surfaces were held in place by walls of dry-laid fieldstone. Fringe benefits of terracing included a reduction in erosion and an increase in groundwater retention. Unfortunately, terraces required great expenditures of cooperative labor to maintain.

They were costly and time-consuming. Without regular attention, terraces deteriorated rapidly, and the combined weight of unanchored soil and tumbled walls could produce devastating landslides.

The first Israelites employed dry farming to grow their crops; that is, they did not irrigate. Thus they were dependent on rainfall to provide the necessary moisture for germinating and maturing their produce. Rain was plentiful during the cool, wet winter months. However, high rates of runoff and evaporation meant that water was not conserved efficiently for the hot summer growing season. Consequently, the rainfall pattern made highland farming a precarious occupation at best.

Another important technology employed by early highland farmers was the widespread use of cisterns to conserve water from the rainy season for human and animal consumption in the dry summer months. Many of the cisterns were lined with waterproof lime plaster. Scholars have often credited the opening of the highland frontier to the widespread use of these water storage facilities coupled with the introduction of iron tools that facilitated the pioneer tasks of clearing forests, plowing fields, and hewing cisterns. However, the technology for building slaked-lime cisterns was available before the Iron Age, and in some areas local geological conditions provided highland farmers with impermeable

bedrock that made waterproof cisterns unnecessary. Moreover, iron did not come into widespread use in the hill country before the tenth century B.C.E. – well after the time of the Israelite settlement. Recent research suggests that the early Israelite farmers adapted to their precarious environment by more subtle means.

To conserve soil resources and maintain fertility, hill country agriculturalists probably employed a variety of procedures. Fields were allowed to stand fallow at regular intervals. Flocks and herds grazed on the fallow grounds, their manure providing excellent fertilizer. Nonetheless, such methods were not very effective. Farmers had to be satisfied with low crop yields (perhaps no better than 1:15 or 1:20), which decreased even more as local soils were depleted by prolonged use.

Communities of farmers in the Early Iron Age highlands adapted to their irregular environments by planting multiple crops in order to avoid depending on a single pattern of rainfall, since there could be great variety from year to year, season to season. Staple cereals and vegetables were mainstays in the highland diet, although tree and vine crops were part of the mix as well. Deut. 8:8 lists wheat, barley, grapes, figs, pomegranates, olives, and dates among the fruits of the land. Archeological investigation has added nuts (e.g., almonds) and legumes (e.g., broad beans, lentils, chickpeas) to the list. This diversity helped farming communities avoid becoming dependent on a single crop that might fail during a given year.

Highland farmers further reduced the risk of their difficult venture by storing the abundance of a good year against future agriculture disasters. Many crops could be preserved; fruit was dried or made into juice and olives were pressed into oil. Large storage jars and household grain pits of the early Israelite period attest to these common practices.

Flocks and herds also served as a way of storing food reserves. Subject to a different set of environmental constraints, these animals stored excess in years of plenty and could be culled when annual crops were inadequate for the community's survival. Sheep and goats contributed to the farm diet by also providing dairy products (e.g., milk for making curds and butter). Livestock husbandry made use of marginal lands and provided much-needed fertilizer. Wool and hides were also important household commodities.

Israelite farming was a corporate venture with labor demands that often went beyond what a single nuclear family could provide. The challenging, risky environment in which the early highland farmers eked out their existence was instrumental in the development of interhousehold and intervillage systems of cooperation and exchange networks. Those systems may well have facilitated the formation of the Israelite nation and its socially conscious religion.

Sowing by hand, still seen today, inevitably leads to some seed being scattered on rocks, high ground, or on the path next to the plowed field, as described in the parable of the sower (Matt. 13:1–9).

Biblical Archaeology Slides, no. 17

ilies probably consisting of from three to eight persons. It appears that limited local trading among settlements took place, with settlements using surplus grain to buy olives, and vice versa (Colorplates 8, 9, 10).

The Literary History of Joshua

In its present form the Book of Joshua is part of the Deuteronomistic History and therefore must date to the final editing of the Deuteronomistic History and the Pentateuch in the sixth–fifth centuries B.C.E. Its content is closely linked with Deuteronomy. Thus, in Deut. 27:1–8 the command that an altar should be built at Mount Ebal after the Israelites have crossed the Jordan is carried out at Josh. 8:30–5. Incidentally, this literary link produces the historical and geographical anomaly that places Joshua and the Israelites in the heartland of Israel without first having conquered it. It is not surprising, therefore, that early Christian attempts to identify Mounts Ebal and Gerizim, such as in Eusebius's fourth-century *Chronikon*, located them in the Jordan Valley to the north of Jericho. The two erroneously identified peaks concerned can be seen clearly today by anyone standing on Tell es-Sultan (ancient Jericho). Other links between Joshua and Deuteronomy are Deut. 19:1–10, whose command to designate three cities of refuge is carried out at Josh. 20:1–6; Josh. 11:21, where the sons of the Anakim mentioned at Deut. 9:1–3 are destroyed by Joshua; and the mention of hornets in Deut. 7:20 and Josh. 24:12.

By means of these links, Joshua is portrayed as the true successor of Moses, who carried out the commands to Moses that applied to conditions in the Promised Land. A summary of this view is found at Josh. 8:35: "There was not a word of all that Moses commanded that Joshua did not read before all the assembly of Israel." This, however, raises questions about the identity of the historical Joshua and the origin of the stories about the conquests attributed to him.

A notice about Joshua's death and burial at Josh. 24:29–30 locates his inheritance at Timnath-serah in the hill country of Ephraim. If this is correctly located at Khirbet Tibnah, then Joshua's home was a large village on an elongated hilltop with an adjacent spring in the southwestern part of Ephraim. Interestingly, it is not too far away from the valley of Aijalon (not more than ten miles), where the battle in defense of Gibeon took place and where Joshua exhorted the sun to stand still (Josh. 10:6–14). The fact that his exhortation is said to be written in the Book of Jashar (Josh. 10:13; possibly an ancient collection of poems) suggests that Joshua was at least a local judgelike leader whose successful military exploits against neighboring Canaanites made a sufficiently strong impression upon Israelite tradition to make him the ideal figure to be portrayed as successor to Moses and leader of the conquest in Israelite storytelling. All history writing and storytelling abhors a vacuum, and where there are gaps the roles of figures prominent in tradition are expanded to fill them.

We can thus suggest the following account of the literary history of Joshua. Although the settlement of the Israelites in Canaan was largely peaceful, there later developed conflicts between the Israelites and other settlers whom we may call Canaanites. In some cases the

Canaanites made common cause with or were allied to the powerful city-states in ancient Palestine. An early prominent and successful Israelite leader was Joshua, around whom stories of the conquest of cities began to gather. In some cases, archeological excavations have shown that cities mentioned in these stories were indeed destroyed, although the dates of destruction cannot necessarily be linked to the time of Joshua nor can the destroyers be identified as Israelites. There may, however, be more genuine historical reminiscence in these stories than is often allowed.

In its earliest form, the Book of Joshua may have been a continuation of the story about the ancestors and the Exodus begun in the Pentateuch and written down during the time of Hezekiah (ca. 727–698 B.C.E.). In this form, its purpose was to relate how all the Israelites entered the land of Israel after journeying through the desert after the Exodus from Egypt. It possibly jumped from what is now the beginning of chapter 13 to what is now the beginning of Judges via the notice of Joshua's death in 24:29–30. Joshua 13:1 speaks of Joshua as "old and advanced in years" and states that much land remained to be possessed. Judges 1 begins with the question, after the death of Joshua, of who will go up to fight against the Canaanites.

The substance of Joshua 1 to 13:1 was linked firmly to Deuteronomy by the passages mentioned above (p. 00). At this stage certain passages were added, such as those that show Joshua carrying out Moses' instructions and those that claim that the whole of the land was subdued and cleared of inhabitants (Josh. 10:40–2). How much of this was done during the reign of Josiah (640–609), when the first and major draft of the Deuteronomistic History was written, we cannot say. But it is likely that chapters 13–21, which record the partition of the land among the tribes, date from Josiah's time, although it must be noted that some scholars date the material in these chapters to the early monarchy (tenth century). Joshua's speech to the assembled Israelites in chapter 23 is similar to other key speeches and passages in the Deuteronomistic History (1 Sam. 12, 1 Kings 8, 2 Kings 17). It seems to be later than Joshua 24, which in turn is closer to Samuel's speech in 1 Samuel 12 than is Joshua 23. Joshua 24 may thus belong to an earlier, and Joshua 23 to a later, Deuteronomistic editing of Joshua.

The Literary Structure and Function of Joshua

The literary structure of Joshua is simple. Chapters 1–11 describe how the Israelites crossed the Jordan and set up camp at Gilgal, and how they defeated Jericho before advancing to the eastern fringe of the Bethel hill country, where they campaigned against Ai and a coalition of kings from the Jerusalem saddle and the Shephelah. An account of a campaign against Hazor in lower Galilee and fighting in the hill country of Judah (chap. 11) leads to a list of kings whom the Israelites defeated (chap. 12). From chapters 13–21 we have the account of the allocation of the land to the tribes. Chapter 22 deals with the special problem of the Transjordanian tribes, and chapters 23–4 are accounts of Joshua's gathering the tribes together and of his addresses to them.

The best way to describe the book's function is to address the problem that most obviously confronts modern readers: the barbarity of a narrative that enjoins the wholesale slaughter of populations in God's name. That the Israelites fought wars in which they believed that God was on their side cannot be doubted. The same is true of Christian European nations in the twentieth century, although that does not in any way lessen the offense. However, in describing war in terms of a crusade to exterminate whole populations, the biblical writers were not depicting reality but were rather following literary conventions. We find the same claim of having destroyed whole populations outside the Old Testament, for example, in the ninth-century inscription of Mesha (*ANET*, pp. 320–1).

In the case of Joshua, this literary convention of the "holy war" is used to present object lessons about what happens when the Israelites obey God and what happens when they disobey him. This is clearly to be seen in the stories of Jericho and Ai (chaps. 6–8), which are notable in Joshua for their literary construction and artistry.

In the story of Jericho's conquest, the Israelites do nothing except march round the city once a day for six days, carrying the ark of the covenant and blowing trumpets but otherwise maintaining silence. On the seventh day they march round the city seven times, and then, on Joshua's command, the people shout and the walls fall down. This successful, if unorthodox, method of warfare contrasts with what happens in chap. 7, where a conventional assault upon a minor town (whose Hebrew name, Ai, means "a ruin") results in disaster for the Israelites. Why? Because Achan had disobeyed the command that no spoil of Jericho was to be kept as a personal possession. Once Achan has been identified as the culprit and has been stoned to death, the fight against Ai is resumed and meets with success.

It is obvious that we are in the realm of religious instruction with these stories, rather than the realm of detached historical description. They show that obedience to God is necessary if the people are to enjoy peace and security. The whole conquest is not a triumph of military strength or skill but is the work of God made possible in particular by Joshua's scrupulous adherence to the law and instructions given to him by Moses. If one of the purposes of the Deuteronomistic History is to present Israel's history as a story of obedience and disobedience and their consequences, for the benefit of those who had returned to Judah from exile, we can see how Joshua plays its part in that scheme. We shall find the same purpose in Judges.

2. Judges

Judges and the Conquest

It has often been suggested that Judges presents a more plausible account of the Israelite conquest than Joshua. This view is based upon Judges 1, in which the tribes go individually to possess the land allotted to them, and where they have only limited success. Thus, to take a typical example, Judg. 1:27 states that

HOLY WAR IN THE OLD TESTAMENT

IN MUCH OF THE OLD TESTAment, Yahweh the God of Israel is cast as a mighty man of war – the Divine Warrior (e.g., Exod. 15:3). Israel's earliest national traditions portray the flight from Egypt into the land of Canaan as the grand march of a heavenly army, arrayed around the children of Israel, and led through the desert by their divine commander-in-chief. During the period of Israel's settlement of the Promised Land, the idea of a Warrior God also played an important role. One of Israel's earliest collections of poetry, now lost, contained a record of the "wars of Canaan" presumably fought during the settlement (Judg. 3:1). Bearing the title the Songs of the Wars of Yahweh, this collection probably contained Israel's songs of praise to the great Divine Warrior who had driven out the inhabitants of the land before them. The Israelite tribes thought of their success as dependent, not so much on their own military prowess, as on their uncompromising trust in Yahweh's ability to give them the victory.

This ideology received an early expression in the Israelite practice of "holy war," an institution of formative Israelite society that reached its fullest development and greatest influence in the settlement period. Some detailed instructions on how to conduct holy war have been preserved in Old Testament texts. Information about the preparation, personnel, conduct, and outcome of holy war is tantalizing but incomplete. Holy war was conducted with the full support of Israelite religious institutions, the priesthood and temple cult. The army apparently underwent a ritual cleansing before a battle (Josh. 3:5), regulations for which seem to have included abstention from sexual intercourse (2 Sam. 11:11).

Deuteronomy 20 pictures three possible outcomes to a holy war. (1) A city about to be attacked had to be offered terms of surrender. If its inhabitants accepted, their lives were spared. The entire population was to be enslaved. (2) If, however, the terms were rejected, the soon-to-be victorious Israelites were instructed to kill all the city's male citizens, taking the city's other inhabitants and their possessions as the spoils of war. (3) The exception to these rules of engagement were cities that lay within the boundaries of the Promised Land. When any of those cities was captured, Israel was to destroy it completely, offering it as a sacrifice to Yahweh.

Holy war ideology was not confined to ancient Israel. Artifactual remains like the Mesha inscription make it clear that other peoples held ideas very similar to those of their Israelite neighbors. Ancient warfare was often cast in terms of a power struggle between the gods of warring nations, and even modern societies tend to use religious traditions to sanctify and legitimize their own sides in times of conflict. Israel's God, however, according to Scripture, refused to identify himself completely with the political aims of the people who worshiped him. Yahweh maintained divine sovereignty over Israel's political ambitions. God's will was absolute over every people and nation.

In monarchical times the old holy war traditions of the conquest and period of the Judges were transformed into instruments of national policy. The declaration of war became a royal prerogative, as opposed to a divine one, and ad hoc armies were replaced by a professional army and organized conscripts. Thus the *institution* of holy war faded away; however, the ideology of sacred warfare continued to play an important part in the traditions of Israel's prophets and its priestly establishment. This ideology forms the background for many biblical presentations and reworkings of themes from the Exodus and conquest, and it is a standard judgment motif in later prophetic and eschatological writings.

Manasseh did not drive out the inhabitants of Beth-shean and its villages, or Taanach and its villages, or the inhabitants of Dor and its villages, or the inhabitants of Megiddo and its villages; but the Canaanites continued to live in that land.

This "realistic" account of the occupation is then contrasted favorably with those passages in Joshua (e.g., 10:40–2) that claim that the whole land was subdued by Joshua and that the indigenous population was destroyed.

However, it is possible to exaggerate the differences between Joshua and Judges 1. Josh. 13:1 acknowledges that the conquest is far from complete, and in the account of the dividing of the land among the tribes, the picture of an incomplete conquest is strengthened. Thus, Josh. 15:63 states that the men of Judah could not drive out the Jebusites, who lived in Jerusalem. Neither, according to Josh. 16:10, could the men of Ephraim drive out the Canaanites from Gezer. Josh. 17:11 lists cities that the men of Manasseh were unable to possess, and it is implied at Josh. 17:16–18 that Ephraim and Manasseh were hindered on the edges of their territory by Canaanite cities whose armies had chariots, which the Israelites could not match.

The issue here is not whether these claims can be verified by archeological or historical research, but rather whether the Book of Joshua envisages a complete and successful conquest at variance with Judges 1. The answer must surely be no. In spite of the fact that a little of the material in Judges 1 repeats what we have in Joshua (most notably the

CHARIOTS

CHARIOTS WERE MORE important and more effective than any other ancient armament, and they played a vital role in the military history of ancient Israel. Moses led the children of Israel across the Red Sea with pharaoh's chariots hot in pursuit (Exod. 14). When the Israelites arrived in Palestine, the Canaanites' chariots of iron were crucial forces in preventing the Israelites from claiming what they considered to be their divine patrimony (Judg. 1:19). Only when David's army acquired chariotry skills did the fledgling nation finally secure its existence against the Philistines (2 Sam. 8:4). Israel's Solomonic golden age was measured in terms of its horses and charioteers (1 Kings 4). The superior chariot power of Assyria and Babylon finally brought an end to Israel's independent existence.

Wheeled vehicles drawn by asses first appear in Mesopotamian art around 3000 B.C.E. By the time of Hammurabi (eighteenth century B.C.E.), chariots equipped with spoked wheels were standard fare. Drawn by people or oxen, chariots were effective military weapons only on smooth, dry ground; they were notoriously slow and clumsy on rougher terrain. The great innovation in chariot warfare came via the Hyksos, the Asiatic people controlling Syria–Palestine and much of Egypt during the Middle Bronze Age (ca. 1500), who introduced the horse-drawn chariot.

The speed and versatility of the new war vehicle gave it great tactical advantages. Two- or three-man horse-drawn chariots became the key to military dominance in the ancient Near East. The advent of equine chariotry made possible the rapid expansions of Egypt's New Kingdom, the Hittite kingdoms, and the Neo-Assyrian Empire. Tribute lists and victory memorials from Egyptian and Assyrian kings indicate the horse-drawn chariot's military centrality. In fact, chariot inventories became an index of political power, and chariots were an integral part of every powerful king's arsenal.

The Old Testament records the use of chariots by foreign rulers (Exod. 14:25, Josh. 11:6, Nah. 3:2). Indeed, Israel's use of chariot technology was closely associated with the rise of the Judean monarchy (1 Sam. 8:11). Chariots, therefore, came to be a symbol of royalty and political sovereignty, even to the point that they became symbols for divine omnipotence (Zech. 6:1 ff.). Yahweh, the God of Israel, was himself portrayed as a mighty king astride his terrifying chariot (Isa. 66:15, Hab. 3:8). A fiery chariot came to symbolize the awesome presence of God (2 Kings 2:11). In his magnificent first vision, the prophet Ezekiel employs a stylized throne–chariot to portray Yahweh's supreme majesty (Ezek. 1:4–28). Ancient Near Eastern gods were commonly pictured riding on powerful beasts or fearsome war vehicles, and Ezekiel, imitating Near Eastern models, combined the two modes of transportation in his vision of a chariot made, not of wood or metal, but of strange living creatures.

account of the conquest of Hebron and Debir in Josh. 15:13–19 and Judg. 1:11–15, 20), we must assume that, as readers, we are expected to see Joshua and Judges as a continuous narrative. In Joshua the land is subdued sufficiently by all twelve tribes acting together for it to be divided among the tribes. In Judges, after the death of Joshua, the tribes go individually into their allotted territories, which still contain pockets of resistance to Israelite rule. How far Judges relates to what we can surmise about what actually happened will now be discussed.

Archeological and Sociological Data on Israel during the Period of the Judges

In the treatment of Joshua, it was argued that recent research indicates that there was a peaceful occupation mainly of the Bethel and Samaria hill country probably during the latter part of the thirteenth century. The occupation was mostly in unpopulated areas and consisted of villages with from 100 to 1,000 inhabitants. A difficult question was whether the settlers would have called themselves Israelites or whether they were people who would later be divided into the two groups that we call Israelites and Canaanites.

The Book of Judges may help to answer this question because it is notable that, apart from the struggle between the Israelite leaders Deborah and Barak and the Canaanite commander Sisera, the oppressors of Israel in Judges are invaders from outside the land. Thus, Ehud resists the Moabites (Judg. 3); Gideon, the nomadic Amalekites and Midianites (Judg. 6–7); Jephthah, the Ammonites (Judg. 11–12); and Samson, the Philistines (Judg. 13–16). Although plausibility is not probability, it would fit well with what we now know about the Israelite settlement if the Israelite villages were subjected to localized threats from groups outside the land that either wanted to settle there or wanted to force Israelite villages to pay tribute in the form of agricultural produce. The "judges," whose stories form the core of the book, would be local heroes who led the Israelites against these oppressors.

The two accounts of internal conflicts are also plausible. The first concerns a coalition of Canaanite city-states led by Sisera against the tribes of Naphtali and Zebulun in lower Galilee and the Jezreel Valley (Judg. 4), providing evidence for a struggle between Canaanites and Israelites for mastery probably during the twelfth century, which the Israelites won. The other exception is Abimelech's attempt, described in Judges 9, to gain control over the Israelite villages, possibly with the

Early Iron Age pillar house at Ai, also known as a four-room house. Typical of ancient Palestine, this is no doubt the kind of house the early Israelites inhabited.

American Schools of Oriental Research, no. 82

FAMILY LIFE IN EARLY ISRAEL

A TYPICAL ISRAELITE household during the Early Iron Age consisted of four to five persons. Because of high infant mortality rates, six births per family were necessary to ensure the survival of the average family's two children. This typical family lived with their livestock in a two-story stone house with about 50 square meters of livable floor space. Their home was located in a cluster of similar domestic buildings that housed other families to whom they were closely related. Families lived crowded together in open settlements, not on individual farming plots. Each day workers walked to the fields early in the morning and returned at night. From ten to twenty extended family units made up the small highland villages. On the average, one of these villages would have been home to fewer than a hundred people.

Of course, such figures are only estimates based on archeological and ethnographic investigation, not a scientfic census of Israelite settlements in the twelfth to eleventh centuries B.C.E. Yet archeology, anthropology, and biblical studies can provide some interesting details about what family life was like in early Israel.

The most common kind of house used by early Israelites had stone walls, plastered floors, and mud- and straw-covered ceilings reinforced with wooden beams. Iron Age dwellings in the highlands were entered through a courtyard. A door led into the most spacious of the house's rooms, a living area often used for food preparation, household crafts, and storage. A narrow room to one side, usually separated by stone pillars that supported low curtain walls of masonry fill, was used as a stable. The back end of the house was formed by a "broad room" running the length of the building.

On the ground floor of these typical "four-room houses" archeologists have found countless storage jars (pithoi), kitchenwares (cooking pots), and implements for processing food (stone saddle querns, chopping blocks, and flint sickle blades) along with evidence of small craft production (e.g., spinning and sewing). Animals shared the first floor with the human inhabitants. Livestock, mainly sheep and goats, would have been brought into the house at night to the flagstone-paved side room through a small passage in the principal domestic quarters. Warmth radiating from them up to the second-story living quarters might also have provided an effective and inexpensive, if somewhat smelly, source of heat. Dining, sleeping, and other activities would have been conducted in second-story rooms built across the timber-supported ceiling of the ground floor. The design was a successful adaptation to farm life by rural families who grew crops and raised livestock.

The early Israelite farmhouses were usually built in clusters, or compounds. Multiple-family compounds comprised two or three private houses, sometimes linked by common walls. Each house in the compound had a separate entrance, usually approached through a shared courtyard enclosure. These multiple- or extended-family groups were the basic socioeconomic unit of life in ancient Israel. They cooperated to procure, process, store, preserve, prepare, and serve food. Sometimes they shared an open-air workshop for metallurgy. The group collectively held land and shared labor needs.

In biblical terminology this social unit is called the *bet 'ab,* "house of the father." An ideal household consisted of a senior couple, their children, and the families of their married sons. Sometimes even after a father's death married brothers continued to live in the same compound working together cooperatively as a single household. Authority was held by the eldest male member, although the household's primary female probably wielded power by virtue of her decision making in allocating the family's resources. Life in such farming villages would have been consumed with meeting the everyday survival needs of their inhabitants. Agricultural and domestic tasks required long hours of hard work. The routine and monotonous seasonal pattern of plowing, sowing, pruning, harvesting, threshing, and gathering set the rhythm for life in each family and in the entire village. Men, women, and children shared household and farm responsibilities as these early Israelite families scratched out their existence on the highland frontiers.

help of non-Israelites in Shechem. It would be unusual for villagers to be allowed to live their lives in peace in twelfth-century Israel, and the picture in Judges of recurrent invasion by groups from outside and of internal attempts to gain power is, unfortunately, completely plausible.

A notable feature of Judges is the almost complete absence of the tribe of Judah. It is true that Judah is the tribe that leads the others in possessing its territory (Judg. 1) and that furnishes a "judge" in the person of Othniel (Judg. 3:7–11). But apart from these passages (and Judah is not mentioned *explicitly* in 3:7–11) and the obvious gloss at 20:18, Judah plays no part in Judges. This accords well with the evidence from the surveys, which shows that settlement in Judah was sparse compared with that in the Bethel and Samaria hills.

How were the villages organized sociologically? Here, it must be confessed, we know less than is often supposed. Over the years, various theories have been put forward about Israel's social organization in the period of the Judges. A very influential theory given classic expression by the German scholar Martin Noth in the 1930s was that Israel was a twelve-tribe amphictyony, that is, a confederation of tribes bound together by mutual obligations and centered upon a particular sanctuary. This view rested partly upon Judges 20–21, in which the tribes unite to punish Benjamin for a moral outrage. Recently, it has been popular to argue that Israel was an egalitarian segmentary society, that is, a society in which there was no central source of power or authority and in which power was distributed horizontally among groups of equal status rather than vertically downward from rulers to subjects. The segmentary theory is probably closer to the truth than the amphictyony theory, so long as we remember that, as will now be argued, the Israelites had powerful local leaders during the so-called period of the Judges without having one single seat of absolute power.

In Judg. 10:1–5 and 12:8–15 we have brief details about so-called minor judges. Of Jair the Gileadite we learn that he had thirty sons and thirty cities (Judg. 10:3–4), while Abdon had forty sons and thirty grandsons, who rode on seventy asses (12:13–14). The conclusion of the story of Gideon (8:29–30) claims that he had seventy sons born to his many wives. Even allowing for exaggeration, it is clear from these passages that the "minor judges" were leading men in their local communities who, in return for the responsibilities that they had assumed for their people, were allowed privileges such as a multiplicity of wives. Their responsibilities probably included the coordination of activities that needed the resources of more than one village (such as the clearing of forests or the building of terraces) and the settling of disputes. Their families were or became dominant in their localities. Whether or not we can call them leaders of tribes is a difficult question because the term "tribe" is very ambiguous, and in the case of ancient Israel we do not know whether tribes were descent groups or territorial areas or both. We also do not know whether the tribes took their names from or gave their names to the geographical areas in which they settled.

THE TWELVE TRIBES OF ISRAEL

THE FINAL EDITORS OF Israel's national religious history present what seems to be a clear picture of early Israelite social organization. From the very moment of the Exodus the people of Israel are said to have been divided into twelve tribes, each descended from one of the sons of their common ancestor Jacob (by Leah: Reuben, Simeon, Levi, Judah, Issachar, and Zebulun; by Rachel: Joseph and Benjamin; by Bilha: Dan and Naphtali; by Zilpah: Gad and Asher). According to Judges 13–22, the tribes were apportioned adjoining territorial allotments in Palestine and the Transjordan. A close examination of the biblical text, however, suggests that this twelve-tribe system is an over-simplification of historical reality in early Israel. Such tribal designations reflected territorial, rather than genealogical, divisions. (Groups that were bound by similar histories and who shared lifestyles and territories often expressed their relationship in terms of belief in a common ancestry.) But even understanding the twelve tribes as inhabitants of twelve separate territories is inadequate. The tribal society of Israel before the monarchy was marked by vague, fluid divisions. Identities and relationships between social units changed from time to time.

It seems that administrative needs from later eras imposed a twelve-tribe system on what was really a rather complicated situation in early Israel. In the north settled the tribe of Manasseh with the associated and perhaps subordinate groups known as

Ephraimites, Benjaminites, and Gileadites. Asher, Zebulun, Issachar, and Naphtali settled in the Galilee–Jezreel region. Calebites, Kenizzites, Jerahmeelites, Kenites, and Simeonites – groups that would come to compose the social entity of greater Judah – lived in the south. The tribes of Reuben and Gad apparently had no fixed territory but roamed about with their herds and flocks. At some point the Danite tribe seems to have migrated from its coastal territory to the region near the springs that feed the Jordan north of the Sea of Galilee. This more accurate picture, drawn from close inspection of narratives in Joshua and Judges, stresses the independence and interrelatedness of various tribal groups. Although they cooperated together loosely and sporadically (especially in the face of military threats), the tribes by and large lived autonomous lives.

For many years scholars reconstructed the history of premonarchic Israel along more formal lines, specifically on analogy to sacred tribal leagues that existed in the Mediterranean world among the Greeks and Old Latins. Israel's tribes were thought to have existed in a close alliance that exhibited many of the same characteristics as these amphictyonies (Greek "inhabitants of the neighboring district"). An amphictyony was an association of autonomous groups organized into multimember confederations (cf. the twelve tribes of Israel). The groups worshiped a common deity at a common shrine (cf. Yahweh's ark at Shechem and later Shiloh), accepted binding sacred law (cf. the Sinai covenant), and submitted to the

rule of a body of officers delegated from the member groups (cf. the Israelite judges). Biblical evidence for such a confederacy in Israel, however, is ambiguous. The twelve-tribe system is a relatively late phenomenon in premonarchic Israel; worship in early Israel was certainly not limited to a single shrine; and the biblical judges were seldom national leaders.

This is not to suggest that some form of cooperation and some kinds of social bonds did not exist between various Israelite tribes before the nation of Israel was established by Saul and David. The Israelite monarchy presupposes some kind of preliminary tribal association, and even an early text like the Song of Deborah (Judg. 5) assumes some kind of pan-tribal organization (although the list of tribes in that passage differs in number and content from the classic formulation of Israel's twelve tribes).

Recently scholars have suggested that the twelve-tribe system familiar to us took shape just prior to the formation of the monarchy. David apparently expanded and reconstituted the system to incorporate the Canaanite populace of his growing territories. David's list represents the roster of administrative districts organized around traditional social groups from which he drew his monthly quotas of military personnel and supplies. Solomon utilized the same names in his program of redistricting the nation that was designed to increase administrative efficiency. Solomon, however, merely used the tribal designations as symbols since his boundaries were drawn according to practical needs and not traditional social divisions. After the separation of the northern and southern kingdoms, the twelve-tribe system became a traditional concept which expressed the unity of all those who worshiped Yahweh rather than actual sociological divisions.

This reconstruction helps explain an anomaly in the biblical presentation of the twelve tribes. The Old Testament actually preserves two different lists with twelve tribes each. One list includes Ephraim and Manasseh as separate tribes, omitting the Levites; the other includes the tribe of Levi and telescopes Ephraim and Manasseh into the single tribe of Joseph. Scholars think that the Ephraim–Manasseh list is older. When the system of twelve tribes became more symbolic than actual, it became necessary to include the priestly Levites as one of the original twelve tribes. In order to retain the traditional number of twelve tribes, two closely related tribes in the north were conflated and given the name of their common ancestor Joseph.

The idea of the twelve tribes of Israel was generalized and used as an encompassing conception read back into the earliest days of Israel's history. It symbolized the unity of the Israelite people from the days of Moses onward. It could even be retrojected into the grand genealogical design of the patriarch Jacob and his twelve sons. In that way a system that took shape in the days of the united kingdom became a way of expressing the cooperation between traditional "proto-Israelite" groups during the time Israel was first settling into the land of Canaan.

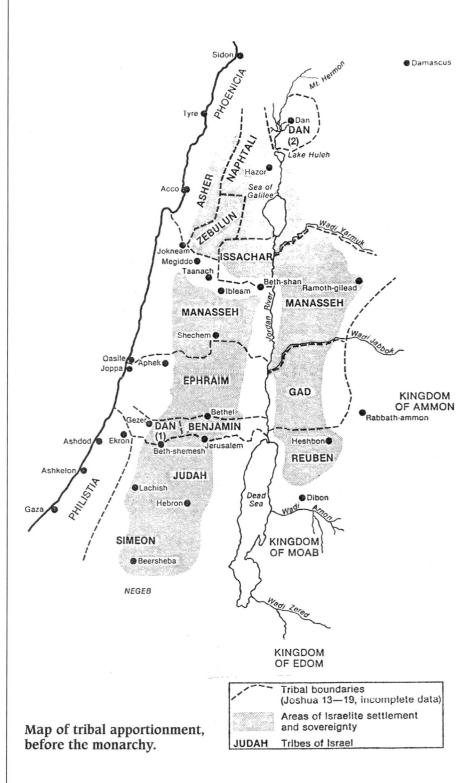

Map of tribal apportionment, before the monarchy.

On the basis of the foregoing we can suggest the following about the life of Israel in the period of the Judges (ca. 1220–1020 B.C.E.). Israel consisted of a number of villages in the Bethel and Samaria hills and in lower Galilee. They were ruled by leading members of dominant families who exercised local control, who were leaders in war, and who adjudicated disputes. Most of the threats from groups outside the land were dealt with by local leaders about whose exploits stories were preserved locally. Sometimes, different Israelite groups would unite to face a common enemy, such as Sisera (Judg. 4–5); but Israelite groups could also quarrel or fight among themselves, as in the case of Gideon of Manasseh's dispute with Ephraim and the men of Succoth and Penuel. Also, the Gileadites under Jephthah had a bitter dispute with the Ephraimites (12:1–6). The attempt of Abimelech to establish centralized control caused much internal strife (Judg. 9).

It is notable that the religious attitudes displayed in Judges differ from what the Old Testament reports about religious practice, say, from the eighth century B.C.E. Jephthah sacrifices his only daughter in fulfillment of a vow to God (11:29–40). Samson's involvement with women seems strange for one who had belonged to the order of Nazirites from birth and who was required to abstain from alcohol. In Judges 18 the men of Dan enlist a Levite to be their priest and acquire by force household gods and a graven image to be part of his cult. If Judges 18–20 reflects the conditions of the period, then the "tribes" were not only pledged to mutual help against a common enemy but pledged to punish any tribe that violated the customs of hospitality and the protection of travelers.

The Literary History of Judges

In its final form Judges claims to describe what happened to the whole Israelite nation from the death of Joshua to the eve of the rise of the monarchy. The narrative is determined by the agenda that all Israel had traveled from Egypt to Israel and had fought against the Canaanites before the tribes had separated to occupy their allotted land. The local leaders are presented as leaders of the whole nation, and the local enemies become the enemies of the whole people.

Twelve judges span the period from Joshua to the eve of the birth of Samuel (ca. 1220–1020):

Othniel	3:7 11
Ehud	3:12 30
Deborah	4:1 23
Gideon	6:1 8:35
Abimelech	9:1 57
Tola	10:1 2
Jair	10:3 5
Jephthah	11:1 12:7
Ibzan	12:8 10
Elon	12:11 12
Abdon	12:13 15
Samson	13:1 16:31

From the above list it is obvious that Judges is based upon two types of material: longer stories about judges who deliver Israel from oppressors (Ehud, Deborah, Gideon, Abimelech, Jephthah, and Samson) and brief notices about powerful local leaders (Tola, Jair, Ibzan, Elon, and Abdon). Othniel probably belongs to the latter group. These traditions have been joined to fill the gap from Joshua to the time of Samuel.

In addition to the notices and accounts of these leaders, Judges is set in a theological framework which interprets the events of the period in terms of disobedience, punishment, and repentance. The people of Israel turn from God and serve other gods. God then gives them into the hand of a particular enemy, who oppresses them. When the Israelites return to God and cry for help, he raises up a deliverer who defeats the enemy and gives the Israelites rest for a period, until the whole process begins again. In some cases it is easy to see how this framework has been added to the stories about the deliverers. This is particularly true of the story of Samson, where 13:1, which introduces the Samson story, has been added to a complete story in which the Philistines only gradually appear as the enemy (13:5b is also an addition). This suggests that Judges went through two or three editions before reaching its present form.

In its first edition Judges probably lacked the theological introduction in chapters 2:1–3:11 as well as the regular references to the disobedience–oppression–deliverance cycle. Although its exact form at this stage cannot be reconstructed, it was probably part of a larger work that included the stories of the ancestors and the conquest and culminated in the establishment of David's kingship. A date for this edition is hard to establish; a plausible time would be the reign of Hezekiah (727–698). Probably during the time of Josiah (640–609) it was adapted into the Deuteronomistic History, where it began to receive its theological framework and Deuteronomistic comments. This process was not completed until the exile (sixth century).

Two special problems are chapter 5, the Song of Deborah, and the so-called epilogue to the book, chapters 19–21 (or 17–21). The date of the Song of Deborah is much disputed. At one end of the scale the song is taken to be one of the oldest parts of the Old Testament, notable for its description of God marching from Edom, its attribution of Israel's victory to the stars of heaven, and its lack of reference to Judah. On this dating, the song is prime evidence for the location and situation of the tribes in the period between 1200 and 1020. Alternative views date its completion to the eighth–seventh centuries. A subsidiary question is the relationship of chapter 5 to chapter 4. In the latter, only two tribes, Zebulun and Naphtali, are involved in the battle, whereas it is implied in the former that Issachar, Zebulun, Ephraim, Benjamin, and Machir (a poetic name for, or a "clan" within, Manasseh) also fought for Deborah and Barak. In favor of the view that the Song of Deborah at least contains ancient material is the nonmention of Judah, the apparent location of Dan near the coastal plain and not in the far north, and the unusual name for Manasseh.

If Judges originally ended at 16:31 with the death of Samson, this would have been an excellent prelude to the story of the birth of Samuel in 1 Samuel. Chapters 17–21 interrupt the sequence and, with their recurring refrain that there was no king in Israel and that everyone did what was right in his own eyes, seem to address a different agenda from that of the rest of the book. They have thus often been treated as having been added at a late stage in the book's composition. On the other hand, as has been noted above, some of the religious practices described in chapters 17–21 seem to be at odds with later practice. Further, if Judges looks forward to and promotes David's kingship, then chapters 17–21 could well have been part of the first edition of Judges, serving to show how necessary it was for a king chosen by God to rule the people.

The Literary Structure and Function of Judges

The book consists of an account of the tribes entering their territories after Joshua's death (chap. 1), after which a theological meditation upon the unfaithfulness of the people to God and how he both punished and delivered them (2:1–3:11) leads to the stories of the deliverer judges, whose numbers are made to add up to twelve by the brief notices of minor judges (3:12–16:31). The epilogue (chaps. 17–21) describes the unsatisfactory moral and religious state of affairs when there was no king in Israel.

The most obvious function of the book is indicated by the Deuteronomistic introduction in chapters 2–3 and by the passages that show the persistence of the disobedience–punishment–repentance–deliverance cycle. Within the Deuteronomistic History the function of this material is clear. If the History is addressed to the Jews who stand poised to return, or have just returned, to Judah and Jerusalem, Judges is telling them that their exile to Babylon was the result of their disobedience to God. Their return has been God's gracious act of deliverance. If they wish to remain in the land in the future, they must heed the warnings contained in Judges and not turn away from God.

But it is possible to see another function in Judges, whether or not we accept that it once existed in a version without its Deuteronomistic trappings. It seems, in several ways, to look forward to David's kingship and ends with the observation that there was no king in Israel. In between, there are accounts of leaders; yet each is in some way flawed and none establishes a dynasty. Ehud is left-handed (regarded as a defect by Israelite society), Barak is not prepared to lead his people unless accompanied by Deborah, and Deborah herself cannot become a king or founder of a dynasty because she is a woman. Gideon is offered the kingship but refuses it; and in any case he has made an idol, which becomes an offense to Israel (8:27). Gideon's son Abimelech does try to become king, but the attempt is a disaster and he is killed while attacking one of his own cities. Jephthah has only one child, a daughter, and she is sacrificed in fulfillment of Jephthah's vow to offer in sacrifice the first person he meets on returning home if God grants him victory. Samson is hardly a suitable candidate to establish permanent leadership given his weakness for dubious women.

After the stories about brave, but flawed, heroes and heroines, the final chapters of the book portray a state of religious and moral chaos in leaderless Israel. Although the Israelite tribes unite to punish the tribe of Benjamin for the outrage perpetrated by one town on a traveler and his concubine, the outcome is out of all proportion to the original crime, serious as the crime is. The losses in the battle between Israel and Benjamin amounted to 40,000 for Israel and 50,000 for Benjamin. This is not the end of the slaughter, for, in order to provide wives for the men of Benjamin, because the other tribes will not provide wives, the males of Jabesh-gilead are slaughtered and four hundred virgins are brought from there to Benjamin. The crime of Jabesh-gilead (in Transjordan) is not to have joined the rest of Israel in fighting Benjamin. Thus the book ends with a vivid account of chaos in Israel, a chaos ascribed to the lack of a king. The books of Samuel tell how that lack was to be met.

3. First and Second Samuel

Archeological and Sociological Data on Israel
Immediately before and during the United Monarchy

As the eleventh century drew to a close, Israel consisted of a number of villages in the Bethel and Samaria hills and in lower Galilee. There were no urban centers exercising local control; but there was local leadership exercised by what we may call chiefs, who were leading members of dominant families who were accorded certain privileges in return for their responsibilities as leaders in battle and judges in case of disputes. The same was true in Judah, which was less densely settled than Israel and which witnessed a slow increase in population in the twelfth to eleventh centuries. It is probable that, certainly in Israel, a social and religious identity had been formed or consolidated during the period of the Judges. How this was expressed is difficult to say. It is going too far to speak of a confederation with officials and a common law, such as was demanded by the theory of the Israelite amphictyony. On the other hand, there was at least a sufficient sense of common interest for the Israelite villages to unite together locally or nationally in the face of threats from outside. This common interest had both a natural kinship element and a religious element, with the latter focused upon the ark of the covenant. This was a portable sacred box which was the pledge of the presence of Yahweh, the God who had freed his people from slavery and who accompanied them in their battles.

As the eleventh century ended, the last, and most serious, threat to Israel from an outside group became manifest in the form of the Philistines. They were part of the Sea Peoples, who had traveled by sea and land from Crete or Asia Minor and had attempted to settle in Egypt a little after 1200. Some succeeded in settling in the coastal plain in the ancient cities of Ashkelon, Ashdod, and Gaza. They then began to expand into the Shephelah, where they founded or occupied Gath and Ekron (the exact location of these two cities is uncertain). Around 1040, they began to exert pressure on the tribe of Dan, which was situ-

THE ARK OF THE COVENANT

MENTIONED SOME 200 times in the Old Testament, the ark of the covenant was perhaps ancient Israel's most important religious symbol. In Exodus 25 the ark is described as a box made of acacia wood, its dimensions 4 × 2 1/2 × 2 1/2 feet. It was covered with gold plate, and to it were attached golden rings through which poles were inserted to carry the ark about. Over the ark was a plate of gold called the *kipporet,* or "mercy seat" (King James Version). Two cherubim, winged sphinxlike creatures, stood at the ends of the *kipporet* covering it with their wings. According to the priestly tradition, the ark was the throne of Yahweh. Similar imagery and ideology run throughout the religious art of the ancient Near East. The tabernacle was built to accommodate the ark, which was central to the worship of the Israelites from the days of their wanderings in the desert until the end of Israel's independent existence.

But like the tabernacle, also described in the Book of Exodus, this picture of the ark probably represents a retrojection back into an earlier age, reflecting the details of Solomon's temple, where the ark stood in the sanctuary's holiest place. The ark seems to have played a key role in some of Israel's earliest nation al traditions, but it is likely to have been at first a simple wooden box designed as a receptacle for some abstract or copy of the covenant law (Deut. 9:9). Ancient covenants were often deposited in special locations related to the presence of the gods in whose names they were made. The ark became the visible sign of Yahweh's presence, an extension of the divine personality (cf. Ps. 132). The ark is found thus in military contexts, a symbol of divine protection in war and adversity (Num. 10:33 ff.). The ark is said to have led Israel over the Jordan and to have figured prominently in the stories of the Israelite settlement of the Promised Land (e.g., at Jericho, Josh. 5–6).

The precise location of the ark of the covenant becomes obscure during the period of the Judges until it reappears at Shiloh under the protection of Eli and his family. Its place in Israel's worship before the monarchy is uncertain. Although the ark may have been important for some groups, it most likely did not serve as the focal point of any tribal confederacy during the days of early Israel. The ark plays a central role again in the Samuel narratives, which culminate with the story of how David brought the ark to Jerusalem. Before the ark achieved its final place of glory in Solomon's temple, it featured in a variety of narratives that emphasize its power and grandeur. The Philistines experienced its effects when a plague of boils struck after they had captured the ark (1 Sam. 5); seventy men from Bet Shemesh were struck down for not rejoicing when the ark appeared (1 Sam. 6:19); and Uzzah's death was viewed as punishment for his having inadvertently touched the ark during its grand procession to the new capital (2 Sam. 6:7).

By moving the ark to Jerusalem David ensured that his new southern-based kingdom was heir to the religious and political traditions of the north. The move symbolized Jerusalem's new role as the religious center of the nation, and David claimed for himself the role of protector and patron of the national cult. The ark was placed in a tent built especially for that purpose until Solomon completed work on its final resting place, the temple of Yahweh. The ark of the covenant probably disappeared during the invasion of Nebuchadnezzar in 587/6 B.C.E., or perhaps it was taken along with the temple's other treasures when the Babylonians exacted tribute from King Jehoiachim ten years earlier. No new ark was made for the second temple (Jer. 3:16), though some scholars understand the *kipporet* – the seat of the divine presence – to be a substitute for it in the postexilic tradition (1 Chron. 28:11; cf. Lev. 16:2, 3). The ark's final fate remains a mystery.

The original ark that held the tablets of the law did not survive into the second temple period. This sculpted decoration from the synagogue at Capernaum shows an early ark as a wheeled chest in the shape of a Greek-style temple. The doors on the front of the temple chest would have opened to give access to the scrolls stored inside.

Biblical Archaeology Slides, no. 132

ated on the coastal plain, the valley of Aijalon, and in the Shephelah to the north of the Philistines. The stories of Samson belong to this phase.

Around 1020, having forced the Danites to migrate to the far north, the Philistines set out to conquer Israel, and they defeated the Israelite forces in two battles in the foothills of Ephraim (1 Sam. 4). An important question is why they turned their attention to the Ephraim hills instead of moving immediately eastward against Judah, a movement that would have been assisted by the fact that the Shephelah is a transitional zone between the coastal plain and the Judean hill country. Judg. 15:9–13 hints that part, at least, of Judah was subject to Philistine raids; this is a story about the Philistines invading Judah to make the men of Judah capture and hand over Samson. Also, the story of David and Goliath raises the question whether, at its core and ignoring its theological elaboration, the narrative contains the memory of a combat between two representatives at a time when the Philistines and the men of Judah were fighting each other in the Shephelah. Further, David is introduced into the entourage of Saul as a man of war (1 Sam. 16:18).

There is no explicit information in 1 Samuel about a Philistine campaign in Judah, and this may be an accident; but there is another way of looking at the matter. Philistine expansion was no doubt inspired by the desire for more power and territory; but expansion also needed to be sustained by adequate food supplies. In this regard, the settlement in Israel (the northern tribes) was more advanced than in Judah. Rainfall is more reliable the further north one goes, and the broad valleys of the Samaria hills and lower Galilee were more suitable for producing grain than the Judean hill country. The move against Israel therefore made strategic sense, and after defeating the Israelite armies, the Philistines established themselves in key ancient cities such as Megiddo and Bet She'an, as well as in small garrisons in the central hill country.

This cult stand was found at Tell Taanach, 8 miles southeast of Megiddo, and stands 3 feet high. The nude female holding two lions by the ear on the bottom register may represent a female deity. Two sphinxes flank the doorway on the next register, and a Tree of Life stands above. The calf on top may represent Baal.

The response to this threat that seemed to have been effective previously, namely, action taken by a local leader, failed on this occasion. The local leader seems to have been Samuel. Although he is credited with victories over the Philistines (1 Sam. 7:5–14), any respite was temporary, and Israel looked to a more powerful type of leadership, that of a "king," to deliver them from the Philistines. Recent discussion of the monarchy in Israel has concluded that it is more accurate to describe Saul and David as chiefs rather than kings and to regard Solomon as the first Israelite ruler to put in place the administrative infrastructure that would make the description "king" appropriate.

This discussion also points to the importance of the personalities of Saul and David and to the essentially family nature of their rule. However, the terminology of "king" will be retained here, while bearing the above points in mind.

The person who became the leader of the northern tribe was Saul, of the tribe of Benjamin. Unfortunately, the accounts of his leadership in 1 Sam. 8–15 leave much that is unclear. We do not know how long he reigned (1 Sam. 13:1 says two years, but gives his age at accession as one year old!) or even how he became king. The reason is that the narrative of 1 Samuel has its sights set firmly on the establishment of David's rule and considerably truncates the story of Saul's leadership. However, it can be deduced from what we have that Saul was associated with the prophetic groups led by Samuel (1 Sam. 10:12; see below), that he was a zealous adherent of Yahweh (1 Sam. 28:3, 2 Sam. 21:1–6), and that he delivered the men of Jabesh-gilead from the Ammonites (1 Sam. 11:1–11), probably prior to becoming Israel's supreme chief in the struggle with the Philistines.

There has been much discussion about why the new form of leadership arose. It has been suggested that the Philistine threat alone is not a sufficient explanation, and underlying social and economic causes have been sought. According to one view, the change of leadership was allied to the inability of the existing social and economic structures to provide food for a growing population. Of the two possible responses to this situation, emigration of surplus population or the adoption of new, more centralizing structures, the latter won the day. Although these explanations are helpful, it remains likely that the Philistine threat was the catalyst for the move to a new type of leadership.

In any event, Saul's leadership gave only temporary respite to Israel, and it was left to David to turn a desperate situation to the advantage of Israel and Judah. Fragments of genealogy such as 2 Sam. 17:25 suggest that David was related through his mother to the rulers of the east Jordanian Ammonites. Indeed, the group from which David was descended may have settled in Judah during the twelfth century, traveling from Ammon via Moab. Judah probably became formally allied with Israel against the Philistines when David, the son of a chief in Judah, joined Saul's entourage (1 Sam. 16:14–23). David soon became close friends with Saul's son Jonathan, and he married Saul's daughter Michal, but Saul's suspicions of his motives led to a breach with David, forcing the latter to become the leader of a powerful group of guerilla fighters before eventually deserting to the Philistines. After Saul's defeat and death at the hands of the Philistines, David quietly consolidated a power base in Judah until he was strong enough to defeat the Philistines, to establish his rule over Israel and Judah, and to inflict defeats upon neighboring peoples such as those in Damascus, Ammon, Edom, and Moab.

Just as there has been discussion about the appropriateness of the term "king" to describe Saul and David, so it has been doubted whether we should speak of a Davidic state or empire. The question is, what sort of infrastructure must be in place for there to be meaningful talk about kings, states, and empires? According to the indices adopted by Jamieson-Drake – public works, size of urban center, literacy, and luxury items – "Judah was a small state in the 8th–7th centuries, but not before" (Jamieson-Drake 1991, p. 139). Using these indices, even Solomon cannot properly be described as a king, although according to Jamieson-Drake, he "should be credited with setting in motion the institutional forces which eventually resulted in state bureaucratic controls accompanied by an intensity of settlement and levels of regional economic activity appropriate to a state" (1991, p. 144).

It seems, then, that we must look at David's achievements in a new light and say that his power in Israel was that of a chief to whom loyalty was forthcoming because he had freed the people from Philistine domination. His war against the Ammonites was probably on behalf of Israelites living in north Transjordan, but his other victories did not result in the establishment of his rule over other territories outside Israel in the form of an empire. Indeed, Jamieson-Drake's researchers indicate that there was no centralized rule over *Judah* from Jerusalem until the eighth century. The personal nature of his rule is indicated by the fact that, according to 2 Sam. 14–15, the king was expected to adjudicate legal disputes. Further, there were two revolts against David, and his commander and nephew Joab was able to disregard David's instructions and even to wield power over him (2 Sam. 3:20–39).

A standard description of Israel's history from 1200 to 1000 B.C.E. has been in terms of the transition from tribal confederacy to dynastic state. Recent research makes these labels inappropriate. One important result of David's reign, however, was the temporary takeover of Israel by Judah. Later, that takeover would become permanent, with significant implications for the form of the biblical writings.

The Literary History of the Books of Samuel

This is a subject on which very diverse views are held. Although it is commonly believed that 1 and 2 Samuel reached their final form as part of the Deuteronomistic History during the exile, experts differ about the antiquity of the material. Twenty years ago it was generally agreed that 2 Samuel 9–20 was part of a court chronicle written during the reign of Solomon. Although the purpose of this composition was argued about – whether it was the story of the succession to David's throne or was a religious and prophetic work centered on the punishment of David's misdemeanors (to name two suggestions) – the date was not disputed. Today, some scholars believe that 2 Samuel 9–20 was written after the exile. The issues are too numerous to discuss here; but it will be assumed here that 1 and 2 Samuel contain at least some material from the time of David and Solomon. This material includes fragments about Saul's leadership (1 Sam. 9–11, 13–15), and the story of David's rise to leadership, which begins in 1 Samuel 16, is intertwined with stories about David and Jonathan before emerging as a clear story line in the closing chapter of 1 Samuel, and continues through to 2 Samuel 20, with some insertions in chapters 2 and 8. The final chapters of 2 Samuel also contain what looks like old material.

Given that in premonarchic Israel there was no circulation of written material in the way we understand it, for whose benefit would the story of David's rise be written down? It is possible, of course, that the material is a written version of stories about David and Saul that circulated orally and that were intended to inform and entertain. One line of approach may be via the question of why the story of David's rise from 1 Samuel 16 is so strongly concerned to absolve David from any guilt in the failure of Saul's rule. For example, David's desertion to the Philistines is presented as a last desperate move on David's part to get out of reach of Saul's manic quest to destroy him. David's nonparticipation on the Philistine side in the battle in which Saul and Jonathan are killed is stressed, while David's elimination of Saul's family in 2 Sam. 21:1–14 is described as necessary to avert famines that are God's punishment for Saul's unlawful slaying of the Gibeonites. That this is not an attempt to present David generally as an exemplary character is shown by 2 Samuel 10–12, where David's adultery with Bathsheba and his cynical maneuver to get her husband, Uriah, killed in battle are narrated without pity, as are the disastrous consequences of these actions.

It is difficult to imagine that these attempts to vindicate David in his dealings with Saul were first penned during the exile (sixth century B.C.E.), when the northern kingdom had not existed for nearly two hundred years. A more likely time is either that of Hezekiah (ca. 727–698), when Judah took over Israel's identity following the demise of the northern kingdom, or the time of Solomon (961–931), when the northern tribes were uneasy about being ruled from Jerusalem by a dynasty that was possibly known to have Ammonite connections. Indeed, it is noted at 1 Kings 14:31 that Solomon's son and successor, Rehoboam, had an Ammonite mother.

Granted that we are in the realm of plausibility not probability, a case can be made for the time of Solomon when stories about David's rise were circulated orally and written down, their purpose being to make David and his son acceptable to the northern tribes. Later, possibly during Hezekiah's reign, this old material was joined with the first edition of the material in Judges and that about the ancestors, Exodus, and wilderness wanderings to show how God's promises to Abraham about his descendants possessing the land of Israel had been fulfilled in David, and that David was the leader chosen by God to establish a dynasty over Israel. In Josiah's reign, 1 and 2 Samuel became part of the Deuteronomistic History and during the exile received passages such as that in 1 Samuel 8 where there is a very negative view of the kinship, the story of the loss and recovery of the ark in 1 Samuel 4–6, and the present form of 2 Samuel 7, with its qualified promise that God will maintain the Davidic dynasty. This view of the literary history of the Books of Samuel explains why David is presented as what we now call a chief rather than a king, hearing and adjudicating cases and ruling through his family. It also explains the fragments of genealogy

KINGSHIP IN THE ANCIENT NEAR EAST

KINGSHIP WAS THE FOUN-dation of civilized life in the great cultures of the ancient Near East. Kingship was the focus of the ancient world's hopes for security, peace, and justice. The king was also the center of religious reality in ancient Near Eastern cultures, for there was as yet no real division between the sacred and the profane. In such social settings the monarch provided a vital contact point between this world and the otherworldly realm of the gods. Human society was viewed as an integral part of the larger cosmos, and it was the king's function to maintain the harmony of that integration.

The precise concept of kingship varied extensively, however, in its specific cultural contexts. An Egyptian monarch was conceived as a divine being actually descended from the gods. Although living among mortals, he or she remained an important part of the divine world, a continual reincarnation of the god Horus, who lived in mysterious communion with his predecessor, Osiris. To the rulers of Egypt were attributed superhuman physical powers, a quality characteristic only of the gods. Egypt's rulers were also living testimony to the community's freedom from fear and uncertainty. When pharaoh ruled on the throne, the world was seen to be functioning as it should; established order was holding back the onslaught of the powers of chaos. The pharaoh enjoyed absolute power, yet he was not to yield it capriciously but to exercise it within the bounds of order, justice, and right (Egyptian *ma'at*). In the early dynasties the Egyptian ruler frequently represented the entire society and embodied the hopes of the members of that society for life beyond death.

In Mesopotamian cultures, the conception of the divine essence of kingship that was so fundamental to Egyptian civilization and religion is absent. Kings in the "Land between the Rivers" were mortals. The Mesopotamian word for "king" literally means "great man." Although the king was a heroic person and leader of his people, he was not essentially different from his fellows. Mesopotamian rulers were elected by the gods, but they did not necessarily enjoy the benefit of special divine counsel. Kings and commoners alike in Mesopotamia were forced to seek knowledge from rites, dreams, and omens in order to perform their respective duties in accordance with the often capricious will of the gods.

Kings in Mesopotamia served three functions: to administer the realm faithfully, to represent the people prayerfully before the gods to ensure prosperity and well-being, and to serve the gods regularly by building temples for them and by officiating at their state festivals. Society and nature were not so well integrated in Mesopotamia as they were in Egyptian ideology; the harmony between the world of the gods and the world of humankind was by no means assured as it was in Egypt. Since the ruler was himself only a mortal, he too stood anxious before the unpredictable will of the gods. As a consequence, however, in Mesopotamia the community maintained considerable independence from the king because of his lack of divine status.

Israel's monarchy developed in the context of these and other ancient Near Eastern conceptions of kingship. The unique Israelite religious and social traditions that were to emerge were characterized by a peculiar royal institution that emphasized the king's dependence on Yahweh and his responsibility to the people and their traditional allegiances. In Israel the monarchy seems to have taken shape at the invitation of the community and under the strain of a national emergency rather than developing as the society's original mode of organization. Still, Israel designed its unique form of kingship by drawing on a common stock of ideas and forms current in other ancient Near Eastern cultures. It is not surprising to find hints of Israelite belief and practice that represent beliefs and practices originating in Mesopotamia and Egypt.

Probably several competing concepts of kingship existed in Israel, some more favorably disposed toward foreign models than others. In some cases the similarities between Israel and its contemporaries may be more numerous than the Old Testament suggests. The final editors of the biblical narratives are also likely to have colored historical accounts with their own perspective, which developed in a time when the monarchy had been generally discredited and was no longer a viable political institution.

with Ammonite overtones (2 Sam. 17:25) as well as the important material in 2 Samuel 23 about David's heroes.

Samuel as Prophet: An Introduction to Prophecy

Part III of this *Companion* deals specifically with the world of Israel's prophets and is concerned with the literature of the three major prophetic books (Isaiah, Jeremiah, and Ezekiel) and the Twelve Minor Prophets. However, those books are not the only ones that document prophetic activities in the Old Testament. Abraham is described as a prophet at Gen. 20:7 by Abimelech, Aaron is called a prophet at Exod. 7:1, and his sister Miriam is accorded the title of prophetess at Exod. 15:20. In Deut. 18:15–22 Moses promises that "God will raise up for you a prophet like me." In an earlier section (p.000) we discussed the non-Israelite prophet Balaam. There is also an interesting incident in Num. 11:16–17, 24–30, in which God takes some of the spirit that is upon Moses and puts it upon seventy elders who are to assist Moses in his governing of the people. When the spirit rests upon them, they prophesy, which means that they speak in a state of ecstasy. Two men who are not with the seventy elders also receive a share of Moses' spirit and they, too, "prophesy." When this is reported to Moses, he replies, "Would that all the LORD's people were prophets, that the LORD would put his spirit upon them."

This passage leads us conveniently to a discussion of 1 Samuel and to the appearance in this book of bands of ecstatic prophets led by Samuel. If the Old Testament is read as literature, and without regard to scholarly conclusions about the dates of the individual books and the history of Israelite religion, then the appearance of ecstatic prophets in 1 Samuel is not a surprise since they have already appeared in Num. 11:24–30. However, if we approach the matter by way of the history of religion in Israel, then it seems that ecstatic prophets first appear in Israel in the eleventh century B.C.E., and that both Samuel and Saul were connected with these groups. Although the material in Num. 11:24–30 was probably written later than 1 Samuel, it articulates a view of what prophets were that is similar to what we find in 1 Samuel, namely, that they are zealous followers of Yahweh, whose spirit causes them to enter ecstatic states in which their speech and behavior depart from what is usual. There is no indication that this "prophesying" involved passing messages from God to third parties, although we must not rule this possibility out. In 2 Samuel we meet a prophet, Nathan, who does speak in the name of Yahweh, and the story of the birth and youth of Samuel in 1 Sam. 1:1–2, 26, and 3:1–4 describes how Samuel passed on messages from Yahweh.

At this point we must address a question of method. In the Old Testament a number of different types of person are traditionally described as prophets. There are the ecstatics of Num. 11:24–30 and 1 Samuel, the court prophets such as Nathan and Isaiah, the "provincial" prophets such as Micah, the opponents of kings and rulers such as Elijah, and figures such as Amos who deny that they are prophets. From the point of view of the editors of the final form of the Bible, these diverse figures were all prophets – men and women inspired by the spirit of God to perform a special task. From the point of view of the history of religion in Israel, we should regard them as distinct phenomena, which the Old Testament also does in its varying terminology. The importance of recognizing this diversity is that it will prevent us from assuming that there was a coherent religious institution in Israel called "prophecy." If we did assume this, we would then wonder how the ecstatic type of prophecy met in 1 Samuel suddenly became the oracular type of prophecy exemplified by Nathan in 2 Samuel. We might draw wrong conclusions about the dates of parts of the material because we conclude that the political, oracular prophecy of Nathan must be a highly developed, and therefore much later, form of what we meet in the ecstatic bands of prophets. The fact is that they are different and unrelated phenomena. This diversity is recognized in the terminology for prophets in the Old Testament. In 1 Sam. 9:9 we are informed that a man who was formerly called a seer (Hebrew *ro'eh*) is now called a prophet (Hebrew *navi'*). But we also find the designations "seer" (Hebrew *hozeh*) and "man of God." It is safest to assume that in Israel there were various types of what have been called, deliberately vaguely, "intermediaries" between God and humans. In some cases these were groups of men who lived on the margins of society, such as the groups led by Elijah and Elisha (2 Kings 1). Other groups were ecstatics. Some intermediaries were thought to possess powers of insight into the future or of divination. Some were employed at court in large numbers, such as the four hundred at Ahab's court (1 Kings 22:6). Some were part of the establishment, and others were opposed to the establishment. Some were probably closely connected with the religious centers. This diversity can be matched elsewhere in the ancient Near East. For example, texts from Mari dating from the eighteenth century B.C.E. indicate the evidence of intermediaries known variously as answerers, cult functionaries, ecstatics, and diviners.

For our purposes in Samuel and Kings, we can say that the prophetic groups were zealous adherents of Yahweh and were prepared to oppose and if necessary depose kings who were unfaithful to God. In 1 and 2 Samuel, Saul is made king and then disowned as king by Samuel, whom we should not regard as an isolated individual in this regard but as the leader of prophetic groups. The saying "Is Saul also among the prophets?" (1 Sam. 10:11–12) indicates that Saul also was, even if temporarily, a member of such a group. Perhaps because of this he instituted religious reforms in Israel (1 Sam. 28:3) and attacked the Gibeonites in an attempt to cleanse the land of foreigners (2 Sam. 21:2).

The importance of 1 Samuel for the religious and political history of Israel is that we meet the prophetic groups for the first time as a significant force. Led by Samuel they probably contributed to the initial success in resisting the Philistines. When they failed, they designated Saul to do the job but were quick to switch to David when it was clear that Saul could not succeed. In the ninth century they would lead the opposition to the dynasty of Omri and Ahab.

The Literary Structure and Function of Samuel

The Books of Samuel can be considered in three unequal sections from a literary point of view: (*a*) 1 Sam. 1:1–15:35, (*b*) 1 Sam. 16:1–2 Sam. 20:25, (*c*) 2 Sam. 21:1–24:25. The first section contains four blocks: the birth and youth of Samuel (1:1 4:1a), the story of the ark (4:1b 7:2), the ministry of Samuel (7:3 8:3), and the story of Saul (8:4 15:35). Although the four blocks are self-contained (i.e., probably once existed independently; e.g., the story of the ark's capture by the Philistines and its return after causing death and panic), they are linked to form a continuous narrative. Thus, although Samuel is absent from the story of the ark, the account in it of the death of Eli and his two sons links it to the story of Samuel's birth and youth, Eli being the priest who brings up Samuel.

Several important themes appear in the first two blocks. A passage in 2:27–36 concerning an unnamed "man of God" introduces a theme that is important in the remainder of Samuel and Kings, that events are shaped by God, especially in the form of disaster in response to the wickedness of leaders. The destruction of Eli's house is foretold, and it is promised that God will raise up a faithful priest. 2 Kings 1:27, in which Abiathar is thrust out from the priesthood, refers back to this promise in 1 Sam. 2:35, binding Samuel and Kings together in the Deuteronomistic History. In the story of the loss and recovery of the ark, which was edited during the exile, it is hard not to see the anticipation of the future fall of Jerusalem and thus a hope that it will be restored, just as the captured ark was returned.

The brief third block dealing with Samuel's ministry casts him as similar to the judges and credits him with victories over the Philistines, which is probably historically true. It is made clear, however, that like the judges, Samuel is not to establish a dynasty. His sons are described in 8:1–3 as judges who perverted justice, and the way is prepared for the story of Saul. This fourth block is confusing. It contains several independent stories that have been woven together in a rough manner. However, we need to remember that the biblical writers did not use footnotes and wanted to preserve and present the material at their disposal. The individual stories are (*a*) 9:1–10:16, 13:8–14; (*b*) 8:4–22, 10:17–27, 15:1–33; (*c*) 11:1–15; (*d*) 14:1–52. It is possible that story *c* was once part of story *a*, but if so it has been edited to fit the sequence of the narrative as a whole. The first two stories describe Saul's elevation to and deposition from the kingship. Story *a* implies that Saul was king for only a period of days before Samuel deposed him (cf. 10:8 with 13:8) because he wrongly offered burnt offerings. In story *b* the deposition results from Saul's refusal to destroy the Amalekite king Agag. Thus, although chapters 8–15 contain no material that historians can use to reconstruct the events of Saul's reign, the biblical account articulates a negative view of kingship in general (8:10–17) and a hostile attitude to Saul in particular. The one narrative of a brave deed (apart from Saul's rescue of the men of Jabesh-gilead in 11:1–11) is that of Saul's son Jonathan in chapter 14.

Beginning in 1 Samuel 16 we have the extensive story of David. Initially, its main lines are obscured by its being interwoven with the

An aerial view from the west of the Old City of Jerusalem. In the center left, the opening in the city wall is the Jaffa Gate. South of the gate, to the right, is the fortress called the Citadel. In the center background of the picture is the golden-hued Dome of the Rock, built by Moslems to commemorate the spot from which Mohammed ascended to heaven.

Biblical Archaeology Slides, no. 62

story of David and Jonathan; but from 1 Samuel 25 it is recognizably a single narrative that then extends to 2 Samuel 20, with a few additions such as 2 Samuel 8. For literary artistry it is matched only by the story of Joseph (Gen. 37–47). For example, in 1 Samuel 31 Saul's death in battle against the Philistines at Mount Gilboa is related. Saul asks his armor bearer to kill him and takes his own life when the latter refuses. In 2 Samuel 1 David is in Ziklag waiting for news of the battle. News is brought by an Amalekite, who says that he killed Saul at Saul's request and was charged to bring Saul's crown and armlet to David.

This is literary artistry at several levels. The reader knows that the Amalekite is lying. The reader also knows from 1 Samuel 30 that while Saul and the Philistines were fighting at Mount Gilboa, David was pursuing Amalekites who had raided Ziklag while he was on his way back from Mount Gilboa, the Philistines having decided that they could not trust him to fight with them against Saul. The Amalekites are thus not popular with David! But it is on his own false testimony that the Amalekite forfeits his life. David has him killed for having done what Saul's armor bearer declined to do – strike dead the Lord's anointed. What about the crown and armlet? Here we must ask literary, rather than historical, questions. It is conceivable that an Amalekite was close enough to Saul in battle to take his crown and armlet when he fell. It is more likely that the biblical writer has used

JERUSALEM BECOMES THE CAPITAL

THE ENIGMATIC STORY OF how David captured the Canaanite city of Jerusalem from the Jebusites is told in 2 Sam. 5:6–10. With that political masterstroke, the Israelite king set in motion a course of events that would transform a relatively unimportant walled village in the Palestinian highlands into the booming capital of a small Levantine empire. From rather humble beginnings Jerusalem grew to enjoy the wealth and prestige of international prominence. It was the organizational and administrative hub from which David and Solomon supervised their expanding territories and consolidated the power of the fledgling monarchy. In time, Jerusalem also became the religious, cultural, and political center of the Israelite nation – especially after the fall of Samaria in 721 B.C.E.

The original Jebusite settlement was limited to the southern spur of Jerusalem's eastern hill, below the temple mount (Haram es-Sharif) of the modern-day Old City. For the most part, the first Israelites to occupy the city simply appropriated the fortifications and town plan that had existed from the Late Bronze Age (fourteenth century). Extensive archeological investigation in this area, properly known as the City of David, has indicated that those responsible for transforming Jebusite Jerusalem into the Israelite capital reused many Canaanite defense walls and support structures.

Surrounded on three sides by deep valleys and provided with a perennial supply of water, Jerusalem was an excellent strategic location. However, its mountainous location required the construction of artificial platforms along the side of the hill in order to provide sufficient area for extensive building activities on its crest. The Canaanite city boasted a series of terraces with stone support walls that served as the substructure of a massive fortress that was built overlooking the Kidron Valley. After David captured that fortress (the "stronghold of Zion," 2 Sam. 5:7), he rebuilt it as his own citadel. The terraced walls that supported the Canaanite fortified precincts were covered with an immense structure of stepped stones, perhaps the biblical *millo* (see 2 Sam. 5:9, 1 Kings 9:15). Over 200 square meters of this stepped-stone structure have been excavated, qualifying it as one of the most impressive monuments of the Iron Age in Israel.

On top of the stepped-stone structure was located a fortified district that became the heart of the monarchy's new capital. The area can be identified as the Ophel (Citadel) of Jerusalem (see Isa. 32:14, 2 Chron. 27:3). The Ophel quarter would have housed the royal palaces, important administrative buildings, military bunkers, and other public structures.

Jerusalem was still a small city with an area of only about twenty acres when David acquired it as his capital. The residential districts of the lower city were home to no more than a few thousand people. But soon Solomon annexed a large area north of the main city to build a monumental palace–temple complex. The new capital was becoming the focus of power and the depository of wealth associated with the increasing prominence of the royal household and the national cult. Within a few centuries future expansions and a growing population would transform Jerusalem into the most important urban center in Palestine.

his imagination to symbolize the passing of the kingship from Saul to David by writing that the crown and armlet were brought from the battlefield to David.

The theme that the kingship has passed finally to David drives the next part of the narratives as David becomes, first, king over Judah in Hebron and, then, king over Israel following the collapse of the attempt to preserve Saul's kingdom by his cousin and military commander, Abner. The narrative here as elsewhere emphasizes that David is innocent of any complicity in the downfall of Saul and his house. The next landmarks are the capture of Jerusalem (2 Sam. 5), the bringing of the ark to Jerusalem (chap. 6), and the dynastic oracle (chap. 7), in which God promises to preserve David's house forever. From 2 Samuel 9–20 we have the so-called court chronicle, a marvellously crafted narrative which describes David's adultery with Bath-sheba, the plot to ensure that her husband falls in battle, the denunciation of David by Nathan the prophet, and the account of the consequent fratricide within David's family and the two revolts against him, one led by his son Absalom. There are so many themes and subplots that they cannot be described here. There is, for example, the ambiguous character of Joab, who is either blindly loyal to David to the point of disobedience when it is in David's interest or a calculating and ambitious individualist with power over David. What is remarkable on any reading is that so soon after the promise to David that God will preserve his dynasty, we have an unflattering narrative that depicts the chosen servant of God with so many human failings.

The final section of the Books of Samuel is a collection of diverse materials interrupting the story of David, which is resumed in 1 King 1. It was an act of literary artistry to place this material here, ending 2 Samuel with scenes of David the poet, David the commander of a band of heroes, and David the initiator in building the temple (by buying the site where it will be built). When he reappears in 1 Kings, David is a feeble old man whose approaching death occasions wranglings for the succession. We can be grateful that 2 Samuel ends with a David that accords with what the tradition claims for him – that he brought Israel from a disaster that threatened its disappearance to a future full of hope.

4. First and Second Kings
Archeological and Sociological Data on Israel and Judah during the period 961–560 B.C.E.

The period covered by the Books of Kings is from the accession of Solomon around 961 to the thirty-seventh year of the captivity of the last surviving Davidic king, Jehoiachin, in 560. This is a period rich in archeological evidence. Generally speaking, we have the results of Jamieson-Drake's analyses, which plot public works, the area of walled cities, and the spread of literacy and of luxury items in Judah. His results show that in the eighth century the work put into constructing walls and public buildings far exceeded that of the preceding or following centuries, whereas the seventh century predominated in the presence of luxury items and in the spread of literacy. The decline of all the indices from the seventh to the sixth century is spectacular.

The following evidence from archeology can also be mentioned. From the time of Solomon there are new city walls and gates at Hazor, Megiddo, Beersheba, and Gezer, as well as other evidence that Solomon undertook extensive fortification of the strong points of his kingdom. In 924 the land was invaded by the Egyptian pharaoh Sheshonq I, called Shishak in the Bible (1 Kings 14:25). A list of towns that Sheshonq claims to have conquered has been preserved at the Amun temple in Karnak (see *ANET*, pp. 242–3), and a fragment of a stela found at Megiddo appears to be part of a victory monument erected by the pharaoh. Although Sheshonq's list is not easy to turn

ROYAL ZION THEOLOGY

WHEN DAVID ESTABLISHED Jerusalem as the capital of his kingdom, he set in motion the development of a theological tradition that surfaces throughout the Old Testament. The so-called royal Zion theology grew up around Jerusalem, the political and religious center of the Israelite realm and the seat of David's dynasty. Royal Zion theology appears first in the context of oracles about the royal installations of David and Solomon (2 Sam. 7:8–17, 23:1–7; 1 Kings 8:46–53, 9:2–9). It can be summarized in five points:

1. Yahweh chose Jerusalem as the place of his own special presence and as the chief city of his people.
2. Yahweh designated David and his descendants to rule from Jerusalem in an unending dynastic succession.
3. The Jerusalem temple was to be the nation's central religious shrine, since it was there Yahweh would "cause his name to dwell."
4. David and his successors were to play a key role as mediators between Yahweh and his people.
5. Jerusalem was secured against the threat of natural or supernatural forces as long as (a) a descendant of David sat on the throne and (b) the people were faithful in their allegiance to Yahweh.

These theological ideas centering on the royal city developed over several hundred years, principally from the reign of Solomon onward through the tumultuous history of the Judean monarchy. Scholars are divided, however, about the tradition's exact origin. Some consider it a continuation of ideas current in the Jebusite city of Jerusalem that David captured, while others understand the concepts as original creations of the Davidic court. A few scholars emphasize the continuity between royal Zion theology and earlier Israelite religious traditions, especially beliefs associated with the ark of the covenant and the cult at Shiloh. These scholars suggest that the complex of ideas surrounding Jerusalem that developed during the monarchy was little more than a transfer of older Israelite theology to a new geographical and political context. Probably aspects of all three suggestions are correct. Royal Zion theology most likely developed as a unique combination of old traditions from Israel that were modified to meet new historical circumstances and colored by religious ideology drawn from the larger world of the ancient Near East.

Several psalms contain important expressions of royal Zion theology cast in the mythological imagery of religions practiced by Israel's neighbors. Rich in Canaanite symbolism, these psalms (especially 46, 48, 76) emphasize Zion as the highest mountain of the north, on which the gods dwell, and picture Zion as the center of the world, from which flows the river of paradise. At Zion Yahweh conquered the watery chaos monster, and there he triumphed over the heathen nations.

Royal Zion theology played an important role in the traditions that grew up around the deliverance of Jerusalem from the Assyrians in 701 B.C.E. Although Hezekiah probably capitulated to spare the city from Sennacherib's vindictive destruction, the fact that Jerusalem avoided any battle or military defeat was later interpreted as a sign of the city's inviolability. This interpretation, emphasizing the special divine providence that attached to Jerusalem, was utilized in other times of national crisis by those who wished to portray the city as safe from any danger of invasion or siege. Ultimately, the prophets castigated individuals who were more committed to a belief in an inviolable Jerusalem than firm in their loyalty to Yahweh.

When the city subsequently fell to the Babylonians, the royal Zion theology was shattered and projected into the eschatological future. These Jerusalem traditions continued to be reinterpreted. Jerusalem in time became the focus of prophetic and apocalyptic hopes for the restoration of Israel in history and beyond. It would be the place

> [to which] all nations shall flow,
> and many peoples shall come
> and say,
> "Come, let us go up to the
> mountain of the LORD,
> to the House of the God of
> Jacob."   Isa. 2:2–3

TRADE IN THE EARLY MONARCHY

IN THE ANCIENT NEAR EAST A country had to have good land and sea communications with other peoples in order to become a commercial center. Usually surpluses of industrial or agricultural products for trade were also necessary. The fledgling kingdom of Israel meagerly fulfilled both these criteria, and during the early monarchy the country apparently began to share wholeheartedly in the commerce of the Near East. Palestine lacked good seaports in first temple times, but the country lay across the main land routes between the major economic powers of Egypt, Phoenicia, Persia, and Mesopotamia. The Way of the Sea and the King's Highway, the most important overland routes of the age, both crossed Israelite territory. References to trade and traders in the Bible suggest that in the early period of Israelite history trade was conducted by foreign merchants passing through the country along these caravan routes (e.g., Gen. 37:25, 28). During the years when Israel had just begun to settle the land, trade in small imported goods and the purchase of local wares for export apparently still lay in the hands of the indigenous people of Palestine. But with the establishment of the monarchy, trade became an important element in the Israelite economy.

Trade was basically a royal monopoly in the ancient Near East, and Solomon seems to have been successful in developing a network of merchants and trading partners of his own (1 Kings 10:28–9). The Solomonic kingdom, although relatively small, maintained economic and diplomatic ties with many of the important rulers of the era, not the least of whom was the Egyptian pharaoh. Solomon also arranged with Hiram, king of Tyre, to build and equip a fleet of ships that could exchange the copper of Ezion-geber for the gold and precious stones of Ophir. The temple of Yahweh in Jerusalem was constructed with labor and materials from Phoenicia that were exchanged for Israelite agricultural products. Although the list is probably exaggerated, 1 Kings 10 details the quantity and variety of valuable goods that Solomon is said to have imported to his kingdom.

Solomon is also credited with establishing a monopoly on the trade of horse-drawn chariots in Syria–Palestine. The Bible presents Solomon as a "middleman" in the ancient arms trade, combining imported horses from Cilicia with chariots from Egypt to produce the most important military weapons of his day. Solomon built up his own chariot army and exported his surplus of these essential armaments to the rulers of petty kingdoms in Syria and Anatolia. The traditional story of the Queen of Sheba's visit to the Solomonic court perhaps indicates how the early Israelite kingdom also shared in the lucrative commercial interests of South Arabia. Frankincense and myrrh, Arabian luxury exports used for a variety of medical, cosmetic, and cultic purposes in the ancient world, are listed among the gifts that the mysterious queen gave to King Solomon.

Exactly how Solomon paid for all his imported goods remains unclear in the Bible. Palestine's most valuable exports were agricultural products: oil, wine, and grain. Tyrian merchants sometimes bought these commodities and sold them throughout the Mediterranean. Tyre may also have bought timber from the northern regions of Israel with which to build ships and make oars (Ezek. 27:17). Solomon provided wheat and oil in exchange for Hiram's assistance in building the temple (1 Kings 5:6, 10–11). Oil was also sold to Egypt (Hos. 12:1). Some stories suggest, however, that Israel's production of agricultural goods and revenues did not provide a sufficient basis for external trade. In 1 Kings 9:11–13, for example, the story is told of twenty Israelite cities that were leased to the king of Tyre.

Most scholars agree that the biblical accounts of Solomon's reign are exaggerated. Yet those narratives suggest that with the development of the monarchy, Israel took its place among the small kingdoms of Syria–Palestine in a flourishing environment of international trade. The young kingdom exchanged its meager surpluses for the accoutrements of empire, eventually overextending its resources in an attempt to prove its legitimacy on the international scene. Yet trade continued between the divided Israelite kingdoms and the larger ancient Near Eastern world. Archeological data have demonstrated continued economic exchange between Judah and Israel and the cultures of Egypt, Syria, Persia, Phoenicia, Africa, and Mesopotamia. The developing city life of Israelite Palestine during the monarchy provided an expanding market for such trade. From the tenth century B.C.E. onward, the process was accelerated by increased international contacts, the alternation of military campaigns with periods of peace, and the opening up of international trade routes throughout the Near East.

into a historical account, it seems that his purpose was to destroy fortified towns rather than to occupy territory. 1 Kings 14:25 says that he came up against Jerusalem, although it is more likely that he received tribute from Jerusalem on condition that he spared it.

The inscription of Mesha, king of Moab, which dates from about 850 B.C.E., mentions Omri, who was king of Israel from 885 to 874 and who built Samaria as the northern kingdom's capital. It relates how Omri had subdued Moab and how Mesha turned the tables on the Israelites after Omri's death. From the same period (885–853) we have archeological evidence from Megiddo and Hazor that impressive water systems were constructed that tapped the deep water table.

The latter part of the ninth century B.C.E. brought Israel and Judah into conflict with Assyria, as shown by the portrayal of the Israelite king Jehu, or his representative, on the Black Obelisk of Shalmaneser III presenting tribute to the Assyrian king. Jehu is described on the obelisk as the son of Omri. In fact, he had destroyed Omri's dynasty and taken over the kingship at the urging of the Israelite Elisha!

For the eighth century, there is much archeological evidence. Within Israel we have the famous seal of "Shema the servant of Jeroboam," which bears the so-called Megiddo lion, named after where it was found. Jeroboam is Jeroboam II (782–747 B.C.E.) and Shema was a high officer in the administration. The Samaria ostraca (potsherds) from the same period record receipts of wine and oil made to the capital from surrounding districts. Assyrian records chart the rise of Tiglath-pileser III (745–727) and his campaigns into Israel, called the "house of Omri" nearly a hundred and fifty years after Omri's death! The conquest of Samaria in 722/1 and its rebuilding by Sargon II are reported in that king's annals (*ANET*, pp. 284–5), and the siege of Jerusalem mounted by the Assyrian king Sennacherib in 701 B.C.E. is reported in

In late ninth century B.C.E., King Mesha of Moab ordered this black basalt stela inscribed to commemorate his achievements. Prominent in the text is the king's version of a war fought with Israel in 850 B.C.E. The official Israelite account of this war appears in 2 Kings 3.

Biblical Archaeology Slides, no. 114

Ancient weapons of war. On the right are bronze and iron arrowheads and knife blades. On the left are sling stones. The background shows Assyrian soldiers using similar weapons in battle.

American Schools of Oriental Research, no. 101

Sennacherib's annals (*ANET*, pp. 207–8). This account mentions "Hezekiah the Jew," who would not submit and who was made a prisoner in Jerusalem "like a bird in a cage." The reference is to King Hezekiah of Judah, and the large tribute paid by him is recorded. From the Jerusalem of this time we have evidence that the city was considerably enlarged, presumably to contain Israelites who had come south to Judah after the fall of Samaria. Hezekiah also probably constructed the shaft known as Warren's shaft, bringing water from a spring outside the eastern walls into the city. The tunnel that is often called Hezekiah's tunnel was probably built five hundred years later.

For the seventh century the most significant finds are the seals and bullae analyzed by Keel and his associates. These show that, in the first part of the seventh century, during the reign of Manasseh, whose reign is described in 1 Kings 21 as a time when paganism flourished, the goddess Asherah, who had previously been represented as a tree, now took on a female form. This striking evidence for the syncretistic religion of the time is to be contrasted with the equally striking fact that seals bearing the names of men known to be associated with Josiah's reform of the cult in 622 B.C.E. are aniconic, that is, have no representations of human or other figures.

The Babylonian Chronicles of the seventh to sixth centuries record the capture of Jerusalem on 16 March 597 by Nebuchadnezzar, the taking of its king into captivity, and the placing on the throne of a king after Nebuchadnezzar's heart (*ANET*, p. 564). The last period of Judah's independence, before the fall of Jerusalem in 587/6, is illuminated by the Lachish letters. These are messages, written on broken sherds, from observation posts to the defenders at Lachish. One mentions that the observers are looking for the fire signals of Lachish because they can no longer see those of Azekah. This latter town was on the main route through the Shephelah to Lachish, and the letter suggests vividly that it had just fallen to the Babylonians. Another let-

These Iron Age Astarte figurines (eighth to sixth centuries B.C.E.) depict the female body with enlarged breasts, possibly emphasizing her role in procreation. They may represent the deity or simply be votive statues.

ter complains that the words of the princes are weakening the hands of the people, that is, undermining their morale (*ANET*, p. 322). This is reminiscent of the charge made against Jeremiah, who advocated surrender to the Babylonians as the will of God (Jer. 38:4). Babylonian records listing the provision of food for prisoners of war dependent on the royal household mention provisions for Jehoiachin, some of his sons, and eight men of Judah (*ANET*, p. 308). The Books of Kings end with Jehoiachin still a captive in Babylon in 560 B.C.E.

For the period of the monarchy from Solomon to Jehoiachin we have the greatest quantity of archeological evidence in the form of excavated remains in cities, inscriptions and letters, seals and bullae. For the sociology of the period we have the results of Jamieson-Drake's analyses, which show that urban centers began to be more dominant in Judah in the eighth century. The same is probably true in the northern kingdom, with Samaria dominating the surrounding area. It is probable that the old patterns of self-subsisting and cooperating villages broke down in the face of increasing centralization, conscription, and imposition of taxes in the form of food products to supply an increasing number of state officials. With such taxes came the inability of some to pay if, for example, there was a bad harvest. Failure to pay would mean, first, indebtedness; then, becoming a day laborer on land one had been forced to sell; and finally, complete loss of freedom. Wealth became concentrated into fewer families, and powerful families formed opposition parties.

The rise of competing powerful families is seen especially in the time of Jeremiah before the fall of Jerusalem in 587/6. The text of 2 Kings and Jeremiah indicates that one powerful family, that of Shaphan, was involved in Josiah's reformation of 622, protected Jeremiah from his opponents, and read Jeremiah's words of warning to the assembled people. Gedaliah, the governor of Judah, to whom

THE CULT OF ASHERAH

SOME FORTY REFERENCES TO the cult of the old Canaanite fertility goddess Asherah appear in the Old Testament. The deity is known from mythological texts at Ugarit as the consort of El, chief god of Canaan's pantheon. In the Bible, her appearance is often confusing and ambiguous. Because Semitic gods were conceived of in generally flexible terms, Asherah sometimes appears to be fused with other personifications of a universal "Mother Goddess" (e.g., with Anath, consort of the storm and fertility god Baal; or with Ashtar/Astarte, an astral deity also involved in the fertility cycle). Ancient scribes further confused the situation by deliberately misvocalizing the deity's name, retaining the consonants but substituting the vowels of the Hebrew word *boshet* (shame) – hence the Hebrew "Ashtoreth" (see 1 Kings 11:5, 33). All these terms are ambiguous. Sometimes they refer to an enigmatic cult image (perhaps a wooden pole or a tree), sometimes to the goddess herself, and sometimes to the general practice of Canaanite religion. Often the name occurs in a plural form (Hebrew *'ashterot, 'asherim*), suggesting that the goddess was worshiped in various local manifestations. To some of those sites she gave her name (e.g., Ashtoroth-Karnaim in Gilead).

Archeologists have unearthed large numbers of small female statuettes throughout Palestine that are probably related to the worship of Asherah. The goddess is usually represented as a naked woman with long hair holding her breasts. Molded of clay, the figurines emphasize the breasts and pudenda. These "Astarte plaques" have been associated mostly with private residences, which suggests that they are symbols of prayers or vows to the goddess of fertility. Perhaps they were made on the principle of imitative magic, to influence the deity and thus achieve conception.

Some scholars argue that the widespread evidence for the cult of Asherah in the Old Testament is simply another expression of the persistence of Canaanite religious practices among the common folk of early Israel. Extending into the later periods of the monarchy, the worship of fertility deities like Asherah enjoyed even official sanction. Furnishings for Asherah's use in the temple of Jerusalem are mentioned in 2 Kings 21:7. Solomon patronized the cult of Asherah (1 Kings 11:5), and she enjoyed a worship place in the Judean royal capital throughout most of the monarchy (2 Kings 23:13). A typical Hebrew blessing found on a tomb inscription at Khirbet el-Qom and similar blessings and some cultic drawings discovered at Kuntillet 'Ajrud suggest that Asherah was even worshiped as Yahweh's female consort. At least in some circles, the Israelite national God Yahweh merely succeeded the Canaanite god El and appropriated El's consort for himself. Apparently this cult was so thoroughly suppressed by the Yahwistic reformers of the eighth to sixth centuries B.C.E. that later interpreters had difficulty understanding allusions to this fertility goddess in the Old Testament.

In such a case archeological data become all the more important in illuminating and clarifying the history of worship in Israel as it has been preserved in the biblical text. The worship of female fertility deities was common in many cultures of the ancient world (e.g., Ishtar in Mesopotamia, Ashtarath from Phoenicia, Qodshu of Egypt, and Aphrodite and Venus in later hellenistic and Roman tradition). It is likely that throughout the Judean monarchy, and well into second temple times, Israel participated in this rich history of fertility worship.

Jeremiah was entrusted after the fall of Jerusalem, was a member of the Shaphan family. Opposed to the family of Shaphan was that of Elishamah, whose grandson Ishmael murdered Gedaliah, probably in 582 B.C.E.

Light is shed on one aspect of social conditions in the seventh century by a letter written on a sherd, most of the pieces of which were discovered in 1960 at Mesad Hashavyahu (Yavneh Yam). It is usually dated to 630, a time when Judah was establishing control over that area as Assyrian power collapsed (see *ANET*, p. 568). The letter is a complaint from a person, whose name is not preserved, to a local military ruler or high official. The complainant is a member of a gang of conscripted laborers whose job is to harvest a particular quantity of grain. He claims to have fulfilled his due quota, in spite of which the overseer, Hoshiah (or Hashabiah), has taken his garment. Hoshiah's action is presumably designed to make the complainant return and do more work in order to get his garment back. The complainant insists that his fellow workers will back up his story, and he appeals to the high official to see that his garment is returned. This sad text shows how far Israelite society had changed from being an association of self-subsistent and cooperative villages ruled by local chiefs to a society in which free men were conscripted to do public work and were at the mercy of overseers and officials. In the light of this, prophetic denunciations of the abuse of power by those in authority are understandable.

Solomon's kingdom: an aerial view of the mound of Megiddo, originally excavated by the Oriental Institute of the University of Chicago (1935–9). Renewed excavations by American and Israeli scholars were begun in 1994.

The Literary History, Structure, and Function of Kings

The preceding section has shown how much evidence is available to scholars who wish to reconstruct the history of Israel and Judah from 961 to 560. A historical outline of the period will now be given, not only to place the extrabiblical evidence into perspective but to show how different a modern reconstruction is from the biblical account.

The reign of Solomon (ca. 961–931 B.C.E.) was a time of consolidation. He made treaties with surrounding peoples, fortified cities in key areas, developed trade, and built a temple and palace in Jerusalem. But there was also unrest because the first steps were being taken to undermine the relative independence that Israelite villages had enjoyed. Taxes were imposed, and villagers were conscripted into gangs of construction workers. To pay for his schemes, Solomon gave away territory and cities to the king of Tyre (1 Kings 9:10–14). Prophetic opposition to Solomon gained strength in Israel, and Jeroboam was encouraged to revolt. He was unable to do this until Solomon's death; but in 931 he led ten tribes in a breakaway to form the northern kingdom of Israel, leaving Solomon's son Rehoboam with Judah and Benjamin. Whatever else the revolt was, it was also an attempt to reestablish Israel as religiously separate from Judah, with its Jerusalem temple and Davidic dynasty.

Relations between the two kingdoms were affected by external factors. The invasion of the Egyptian pharaoh Sheshonq in 924 seems to have damaged the larger Israel more than the smaller Judah; even so,

SOLOMON'S REORGANIZATION OF THE KINGDOM

THE KINGDOM OF DAVID and Solomon was not a simple, self-contained nation-state. It was rather the seat of an empire, modest in size when compared with the traditional imperial regimes that held sway in the ancient Near East but existing under similar dynamics. David was the first Israelite emperor – the charismatic warrior who brought the tribes together under unified rule and extended his sovereignty over a succession of surrounding territories. Solomon's function as king was the maintenance of this miniature empire. To that end, he imposed stronger administrative and economic controls over the internal matters of his kingdom. Solomon implemented a redistricting plan for Israel that cut across traditional tribal boundaries (1 Kings 4:7–19). The new system provided a more even distribution of responsibility for provisioning the expanding Jerusalem court and for fulfilling the labor demands of royal building programs. Demonstrated bureaucratic rationality rather than age-old tribal affiliations was the basis for the new division of territory. Royal control of the districts was ensured by court-appointed administrators who were loyal to the crown rather than to traditional tribal authorities.

Solomon also reorganized the royal cabinet, elaborating the civil bureaucracy and streamlining the military establishment. The list of Solomonic officials in 1 Kings 4:1–6 indicates that in comparison with similar rolls from the time of David, a consolidation of the royal armies and a decrease in the importance of military affairs took place. New officers were added to aid the king with the growing complexity of administering his empire.

These efforts by Solomon to reorganize the kingdom of Israel were directed toward keeping control of the labor force and economic resources that had been captured by David's military exploits. Solomon was faced with the task of maintaining the loyalty of his own bureaucracy and sustaining the tributary status of vassal states. Solomon's ability to exact taxation and tribute rested upon the notion of his dynastic supremacy. He refashioned Jerusalem as the center of the empire and set about developing the small Davidic city into a symbol of his dynasty's splendor, might, and right to rule.

Solomon also recast intertribal Yahwism in nationalistic terms that had international implications. The worship of Yahweh became private celebration surrounding a dynastic deity. As such, it was a useful symbol for differentiating Israel from its conquered peoples. Solomon's construction of an elaborate temple complex was the symbolic representation of Yahweh's presence in Jerusalem. It served as the visible focus of Israel's identity as the people of Yahweh to the people dominated by the short-lived united monarchy.

Enhancing the grandeur of Jerusalem was a further dramatic symbol, available for all to see, that demonstrated Yahweh's legitimization of Solomon's rule. Solomon's reputation in international trade, however exaggerated it may be, is related to the symbolic role of Jerusalem as both the political and the symbolic center of the empire. The eclectic styles of royal construction along with the accumulation of costly and exotic goods in the royal temple treasuries were concrete portrayals of how the empire's center was a dominating microcosm of all the peripheral areas around it.

Maintaining Jerusalem as the center of an empire and demonstrating the strength necessary to legitimize his right to rule demanded that Solomon extract heavy taxation, tribute, and forced labor (corvée) from his kingdoms. The mechanics of empire depended also on the construction of store cities, administrative centers, and military outposts throughout the land. Solomon executed a successful plan of reorganization and capital improvements that met the needs of empire after the Davidic conquests had exhausted the supply of captive workers and expended the spoils of war. But the cost to Israel and its conquered peoples was considerable. Most of the territories they inhabited were not naturally suitable for yielding economic surpluses. Thus, after Solomon's reign the royal heirs were no longer able to exploit the overextended resources necessary to maintain Israel's imperial status. Both the empire and the united nation at its center fell apart.

Aerial view of the multichambered gate (*right foreground*) at Hazor attributed to Solomon. A casemate wall runs to the left. The large pillared building probably was used as a storehouse; it is now dated to the ninth century B.C.E., the time of Ahab.

Judah needed to make alliance with the Syrians to the north of Israel in order to curb the ambitions of Israel. In 885 the accession of Omri as king of Israel after a bitter civil war enabled Israel to gain control over Judah, Moab, and possibly Damascus. Omri built a new capital at Samaria, and his son Ahab fortified many cities. During Ahab's reign, Elijah and Elisha were the focus of prophetic opposition to Omri's dynasty, which ended with a revolution in which Jehu seized the throne and destroyed Omri's dynasty. However, this internal strife weakened Israel's ability to withstand invasions from Damascus; and

This large rectangular building with its double row of pillars, uncovered at Hazor and initially thought to be stables, is more likely a royal storehouse built under King Ahab's rule in the ninth century B.C.E.

Biblical Archaeology Slides, no. 55

with the appearance of the Assyrian Shalmaneser III, Jehu was forced to pay heavy tribute. This led to impositions on the ordinary people.

Around 800, Damascus was crushed by the Assyrians, and Israel and Judah suddenly enjoyed a period of peace and prosperity, albeit one in which the rich and powerful benefited at the expense of the poor. Around 750, the prophets Hosea and Amos began to warn the people of approaching judgment. The second half of the eighth century saw the reassertion of Assyrian power under Tiglath-Pileser III (745–727). In 734/3, the Assyrians annexed large parts of Israel, leaving only the rump of the northern hill country with its capital Samaria. In 722/1 Samaria fell, the history of the northern kingdom came to an end, and many people loyal to Yahweh fled south to Judah, where, under Hezekiah (727–698), the traditions of Judah and Israel began to be combined.

Hezekiah tried to extend the influence of Judah over parts of the former kingdom of Israel. His ambitions brought him into conflict with Assyria, however, and at the end of his reign he was forced to pay a large sum of tribute to Sennacherib following the latter's invasion of Judah. Under the long reign of Hezekiah's son Manasseh, Judah was a vassal of Assyria, and the religious reforms that Hezekiah had attempted were undone. Local paganism, possibly reinforced by Assyrian religious practices, became rife, and this was a dark period for those loyal to Yahweh. When Manasseh died in 642, his son Amon reigned for less than two years before being assassinated. The "people of the land" put the assassins to death and made Amon's son Josiah king. He was eight years old. The "people of the land" were presumably powerful landowners who favored opposition to Assyria, and as Assyrian power waned Judah began to extend control into the former northern kingdom. The "discovery" of the book of the law in the temple in 622 was the occasion for a far-reaching religious reform that included closing down sanctuaries other than Jerusalem and elevating Jerusalem to the status of a national sanctuary.

The hopes generated by all this were short-lived. Josiah was killed in battle at Megiddo by the Egyptian pharaoh Necho II in 609, his reforms collapsed, and Judah faced the menace of the expansion of Babylon, which had taken Assyria's place as the great power of that part of the world. In 597, Nebuchadnezzar captured Jerusalem and exiled the king and the nobility and key craftsmen to Babylon. King Jehoiachin was eighteen and had been king for only three months. His uncle Zedekiah was placed on the throne by the Babylonians. When Zedekiah rebelled in 589/8, the Babylonians invaded once more, capturing and destroying Jerusalem in 587/6. The history covered by the Books of Kings ends here, except for the reference to the favorable treatment of the exiled Jehoiachin in 560.

In considering the Books of Kings we must inquire first about their sources. According to their own claims, the sources for Kings were the "book of the acts of Solomon" (1 Kings 11:41), "the Book of the Chronicles of the Kings of Israel" (1 Kings 14:19), and "the Book of the Chronicles of the Kings of Judah" (1 Kings 14:29). We do not have these sources today, but we can detect excerpts from them in 1 and 2 Kings. The first of these sources is probably an account of the building of the temple (1 Kings 6) and may be contemporary. It is noteworthy that, in two places, it uses Canaanite names for months of the year (Ziv and Bul in 1 Kings 6:1 and 37–8); later compilers added explanatory glosses for later readers, in whose time these names were no longer used. Material such as the list of Solomon's officials and of his administrative districts (1 Kings 4:1–19) may also come from this source. The Chronicles of the Kings of Judah and Israel were probably administrative archives compiled and preserved in Jerusalem and Samaria.

Those mentioned in Kings are independent works on which the bib-

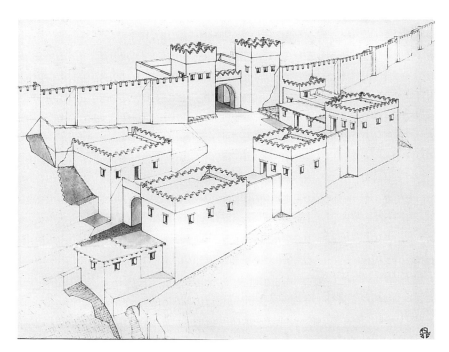

Megiddo, reconstruction of the Stratum IV gate, perspective view from the northeast.

SIEGEWORKS IN ANCIENT NEAR EASTERN WARFARE

THE POWERFUL ARMIES commanded by the great empires of the ancient Near East left small kingdoms little recourse beyond seeking protection behind their fortified city walls. Toward the middle of the Iron Age these fortifications encircled entire cities at a height of up to twelve meters. Sometimes six meters thick, the walls were further strengthened by bastions and salients. They were crowned with balconies and crenellated parapets, from which soldiers defended the city when it was under attack. The city was often protected by a stone glacis, which made any approach to the wall's lower reaches impractical. Yet these fortifications were still vulnerable to assault and siege. Enemies mounted attacks by storming the ramparts, breaching the walls and gates, scaling, tunneling, and sometimes even using psychological warfare.

It was apparently the Assyrian army that introduced battering rams, the scourge of fortified cities, to the ancient arsenal. The first machines were heavy objects with limited mobility. They moved on six wheels with a body built over a wooden frame. Wicker shields covered their sides. In the front stood a tall, round-domed turret. From the turret hung a rope on which the battering beam was attached like a pendulum. The warriors operating the ram were, however, perfect targets for defending archers above. Their own bowmen, perched on mobile towers nearby, gave the attacking soldiers covering fire. In time advanced types of battering rams were developed, light-bodied with four wheels. Metal ramming rods were attached that could be manipulated to wedge out chunks of the wall weakened by the battering beam. Sennacherib's battering rams were made of easily assembled and dismantled materials, covered with leather. His machines were easily maneuverable, and they could be used alone or in groups.

The city gate was an attacking army's focal point of assault. The gate was the wall's weakest point, and battering rams could be wheeled up the path which led to it without requiring the construction of a special ramp. But ramps were constructed in other situations to overcome a city's natural strategic setting when the preferred point of breach lay somewhere along the wall itself.

Direct warfare was costly, so passive siege was often used as a method of reducing a walled city. Starved for water and food, besieged cities were often forced to capitulate (see the account of the fall of Samaria after a siege of three years in 2 Kings 6:25). A city's ability to withstand siege depended on its ability to feed and provide water for its inhabitants. To that end the kings of Judah built store cities and in several important sites engineered impressive underground water systems that could provide a constant supply of water should those cities fall under siege. But when a city was starved for water or food, it was forced to capitulate. Loss of morale among the defenders was also a problem during a prolonged engagement. Throughout the siege the attacking army also engaged from time to time in ruses and stratagems designed to draw the defenders out of the city or gain access for their own forces. They also employed threats and psychological manipulation to undermine the confidence of the besieged defenders, rousing the people and army to overthrow their leaders by the threat of severe action if they refused and the promise of great rewards if they acquiesced (see the account of Sennacherib's siege of Jerusalem in 1 Kings 18–19).

The art of siege was perfected by the Assyrian and Babylonian Empires and used with great effectiveness against the fortified cities of Iron Age Israel. Lachish and other important cities of Israel and Judah were destroyed by Assyria late in the eighth century B.C.E., a campaign remembered in the great reliefs from the palace of Sennacherib. Jerusalem was besieged but miraculously spared, but only for a time. Lachish rose again only to fall a little more than a century later, this time together with Jerusalem, to the siege and attack of Nebuchadnezzar of Babylon.

lical authors relied and from which they occasionally quoted in producing their own narrative. In addition to these "official" sources, there is a large block of material from 1 Kings 17 onward dealing with the prophets Elijah and Elisha. It was suggested above (p. 88) that there was a link in the northern kingdom between the prophetic groups led by Elijah and Elisha and the scribal high official Obadiah. We can assume that the Elijah/Elisha stories were preserved by the circle of Obadiah and brought to Judah together with the Chronicles of the King of Israel after the fall of Samaria in 722/1.

The most striking feature of the Books of Kings is the presence of Deuteronomistic material and a Deuteronomistic scheme (see above, p. 88ff.). Scholars disagree whether the Books of Kings were composed in several stages – the main part during the reign of Josiah and the rest during and after the exile – or in one stage during and after the exile. However, it is generally agreed that the Books of Kings are a Deuteronomistic compilation, although a pre-Deuteronomistic first draft completed in Hezekiah's reign (727–698) cannot be ruled out.

The Deuteronomistic material is of two main kinds. First, there is a "prophecy and fulfillment" scheme that provides a basic framework from 1 Kings 12 onward. Second, there are two "extended reflections" that articulate the theology of the final form of Kings. These two types of material are not unique to Kings. The prophecy and fulfillment material makes a brief appearance in 1 Sam. 2:27–36, with a sequel in 4:12–22, and there is an extended reflection at 1 Samuel 12. However, the impact of these two types of Deuteronomistic material is greater in Kings than elsewhere.

The prophecy and fulfillment scheme in Kings can be set out as follows:

1. 1 Kings 11:29–39. Ahijah prophesies that Jeroboam will rule over ten tribes in the divided kingdom. The narrative sequel is 1 Kings 12:1–20.
2. 1 Kings 13:1–3. A man of God prophesies that Josiah will tear down the altar at Bethel. The narrative sequel is 2 Kings 23:15–20.
3. 1 Kings 14:4–16. Ahijah prophesies the destruction of Jeroboam's dynasty and the exile of the northern kingdom. The narrative sequels are 1 Kings 15:27–30 and 2 Kings 17:1–6.
4. 1 Kings 16:1–4. Jehu son of Hanani prophesies the destruction of the dynasty of Baasha. The narrative sequel is 1 Kings 16:8–13.
5. 2 Kings 14:25. Jeroboam II restores the borders of Israel in accordance with the prophecy of Jonah son of Amittai.
6. 2 Kings 21:10–15. God's prophets prophesy the exile of Judah because of Manasseh's wickedness. The narrative sequel is 2 Kings 25.
7. 2 Kings 22. Huldah prophesies that God will punish Jerusalem and that Josiah will "be gathered to his grave in peace." The narrative sequel for Jerusalem is 2 Kings 25. Josiah was killed in battle (23:29–30).

It will be noticed from this scheme that there is a large gap between sections 4 and 5 and a smaller one between sections 5 and 6. This is because the stories centered on Elijah and Elisha occupy much material between 1 Kings 17 and 2 Kings 10, and because Isaiah is prominent in 2 Kings 19. When taken with the prophecy and fulfillment scheme, these chapters show that the history presented in Kings as a whole is bound up with the word of God as spoken by his prophets.

It would be wrong to suppose that this history is "driven" or determined by the prophetic word, or that there is an inexorable, impersonal law of retribution at work. Rather, the prophets testify that God is at work in the historical process and that the obedience or self-will of kings leads to blessing or punishment. For example, Jeroboam is promised that if he walks in God's ways and observes his statutes, God will build a sure house for him (1 Kings 11:38). Thus, it is not God's will that evil should come upon the northern kingdom. It results from Jeroboam's disobedience.

A modern reader may well object that all that is happening here is that the writers are projecting their own ideology back onto the past. They are writing from the perspective of Judah, they know that the northern kingdom was destroyed and that Jeroboam's dynasty lasted but briefly, and they are rationalizing the events accordingly. There is probably much truth in this, but there can be little doubt that prophetic groups under Elijah and Elisha waged a bitter war against the dynasty of Omri in the name of the God of Israel, who stood for justice. In these groups, the word of God became action against a religion and politics that glorified power and rode roughshod over the weak. The overthrow of Omri's dynasty by the prophetically backed Jehu (2 Kings 9) was a victory for faith in the God of liberation and justice. What the compilers of the final version of Kings were seeking to do was to show that the history of Israel and Judah was not the history of a secular people but the history of the people of God; a people chosen for God's purpose, who could not opt out of this purpose by trying to go their own way. While Israel and Judah existed politically, this perspective was probably of little interest to most Israelite and Judahite monarchs. When 1 and 2 Kings reached their final form, during the exile, when the nation no longer existed politically, this perspective took on a new significance. If Israel and Judah really were the people of God and could not opt out of God's purposes, then perhaps there was hope for the future, especially a future that would learn from the mistakes of the past. Thus, in their postexilic final form the Books of Kings articulated hope for the future combined with warnings about the past.

Nowhere was this dual purpose – future hope based on past warnings – more powerfully articulated than in the major of the two extended reflections, 1 Kings 8:12–53. The other such passage, 2 Kings 17:7–23, is concerned mainly with why the northern kingdom was destroyed by the Assyrians. Solomon's prayer at the dedication of the Jerusalem temple, in 1 Kings 8:12–53, is significant because it was probably written after the temple's destruction by the Babylonians.

The prayer begins by summarizing why the temple was built (vv. 15–21) and extols God's faithfulness (vv. 22–6); but it then goes on to speak of the redundancy of the temple:

THE TEMPLE OF SOLOMON

IN THE COURSE OF HIS REIGN, Solomon launched an extended building campaign across the kingdom of Israel. Nowhere were his efforts more impressive than in Jerusalem. And perhaps none was more important than the temple of Yahweh that Solomon erected in a complex of royal buildings that took altogether twenty years to construct (1 Kings 7:1–12, 9:1). Work on the temple itself spanned seven years according to the Bible (1 Kings 6:37). Begun in the fifth year of Solomon's reign (ca. 957) during the first month of the dry season that was suitable for building, the first temple served basically as a royal chapel. However, the temple also had public and national significance – increasingly so as Israelite political and religious institutions developed.

Solomon's temple, like other temples in the ancient Near East, was intended for ritual activities that were the exclusive domain of a special priestly order, though the ruling monarch also played a significant role in the cult. Common worshipers were not allowed to enter. The temple's religious services, described in some detail in Leviticus, included the acceptance of tithes and offerings to support the needs of temple personnel and to accomplish the daily sacrifices. Also a focus for public worship, the temple became an important pilgrimage center where the masses assembled, prayed, and offered sacrifices on key holidays and other ritually prescribed occasions. The temple also seems to have served as the royal treasury.

Surprisingly, no remains of the Solomonic temple have been recovered archeologically, so modern conceptions of its appearance must be drawn by examining the biblical text and by inferring certain features from analogous structures. Extensive descriptions of the temple are given in the Old Testament, the most detailed in 1 Kings 5–8. A parallel account in 2 Chronicles is more exaggerated but contains a few important additional details. Ezekiel's description of the temple is a visionary depiction of a future temple following the first temple's destruction in 586 B.C.E., yet some argue that his narrative also contains relevant information about the actual preexilic structure. Most scholars agree that the priestly writer's (P source) description of the desert tabernacle also owes some of its features to the Solomonic house of worship. From these diverse sources scholars have attempted to reconstruct an accurate picture of Solomon's temple.

The building's exterior measurements are said to have been 60 × 20 × 30 cubits (about 90 × 30 × 45 feet). The temple was constructed of hewn stone and cedar (masonry locked together by beams), a common, archeologically attested building method. Structurally, Solomon's temple was divided into three parts: the 'ulam ("porch, portico, vestibule, entrance hall"), the hekhal ("main room, holy place, temple proper, nave"), and the devir ("Holy of Holies, shrine, most holy place, inner sanctuary, adytum"). Such a tripartite division was a common feature of worship structures in Syria–Palestine, familiar to archeologists from Hazor, Megiddo, Bet She'an, Arad, Lachish, Shechem, and Tell Tayinat (ancient Hattina, located in northern Syria). In general, the Solomonic temple was constructed according to this "Phoenician," or Canaanite, plan. The biblical texts also preserve the memory of how Solomon relied on craftsmen from Tyre to construct and decorate the building (1 Kings 5:5).

Like most Semitic sanctuaries, the temple stood in the middle of an enclosed court used for public assembly and sacrifice. A small porch ('ulam) separated the sacred temple grounds from the profane world. In the main hall (hekhal), lit by means of recessed frame windows, most of the priestly ritual was performed. All along the outside of the building (except the porch) ran a three-storied structure (the yaziq, "side building") that buttressed the temple's external walls and provided storage space for cultic paraphernalia (post, shovels, sprinkling bowls, lamps, tongs, snuffers, etc.) and the temple treasury. The temple gates and its interior were lavishly decorated with fine sculpture, metal work, and embroidery. Its appointments were made from rare woods, expensive metals and jewels, and fine fabrics. Remains from other monumental buildings of the Iron Age and common oriental imagery give modern artists some idea of how the temple was decorated.

In front of the temple stood two tall (nearly 40 feet) bronze pillars enigmatically named Jachin and Boaz. A bronze or stone horned altar stood in the courtyard along with the great "Molten Sea," a fantastically immense bronze basin that held water for the priests' ritual purifications. According to the biblical account, this huge tank's capacity was

(continued on p. 148)

(continued from p. 147)

about 10,000 gallons. It was supported by twelve bronze bulls arranged in groups of three. Each group faced a cardinal point of the compass.

Many of the temple's auxiliary features reflect a rich, almost sacramental symbolism that Israel shared with other cultures of the ancient Near East. The bronze pillars hearken back to the common erection of sacred stone pillars (*maṣṣebot*) by the Canaanites. In the context of Solomon's temple, they probably stood for the power supporting the Davidic dynasty and the Jerusalemite religious establishment. The Molten Sea, too, probably had a symbolic significance, representing the great primordial waters of chaos that Yahweh conquered when he created the earth. Bulls supported the basin, and they were usually representative of virility and fertility among the peoples of the Mediterranean basin. The Canaanite storm god Baal, by no means unfamiliar to the Israelites, was often pictured as a bull. Solomon's temple was most likely oriented toward the rising sun,

perhaps indicative of solar elements in the religions that influenced the Israelite cult. All in all, the temple was conceived of as the abode in this world of a god who dwelled in the heavens – a microcosmic earthly representation of Yahweh's heavenly dwelling place.

However Solomon's temple may have looked originally, it did not remain that way for very long. In the course of Israel's history various kings altered and improved it. Some utilized it for the worship of deities other than Yahweh. A few were forced to convert its wealth to tribute money for foreign kings (e.g., Ahaz to Tiglath-pileser of Assyria, 2 Kings 16:7–8); sometimes foreign kings plundered it for themselves (e.g., Pharaoh Shishak/Sheshonq, 1 Kings 14:25; King Jehoash of Israel, 2 Kings 14:11–14). These historical developments are not clearly outlined in the Bible's pastiche of temple descriptions. The first temple was emptied of its treasures and finally destroyed by Nebuchadnezzar and the Babylonians in 587/6.

Even heaven and the highest heaven cannot contain you; much less this house that I have built! (V. 27)

The temple will function as a place toward which people pray. There then follows a series of possible situations in which people will pray toward the temple. Apart from verse 31, where the example is of someone coming to swear an oath before the altar (something that could be done in the ruined temple), there is no mention of any ceremony or service taking place in the temple. There is no mention of sacrifices, which in postexilic Judaism could only be offered in the rebuilt temple. All the examples (save for v. 31) concern praying toward the temple; and they conclude, significantly, with the example of the people taken captive to a foreign land.

. . . if they come to their senses in the land to which they have been taken captive, and repent. . . . then hear in heaven your dwelling place their prayer and their plea, maintain their cause and forgive your people (Vv. 47, 49–50)

The prayer reminds God that they are his people, whom he delivered from Egypt (v. 51).

The dedication prayer, then, holds out hope to the people whose history is described in the Books of Kings and which, in a sense, had come to an end when these books reached their final form. Even in captivity there is hope for the future. True repentance and the desire for God, expressed in prayer toward the ruined temple, will bring a response from the God whose word was active in Israel's history, even to the point of being responsible for the very destruction of the temple!

B. THE CHRONICLER'S HISTORY

1. Identity of the Chronicler; the Books of Chronicles, Ezra, and Nehemiah

The term "Chronicler" is widely understood to describe an author or authors responsible for the composition of 1 and 2 Chronicles and of Ezra and Nehemiah. Although the view taken here is that Ezra and Nehemiah are not the work of the Chronicler, all four books will be discussed in this section. Indeed, this is necessary; for although the events described in 1 and 2 Chronicles precede those in Ezra and Nehemiah, the latter two books were written before Chronicles. Indeed, the Books of Ezra and Nehemiah are our main source of evidence for the history and social conditions that led up to the time of the composition of Chronicles. Thus, we have to begin with Ezra and Nehemiah.

Unfortunately, Ezra and Nehemiah present some of the most difficult critical questions to be found in Old Testament studies, with no overall scholarly agreement. The Book of Ezra begins with a decree of Cyrus the Great (likely historical date 539 B.C.E.) allowing the Jews in exile in Babylon to return to Jerusalem and rebuild the temple. Led by Sheshbazzar (a leader mentioned only in Ezra, about whom nothing is otherwise known), a first group of exiles returns, bringing with them more than five thousand vessels of gold and silver (chap. 1). According to chapter 2, almost 50,000 people returned (Ezra 2:64–5). Chapters 3–6 (of which 4:8–6:18 is in Aramaic) tell of efforts to rebuild the temple under the leadership of Jeshua the priest and Zerubbabel. However, these efforts are frustrated by the "adversaries of Judah and Benjamin," and the work is completed only after Cyrus's decree is found in the archives during the reign of Darius (522–486 B.C.E.). The temple is completed in Darius's sixth year (516; Ezra 6:15) and the temple is dedicated. Jeshua and Zerubbabel are not mentioned in connection with the completion and dedication.

Ezra 7 introduces us to Ezra, the "scribe skilled in the law of Moses" (Ezra 7:6), and dates his journey from Babylonia to the seventh year of Artaxerxes, king of Persia, probably referring to the first of several kings of that name, who reigned from 465 to 424 B.C.E.. His mission is authorized by a letter from the king (Ezra 7:11–26). Ezra 7:27–9:15 gives a first-person account of Ezra's work: those who accompanied him (8:1–14), how he journeyed with his party (8:15–31), his arrival in Jerusalem (8:32–6), and his shame at what he found there (9:1–15). The cause of Ezra's shame was that the Jews in Jerusalem, including priests and Levites, had intermarried with non-Jews. Chapter 10 is a third-person account of how Ezra assembled the people and had them make a covenant to "put away" the foreign wives and children. A list of those who did so concludes the book (10:18–44).

The Book of Nehemiah begins with a long first-person account of how Nehemiah obtained permission from Artaxerxes to go to Jerusalem as governor in that king's twentieth year, after learning that Jerusalem's wall was broken down, that its gates were destroyed by fire, and that the returnees were in great trouble (Neh. 1:3). Chapters 1–6 describe Nehemiah's journey, his inspection of the city, and his rebuilding of its walls in spite of the opposition of Sanballat (governor of Samaria), Tobiah the Ammonite, and Geshem the Arab. In chapter 7, Nehemiah decides to enroll the people by genealogy, in the course of which he discovers the list of those who first returned from exile. This list (Neh. 7:6–69) is almost identical with Ezra 2:1–67. In chapter 8 there is the sudden appearance in the narrative of Ezra, who reads "the

CYRUS THE GREAT AND THE EDICT OF RELEASE

TOWARD THE MIDDLE OF the sixth century B.C.E. a new ruling power arose in the ancient Near East. The Persians, an Indo-European people whose homeland lay to the northeast of the Fertile Crescent, speedily established the most comprehensive empire in the Near Eastern world until that time. Cyrus ("the Great") of Anshan was the architect of this new empire. Taking advantage of the weakness of Babylon, Lydia, Media, and Egypt, Cyrus appealed to those who favored an international power in place of the limited ethnic kingdoms that had held sway since the demise of the Assyrian Empire. Cyrus was the founder of an important dynasty that eventually controlled most of Anatolia, the Fertile Crescent, and the Mediterranean basin. He proclaimed himself "king of the world, great king, legitimate king, king of Babylon, king of Sumer and Akkad, king of the four rims (of the earth)." Cyrus's son, Cambyses, added Egypt to the Persian holdings. His grandson, Darius I, further expanded the huge empire and improved its internal organization. Syria–Palestine and the Jewish community in Judah were a part of this Persian hegemony for more than two centuries, from the capture of Babylon in 539 until the fall of Tyre to Alexander the Great in 332 B.C.E.

It was during the reign of Cyrus the Great that Jewish exiles began to return to Palestine from their captivity in Babylon, that reconstruction began on the second temple, and that the city of Jerusalem began to be refortified.

These key events in the life of Israel are part of a larger Persian policy, instituted by Cyrus, that exhibited tolerance and benevolence to subject peoples. In the age-old royal tradition of the Near East, Cyrus promoted himself as "gatherer of the dispersed" and "restorer of the gods and their sanctuaries." Cyrus played the role of liberator, accepting and acknowledging the patronage of the gods worshiped by those capitulating to and supporting him. This Persian policy of permitting relative cultural autonomy among the separate peoples of their realm was actually an excellent method of political control. Contented regions were less likely to rebel.

Both the biblical picture of Cyrus and ancient historical portraits of the great ruler are somewhat idealized. His treatment of groups that had been deported and settled throughout the empires of Assyria and Babylon probably varied from case to case. When it was politically expedient, the Persians did not hesitate to take harsh action against their subjects and the cultic centers in which they participated. Nonetheless, it was an edict from Cyrus in 539 B.C.E. that permitted the Jewish exiles to return from Babylon. Thus Cyrus was hailed by the prophecies of Deutero-Isaiah (see p. 175) as the savior and redeemer of Israel, chosen by Yahweh. Cyrus is even called "messiah," the one "whose right hand [Yahweh] has grasped, to subdue nations before him and ungird the loins of kings" (Isa. 45:1).

Although there is no Persian record of the edict of release, it is found in two versions in the Old Testament. The edict recounted in Ezra 1:2–4 is in Hebrew. It may represent the original message of Cyrus's new policy related to various Jewish communities by official heralds. Ezra 6:3–5 is preserved in Aramaic, the *lingua franca* of diplomatic relations in the Persian period. Focusing on details of the temple's reconstruction, perhaps this second record represents an official memorandum stored in the royal Persian archives. The edict describes the temple's dimensions, provides for Persian support for defraying the cost of rebuilding, and assures the return of the temple's cultic vessels from their storage in the treasuries of Babylon.

These decrees do not represent Persian favoritism toward the Jews. Such actions were typical of Cyrus when they were judged in the best interest of his empire. The political realities of Cyrus's southwestern border conflicts with Egypt made expedient such a friendly and supportive gesture. The biblical records of Cyrus's edict of release portray him as a devotee of Yahweh, to whom Cyrus attributed his good political fortune. But in a different context, Cyrus made similar affirmations about the Babylonian god Marduk. In the end, the edict of release was more Persian propaganda – of which Cyrus was a master – than historical reality. It did not require or allow a massive ingathering of the Jewish Diaspora scattered throughout the Persian Empire. No return *en masse* was envisioned, and it would be many years before the Jews of Palestine would be able to establish firm political, religious, and economic foundations in the postexilic period.

book of the law of Moses" to the assembled people. The main outcome is the observance of the Feast of Booths (8:13–18), after which the assembly confesses its sins (9:1–2) and Ezra utters an extended prayer and meditation on Israel's past history (9:6–37), concluding with the moving words: "Here we are, slaves to this day – slaves in the land that you gave to our ancestors. . . . Its rich yield goes to the kings whom you have set over us because of our sins" (9:36–7).

Chapter 10 lists those who made a covenant to undertake various things: to abstain from marriages with foreigners, to observe the Sabbath and the Sabbatical year, not to exact debts, and to make various offerings for the support of the priests and Levites. In chapters 11–12 there are further lists of people, especially of temple officials, after which Nehemiah's first-person account resumes at 12:31. This relates how Nehemiah organized a thanksgiving and made provision for the support of the priests and Levites. Chapter 13 relates how, after returning to Jerusalem in the thirty-second year of Artaxerxes, Nehemiah had to deal with the following abuses: nonprovision of support for the Levites and singers (13:10–14), nonobservance of the sabbath (13:15–22), and marriages with foreigners (13:23–7).

Among the problems of Ezra and Nehemiah implied by this outline are the "disappearance" of Sheshbazzar in connection with rebuilding the temple and the appearance of Jeshua and Zerubbabel in connection with its dedication; the repetition of the list of returnees in Ezra 2 and Nehemiah 7; the meager description of Ezra's reforms in the Book of Ezra and the fuller account of his work in the Book of Nehemiah; and the remarkable overlap in the reforms carried out by Ezra and Nehemiah (indeed, Neh. 13 lists precisely the issues that Ezra had already dealt with: the Sabbath, provision for temple officials, and mixed marriages). To these can be added the further problem that, in Ezra 4–5, letters from the reign of an Artaxerxes (of which the first king of that name reigned from 465 to 424) are placed between the reigns of Cyrus (559–529) and Darius (522–486)! A solution to these literary problems, together with a tentative history of the period 539–420, will now be sketched.

The author of Ezra and Nehemiah probably worked in the fourth century B.C.E. Exactly where he should be placed is difficult to determine; but even if we date him as early as 400 B.C.E., this is 140 years after the beginning of the return from exile. This is equivalent to a historian in 1993 describing events that began in 1853. Compounding the ancient author's problem were the comparatively meager sources with which he had to work. His sources were (a) the prophetic books of Haggai and Zechariah 1–8, (b) miscellaneous official documents from the reigns of Cyrus, Darius, and Artaxerxes (presumably Artaxerxes I), (c) various lists of citizens and temple officials, and (d) the so-called Nehemiah memoirs, that is, the first-person narrative in Neh. 1:1–7:5 and 12:31–13:31. Some scholars believe he also had an Ezra memoir and that it is to be found in the first-person narrative in Ezra 8–9, but this view is not followed here.

From the official Persian documents the author knew that Cyrus had authorized a return of Jews to Jerusalem to rebuild the temple and that a certain Sheshbazzar was entrusted with the task. This royal decree was consonant with Cyrus's policy toward subject peoples, as expressed in the cuneiform text called the Cyrus Cylinder. From the Books of Haggai and Zechariah 1–8 the author knew that the rebuilding had not gone well. Haggai records that, in Darius's second year (i.e., 520 and thus probably nineteen years after Cyrus's authorization of the rebuilding), the people were saying "the time has not yet come to rebuild the house of the LORD" (Hag. 1:1–2). From the two prophetic books the author learned that the leaders in Jerusalem were Zerubbabel and the high priest, Joshua (the difference between this form and "Jeshua" is not significant), although he knew nothing about who had appointed them or whether they had replaced Sheshbazzar. He also had official documents from a much later period (the reign of Artaxerxes) which concerned attempts to build, not the temple, but the city walls of Jerusalem, an attempt that was ordered to be stopped (Ezra 4:7–23). In composing the first six chapters of Ezra, the author freely adopted the official documents and used the correspondence about stopping the building of the city walls in the fifth century to explain why building some of the temple had taken so long in the sixth century! He also used a census list from a later period to detail the names and numbers of those who returned with Sheshbazzar in 539.

If those seem harsh judgments on the author, they are not meant to be. Anyone who tries to reconstruct the past has to make informed guesses; this is as true of the present writers as it was of the author of Ezra and Nehemiah. The latter was doing his best with the material available to him. At Ezra 7 the author introduces Ezra, who was known to him only from a document from the reign of Artaxerxes which commissioned Ezra to go to Jerusalem and to teach the people the Jewish law. Having no other information about Ezra, the author freely composed an account of Ezra's mission by basing it upon what Nehemiah claimed to have done in his memoirs together with some of the census lists that were available. This explains the overlap in the work of the two men.

At the time the author wrote, the Book of Nehemiah was already largely in existence in the form of the memoirs. Into this the author inserted freely composed material relating to Ezra (chaps. 8–10) and various other lists of civic and religious functionaries (11:1–12:26).

Social and Historical Data on the Period 539–420 B.C.E.

The Judah to which the decree of Cyrus permitted Jews to return in 539 was smaller than the Judah that had been conquered by the Babylonians in 597 and 587/6. To the north it included the territory of Benjamin as had preexilic Judah; but its southern boundary ran only to the north of Hebron. Thus Hebron, the old capital of Judah, was no longer part of it, the southern portion of the land having been occupied by Edomites. The population of Judah prior to the return is unknown. Because those deported to Babylon in 597 and 587/6 were the nobility and the skilled classes, those remaining were ordinary farmers; and because their settlements did not include areas where grain was best grown, it is likely that they concentrated upon the production of oil and wine.

How many Jews returned, we cannot say. There were flourishing Jewish communities in Babylonia, some of whose inhabitants were well integrated with the larger society (as indicated by the Murashu tablets) and many probably did not wish to return. We must assume that those who did return with Sheshbazzar in 539 had insufficient resources to do more than minimal work on the temple. Only in this way can we understand why little work was done on the temple from 539 to 520.

The prophetic books of Haggai and Zechariah 1–8, which date from this period (see below, p. 223), indicate new activity under Zerubbabel and Joshua in 520 and suggest that a series of agricultural disasters was partly to blame for the lack of progress. Zerubbabel is credited at Zech. 4:9 with having laid the foundation of the temple, and it is promised that he will complete it. The tone of both books is highly eschatological. The rebuilding of the temple will usher in a new era. Nations will be overthrown and Zerubbabel will be given a position of great power (Hag. 2:23, Zech. 3:6–10). These hopes were disappointed. Zerubbabel was not even present at the rededication of the temple, if

THE MURASHU ARCHIVE

UNCOVERED AT THE BABYlonian city of Nippur in 1893, the Murashu archive represents the single most important source available for understanding the life of Jews living beyond the borders of Palestine during the exilic and postexilic periods. The collection includes about 730 clay tablets inscribed with cuneiform Akkadian. The tablets belonged to the banking family of Murashu. The family records date from the reigns of Artaxerxes I (464–424 B.C.E.) and Darius II (424–404 B.C.E.).

Little is known about how the exiled Jews fared after the destruction of Jerusalem. Jeremiah urged the exiles to make a good home for themselves in Mesopotamia (Jer. 29:4–7), and some cuneiform records list rations sent to the exilic community. The Murashu archive yields

more than just an account of the Jewish presence in Babylon. These records reflect a vibrant, cosmopolitan city with many different national/ethnic groups engaged in cooperative trade. Personal names in the Murashu archive reflect Babylonian, Persian, Median, Egyptian, and semitic ancestry. Some of the names can be identified as specifically Jewish in origin.

Records of transactions between the Murashu family and persons clearly bearing Jewish names reveal some interesting facts. Jews at Nippur seem to have been engaged in the same kinds of commerce that occupied the lives of non-Jews. Interest rates were no different for the banking family's Jewish customers. No group apparently suffered discrimination on religious grounds. At least two Jews mentioned in the archive appear to have obtained prestigious positions in the Nippur financial

community.

The personal names attested in the Murashu archive provide clues to beliefs and customs of the Jewish community in Nippur, as well as an idea of the social pressures with which they were faced. Many Jews in the Babylonian Diaspora gave their children Babylonian names (e.g., the royal governors Sheshbazzar and Zerubbabel). Analysis of the changes in Jewish name-giving in Nippur, in Judah, and in the narrative literature of the Hebrew Bible suggests that the Jewish community was increasingly assimilated to the culture of Babylon. By the fifth century B.C.E., the Jews at Nippur seem to have fully integrated themselves into the life of a foreign city that had initially been a place of exile. The community appears to have heeded Jeremiah's advice – perhaps even more than the prophet intended.

Ezra 6:15–18 is to be taken literally. He may have been removed from his position as governor by the Persians, or he may have died or left Jerusalem.

From 516 to 458 we know nothing of events in Judah, or Yehud, as the Persians called the province. The next event is the mission of Ezra, which began in the seventh year of Artaxerxes I (465–424) according to Ezra 7:7. Much ink has been spilled on the respective dates of the missions of Ezra and Nehemiah, with some scholars arguing that Ezra came to Jerusalem in the seventh year of Artaxerxes II (404–359), and others arguing that he came in the thirty-seventh year of Artaxerxes I (i.e., 428), emending "seventh" to "thirty-seventh" at Ezra 7:7. The main reason for proposing these later dates is that these hypotheses slightly ease the problem of the overlap of activity of Ezra and Nehemiah. However, the view taken here is that the account of Ezra's activities in Ezra 8–9 and Nehemiah 8–10 is a free composition based upon Nehemiah's memoirs; in which case we know nothing of the exact nature, length, or outcome of Ezra's mission.

With Nehemiah we seem to be on firmer ground, having his first-

BULLAE FROM POSTEXILIC JUDAH

BULLAE ARE SMALL LUMPS of clay that were used to seal letters and other documents. They were pressed on knotted string or cord that tied a rolled papyrus or leather scroll and then stamped with a seal. A collection of seventy such bullae came to light in 1974. Scholars obtained them from an antiquities dealer who could identify them only as having been found in a pottery vessel somewhere in the region around Jerusalem. More than likely, the documents which they sealed had long ago disintegrated. When such ancient artifacts become removed from their archeological context, much information is lost. Nonetheless, scholars have been able to identify these bullae as the remains of a late-sixth-century archive of official documents from the Persian subprovince of Yehud (Judah).

The bullae are inscribed in the Hebrew language using an Aramaic script that became wide-ly used following the return of the Jewish exiles from Babylon. They record activity by fourteen persons with twelve different names. Most of the names also occur in the books of Ezra and Nehemiah for biblical characters who would have been active during this period of Jewish history. Among the persons named on the bullae is Elnathan, who bears the title "governor." Some scholars suggest that Elnathan held office sometime between the administrations of Zerubbabel (515 B.C.E) and Nehemiah (445–433 B.C.E). The name of Elnathan's "maidservant" (possibly his wife), Shelomith, also appears on one of the bullae. Her high position of responsibility is somewhat unusual for a woman in the biblical period. Whether she held such a position by virtue of office or by her personal relationship with the governor is unclear. The bullae also record activity by a professional scribe and various other officials or private individuals. Some of the people represented may have been owners of estates, for example, who affixed their seals to legal documents, records of commercial transactions, or important public communications.

Many of the bullae bear the official provincial stamp "Yehud," the name by which the land of Judah was known to the Persian administration. The bullae present further evidence that Judah existed as a separate Persian subprovince beginning in the sixth century, a distinct administrative unit with its own autonomous internal rule. Other archeological evidence corroborates that conclusion. Storage jars found at a variety of sites in the country bear similar stamps. The stamp gave official sanction to the jars, whose contents were used to pay taxes in kind. One name, Hanana, actually appears both on one of these jars and on one of the sixth-century bullae. Small silver coins stamped with the Yehud legend also testify to Judah's provincial administrative autonomy under Persian rule.

hand account to rely on. But even here there are unanswered questions. Why were the city walls of Jerusalem broken down nearly a century after the return from exile (Neh. 1:3)? A partial answer is given in the correspondence between the governor of Samaria and the Persian court that has been preserved, but misplaced, at Ezra 4. The rebuilding of the walls had been officially stopped because Jerusalem was a rebellious city and because rebuilding would encourage further disobedience (Ezra 4:13–16). This may suggest that there had been a rebellion in Judah, of which we otherwise know nothing, which had reduced Jerusalem to a parlous state and which made local officialdom regard it with suspicion. How Judah was being administered when Nehemiah arrived in Jerusalem in 445 is not known. It has been widely thought that it was ruled from Samaria, and that this is why Sanballat of Samaria opposed Nehemiah's appointment as governor of Judah and his work of rebuilding. The fact that one of the Elephantine papyri (letters to Judah from a Jewish colony at Elephantine on the

JEWS AT ELEPHANTINE

SEVERAL CACHES OF ARAmaic papyri unearthed around the beginning of this century reveal the presence of a thriving colony of Jews from the Persian era on the upper Nile River, opposite modern-day Aswan. Many of the documents are legal texts reflecting a variety of situations in the colonists' everyday lives. Transfers of property, loans, marriage contracts, and writs of adoption and manumission are all represented. The texts derive principally from the archives of two families. These Aramaic-speaking Jews also left behind numerous letters, some of which have important ramifications for the study of the history of Israel and the early development of the Jewish religion.

The Jewish community at Yeb (Elephantine) may have had its origin in the sixth century B.C.E. when Israelites displaced by the Babylonian exile took up residence there. A large entourage accompanied exiled King Jehoahaz II to Egypt (2 Kings 23:34). Jeremiah and others fled to Egypt after the assassination of Gedaliah, and Jeremiah knew of an active Jewish community in Egypt during his days. On the other hand, the Jews at Elephantine may have been members of a military colony whose roots might go back as far as the eighth to seventh centuries, when Judean rulers traded Israelite mercenaries for Egyptian political support and military supplies. Israel had a long history of mercenary activity in Egypt (Deut. 17:16, 2 Sam. 10:6, 1 Kings 15:18).

A striking feature of Jewish life at Elephantine was the existence of a temple to their ancestral God *yhw* ("Yahu" or "Yaho"). One document claims the temple had been in existence before the Persian king Cambyses' invasion of Egypt in 525 B.C.E. Priests of the Egyptian god Khnum, with the help of the local Persian commander, destroyed the temple in 410 B.C.E. A famous letter from the leaders of the Elephantine Jews to Bagoas, governor of Judah, requests his help in restoring the temple. This letter, dated 407 B.C.E., also contains a reference to Sanballat and the high priest Johanan (Neh. 12:22, 13:28) – key figures in the problems of establishing dates for the work of Ezra and the Samaritan schism. The Jewish leaders in Palestine apparently counseled their Egyptian counterparts to rebuild the temple and resume its cultic practice, with the exception of animal sacrifice, which was to remain the sole prerogative of the main temple in Jerusalem.

Jewish religion at Elephantine seems to have tended toward syncretism. A list of temple contributors shows that the treasurer had collected funds for the gods Eshem-bethel and Anath-bethel as well as for Yahu. Epistolary salutations often refer to "the gods." In one legal text, a Jewish woman swears by Egyptian gods during a court procedure. Nonetheless, the Jews at Elephantine probably observed the weekly Sabbath festival as well as the annual feast of Passover. One papyrus from the archive is an order issued under the auspices of Darius II (ca. 419) and Arsames, the governor-general of the Egyptian satrapy, which instructs the colony to observe the Feast of Unleavened Bread.

upper Nile) is addressed to the sons of Sanballat, governor of Samaria, as well as to Bagoas, governor of Judah, is cited as evidence in favor of Samaria's erstwhile control over Judah (see *ANET*, p. 492). However, it is increasingly believed that Judah did indeed have its own governors, including Sheshbazzar and Zerubbabel, and that the list can be supplemented by bullae, jars, and jar handles that have on them the word "Yehud," the word for "governor," and a personal name.

One thing that does seem to be clear is that the exile produced a new basic form of social organization among the Jews: the *bet 'avot*. Literally translated it means "house of fathers." In practice it was probably a descent group named after a particular ancestor. In the list at Ezra 2 (Neh. 7:6–73) we have

> sons of Parosh, 2,172
> sons of Shephatiah, 372
> sons of Arach, 652
> sons of Pahat-Moab belonging to the sons of Joshua and Joab, 2, 818 . . .

This new social pattern was probably the result of the destruction of old kinship ties when the exiles were scattered in Babylon. A new organization emerged in which people belonged to groups initially headed by and later named after prominent leaders. When these groups returned to Judah, they retained these social identities, possibly in contrast to those who had not gone into exile and who were identified by the names of the villages in which they now lived (see Ezra 2:27–8). Another generally agreed upon point is that the postexilic community of the fifth century and later was dominated by the life and organization of the Jerusalem temple. Possibly a third of the entire community were priests, Levites, and other temple officials.

Nehemiah 5 records a situation in which some landholders were forcing other landholders into debt and slavery. Verse 4 mentions some who have borrowed money to pay the king's tax and that this has forced them into debt and into selling their sons and daughters as slaves. This is a situation that could easily be brought about by a succession of drought years. The complaint made to Nehemiah in his capacity as governor is that, far from helping each other, Jews are profiting at the expense of fellow Jews. Nehemiah deals with the problem by ordering all fields, vineyards, and olive orchards to be returned to their owners, and for loans to be free of interest. Unfortunately, we do not know whether those who were losing their lands were descended from returnees or from those who had remained, or whether both groups were affected.

A clear aim of Nehemiah's policy was to dissolve marriages between Jews and non-Jews and to give the Jewish community in Judah a clearer identity. The Books of Ruth and Jonah indicate that some people were more ready to accept non-Jews as members of the community; and passages in Isaiah 56–66 seem to imply a conflict between those hostile to and those in favor of non-Jews (e.g., Isa. 56:3–8, 63:15–19). What motivated the "hostile" attitude is hard to say. Perhaps the writer of Ezra and Nehemiah (as distinct from, but not in opposition to, the historical Nehemiah) believed that abolishing mixed marriages would lead to more faithful observance of the Jewish law, which in turn would bring blessing upon Judah and free the people from subservience to Persia (see Neh. 9:36–7). If this was also the view of the historical Nehemiah, the opposition of people such as the governor of Samaria, Sanballat, is understandable. They desired a less religious regime and one that accepted non-Jews. The rebuilding of the city walls and the consolidation of the Jewish religious community of Judah would have been a threat to their position.

The Literary Purpose of Ezra and Nehemiah

The writer of Ezra and Nehemiah probably lived at a time when Nehemiah's reforms were beginning to produce a more exclusively religious community without, however, this leading to the throwing off of the Persian yoke. The writer's attitude to the Persian Empire was ambivalent. On the one hand, Persian kings had decreed a return to Jerusalem and the rebuilding of the temple and had authorized Ezra and Nehemiah to reform the community. On the other hand, a Persian king (the same one who authorized Ezra and Nehemiah!) had ordered a stop to the rebuilding of Jerusalem's walls; and Persian kings levied a tax on the land, which sometimes caused hardship to the farmers. Further, this symbol of foreign possession of the land was a sore point for those who believed that God had given the land to the Israelites as a possession (Neh. 9:24–5).

The tone in Ezra and Nehemiah is one of penitence before a God who is in control of nations, who has worked to bring about a partial restoration of his people's fortunes, but who, it is hoped, will restore them completely. This tone is found in Nehemiah's memoirs, with their appeals to God "to remember for good" what Nehemiah has done, and in the extended prayers composed by the writer and attributed to Ezra. Here, then, is literature of a people penitently and expectantly waiting upon God to restore their fortunes completely. They have rebuilt their temple, restored and repopulated the city, dissolved mixed marriages, and arranged for the Sabbath to be observed and the temple officials to be supported. It is now up to God to exert his sovereign power on their behalf.

The Books of Chronicles

The situation just sketched is one in which the Books of Chronicles can be placed and which helped to shape their distinctive account of Israel's history. These books, written in the fourth century, are unique in the Old Testament in that we possess many of the sources on which they are based. The writer made use of the Books of Samuel and Kings, and although his version is not completely identical with Samuel and Kings as we now have them, it is very close. This is the standard view; but it has recently been argued that the writer of Chronicles did not use Samuel and Kings but a source to which the writers of Samuel and Kings also had access. The author also used parts of Psalms 96, 105, and 106; a list from Nehemiah 11; and genealogical material based on Genesis.

Chronicles begins with Adam, and the first eight chapters are genealogies, which, in the case of the family of David, bring the descent line from Adam to close to the time of the writing of Chronicles. In 1 Chron. 3:10–24 the genealogy of descendants of Solomon lists seven generations following King Jehoiachin, who was exiled to Babylon in 597 and was still alive in 560 (2 Kings 25:27). If we reckon 25 years for a generation, seven generations will add up to 175 years and bring the seventh generation into the fourth century. We might suppose that this was intended to keep alive hopes of a restoration of the Davidic dynasty; and so it might have been. But perhaps more important for the writer of Chronicles was his belief that David had been responsible for instituting the arrangements for worship in the first temple. The continuance of the line of David after the exile helped to stress the continuity between the first and the second temples – an issue of significance for a small community dominated by the temple.

Chapters 1–8 of 1 Chronicles also contains genealogies of tribes from the northern kingdom, which had ceased to exist nearly four hundred years before the book was written. The author evidently had no information about Dan and Zebulun), but all the other tribes are represented, including Reuben (a tribe early absorbed into other tribes) and the east Jordan tribe of Gad. The reason for including northern (and eastern) tribes was that the writer believed that the Judah of his day represented the whole of Israel as it had once been. This is true even though, in his sketch of Israelite history later in Chronicles, the writer largely ignored the material in the Books of Kings about the northern kingdom.

From 1 Chronicles 10 the story of Israel begins to be told, beginning with Saul and concentrating, from chapter 11 to the end of 1 Chronicles, on the reign of David and his ordering of the temple worship. Much of the material from chapters 11–21 is based upon the Books of Samuel, and the psalms mentioned above are also used. Material unique to Chronicles is in chapter 12, which claims that although David was a Philistine vassal in Ziklag, he received support from men from the tribes of Benjamin, Gad, Manasseh, Issachar, Zebulun, Naphtali, Dan, Asher, and Reuben. As in the case of much of the material found only in Chronicles, it is difficult to know whether the writer was using an ancient source not otherwise known to us or whether he was freely composing. There is no agreement among scholars on this point. One interesting feature of 1 Chronicles 12 is the "charismatic inspiration" of a leader of the Benjaminites as they come to pledge loyalty to David. He proclaims

> We are yours, O David;
> and with you, O son of Jesse!
> Peace, peace to you,
> and peace to the one who helps you!
> For your God is the one who helps you.

Because we can compare passages in Samuel and Kings with how they have been used in Chronicles, we can arrive at securely based conclusions about the author's outlook and intentions. The following points can be made.

1. Chronicles gives an explicit "all Israel" flavor to the narratives. This is clear from a comparison of the narratives of the bringing of the ark to Jerusalem in 2 Samuel 6 and in 1 Chronicles 13. In the former, David simply goes with "all the people who were with him" to bring the ark up from Baale-judah. In the latter, David consults with all the commanders and leaders in Israel as well as with the "assembly of Israel," resolving to summon all Israelites, especially priests and Levites, "in cities that have pasturelands" to come together to bring up the ark.

2. Where it suits the writer, the order of events in his sources is disregarded. Thus 2 Samuel 6 (the bringing up of the ark) is placed before 2 Sam. 5:13–25 (David's wives and concubines in Jerusalem and the defeat of the Philistines).

3. The writer presents David's character in a more favorable light than in Samuel by omitting the whole of the narrative about David's adultery with Bath-sheba, his successful plan to have her husband, Uriah, killed in battle, and the subsequent turmoil in his family and kingdom.

4. From 2 Chronicles 13 onward, speeches made before battles and other incidents are prominent in the narratives. Thus, in 2 Chron. 13:4–12 Abijah speaks before encountering Jeroboam. In 14:11 Asa prays to God before defeating the Ethiopians. In 15:2–7 the prophet Azariah encourages Asa to carry out a reform. In 20:6–12 Jehoshaphat prays before the assembly prior to fighting the Moabites and Ammonites and is further encouraged by an inspired utterance from the Levite Jahaziel (20:15–17). The people go into battle fortified by a further brief exhortation from the king (20:20) and by singing

> Give thanks to the LORD,
> for his steadfast love endures forever.

In these, and similar passages, we can perhaps see and hear the community of the writer of Chronicles at worship. It is a community that draws upon its spiritual heritage of psalms and is encouraged by inspired outbursts of Levites and others. It has a firm belief in the sovereignty of God, who, having delivered his people in the past in response to their faithful obedience to the law and their trust as expressed in worship, will do the same in the present and future.

5. One of the most striking things about Chronicles is the way in which it reverses the verdict upon kings of Judah as compared with the account of them in the Books of Kings. This is most striking in the case of the kings adjudged "bad" according to the outlook in the Books of Kings.

Abijam, as portrayed in 1 Kings 15:1–8, is a "bad" king. "He walked in all the sins which his father did before him; and his heart was not wholly true to the LORD his God" (15:3). Yet, as we have seen above, Abijah (as he is called in Chronicles) gives an address before defeating Jeroboam. In the address he claims that he and his people have not forsaken God and that God is with them (v. 10). No negative verdict is passed on Abijah in Chronicles.

The most striking transformation is in the case of Manasseh. Chapter 21 of 2 Kings has such a negative view of him that, in verses 10–15, God's prophets warn that his evil reign will be the reason why Jerusalem will be destroyed, as Samaria was destroyed. Chapter 33 of 2 Chronicles begins in similar vein but then, unexpectedly, tells us that when Manasseh was taken by the king of Assyria to Babylon, he humbled himself and prayed to God, and God, hearing his prayer, brought him back to Jerusalem (vv. 10–13). We are then told of a reformation carried out by Manasseh in which foreign gods and idols were removed from the temple and destroyed (v. 15). Whatever our views about the historicity of Manasseh's repentance and reform, we cannot escape from the fact that the writer of Chronicles believed that God would honor the sincere repentance of the most wicked offender.

If Chronicles is generous to wicked kings who repent, it is hard on some of the "good" kings in the accounts in the Books of Kings and in its own material. We have seen how Asa prayed to God and was encouraged by a prophet (2 Chron. 14:11, 15:2–7). But at the end of the narrative concerning him, he is condemned by a prophet for making an alliance with Damascus instead of relying upon God. This prophet is imprisoned for his utterances (16:10) and Asa's reign ends partially under a cloud.

The account of Jehoash's reign in 2 Kings 11:21–2:21 is in terms of him being a good king. A different perspective is given in 2 Chronicles 24. After the death of the priest Jehoiada, Joash (as he is called in Chronicles) forsakes God, and the son of Jehoiada is stoned to death on Joash's orders because he warns the people, in an inspired utterance, that they have forsaken God. Joash's assassination is described as retribution for this act.

Changes are also made in the case of Josiah. In 2 Kings 22–3 he is given an outstanding portrait as a good king, ending with the words:

> Before him there was no king like him, who turned to the LORD with all his heart, with all his soul, and with all his might . . . nor did any like him arise after him. (2 Kings 23:25)

However, in 2 Chronicles a sour note is introduced. When Josiah goes up to his fatal encounter with the Egyptian pharaoh Necho, the latter is inspired by God to warn Josiah off (2 Chron. 35:21–2). Josiah takes no notice. Thus his death as described in Chronicles is the result of his refusal to listen to God's word. Even a very good king can be flawed in his attention to God, and suffer the consequences.

In Chronicles, the past history of Israel is perceived and presented from the viewpoint of a worshiping, temple-based community. This sense of the sovereignty of God is such that there is a scaling down of human achievements and an exaltation of what God can do with even the most unpromising material. Thus, a Josiah can err and a Manasseh can repent.

The community's hope that, in due time, God will reward their faithfulness and trust is best summed up in two of the prayers uttered by two kings. In 2 Chron. 20:12 Jehoshaphat, faced by overwhelming enemy armies, prays:

> we are powerless against this great multitude that is coming against us. We do not know what to do, but our eyes are on you.

At 1 Chron. 29:14–15, David prays:

> But who am I, and what is my people, that we should be able to make this freewill offering? For all things come from you, and of your own have we given you. For we are aliens and transients before you, as were all our ancestors; our days on the earth are like a shadow, and there is no hope.

If this piety was the outcome of Nehemiah's attempt to abolish mixed marriages and to reconstitute Judah as a community faithful to God's laws, his actions cannot have been entirely misconceived.

III. THE WORLD OF ISRAEL'S PROPHETS

A. THE ORGANIZATION OF THE PROPHETIC WRITINGS

1. The History of Prophetic Literature
The Forms of Prophetic Speech

We are familiar with written books in the Bible attributed to named prophets such as Amos, Isaiah, or Jeremiah. In fact, as we shall see, many such books contain some material that did not emanate from the prophet after whom the book is named, and the reason for this is that the prophets themselves were not writers but speakers. Theirs was not the power of the pen but the power of the spoken word as they confronted kings, princes, and ordinary people of their time with oracles often prefaced by the phrase "thus says (or said) the LORD."

Before the types of speech used by the prophets are discussed, it is necessary to point out that we must not suppose that there was a uniform or typical "thing" in ancient Israel that we can call prophecy; neither were prophets people who necessarily belonged to a distinctive guild or profession. They were very different types of people from quite different backgrounds. Ezekiel was a priest, Isaiah was close to the royal entourage, and Micah was a provincial leader with some enmity to the establishment. Amos denied that he was a prophet (Amos 7:14); and it is only because scholars have been determined to see prophecy as an identifiable institution within ancient Israel that they have often refused to take his disclaimer seriously. It has been argued that Amos was saying that he was not a professional prophet or a member of a guild; or even that his words "I am no prophet" were a way of saying that he really was a prophet! The only thing that people whom we call prophets had in common in the preexilic period was their conviction that God had spoken to them and that they were impelled to communicate to the king or the people what he had said.

> The lion has roared;
> who will not fear?
> The Lord GOD has spoken;
> who can but prophesy?   (Amos 3:8)

If we ask how the prophets believed that God had spoken to them, we have a few clues, but they certainly do not tell the whole story. In several passages the use of puns suggests that seeing an ordinary object triggered an association and message in the prophet's mind. Thus Amos sees a basket of summer fruits (Hebrew *qayits*) and thinks of the similar word for "end" (Hebrew *qets*; Amos 8:1). Jeremiah sees an almond tree (Hebrew *shaqed*) and thinks of the word for "watching" (*shoqed*; Jer. 1:11–12). The observation of everyday happenings could also trigger a message, as when Jeremiah saw a potter at work (Jer. 18:1 ff.) or when Amos saw locusts eating grass (Amos 7:1–3). Prophets were clearly people who had an intimate relationship with God and who, in prayer and visions, as well as daily experiences, believed that they were being given a message to proclaim.

In order to get their message across they used a variety of devices. A famous example is the messenger formula, which was used by kings to convey messages to each other. A messenger would stand in the king's presence while the king spoke the message to be conveyed to another king. The messenger would go to that king and repeat exactly what he had heard. There is an example of this in Judges 11, where Jephthah sends messages to the king of the Ammonites. His message in verse 14 begins "Thus says Jephthah." When the prophets delivered a message that began "Thus says (or said) the LORD," they were implying that they had stood in God's presence and had heard him say the words they were now repeating. Of course, they had only stood in God's court metaphorically or in a vision; but the effect of their use of the messenger formula must have made a great impact. The messenger formula was quite stylized and took the form of an introduction describing how a state of affairs had developed, followed by a statement of what the king demanded or was about to do, preceded by the word "therefore."

Another common form was that of the legal accusation. The prophet would call heaven and earth, or the citizens of surrounding nations, to hear an accusation that God was bringing against his people. A good example is at the beginning of Isaiah:

> Hear, O heavens, and give ear, O earth;
> for the LORD has spoken:
> "Sons have I reared and brought up,
> but they have rebelled against me.
> The ox knows its master,
> and the ass its master's crib;
> but Israel does not know,
> my people does not understand."   (Is. 1:2–3)

Another device was to use the type of lamentation with which a death was mourned. The prophets often spoke in poetry, and the lamentation has a distinctive pattern: a line of three stressed syllables followed by a line with two stresses. This is not easy to reproduce in English, but an example is Amos 5:2–3, where the poem is even introduced as a lament. The stresses are marked:

> Fall′en, no m′ore to ri′se,
> is the vi′rgin Isra′el;

forsak´en o´n her la´nd,
with no´ne to raise h´er up.   (Amos 5:2)

In Isa. 5:1–2 the prophet used the form of a love poem to convey his message:

Let me sing a song for my beloved
a love song concerning his vineyard.   (Is. 5:1)

At the end of the passage there is another device – the use of similar-sounding words with different meanings:

and he looked for justice [*mishpat*]
but behold, bloodshed [*mispah*];
for righteousness [*tsedaqah*],
but behold, a cry [*tse aqah*].   (Isa. 5:7)

In Micah 1 there is an extended speech in which puns are made on the names of cities to warn their inhabitants. The poem is badly preserved, but the following modernization conveys the flavor:

1:10b   In Dustville, roll yourselves in the dust.
1:11b   Do not go out, citizen of Out-town.
1:13a   Harness the chariot to the horse, citizens of Horseville.
1:14c   The homes of Deceitville are deceitful.

Mention must also be made of what has been called "prophetic symbolism." This was an action of a prophet which included both an oracle and a physical performance designed to give dramatic expression to the words spoken. One of the best-known examples of prophetic symbolism is recorded in 1 Kings 11:29–39. The prophet Ahijah meets Jeroboam on the road and takes his own new garment and tears it into twelve pieces, giving Jeroboam ten of them. This dramatically symbolizes his words:

Behold I am about to tear the kingdom from the hand of Solomon, and will give you ten tribes. (1 Kings 11:31)

In Isa. 8:1 the prophet writes on a large tablet the name to be given to the son of a prophetess: *maher-shalal-hash-baz*, meaning "the spoil speeds, the prey hastes." This dramatically reinforces the prophet's warnings to Damascus about its imminent fate. It is also possible that the difficult first chapter of Hosea is to be understood as prophetic symbolism, in which case the prophet's family acts out the command to the prophet to marry a prostitute and to have children by her. This, however, is only one of several ways of interpreting this intriguing passage.

Prophetic symbolism is met most frequently in the prophetic books in Ezekiel. In chapter 4 the prophet draws on a brick a picture of Jerusalem surrounded by siege works. He is instructed to lie on his left side for 390 days, symbolizing the years of the punishment of Israel (the northern kingdom), followed by 40 days on his right side, representing the years of the punishment of Judah. Whether Ezekiel actually lay in public view on his left side for a year and a month we do not know. Would his viewers have kept count? It has been plausibly suggested that, here and elsewhere, Ezekiel was performing street theater, and that in this way, in the example given, he acted a part as though he was lying on his side for 390 days. Whatever the truth, the fact is that prophetic utterance not only drew upon many oratorical devices but in some cases backed these up with dramatic actions.

From Oral to Written Prophecy

We have little direct information about how the spoken (and acted) words of prophets reached the form in which we have them in the prophetic books. The older theory, that prophets wrote the books that bear their names, began to be abandoned in the eighteenth century when passages or sections demonstrably later than the time of a given prophet were identified. For example, in the 1770s chapters 40–66 of Isaiah were ascribed to a prophet who lived two hundred years later than the Isaiah of 1–39. Further research indicated that sections of Isaiah 1–39 were also later than the time of Isaiah of Jerusalem (the "author" of Isaiah 1–12, who lived in the second half of the eighth century B.C.E.). In the nineteenth century the prophets were "rediscovered" as speakers rather than writers, as inspired figures who proclaimed "thus saith the LORD" to their contemporaries. So how did these spoken words come to be written down?

Jeremiah 36 describes how Jeremiah dictated his oracles to the scribe Baruch son of Neriah. Attempts to discredit this information are surely weakened by the publication by Avigad in 1986 of a seal bearing the name "Barachiah son of Neriah the scribe." Thus we know one way in which oracles were written down. It would be wrong to conclude that all prophetic books were produced in the same way, but the Jeremiah incident indicates the vital fact that prophets were not solitary figures but had supporters and disciples. In most cases the sources are silent about who these were; but studies of "intermediaries" by social anthropologists indicate that "support groups" are important for prophets, whether these groups function at the center or the periphery of a society. The stories of Elijah and Elisha in 1 Kings 17 to 2 Kings 10 indicate that they presided over groups called "sons of the prophets," and there are hints in Isa. 8:16–18 that Isaiah had disciples. Obviously, we must not forget what was said earlier about the danger of overlooking the diversity that existed among those we call prophets, but it is safe to assume that none was an isolated individual.

Isa. 8:16–20, although not an easy passage to understand, suggests that prophetic oracles were written down, sealed, and kept by disciples so that they could be used on subsequent occasions to seek the word and will of God. This is probably the best clue about how and by whom the oracles were recorded and transmitted. How were they later arranged into a collection? There were various principles. The most obvious was the thematic principle, indicated by the blocks of oracles against foreign nations in Isaiah 17–19, Jeremiah 46–51, and Ezekiel 24–32. In other cases, short collections such as Amos 3, 4, and 5, each of which begins with the formula "hear this word," were put together to form a larger block. Another principle was the "catchword" principle, whereby an oracle beginning with a particular word, name, or phrase would be linked to an oracle with a similar ending. However, not many clear examples of the catchword arrangement can be found.

The work of the collectors and arrangers did not stop with merely arranging the material at hand. Commentators on most prophetic books have found evidence that original oracles were reworked and/or expanded. The reason for this was that the word from God that the oracles contained was believed to be relevant not only for its original occasion of speaking but for later situations. Prophecy was therefore a living tradition, begun by individual prophets but sustained by generations of disciples engaged in the interpretation of their words.

A decisive event in the writing of prophetic books was the Babylonian exile (sixth century B.C.E.). Israel's survival of this catastrophe was made possible by prophetic groups who saw the fall of Jerusalem as God's punishment of his people's unfaithfulness and who believed in a restoration of Jerusalem. The exile seems eventually to have brought all the existing prophetic traditions under the control of the priestly–scribal authorities in postexilic Judah, though not, as we shall see, without protest (see the discussion of Malachi below, pp. 226–228). It was in this context that the prophetic books reached their final form and that the diversity that once existed among prophets and their followers was flattened into uniformity.

One effect of this was that prophets hostile to Israel and Judah to the point of offering nothing beyond God's annihilating judgment had oracles of hope added to their books. The concluding verses of Amos (9:1–15) speak of raising up the booth of David that is fallen and thus presuppose the fall of Jerusalem. Because this happened 150 years after the time of Amos, these verses are an addition designed to mitigate the book's uncompromising message of judgment. Micah has been treated even more drastically, with oracles of salvation interspersed among his oracles of destruction. If we regard this practice with distaste, we must remember that the final editors of the prophetic traditions viewed the history of Israel and Judah from a larger perspective than was possible for any individual prophet. Amos and Micah had been proved correct in their warnings of coming judgment, but there had also been a restoration, and the final editors set the messages of Amos and Micah in that context. This process was a vital part of the move from oral to written prophecy.

The Organization of the Prophetic Books

In our translations of the English Bible, the prophetic books are Isaiah, Jeremiah, Ezekiel, Daniel, and the Twelve Minor Prophets. They come at the end of the Old Testament, so that the closing words of Malachi, which speak of the coming of Elijah, form a fitting prelude to the New Testament and the Elijah-like activity of John the Baptist. In the Hebrew Bible Daniel belongs to the section known as the Writings, and the remainder of the prophets are designated Latter Prophets and follow the Former Prophets (Joshua, Judges, Samuel, and Kings). In Jewish reckoning there are four Latter Prophets – Isaiah, Jeremiah, Ezekiel, and the Twelve Minor Prophets (regarded as one book) – and it has been suggested that the length of each corresponds to what could be written on a scroll. The traditional Jewish enumeration gives the following numbers of verses: Isaiah, 1,295; Jeremiah, 1,365; Ezekiel, 1,273; the Twelve, 1,050. Of the three "larger" prophets, the Book of Isaiah is unique in consisting of three blocks of material from three quite different periods: chapters 1–39 (with later additions) from the eighth century B.C.E., chapters 40–55 from the sixth century, and chapters 56–66 from the fifth century. It may be that the whole book is the work of an Isaiah "school" over many generations.

There has been much speculation about the order and arrangement of the Twelve Minor Prophets. One influential theory has been that they were basically arranged according to the dates of the prophets after whom they were named. Thus, Hosea, Amos, and Micah (eighth century) preceded Nahum, Habakkuk, and Zephaniah (seventh century), who in turn preceded the fifth-century Haggai and Zechariah 1–8 and the fourth-century Malachi. In the third century chapters 9–14 were added to Zechariah, and Joel and Obadiah were composed. The positions of Jonah, Joel, and Obadiah were determined as follows. Jonah was placed before Micah because of the reference in 2 Kings 14:25 to a Jonah who prophesied during the reign of Jeroboam II (eighth century). Joel was placed between Hosea and Amos because Joel 3:16a (Hebrew Bible, 4:16a) was similar to Amos 1:2, and Joel 3:18a (4:18a) was similar to Amos 9:13. Obadiah was placed after Amos because it concerned Edom and thus followed naturally from the end of Amos 9:12 with its reference to Edom (before the addition to Amos of 9:13–15). In other words, we have both a date and a "catchword" principle operating in the arrangement of the Twelve.

A striking difference between the Three and the Twelve is that, apart from Jonah, we know almost nothing about the prophets named in connection with the Twelve, whereas Isaiah, Jeremiah, and Ezekiel contain some biographical material. It has been suggested that the biographical information about the Twelve was omitted in the redaction process for two reasons: to shorten the material so as to occupy one scroll and to remove historical details so that the oracles would be applicable to situations beyond their original setting. These are suggestions only and cannot be proved.

2. Prophecy in Israelite History

The Monarchical Period (Eleventh to Sixth Centuries B.C.E.)

It was pointed out earlier that we must be careful not to assume that prophets were all of a piece in ancient Israel or that they belonged to a recognizable "institution." In 1 Sam. 9:9 there is an indication that different kinds of intermediaries (to use a neutral term) were known:

> Formerly in Israel, when a man went to inquire of God, he said, "Come, let us go to the seer"; for he who is now called a prophet was formerly called a seer.

The setting of 1 Samuel 9 is Saul's search for some lost asses, and the purpose of consulting the seer is to obtain supernatural information about the journey that Saul and his servant have undertaken. It is believed of this seer (Samuel) that "all that he says comes true" (1 Sam. 9:6). As presented in 1 Sam. 9–10 and 19:18–24, Samuel is the head of a group of "prophets" whose distinctive characteristic is their ecstatic behavior, which included lying naked on the ground for hours on end. Samuel is also presented as a powerful figure in his society, with authority both to anoint a "king" and to reprove him. This authority no doubt derived from popular belief that he was in direct communication with God.

The type of prophecy represented by Samuel seems to be continued in Elijah and Elisha. They, too, preside over groups of prophets, although we are not told that these groups were ecstatic, and the Elijah/Elisha stories concentrate on these men as wonder-workers who can restore the dead to life (1 Kings 17:17–24, 2 Kings 4:18–37), cause vessels never to be empty (1 Kings 17:8–15), and make iron axheads float (2 Kings 6:1–7). These prophets also perform what seem to be immoral deeds. Elijah destroys men seeking to arrest him by calling down fire from heaven (2 Kings 1:9–12), and Elisha curses small boys who call after him "Go up, you baldhead," and they are killed by two she-bears (2 Kings 2:23–5). Along with these strange stories is evidence that Elijah and Elisha were active in national affairs, opposing Ahab and Jezebel and anointing Jehu to carry out a revolution by overthrowing Ahab's dynasty. There is also a recognition in the account of Elijah's contest with the prophets of Baal (1 Kings 18:17–40) that prophets were not peculiar to Israel. The narrative describes the Baal prophets as cutting themselves with swords and lances and limping and raving in order to prevail upon their god.

If Elijah and Elisha (and Samuel?) operated from the margins of society in championing traditional faith in the God of Israel, albeit with support from powerful sympathizers at the center of power (see 1 Kings 18:3–4 and p. 145, above), there were also prophets employed officially at court. Nathan was apparently a prophet at David's court; he reproved David's adultery with Bath-sheba and his "murder" of Uriah (2 Sam. 12:1–15) and played an important part in the succession of Solomon to the throne (1 Kings 1:22–40). In 1 Kings 22:5–12, 400 prophets gather to advise Ahab whether to fight at Ramoth-gilead. They seem to be ecstatic prophets, if this is a correct inference from verse 10: "All the prophets were prophesying before them." Other prophets mentioned in the period from Saul (eleventh century B.C.E.) to the end of the ninth century include Ahijah, who encouraged Jeroboam's rebellion against Solomon's son Rehoboam (1 Kings 11:29–39), and Micaiah, who foretold the death of Ahab, contradicting the view of the 400 prophets who foresaw Ahab's success (1 Kings 2:13–23). The picture that begins to emerge from this diversity is that there were prophets who, whatever their other differences, played an active role in the religious and political affairs of Judah and Israel, helping to set up and to bring down kings and zealously defending faith in the God of Israel.

In the eighth century we have the first of the prophets to whom prophetic books are attributed. Their diversity must not be overlooked. Isaiah seems to have been a court prophet, whereas Amos and Micah were from small provincial towns in Judah, and Amos insisted that he was not a prophet (Amos 7:14). Of Hosea we know nothing but presume that he came from the northern kingdom, Israel, because his oracles are concerned with Israel (but then, so are most of Amos's, and he is usually held to have come from a southern town). These eighth-century prophets did not, so far as we know, try to overthrow kings; but their oracles were often concerned with God's coming judgment upon Israel and Judah because the people and their rulers had forsaken God. The seventh-century prophets – Zephaniah, Nahum, and Habakkuk – add little to the picture. We know nothing about them. Nahum stands out from the rest in that the oracles of this book are directed not against Judah but against Nineveh. Jeremiah's ministry dates from the end of the seventh century to the beginning of the sixth and was concerned with Jerusalem's impending destruction. He exemplifies the type of prophet who operated from the margins of society but who nonetheless had supporters close to the seat of power.

Scholars have debated two main questions regarding prophets in the monarchical period. Did they create the faith of Israel, and how were they related to institutions such as the temple cult? The view that the prophets created the faith of Israel became influential in the second half of the nineteenth century. The prophets were seen as the originators of ethical monotheism, who preached this religion to an Israel that was barely distinguishable from its Canaanite neighbors. Prophetic religion was, in this view, embodied in the Deuteronomistic law and enacted in the reforms of Josiah, only to be swamped in the postexilic period by an emergent priestly–scribal religion that gave preeminence to the law.

There is some truth in all of this. The law did not reach its present form until after the exile, when priestly–scribal religion predominated, and a link between prophetic witness and the Deuteronomistic tradition is very likely. Also, the contribution of preexilic prophecy to the upholding and developing of Israel's religion cannot be overestimated. However, it is probably incorrect to see the prophets as the inventors of Israel's faith in Yahweh. Some of the traditions preserved in Deuteronomy probably have their origin in the premonarchical period and imply a simple form of agreement that bound Israelite groups to Yahweh. If, as is likely, Jeroboam's revolt against Solomon and his son was partly a prophetic-led revolt of the "old" faith against the new-fangled temple cult in the lately elevated Jerusalem, this shows that prophets preserved and did not simply invent traditions that expressed the people's faith in Yahweh.

We do not know exactly how the prophets related to the temple cult or other institutions. That Isaiah received his call while in the temple (Isa. 6:1–10) and that Jeremiah preached in the temple court (Jer. 7:1–4) may mean little or much according to one's prejudices. Discussion has centered on the theme of the "Day of Yahweh," which is found in Isaiah, Amos, and Zephaniah and possibly (by implication) in Nahum and Habakkuk. This "day" is one of judgment and wrath for the ungodly in Judah and Israel and elsewhere, when God acts to assert

THE DAY OF YAHWEH

THE DAY OF YAHWEH (or the Day of the Lord) is a familiar concept in the Hebrew Bible, especially in the prophetic canon. However, the idea probably originated much earlier in Israel's history. Scholars have debated its exact origin, and several theories have been proposed. The eminent scholar Gerhard von Rad argued that the prophets' Day of Yahweh grew out of Israel's historical and theological experience of holy war, described vividly in Joshua and Judges. Sigmund Mowinckel sought a more cultic origin, locating the concept as part of a hypothetical Israelite celebration of the New Year when Yahweh was ritually re-enthroned annually. Others have suggested that the idea of an awesome divine epiphany is a holdover from Canaanite mythology. In any case, the Day of Yahweh began as the promise that Israel would be vindicated by Yahweh. When Yahweh appeared, the enemy fled, the universe returned to order, and peace and security were assured for the whole people of Israel.

By the time of the eighth-century B.C.E. prophets, the Day of Yahweh had taken on an entirely different meaning. In the speeches of Amos (5:18–20), Isaiah (2:9–19), and, later, Zephaniah (1:7–16, 2:2–3), the Day of Yahweh is anticipated as a day of destruction for Israel and Judah. When Yahweh appears, his purpose is to punish the people for their sins and bring them to repentance. Although warnings about the impending Day of Yahweh often paint its coming in fearful poetic images, the classical prophets generally had in mind real catastrophes which were about to befall their people. Agricultural and military disasters are the most commonly threatened calamities. Some prophets found the fulfillment of oracles about the Day of Yahweh in the sixth-century B.C.E. destruction of Jerusalem. Ezekiel (34:12) and Lamentations (1:21) understand the Day of Yahweh as an event that had already come to pass.

Apocalypticism influenced the theological development of the Day of Yahweh in the Hebrew Bible's latest writings. In Zechariah (14) and Joel (English translation, 1–2, 3:14–15), the Day of Yahweh is depicted as a period of cosmic cataclysm that marks the end of history. The final battle between good and evil is fought on that terrible day in the midst of universal upheaval and natural destruction. On this apocalyptic Day of Yahweh, the people of God will triumph over all their enemies, and every surviving nation will worship the king, Yahweh of Hosts.

The exact phrase "Day of Yahweh" disappears from Jewish literature in the postbiblical period, although the idea it expresses remained an important concept in Jewish thought. The rapidly approaching Day of Final Judgment holds an important place in apocryphal, pseudepigraphic, and rabbinic works. In the New Testament, however, the effect of terminology inherited from Jewish tradition is pronounced. The Day of the Lord is recast in christological terms and taken up by the Gospels (Luke 17:24; cf. John 8:56), the Pauline epistles (1 Thess. 5:2, 2 Cor. 1:14), and the Apocalypse of Saint John (Rev. 16:14).

his sovereignty. Whether the Day of Yahweh is to be located in the temple cult and connected with an annual or periodic celebration of the universal kingship of God, or whether it derives from the institution of holy war, is a matter of scholarly disagreement. This disagreement arises partly from a dearth of evidence; but the fact that three prophets invoke the theme of the Day of Yahweh indicates that they were operating in the context of traditions or institutions, even if we can say little more than that. We are probably on firmer ground with the so-called Zion theology. This theology uses phrases such as "Lord of Hosts" and stresses righteousness. It can probably be found in Isaiah and also occurs in Psalms (e.g., Pss. 24, 46).

The Exilic Period (Sixth Century B.C.E.)

Two prophets dominate the exile: Ezekiel and the unknown prophet of Isaiah 40–55. Ezekiel and Isaiah 40–55 are substantial works written during this period and bring to a high point Israel's faith in the sovereignty of God. Ezekiel's certainty that God must destroy Jerusalem before there can be any hope of restoration of the nation is expressed in visions of Jerusalem's abominations and of God's judgment against nations that might come to Judah's help, especially Egypt. Only when news reaches Ezekiel that Jerusalem has fallen does he begin to speak of restoration. In Ezekiel 37 the prophet has a vision of dry bones being clothed with flesh and becoming an army of living people. This is a powerful metaphor for how an utterly hopeless situation from a human standpoint can be redeemed by the power of God.

Isaiah 40–55 has two main themes: the lordship of God over historical events and the power of vicarious suffering to bring repentance to wrongdoers. The prophet sees the victorious march of the Persian king Cyrus toward Babylon as God's action prior to restoring his people. But these chapters also speak of the sufferings of the mysterious "Servant of the Lord" (the prophet himself or the prophet and his disciples, who are the true remnant of Israel), sufferings that make the people recognize their wrongdoing and the possibility of renewal. These two exilic prophets deepen immeasurably Israel's understanding of the nature and ways of God.

The Restoration Period (Late Sixth to Fifth Centuries B.C.E.)

The restoration period (which began in 539) brought great changes in prophetic activity without eliminating its diversity; and we can often only speculate about how to connect the diversity. The earliest restoration prophets are Haggai and Zechariah 1–8, and we have discussed above (p. 153) their central role in encouraging the rebuilding of the temple. This fact at once separates them from Micah, who probably envisaged the temple's permanent destruction (see below, p. 210); Isaiah 1–12, who fiercely attacked the cult; and Jeremiah, who foretold the temple's destruction. Haggai and Zechariah are closer to the final chapters of Ezekiel, which foresee a restored temple, although Ezekiel is also unsparing in his denunciations of the cult in the first temple. The association of prophets with, rather than against, the cult is seen most strongly in Chronicles, when, in 1 Chron. 25:1, we are told of "certain of the sons of Asaph, and of Heman, and of Jeduthun, who should prophesy with lyres, with harps, and with cymbals." This looks like an attempt to absorb prophets into temple personnel responsible for leading worship and reflects the changed circumstances of postexilic Judah – a small community dominated by the temple.

However, we find a note of dissent from this loyalty to the temple in Isaiah 56–66. It is true that chapters 60–2 contain positive sentiments about the restoration of Jerusalem, but nothing is said in these passages about the temple, and elsewhere there are sharp attacks on the cult. Chapter 58 contrasts religious observance unfavorably with the practice of social justice, while 66:11–12 seems to repudiate the need for a temple. Also, in chapters 56–66 we find opposition to the redrawing of the boundaries of the Jewish community in narrow, exclusive terms (see especially 63:15–19 and 56:6–8, which calls the temple "a house of prayer for all peoples").

Exactly how we should position Isaiah 56–66 within postexilic Judah is hard to say. The same is true of passages such as Zech. 13:2–6. This remarkable piece, which includes a parody of Amos's denial that he was a prophet (Zech. 13:5; cf. Amos 7:14), envisages a period when God will remove "the prophets and the unclean spirit" from the land. It seems to take to an extreme a problem that is wrestled with in Deuteronomy (13:1–5) and Jeremiah (28:1–16) as well as in the Micaiah incident in 1 Kings 22 – the problem of false prophecy and of how to distinguish it from true prophecy. It seems to be saying that any person who claims to be a prophet is suspect. Similarly, Joel and Malachi imply that prophecy is something not to be expected now, but that it will occur in the Latter Days. Thus Joel 2:22 (Hebrew Bible, 3:1) looks forward to the time when God will pour out his spirit on all flesh and when "your sons and your daughters shall prophesy." Malachi anticipates not so much the renewal of prophecy as the coming of a particular prophet, Elijah, who will prepare the people for the coming Day of Yahweh (Mal. 4:5–6; Hebrew Bible, 3:23–4).

However these diverse elements are to be related, the fact is that they were collected together and formed into the prophetic collections as we have them. In this process, a pro-temple view triumphed without the anti-cult passages being excised. Thus, as we have seen, the most uncompromising critic of the temple, Micah, was edited in such a way that his polemic was softened. Also added to the prophetic literature were apocalyptic elements such as Isaiah 24–7 and Zechariah 9–14. "Apocalyptic" will be treated as a separate subject (see below, pp. 000–000). Suffice it to say here that it has been suggested that the apocalyptic literature originated from circles such as those represented by Isaiah 56–66 that were hostile to the temple-based community.

B.   ISAIAH

1.   Isaiah 1–39
History of the Period

The division of Isaiah into three blocks – 1–39, 40–55, and 56–66 – wrongly gives the impression that chapters 1–39 belong to the eighth-century "Isaiah of Jerusalem." In fact, chapters 12–13, 15–16, 19, 21, 23–7, and 33–9 were written later than the eighth century. If we concentrate on what can be determined about this Isaiah (an operation that goes against the current and justifiable interest in the final form of the text), we can say the following about the prophet and the history of his period.

Isaiah was called to be a prophet in the year of King Uzziah's death (ca. 739 B.C.E.) and was active during the reigns of Jotham, Ahaz, and Hezekiah; although a different view is that Isaiah was active also during Uzziah's reign and that chapter 6 concerns not a call to be a prophet but a special commission. The latest date that can be associated with Isaiah's work is 701, the time of Sennacherib's invasion of Judah. Thus, Isaiah lived through the collapse and destruction of the northern kingdom, the influx of refugees who settled in Judah after

722/1, Hezekiah's attempts to establish Judah's independence from Assyria, and his failure when the Babylonian king Sennacherib invaded in 701 and devastated Judah.

Isaiah's work as related to his oracles can be divided into five main periods. First is the period of Jotham (or Uzziah and Jotham), from 739 (or, possibly, 745) to 734. In this period Isaiah attacked the social injustice which had come about during the long and (for some) prosperous reign of Uzziah. Powerful landowners had been able to dispossess their poorer neighbors, justice had not been practiced, and the rich had followed an indulgent lifestyle (see the description of the wealthy "daughters of Zion" at 3:16–26). In this situation Isaiah looked for a coming Day of Yahweh, when human achievements would collapse before God's majestic intervention (chap. 2).

The second period concerns the so-called Syro-Ephraimite crisis of 734–3. The kings of Israel and Syria declared war on Judah and evidently besieged Jerusalem (Isa. 7:1–2). It is often assumed that their purpose was to force king Ahaz (ca. 734–727) to join an anti-Assyrian coalition, although there is no direct evidence for this. Isaiah confronted Ahaz and urged him to put his trust in God for deliverance (7:3–16), giving him the sign of the Immanuel child. A pregnant woman would give birth, and the land would be free from the two kings before the child could choose between good and evil (7:14–16). However, Ahaz turned instead to the Assyrian king Tiglath-pileser III for help (2 Kings 16:5–16), who attacked Syria and Israel, leaving to the latter only the rump of Samaria. During the third period, before 722/1, Isaiah prophesied against the northern kingdom, warning of its fate. Material pertinent to this period includes 9:8–21, 17:3–6, and 28:1–4.

The fourth period is that of the rebellion of Ashdod against the Assyrian king Sargon in 711. Material from this period includes 20:1–6 and 18:1–2. The fifth period is that of Sennacherib's invasion of 701 in response to Hezekiah's rebellion. Jerusalem survived the siege, thanks to Hezekiah's fortifications and the construction of "Warren's shaft" to secure the water supply; but the rest of the land suffered grievously. The conquest of Lachish, Judah's second city, was recorded by Sennacherib on the famous reliefs now in the British Museum in London, and Hezekiah was forced to pay heavy tribute. This incident is reflected in some of the material in chapters 28–32 (especially where dependence on Egypt is denounced) and in 1:4–8 and 22:1–14. Chapters 36–9 also tell of this period, in material similar to 2 Kings 18–19.

Literary Structure and Contents of Isaiah 1–39

Isaiah 1–39 can be divided roughly into five sections: 1–12, 13–23, 24–7, 28–32, and 33–9.

Isaiah 1–12 Chapter 1 begins with a complaint against the nation's faithlessness (vv. 2–3) and then describes its situation at the time of Sennacherib's invasion (vv. 4–9). The catchwords "Sodom" and "Gomorrah" (vv. 9–10) introduce a section that castigates Jerusalem's failing in both worship and justice and that looks forward to the city's cleansing (vv. 10–31). This hope is endorsed by the famous vision of an exalted Jerusalem as a place of pilgrimage of the nations (2:1–4[5]; cf. Mic. 4:1–4[5]):

> In days to come
>   the mountain of the LORD's house
> shall be established on the highest of the mountains,
> and shall be raised above the hills;
>   all the nations shall stream to it.
> Many peoples shall come and say:
> "Come, let us go up to the mountain of the LORD,
> to the house of the God of Jacob;
> that he may teach us his ways
>   and that we may walk in his paths."   (Isa. 2:1–2)

The theme of judgment returns, in terms of the Day of Yahweh (2:6–22). Future judgment will totally destabilize a corrupt society, including the rich women of Zion (3:1–4:1), but there will be a future hope for Zion and its women (4:2–6). In 2:1–4 and 4:2–6 we have indications of later editors "layering" oracles of hope into oracles of judgment. Isa. 5:1–30 denounces social injustices, a theme continued in 10:1–4. Isa. 9:8–21 denounces Israel, including a refrain found also in chapter 5 (cf. 5:25b; 9:12b, 17b, 21b – possibly originally one passage?), and 10:5–34 both summons Assyria to be God's instrument of punishment on Israel and Judah and speaks of punishment of Assyria on account of its pride.

Into the section consisting of chapters 5 and 9–10 have been inserted chapters 6–8, which deal with Isaiah's call (or special commission) and describe the Syro-Ephraimite crisis. A famous passage is 9:1–7

A depiction of the most ambitious Israelite water system ever discovered, the tunnel cut beneath the Ophel Hill in Jerusalem.

Biblical Archaeology Slides, no. 58

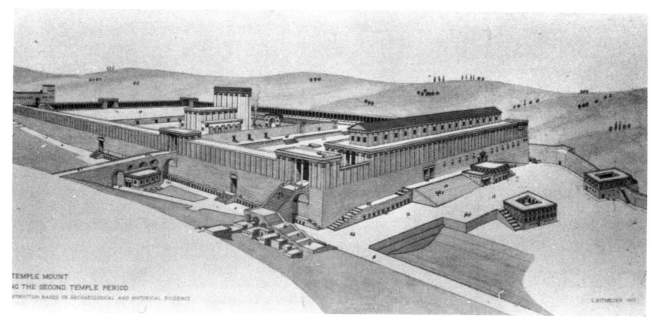

TEMPLE MOUNT
IG THE SECOND TEMPLE PERIOD
TRUCTION BASED ON ARCHAEOLOGICAL AND HISTORICAL EVIDENCE

(Hebrew Bible, 8:23–9:6), which contains the words "For a child has been born for us." Whether this and 11:1–9 belong to the time of Isaiah or later is disputed. Isa. 11:1–9 seems to imply that the tree of the house of Jesse (David's father) has been cut down, that is, that the fall of Jerusalem in 587/6 has happened. It is probable that chapter 11 and the hymn of praise in chapter 12 are exilic or postexilic. Isa. 9:1–7 is harder to date. Verse 1 looks forward to the restoration to Israel of areas lost to Tiglath-pileser III; verses 2–7 may or may not be connected to verse 1. Isa. 9:2–7 combines two themes: a holy war of restoration of God's people and the birth (or coronation) of a prince of five names (of which the last is not preserved, although there are traces of it in the Hebrew). If these verses come from Isaiah, who is the prince? The lack of precise detail, which may be deliberate, allows for various candidates (e.g., Hezekiah, Josiah) but no agreement among commentators.

Isaiah 13–23 These are oracles against the nations: Babylon (13, 14:1–23), Assyria (14:24–7), Philistia (14:28–31), Moab (15–16), Damascus and Israel (17), Egypt and Ethiopia (18–20), Edom (21), Jerusalem (22), and Tyre (23).

Isaiah 24–7 This is often called the "little apocalypse" but the name is a misnomer. It certainly contains apocalyptic motifs, such as in 24:21–4 (the heavenly host will be punished, they will be imprisoned for many days, the sun and moon will be confounded and ashamed), 26:19 (resurrection of the dead), and 27:1 (the slaying of the sea dragon Leviathan); but it is not an apocalypse. Chapter 24 envisages the punishment of earth and heaven before God reigns in glory in Jerusalem, while chapters 25–6 are mostly hymns of praise to God for what he has done and will do for those who are faithful to him. Chapter 27 also expresses hope for the future, using the theme of the vineyard which God protects (possibly a deliberate contrast with the Song of the Vineyard at 5:1–7).

Isaiah 28–32 These oracles date mostly from the time of Sennacherib's invasion in 701 (although they begin with an oracle against the northern kingdom to be dated around 722) and include condemnations against trusting in help from Egypt, as well as oracles of hope and encouragement (e.g., 29:13–14, 15–16, 17–21, 22–4).

Isaiah 33–9 Chapters 36–9 parallel 2 Kings 18–20 and are considered by some commentators to be earlier than the 2 Kings material. They relate in prose Hezekiah's rebellion against Sennacherib and the besieging and deliverance of Jerusalem (36–7) and Hezekiah's illness and recovery and the embassy from the Babylonian king Merodach-baladan (38–9). Chapter 33 includes a prayer to God for hope (vv. 2–4) and a divine response (vv. 10–12), followed by a summons of encouragement to those who hope for a purified Jerusalem (vv. 13–24). Chapter 34 is an oracle against Edom, and chapter 35, which is strongly reminiscent of chapters 40–55, envisages the return of the exiles to Jerusalem.

Is the whole collection haphazard or coherent? The answer is: something of both. An uninstructed "first reader" will find Isaiah 1–39 incoherent, a collection of inspiring and puzzling passages. On further reflection, Jerusalem emerges as a recurrent theme. Chapter 1 introduces it as an unfaithful city; and in Ahaz it has an unfaithful king. But there are also hopes for a restored and cleansed city, and those hopes are partly centered on a faithful king, Hezekiah. Those who threaten Jerusalem, such as Israel and Damascus, will be punished, as will the chosen instrument of God's judgment upon Jerusalem (Assyria). Judah's dependence upon God, and not upon other nations such as Assyria and Egypt, is enjoined; and Hezekiah's virtue, as opposed to Ahaz's vice, was just such dependence on God. Where there is trust in God, there is sure hope of restoration.

Although it is customary to see a break between chapters 39 and 40, it is arguable that 39:5 – "Days are coming when all that is in your house . . . shall be carried to Babylon" – is an introduction to the restoration theme, with which chapters 40–55 are concerned.

2. Isaiah 40–55

Archeological and Sociological Data on the Period

It is today generally accepted that Isaiah 40–55 (often referred to as Second Isaiah or Deutero-Isaiah) is the work of an unknown prophet who lived in exile in Babylon toward the end of the reign of Nabonidus (555–539, and probably into the early part of the reign of the Persian king Cyrus, who conquered Babylon in 539). The book is addressed to an audience that is away from Jerusalem and promises a return. Their location is Babylon, whose religious processions are described in chapter 46 and whose fall is anticipated in chapter 47. The freeing of the people will be accomplished by Cyrus, whose victories over the Babylonians are God's work (41:2–4), and who is called God's anointed (45:1), with the task of subduing kings.

That the setting of chapters 40–55 was Babylon of the sixth century has long been recognized, but as long as prophets were believed to be writers inspired by God who could predict events centuries in the future, there was no difficulty in ascribing to the eighth-century Isaiah of Jerusalem these chapters concerned with sixth-century Babylon. In the eighteenth century it was first suggested that these chapters were actually written in the sixth century in Babylon. To some, this is seen as a denial of God's power to inspire prophets to foretell the future. A better way of seeing it is to accept that a prophet spoke God's word to the exiles in sixth-century Babylon, as opposed to an eighth-century prophet writing passages that had no relevance to his own circumstances.

Descriptions of the social setting of Isaiah 40–55 often speak of the condition of the exiles in Babylonia as a whole. There are names of places where the exiles are located in Ezra 2:59 (Tel-melah, Tel-harsha, Cherub, Addan, Immer), and Ezekiel mentions Telabib by the river (probably a canal) Chebar. Reference should also be made to the Murashu documents (see p. 153), which date to about 455–404 and are from an archive of a business in Nippur, some of whose senior members were Jews. They contain information about where Jews were settled in the Nippur region and what trades they practiced. However, it is arguable that what is most pertinent to the background of Isaiah 40–55 is a description of Babylon itself. This great city seems to be the focus of the unknown prophet's concern.

Under Nabopolassar (625–605) and Nebuchadnezzar II (604–562) Babylon was restored as a capital worthy of a great empire. The Euphrates River flowed through its center, dividing the western from the eastern part of the city. Moats from the river enclosed the city, within which were walls and gates. The walls enclosed an area of five square miles. Among Babylon's wonders were the hanging gardens and the Ishtar Gate, through which passed the processional way from the temple of Marduk to the *ahitu* temple (where the symbolic sacred marriage of the king, who represented the god, took place during the *ahitu* festival, celebrated at the New Year). The glazed-brick walls of the processional way portrayed lions over three feet high; bulls and dragons incorporating features of lions, snakes, and eagles decorated the Ishtar Gate.

Any exiles from Judah who visited or lived near Babylon would have been overwhelmed with what they saw. Here was evidence of a mighty nation which had crushed their own nation and of mighty gods superior to their own. Jerusalem must have seemed a tiny irrelevance compared with Babylon's size and magnificence.

But Babylon was destined to remain Babylonian for only a few years. After Nebuchadnezzar's death, his son Amel-Marduk (who appears as Evil-Merodach in the Bible at 2 Kings 25:27–30) reigned only from 561 to 560. Between 560 and 555 (when Nabonidus began to reign) were two kings, the second of whom was assassinated after only two months. Nabonidus (555–539) was a deeply religious man who worshiped the god Sin and rebuilt the temples of Sin in Ur and Haran. His loyalty to Sin brought him into conflict with the priests of Babylonia's holy cities, such as Babylon, Nippur, and Ur. Possibly in obedience to a dream or oracle, Nabonidus spent a long period (possibly ten years) at Taima in northwest Arabia. During this time his son Belshazzar ruled in Babylon. When Nabonidus returned from Taima to Babylon, sometime between 544 and 540, his kingdom was doomed. In 559 Cyrus became ruler of the Persians, who, at that time, were vassals of the Medes. Around 550 Cyrus overcame the Medes and ruled over a vast empire to the north of Babylonia. In 539, after defeating the Babylonian army at Opis, the Persian army entered Babylon without a fight, and Nabonidus was taken prisoner. From being hopeless exiles, the Jews became the recipients of Cyrus's benevolent treatment of captives of Babylonia and were allowed to return home. For the prophet of Isaiah 40–55, this was the work of the God of Israel, the lord of creation and of history.

Literary Structure and Contents of Isaiah 40–55

Isaiah 40–55 begins with the words "Comfort, comfort my people" (40:1). They set the tone of a series of passages from which denunciation and threats of imminent judgment, familiar from the preexilic prophets, are absent. The people are reassured. Their time of punishment is over (40:2); they have not been forgotten or forsaken by God; they must be afraid no longer but must trust in the power and the word of the incomparable lord of creation. This word will accomplish its purpose as surely as rain and snow allow plants to grow from which food is provided (55:10–11). Because there is so much stress on comfort and reassurance, as well as hymnic passages celebrating God's lordship in creation, readers will inevitably be reminded of passages in those Psalms that speak of reassurance to those who seek God when in trouble and that rehearse that God is lord of creation. However, there are no close similarities in actual content between Isaiah 40–55 and these Psalms.

It is not easy to discern a literary structure in these chapters. The work probably begins with a prophet's call when he hears a voice (in the heavenly court?) say, "Cry," and responds, "What shall I cry?" in words possibly deliberately reminiscent of Isa. 6:8–11. The work ends with an assertion of the power of God's word. Some commentators have suggested a change in mood between 40–48 and 49–55, with the second section postdating Cyrus's decree for exiles to return. However, this is not obvious. An important question is whether the so-called Servant Songs (42:1–4, 49:1–6, 50:4–9, 52:13, 53:12) are later additions to the text or are fully integrated into it. The fact that both positions can be advocated indicates that no clear literary scheme is present. This being so, the material will be discussed under some main themes.

God's Superiority over Other Gods   In these chapters, the belief that other gods are at best powerless and at worst nonexistent is strongly articulated. The idol maker's work is ironically sketched in 40:18–20, 41:7, and 44:9–20, emphasizing that idols are no more powerful than their human makers. In 46:1–7, possibly alluding to processions in which the images of gods were solemnly carried on carts through Babylon, a contrast is drawn between gods that need to be carried and God, who carries his people.

God, the Lord of History   The events of Cyrus's victories are seen as God's doing, bringing new things to pass. In a trial scene in 41:1–4, the peoples are summoned to answer who it is who has stirred up someone in the east, "whom victory meets at every step." Not only has God stirred up Cyrus, but he has declared what will happen before it occurs (41:25–9). The peoples and their gods cannot match this (41:21–4). In 44:24–45:7 the coming victories of Cyrus are connected with God's power over nature and human events and with his determination to restore Jerusalem, reform its temple, and rebuild the cities of Judah. A lament over the imminent fate of Babylon, pictured as a virgin daughter, shows how powerless human greatness is in the face of God's action (chap. 47).

God the Creator   These chapters contain the most sublime language about God as creator and lord of nature anywhere in the Old Testament. The nations are like a drop in a bucket, and compared with him "who sits above the circle of the earth, its inhabitants are like grasshoppers" (40:12–17, 21–4). Human questioning of the creator's actions is like the clay questioning a potter (45:9–13). God the creator is the incomparable one, the first and the last (48:12–13).

God's Purposes Embrace the Nations Because God is the incomparable lord of creation and history, his purposes, although centered on Jerusalem, affect other nations. They will recognize that Cyrus's victories are God's doing and will fear (41:5–6), and when Israel is saved, nations will do homage to God's people (45:14–17). They will bring back to God's people those scattered in exile (49:22–6).

Israel's Past Traditions These chapters are noteworthy for their references to Abraham (41:8, 51:2), Sarah (51:2), the Exodus (43:16–17), the wilderness wanderings (43:19–21), and the Flood and deliverance of Noah (54:9–10). The references to Noah and to the wilderness wanderings are quite explicit. For example, for the wilderness wanderings: "they did not thirst when he led them through the deserts; he made water flow for them from the rock" (Isa. 48:21; cf. Exod. 17:2–7, Num. 20:2–13). This reference to older traditions is part of a contrast between old things and new things. Not only is the guarantee of God's promise to restore the people grounded in the new things he is doing, such as the victories of Cyrus, but it is grounded in what he did of old. And the return of the people to Jerusalem will be, in effect, a new Exodus (51:9–11).

The Servant Songs The term "servant" occurs many times in Isaiah 40–55. The servant is Israel (41:8), who is now a worm but will become a threshing sledge (41:14–16) when God vindicates him. He is reassured if he feels that God has forgotten or forsaken him (40:27–31, 49:14–21). He has sinned (42:21–5) but is now forgiven (43:25–8).

In the Servant Songs (42:1–4, 49:1–6, 50:4–9, 52:13–53:12) we have a different picture, which is why scholars have treated these passages separately from the rest of Isaiah 40–55. If the servant is Israel (49:3 is the only direct identification in the Servant Songs), this fact is not prominent. The servant is passive (42:2–3) and has a mission to Israel (49:6) and possibly to the nations (49:6). If he needs reassurance, it is not because he thinks God has forgotten him but because he feels he has labored in vain (49:4). Rather than having been justly punished and now forgiven, the servant has suffered innocently (50:6), and his suffering will bring about forgiveness for others (53:3–6).

Given that the Songs are not together in one section (see above) but are distributed throughout the chapters, it could be argued that the editor or author intended readers to connect the servant in the Songs with the servant elsewhere in the chapters. Israel, it could be argued, is a complete entity, consisting of a faithful remnant that suffered vicariously and the larger body that had been justly punished and that is now reassured. However, even if this is right, we are still justified in asking the identity of the remnant, that is, the group or individual that suffers vicariously.

A widely held view, and the one adopted here, is that the servant in the Songs is the prophet himself and that the Songs describe the prophet's ministry. We can assume, from 50:6, "I gave my back to those who struck me," and 53:4, "we accounted him stricken, struck down by God and afflicted," that the prophet had some physical or other disability and that his mission was badly received. Opinions are divided about the interpretation of 53:9, "they made his grave with the wicked." Does this indicate an actual death (in which case the fourth Song was composed by a disciple after the prophet's death), or should we compare it to one of the psalms (e.g., 22) in which the psalmist came close to death and survived? In either case, the prophet's mission succeeded when his rejection and his suffering brought his detractors to the realization that he was truly God's servant (see 53:4–11). Although an understanding of the servant as an individual provides the most convincing reading, there is also an argument for a corporate identity. Just as the servant prophet was, outwardly, an unlikely vehicle for God's work (see 53:2–3), so the servant people were, in the eyes of the nations and perhaps in their own eyes, an unlikely vehicle for God's work. This was why the people needed constant reassurance of God's concern for them. Thus there is a symmetry between the servant prophet and the servant people, which indicates that "God chose what is foolish in the world to shame the wise" (1 Cor. 1:27).

The way in which the oracles about the servant prophet are woven into those about the servant people is characteristic of Isaiah 40–50 as a whole. The continual juxtaposition of recurring themes brings about a rich and exciting kaleidoscope effect. The chapters should be read through, not in order to discover a plan or structure, but to experience the shifting patterns of its uniquely rich material.

3. Isaiah 56–66

Archeological and Sociological Data on the Period

When we pass from chapters 40–50 to 56–66, we find ourselves in a different world. Gone is the continual interplay between doubt and reassurance and confident and hymnic affirmation in response to the uncertainty of the people. Instead, we have denunciations of leaders, of injustice, and of insincere worship. If the people complain, it is about their present plight, and not that God has abandoned or forgotten them. There are, it must be said, passages of divine reassurance and, at 61:1–4, an oracle that is reminiscent of the Servant Songs of chapters 40–55 and that was used by Jesus in his sermon in Nazareth (Luke 4:16–29). There are also passages similar to those in chapters 40–55 that speak of God's lordship over the universe and history; but the overall impression is quite different from that in chapters 40–55.

The diversity of the material has left scholars divided about whether the chapters are the work of one prophet at one period or of several prophets over a time span of two hundred years. For example, 64:10–11,

> Your holy cities have become a wilderness,
> Zion has become a wilderness,
> Jerusalem a desolation.
> Our holy and beautiful house,
> where our ancestors praised you,
> has been burned by fire,

implies that the temple is still in ruins. A date of 539–520 B.C.E. is therefore suggested. On the other hand, material in chapter 56 would fit well with the situation described in Nehemiah (late fifth century). Foreigners who have joined the community must not say, "The LORD will surely separate me from his people" (56:3). Membership in the community will not depend on birth but on faithfulness to God's covenant (54:6) – a view contrary to that in Ezra and Nehemiah and thus possibly a stand by a prophetic group opposed to the policies of Nehemiah that were hostile to non-Jews.

Even if the chapters are assigned to one prophet and one period, the historical setting they depict is impossible to determine with certainty. Is it a situation similar to that implied in Haggai and Zechariah 1–8, in which a small, dispirited community copes with economic hardship and is ambivalent about rebuilding the temple? Or are those correct who have envisaged a deep split in the community between a priestly, temple-centered group and a prophetic–apocalyptic group whose views come to expression in support of faithful foreigners (56:3–8), in criticism of the temple cult (58:1–9), and in doubting the need for a temple (66:1–4)? Yet another possibility is that these chapters are to be read, not in the context of an assumed social and historical setting, but in the light of Isaiah 1–55, on which these chapters are to some extent a commentary.

In view of so much uncertainty it would be rash to take a strong stand, but it is better to offer some orientation to readers rather than none. Accordingly, the view taken here will be that the chapters make most sense if set in the period between 539 and 520 B.C.E. The prophet has returned from Babylon with a group who had been encouraged by the prophecies of chapters 40–55. The reality that the community faces is different from what was expected. The temple is still in ruins, there is social injustice, and the leadership is ineffective. There is uncertainty about who is entitled to membership in the covenant people. In this situation the prophet affirms his commission to "build up the ancient ruins" (61:4), enjoins the people to practice social justice, and gives hope to the people on the basis of God's sovereign power.

Literary Structure and Contents of Isaiah 56–66

It is generally agreed that the core of chapters 56–66 consists of chapters 60–2, which are words of hope and consolation. They are sandwiched between two communal laments: 59:9–20 and 63:7–64:12. An outer framework is provided by 56:9–59:8 and 65:1–16, 66:1–16, which are oracles of judgment. The scheme can be represented as follows:

56:9–59:8	oracles of judgment
59:9–20	lament
60:1–62:12	oracles of hope
63:7–64:12	lament
65:1–16, 66:1–16	oracles of judgment

Outside this scheme fall 56:1–8 (concerning faithful foreigners), 63:1 6 (God's wrath against the nations), 65:17–25 (vision of a new heaven and earth) and 66:17–24 (a seemingly miscellaneous collection).

Isaiah 60–2 Central to the core is 61:1–4, beginning with the words "The Spirit of the Lord GOD is upon me." Here, the prophet speaks of his commission to set the people free so that the ancient ruins may be rebuilt. The section begins with the encouragement "Arise, shine; for your light has come" (60:1). God will bring back Zion's captives, and the nations will serve God's people. The glory of the people will be restored (60:17–18), and they will possess the Promised Land forever (60:21–2). In chapter 62 Zion is promised that "she" will be called "married" and "sought out." The theme of hope and confidence is strongly maintained throughout.

Isaiah 59:9–20 and 63:7–64:12 The first lament complains that, while the people look for light, all they see is darkness. Is there an allusion here to 60:1? The sins of the community are confessed: transgression of the law, denying God, prevention of justice, lack of truth. Divine action is promised.

The second lament draws upon Israel's past history, including the Exodus and wilderness wanderings (63:11–14). God did mighty things in the past and "no eye has seen any God besides you" (64:4). Will you restrain yourself, and keep quiet, ask the people (64:12)?

Isaiah 56:9–59:8 These oracles of judgment condemn the leaders (described as watchmen and shepherds in 56:9–11) and imply that the sons of sorceresses and adulterers are in charge (57:1–4) and that idolatry is rife (57:4–10). Isa. 58:1–9 condemns fasting that is merely an outward observance, coexisting with injustice and strife. God will hear his people only if they practice social justice. Isa. 59:1–8 condemns the perversion of justice.

Isaiah 65:1–16 and 66:1–16 The first passage condemns religious perversions such as eating swine's flesh and burning incense (presumably to idols: 65:3–4). These unfaithful people will starve and suffer (65:13–16). The second condemnation is also about worship but implies that formally correct worship can also be an abomination when done insincerely: "he who presents a cereal offering [is] like him who offers swine's blood" (66:3). It ends with words of consolation to Zion based on God's indignation against his enemies.

Isaiah 56:1–8, 63:1–6, and 66:18–21 These passages deal, in different ways, with non-Israelites. In the first, there are promises for foreigners who are faithful to God's covenant. The second vividly describes God's judgment on the neighboring nations using the figure of a man treading the grapes of wrath. The third passage speaks of the nations acknowledging God's glory and of giving up the Jewish captives, some of whom God will take for priests and Levites (66:21).

Isaiah 65:17–25 This magnificent passage is a vision of the future when God creates a new heaven and a new earth. All the pain and ambiguity will be removed from creation. The closing verse, very similar to Isa. 11:6–9, reintroduces the vegetarian creation implied in Gen. 1:26–30 – a creation different from that of our experience.

4. The Book of Isaiah as a Whole

The previous three sections have indicated that Isaiah did not reach its present form in three simple stages: composition of 1–39, addition of 40–55, addition of 56–66. We have seen that chapters 1–39 contain much material that is later than "Isaiah of Jerusalem," while 66:24 echoes 1:6–9. Although we can only guess about the actual process, it is arguable that the person or persons who put the book into its present form intended certain themes to run through the whole. Some of these will be identified.

The Daughter of Zion In 1:8 the daughter of Zion is described as an isolated booth in a vineyard and as a besieged city. In 49:11–26, Zion complains that she has been forsaken. Her consolation and restoration are dealt with several times in chapters 56–66 (e.g., 62:1–12, 66:12–14).

Jerusalem, the City of Injustice and Justice Isa. 1:21–8 explores the theme of Jerusalem's lost justice and the restoration of its justice. Establishment of justice is promised at 54:14, and 60:21 states that Zion's people will be righteous.

God's Glory At Isaiah's call or commissioning, he hears the seraphim praising God's glory (6:3). The glory of God will be made clear for all to see (40:5), and the people are promised that "the glory of the LORD has risen upon you" (60:1).

Comfort At 12:1 Israel is told that they will say, "you comforted me." Isa. 40:1 begins with the famous words "Comfort, comfort my people."

Insincere Worship This theme figures largely in Isa. 1:12–20. Sacrifice without social justice is an abomination to God. The theme returns strongly in 56–66. Thus 58:1–9 speaks of the uselessness of fasting without social justice, and 66:3–4 (reminiscent also of 1:10–11) says that formal worship by those who do evil is no better than murder or idolatry.

These points could be elaborated; but it is hoped that they will suffice to show how many of the themes of Isaiah 1–11 run through the whole book and to indicate the value of a thematic reading of the whole.

C. JEREMIAH

1. Archeological and Sociological Data on the Period

Jeremiah 1:2–3 gives the period of Jeremiah's ministry as from the thirteenth year of Josiah (627) to the eleventh year of Zedekiah (587/6). However, chapters 39–44 record Jeremiah's activity in the period after Zedekiah's final capitulation to the Babylonians in 587/6 and describe how Gedaliah was appointed governor of Judah, how he was assassinated, and how Jeremiah was taken unwillingly to Egypt. A final date for Jeremiah's ministry can only be conjectured; 585 is a generally accepted proposal. The period thus delineated covers the reigns of Josiah (640–609), Jehoahaz (609), Jehoiakim (609–598), Jehoiachin (598–560, almost all of which was spent in exile in Babylon), and Zedekiah (597–587/6) and part of the exile (to ca. 585).

When Josiah ascended the throne in Judah at the age of eight, Ashurbanipal, king of Assyria, was in the second half of his long reign (668–627). Ashurbanipal had, by 640, quelled a civil war initiated by his brother, who was king of Babylon, and had dealt with other rebels in an empire that stretched from Egypt, through Syria and Palestine, to the Persian Gulf. He had also established a library in Nineveh, which he stocked with texts collected from temples and scribal schools throughout Babylonia. He claimed to be able to read texts in Sumerian and Akkadian. When he died, probably in 627 (the date is not certain), civil war again broke out between Assyria and Babylonia, which hastened the demise of the Assyrian Empire and saw the emergence of a new Babylonian Empire. Nabopolassar became king of Babylon in 626, and by 616 he had secured Babylon's independence from Assyria and began to threaten Assyria. In 612, in alliance with the Medes, the Babylonians captured and destroyed the Assyrian capital, Nineveh. A last stand was made by the Assyrians at Haran, but they were defeated in 609.

Assyria's decline gave Egypt the chance to expand. The Egyptians had been the allies of Assyria, and in 610–609 they came to the aid of Assyria. Josiah tried to check their progress at the strategic pass commanded by Megiddo, but he was killed by the Egyptian Necho II, who also deposed Josiah's heir, Jehoahaz, replacing him with Jehoiakim. The Egyptians now occupied Palestine and Syria as far as Carchemish, but they were defeated at Carchemish by the Babylonian crown prince Nebuchadnezzar in 605. Soon after this, Nebuchadnezzar succeeded to his father's throne and resumed his campaign against the Egyptians. By 601 he was in control of Syria and Palestine and was fighting on Egypt's frontiers. A battle on these frontiers in 601 was indecisive, perhaps even a defeat for Babylon. This probably encouraged Jehoiakim to rebel, as a result of which the Babylonian army invaded Judah and captured Jerusalem on 16 March 597. Jehoiakim's son Jehoiachin, who had been king for only three months, was deported to Babylon together with nobles and craftsmen. His uncle Zedekiah was placed on the throne by Babylon. When Zedekiah later rebelled, the Babylonians again attacked, and this time they destroyed Jerusalem. The year was 587/6. The Babylonians then appointed a Judahite, Gedaliah, governor of Judah in Mizpah, but he was assassinated by Judahites sympathetic to Egypt. These Judahites fled to Egypt, taking Jeremiah with them.

Against this general background, the specific history of Judah can be sketched as follows. In 627, the likely year of Ashurbanipal's death, Josiah "began to seek the God of David his father" according to 2 Chron. 34:3. He set in motion a reform which involved closing down Judah's high places and destroying the altars of Baal and other offensive cult objects. A different view emerges in 2 Kings 22:3–23:14. According to this account, it was only after the discovery of the "book of the law" in the temple in Josiah's eighteenth year (622) that the reformation began to be carried out. The main difference between the two accounts is that in Chronicles, Josiah initiated the reform, whereas in Kings he merely ordered the repair of the temple and then carried out the reform after the book of the law was found. Whatever the truth, the reign of Josiah saw a religious reformation whose effects have been confirmed by Keel's researches into the iconography of Israel and Judah. Seals bearing the names of men connected with the reform, such as Gemariah son of Shaphan (Jer. 36:10), are aniconic, in contrast with seals earlier in the seventh century, which bear religious symbols (see above p. 92). The reform was supported by the powerful family of Shaphan, with whom the Deuteronomistic groups were also connected.

After the death of Josiah in 609, a split developed between the Shaphan family, who supported Jeremiah and became pro-Babylonian, and the family of Elishama (36:12), who looked to Egypt for help. In the immediate aftermath of Josiah's death, the pro-Egypt party probably gained the upper hand. After the battle of Carchemish and until 597, when the Babylonians first captured Jerusalem, the struggle between the two sides was probably equal. When Zedekiah rebelled against Nebuchadnezzar, the Egypt party gained strength with the prospect of a relief army against the besieging Babylonians (Jer. 37:6–12). Their temporary ascendancy enabled them to arrest and imprison Jeremiah (37:12–38:16).

The final days of Judah have been illumined by the Lachish letters – messages discovered in a guardroom at Lachish and consisting of reports from a lookout post that could evidently observe fire signals from both Lachish and Azekah. They are usually dated immediately before the siege of Lachish in 589 or 588. There are some interesting parallels between Jeremiah and these letters. Letter 3 speaks of a letter that came "through the prophet." Although the prophet's name has not survived in these texts, this letter indicates that prophets were playing an active role in the events of Judah's demise, though whether this was for or against the "establishment" cannot be said. The same letter mentions a commander who has "come down in order to go into

Egypt" (*ANET*, p. 322). This agrees with Jer. 37:3–10 that there was support for Judah from Egypt. Letter 6 contains a complaint that the words of the princes "weaken our hands" (i.e., weaken morale) and "slacken the hands" of others (*ANET*, p. 322). A similar charge is brought against Jeremiah (Jer. 38:4), using the phrase "weakening the hands of the soldiers" (New Revised Standard Version: "discouraging" the soldiers). In letter 4 the observers say that they can no longer see (the fire signals of) Azekah. At Jer. 34:7 we are told that, apart from Jerusalem, only Azekah and Lachish remained of Judah's fortified cities following the Babylonian attack upon Judah. Lachish letter 4 evidently derives from the moment when Azekah, too, fell. When Lachish was captured by the Babylonians, the city was destroyed by fire.

2. The Literary History of Jeremiah

The book of Jeremiah is unique in the Old Testament in giving details about how it was written. Chapter 36 records that Jeremiah dictated all his words that he had spoken against Israel and Judah to Baruch the scribe. This scroll was then burned by King Jehoiakim, after which Jeremiah redictated the words, adding to them further words (36:32). At 51:60 we are told that Jeremiah himself wrote the oracles against Babylon and gave them to Seraiah (apparently Baruch's brother) to read in Babylon when he accompanied Zedekiah thence in the latter's fourth year of his reign (605).

Differing estimates of this information are made by scholars. One view accepts that Jeremiah had learned the scribal arts and that he wrote parts of his book. His link with the scribal family of Shaphan is thus underlined. It also accepts that Baruch played a role in the genesis of the Book of Jeremiah. An opposite view notes the oddity that, if Jeremiah was himself a scribe, he needed the services of Baruch to write down his words. Granted that Jeremiah was debarred from going to the temple (Jer. 36:5–8) and thus needed Baruch to read his words for him in the temple, why did Jeremiah not write the scroll himself and then get Baruch to read it in public? Further, the Seraiah incident creates the difficulty that Jeremiah both publicly condemns Babylon in 605 and then spends the remainder of his ministry proclaiming that God has given Jerusalem into the hands of Nebuchadnezzar, king of Babylon! The conclusion drawn is that the information about Baruch and Seraiah belongs to a period when a Jeremiah legend was being created and that we cannot rely on this material for the facts.

Another matter of dispute concerns the prose speeches in Deuteronomistic style (e.g., chapters 7–8). Are they the work of Jeremiah, and can their Deuteronomistic style be attributed to Jeremiah's close links with Deuteronomistic circles; or are they the work of exilic Deuteronomists who put the book into its present form? The discussion is further complicated by the two versions of Jeremiah: that in the traditional Hebrew text and that in the Greek translation of the third century B.C.E., the Septuagint. The order of the material differs significantly in the two versions. Although the literary questions here are highly complex, it can be said generally that the Greek version numbers the oracles against the nations (chaps. 46–51 in the Hebrew) as chapters 26–32 and that thereafter chapters 26–45 in the Hebrew are chapters 33–51 in the Greek. In addition, the Hebrew text contains many expansionary glosses compared with the Greek. The discovery of fragments of a Hebrew text of Jeremiah at Qumran that support the shorter, Greek readings indicates that the Greek translation was made from a shorter Hebrew text.

The existence of the two versions invites various possible answers about the literary history of Jeremiah. Assuming that the Greek translation was done in Egypt, does this mean that Jeremiah took an almost complete Hebrew text with him to Egypt (or put an almost complete text together while in Egypt), which was then translated into Greek? If, on the other hand, the Deuteronomists compiled the shorter Hebrew text (found at Qumran), at what stage was this taken to Egypt, and where and when was this shorter text expanded into the longer, traditional Hebrew text?

The view that will be taken here is that the shorter Hebrew text was compiled by the Deuteronomists. These included members of the family of Shaphan, who supported Jeremiah. His importance for them was that he both predicted the coming destruction of Jerusalem and believed that the God who was about to punish his people in this way also had a future for them. Preserving Jeremiah's sayings and telling his story were one way of coping with the shock and upheaval of the fall of Jerusalem, and it was necessary for the survival of the people that a sufficiently powerful group could tell this story. No doubt, in the process, the figure of Jeremiah was idealized. Such is the nature of tradition looking back to a hero. But it does not follow that the man Jeremiah is entirely the creation of the tradition. We have various checks upon the tradition such as the seals and the Lachish letters. There is also no reason why Jeremiah should not have dictated some and written some of his oracles, although it is doubtful whether it is possible to recover the exact processes involved. It is common to distinguish three types of material in Jeremiah: (a) oracles and first-person narratives, which may be the work of Jeremiah. These are mainly in chapters 1–26 (but by no means account for everything in these chapters); (b) narratives about Jeremiah in the third person (the work of Baruch?), comprising 19:1–20:6 and chapters 26–9 and 36–45; (c) Deuteronomistic prose speeches, including 7:1–8:3, 11:1–14, 18:1–12, 21:1–10, 22:1–5, 25:1–11, 34:8–22, and chapter 35. Disputed are chapters 30–3, the so-called Book of Comfort. They probably consist of material that derives from Jeremiah but that has been expanded by postexilic editors. It is to be noted that chapters 1–25 are mainly in poetry, and chapters 26–45 are mostly in prose. Whether or not this indicates that the scroll dictated to Baruch included much of chapters 1–25 is debated.

3. The Literary Structure and Contents of Jeremiah

The three main blocks of Jeremiah are chapters 1–25 (mostly in poetry), 26–45 (mostly in prose), and 46–51 (oracles against the nations). Chapter 52 is an appendix. These blocks can be subdivided as follows:

Jeremiah 1:1–10:25

These chapters begin with Jeremiah's call and consist mostly of oracles of coming judgment, which have an intensity hardly matched elsewhere in the Old Testament. The prophet "sees" the ruined city of Jerusalem, "hears" the sounds of its destruction and subsequent despair, and himself experiences a participant's anguish. The passages are often dated to 627–622, in which case the vivid portrayals of Jerusalem's imminent doom would have led to the prophet's becoming totally discredited when no "foe from the north" (Jer. 1:14) materialized. It used to be argued that the foe did come, in the form of Scythian hordes as described by the Greek historian Herodotus; but few experts now believe this claim. It is, of course, also possible that all or much of this material belongs to a later period, such as that following Josiah's death.

Jeremiah 11:1–20:18

This section differs from the preceding one in two ways. First, it contains much more third-person material (e.g., 19:1–20:6), some of which (e.g., 11:1–14, 18:1–12) is probably Deuteronomistic. It also contains the personal laments that have been called the Confessions of Jeremiah (11:18–20, 15:10–21, 17:14–18, 18:19–23, 20:7–18). These Confessions are unique in the prophetic literature in uncovering the personal fears, anguish, and even bitterness of the cost to the speaker of being a servant of God. The most poignant poem is in 20:7–18, where the speaker agonizes over the two unenviable paths, one of which he must take: either speaking in the name of God and thereby evoking derision from his fellow citizens, or keeping quiet and feeling the unspoken word of God like a burning fire shut up in his bones. The poem concludes, in words similar to those in Job 3:3–13, with a curse upon the day that the speaker was born.

Jeremiah 21:1–24:10

The oracles in this section are mostly warnings to officials and leaders in Judah of coming judgment. The material is of various dates: 21:1–10 from the time of Zedekiah (597–587/6, probably toward the end of that period), 22:11–12 probably from soon after Josiah's death and the deposition of his son, 22:24–30 and 24:1–10 probably from soon after Jehoiachin's exile to Babylon in 597.

Jeremiah 25:1–38

This is the conclusion of the first main section (1–25) and is a declaration of impending judgment not only on Judah but also on the surrounding nations and empires.

Jeremiah 26–9 and 34–45

These chapters are a third-person narrative about Jeremiah's work from the beginning of Jehoiakim's reign (609–598) to when Jeremiah was taken to Egypt after the assassination of Gedaliah. The material is not entirely in chronological order, but chapters 37–44 are a consecutive narrative from the last two or three years before the fall of Jerusalem in 587/6. The narrative provides an important supplement to the bare account of the events leading up to the fall of Jerusalem found in 2 Kings 24:18–25:2. The story of the dictating and burning of Jeremiah's prophecies is also recounted here (chap. 36).

Jeremiah 30–3

The so-called Book of Comfort is a mixture of poetry and prose, with emphasis upon hopes of restoration. Some of the oracles (e.g., 30:10–11, 18–22; 31:2–6, 7–9, 10–14) are reminiscent of material in Isaiah 40–55. A famous passage promises that God will make a new covenant with Israel (31:31–4). Scholars are divided as to whether the passage comes from Jeremiah or from exilic editors, but this decision hardly affects the important content of the verses. Chapter 32 is the story of Jeremiah buying a field in Anathoth in order to demonstrate, at the time of the siege of Jerusalem (588–587), that "houses and fields and vineyards will again be bought in this land" (32:15).

These chapters are in an important position in the book as a whole. There are earlier promises of restoration (e.g., 16:14–15), but chapters 30–3 set the grim story of the following chapters in a context of hope. The God who is about to execute judgment is the God who had already promised to restore.

Jeremiah 46–51

Oracles against the nations are directed against Egypt (46:1–12, 13–24), Philistia (47:1–7), Moab (48:1–47), Ammon (49:1–6), Edom (49:7–22), Damascus (49:23–7), Kedar (inhabitants of the desert, 49:28–33), Elam (49:34–9), and Babylon (50:1–51:58). Whatever the exact circumstances that occasioned each of these oracles, their collection together and placement here reinforce the point that the God who destroyed Jerusalem is the sovereign Lord of the nations, not a local God. Contained within these oracles of judgment are promises of restoration (e.g., 48:47, 49:39).

Jeremiah 51:59–52:34

The appendix to Jeremiah repeats much of 2 Kings 24:18–25:30 and is an account of the destruction of Jerusalem (already given at 39:1–10), ending with the release of Jehoiachin from captivity in 560.

D. EZEKIEL

1. Archeological and Sociological Data on the Period

At first sight, the background to the Book of Ezekiel will seem to be the same as that to Isaiah 40–55. Like the unnamed prophet of those chapters, Ezekiel was an exile in Babylonia, living with a community of fellow exiles. His location, at or near the river or canal Chebar (Ezek. 1:1), cannot be identified. However, Ezekiel's circumstances and background differed markedly from those of "Second Isaiah," apart from the fact that Ezekiel's prophecies probably ended

---

THE DIASPORA

DURING NO PERIOD OF Israelite or Jewish history have all Jews or their predecessors been resident in Palestine. During the great expansion of the united monarchy, David and Solomon sent Israelites to various parts of Asia and Africa as government colonists or private tradesmen. Some of them undoubtedly settled in those places permanently. A minor deportation of prisoners of war may have taken place during the invasion of Pharaoh Shishak/Sheshonq (ca. 918 B.C.E.). But, of course, the greatest cause of dispersion was the series of exiles imposed on Israel and Judah by the Assyrian and Babylonian Empires.

The Hebrew term for these most important dispersions is *galut,* "exile." In Greek translations of the Hebrew scriptures, this term and several similar nouns referring to Jewish people living outside the borders of the land of Israel were rendered by the word *diaspora,* which means "scattering." Following the destruction of Jerusalem in 586 B.C.E., the Diaspora became one of the distinguishing features of the Jewish people. The Diaspora grew geographically and numerically as

people were banished from Israelite Palestine. Political and religious pressures there and economic prospects emerging in other, more prosperous countries added to the Diaspora's extent and population.

Babylon was the most heavily settled Jewish center outside Palestine during the Persian and Greco-Roman periods. It was there that the Bible was first redacted and where the antecedents of synagogue Judaism appeared. The long-term importance of this Diaspora for Judaism is evident in the fact that the successors to the great Palestinian sages (Tannaim) were the Babylonian Amoraim ("interpreters"; lit. "speakers"). The Babylonian Talmud is today considered the authoritative interpretation of the Jewish legal tradition preserved in the Mishnah. Next in importance was the dispersion in Egypt, an early (sixth century B.C.E.) and well-settled center of Jewish population. By the beginning of the common era, Philo Judaeus reported that the Jewish population of all Egypt, from the border with Libya on the east and with Ethiopia to the south, was "no less than one million." Two of Alexandria's five districts were predominantly Jewish. At the

height of the Greco-Roman period the Diaspora reached to such far-flung places as Phoenicia, Syria, Pamphylia, Bithynia, Greece, Italy, Cyprus, Crete, Egypt, and almost every country west of the Euphrates.

The Diaspora brought Jews into close contact with Greco-Roman civilization, which thus considerably influenced the development of Judaism during the hellenistic period. Where their numbers permitted, the Jews of the Diaspora played a role in the political life of their adopted countries. They were accorded religious tolerance in most cases, permitted to organize their own communities, and allowed to maintain contact with the political–religious center in Jerusalem. Most scholars suggest that the Diaspora gave birth to the Jewish synagogue and was responsible for the translation of the Hebrew scriptures into Greek. During the first centuries of the common era, the Diaspora facilitated the early and rapid spread of Christianity. It provided a network of people who were familiar with the scriptures and who shared the messianic expectations that the Christian missionaries claimed had been fulfilled by Jesus of Nazareth.

---

some forty years before those of Isaiah 40–55. Whereas the unnamed prophet was probably an unrecognized, or even excluded person (see above p. 170), Ezekiel belonged to a priestly family, was exiled in 597 along with the noble, skilled, and influential people, and was probably regularly consulted by the elders of his community (Ezek. 8:1). It is also possible that he conducted, or spoke in the context of, worship in his community.

It has been suggested that Ezekiel's community numbered about 3,000 people, many of whom had supported Jehoiakim's rebellion against Nebuchadnezzar. If this is so (although it is legitimate to question whether the Babylonians would have concentrated, rather than dispersed, such rebels), there would have been lively hopes among Ezekiel's fellow exiles that their fortunes would soon be reversed and that Egypt would defeat Nebuchadnezzar. Such a situation would explain the number of anti-Egyptian oracles in Ezekiel since the prophet believed that no human agency or nation could save Jerusalem from destruction.

A unique feature of the book is the description of worship in the Jerusalem temple of the period (e.g., Ezek. 8). The description concentrates upon abominations which one would not have expected to find: the "image of jealousy" north of the altar gate (8:5), portrayals of "creeping things, and loathsome animals," on a wall (8:10), women weeping for Tammuz (8:14), and men worshiping the sun (8:16). Is this an exaggerated picture of the sum of Judah's provocations against God, or is it in some sense an accurate reflection of what was happening in the temple between 597 and 587? If it is the latter, it probably indicates that Josiah's religious reformation in 622 had hardly touched the "folk religion" of the ordinary people. It was a "top–down" reformation, which, by suppressing local shrines, meant that Jerusalem became a center into which popular religion was introduced after Josiah's death. At the very least, the worship of the sun can be ascribed to the continuance of Egyptian influence, which was reemphasized after Necho II defeated and killed Josiah in 609.

Keel's research has shed light on Ezekiel's visions of God in chapters 1 and 10. In particular, two pieces of artwork found in Arad and Bethlehem show a God in human form shrouded by a lotus plant, in concentric circles, giving a chariot-wheel effect. Ezekiel's visions clearly owed something to the iconography of his times; and his apparent knowledge of the mythology of foreign nations (as in the oracles against Tyre and Egypt in chaps. 28 and 31) shows how, among intellectual circles, such mythologies were learned as part of one's education.

2. The Literary History, Structure, and Contents of Ezekiel

Ezekiel is unique in the Old Testament in the number of dated oracles that it contains. From their position in the book, much can be deduced about the book's literary history. The following information is based upon Bernhard Lang.

Reference	Date in Ezekiel (day/mo.-yr.)	Modern date (day/mo.-yr.)	Subject
1:1	5/4/30	24/7/568	opening verse
1:2	5/?/5	593/2	opening vision
8:1	5/6/6	17/9/592	address to elders
20:1	10/5/7	14/8/591	address to elders
24:1	10/10/9	5/1/587	against Jerusalem (see 2 Kings 25:1; Ezek. 24:1 is dated to the beginning of the siege of Jerusalem in the reign of Zedekiah)
26:1	1?/11 (Septuagint: 12)	586 or 585	against Tyre, which was besieged ca. 585–572
29:1	12/10/10	7/1/587	against Egypt
29.17	1/1/27	26/4/571	against Tyre
30.20	7/1/11	29/4/587	against Egypt
31:1	1/3/11	21/6/587	against Egypt
32:1	1/12/12 (Septuagint: 11)	3/3/586 or 585	against Egypt (after the fall of Jerusalem but before the news reached Ezekiel)
32:17	15/?/12	27/4/586–17/3/585	against Egypt
33:21	5/10/12	8/1/585	against Israel (immediately after receiving news of Jerusalem's fall)
40:1	10/1/25	28/4/573	vision of restored temple

A glance at the above shows that the oracles are not in exact chronological order. In particular, the two oracles against Tyre (26:1 | ff, 29:17) disturb the order and indicate that the oracles against foreign nations were artificially placed together, as we also find in Isaiah (13–23) and Jeremiah (46–51). This suggests that the book reached its final form at the hands of editors.

It is also generally agreed that chapters 38–9 and parts of chapters 43–4, which give details about sacrifices, are later additions. The arguments about chapters 43–4 are too complex to be addressed here. Regarding chapters 38–9, it can be said that these chapters (which break the connection between 37:28 and 40:1) date from a period when the hopes of restoration expressed in Ezekiel had not been fully realized. They envisage a future period of conflict when Gog of the land of Magog will be brought by God against the Israelites reassembled in their land (38:8). The attack of Gog against Israel will cause God to defend his people, and in so doing he will manifest his glory among the nations (39:21). God's people will also recognize his power and understand his purposes (39:25–9).

The remainder of the book can be understood generally according to the following scheme:

Section A	Transition	Section B
(a) 1–3: The call of the prophet		(a) 33:1–20, 21–33 The call of the prophet
(b) 4–7, 12–15; prophecies of judgment against Jerusalem and its leaders	(d) 16–19 Parables of judgment and hope	(b) 34–7; prophecies of judgment against and hope for Jerusalem and its leaders.
(c) 8–11; visions in Jerusalem of its abominations; the "glory" departs (11:22–3)	(e) 20–32: prophecies of judgment against Jerusalem, Samaria, Ammon, Moab, Edom, Philistia, Egypt.	(c) 40–8; visions in Jerusalem of its restoration; the "glory" returns (43:1–5)

This scheme is meant to help the modern reader but it is not claimed that the editor of Ezekiel intended this structure. On the other hand, it is not entirely arbitrary. The departure of the "glory" (God's presence) from the temple and city at the end of chapter 11 is balanced by its return at 43:1–5. Also, the gathering together of the oracles against the nations into chapters 20–32 yields the result that after the renewal of the call to the prophet in chapter 33, the final section (34–7, 40–8) is able to concentrate on the theme of the restoration of Jerusalem uncluttered by oracles against foreign nations.

It is also noteworthy that there are few oracles of hope (the exceptions are in chaps. 16–19) in Ezekiel until after he has received the news of Jerusalem's fall (3:21–2). From that point onward, oracles of hope and restoration abound. It is reasonable to assume that this corresponds to Ezekiel's actual ministry: as long as people hoped that a foreign power (Egypt, in particular) would defeat Babylon and restore them to Jerusalem, Ezekiel's oracles against foreign powers were insistent. (Some against Tyre were given much later, of course; see 26:1 | ff, 29:17 | ff.). From the time that the destruction of the temple was known, Ezekiel began to speak predominantly in terms of hope. It was no longer possible to trust in human intervention to save Jerusalem. Restoration could now come only from God.

The literature of Ezekiel has several unique features. The prophet's strange actions in lying on his side for long periods (4:1–17), shaving his head and beard and burning some of his hair (5:1–3), and his dumbness (3:26–7, 24:25–7, 33:21–2) have led to theories ranging from postulating illnesses such as catalepsy to the proposal that he was indulging in street theater. His visionary shifts from Babylon to Jerusalem and back have led some to argue that some of his ministry was actually spent in Jerusalem. His visions of the glory of God in the form of a chariot supporting a throne are remarkable in their own right.

EZEKIEL AT DURA-EUROPOS

IN 1932 AN EXTRAORDInarily well preserved synagogue dating to the third century C.E. was uncovered at Salahiyeh in Syria. This site on the upper Euphrates River was identified as the ancient city of Dura-Europos. Dura-Europos was established by the Seleucid ruler Nicator I about 300 B.C.E. Although it was dominated by several different invading armies, the city retained its hellenistic character until it fell to the Sassanids in 256 C.E. Only a few years before the city's destruction, at least two artists decorated the upper story of a small synagogue with two-tiered panels of exquisite paintings depicting mostly biblical scenes. These scenes were often supplemented with details drawn from the rich world of Jewish homiletical tradition, some of which has been preserved in the Talmud and in early Christian works that have incorporated or have been influenced by Jewish tradition. These paintings also used figures, forms, and symbols from the Greek and Persian worlds. Scenes from the life of Moses, Elijah, and David are combined with pictures of Greek gods and goddesses to present a Jewish–hellenistic fusion of Eastern and Western art.

Along the synagogue's northern wall on the lower panel is the longest painting. It depicts a pageant of events from the life of the prophet Ezekiel. He is presented in three great scenes that are separated by two large mountains. The painting's design is read left to right, away from the west wall, where it adjoins the scene of the infancy of Moses. At the painting's extreme left is a tree drawn in a familiar classical style. To the tree's right is a row of bushy-haired, lightly bearded figures in different poses but in identical dress. Clad in Persian costume, the figures wear white soft boots, reddish brown smocks covered with elaborate embroidery, and green trousers. All three men have been taken to be the prophet Ezekiel. At their feet are a number of human heads, arms, and legs. A heavenly hand lifts the first Ezekiel by the hair of his head into this place of human fragments. The artist thus portrays God bringing Ezekiel into the famous valley of dry bones (Ezek. 37) by the means described in an earlier vision (Ezek. 8:2–3). The second Ezekiel is prophesying to the bones, and the third points to a strange mountain beside him.

A second mountain, topped by a fruit tree, divides this scene of heavenly triumph from the final panel, which depicts the legendary execution of Ezekiel. The panel shows a figure in Persian clothing who has been dragged away from an altar by the hair of his head. He stands at the mercy of a royal military figure by whom he is about to be beheaded. Jewish–Christian tradition suggests that perhaps Ezekiel was martyred at the request of the head of the Babylonian Jewish community, a descendant of the Davidic line, whose apostasy the prophet had continually upbraided.

The Dura-Europos Ezekiel cycle was constructed from various details as an original series of scenes from the prophet's career. Mountains, for example, repeatedly appear in Ezekiel's prophecies (e.g., Ezek. 6:2–7, 32:5, 35:1–8, 36:1–7, 38:20, 40:40–1). The Dura-Europos paintings present selections from the legend and text of Ezekiel according to an established iconographic tradition. Little other tradition about Ezekiel himself has survived, so interpreting these paintings is difficult. Nonetheless, the paintings probably reflect the prophet's ascent into the heavenly regions (the central panel), followed by a return to the sorry world of earthly reality and death, which has been cast in terms of Ezekiel's description of the valley of dry bones. This cycle of earth, heavenly glory, and then return to earth, though ostensibly inspired by the prophet's life, was also a prominent theme in some strands of early Jewish mysticism. To the person or persons who designed the wall, Ezekiel seems to have been a great mystic guide of the soul, able to lead humankind to the highest perfection. In any case, the Ezekiel cycle is eloquent testimony to the continuing vitality of Old Testament traditions toward the end of the Greco-Roman era both in Judaism and in Christianity, which shared many of the same interpretations and iconographic conventions.

These third-century C.E. reconstructed frescoes are from the ancient synagogue at Dura Europos. The niche to the left is where the Torah scroll was displayed during worship.

Some of his "parables" are also remarkable. In chapter 16 Jerusalem is likened to an abandoned female baby, whom God saved from death and married when she was physically ready for love. Her subsequent harlotries are an illustration of Israel's turning to other gods; but the thought and imagery are daring. Again, the vision of the valley of dry bones in chapter 37 is a powerful statement of God's power to bring hope to the most impossible situation.

Another famous passage is at 28:11–19, an oracle against Tyre in which its king is said to have been placed in the Garden of Eden and to have been blameless until pride and violence caused a guardian cherub to drive him from the Garden. The similarities with Genesis 3 have long been noted, together with speculation about the literary or other dependence of the two passages, if any.

When Ezekiel is compared with his younger fellow prophet of the Babylonian exile, Second Isaiah, the diversity of Old Testament prophecy becomes apparent. The one is a respected priestly visionary given to strange behavior and insistent that there is no hope of restoration apart from God. The other is a prophet of consolation, probably persecuted and despised in his lifetime and recognized as God's servant only by way of hindsight.

E. HOSEA

1. Archeological and Sociological Data on the Period

According to Hosea 1:1 the prophet of that name was active in the reigns of Uzziah, Jotham, Ahaz, and Hezekiah (kings of Judah) and Jeroboam II (king of Israel). The Judahite kings reigned from around 767 to 698, and Jeroboam's reign was from 782 to 747. This overall period of more than eighty years is obviously far too long. In fact, scholars are generally agreed that echoes can be found in Hosea of the anti-Assyrian coalition between Israel and Damascus in 733/2 and its aftermath (Hos. 5:8–14), and that there are possible references to the period from the death of Tiglath-pileser III (727) and the fall of Samaria (722/1), when there was hope of help from Egypt (11:5, 12:1 [Hebrew, 12:2]). The oracles of chapters such as 2 and 4:4–5:7 are placed in the period before the anti-Assyrian coalition of 733; but it is hard to say how much earlier than this Hosea's work began. On the evidence of the book apart from 1:1, Hosea's period of activity was thus roughly 750–720 B.C.E.

Hosea is a northern prophet concerned almost entirely with the northern tribes that constituted the kingdom of Israel after Jeroboam's revolt against Rehoboam in 930. If he began his work in Jeroboam II's reign, it was in a time of peace and prosperity. According to 2 Kings 14:28, Jeroboam greatly extended the boundaries of the northern kingdom, from which we can infer that the northern kingdom Israel enjoyed increased trade, economic activity, and political influence. If this led to an increase in prosperity for the powerful and oppression for the weak, this is hardly reflected in Hosea. The emphasis is overwhelmingly religious. Hosea (4:2) complains of the occurrence of "swearing, lying, killing, stealing, and committing adultery" (words that may reflect a knowledge of the Ten Commandments), but these words are not typical of the book. The overwhelming emphasis is upon Israel's *religious* apostasy: its desertion of Yahweh and its predilection for the Canaanite god Baal.

Keel argues, on the basis of his iconographical research, that in the Israel of this period Yahweh and Baal fulfilled for the people identical functions and that they were interchangeable. This does not mean that they were identical theologically. Keel stoutly maintains that, whereas Baal had a female consort, Yahweh did not. The point is that whatever the prophetic guardians of "pure" faith in Yahweh maintained, the religion of Israel's sanctuaries was syncretistic. No doubt this was encouraged by the ruling dynasty, as it led to a legitimizing of the use and abuse of power by the Israelite kings. In this regard, there is a link between Hosea and the guilds led by Elijah and Elisha in the ninth century B.C.E. They, too, were opposed to the official encouragement of the cult of Baal and waged a primarily religious war with political

> ## KNOWLEDGE OF GOD
>
> THE CONCEPT OF THE "knowledge of God" (*da'at 'elohim*) occurs throughout the prophetic literature of the Hebrew Bible. This phrase is particularly important in the Book of Hosea (e.g., "knowledge of God is better than sacrifice," Hos. 6:6). In theological terms, the Hebrew Bible presents the knowledge of God as being derived from momentous historical events through which God has been revealed to the chosen people Israel. Individuals display this knowledge of God by proper conduct in everyday life – doing justice, working righteousness, judging the case of the poor and needy, remaining upright of heart, trusting in divine wisdom. In some passages, knowledge of God appears parallel to the concept of "fear of Yahweh" as a description of authentic Israelite religion (Isa. 11:2, Jer. 22:16).
>
> Hosea identifies the knowledge of God as a constitutive element of the covenant faith. The term appears alongside the central concepts of faithfulness (*'emeth*) and mercy (*hesed*). In this context, knowledge of God refers to an understanding of the ways of God as revealed in the covenant. When the Israelite community did not possess the knowledge of God (i.e., when they did not uphold the covenant), there was religious decline and apostasy. Theft, adultery, murder, perjury, and blasphemy were the inevitable accompaniments leading to the people's eventual destruction (Hos. 4:1–6).
>
> Some passages suggest that the absence of knowledge of God can be the result of inexperience (Gen. 17). Other texts imply that outside the community of Israel knowledge of God did not exist. The gentiles had no knowledge of God and consequently could not enjoy a right relation to Yahweh (Ps. 79:6, Jer. 10:25). However, the technical term *da'at 'elohim* has a less exclusive connotation. *'Elohim*, the creator, is God of the whole world.

weapons. On the other hand, Hos. 1:4–5 seems to condemn the revolution of Jehu, who was anointed by one of Elisha's servants in order to destroy the dynasty of Omri and Ahab (2 Kings 9), a dynasty that favored Baal over Yahweh.

An interesting feature of Hosea is its references to the ancient traditions of Israel. Possible allusions to the Ten Commandments have been mentioned already. There are allusions to Exodus traditions (2:15; 8:13; 9:3, 10; 11:1–4; 12:9, 13–14; 13:4–5) as well as to the story of the Israelite hero Jacob (12:3–4, 12:12). Such allusions support the theory that, in prophetic circles in Israel, the Jacob and Exodus traditions were known or being composed prior to their being brought south after the fall of Samaria in 722/1.

2. The Literary Structure and Contents of Hosea

The book can be divided into the following sections: (*a*) 1–3, (*b*) 4:1–5:7, (*c*) 5:8–6:6, (*d*) 6:7–9:9, (*e*) 9:10–13:16 (Hebrew, 14:1), and (*f*) 14:1–9 (Hebrew, 14:2–10).

Hosea 1–3

Chapters 1–3 begin with God's command to Hosea to "take a wife of whoredom and have children of whoredom" (1:2). The prophet married Gomer, and two sons and a daughter are born to them, each of whom is given a symbolic name. The elder son's name, Jezreel, is a sign that God will soon bring to an end the dynasty of Jehu, whose descendant Jeroboam II is. The connection between Jehu's dynasty and the name Jezreel is that it was in the city of Jezreel that Jehu received the heads of seventy sons of king Ahab slaughtered on Jehu's instructions (see 2 Kings 10:1–11). The daughter is named Lo-ruhamah, which means in Hebrew "not pitied." The younger son is named Lo-ammi, meaning "not my people." The whole passage (1:2–9), with its declaration that God will destroy his people without pity, is followed (vv. 10–11; Hebrew, 2:1–2) by a prophecy of the restoration of Israel and Judah.

Chapter 2 (Hebrew, 2:3–25) is a long poem that is difficult to summarize. A speaker in the first person commands at least two people (the Hebrew imperative form used is for two or more people) to tell their brother Ammi (my people) and sister Ruhamah (pitied) that they must plead with their mother, telling her that the speaker is no longer her husband. She has committed adultery and he will expose and punish not only her but her children. Further, she will be punished when she tries to pursue her lovers. There is then a tender passage in which the speaker promises to woo back his rejected wife so that their relationship will be as it was when she was young, when she came out of the land of Egypt. These verses indicate that the speaker is God and that the wife is the people of Israel and that the whole passage is contrasting Israel's faithfulness to God in the wilderness after the Exodus with its unfaithfulness after it enters the land of Canaan. (The wilderness wanderings stories in the Books of Exodus and Numbers mostly stress Israel's unfaithfulness during the wilderness period!) Chapter 2 ends with a promise of future blessing when Israel will be completely faithful to God.

In chapter 3 the prophet is commanded to "love a woman who has a lover and is an adulteress" (3:1). The prophet buys a woman for fifteen pieces of silver plus measures of grain and wine. He tells her that she is to have no intercourse with any man, including him. This symbolizes a period when Israel will have no king or sacrifices.

These very difficult chapters have given rise to a number of interpretations, of which the best known is as follows. The chapters reflect Hosea's personal experience when he married a woman who became a prostitute and was sold into slavery. Hosea bought her back from slavery and made her his wife once more. Another view is that when Hosea was commanded to marry "a wife of whoredom," he and his wife and children were to act out a dramatization in which they took the parts of a prostitute and her children. Many interpreters have asked whether God is likely to have ordered the prophet to do an immoral act such as marrying a prostitute (1:2) or loving an adulteress (3:1). Another difficult question is whether the prostitute and the adulteress are the same woman or two different women. Given these uncertainties, it is better not to speculate about whether the chapter reflects Hosea's personal experiences. What is clear is that chapter 2 uses the imagery of prostitution and divorce to describe Israel's apostasy from God and his determination to win his people back to faithfulness after he has punished them.

Hosea 4:1–5:7

This material is a series of oracles of judgment in the form of legal accusations. God has a controversy with his people (4:1), and he is the one who will press the case (4:4). Among those singled out for condemnation are the leaders: the priests (4:4–6, 5:1) and the king (5:1).

Hosea 5:8–6:6

This section is usually connected with the Syro-Ephraimite war of 733/2, when Judah appealed to the Assyrian king, Tiglath-pileser III, for help when threatened by Israel and Damascus.

Hosea 6:7–9:9

Here Hosea denounces the corruptions of human leadership and of false worship. Wickedness gladdens the king and his nobles (7:3), and the present kings are not approved by God (8:4). The nation seeks help from foreign countries (7:11, 8:9–10) and false gods (7:16, 8:5b). Not only do the people not seek God, but they reject the prophets whose task it is to warn the people of the consequences of their deeds (9:7–9).

Hosea 9:10–13:16

In this section we have the allusions to Israel's patriarchal and Exodus traditions. Those traditions are a continuous story of Israel's backslidings in spite of being freed from slavery and guided through the desert to the accompaniment of signs and wonders. It provides rich allusions for this part of Hosea, central to which is 11:1–9, in which God declares that he cannot and will not abandon the child he called out of Egypt, in spite of that child's apostasies.

Hosea 14:1–9

Hosea ends with a plea to the people to return to God, even to the point of providing words with which to seek God's mercy (14:2–3). An assurance that mercy will be forthcoming is concluded with a verse in the "wisdom" tradition of Israel (14:9).

F. JOEL

The Book of Joel contains no material that enables it to be linked with any known event or to be placed within any certain historical or social context. It is not clear whether the book was written mainly by one author, whether there were two authors from different periods whose work was joined together, or whether a second, later author composed the second half of the book in deliberate response to the first part. In view of these uncertainties, it is not possible to treat separately the matters of historical and social setting, literary history, and structure and content.

The division of material in Joel into chapters and verses differs in the Greek translation from that in the traditional Hebrew text. The differences are as follows:

Hebrew chap. 1 equals Greek chap. 1
Hebrew chap. 2 equals Greek 2:1–27
Hebrew chap. 3 equals Greek 2:28–32
Hebrew chap. 4 equals Greek chap. 3

The standard English translations follow the Greek numbering, which will be used here.

Joel can be divided into two parts: 1:2–17 and 2:20–3:21. Verses 2:18–19 form the bridge between the two parts. The overwhelming message of part one is of imminent disaster, which repentance on the part of the people may possibly avert. After the opening verse, which names, but does not date, Joel, there is a devastating account of the effects upon the land of a plague of locusts (1:4–7). The effects are so comprehensive that not only are crops, vines, and fruits ruined, but even the temple service has been deprived of cereal and drink offerings (1:8–13). The situation demands a national fast and a solemn assembly (1:14). Further, it heralds the "Day of Yahweh" – that awesome day when God will bring his armies to execute justice on his people (1:15–20).

Chapter 2 warns the people of the approach of the Day of Yahweh and pictures its arrival in apocalyptic language. There will be blackness and thick darkness, the enemy will be preceded by fire, the earth will tremble, and the sun and moon will be darkened (2:1–11). This grim prospect is the occasion for a call for repentance, accompanied by fasting and weeping, led by the priests in the temple. God, who is gracious and merciful, must be implored to spare his people (2:12–17).

Devastating plagues of locusts were experienced in Palestine from time to time, even up to the present century. We cannot date the one that Joel saw. In Joel 2, the imagery of the advancing army of locusts is used to describe the advent of the armies that God will summon to be part of his "Day."

It is understandable that older commentators identified this imminent army with the Syrians of the ninth century or with the Assyrians and Babylonians of the eighth and seventh centuries respectively. However, the following considerations suggest a postexilic date: there is no mention of a king, the prophet's attitude to the priests and the temple cult is positive (in contrast to the severe criticisms of the preexilic prophets), and the material would fit well with a small community dominated by the temple. It may therefore be dated between 450 and 400 B.C.E.

The bridge to part two is a declaration that God responded to his people's prayers and answered them favorably (2:18–19). The remainder of the book, in contrast to part one, is characterized by consolation for God's people. Even the Day of Yahweh is transformed from a day of judgment for God's people to a day of deliverance (3:9–21). Whereas part one speaks of the devastation caused by the locusts, 2:23–7 speaks of the abundance of produce which the land and the people will enjoy. Joel 2:28–9 is the famous passage about the outpouring of the Spirit of God that is quoted in Peter's speech in Acts 2:17–21:

Then afterward
I will pour out my spirit on all flesh.

A reference in 3:4–8 might date this part of the book. Tyre, Sidon, and Philistia are accused of selling God's people to the Greeks. This could date the material to the late fourth century, but many scholars see 3:4–8 as an even later addition to Joel.

A feature of part two is its apparent allusions to other prophecies. The words

> beat your plowshares into swords
> and your pruning hooks into spears   (3:10)

immediately recall Mic. 4:3 and Isa. 2:4. But there are other allusions too. "The LORD roars from Zion" (3:16) recalls Amos 1:2 while 3:18 seems to combine themes from the closing verses of Amos (9:13) and Ezekiel (47:1–12). For this reason, Joel has been called a *Schriftprofet*, that is, one who is essentially a user and interpreter of earlier prophecies.

In spite of its complicated history of composition, the book can be seen as a literary unity. The fears of coming judgment engendered by the plague of locusts are transformed into hope for Jerusalem and Judah. Because God is faithful to his people, their want will be turned to plenty, and the judgment they fear will become their vindication in the eyes of their enemies.

G.   AMOS

1.   Archeological and Sociological Data on the Period

According to Amos 1:1, Amos was active during the reigns of Uzziah of Judah (ca. 767–739) and Jeroboam II of the northern kingdom of Israel (782–747). This places him in the first half of the eighth century and before the fall of Israel's capital, Samaria, in 722/1. There is also a reference to an earthquake in 1:1, and Amos is said to have spoken two years, or during the two years, before this event. Evidence of a massive earthquake has been found at Hazor; but this does not help us to date Amos, because the archeologists have used Amos to date the earthquake!

Archeological investigations in the northern kingdom of Israel, where Amos performed most of his ministry, indicate that the first part of the eighth century witnessed little, if any, building activity. This was because important works had been undertaken in the ninth century in the major cities, which concentrated on the provision of massive fortifications. These fortifications served the cities through the eighth century, until the Assyrians began to conquer the land in about 734. In the case of Hazor, where the earthquake caused buildings to collapse, they seem to have been rebuilt on the same lines as before; and we can assume that this was also true of other cities affected by the tremor.

According to 2 Kings 14:25 Jeroboam II "restored the border of Israel from Lebohamath as far as the Sea of the Arabah"; verse 28 adds that he recovered Damascus and Hamath for Israel. These claims imply an enormous extension of Israelite power to the north, and most commentators assume that the claims are exaggerated, or employ ideal boundary terminology. The credibility of the passage is not helped by verse 26, which describes the bitter distress of Israel and that "there was no one left, bond or free, and no one to help Israel." How this is to be squared with the usual view of Israel at this time, as enjoying unparalleled prosperity, is hard to see. However, even if these details are exaggerated, the summary of Jeroboam's reign insists that the king fought his enemies, and if we take this seriously, it affects our estimate of the sociology of the period, since war entailed conscription of labor and the levying of taxes to support men who were not agriculturally productive.

Among the archeological discoveries of this period are the Samaria ostraca, which are accounting records of the receipt of jars of oil or wine sent to Samaria from a number of towns mostly between four and eight miles from Samaria. They are usually dated in the reign of Jeroboam II and are believed to indicate, not a nation-wide system of taxation, but rather sources of wine and oil that were used to supply the needs of the capital city. No doubt these supplies were a kind of local tax which supported the luxurious lifestyle of those who lived in Samaria, a lifestyle that Amos condemned (4:1).

A disputed point among experts is whether Jeroboam's reign was one in which general prosperity enabled the rich to grow more powerful at the expense of the poor or whether it was a period of declining wealth in which the attempts of the rich to retain their standard of living bore heavily on the poor, causing them greater hardship. Whatever the truth, the poor certainly suffered, and this is reflected in passages such as 2:6–8 and 8:4–6. These passages indicate that justice was being perverted, that pledges taken in lieu of loans were not being properly honored, and that there was dishonest trading. Yet it must be noted that these accusations are general rather than specific and give no information that would allow us to reconstruct the sociology of the period.

SAMARIA

SAMARIA WAS THE CAPITAL of the northern kingdom of Israel. Although archeological excavations at the site have shown some signs of very ancient occupation, the city owed its construction primarily to the collapse of the united monarchy following the death of Solomon. David's capital, Jerusalem, was retained by rulers of the southern territory of Judah, and the kings of Israel needed an administrative center of their own further north.

The city was built during the Early Iron II period (900–800 B.C.E.) during the reigns of Omri and Ahab. Located on a hill over-looking fertile valleys, Samaria was from the outset a well-designed and beautiful city. It became a showcase for the wealth and power of Israel. Most of the city's remains have been destroyed by quarrying and later construction. However, archeologists have found more than five hundred fragments of ivory inlay near the city's summit, where the royal palaces were located (cf. the reference to Ahab's house of ivory in 1 Kings 22:39). The city's riches drew the wrath of prophets like Amos, who protested against rulers amassing wealth at the expense of the ruled (Amos 6:4 ff.).

Samaria survived revolution, assassination, and prophetic ire – but not the Assyrian army. The city fell in 722/1 B.C.E. and was burned to the ground by the army of Sargon II. However, it took the powerful Assyrian military machine three hard-fought years to capture Samaria, eloquent testimony to the effectiveness of the city's strong three-ringed defense system. The people of Israel were deported, in line with the Assyrian policy of transplanting the populations of captured territories in order to prevent future nationalistic revolt. The northern kingdom of Israel disappeared from history.

The city of Samaria nevertheless outlasted the kingdom of Israel. Samaria was resettled by Assyrian captives from Babylon, Ananth, Ava, and Hamath. These new Samaritans gradually adopted a modified form of Yahwism and worshiped at a temple on Mount Gerizim, and the enmity that developed between them and the inhabitants of Judah extended into the common era. The city itself went on to serve as a provincial capital for the Persian, Greek, Roman, and Arab rulers of Palestine.

Samaria ivory: ivory sphinx in lotus thicket, ninth century B.C.E.

If the period is to be described sociologically, it has to be done in the following general terms. Jeroboam II inherited a kingdom that was recovering from the hard times of the latter part of the ninth century, when Israel had been hard-pressed by both Assyria and Damascus. A period of relative peace and freedom from interference by Assyria probably enabled Jeroboam to settle some old scores against Damascus. Possessions in the area of Transjordan south of Damascus were always in dispute between the two kingdoms, and Jeroboam probably either seized several that had been lost to Israel or allowed them to remain in Syrian hands in return for trading concessions in Damascus. There is no doubt that even small-scale wars, together with the demands of supplying food and drink to Samaria, bore heavily on small landowners. Although the rainfall was more secure than in Judah, there could be droughts and bad harvests. Such natural disasters added to conscription for military service and to royal taxes could reduce small landowners to hired laborers on their own landholdings. The gap between rich and poor thus became greater and greater.

2.   The Prophet Amos and His Book

Amos is usually regarded as a "prophet" from the town of Tekoa in Judah, on the edge of the wilderness that slopes down to the Dead Sea (Amos 1:1). This identification raises questions. If he was a man of Judah, why did he prophesy mostly in Israel? How did he know about conditions in Israel and in the capital, Samaria? A further problem is that, if he was a dresser of sycamore trees (Hebrew *shiqmah;* plural, *shiqmim;* (Amos 7:14), these certainly did not grow near Tekoa in Judah. Accordingly, a northern location for Tekoa has been suggested at Horvat Shema', which is not far from Meron, several miles northwest of Tsephat.

The fig sycamore (*shiqmah*) grew in lower Galilee in the north of Israel according to the Mishnah (second century B.C.E.) at *Sheviith* 9:2. However, the northern location for Tekoa has not found great favor among scholars, and the southern location is defended as follows. First, the fig sycamore grew in Jericho according to a discussion in the Babylonian Talmud (*Pesachim* 56, a–b). Amos could easily have traveled thence from Tekoa. Further, as a shepherd (1:1) he would be likely to move with his flocks and would thus be aware of events in the northern kingdom. However, this does not answer all the outstanding questions. In particular, if Amos was an owner of cattle as well as sheep (cf. 7:14), would he have traveled extensively with his animals, and was it possible for shepherds from Judah to move freely to the northern kingdom and use pasturage there? Perhaps we should admit that we know less about Amos than has often been assumed.

Another question concerns whether or not Amos regarded himself as a prophet. In the incident in 7:10–17, in which he was reproved for speaking at or against the sanctuary of Bethel, Amos averred that he was not a prophet. However, verse 14 can be translated in two ways:

1. I was not a prophet . . .
2. I am not a prophet . . .

The first would imply that, before his call, Amos was not a member of a prophetic guild or family, and that he owed his status as prophet to his call from God. The second would imply that he was not now, and had never been, a prophet in the technical sense. If the second approach is followed, this does not mean that Amos was a solitary speaker of God's words. Someone must have preserved what he had said or written; and presumably, the belief that he had spoken shortly before the earthquake must have been a tradition within a circle of followers or friends.

To the historical Amos it is usual to ascribe at least the following parts of the book:

1. The oracles against Damascus, Gaza, Ammon, Moab, and Israel (1:3–8, 13–15; 2:1–3, 6–16)
2. The five visions of 7:1–3, 4–6, 7–9, 8:1–2(3); 9:1–2
3. Three collections of sayings beginning with "hear this word," at 3:1–15, 4:1–13, 5:1–6
4. Three small collections beginning with the word "woe," at 5:7, 10–17, 18–24; 6:1–7

This by no means covers all the Amos material but suffices to indicate that the book is based upon a number of collections with formal, rhetorical features. Thus, the opening oracles against the nations begin

For three transgressions of X,
and for four, I will not revoke the punishment.

Three of the visions begin with the phrase "This is what the lord GOD showed me." In 3:1–6, 8, a series of questions expecting the answer "no" leads to a climax.

Although we can only guess intelligently about the literary history of the book, what follows is plausible. The first main collection was chapters 3–6, excluding the hymnic passages at 4:13 and 5:8–9. The oracles against the nations were added at the beginning and the visions at the end. The series of visions was interrupted by the addition of the story of Amos's reproof by Amaziah (7:10–17) and a passage of social critique at 8:(3)4–14, which is extended in 9:2–4, 7–10.

The second stage of the book's growth involved the addition of the oracles against Tyre, Edom, and Judah (1:9–12, 2:4–5) perhaps during the early exilic period (sixth century B.C.E.). At some stage the three hymnic passages at 4:13, 5:8–9, and 9:5–6, which have a distinctive style in Hebrew, were added.

The final addition was 9:11–15, and this gave the book a different flavor. Whereas the message of the rest of Amos is almost entirely without hope, the epilogue, set in a time when the "booth of David" is fallen (i.e., the southern kingdom has fallen), looks forward to a time of restoration. As in the case of Micah, the postexilic community was able to set grim words of judgment into a new context. The judgment had indeed come; but so had a restoration, through God's mercy.

We can thus perceive three main stages in the composition and sense of the book. The first stage was a collection of oracles of judgment delivered by a man who was not a professional prophet but who had been commissioned by God to warn the northern kingdom of Israel of impending doom. In the second stage the words of judgment were seen to be applicable to Judah as well as Israel. The third stage, following the fall of both nations, expressed hope for a future restoration.

3.   The Literary Structure and Contents of Amos

The content of Amos can be considered from several angles. If it is divided into two very unequal parts, 1:1–9:10 and 9:11–15, it follows a pattern found elsewhere in the Minor Prophets of oracles of judgment followed by words of hope and restoration. Another view is that it is unique in placing its oracles against the nations at the beginning, the usual place being the middle or toward the end. In the present work Amos will be considered under the following headings: (*a*) oracles against the nations (1:2–2:16), (*b*) material concerning prophecy (3:1–8, 7:10–17), (*c*) general words of judgment (3:9–6:14, 8:[3]4–14, 9:2–10), (*d*) the five visions (7:1–3, 4–6, 7–9; 8:1–2[3]; 9:1–2), and (*e*) the epilogue (9:11–15).

Oracles against the Nations

It was pointed out above that the oracles that derive from Amos himself are those against Damascus (1:3–5), Gaza (1:6–8), Ammon (1:13–15), Moab (2:1–3), and Israel (2:6–16). The first four have a formal, recurrent structure. The opening mentions three and four transgressions for which punishment will not be revoked, but in fact only one offense is detailed. God then threatens to send a fire against the nation which will destroy the strongholds of a king or principal city, after which more general punishment will fall on the people. In each case, the offense mentioned is what we would today call a war crime: drawing threshing sledges across the backs of prisoners (1:3), exiling whole communities (1:6), ripping open pregnant women (1:13), and denying burial to a defeated king (2:1).

The importance of these passages is twofold. First, their opening and closing words, "Thus says the LORD" and "says the LORD," place them in a religious context which indicates that cruel acts of humans against other humans outside Israel are an affront to God and punishable by him. God is concerned not only with Israel but with all nations. Second, the prophet is appealing to what we can call "natural morality" and is assuming that there are international conventions of right and wrong that should not only be accepted by all humans but are standards that God expects them to observe.

The oracle against Israel, with which the series originally concluded, was intended to shock Amos's listeners. It differs from those that precede it in that it presupposes, not general standards of morality, but a special relationship between God and Israel. The Exodus and wilderness wanderings are appealed to (2:10), and God addresses Israel in the first person. The offenses include the corruption of justice, the affliction of the poor, and the disregard of holy things (2:2–8). The coming judgment mentions that the strong and powerful, in particular, will not escape (2:13–16). The implication here, as elsewhere in Amos, is that the God of the nations expects an appropriate response of loyalty to his laws from the nation that he has specially chosen, and that it will not be exempted from judgment.

The oracles against Tyre (1:9–10), Edom (1:11–12), and Judah (2:4–5) do not entirely reproduce the form of the other oracles against the nations (except for the oracle against Israel) and do not mention fire devouring a principal city. In the case of Judah there is no hint of a special relationship with God, and the offense is that Judah rejected God's law and has not kept his statutes. In context, these three oracles apply God's concern for justice to more peoples and in this regard constitute a proper extension of Amos's message. The first two chapters set the tone for the remainder of the book.

Material Concerning Prophecy

Chapter 3 begins with two verses that sum up chapters 1–2: knowledge of God entails his judgment not his indulgence. A passage about prophecy follows. A series of rhetorical questions expecting the answer "no" leads to a verse in which the implied question, Is it possible to be silent if spoken to by God? is expressed poetically as

> The lion has roared;
> who will not fear?
> The Lord GOD has spoken;
> who can but prophesy?

This passage is probably Amos's justification for his prophetic activity, and it is of a piece with 7:10–17, in which Amos denies that he is, or has ever been, a prophet in the human or professional sense. He owes his work entirely to the call of God and rejects the idea (7:16) that any human has the authority to tell him to be silent. The God who has called Amos, we must note, is the awesome God of the opening chapters, who judges the nations. A verse inserted during editing at 3:7 interrupts the sequence of rhetorical questions leading to the climax at 3:8 and has the effect of claiming Amos as a prophet after all! In a sense, of course, the verse is correct.

General Words of Judgment

These oracles, in chapters 3–6, 8, and 9, amplify the words against Israel in chapter 2. What is condemned is perversion of justice (5:7, 10;6:12), oppression of the poor (3:10, 5:11, 8:4–5), and abuse of worship (4:4–5, 5:21–4). A new theme is the vicious denunciation of the rich in Samaria (4:1, 6:1b–6). However, the message is presented with great artistry. In 4:6–12, a poem with the refrain "yet you did not return to me" at the end of each of five verses leads to the climax "Prepare to meet your God!" The poem details various setbacks faced by Israel: famine, drought, blight, illness, and war (raising here, and at 5:3, the question of how peaceful Amos's times really were). The background to the poem may well be the covenant promises and curses as we find them now in passages such as Deut. 28:20ff, with the implication that the curses are now coming upon Israel.

In Amos 5:1–2, the words of judgment are introduced by a dirge, such as might be sung at a funeral. Amos 5:18–20 is a famous passage about the Day of the Lord, which Amos portrays, not as a day on which God's armies will fight *for* Israel, but as a day of gloom and darkness for Israel. Amos 9:2–44 is a poem that reads like a negative version of Psalm 139 and that may be a deliberate parody of the psalm or a similar passage. The idea that God's presence is everywhere, even in Sheol (the underworld), is given a sinister twist: there is no hiding place from God's judgment. The material is punctuated by three hymnic passages (4:13, 5:8–9, and 9:5–6), which, if they are later additions, have been superbly placed. They celebrate the might of God the creator and complement the opening two chapters. The other material in this section consists of various descriptions of coming judgment.

The Five Visions

Of the first four visions, two are of ordinary events that Amos sees, or is shown to have deeper meaning. In the first, the threat of locusts to the harvest indicates coming judgment which Israel will be too weak to withstand. In the fourth, the similarity between the Hebrew words for "summer fruit" (*qayits*) and "end" (*qets*) yields the message that the end of Israel is near. Visions two and three are more mysterious, involving a fire that consumes the deep (Hebrew *tehom*; cf. Gen. 1:2) and a vision of God holding a plumb line against a wall. Yet in spite of the more mysterious nature of these two visions, there is none of the exotic imagery of Zechariah 9–14 or Daniel and no angelic interpreter. God himself shows the visions and questions Amos. In the first two visions there is a hope that God will relent; but this is not to be, and the fifth vision involves no dialogue with the prophet. God commands judgment to be carried out, and no one will escape.

The Epilogue

The book ends on a note of hope, with the promise that David's fallen booth (his kingdom and dynasty) will be raised up. This unexpected Judahite perspective is, as already noted, a later addition. It places the Book of Amos in the context of the community that is now on the yonder side of the judgment that Amos foresaw for Israel, and that his editors extended to Judah.

H. OBADIAH

This book of only twenty-one verses is concerned with Edom, the kingdom in Transjordan roughly south and east of the Dead Sea (Obad. 1, 6, 8, 18, 19, 21). The first nine verses envisage the coming devastation of Edom. Its cities built upon high and inaccessible rocks will not escape, nor will its fabled wisdom avail. The reason for the coming disaster is given in verses 10–14. Edom was not loyal to its brother Jacob when Judah and Jerusalem were plundered. Indeed, instead of aiding its brother, Edom gloated over the disaster and joined in the looting.

Verses 15–16 are a transition to the final verses, which describe a time when the dispossessed Israelites will return and will repossess their land. Edom will be destroyed, and Israelites will occupy the land from Edom and the Negev north through the Shephelah to Ephraim, Samaria, and Gilead (northern Transjordan), and as far as Phoenicia. This is roughly the extent of David's empire as described in 2 Samuel 8. According to verses 15–16, this time of reversal is near, when those nations that wronged Jerusalem and Judah will receive due punishment.

The lack of specific historical detail in Obadiah makes it difficult to identify the occasion of Edom's complicity against Jerusalem, although most scholars believe that the most likely event was the destruction of Jerusalem in 587/6. Indeed, on the basis of Obadiah it has been supposed that the Edomites joined in the plundering of Jerusalem and Judah, and although this may be correct, we must note that Jer. 40:11 says that after Jerusalem's fall, some men of Judah took refuge in Moab, Ammon, and Edom. If this is accurate, we may well ask why Judahites went to shelter in a country that had attacked Judah and Jerusalem. We must not rule out the possibility that verses 10–13 refer to the occupation of the southern part of Judah by the Edomites during the postexilic period, and that there has been some telescoping of this movement with the fall of Jerusalem in 587/6.

Of the prophet Obadiah and his circumstances we know nothing; and there is the complication that parts of the book can be paralleled from elsewhere in the Old Testament. Most striking is the fact that verses 1b–9 have close parallels with parts of Jer. 49:7–16, which is also an oracle against Edom. Verses 1b–4 are close to Jer. 49:14–16, and verse 5 resembles Jer. 49:9. In these examples, the verbal agreement is very high. Other parallels, with less extensive but significant verbal agreement, are Obadiah 8 and Jer. 49:7, where there are references to Edom's wisdom, and Obadiah 16 and Jer. 49:12, where the common ideas are about drinking the cup and its relation to punishment. Parallels can also be drawn between Obadiah and Joel, with particular regard to Obadiah 15, 16, 17, and 18 and Joel 1:15, 3:17, 2:32, and 2:5.

What are we to make of these parallels? Has Obadiah (assuming him to have been a prophet) drawn upon a common stock of ideas used also in Jeremiah 49 and Joel or was he dependent upon Jeremiah and Joel? Is it possible, advancing the most extreme point of view, that the Book of Obadiah was compiled by the editors of the book of the Twelve Minor Prophets out of already existing material in order to bring the number of Minor Prophets to twelve? We cannot answer these questions; but they indicate how this short book, which expresses the hope of a bright future arising from the ashes of disaster, presents the reader and the interpreter with an intriguing set of problems.

I.   JONAH

Jonah is unique among the Minor Prophets in that it is a narrative and it incorporates a psalm. Its story is simple and well known. Its interpretation raises many questions.

The book opens with God's command to Jonah, son of Amittai, to go to Nineveh, the capital of Assyria, and to prophesy against it. A prophet of this name is known to us from 2 Kings 14:25. He was active during the reign of Jeroboam II of Israel (782–747) and appears to have prophesied that Jeroboam would restore Israel's borders to their fullest extent. However, most scholars hold that the author of Jonah was not that prophet and that the Book of Jonah is to be dated later.

The story proceeds with great skill and irony. Jonah disobeys God by setting off by boat to Tarshish instead of traveling over land to Nineveh. A dreadful storm arises, during which Jonah sleeps while the crew desperately try to save the boat. Lots are cast to see who is to blame for the storm. Jonah is identified as the cause and confesses that he worships the "God of heaven, who made the sea and the dry land" (1:9). The irony that he nonetheless hoped to evade the command of such a God is apparent. He requests that he be cast into the sea, where he is swallowed by a great fish. Another irony of chapter 1, and an anticipation of what is to come, is that the non-Israelite seamen fear and sacrifice to Yahweh.

Chapter 2 is Jonah's psalm while in the belly of the fish. Even if it was added later to the book, this was done with skill; the psalm has the dramatic effect of bringing the first main scene to an end. The psalm contains phrases that echo the Book of Psalms. In particular, metaphorical phrases that speak of God's anger in terms of being overcome by floods or being taken down to the grave are given a new, somewhat more literal content without losing their metaphorical power. Indeed, the psalm is a powerful assertion of what Jonah confessed when the casting of lots identified him as the cause of the storm: that he worships the God who made the seas and the dry land. Even while he is in the depths of the sea, he is not cut off from God, who hears his prayer and grants him deliverance.

Deliverance, however, means the resumption of duty, and the command to go to Nineveh comes a second time (chap. 3). The result of Jonah's preaching of imminent judgment is that the people of Nineveh (who are Assyrians) repent, from the king downward. God decides not to bring judgment upon them. Again, the irony is profound. If Jonah had been preaching in the capital of Israel, for instance, would the result have been the same? Chapter 4 records Jonah's anger that God did not punish Nineveh. The book closes with God making the point that he cares for the people and also the animals of Nineveh and would not delight in their needless destruction.

This simple story can be read at many levels. Older scholarship dated it in the time of Ezra and Nehemiah because the book was seen as a protest against their nationalistic policies. This date, in the fourth century B.C.E., may well be right. But it is arguable that God's willingness to be gracious to non-Israelites is not the book's main point, even though the importance of this theme must not be overlooked. The central problem seems to be that of true and false prophecy. Jonah turns out to be a false prophet on the criterion of Deut. 18:22; a prophet is false if what he says does not take place. Jonah was told by God to say that Nineveh would be overthrown in forty days. Jonah feared that

JONAH IN JEWISH AND CHRISTIAN TRADITION

ARTISTS AND STORY-tellers have long been attracted to the colorful tale of Jonah and the whale. The reluctant prophet became an important figure in the traditions of both Jewish and Christian communities of faith. Jonah occupies a place in the folklore, theology, art, and liturgy of Jews and Christians alike.

Classical Judaism was the setting for fantastic embellishments of Jonah's story. According to one tradition, Jonah was the son of the widow of Zarephath whom Elijah restored to life (1 Kings 17). His fury at the worm and his flight from God notwithstanding, Jonah came to be known as one of the few perfectly righteous men the world had ever known. A rabbinic Haggadah preserves the tradition that when Jonah fled toward Tarshish, he was acting in the best interests of his people: were the heathen Ninevites to repent at the words of a lone prophet, surely God would punish recalcitrant Israel. The chosen people had remained impenitent in spite of the many holy men

from God who preached repentance to them. The rabbis understood Jonah as one who sacrificed his life for the sake of his fellow Israelites.

The New Testament mentions two events from the life of Jonah: his stay in the belly of the great fish (e.g., Matt. 12:40) and his successful preaching of repentance in Nineveh (e.g., Luke 11:32). Also, the evangelists seem to have cast the story of Jesus' stilling the storm (e.g., Mark 4:35–41) in language that recalls Jonah's adventures on the stormy sea. In the early church, Jonah was regarded as proof that salvation was available to the gentiles and that God had indeed intended that they should be saved. Jonah's tale also found a place in the early Christian polemic against Judaism. The repentance of the Ninevites became a symbolic warning and threat to the Jews: at the Day of Judgment, the men of Nineveh would accuse and condemn those who would not heed the words of Jesus – a prophet even greater than Jonah (Luke 11:32).

Both Matthew and Luke mention "the sign of Jonah," a concept which played an important

role in early Christian theology. This enigmatic phrase may refer to Jonah's miraculous deliverance from the great fish or to his effectiveness in persuading gentiles. This miracle stood as God's validation of Jonah's message. The early Christian community understood that God had also authorized Jesus as a divine messenger by similarly delivering him from death. The Gospel writers were quick to draw a parallel between Jesus' time in the tomb and Jonah's three days in the great fish. Accordingly, scenes from the life of Jonah became a key feature of Christian funerary art. Jonah's theme of human repentance and divine mercy found a significant place in the liturgies of both church and synagogue. Jews read Jonah during the Days of Awe at the afternoon service of the Day of Atonement (Yom Kippur). According to the Mishnah, the Book of Jonah was chosen for that occasion because it illustrates the power of repentance and shows that there is no escape from God. The traditional liturgy for Ash Wednesday, the beginning of the Christian season of Lent, also includes a reading from Jonah.

what he was told by God to say would not come to pass, and this was why he refused to go to Nineveh (4:2). Indeed, Nineveh was not overthrown. In other words, the Deuteronomistic criterion is too simplistic; and it certainly does not account for the inner conflict and pain experienced by prophets; it treats them as though they were merely mouthpieces without feelings or emotions. In that it portrays the conflicted inner life of a prophet, Jonah as a book is similar to Jeremiah.

The Book of Jonah asserts that God does not delight in destruction but in repentance. It has a generous attitude to non-Israelites. Its choice of Nineveh as the recipient of mercy is remarkable, given the harsh words about Nineveh in Nahum and Zephaniah. Within the book of the Twelve Minor Prophets, however, it clarifies why later editors added oracles of hope to prophetic words of doom. By the criterion of Deut. 18:22, Micah was a false prophet if he envisaged the destruction of Jerusalem and that it would not be rebuilt (Mic. 3:12). Amos was a false prophet if he saw no hope for Israel. Yet in both these books (and also at the end of Zephaniah) oracles of hope were added by the post-exilic editors to show that after judgment came restoration.

Jonah shows us the pain and anxiety involved in responding to the divine call to prophesy. It warns against oversimplifications and is a message to its readers that God responds graciously to repentance; and it explains why prophetic books originally concerned mainly with judgment had oracles of hope added to them by editors living at the time of the restoration that followed Jerusalem's fall.

J.   MICAH

1.   Archeological and Sociological Data on the Period

According to Mic. 1:1, the prophet was a native of Moresheth in Judah and was active in the reigns of Jotham, Ahaz, and Hezekiah, that is, between 740 and 698 B.C.E. The full name of Micah's town is usually said to be Moresheth-gath (Mic. 1:14), meaning "possession of Gath." However, if scholars are correct in identifying Moresheth with Tell ej-Judeideh (Tel Goded) one wonders why such a large and prominent settlement should be named as though it was a mere suburb of Gath. Perhaps the equation with Moresheth-gath is wrong or the location at Tell ej-Judeideh is wrong. However, if we accept that location, then Micah's home was a large site overlooking the important route through the Shephelah from Bet Shemesh to Lachish. (Today it is to be found on the left-hand side of the road just north of Bet Guvrin.) Even if this location is wrong, the poem of 1:10–16 locates Micah's home somewhere on the Bet Shemesh–Lachish route, since the following identifiable sites in that area are mentioned in the poem: Gath, Adullam, and Lachish.

Micah's location is important for his message and setting. He was not a Jerusalemite but a provincial man, possibly an elder of his town. He lived in an area that was both fertile and strategic; strategic in that anyone invading Judah would use the route from Bet Shemesh to reach Lachish, Judah's second city after Jerusalem. In 701 the Assyrian king Sennacherib besieged and captured Lachish and recorded his triumph on the reliefs now in the British Museum. The poem in 1:10–16 implies an impending attack along the route to Lachish, although its date cannot be fixed. In 2:1–11 there may be reference to the militarization of the towns along the route, involving the seizing of houses and fields (2:2) and the eviction of their inhabitants (2:9). This poem may, of course, refer to the acquisition of property by the imposition of taxes that could not be paid, resulting in the indebtedness and ultimate dispossession of the landholders; but the forcible militarization of the area would also explain the bitterness that Micah felt toward Jerusalem.

If it is accepted that Mic. 5:2–5a (Hebrew, 5:1–4a) comes from the prophet (and many scholars would deny this), we have an important alternative view to that manifested in many parts of the Old Testament that glorify Jerusalem. At the end of chapter 3, Micah announces that Jerusalem will be destroyed and never rebuilt (it will become a wooded height). If his words originally continued in 5:2ff., then he was looking for a new beginning that would switch the center of God's activity from Jerusalem to Bethlehem. Because the line of David had become corrupted in Jerusalem, it would be replaced by a new line issuing from the small village of Bethlehem. Just as a leader from Bethlehem (David) had once delivered his people, so a new leader from that town would deliver them now. Even if this viewpoint is too speculative, we have sufficient material in Micah 1–3 that is universally accepted as coming from Micah to see this prophet as a provincial champion of oppressed small farmers in Judah, protesting against their treatment by the central government in Jerusalem at a time when Judah was threatened with invasion from Assyria.

2. The Literary History of Micah

There is little agreement among scholars about the material in Micah that can be attributed to the prophet. A common view is that only chapters 1–3 can be attributed to him. Criteria for deciding such matters are very subjective, and a maximalist view would be that, in addition to chapters 1–3, the following material may derive from Micah: 5:2–6 (Hebrew, 5:1–5), 10–15 (Hebrew, 9–14); 6:9–16; and 7:1–7. If this was the original core of the book, additional material was added during and after the exile (sixth–fifth centuries B.C.E.). The oracle of 4:1–5 is very close in wording to Isa. 2:2–4. It was probably added in order to soften the prediction about Jerusalem's fall in 3:12 and to reflect the fact that Jerusalem and its temple had been rebuilt at the end of the sixth century B.C.E. Mic. 4:6–5:1 (Hebrew, 4:6–14) implies that the Babylonian exile is imminent or has happened. The command to Zion to thresh her enemies is similar to Isa. 41:15. In 5:7–9 (Hebrew, 5:6–8) the people are described as a remnant surrounded by the gentile nations. This suggests the exilic or postexilic community.

With 6:1–8 we have the famous passage in which God tells his people "to do justice, and to love kindness, and to walk humbly with your

God" (6:8). Whether this whole passage is Micah's or not depends on whether we believe that the references to Moses, Aaron, Balak, and Balaam (6:4–5) imply that the Pentateuchal traditions have reached something like their final form and are being quoted here (which did not happen until the fifth century B.C.E.). In favor of attribution to Micah could be the anti-temple cultic stance of 6:6–8. Micah's opposition to Jerusalem, whose "priests teach for a price" (3:11), could entail opposition to its cult. The conclusion of the book implies that Jerusalem is fallen and warns its enemies not to rejoice at its fate (7:8–10). There follows a prophecy of restoration (7:11–17) and an assertion (7:18–20) of God's pardoning love. The implied setting and the sentiments of the conclusion are appropriate to the situation of the exile rather than to Micah's complaint against Jerusalem.

3. The Literary Structure and Contents of Micah

It is generally accepted that the book as we have it is structured in alternate layers of judgment and promise of salvation:

Judgment	Promise of Salvation
1:1–2:11	
	2:12–13
3:1–12	
	4:1–8
4:9–5:1 (Hebrew, 4:9–14)	
	5:2–9 (Hebrew, 5:1–8)
5:10–6:16 (Hebrew, 5:9–6:16)	
	7:1–20

The Book of Micah puts the words of the prophet into a form that makes the work a dramatic whole. It opens with a dramatic picture of the majestic coming of God to judge Samaria. The mountains and valleys are obliterated, and the magnificent buildings on the hill of Samaria are tossed into the valley below. However, it is not only Samaria that is targeted; Jerusalem is also under the threat of judgment, and this is bad news for the towns of the Shephelah, along the road that has been fortified to protect the hill country of Judah. The poem of 1:10–16 is full of wordplays, of which some idea can be given by the following rendering:

in the house of Aphrah [*bet le ʿaphrah*]
roll yourselves in the dust [*ʿaphar*]   (1:10)

Harness the chariots to the steeds [*rekhesh*]
inhabitant of Lachish [*lakhish*]   (1:13)

The houses of Akhziv [*ʾakhziv*]
will be a deception [*ʾakhzav*]
to the kings of Israel   (1:14)

Chapter 2 condemns those who are dispossessing the inhabitants from their lands (2:1–5) and contains a poem about an attempt to prevent the prophet from speaking, which opens and closes with the verb "to preach" (2:6–11; cf. vv. 6 and 11). After a small postexilic addition (2:12–13), chapter 3 introduces some of the toughest language found anywhere in the Bible in condemning injustice. The rulers are depicted as cannibals, cooking the flesh and bones of the people to devour them (3:2–3); Zion is built on blood (3:10); Jerusalem will be destroyed and never rebuilt (3:12).

Micah's harsh words are then softened by the oracles about the exaltation of Jerusalem in the latter days (4:1–5) and a promise of gathering together those who have been scattered from Zion (4:6–7). A new deliverer from Bethlehem is promised (5:2–6; Hebrew, 5:1–5), and Jacob is described as a lion among its enemies.

Chapters 6–7 are dominated by passages in the first person. God asks his people why they have become weary of him (6:3–5), and a representative of the people replies (6:6–7). God cries out that he cannot tolerate injustice (6:9–16). At 7:1–10 desolate Zion speaks, and after being reassured that she will be vindicated (7:11–17), she rejoices in God's pardoning love (7:18–20).

The drama of the book as thus outlined moves from the awesome description of God's coming in judgment to the moving affirmation of his graciousness; from the objective description of the divine judgment on injustice to the personal and intimate discourse of God and Zion. There is a movement from outer to inner and from judgment to hope. No doubt this is far from the original sentiments of the historical Micah, who was expressing outrage at the unjust treatment of his people; but the tradition has given this outrage a deeper dimension that has not suppressed the words of Micah but has created new ways of appreciating them.

K. NAHUM

It is usually asserted that the Book of Nahum is a collection of prophecies directed against Nineveh, the capital of Assyria, which fell in 612 B.C.E. There is justification for this assertion. Nineveh is mentioned at 2:8 (Hebrew, 2:9) and 3:7. Assyria is mentioned at 3:18, and the heading of the book reads "An oracle concerning Nineveh." However, if it were not for this heading, readers would be disposed to see the book in a different light.

In 1:2–14 we have a poem that is an awesome statement of the avenging majesty of God. Not only does it draw upon stock imagery, such as God's coming in the whirlwind and storm (1:3), with the resultant terror on the part of the mountains (1:5); but it is also an incomplete acrostic poem (i.e., a poem in which the first word of each verse follows an alphabetical sequence), in which verses 2, 4, 5, 7, and 10 begin with the Hebrew letters aleph, gimel, he, tet, and kaph, with the intervening letters bet, vav, zayin, and het appearing at 3b, 5b, 6a (the second word), and 6b. (The complete sequence would be aleph, bet, gimel, dalet, he, vav, zayin, het, tet, yod, and kaph.) If we were not predisposed by 1:1 to read it in connection with Nineveh, we would see it as a general poem about God coming in judgment and the impossibility of human resistance.

After this first poem, the division of the material is crucial. The Hebrew numbering of chapters and verses begins chapter 2 at 1:15 in our English Bible. This contains a reference to Judah; and if what immediately follows is a continuation of 1:15, then the country being addressed in chapter 2 appears to be Judah, not Assyria. It is true that Nineveh is mentioned in 2:8 (Hebrew, 2:9), but the Hebrew of this verse is very obscure (lit., "and Nineveh is like a water pool, she is from the days; and they flee. Stand! Stand! But no one turns."), and it is not obvious that Nineveh's destruction is being described or predicted, although a case can be made for reading the material in that way.

Because of these facts, it is not surprising that some commentators have doubted whether chapters 1–2 were composed with the destruction of Nineveh in view. An attempt has even been made to argue that oracles originally addressed to Judah and Jerusalem have been reapplied to Nineveh.

In chapter 3, the material seems to be directed more toward Nineveh, and verse 7 reads:

> Nineveh is devastated;
> who will bemoan her?

There is also a reference to the sleeping shepherds (i.e., rulers) of Assyria in verse 18. Yet even in chapter 3 there is not any detail that connects the material with Assyria and Nineveh in such a way as to rule out other possible identifications.

All this is a way of saying that we must not regard the interpretation of Nahum as being straightforwardly bound up with the fall of Nineveh in 612, so that the only critical question that needs to be discussed is whether the book was composed before or after 612; or, in other words, whether it is a forecast or a subsequent description of the fall of Nineveh. A cautious view would be that chapters 2–3 are a forecast or description of Nineveh's fall, containing a reference, at 3:8, to the fall of Thebes, which was finally captured by the Assyrians in 661. In this case, chapters 2–3 would predate 612. To these poems, it could be argued, was added a part or the whole of an acrostic poem describing the awesome vengeance of God. This could have been added before or after 612. The heading then made it clear that the whole book concerned the fall of Nineveh.

Even if this cautious view is accepted, it must be noted that the book shows signs of reaching its final form during the Babylonian exile (sixth century). The word of comfort to Judah at 1:15 (Hebrew, 2:1),

> Look! On the mountains the feet of one
> who brings good tidings,
> who proclaims peace!

has been compared with Isa. 40:9 and 52:7 (which date from the sixth century), and this raises the possibility that 1:2–15 was originally addressed to Judah to promise deliverance from her Babylonian oppressor.

Within the book of the Twelve Minor Prophets Nahum presents an interesting contrast to Jonah. The latter book used Nineveh as an object lesson to show how unresponsive Israel had been to the preaching of the prophets. It portrays a God of compassion who desires not to destroy Nineveh if he can avoid it, for the sake of the animals as well as the humans. In Nahum God's vengeance must be worked out upon a people that is, by implication, unrepentant, and who use animals as instruments of war. It is interesting that, in the Greek Bible, Nahum follows Jonah.

In the context of the book of the Twelve, then, Nahum is an example of the variety and creativity within Old Testament tradition. Some of its poetry is among the most vivid in the Old Testament, especially at 2:3–5 and 3:3–4. Its view of the majestic power of God over a mighty foreign nation is sublime. Its explicit references to Nineveh require it to be read together with the completely different Book of Jonah. It thus supports the growing opinion that the individual Minor Prophets must be taken together as a single book, even if we do not, as yet, have as many clues as we should like as to how to account for their common features.

L.   HABAKKUK

Habakkuk is unusual among the Minor Prophets because of its similarity to the Book of Psalms. Chapter 3 is mainly a psalm (headed "A prayer of the prophet Habakkuk"), complete with a musical direction ("to Shigionoth"), and 1:2–4 and 12–17 are similar to laments of the individual (see below p. 263). Chapter 2 presents the reader with some difficulties, especially at verses 6–17. This is a poem with four sections, each introduced by the word "alas" and containing a criticism of a social abuse. The obvious immediate reference is to abuses in Jerusalem such as those summarized in 1:2–4. Yet as each section continues, it seems to refer not to Jerusalem but to an imperial nation. It has thus been argued that 2:6–17 was originally a denunciation of social abuses in Jerusalem and that the material was expanded to apply it to Babylon. This view will be accepted here and will be used to indicate how Habakkuk reached its present form.

The book begins with a complaint of the prophet in the form of a lament (1:2–4). It is asserted that the law is slack, that justice is not effective, and that the wicked surround the righteous. Such a complaint could have been made on many occasions in the history of ancient Israel; but a possible dating is given in 1:5–11 when God's reply says that he is rousing the Chaldeans (i.e., the Babylonians), with the implication that this is his way of addressing the situation complained of by Habakkuk. This suggests that the prophet was a contemporary of Jeremiah and that, like Jeremiah, he regarded the Babylonians, initially at any rate, as God's instruments for justice. A date between 610 and 600 B.C.E. is indicated.

The language of the prophet's reply to God (1:12–17) and the oracle in 2:6–17 do not make it clear whether they are renewals of the complaint about injustice in Jerusalem or are complaints about the Babylonians. Modern translations are divided. The Hebrew word "he" in 1:15 (which is not expressed separately but is included in the verb form) is translated as "the wicked" by the Revised English Bible and as "the enemy" by the New Revised Standard Version. In other words, the Revised English Bible translators think that the complaints are against wicked people in Jerusalem, and the translators of the New Revised Standard Version think that the complaints are against the Babylonians. A solution to the difficulty is that the prophet initially welcomed the Babylonians in 610–600 as God's punishment for justice but then was appalled at their brutality. He then reapplied to the Babylonians his original complaint about the behavior of wicked people in Jerusalem. It is also possible that a later editor reapplied Habakkuk's words.

In reply to Habakkuk's complaint in 1:12–17 God tells him to write down on tablets a vision for the end time in which pride and wealth will perish and those who are righteous will be sustained by their faithfulness (2:2–5). There follows the powerful poem of 2:6–17, which condemns creditors, those who gain unlawfully, those who build by means of bloodshed, and those who make their neighbors get drunk (a vivid description of despoiling them). These accusations are applied implicitly to Babylon. This assessment is reinforced at 2:18–20, which condemns idols and their makers in terms very similar to Isa. 40:18–20 and 42:17, where Babylonian idolatry is attacked.

Chapter 3 is entirely different. It is a psalm in the tradition of Psalm 68, speaking of God's coming from the south (Teman and Mount Paran) in warlike majesty to rescue his people. It is similar to other passages in the Old Testament that celebrate God's warlike deeds in the past (e.g., Judges 5, Ps. 68). Its implications are clear for the book as a whole (whether or not it is a later addition): God's justice executed through human agency will be less than perfect and may bring no improvement. God's own assertion of his just rule is required and will happen in the future as it did in the past. This brings the response that is the climax of the book's expression of hope:

> Though the fig tree does not blossom,
> and no fruit is on the vines;
> though the produce of the olive fails,
> and the fields yield no food;
> though the flock is cut off from the fold,
> and there is no herd in the stalls,
> yet will I rejoice in the LORD;
> I will exult in the God of my salvation.   (3:17–18)

M.   ZEPHANIAH

According to the heading in Zeph. 1:1, the prophet Zephaniah was active during the reign of Josiah (640–609). The contents of the book are largely consistent with this information, if we assume that Zephaniah's ministry fell within the early part of Josiah's reign, before he began to reform his nation's religion in 622. Judah and Jerusalem are portrayed as places where there were idolatrous priests and where

HABAKKUK AT QUMRAN

ONE OF THE MOST INTEResting sectarian documents found at Qumran is the *pesher* on Habakkuk. (The Hebrew word *pesher* means "commentary" or "interpretation.") Among the first scrolls to be published, the Habakkuk Pesher consists of twelve columns of running commentary on nearly the whole text of Habakkuk 1–2. The scroll has had important consequence, for the textual study of the Hebrew Bible, for the literary study of Habakkuk, and for our knowledge of the history and practice of the Qumran community.

Text critics who have studied the Habakkuk Pesher found nearly 135 distinct occurrences where the Qumran scroll's text varied from the received text of the Hebrew Bible. Some of the discrepancies resulted from simple scribal errors. However, many differences seem to indicate that the biblical text represented in the Qumran scrolls is based on an entirely separate textual tradition from the traditional Masoretic text. (The Masoretic text was established ca. 800 C.E. by a group of Jewish scribes who added vocalization to the consonantal Hebrew text.) Scholars have used material like the Habakkuk Pesher in their attempts to unravel the complicated textual traditions of the Hebrew Bible in the period before the text became standardized.

The Habakkuk Pesher does not include the text of Habakkuk's third chapter, a fact which some scholars have used to support the hypothesis that the liturgical poem in Habakkuk 3 was a much later addition to the book. Biblical critics have long suspected that

Habakkuk's third chapter was not original to the book, but specialists in the literature of Qumran are hesitant to use information drawn from the Habakkuk Pesher as evidence in this ongoing debate. They speculate that the textual tradition from which the Qumran sectarians drew their scriptures may not have included the third chapter, or that perhaps the Qumran interpreters simply did not care to comment on the third chapter since it did not lend itself well to the style of exposition they had used for chapters 1 and 2.

The commentary on Habakkuk is only one example of the literary genre *pesher,* which was very popular at Qumran. Researchers have also found extensive *pesharim* (plural of *pesher*) on Nahum and the Psalms. Fragmentary texts exist with running commentary on parts of Isaiah, Hosea, Micah, and Zephaniah. These scrolls and fragments are verse-by-verse commentaries on lengthy blocks of biblical text. Usually they quote a passage from the Bible and then follow with explanatory remarks formally introduced by the words "the interpretation of the passage is" (*pesher haddabar*). The purpose of *pesharim* was to disclose historical and eschatological events in biblical prophecies. A gap existed between the biblical text's literal meaning and the community's interpretation of it. Thus, the Qumran community used a series of hermeneutical devices to extract from ancient texts predictions relevant to their own historical existence. The leaders at Qumran tried to interpret "mysteries" which had come to pass at "the end of time," in which they believed they were living. With

divine revelation, they thought themselves able to understand cryptic references to contemporary events that had been hidden in prophetic texts.

Three historical persons or groups play a prominent role in the Habakkuk Pesher. The central personality is the Teacher of Righteousness, the apparent leader of the sect. Much of the scroll relates the conflict between this figure and his opponent, the Wicked Priest. Scholars have attempted to draw a portrait of the Qumran congregation's early history from this conflict. Sometime during the rule of the Wicked Priest, the Teacher of Righteousness seems to have spawned a religious controversy, perhaps over the interpretation of Scripture and halakah (legal material from the Old Testament or from postbiblical Jewish literature). In the midst of this ongoing political rivalry, the Teacher of Righteousness and the community gathered around him endured persecution at the hands of the Wicked Priest. The text creates a typology of good and evil characteristic of the Qumran sectarian mentality: the archvillain Wicked Priest/Man of Lies heads a "congregation of falsehood," while the poor and persecuted but just Teacher of Righteousness leads "the congregation of his elect."

The scroll's other major emphasis is to describe the appearance of the Roman army in Palestine. The Romans appear in the Habakkuk Pesher under the name "Kittim," a fearful warlike people who come from the islands of the sea to subjugate Israel cruelly. The term "Kittim" is taken from Balaam's prophecy in Num. 24:24, where it designates a

(*continued on p. 218*)

(continued from p. 217)

group that will play a major role in the Last Days. The Kittim are sent by God to punish the wicked priestly establishment in Jerusalem. The commentary vividly describes the irresistible Roman legions which ground out their victories with merciless ferocity.

Habakkuk Pesher's description of the Roman army bears the marks of fresh memory, and most scholars date the document to ca. 30 B.C.E., the period when Rome gained political control of Palestine. Identifying the Wicked Priest has been a more controversial endeavor. Most specialists of Qumran literature nominate either Jonathan or Simon Maccabee, the first two Hasmonean priests (152–134 B.C.E.). In light of the existing data from published texts, an identification of the Teacher of Righteousness does not seem possible.

the Canaanite god Baal (1:4) and the host of heaven (i.e., sun, moon, and stars) were worshiped. It is implied that the officials adopt foreign (Assyrian?) dress (1:8) and that the wealthy trading classes act unjustly (1:10–13). A particularly strong attack upon those in authority occurs in 3:3–5. The officials and judges are described as lions and wolves, the prophets are faithless, and the priests have profaned what is sacred. All this fits well with what the Old Testament tells us elsewhere about the reign of Manasseh (698–642), who preceded Josiah (Manasseh's son Amon reigned for only two years, 642–640). It was a time when paganism and injustice were rife (2 Kings 21:1–18). Part of the reason for this was Judah's subjugation to Assyria, against which there is an oracle of judgment in Zeph. at 2:13–15.

The bulk of the book fits plausibly into the period when the boy Josiah had begun to reign but when many abuses from Manasseh's rule persisted. It is also apparent that Zephaniah contains some postexilic material. In particular, 3:14–20 has strong echoes of Isaiah 40–66, and this section's command to Zion to rejoice because God's judgments against her have ceased provides Zephaniah with an optimistic ending.

The remainder of the book has a quite different thrust. Chapter 1 contains in verses 14–18 an important passage about the imminent Day of Yahweh, normally understood as a time when God will defeat the enemies of his people. The idea that the God of Israel commands

Aerial photo of Qumran, site of the Dead Sea Scroll community. Located south of Jericho and just west of the Dead Sea, the community is most often associated with the Essenes.

heavenly armies that fight against Israel's enemies can be found in early poems such as Judges 5 and Psalm 68, and it helped to shape the final form of the accounts of Joshua's battles. For example, in Joshua 6 the Israelites did almost no fighting against Jericho; they merely obeyed God's instructions, and he ensured the victory. But in the hands of the prophets, the idea of the Day of Yahweh, when God would defeat Israel's enemies, was turned on its head to become a day of judgment against Israel. In Zeph. 1:14–18 the military imagery is unmistakable; and this poem follows a passage that also portrays the coming judgment of God in awesome terms. This poem is directed against Judah and Jerusalem, as is the passage in 3:1–7.

What is unusual about Zephaniah among the Minor Prophets is that it also includes a series of oracles against foreign nations: Gaza, Ashkelon, Ashdod, and Ekron (2:4), other parts of the coastal plain (2:5–7), Moab and Ammon (2:8–11), Ethiopia (2:12), and Assyria (2:13–15). The details in these oracles are vague, so that it is impossible to link them with specific historical events. For example, Moab and Ammon have "made boasts" against Israel's territory (2:8); but this must have happened on many occasions.

In chapter 3, God expresses the vain hope that Jerusalem will turn to him to accept correction (3:7). Is there a contrast here with Nineveh's repentance in Jonah? Zeph. 3:8–13 speaks of a coming judgment of nations which will herald a new order. All nations will speak one language and will worship Yahweh, who will leave in Jerusalem a purified remnant worthy of the new order.

Thus, Zephaniah, about whom we know nothing except that he was possibly a descendant of King Hezekiah (1:21), indicates the diversity of those servants of God to whom we apply the blanket term "prophet."

N.   HAGGAI

In contrast to most of the so-called Minor Prophets, Haggai (like Zech. 1–8) is furnished with precise dates. According to 1:1, God's word came to Haggai on the first day of the sixth month of Darius's second year (i.e., 520 B.C.E.). Further datings at 2:1, 10, and 20 take us to the twenty-first day of month seven and the twenty-fourth day of month nine. There is also a date at 1:15 (the twenty-fourth of the sixth month) that is not easy to fit into the context. Thus, Haggai's recorded oracles fit into a period of about four months in 520 B.C.E.

The subject matter of the book is mainly concerned with the rebuilding of the temple. In 1:2 the opinion of the people that "the time has not yet come to rebuild the LORD's house" is recorded in order to be contradicted. The prophet replies (1:4–6, 7–11) that recent bad harvests have come about because the people have been more concerned with their own houses than with rebuilding God's house. In response, the people, led by Zerubbabel and Joshua, the high priest, begin work on the temple (1:12–14). In 2:1–9 there is encouragement from God for this work. The results so far are apparently disappointing (2:3); but God promises that he will shake the heavens, the earth, the sea, and the nations, and that the latter splendor of the temple will be greater than the former.

The mood changes in 2:10–14. Haggai asks the priests for a ruling on the relative potency of clean and unclean objects. The answer is that unclean things can defile holy things but that clean things cannot purify defiled things. The application is then made to the people's situation. Their holy task – presumably, rebuilding the temple – can become defiled if what the people offer is unclean. This cryptic passage has been seen by some as a reference to the involvement of "outsiders" such as Samaritans in the rebuilding work. But this entails reading into the text what is not there. Two possible interpretations are more likely: first, that the unclean work by the people is their lack of justice (cf. Isa. 1:12–17); second, that their offerings (e.g., of grain) are ritually impure. Hag. 2:15–19, which links bad harvests to the failure to rebuild the temple and draws attention to the immediate benefits following the beginning of work on the temple, is probably an expansion of the sentiment of chapter 1. The book concludes with another promise of imminent divine cosmic action when nations will be overthrown and Zerubbabel will be made "like a signet ring" (2:23).

Haggai (and Zech. 1–8, which shares a common editorial frame-

---

ZERUBBABEL AND THE DAVIDIC LINE

ZERUBBABEL, WHOSE NAME means "the offspring of Babylon," was a leader of the Jewish community in Babylon mainly during the reign of Darius I. His ancestry and achievements are variously reported in historical sources from the early postexilic period. Zerubbabel most likely led a second wave of settlers back to Palestine from the Babylonian exile. Zerubbabel was closely associated with the program of his elder brother or uncle Sheshbazzar. By the year 520 B.C.E., Zerubbabel had assumed complete leadership.

Zerubbabel owed whatever prominence he enjoyed to his royal lineage. He was the grandson of Jehoiachin, the Judean king who had been exiled to Babylon in 597. The prophets Haggai and Zechariah may allude to the fact that Zerubbabel was the Davidic scion and messianic figure promised from of old (Isa. 11:1; cf. Hag. 2:20–3, Zech. 3:8, 6:12). To Zerubbabel belonged the mantle of David's ideal kingship. Some scholars have understood Zerubbabel as the focus of Jewish nationalistic hopes during the early postexilic period, suggesting that his followers were a threat to the Persian Empire's control of Palestine (cf. Hag. 2:21–2, Zech. 4:6–7).

More likely is the possibility that Zerubbabel was groomed for his position (like Nehemiah) in the Persian court. Zerubbabel may well have been named governor in order to conciliate the citizens of Yehud (Judah), who were hoping for the restoration of the temple. It was in the Persians' best interests not to give full independence to the population occupying the land between Asia and Africa.

For the prophets, Zerubbabel's essential role was as the monarchical representative necessary for the laying of the foundations of the temple. The notion of an ideal Davidic king sitting on the throne in Jerusalem was only a future hope in the view of Haggai and Zechariah. Zerubbabel's limited authority had only the *potential* to become at some later time the legitimate kingship of an independent state.

Zerubbabel may not have been the last of the Davidic line to be associated with the governor's office in the Persian subprovince of Yehud. Elnathan, Zerubbabel's successor, apparently strengthened his position as governor by marrying into the Davidic line. A recently discovered seal identifies Elnathan's wife (lit., "maidservant") as Shelomith, a name known from 1 Chron. 3:19 as a daughter of Zerubbabel.

work) is usually interpreted in terms of Ezra 2:2, 3:1–13, 4:1–3, 5:1–2, and 6:13–15. According to this information in Ezra, Zerubbabel and Jeshua had returned from exile in Babylon and were encouraged by Haggai and Zechariah to rebuild the temple, which task was completed in the sixth year of Darius (516 B.C.E.; Ezra 6:15). However, this comparative approach is not without difficulty. According to other information in Ezra, the exiles returned from Babylon in 539 and were led by Sheshbazzar, who laid the temple's foundation (Ezra 1:8, 11; 5:16). No doubt it is possible to harmonize Ezra and Haggai; but it still needs to be asked why nearly twenty years elapsed between Zerubbabel's return and the surge of building activity inspired by Haggai and Zechariah. A further question is whether Ezra 3 implies that Zerubbabel began work immediately (i.e., in 539/8), and how we can reconcile the impressive contribution to the rebuilding described in Ezra 3 with the implied meager progress in Haggai 2:1–9 by 520.

In view of these questions it has been argued that the writers of Ezra (which was composed around 400 B.C.E.) used Haggai and Zechariah (which were written around 520 B.C.E.) as sources for a general reconstruction of the period. Although the reconstruction in Ezra was in no sense a deliberate falsification, it was nonetheless inaccurate (see above on Ezra, p. 154).

Even if we accept that the writer(s) of Ezra made mistakes in working out what had happened on the basis of the information available, we must agree that the use made of Haggai was not unreasonable. Haggai says nothing about a return from exile; but a change in the political circumstances of Judah must lie behind the prophet's activity. To have attempted to rebuild the temple while Judah was part of the Babylonian Empire would have been regarded as rebellion. Only with the defeat of Babylon by Persia in 540 did rebuilding become an option. The existence and encouragement of that option needed to be made known to those living in Judah. This would most likely come from returnees from Babylon or from a newly appointed governor.

There are still unanswered questions. Why was Joshua, the high priest, apparently content to be priest of a ruined (or, at any rate, unbuilt) temple? Why were the people satisfied with this situation? Even if these questions must remain unanswered, Haggai contains sufficient information for us to glimpse this situation. A series of catastrophic harvests enabled Haggai to counter the general view that the time was not right for rebuilding the temple. In a situation where self-interest had concentrated people's attention on their own welfare, perhaps to the neglect of social justice for the poor, the prophet was able to urge the people to turn to God by way of joining in the work of rebuilding the temple. The result was that the harvests improved, and Haggai senses a renewal of hope that would lead swiftly to divine action to crush the nations and restore the glory of the temple. Even if these hopes were not immediately realized, they played their part in the reestablishing of the Jewish community in Judah in the late sixth century.

TEMPLE BUILDING IN THE ANCIENT NEAR EAST

A TEMPLE IN THE ANCIENT world was conceived of as a residence, house, or palace for the deity. It was not a house of worship for the general public. As befits a dwelling place, a temple contained all the furnishings that a royal resident might require. As the abode of a god, the temple had to be constructed of materials suitable to its divine inhabitant. Furthermore, the needs of the resident deity had to be met. Temple sacrifice and other cultic acts in Near Eastern religions can be explained in part as the ritual provision for all the needs of the god.

However, it would be a mistake to assume that the temple's role was confined to its cultic functions. Temples were central to the existence and vitality of political states in the ancient world. They were often bound up with the founding or legitimizing of nations. No human king could claim authority to execute justice, levy taxes, and conscript armies without the approval of the stronger forces of the cosmos. Building a temple in which the god took up residence was a powerful symbolic statement signifying that the god sanctioned the dynastic power. The local citizenry could not oppose the dictates of rulers who had the approval of the resident deity. Erecting a temple in an administrative center was therefore an integral part of establishing the authority of a political regime.

Once erected on its specifically prepared spot in the capital city, the temple became part of the economic, political, and legal life of the nation and dynasty that were responsible for its existence. The king was the chief officer of the state, but the officers of the temple were also important administrators. Palace and temple together constituted the administrative core of the realm. Thus any decision to build a temple was generally thought of as monarchic prerogative. Building a temple was of momentous national importance.

Because of its key role in ancient societies, invading armies were always careful to destroy the temple of a conquered territory. Refounding a temple that had been destroyed made a bold statement that a nation was once again claiming for itself at least a semi-autonomous existence. Physical continuity between the old and new orders was expressed symbolically when a temple was refounded. The temple was usually rebuilt on the same site. Sometimes great effort was necessary to prepare a devastated site for new construction. In addition, a unit of building material removed from the former temple ruins became a symbolically important part of the new building. (This foundation stone is known by the technical term "first brick" or "premier stone.") Placing the foundation stone marked the completion of the preparatory labors mandated for the reconstruction of a ruined building. A deposit of metal nails or tablets ("tin stone," Zech. 4:10a) was also laid in the new temple's foundation. This "peg deposit" was the symbol of the temple's future existence, a statement of optimism that the structure would endure for many years.

Ancient Near Eastern kings and queens were directly involved with the construction of temples in their realms. In Mesopotamian practice the king carried the bricks to be used in the new building and even formed some of them. The actual ceremony of refoundation was a joyous occasion. It was a celebration filled with much ceremonial rejoicing by the priestly establishment and the temple's professional musicians. The public also participated by expressing their support with loud exclamations of approval during the ceremony.

Zech. 4:6–10 and Ezra 3:10–12 recount this occasion in the life of the postexilic community of Judah. The refounding of the temple of Yahweh shares extensively in the heritage of temple-building practices common throughout the ancient Near Eastern world.

O.   ZECHARIAH

Zechariah has the most chapters (fourteen) of any of the Minor Prophets; but a brief glance indicates that the book has two quite distinct parts. Scholars see the dates given at 1:1, 1:7, and 7:1 as a continuation of the scheme in Haggai. In Haggai, the oracles were dated between the sixth and ninth months of Darius's second year (520). Zechariah's visions are dated to the eighth month of 520 (1:1), the twenty-fourth day of the eleventh month of 520 (1:7), and the fourth day of the ninth month of 518 (7:1). With chapter 9 we have a complete change. The material is not dated and is introduced by the heading "An Oracle," as is the material in chapter 12.

These considerations have led to the view that Zechariah should be divided into two "books," chapters 1–8 and 9–14, or even into three, chapters 1–8, 9–11, and 12–14. The division into two books will be followed here, even though this implies that the material has been compiled in a simpler manner than may be the case.

1.   Zechariah 1–8

The core of the book is a series of seven visions, whose original form was probably as follows:

1. Four horsemen who have patrolled the earth and found it at peace (1:8–12)
2. Four horns that scattered Judah, and four blacksmiths come to strike them down (1:18–21 [Hebrew, 2:1–4])
3. A man measuring Jerusalem with a measuring line (2:1–5 [Hebrew, 2:5–9])
4. The lampstand with seven lamps, and two olive trees (4:1–6a [to "he said to me"], 10b [from "these seven"]–14)
5. The flying scroll, which is a curse (5:1–4)
6. The woman in the basket taken to Shinar (5:5–11)
7. Four chariots representing four winds or spirits patrolling the earth (6:1–8)

A symmetrical pattern is probably implied:

1. Four horsemen patrolling the earth
   2. Judah's enemies defeated
   3. Jerusalem restored
   4. The two anointed ones
   5. The wicked cut off from the land
   6. The land's guilt removed
7. Four chariots patrolling the earth

Taken in this way the visions center on the two anointed leaders. The two preceding visions concern the defeat of Judah's enemies and the rebuilding of Jerusalem, and the two following visions depict the spiritual and moral cleansing of the land. The visions set the events in the context of God's universal rule.

We do not know whether the date of the visions given at 1:7 (the twenty-fourth of the eleventh month of Darius's second year, i.e., 520) is the date on which the visions were seen. If it is, then the year 520 seems to be late for visions of restoration, because the Jews had already returned to Jerusalem from Babylon in 539. We could surmise that the visions were composed in Babylon shortly before Cyrus of Persia conquered the city and released the Jews from captivity in 539. The visions would thus have been written slightly later than Isaiah 40–55; and it is noteworthy that a passage such as 2:6–12 (Hebrew, 2:10–16) has many similarities with Isaiah 40–55.

In the form in which we have Zechariah the visions (whenever seen) have been set in the context of the events of 520, when the prophets Haggai and Zechariah encouraged Zerubbabel and High Priest Joshua to rebuild the temple. The temple as such does not have the prominence in Zechariah that it does in Haggai; instead, the main themes are restoration and cleansing. Whoever the two anointed figures in Zech. 4:14 were originally intended to be, in the final form of Zechariah they are Zerubbabel (explicitly) and Joshua (implicitly). In the central vision of the seven visions, an expansion refers explicitly to Zerubbabel (4:6b–10a). But it is also possible that, by the time the book reached its final form, Zerubbabel had disappeared from the scene and only Joshua remained. This possibility is suggested by chapter 3, which breaks the sequence of the visions (it takes the form of a vision, but differs from the seven; e.g., it has no interpreting angel). Joshua alone appears and is promised that God's servant, "the Branch," will come (3:8). "The Branch" is, perhaps, a coming royal figure. In 6:9–14 the prophet is told to collect silver and gold in order to make a crown according to the Greek and Syriac versions, and crowns according to the Hebrew. However, only one crown is used in the narrative and is placed on the head of Joshua, the high priest. But the high priest is not the focus of the passage. The focus is again "the Branch" (6:12), who has royal honor and will sit on his throne with a priest at his side.

The obscurity of this passage has led to much speculation. Was there an attempt to crown Zerubbabel as king, and was he removed or executed by the Persians? Was the passage reworked when Zerubbabel simply died or moved away before the hoped-for glory had materialized? We do not know, and Zechariah 1–8 remains a tantalizing text as a result.

The visions are confined to chapters 1–6. Chapters 7–8 are different in content and are possibly a bridge to the material in chapters 9–14. Zech. 7:1–7 concerns a question about fasting, and the answer given there and in 7:8–14 appears to condemn insincere fasting and to command social justice. The similarity of this theme with Isaiah 58 is striking. Chapter 8 continues the theme of fasting (8:18–19) and justice (8:16–17) and looks forward to hopeful days for the Jerusalem community. The strong impression gained from this chapter is that although the foundation of the temple has been laid, times are still hard for the people of Judah.

2. Zechariah 9–14

Chapters 9–14 contain much material that is strange and fascinating. For Christian readers it is interesting because it contains passages associated with the Passion of Jesus. In 9:9 there occurs the promise of the king riding into Jerusalem on a donkey that is taken up by the Gospel writers in connection with Jesus' entry to Jerusalem on Palm Sunday (cf. Matt. 21:5). Zech. 11:12 is part of an obscure passage in which a "shepherd" is paid his wages: thirty shekels of silver. The New Testament mentions an identical sum of money as the price paid to Judas for betraying Jesus (Matt. 26:15). Also in the narrative of the Passion of Jesus is the quotation at Matt. 26:31,

> I will strike the shepherd,
> And the sheep of the flock will be scattered,

which is taken from Zech. 13:7. It is also noteworthy that in Zech. 12:10–14, in the context of the promise of God to "pour out a spirit of compassion and supplication on the house of David," there is an obscure reference to "one whom they have pierced." This reminds Christian readers of the piercing of the side of Jesus in John 19:34.

Apart from these passages, which were drawn upon by the writers of the New Testament, Zechariah 9–14 contains the following main themes:

1. The restoration of Judah and the gathering of exiles (9:11–17, 10:7–12)
2. Battles of the nations against Jerusalem (12:1–9, 14:1–15)
3. Divine condemnation of the "shepherds" (i.e., leaders; 10:3–5, 11:4–17, 12:7–9)

These main themes indicate the difficulty of dating and interpreting these chapters. On the one hand, the passages about gathering the exiles and restoring Judah could be exilic, and thus earlier than the dates given for Zechariah 1–8 (520–500). On the other hand, the material about the nations warring against Jerusalem gives the impression of being later postexilic, perhaps fourth century. But there is a further factor, and that is that Zechariah 9–14 seems to contain echoes, perhaps deliberate allusions, to others parts of the Old Testament.

The theme of the "shepherds" is one that occurs in Ezekiel 34; and the passages about the wars against Jerusalem have the same flavor as Ezekiel 38–9, the threat of Gog of Magog. Another hint of Ezekiel is at 14:8, which reads, "On that day living waters shall flow out of Jerusalem" (cf. Ezek. 47:1ff.). A remarkable allusion is at 13:5, in a passage that promises the removal of prophets from the land (and idols and unclean spirits). Any who prophesy must be pierced through by their parents (13:3), and there is a promise that on the day that God acts decisively, prophets will no longer deceive but will say, "I am no prophet; I am a tiller of the soil" (13:5). This is a clear reference back to Amos 7:14, where that prophet (supposedly) declares that he is not a prophet.

In view of the above, we have to face the possibility that Zech. 9–14 is a collection of disparate material dating from the exile (sixth century B.C.E.) to perhaps hellenistic (fourth century B.C.E.) times. It is possible, of course, to date one of the oracles about gathering in the exiles to the Greek period, given the explicit reference to Greece at 9:13. Attempts have also been made to see a reference to the split between Jews and Samaritans at 11:14, where the prophet breaks the staff named Unity. But we do not know exactly when this split took place. Meyers and Meyers (1993, pp. 26–8) place Zech. 9–14 in the first half of the fifth century, although they allow that some material may be older.

Can anything be said about the community or circle that produced Zech. 9–14? The view that the "apocalyptic" nature of the material indicates its setting in an anti-establishment "eschatological" group is not followed here (see below on apocalyptic p. 271ff.). Indeed, a case can hardly be made for the material being apocalyptic. The strictures against the "shepherds" could indicate an anti-establishment group; yet condemnation of rulers is found in many prophetic books of the Old Testament, even from such obviously "establishment" figures as Isaiah (cf. 1:10ff.). Of more interest is the polemic against prophets in chapter 13. Does this indicate a setting in an established, literary, possibly priestly circle devoted to interpretation of what is written, as opposed to the unscripted words of prophets? Meyers and Meyers do not accept this suggestion. They attribute Zech. 9–14 to several individuals who spoke within the framework of earlier prophecy and who emerged in the shadow of the prophet of Zech. 1–8. They also believe that these speakers adapted the main themes of Zech. 1–8 to their own situation. This was a situation of Greco-Egyptian rebellion against Persia, the consequent firmer control exercised by Persia over areas such as Judah, and a general movement away from spoken communication to written communication.

P.   MALACHI

Most commentators agree that Malachi is not the name of a prophet but the Hebrew for "my messenger." The opening verse (1:1) picks up the beginning of 3:1, "See, I am sending my messenger," and was probably added by an editor as a heading. The opening of Malachi ("An oracle. The word of the LORD to Israel by Malachi") is similar to the headings of Zechariah 9:1 and 12:1.

In its literary form, Malachi is unique in the Old Testament in that it quotes and answers a series of questions that were important to the people or their priests. The questions are

1:2   How have you [God] loved us?
1:6   How have we despised your name?
1:7   How have we polluted it [the altar]?
2:14   Why does he [God] not (accept our offering)?
2:17   How have we wearied him?
3:8   How are we robbing you?
3:13   How have we spoken against you?

In some cases, the questions are answered by a further quotation from the people or their priests. At 1:13 the priests have said, "what a weariness this is," concerning the exact observance of the regulations about offering pure animals to God in sacrifice. At 2:17 God has been wearied by people saying, "All who do evil are good in the sight of the LORD, and he delights in them," and "Where is the God of justice?" The words with which God was spoken against in 3:13 were "It is vain to serve God. . . . when [evildoers] put God to the test, they escape" (3:14–15).

From these words spoken against God we can build up a picture of the community being addressed in Malachi. Their main concern was that evil and injustice were not being punished, either by the leaders or by God. Mal. 3:5 lists as wrongdoers who are soon to be judged by God the following: sorcerers, adulterers, those who swear falsely, and those who oppress hired workers, widows, orphans, and aliens. If this list accurately reflects wrongdoers at the time (it may be a conventional list of wrongdoers), then the period concerned is most likely to be the first part of the fifth century B.C.E. before the reforms of Nehemiah. However, in agreeing with the majority of scholars in this regard, we must note that we really know little about this period.

The lack of justice and fairness seems to have led to disillusionment: "It is vain to serve God" (3:14). The offering of animals as sacrifices was being done in a grudging manner which disregarded the regulations of the temple (1:6–14). The expansion of Edom in southern Judah (if this is the background to 1:2–5) produced despair. Divorce laws, intended to protect wives, were being ignored (2:13–16). There was a refusal to pay tithes to the temple and to give offerings to support the priests (3:8–12). All this was probably acted out against a background of bad harvests (3:10–12).

In this situation of disillusionment and frustration, the prophet does two things. First, he insists in various ways that the people are in the wrong in their attitude to God and the proper worship of him. Second, he promises that God will send his messenger, who will be like a refiner's fire and fuller's soap, and who will both purify the service of the temple and put right the social injustices (3:12–15). This emphasis on the messenger coming to the temple reminds us how much of Malachi is concerned with temple cultic matters. The text is clearly the product of a temple-based community in which both religion and justice had become corrupt. The identity of the messenger who will come and cleanse the temple and society is not revealed, and there is no way for us to know what or whom the writer intended.

Those who put the book into its final form, however, were more explicit. It is generally accepted that the famous closing words about God sending the prophet Elijah (4:5–6, Hebrew, 3:23–4) belong to a later, editorial phase and indicate a time when legends about Elijah were beginning to multiply.

> Lo, I will send you the prophet Elijah before the great and terrible Day of the LORD comes. He will turn the hearts of parents to their children and the hearts of children to their parents, so that I will not come and strike the land with a curse.

In 2 Kings there is an account of Elijah being taken up into heaven. This led to the belief that he did not die and that he would be sent back to earth to herald the coming Day of the LORD. The enigmatic reference to "my messenger" in 3:1 has been elaborated in terms of the Elijah legend.

In Christian Bibles that do not have an intervening Apocrypha, Malachi is the last book of the Old Testament and thus forms a fitting prelude to the New Testament. It means that the last passage in the Old Testament foresees the coming of Elijah, while the gospels portray John the Baptist as an Elijah-like figure who acts as the herald of the mission of Jesus. The book order of the Bible in Hebrew is different. Malachi ends the section known as the Latter Prophets, which is part of the second division, the Prophets. Malachi gives us a unique picture of the community that lived around the rebuilt temple, in terms that very much echo many modern-day problems.

IV.   THE WORLD OF ISRAEL'S WORSHIP

A.   WORSHIP, SACRIFICE, AND RITUAL

In its final form the Old Testament is the product of a temple-based community living in and around Jerusalem in the fifth to second centuries B.C.E. Gathered together and systematized in the Old Testament is material about worship and sacrifice that predates by many centuries the time of this final compilation; and this material originated not only from Jerusalem but from the northern kingdom of Israel, and not only from specifically religious centers but from the celebrations of towns and villages at great occasions such as harvest festivals. The writers of the Old Testament effected their systematization by designating Moses as the founder of the priestly and sacrificial cult and David as the founder of the musical and liturgical organization of the temple. Any attempt to describe the historical development of worship in Israel and Judah has, therefore, to unscramble the coherent way in which the relevant material has been assembled. Complete agreement among scholars about the resulting reconstructions cannot be expected.

1.   Worship and Sacrifice in Israel and Judah prior to the Reforms of Hezekiah (727–698 B.C.E.) and Josiah (640–609 B.C.E.)

It is evident from the Old Testament that prior to the seventh century B.C.E., God was worshiped at many holy places. Abraham and Jacob are described as building altars at Shechem (Gen. 12:7, 33:20) and Bethel (Gen. 12:8, 35:1–2), and Jacob exclaims after his dream at Bethel, "This is none other than the house of God" (Gen. 28:17). In the stories of Saul and Samuel the following holy places are mentioned where sacrifice is offered to God: Shiloh, Gilgal, Mizpah, and Nob. In the story of Absalom's revolt against David, he offers sacrifices at Hebron (2 Sam. 15:7–12), and David pauses at the summit of the Mount of

WORSHIP IN EARLY ISRAEL

IN THEIR FINAL FORM THE biblical narratives present a very idealistic picture of the religious beliefs and practices of the Israelites who first settled in the land of Canaan. The eleven secular tribes were led in worship by the priestly tribe of Levi. The Levites championed the faith of Yahweh, which contrasted sharply with the native Canaanite religions. Shechem and Shiloh are presented as the central cultic shrines where the twelve tribes joined together to worship the national God of Israel.

Biblical and archeological evidence suggests the situation was not quite so clear-cut. There was apparently a large degree of continuity between the early Israelite cult and the religions practiced by the indigenous population of Syria–Palestine. The age-old practices and symbolism of Canaan were thus popular in the worship of early Israel. Numerous shrines, high places, and altars were scattered throughout the territories of the Israelite clans. Although some would have been of greater renown than others and therefore enjoyed a broader constituency, no single exclusive cultic center existed in premonarchic times.

Moreover, no single priestly family seems to have had a monopoly on cultic leadership. In fact, priestly families and guilds probably competed against each other actively. Perhaps most important, the early religion of Israel is likely to have been quite syncretistic. Even late in the history of the Israelite kingdoms, those who championed the worship of Yahweh alone faced a considerable challenge – sometimes even from the royal establishment and almost always on a popular level. Yahwistic religion played some role in the settlement period, but no uniform faith held the allegiance of all Israel in the days before the monarchy.

Yahweh likely would have been worshiped along with other gods from the pantheon of Syria–Palestine (e.g., Baal, El, Astarte) and in a similar fashion. Local groups or families of priests oversaw cults that were organized around making sacrifices, celebrating ritual meals, and seeking divine oracles. Religious celebrations often involved music and solemn processions. Several narratives in Judges mention sacred objects associated with this kind of worship: the ephod (Judg. 8:27), teraphim, and various molten and graven images (cf. Judg. 18:14).

In addition to the more elaborate sanctuaries adapted from the Canaanite world, the early tribes of Israel would probably also have worshiped in open-air holy places known in the Old Testament as *bamot* (singular, *bamah*, "high place"). These country shrines were usually built on a height or mound, sometimes on a natural outcropping of rock. They were used for making seasonal offerings and sacrifices similar to those of the fertility cults of the Canaanites or perhaps for ceremonies connected with clan memories of revered ancestors. Often marked by a tree or group of trees, high places were generally provided with altars. A sacred wooden pole (*'asherah*) and stone pillar (*maṣṣebah*) were associated features.

In general, early Israel's worship was quite pluralistic. On the level of popular religion, and sometimes with official endorsement, this pluralism continued well into the monarchy. However, the increasing importance of monotheistic Yahwism in the later kingdom left its impression on the texts concerning the beliefs and practices of Israel during the settlement period. The orthodoxy those texts imply is more a later ideal than a historical reality.

Olives, "where God was worshiped" (2 Sam. 5:32). Solomon, prior to building the temple in Jerusalem, offered many sacrifices at Gibeon (1 Kings 3:4). Amos condemns the insincere worship offered at Beersheba in addition to that at Bethel and Gilgal (Amos 5:5). There was also an Israelite sanctuary at Dan in the far north (Judg. 18:27–31, 1 Kings 12:29), and excavations at Arad in the far south have uncovered an Israelite temple that was originally thought to date to the tenth century but that is now thought to be somewhat later.

The picture yielded by these texts and by excavations is of many sanctuaries serving the needs of local populations, although we know little about what went on at these sanctuaries. Perhaps they served mainly the particular needs of families and individuals, who would

This well-preserved high place from Megiddo dates to the Early Bronze Age (ca. 2500 B.C.E.) and was used until ca. 1950 B.C.E. The mound of rocks functioned as an altar.

(*below*) Tel Dan High Place. This open-air shrine covers nearly a half acre and comes from the tenth to eighth centuries B.C.E. The original shrine may be related to Jeroboam I (920 B.C.E.); the latest, to Jeroboam II.

SANCTUARIES IN EARLY ISRAEL

THE TYPICAL SANCTUARY OF the Israelite tribes was a local operation serving one or more clans or villages, or perhaps one or two tribes at most. Individual families could even set up their own shrines, altars, or temples. Although the compilers of Genesis–2 Kings present Shiloh as the principal religious and political center of premonarchic Israel, important sanctuaries seem to have been located in several towns during the settlement period. These early cultic centers include Shechem, Shiloh, Nob, Kadesh, Beersheba, Dan, Penuel, Bethel/Mizpah/Gilgal, Hebron, Gibeon, and Ophra.

Israel's first sanctuaries were likely patterned after the Bronze Age worship places of the land's indigenous peoples. Archeological evidence suggests, for example, that the Canaanite sanctuary at Shechem was also used by the Israelites during the Iron Age. In Near Eastern culture the sanctity of holy places frequently outlasts the physical structures built on them. Built originally ca. 1600 B.C.E., the temple–fortress at Shechem contained a massive earthen altar that was flanked by a pair of sacred pillars. The altar was positioned so that it would have been visible from almost any place within the city. In the Late Bronze Age (ca. 1500 B.C.E.) the temple was renovated. A new pillar was erected in the front of the structure, which had been rebuilt so as to be oriented toward the rising sun. Another change came about 1150 B.C.E., when a new stone altar replaced the earlier earthen construction. This newly modified structure is probably to be identified with the "House of Baal Berith" (the temple of the Lord of the Covenant) mentioned in Judges in association with the story of Abimelech. The standing stone of Josh. 24:26 is also likely to be related to these structures.

A key feature of early Israelite sanctuaries were such stone pillars, known in Hebrew as *masṣebot* (singular, *masṣebah*). *Masṣebot* have survived in a wide variety of archeological sites related to the Israelite settlement period. They were common constructions in the sacred architecture of Syria–Palestine. The Gezer High Place, for instance, dates to around 1600 B.C.E., and its impressive arrangement of ten enormous stone stelae could well have been known to the early Israelites. The stones, some more than nine feet high, were set in a north–south line just inside the city wall. *Masṣebot* were central cultic objects that may have served as memorials for important ancestors, as witnesses to an experience of theophany, or as remembrances of a solemn covenant. They were sometimes set up on hallowed ground in the countryside, especially in association with sacred trees.

Erecting commemorative stones is an ancient practice that appears in many geographical and cultural contexts. Sometimes the *masṣebah* even served as an object of worship, especially in early Israel, when the cult of Yahweh would have been but one of many religious traditions sharing the same symbols and practices. Orthodox Yahwism rejected that particular understanding of the *masṣebot,* though such conceptions persisted on a mostly popular level. The Bible depicts Israelites as often erecting *masṣebot,* but never ascribing divine power to them (Exod. 24:4, Gen. 35:14). Nevertheless, in Israelite tradition the *masṣebah* continued to be a monument of Yahweh's actual presence and as such a sacred object.

offer sacrifices in time of illness or give thanks for the birth of a child. Perhaps the local sanctuary was where a slave affirmed his lifelong loyalty to his master (Exod. 21:5–6), or where people took legal disputes that could not otherwise be settled. We gain a glimpse of what went on at a local sanctuary in the opening chapters of 1 Samuel. Elkanah used to go up each year to offer sacrifice at Shiloh (1 Sam. 1), and other worshipers also brought sacrifices, from which the priests (wrongly) profited (1 Sam. 2:12–17). However, these glimpses provide little hard information.

Israelite worship did not always take place at local sanctuaries. The historical original of the Passover can only be guessed at. If it is correct to assume that the Passover was observed as a family celebration in the northern kingdom of Israel until Hezekiah (2 Chron. 30) and Josiah

Horned incense altar from Megiddo, tenth century B.C.E.

(2 Kings 23:21–3) made it a national festival for Judah (and, by implication, Israel) celebrated in Jerusalem, then until that time it was an important community- or family-based act of worship. Passover was observed at the same time as the harvest festival for the barley harvest (March/April), when the use of unleavened bread marked the transition from the use of the old barley to the use of the new. Other harvest festivals were held for the wheat harvest (May/June) and the fruit harvest (September/October). In the Old Testament these festivals are associated with the story of Israel's release from slavery in Egypt; for example, the autumn harvest festival, the Feast of Booths, commemorates the wilderness wanderings. However, these harvest festivals were originally times of communal celebration and thanksgiving in towns and villages. The Book of Ruth (Ruth 3) implies that such festivals were also a time for wooing.

Other occasions of worship of which we catch glimpses are an annual festival at Shiloh at which the young women danced in the vineyards (Judg. 21:19–21), a new moon feast presided over by Saul (1 Sam. 20:18–24), and a family sacrifice in Bethlehem for David's family (1 Sam. 20:27–9). There is also mention of new moon and Sabbath festivals at which it could be appropriate to visit a holy man (2 Kings 4:23). At what point the Sabbath became a day of rest and of worship in the way that Jews and Christians today regard the Sabbath and Sunday we do not know. There may also have been national festivals, especially in the northern kingdom, at which the covenant law was read to the assembled people. Traces of this may be seen in Deut. 27:11–26, where the Shechemite Dodecalogue (Twelve Commandments) is rehearsed, and Deut. 31:7, where a reading of the law every seventh year at the Feast of Booths is enjoined.

2. Worship and Sacrifice from the Reforms of Hezekiah (727–698 B.C.E.) and Josiah (640–609 B.C.E.) to the Exile (597/6 B.C.E.)

Beersheba horned altar. This is the first large horned altar for animal sacrifice ever discovered in an Israelite setting.

In 722/1 the northern kingdom of Israel fell to the Assyrians and ceased to exist as an independent entity. Refugees from the former northern kingdom made their way south to Jerusalem. Among them were the guardians of traditions about Israel's law and prophets. The bringing of these traditions to Jerusalem brought about changes in how Israel's religion and worship were understood in Jerusalem. Hezekiah, king of Judah, used his power to effect a reformation that would free the worship of the people from practices that were now regarded as abuses. The worship of many ordinary Israelites at local sanctuaries had not been "pure" from a strictly orthodox point of view. The worship of the God of Israel was accompanied by popular superstitious practices, including fertility rites intended to assist the growth of crops and consultation with mediums. There are many hints of such practices in the Old Testament condemnations of them (e.g., 1 Sam. 28:3–25, Isa. 8:19, Mic. 1:7) as well as in Othmar Keel's impressive evidence for "popular religion" as illustrated from iconography. We must not overlook, either, the prophetic criticism of official religion that offered sacrifice and ignored justice (Amos 2:6–8, 5:21–4; Hos. 6:6; Mic. 6:6–8).

Hezekiah tried to effect a reformation by suppressing all holy places other than Jerusalem (1 Kings 18:4–5, 22) and by commanding the observance of the Passover as a national festival (2 Chron. 30). His aim was to remove the "abuses" from local sanctuaries by closing the sanctuaries. How far he was successful we do not know; and in any case, his reforms were short-lived, because during the long reign of his son Manasseh (698–642) many local pagan and foreign religious practices reasserted themselves. Josiah (640–609) tried again to centralize worship in Jerusalem so as to have control over it. No doubt such a reformation also consolidated his power and brought economic advantages; but it would be unfair to say that the reformation was motivated by purely secular considerations. It was also the work of religious reformers.

For our purposes, the effect of the reformation was to begin the process of producing a coherent story out of the diverse phenomena that constituted Israel's worship in the pre-exilic period. Unfortunately, we do not know whether any of the psalms, liturgical practices, or rituals of sanctuaries other than Jerusalem were preserved during this process, or whether it was only Jerusalem practice that was used as the basis for the regulations for worship and sacrifice in books such as Chronicles and Leviticus. Attempts have sometimes been made to see some psalms (e.g., 42–5) as originating in sanctuaries other than Jerusalem; but there can be no certain proof. After the return from exile there was only one sanctuary, Jerusalem, so that the history of the Israelite cult was written from that perspective.

3. Sacrifice in Ancient Israel

According to the final form of the Old Testament, a complete system of priesthood and sacrifice was instituted by Moses at Mount Sinai. Instructions about these matters are found from Exodus 25 through to Leviticus and parts of Numbers. Moses is not said to have commanded the building of a temple, although the account of the construction of the tabernacle and its appurtenances in Exodus 25–30 and 36–40 is written in the light of the arrangements in the second temple, which was completed in 516 B.C.E. after the return from exile.

An attempt has been made above to indicate that the history of worship in Israel was more complex than the final form of the biblical text allows. The same is true of the history of sacrifice. The Old Testament says that non-Israelites and Hebrews before the time of Moses offered sacrifices. Thus, Cain and Abel made offerings (Gen. 4), and Noah made burnt offerings of all clean birds and animals after the Flood (Gen. 8:20–1). We have already noted that Abraham and Jacob built altars. The non-Israelite Job made burnt offerings for his children in case they had sinned (Job 1:5). The Moabite king's offering of his first-born son as a burnt offering upon the wall of Kir-hareseth is said to have brought great wrath upon the invading Israelites (2 Kings

3:26–7). The Old Testament recognizes, then, that sacrifice in the ancient world did not originate with Moses. Rather, the designation of Moses as the founder of Israel's cult situates the sacrificial system within the story of Israel's election as the covenant people.

Insofar as we can guess about the history of sacrifice in Israel before the exile, we can say with certainty that the whole burnt offering, in which a whole animal was burnt, was widespread and offered for a variety of reasons. Job, as we have seen, is credited with using it in case his children had sinned; but we must recognize that "sinned" probably refers to ritual, rather than moral, acts. The whole burnt offering is also used before armies go to war (1 Sam. 13:8–12), as well as during war as a desperate measure (2 Kings 3:26–7). In the story of Noah the burnt offerings are a thanksgiving after the Flood.

In the material relating to sacrifices in Exodus, Leviticus, and Numbers the attempt is made to present the system as a coherent whole. Although in its final form the material dates from the fifth to fourth centuries B.C.E., it does not follow from this that the sacrifices described date only from this period. Priestly tradition about rituals, especially in oral form, is very robust, and the information that we have about sacrifices in the Old Testament almost certainly goes back to a time long before the exile. This does not rule out, however, its reshaping and reuse after the exile.

Because the material is so complex, a summary of main types of sacrifices follows. The burnt offering has been discussed more generally above. The details about this ritual are contained in Leviticus 1, from which it appears that any clean animal or bird can be offered. The sacrifice is described as providing a "pleasing odor" to God, a phrase that probably reflects the antiquity of this type of offering. It is unlikely that the final editors of the Old Testament believed that God had a sense of smell that could be satisfied with the odor of burning flesh.

Peace offerings (Hebrew *shelamim*), described in Lev. 3 and 7:11–34, compose the second class of animal sacrifices. Only certain parts of the animal are burnt in sacrifice, to which may be added unleavened cakes or wafers. Most of the flesh of the animal is eaten by the worshipers. This class of offerings appears to be connected with acts of thanksgiving, followed by a communal meal.

By far the biggest and most complex offerings are the sin offerings, described in Lev. 4:1–5:13, 6:24–30, 8:14–17, 16:3–22. These sacrifices are required when commandments are unintentionally broken (Lev. 4:2), and the type of animal offered depends upon the status of the offender. If the offender is the high priest or the whole congregation, a young bull is offered. For a leader of people it is a male goat, for an ordinary person it is a female goat or sheep, and poor people may offer a dove or a pigeon. The very poor may offer a measure of fine flour. The offender's status also affects how and where the animal is used. The higher the status, the more holy are the objects in the tabernacle to which the blood of the sacrifice is applied. Thus, in the offering for the congregation, the blood is sprinkled in front of the curtain and applied to the "altar that is before the LORD" (Lev. 4:17–18), whereas in the case of an ordinary Israelite, the blood is applied to the altar of burnt offering.

The fourth type of offering, usually called a guilt offering but better regarded as a restoration offering, is described in Lev. 5:14–6:7 (Hebrew, 5:14–26), 7:1–6. It is the only offering that includes deliberate moral offenses among the actions it seeks to remedy. The examples given (Lev. 6:1–6, Hebrew, 5:20–5) include fraud and robbery. The offerings, of a ram or lamb, the flesh of which is eaten by the priests (Lev. 7:6), are made only after the damage incurred by the fraud or robbery has been made good plus 20 percent.

This last point is a reminder that for many offenses that we regard today as serious moral offenses, no sacrifices were prescribed in the Old Testament because the penalty was the death of the offender. Such capital offenses included intentional murder, striking or cursing a parent, kidnapping (for all these see Exod. 21:15–17), adultery, and raping a betrothed woman (Deut. 22:23–7). To what extent these penalties were carried out we do not know. David escaped with his life after committing adultery and arranging for the offended husband, Uriah, to be killed in battle, even if he did not escape consequent disasters (see 2 Sam. 12–20); but we must assume that if the death penalty was carried out for the prescribed offense, then it was a form of sacrifice that was believed to purge evil from the people (see Deut. 13:5).

How were sacrifices believed to be effective? There are various possibilities, some of which have been influenced by general theories of sacrifice put forward by social anthropologists. Thus, the communal meal as part of the "peace offerings" may have been a fellowship meal with God; the eating of the flesh of the "guilt offering" by the priests may have been an act of "sin eating." Another view suggests that sacrifices were offered in order to cope with and to prevent violence within the postexilic community (Lohfink 1983).

From the Old Testament itself the following points can be made. In regard to the sin offering, the offense was thought to pollute the sanctuary, hence the need to cleanse the most sacred parts of the Tabernacle if the offender was the high priest or the congregation. In the rituals for the consecration of a priest and the readmission of a cured "leper" to the community (Lev. 8:22–35, 14:2–32), certain common acts suggest that the ritual enabled the person to change status. The priest is removed from the sphere of the everyday into that of the holy, whereas the "leper" (the sufferer from one of several skin diseases) is brought back into the community from which he or she had been excluded. Noteworthy in both cases is the transitional period of seven days spent in the camp at the entrance of the tent of meeting (Lev. 8:33–5, 14:11). This transitional period, together with the other offerings, effects a crossing of boundaries: in the one case into the sphere of the holy, in the other case into the sphere of the everyday. A similar use of the spatial categories of holy, everyday, and outside the community is evident in the ritual for the Day of Atonement (Lev. 16). The goat chosen to bear the sins of the community is led from the holy place, through the camp, to the wilderness outside the camp (Lev. 16:21–2),

---

THE TEMPLE SCROLL

AMONG THE MANY IM-portant documents recovered from the Qumran community, the Temple Scroll ranks as one of the most significant. It is the longest of the Dead Sea Scrolls, consisting of nineteen parchment sheets sewn together to form a rolled document over twenty-eight feet (= 8.148 m) long. The scroll was acquired in 1967 by the late Israeli scholar Yigael Yadin. Paleographic experts date the scroll to ca. 135 B.C.E. and credit its composition to the Essenes, one of the three major sectarian groups of Jewish antiquity known to us primarily through the wri-

tings of the historian Flavius Josephus.

The scroll survives in varying states of preservation. Unfortunately, the entire first section of the scroll is missing. In terms of content, the scroll describes in minute detail the plans for a new Jerusalem temple: its courtyards, sacrifices, cultic ritual, and purity regulations. The scroll makes extensive use of biblical and nonbiblical material, and the work is broadly patterned after the Books of Exodus and Deuteronomy. Surprisingly, Moses is usually referred to in the first person as if he were intended to be understood as the scroll's author. Large sections of the scroll

are simply recapitulations of canonical texts from the Hebrew Bible. Frequently, however, scriptural portions have been modified, elucidated, harmonized, or expanded.

Some scholars believe the scroll served the Qumran community as a supplement to the canonical Torah (Genesis to Deuteronomy), legitimizing the covenanters' special cultic beliefs and festal calendar. Divergences between the Temple Scroll and the laws set forth in the Masoretic text of the Hebrew Bible suggest that this work represents the establishment of a halakah (legal prescription of behavior) unique to the sectarians at Qumran.

---

thus symbolizing the removal from the community of the sins that have been confessed.

This section offers only a summary of a complex matter. Rituals such as that of the red heifer (for providing ashes that will medicate water used for washing people who have touched a dead body; see Num. 19) have not been detailed. Neither has the question of the so-called spiritualization of sacrifice, the tradition that true sacrifices are the inward offering of heart and soul, been developed. See Psalms 50–1 for statements of that view.

B. PSALMS

1. The Nature of Israelite Poetry

All of the psalms in the Old Testament are in poetry; but Israelite poetry is not confined to the psalms, nor is the type of poetry found in the Old Testament peculiar to ancient Israel. Other books that contain large amounts of poetry include Job, Proverbs, Isaiah, and Jeremiah, and the so-called Minor Prophets are largely poetic. Poetry can also be found in Song of Songs and Lamentations and is scattered through the remainder of the Old Testament. Thus, the judgment pronounced by God on Adam and Eve in Gen. 3:14–19 is in poetry, as is the song of Lamech in Gen. 4:23–4. Notable poems outside the main poetic books include the Blessings of Jacob and Moses (Gen. 49, Deut. 33), the Song of Moses (Deut. 32), the Song of Deborah (Judg. 5), and David's lament over Saul and Jonathan (2 Sam. 1:19–27).

Hebrew poetry is characterized by parallelism, of which three types have traditionally been recognized: synonymous, antithetic, and syn-

Temple Scroll fragment. The Temple Scroll, the largest of all the Dead Sea Scrolls, was acquired by the Israelis after the 1967 war.

thetic. Synonymous parallelism repeats the same, or almost the same, sense in a second line using different words from those in the first line:

For I was envious of the arrogant;
I saw the prosperity of the wicked.   (Ps. 73:3)

Antithetic parallelism introduces a second line with an opposite point to the first:

For the LORD watches over the way of the righteous,
but the way of the wicked will perish.   (Ps. 1:6)

Synthetic parallelism continues in a second line the thought of the first, without correspondence of words:

The LORD looks down from heaven on humankind
to see if there are any who are wise, who seek after God.   (Ps. 14:2)

Recent researches have made these basic distinctions more complex and have also suggested different ways of describing the material. Thus, from the standpoint of transformational grammar (the theory that surface structures are transformations of kernels in the "deep structure"), a verse such as

> For he who avenges blood is mindful of them;
> he does not forget the cry of the afflicted   (Ps. 9:12)

can be described as follows. The deep structure, "he who avenges blood remembers the cry of the afflicted," is transformed into two lines in which the parallelism is effected by contracting "he who avenges blood" to "he" and by expanding "them" into "cry of the afflicted."

Another approach is to look for pairs of words that commonly occur together and that are used in different lines. For example,

> For the *needy* shall not always be forgotten,
> nor the hope of the *poor* perish forever.   (Ps. 9:18)

> Why do the *nations* conspire
> and the *peoples* plot in vain?   (Ps. 2:1)

An excellent example of wordplay using an *a-b-b-a* pattern is found at Ps. 9:19–20:

> Rise up, O LORD! Do not let *mortals* [*enosh*] prevail;
> let the *nations* [*goyim*] be judged before you.
> Put them in fear, O LORD;
> let the *nations* [*goyim*] know that they are only *human* [*enosh*].

Hebrew poetic style has generated an extensive literature in the past twenty years. The summary here should help readers be sensitive to their own reading of Hebrew poetry. It is essential for readers to use a modern translation in which the poetry is set out as such. This was not done, for example, in the King James (Authorized) Version of 1611.

2.   The Literary History of the Psalms

There are two ways of numbering the psalms. Non-Catholic English translations follow the system in the Hebrew Bible; but the ancient Greek translation known as the Septuagint uses a different numbering. There, Psalms 9–10 are taken as one psalm, with the result that Psalms 11–113 in the Hebrew order are 10–112 in the Greek order. The material from 113–16 presents the following differences:

Hebrew	Greek
114–15	113
116:1–9	114
116:10–19	115

After this, Hebrew 117–46 equals Greek 116–45. The following final difference:

Hebrew	Greek
147:1–11	146
147:12–20	147

enables the two psalters to agree for the final three psalms. There is also a Psalm 151 in the Greek, of which a Hebrew version has been found among the Dead Sea Scrolls and which is included in the Apocrypha section of the New Revised Standard Version.

The psalms are divided into five books (the Hebrew numbering is used in what follows): book 1, Psalms 1–41; book 2, Psalms 42–72; book 3, Psalms 73–89; book 4, Psalms 90–106; book 5, Psalms 107–50. There is some indication that the division resulted from the way the psalms were collected. Thus, most of the psalms of book 1 are entitled in Hebrew *le david*, meaning that they were attributed to David or belonged to a collection associated with his name. Book 2 begins with eight psalms of the sons of Korah (42–9), and book 3 begins with eleven psalms of Asaph (73–83). Most of book 4's psalms have no attribution (an exception is Psalm 90, attributed to "Moses, the man of God"), and book 5 has a collection of "Songs of Ascents" (120–34) and a group of David psalms (135–45).

The books end with doxologies: book 1 with Ps. 41:13; book 2 with Ps. 72:18–19, plus the words of 72:20, "The prayers of David son of Jesse are ended"; book 3 with Ps. 89:52, and book 4 with Ps. 106:48. In the case of book 5, Psalm 150 can be taken as the doxology to this book and to the collection as a whole.

There is evidence that some of the books existed independently as collections before being made into the Book of Psalms. Beginning with Psalm 42 and extending to Psalm 83 there has been systematic substitution of the divine name "God" (Hebrew *'elohim*) for the original "LORD" (Hebrew *yhwh*). This can be seen by comparing Psalms 14 and 53, which are identical apart from the divine names, and by reading Psalms 42–83 and noticing the overwhelming preponderance of the name "God." There thus probably existed an "Elohistic" collection (one using the Hebrew name *'elohim*) that included most of what are now books 2 and 3, whereas Psalms 3–41 were a separate Davidic collection.

It is also probable that the collections of psalms were added to as they grew into the whole Psalter as we know it. The Psalms Scroll from the Dead Sea Scrolls (11QPsᵃ) has an irregular order between Psalms 100 and 150. Psalms 106–8 and 110–17 are omitted, and the following deviations from the traditional Hebrew order occur: 103, 109, 118, 104, 147, 105, 146; and 132, 119, 135; and 93, 141, 133, 144, 155 (one of ten noncanonical pieces in the scroll), 142–3, 149–50. In some cases, this order is the result of grouping psalms that contain *hodu* (praise) or hallelujah (praise the LORD) in their superscripts or postscripts. This accounts for the grouping of 118, 104, 147, 105, and 146. Although care must be taken in drawing conclusions from this scroll, it seems to indicate that, by the first century C.E., when the Psalms Scroll was written, the order of books 1–3 was fixed while that of books 4–5 was still fluid.

Fragment of the Psalms Scroll from cave 11 at Qumran. Here the name of God – the tetragrammaton (YHWH) is written in paleo-Hebrew letters.

Recent study has drawn attention to the fact that Psalm 1 is less about worship than about meditation on God's law, a theme even more prominent in Psalm 119. It has been suggested that, in its final form, the Psalter was intended for private meditation as well as for use in worship. The division of the collection into five books, even though this process may well have predated the final form, would make the psalms correspond to the five books of the Pentateuch, or Torah (law).

The literary history of the psalms can only be hypothetical, based on the clues from the psalms themselves. We can identify separate collections and editorial processes such as the changing of the divine name in Psalms 42–83. We can note that the order of Psalms 100–50 may have been fluid as late as the first century C.E. and that the final form of the collection as a whole stresses meditation upon God's law.

3.   The Psalms in Israelite Worship

As with the literary history of the psalms, we have little firm evidence about the use of psalms in Israel's worship. In the Old Testament itself, the Books of Chronicles cite certain psalms in connection with worship. Thus, at 1 Chron. 16:8–36 in connection with bringing the ark of God to Jerusalem, David is said to have appointed Asaph and his kindred to sing a psalm made up of what we know as Pss. 105:1–15, 96:1b–13, and 106:1, 47–8 (the last verse being also the doxology that ends book 4). In the context of Solomon's prayer of dedication (2 Chron. 6:41–2), Psalm 132:8–10 is quoted. The refrain

For he [God] is good,
for his steadfast love endures forever,

MUSIC AND MUSICAL INSTRUMENTS

MUSIC APPEARS VERY early in the Bible, with a reference in the primeval genealogy to "Jubal, who was the father of all who play the lyre and pipe" (Gen. 4:21). This suggests that the Israelites conceived of music as one of the first developments of culture, and that music played an important part in Israel's life from the beginning. Music served a variety of purposes. With music Israel's warriors and kings celebrated their victories. Musicians aided in worship and helped those who mourned the dead.

In Israel's early history, women appear to have been the primary musicians, as in Miriam's exultation over pharaoh's army (Exod. 15:20; cf. Deborah in Judg. 5) and the women's celebration of David's victory over the Philistines (1 Sam. 18:6–7). Israel's musical traditions included a special place for women who played portable frame-drums and performed dances. Female hand-drummers accompanied and led joyous singing and dancing for many occasions, but their artistry is particularly associated with a distinctive Israelite musical genre known as the "victory song" (see Exod. 15:20, Judg. 11:34, 1 Sam. 18:6, Jer. 31:4).

With the construction of the temple, music became a part of Israel's official cult. As such, it was controlled by the priestly establishment. The Chronicler credits David with organizing the temple musicians (1 Chron. 15), but the consolidation of temple music into the hands of the Levites was probably a more gradual development. By the postexilic period, Levites were almost exclusively associated with the musical service of the temple. Music was a central component of the Jerusalem cultus both before and after the exile (cf. 1 Sam. 10:5, Ps. 81:3, Isa. 5:12). Many psalms associate the praise of God with melody and song (e.g., Pss. 33:1–3, 150:3–6). Psalm 137 suggests that even Israel's Babylonian captors knew of their captives' musical reputation.

The royal court was another musical venue. David soothed Saul's troubled spirit with song. The aged Barzilai regretted not being able to enjoy the music of David's palace. In the eighth century B.C.E., Sennacherib carried off male and female singers from Jerusalem as the spoils of war.

Music also played a part in the everyday life of the community. Particularly noteworthy are the associations of music with laments for the dead. David lamented Saul and Jonathan with a song (2 Sam. 1:19–27). The people similarly mourned the death of Josiah with music (2 Chron. 35:25). Music was apparently a pastime for laborers (Isa. 16:10) and an integral part of wedding ceremonies (Song of Sol. 5:12–16). The prophets, however, associated music with the life of luxury, which they condemned (Amos 6:5–4).

Musical instruments in the biblical period were of stringed, percussion, and wind varieties. The harp and lyre are frequently mentioned, as is the drum. Musicians also employed the flute and trumpet. The sound of music in the biblical period is not recoverable, although some evidence suggests that remnants of liturgical and popular music were preserved in the chants and songs of secluded Jewish communities in Africa and Mesopotamia.

which occurs in Psalm 136, is referred to in 2 Chron. 5:13 and 7:3 and is evidently a response sung by the people, perhaps after each verse of certain psalms, as in Psalm 136. From the titles of the psalms themselves we gain little information about their use, partly because the titles are affected by the process of linking some psalms to incidents in the life of David, perhaps to assist their use in meditation. Psalm 30 is described in its title as "A Song at the Dedication of the Temple," but for most readers today the content of the psalm hardly justifies the title.

Given the lack of evidence in the Old Testament itself, scholarship has resorted to conjecture about the use of the psalms in Israel's worship. Medieval Jewish scholars linked certain psalms with worship events in the life of David and Solomon such as the dedication of the temple. The seventeenth-century Puritan commentator Matthew Poole noted that Psalm 2 had been connected with David's inauguration as king, whereas Psalms 24, 47, and 68 were reportedly composed when David brought the ark of God to Jerusalem (cf. 2 Sam. 6).

With the abandonment by critical scholarship in the eighteenth century of the belief that David had composed all or most of the psalms, the way was opened to suggest royal ceremonies other than ones connected with David in which the psalms were used. This possibility was exploited particularly in the present century, with attention focused upon so-called royal psalms, and especially upon Psalms 93 and 96–9. These celebrate the universal kingship of God over the world and the nations, and it is widely believed that they were used at an annual New Year festival or at the anniversary of the king's coronation. Their opening acclamation (in Pss. 93, 97, and 99), "The LORD is king!" is seen as the culmination of a ceremony that enabled the worshipers to act out their belief in God's kingship in a dramatic way and that also reinforced their hopes and beliefs about God's kingship in the future. Precisely what form the ceremony took, we do not know. One view, much less popular today than forty years ago, is that the king, representing God, suffered ritual combat, humiliation, death, and rebirth, and that the ceremony was believed to promote stability and prosperity for the following year. In this view, psalms such as 2 and 110, with their assurances of victory over enemies, preceded the ritual combat, while the many psalms of lamentation accompanied the combat (e.g., Pss. 3, 11, 12). This approach was deeply influenced by theories about the Babylonian New Year festival.

We are probably on firmer (but still conjectural) ground if we assume that there was a regular, possibly annual, ceremony associated with the ark that celebrated God's "coming" to Jerusalem and that proclaimed his universal rule from that city. Psalm 132 appears to describe a search for the ark and its triumphant entry into Jerusalem, where it is solemnly installed in its appointed place with the words,

> Rise up, O LORD, and go to your resting place,
> you and the ark of your might.   (Ps. 132:8)

Psalm 47:5–7 may indicate the acclamation of God's universal kingship following the solemn installation of the ark:

> God has gone up with a shout,
> the LORD with the sound of a trumpet.
> Sing praises to God, sing praises,
> sing praise to our king, sing praises.
> For God is king of all the earth.

Another part of the liturgy may be Psalm 24, which contains a series of challenges to the doorkeepers to admit "the king of glory." Perhaps these words were spoken as the ark was brought into the city after having been carried in procession round it (cf. Josh. 6:1–7).

Psalms such as 2 and 110 were probably used at the coronation of kings. In both of them, the king is designated as the special representative of the God of the nations. In Psalm 2 the king is given a protocol from which he reads,

Egyptian musicians, from the tomb of Mereruka at Saqqara. Male and female dancers and people keeping time by clapping their hands are depicted performing before the statue of Mereruka.

> You are my son;
> today I have begotten you.   (Ps. 2:7)

This means that he has been adopted into a special relationship with God (cf. Isa. 9:6–7, where the birth may mean the coronation and adoption of a king). Other royal psalms may be 44, used by a king prior to a battle, and 45, used at a royal wedding.

However illuminating these suggestions may be, a word of caution is in order. If these ceremonies did take place, we do not know whether they were performed in a private royal sanctuary or to what extent the people as a whole joined in. Further, these royal psalms imply a date and setting in the first temple period (ca. 960–587/6), whereas some recent scholarship locates the use of the psalms in the second temple period (516 B.C.E.–70 C.E.) and in communal worship apart from the temple (Gerstenberger 1988). This leads to another matter, the so-called form-critical study of the psalms.

In his 1811 commentary on the psalms, the German scholar W. M. L de Wette (1780–1849) noted that over a third of the whole collection were laments, comprising national laments (thirty-two psalms) and individual laments (twenty-six psalms). The laments constituted the heart of the Psalter, expressing the religious doubt and struggles of the nation and its individuals. In the present century scholars have analyzed the form (i.e., recurring typical patterns) of psalms and have classified them more precisely into laments, thanksgivings, and royal psalms. Attention has been focused especially upon typical features of laments. They usually begin with a cry to God for assistance and continue by specifying particular troubles experienced by the psalmist before ending with an affirmation of confidence in God. However, the circumstances of the psalmist's troubles are never so specifically stated as to allow their precise identification. Instead, we have general references to wrongdoers, enemies, sickness, or doubt.

This has raised the following questions, to which no firm answers can be given. Did the authors of the laments make them deliberately general so that they could be used by worshipers in a variety of situations – in which case, how were they preserved and made available to worshipers? Or is their general nature the result of the growth of the Book of Psalms as literature, with specific details being generalized so that the psalms gain in usefulness? Did worshipers in ancient Israel use existing psalms to express their feelings or did they compose their own psalms based on conventional patterns? Whatever the answers, the psalms are deeply rooted in national and individual worship and prayer in ancient Israel and have been preserved in such a way that they continue to be appropriate to the needs of worshipers in different ages and cultures.

4.   The Contents of the Psalter

In the listings that follow (which are based upon Rogerson and McKay's *Cambridge Bible Commentary*, 1977), some psalms appear under more than one heading. This usually means that they are adaptable for use in different situations, but occasionally it means that their interpretation is open to debate.

Hymns

In praise of God for what he is, good, loving, faithful, etc.: 103, 111, 113, 145–6, 150
To God the creator: 8, 19, 24, 29, 104
To God the bounteous provider: 65, 84, 144, 147
To the Lord of history: 68, 78, 105, 111, 114, 117
To God both as creator and as Lord of history: 33, 89, 95, 135–6, 144, 148
To God the mighty, the victorious: 68, 76, 149
On the final victory of God and his people: 46–8, 68, 93, 96–9
"The LORD is king": 47, 93, 96–9.
"Songs of Zion" (cf. 137:3): 46, 48, 76, 84, 87, 122
Suitable for use by pilgrims: 84, 121–2, 125, 127

National Psalms

Prayers for deliverance or victory: 44, 60, 74, 79–80, 83, 85, 89, 108, 126, 129, 137, 144
Prayers for blessing and continued protection: 67, 115, 125
General prayers for mercy or restoration: 90, 106, 123
Psalms that call the people to obedience: 81, 95
Royal psalms: 2, 18, 20–1, 45, 72, 89, 101, 110, 132
Other psalms that include prayers for the king: 61, 63, 80, 84
Other psalms that make reference to the king: 78, 122, 145

PSALMS AT QUMRAN

LIKE ALL JEWISH COMMUNIties in the first century of the common era, the Qumran sectarians used biblical psalms as a part of their scriptures. Psalms probably played an important part in the Qumran community's corporate worship and private devotions. Discoveries near the Dead Sea have unearthed many parts of the Qumran psalter, literature that includes biblical psalms, psalms known from apocryphal collections, and some compositions that were apparently unique to the Qumran community.

Archeologists have retrieved over thirty scrolls and fragments of psalms from eight different caves. The most important manuscript, called the Psalms Scroll (11QPsª), was found by Arab Bedouin in February 1956, nearly a decade after the discovery of the first of the Dead Sea Scrolls. Scholars unrolled and translated the scroll in 1961. Analysis of its writing reveals that the scroll dates from the period 30–50 C.E. Altogether, the scrolls preserve readings from 120 of the Hebrew Bible's 150 canonical psalms.

The Psalms Scroll contains numerous variants from the traditional text of the Hebrew Bible. Among other variations, the scroll contained David's poetic speech, which the Hebrew Bible preserved in 2 Sam. 23:1–7, as one more in the collection of Davidic psalms. In most early manuscripts, the sequential order of biblical psalms is quite traditional, especially in books 1 and 2 (Pss. 1–72). The Psalms Scroll contains material from only books 4 and 5 (Pss. 90–150), and the order of the compositions it preserves is quite different from that in the canonical Hebrew Bible. Scholars have used information like this to point out the complex history of the Psalter's standardization, a process not likely completed before the end of the first century C.E.

In addition to these canonical materials, the Psalms Scroll preserves eight compositions that did not come to be a part of the Hebrew Bible. Four of the ancient poems are known from ancient translations like the Greek Septuagint or the Syriac Psalter or from medieval Hebrew manuscripts of apocryphal literature. The other four compositions were unknown before the Psalms Scroll was found. They include a prayer for eschatological deliverance addressed to the city of Zion, a prayer asking for liberation from evil influences, a wisdom hymn to the creator, and a prose composition about David's wisdom and prophetic inspiration. Apparently the scribe who wrote down these psalms and those who read and appreciated them believed that the whole scroll was Davidic in origin and authoritative for the community.

A number of other scrolls surviving from the Qumran community contain psalmlike material. The most famous are the so-called Thanksgiving Hymns (1QH; the Hymn Scroll). These *hodayot* (praise songs) date from the first century B.C.E. Many of them are very similar to biblical psalms, although their style is quite eclectic. Some of the *hodayot* are very personal – almost biographical – hymns, which some scholars have attributed to the community's leader, the Teacher of Righteousness. Others seem to be expressions of the community as a whole. These psalms reflect many of the Qumran sect's fundamental ideas: dualism, predestination, election, and grace. A few specialists have suggested that the *hodayot* served some liturgical function, though most think they were more likely used for edification and reflection. Several clearly liturgical texts from Qumran also preserve hymnic material, including various supplications and expressions of praise.

Prayers of the Individual in Time of Need

For protection, deliverance, or vindication in the face of persecution: 3, 5, 7, 12, 17, 25, 35, 40–1, 54–7, 59, 64, 70, 86, 120, 123, 140–3

For use in time of suffering and dereliction: 6, 13, 22, 28, 31, 38–9, 42–3, 69, 71, 77, 88, 102, 143

For justice or personal vindication: 7, 17, 26, 35, 69, 94, 109

For forgiveness: 6, 25, 38, 51, 130

Expressing a deep longing for the nearness of God: 22, 25, 27, 38, 42, 51, 61, 63, 73, 77, 84, 130, 143

Expressing confidence or trust: 4, 11, 16, 23, 27, 52, 62, 91, 121, 131

Suitable for use in a night vigil: 5, 17, 22, 27, 30, 46, 57, 59, 63, 108, 143

The "Penitential Psalms" in Christian tradition: 6, 32, 38, 51, 102, 130, 143

Thanksgiving Psalms

For national deliverance: 118(?), 124

For personal deliverance: 18, 30, 34, 66, 116, 118, 138

For forgiveness: 32

For the knowledge of God's continuing love and care: 92, 107

See also under Hymns

Psalms Giving Instruction or Containing Meditations on Various Themes

On the law: 1, 19, 119

On the qualities required in the citizens of God's kingdom: 15, 24, 101, 112

On corruption in society: 11–12, 14, 53, 55, 58, 82, 94

On the lot of humanity, the problem of evil and suffering, the ways of the godly and the wicked: 1, 9–10, 14, 36–7, 39, 49, 52–3, 58, 62, 73, 90, 92, 94, 112

On God's judgment: 50, 75, 82

On God's blessings: 127–8, 133

On God's omniscience: 139

Psalms Generally Accounted Messianic in Christian Interpretation

The royal Messiah: 2, 18, 20–1, 45, 61, 72, 89, 110, 118, 132

The suffering Messiah: 22, 35, 41, 55, 69, 109

The second Adam, fulfiller of human destiny: 8, 16, 40

Psalms describing God as king, creator, etc., applied to Jesus in the New Testament: 68, 97, 102

Special Categories

Acrostics: 9–10, 25, 34, 37, 111–12, 119, 145

Songs of ascent: 120–34

Hallel: 113–18

Hallelujah: 146–50

V.   THE WORLD OF ISRAEL'S SAGES AND POETS

A.   THE NATURE OF "WISDOM" AND THE WORLD-VIEW OF THE SAGE

Most, if not all, modern introductions to the literature of the Old Testament assume that there is a category of "wisdom literature" to which the Books of Proverbs, Job, and Ecclesiastes are to be assigned. This was not the view of most of the nineteenth-century introductions, which designated these books, with others, as poetic literature. In Eduard Riehm's introduction of 1890, these three books were still discussed under the general heading of poetic books but in a special section devoted to "didactic poetry." They were also connected particularly with "the wise," and "wisdom" was seen to be one of their main themes.

In the present century Egyptian and Babylonian texts have been published that contain material similar to that in Proverbs, Job, and Ecclesiastes. Indeed, the Egyptian Instruction of Amen-em-Opet (*ANET*, pp. 421–4), dating perhaps from 1100 B.C.E. is so similar to Prov. 22:17–24:22 that many scholars believe that the Proverbs material is dependent in some way on the Egyptian text. Other texts that have attracted attention include the so-called Babylonian Ecclesiastes (*ANET*, pp. 439–40), in which a sufferer seeks comfort from a friend, and "I will praise the Lord of Wisdom" (*ANET*, pp. 434–7), in which a person of high rank describes his misfortunes, protests his innocence, and describes his ultimate deliverance. These discoveries suggested

---

EGYPTIAN WISDOM

BECAUSE OF ITS PROXIMITY, its political power, and its important trade relations, Egypt had a pervasive cultural influence over Palestine during much of the biblical period. Among these influences was the ancient and acclaimed Egyptian wisdom tradition.

Egyptian literature provides striking parallels to the wisdom traditions of the Hebrew Bible. In both Egypt and Israel, wisdom writings were of two general types: optimistic works that taught traditional morals and practical lessons from experience (like the Book of Proverbs) and more pessimistic works that asked weighty questions about the meaning of life and challenged established tradition (like Job and Ecclesiastes).

In the first category are the Egyptian Instructions. This significant body of literature, with the special title *sebayit*, "teaching", spans a period from 2800 to 100 B.C.E. About a dozen works of instructions, each known after the name of its author, have been preserved. Among the most famous is the Instruction of Amenemope(t), which closely

resembles parts of Prov. 22:17–24:22. These teachings are directed toward the training of young men for court life. They propound the bureaucratic virtues of correct speech, proper relations with women, correct dealings with superiors and inferiors, rules of etiquette, diligence, reliability, self-control, etc. These ideals have a marked similarity with the teachings of many biblical proverbs.

Central to the Instructions is the important Egyptian idea of *ma'at*, a comprehensive divine reality of order, truth, goodness, and justice which created and supported both the cosmos and human society. The cosmic order and the moral order were united, and the goal of human activity was to live in accordance with that order through wise thought, speech, and action. Living according to the principle of *ma'at* paid off with tangible blessings, just as conduct that varied from this divine order resulted in adversity.

Another branch of Egyptian wisdom literature offered a significant protest to these earlier expressions of confidence in the natural and moral order. This tradition ranges from pessimistic complaints about intractable

social forces to a hedonistic grasping after pleasure at any cost. Works like The Dispute over Suicide and the Harper's Songs show the same preoccupation about the central problems of life that is common to Job and Ecclesiastes. Hori's Satirical Letter shares the same tone of questioning that God directs against Job (38:4 ff.).

Some scholars have suggested that another genre of Egyptian wisdom literature also finds expression in the Hebrew Bible. Onomastica, or name lists, were encyclopedic catalogues of various objects and were used for the training of scribes. The Onomasticon of Amenemope(t), for example, lists the 610 things that the god Ptah created. They are listed in an orderly classification of divine and human beings, animate creatures, inanimate objects, natural objects, meteorological phenomena, cities, buildings, food and drink, etc. Lists of created things in Job 38–9, Psalm 148, Wisdom of Ben Sira 43, and the Song of the Three Youths (inserted in the Greek version of Daniel 3) may reflect Egyptian influence.

that "wisdom" was an international genre, in which Israel's literature shared.

Further, the investigation of scribal schools in the ancient Near East, in which scribes learned their craft by copying short proverbs and longer texts, indicated a link between wisdom traditions and royal scribal schools. Given the traditions in the Old Testament linking King Solomon with proverbs and songs (1 Kings 4:29–34, Prov. 1:21), it was natural to infer that Israelite wisdom literature was the product of a royal scribal school dating from at least the time of Solomon. A distinct class of scribal sages was identified from texts such as Isa. 29:14, "The wisdom of their wise shall perish," and Jer. 8:8–9, "The wise shall be put to shame." In this view Israelite wisdom was part of a larger, international phenomenon, mediated by scribes whose profession necessitated contact with other nations. This explains why the literature contains no references to the distinctive story of Israel's redemption as connected with the patriarchs, the Exodus, or the Sinai covenant.

Unfortunately, this neat picture has been criticized from various angles. The following points can be made.

1. We must be cautious in speaking of "wisdom" as an international phenomenon. In fact, the designation "wisdom literature" has been taken from Old Testament studies and applied to Egyptian and Babylonian texts. It is doubtful whether these extrabiblical texts would have been designated thus by modern scholars had it not been for the initiative from biblical studies.

2. The wisdom literature of the Old Testament does not necessarily have its setting in life in scribal or intellectual circles. Some of the proverbs have been compared with those found among contemporary African peoples, and these studies have reinforced the view that there was such a thing as folk wisdom in ancient Israel – practical observations on everyday life built into a simple but robust ethical code and operating at the level of family and village circles.

3. The evidence for scribal schools in ancient Israel is slender, and we cannot be sure that they existed in Judah earlier than the time of Hezekiah (727–698 B.C.E.). Further, it has been maintained above (pp. 88-92) that some of the influential families prominent in the administration of Israel and Judah and thus involved with or members of scribal schools were closely connected with the prophetic and Deuteronomistic movements. This means that we cannot identify such groups as interested in international culture to the exclusion of the traditions about the saving activity of God in Israel's history.

4. The books designated as constituting Israel's wisdom literature are, in fact, so diverse that it is hard to see them as the work of one class or group of people.

The upshot of these and other discussions is that we must avoid the mistake of positing certain sociological classes and conditions on the basis of literary texts, and of then using the sociological reconstructions to interpret the texts from which we began. We must not rule out the possibility that there were scribal schools in Israel and Judah and that these played a part in copying and transmitting proverbs; but we must also allow that some of the "wisdom" material had its origin in the folk wisdom of family circles.

If, as is likely, many proverbs existed orally before being written down and collected together, this very action affected their understanding. We can see this from our own culture if we place together the following two, apparently contradictory, proverbs: "he who hesitates is lost" and "look before you leap." Their juxtaposition produces something that is greater than the sum of their parts. Something similar happened when separate proverbs were collected together and written down in ancient Israel.

Our one certain datum is the literature of Proverbs, Job, and Ecclesiastes. In these books we find out much about daily life, including the actions of kings, traders, guests, and women managing their houses. We hear of the enemies of ordinary decent people – usurers, deceitful traders, oppressors, slanderers – as well as the bad habits of laziness, greed, flattery, bad temper, and uncontrolled utterances. The advice given is based on common sense and experience. It is also based on the view that the readers and listeners live in the kind of "moral universe" in which virtues and decency will ultimately be rewarded and vice and wickedness will be punished.

Yet this simple, perhaps simplistic outlook is tempered with deeper realism. The Book of Job argues against a simple equation between goodness and reward, while Ecclesiastes seems to find the whole "wisdom" outlook at best boring and at worst unrealistic. The wisdom texts are "humanistic" in the way that they explore the dilemmas of life without introducing God as an easy solution to all problems. Yet this kind of humanism is set in an implicit, if not explicit, religious, even Israelite religious, framework. The world is God's world, and from God comes true wisdom, insight, and understanding. God is also ultimately the guarantor of justice, in spite of experiences that seem to contradict this. One of Job's contentions is that if he could only get a fair trial before God, he would be able to prove his innocence. The wisdom literature is also aware of the frailty and transience of humanity in contrast to the enduring nature of God's world.

In older scholarship of this century, wisdom literature was an impediment to attempts to construct Old Testament theology in terms of the covenant, or the history of Israel's salvation. In the past twenty years the realistic humanism of this material within its wider religious context has won for it renewed interest among those seeking to read the Old Testament in the light of today's world.

B. PROVERBS

The Book of Proverbs is divided into a number of sections by a series of headings as follows:

1:1   The proverbs of Solomon son of David, king of Israel
10:1   The proverbs of Solomon
22:17 The words of the wise

24:23   These also are sayings of the wise
25:1   These are other proverbs of Solomon that the officials of King Hezekiah of Judah copied
30:1   The words of Agur son of Jakeh
31:1   The words of King Lemuel. An oracle that his mother taught him.

These headings are indications of separate collections. For example, the headings at 22:17 and 24:23 mark off precisely that section (22:17–24:22) which is so similar to the Egyptian Instruction of Amen-em-Opet. On the other hand, 31:10–31, the acrostic poem about the capable wife is an appendix to Proverbs and does not have a heading, while Agur's words are actually found in 30:1–14 only. In the Greek translation, the Septuagint, some of the material is found in a different order (e.g., 30:1–14 follows 22:17–24:22) and there is additional material not found in the Hebrew text.

The first collection, 1:1–9:18, contains a series of poems that begin with the admonition "my child." These poems are 1:8–19, 2:1–22, 3:1–12, 3:21–35, 4:1–9, 4:10–27, 5:1–23, 6:1–5, 6:20–35, and 7:1–27. They advise the child ("son" in the Hebrew) to avoid sinners, to seek wisdom in order to escape from evildoers and "loose women," to trust God and honor him with one's wealth, to do good to others, to learn from the example of parents, to avoid indebtedness, and to avoid the temptation to commit adultery or to resort to prostitution. The address of parent to child has prompted the suggestion that some kind of formal instruction is the background here, but if this is so, the concentration upon matters of sex suggests instruction within the family rather than something organized on a wider scale.

The remainder of 1:1–9:18 is devoted mostly to the subject of wisdom personified as a woman. Prov. 1:2–7 sets out the purpose of the book, and following the first poem addressed to "my child," Wisdom is introduced as standing in the street and calling out to scoffers and fools (1:20–33). This theme is resumed at 8:1 – "Does not wisdom call?" – where Wisdom claims that kings reign by her and rulers decree what is just (8:15), before the passage reaches its climax in the famous section (8:22–31) in which Wisdom claims to have been created at the beginning of God's work, before the creation of the earth:

> The LORD created me at the beginning of his work,
>   the first of his acts of long ago.

This poem is clearly the result of sophisticated theological reflection and is a claim about the nature of the world of human experience: that it is a moral and rational world in which virtue, industry, and faithfulness to God are rewarded. Chapter 9 opens with the verse made famous in T. E. Lawrence's title *Seven Pillars of Wisdom:* "Wisdom has built her house, she has hewn her seven pillars." It contrasts the delights of following Dame Wisdom with the dangers of heeding Dame Folly.

With the large section 10:1–22:16 we come to material that consists mostly of individual, two-line proverbs. They are too diverse to summarize, but their characteristic types can be noted. Very prominent are antithetical comparisons such as

> A slack hand causes poverty,
> but the hand of the diligent makes rich. (10:4)

Indeed, most of chapters 10–15 are devoted to such antithetical comparisons. From 16:1 there are other forms, such as statements that contain advice:

> Casting the lot puts an end to disputes
> and decides between powerful offenders; (18:18)

and statements that imply condemnation and warning:

> A perverse person spreads strife,
> and a whisperer separates close friends. (16:28)

There are comparisons:

> Better is a dry morsel with quiet
> than a home full of feasting with strife; (17:1)

as well as statements that relate daily living to God:

> All deeds are right in the sight of the doer,
> but the LORD weighs the heart.
> To do righteousness and justice
> is more acceptable to the LORD than sacrifice. (21:2–3)

Although verses such as 21:2–3 are not in any way dominant in 10:1–22:16, they are a reminder that, in its final form, this section is far from being totally secular.

The section 22:17–24:22 is strikingly similar to the Egyptian Instruction of Amen-em-Opet. How similar? This is best decided by readers themselves. The *order* of the material in Proverbs and the Instruction is quite different (see the table of comparison in *ANET,* p. 424 n. 46), but there are verbal similarities, such as:

Proverbs	Instruction (*ANET,* pp. 423–4)
Have I not written for you thirty sayings of admonition and knowledge? (22:20)	See thou these thirty chapters: they entertain; they instruct. (27:7–8 [chap. 30])
Incline your ear and hear my words, and apply your mind to my teaching, for it will be pleasant if you keep them within you, if all of them are ready on your lips. (22:17–18)	Give thy ears, hear what is said. Give thy heart to understand them. To put them in my heart is worthwhile, (but) it is damaging to him who neglects them. (3:9–11 [chap, 1])

Do not eat the bread of the
　　stingy;
do not desire their delicacies;
for like a hair in the throat so
　　are they.
"Eat and drink!" they say to
　　you;
but they do not mean it.
You will vomit up the little
　　you have eaten,
and you will waste your pleas-
　　ant words.　　(23–6–9)

Be not greedy for the proper-
　　ty of a poor man.
Nor hunger for his bread.
As for the property of a poor
　　man,
it is blocking to the throat.
it makes a *vomiting* to the gul-
　　let.
If he has obtained it by false
　　oaths,
his heart is penetrated by his
　　belly.
The mouthful of bread (too)
　　great thou swallowest and
　　vomitest up,
and art emptied of thy good.
　　(14:5–10 [chap. 11]

Although the above comparisons do not prove that the compiler(s) of Proverbs copied from the Instruction, it cannot be doubted that there is some form of dependence, or possibly, reliance of both texts on a common source.

The later sections of Proverbs introduce some new forms. Similes are common in chapters 25–6. An example is

Like cold water to a thirsty soul,
　so is good news from a far country.　　(25:25)

Chapter 30 contains several numerical sayings, such as

Three things are too wonderful for me;
　four I do not understand:
the way of an eagle in the sky,
the way of a snake on a rock,
the way of a ship on the high seas,
and the way of a man with a girl.

They have a riddlelike quality with no clear answer. Another form is the acrostic poem (each verse beginning with a successive letter of the alphabet), with which the book ends.

In its final form Proverbs dates from after the exile (after 540 B.C.E.); but most experts allow that a good deal of the material is pre-exilic in origin. This is most likely true of the central collection 10:1–22:16, to which were subsequently added the smaller collections from 22:17 onward, while the whole was prefaced with the poems of 1:8–9:18 and the introduction (1:1–7).

C.　JOB

The questions raised by the Book of Job and the scholarly literature that has been generated are so vast that any brief treatment can only be superficial. The book itself has a clear structure. A prose prologue and a prose epilogue tell a complete story. Between this prose material are placed poems in which a speech by each of Job's "comforters" is answered by a speech of Job. There are two complete series of these speeches, but the third series is incomplete and is rounded off by a hymn to wisdom (chapter 28) and a concluding speech by Job. There is then a long intervention by a previously unmentioned fourth "comforter," Elihu, before several speeches by God and a brief response by Job bring the poems to an end. The scheme is as follows:

1. Narrative framework		1:1–2:13
2. Lament of Job		3
3. First cycle	Eliphaz	4–5
	Job	6–7
	Bildad	8
	Job	9–10
	Zophar	11
	Job	12–14
4. Second cycle	Eliphaz	15
	Job	16–17
	Bildad	18
	Job	19
	Zophar	20
	Job	21
5. Third cycle	Eliphaz	22
	Job	23
	Job?	24
	Bildad	25
	Job	26–7
6. Hymn to wisdom		28
7. Job's final words		29–31
8. Elihu's speech	32–7	
9. Speeches of God		38:1–41:34 (Hebrew, 41:26)
10. Job's response		42:1–6
11. Narrative framework		42:7–17

The narrative framework tells of a rich man of exemplary piety who is the victim of a wager between God and Satan. Satan is one of the heavenly beings at God's court and does not believe that any human can be loyal to God for God's own sake. God puts his faith in Job's integrity and allows Satan to bring terrible disasters upon Job. In spite of everything, Job maintains his integrity, and at the end of the narrative framework his wealth is restored and seven sons and three daughters are born to him to replace those who perished at Satan's hand. As we have it now, this story is not complete. The epilogue does not mention Satan and it also implies that the "comforters" have spoken – which they have done in the poems but not in the narrative framework.

In the poems we meet with a Job quite different from the submissive, pious Job of the prologue who reproves his wife's insistence that he should curse God, saying, "Shall we receive the good at the hand of God, and not receive the bad?" (2:10). The Job of the poems is combative, and even bitter against God. He curses the day on which he was born (chap. 3) and requests God to kill him (6:8–9). He muses upon the hard lot that has to be endured by humans (chap. 7) and contrasts the nothingness of his own existence with the sovereign power of the creator (chap. 9). He appeals to God, who made him, to make allowance for his frailty, and he asserts his innocence (chap. 10). He attacks the arrogance of his friends and accuses them of self-deception (chap. 13). Two chapters (16–17) that describe his desolation lead unexpectedly to his famous affirmation in 19:25–7 that he knows that his vindicator lives and that he will see God on his side. This is not an affirmation of life after death, but it is an affirmation of vindication and hope based on the only ground for hope, namely, God himself. In his final speeches Job draws attention to the prosperity of the wicked (chaps. 21, 24) and complains about the elusiveness of God (chap. 23). He asserts his innocence (chap.31) and contrasts his present unfortunate state with his former prosperity (chaps. 29–30).

The "comforters" offer the following advice. Eliphaz insists that wickedness is punished, that Job's plight must be due to some evil, and that this is a truth attested by many generations. Bildad insists on the just nature of God and that he will not reject a blameless person. He describes vividly the terrors of the wicked. Zophar similarly reflects on the experiences of the wicked (chap. 20) and insists that God's ways are inscrutable (chap. 11). Elihu (chaps. 32–7) summarizes what has been said and criticizes the three comforters as well as Job. His positive contribution is to stress the redemptive aspect of suffering, which he accuses Job of ignoring (36:15–23).

When God speaks out of a whirlwind, he makes no attempt to deal with Job's complaints. Instead, we have a series of rhetorical questions that concern the world in its awesomeness but also in its apparent triviality. Alongside the question "Where were you when I laid the foundation of the earth?" (38:4) is the question "Is the wild ox willing to serve you?" (39:4) and statements such as

> The ostrich's wings flap wildly,
> though its pinions lack plumage.   (39:13)

Chapters 40–1 extol the virtues of Behemoth (possibly the crocodile) and Leviathan (possibly a dolphin). The material may be out of order, with 40:15–24 and 41:7–34 (Hebrew, 40:31–41:26) describing Behemoth, and 41:1–6 (Hebrew, 40:25–30) describing Leviathan. This unexpected divine response draws from Job the confession

> I had heard of you by the hearing of the ear,
> but now my eye sees you;
> therefore I despise myself,
> and repent in dust and ashes.   (42:5–6)

In reviewing the book as thus described, three main questions must be addressed: what is its literary history, what is its setting, and what is its meaning? Regarding its literary history, it seems that the writer of the major part of the poems composed or adapted a popular story to be the context for the poems. Adaptation is more likely, given the incompleteness of the narrative framework as noted above. Whether this author wrote three complete cycles of speeches of which the third was later disturbed when other material was added we do not know, but this seems likely. The Elihu speeches were probably added later, but not entirely crudely, as their closing words (37:14–24) anticipate the speeches of God. Job evidently had at least two authors.

The book is usually dated in the fifth to fourth centuries B.C.E., but there is little to go on in suggesting a date. Does the book belong to or constitute an attack on "wisdom"? This depends on what we understand by "wisdom." It is doubtful whether there existed a specific class of people whose worldview was that of the wisdom books; nor, in spite of comparisons that can be made with Babylonian works which wrestle with the problem of suffering, can we speak with confidence of an international "wisdom" movement. The most that we can say is that Job certainly attacks some of the views propounded in Proverbs and that the comforters uphold some of these views.

It is possible to locate Job in the literature of the psalms. We have

THE BABYLONIAN JOB

THE PROBLEM OF UNJUST suffering elicited early protests in the literary traditions of Mesopotamia. The Sumerian poetic essay "A Man and His God" proposed that personal suffering was the result of a basic flaw in humans, one with which the gods had burdened the human race. Nevertheless, the poem is more concerned to prescribe the proper attitude and conduct for victims of undeserved misfortune than to explain the cause of their cruel suffering. The author cites the case of an unnamed man who was wealthy, righteous, and wise, blessed with friends and family. When sickness and suffering overwhelmed him, he did not blaspheme his god. Instead, the man came humbly before his god with tears and lamentation, praying with earnest supplication. The god was moved to compassion, heeded the man's prayers, removed his misfortunes, and turned his sufferings into joy.

The same theme recurs in a later text from Babylon entitled Ludlul Bel Nemeqi (after its opening line, "I will praise the Lord of Wisdom"). Because of its affinities with the Hebrew Bible's story of the righteous sufferer, some scholars have christened this work the Babylonian Job. The text was written in Akkadian around the year 1000 B.C.E., although its origins may be long before that date. It is a psalm of thanksgiving from a nobleman whom the god Marduk had rescued from a complete reversal of fortune. Socially ostracized and seriously ill, the hero of the story seeks the reason for his misfortune. Although he consults the gods, he finds no answer. He is convinced that evil has befallen him through no fault of his own; he recounts his exact observance of cultic regulations and his acts of pious devotion. He resigns himself to the conclusion that mortals cannot understand the gods. He gives a long and gruesome description of his disease, which leaves him incapacitated and wallowing in his own waste. He attempts a cure through exorcism, but to no avail. He confesses his trust that the gods will ultimately restore his fortunes, which they do after the hero experiences three divine visions.

The biblical Book of Job differs from this Babylonian composition in setting, literary form, and emphasis. The Akkadian poem is a poetic monologue, whereas Job's form is a dramatic dialogue between several people that is placed between a prose prologue and a prose epilogue. The Babylonian sufferer emphasizes ritual, rather than moral, purity. The author of Job may have been familiar with Ludlul Bel Nemeqi and other similar works from the Mesopotamian tradition. An acrostic poem known as the Babylonian Theodicy (also called the Babylonian Ecclesiastes) and a later composition entitled the Dialogue of Pessimism deal with similar themes. However, there is no evidence that Job's author or authors were directly dependent on any Babylonian literature.

seen that over a third of the psalms are laments and that a feature of a lament is a word or expectation of deliverance. Job could be a very complex and expanded lament, with the comforters expanding the words of enemies in the laments (e.g., 10:5–7). The psalms certainly concern themselves with the problem of innocent suffering. Indeed, psalms such as 37 and 73 have been called "wisdom psalms" on this account! Again, there is much in the psalms about the marvels of the created order (see Ps. 104). Ultimately, it is probably going too far to locate Job entirely within the psalms tradition, but comparisons between Job and psalms can be illuminating.

It has to be admitted that we know nothing about Job's authors and their setting. They *may* have been wealthy Jews who were suffering from the hardships of post-exilic Judah. They were certainly highly educated and philosophically sensitive. Their lack of mention of the traditions about God's action in Israel's history since the Exodus leads to discussion of our final topic, the book's meaning.

On the face of it, Job is an attack on the simplistic view that all suffering is deserved and that the universe is a moral universe. It is here that the absence from Job of reference to other Old Testament traditions becomes an acute problem. Elsewhere, the Old Testament is perfectly aware that innocent people suffer. In the story of David alone we can note the following victims. Abner, is murdered by Joab (2 Sam. 3:22–34) because Abner killed Joab's brother Asahel in battle. Tamar is raped by her half-brother Amnon (2 Sam. 13:1–22). David arranges Uriah's death in battle (2 Sam. 11:14–25). The list could be greatly expanded. There is the further point that people such as Moses, Jeremiah, and the Servant of Isaiah 40–55 suffer by being caught between God's gracious purposes and the half-hearted response of the people. In the light of all this, Job seems to be a discussion that takes no account of an important dimension in the Old Testament and stands closer to the ideology of the Book of Proverbs than even to that of the psalms.

Granted this, is Job a discussion about suffering or the record of an experience of suffering that brought Job a new awareness of God? If it is the former, it sets up some intriguing possibilities. The first, as Philip Davies has pointed out (Rogerson and Davies 1989, pp. 302–3), is that Satan's wager with God means that whether righteousness really exists or not depends not on God but on Job. If Job fails the test, Satan's view, that people only do good for the sake of reward, is vindicated; and although this does not make the world immoral, it makes it cynical and calculating. If Job succeeds, then God is vindicated, but vindicated by a human! This is an important point in view of the assumption that is often made, with some justice, that the effect of the divine speeches is to move Job away from his concern for himself and to make him contemplate the creation. This may be what the poems say; the narrative framework, on the other hand, remains stubbornly human centered.

Another question, which is raised by taking the narrative and the poems together, is whether the restoration of Job's wealth undermines the book as a whole. After all, Job's comforters had argued all along that righteousness is rewarded and wickedness is punished. Job had opposed this; but does not the restoration of his wealth show that the comforters were correct? This is surely not the book's sole intention; part of its greatness is its ambiguity and the many possible answers it generates to the question of suffering.

Job can also be read as the record of an experience of great and undeserved suffering whose outcome was a new awareness of God. Although many writers have stressed the universality of Job's experience and questioning, we must not rule out the possibility that the book is in some way autobiographical. If this is so, it was written on the yonder side of the suffering, with the conversations with the comforters representing issues that were discussed at the time. From this standpoint, the book stands for experience as opposed to theory: the mystery and almost irrationality of encounters with God as opposed to a view of God formed by human logic; for the importance of human honesty as opposed to attempts to coerce submission to what one's conscience denies. It argues for belief in righteousness and justice in an ambiguous world, and against a superficial view of reality that produces a fatal reliance upon human resources. Whatever approach we take, Job is one of the greatest pieces of writing in the Bible and in world literature.

D.   ECCLESIASTES

The Hebrew name for this book is Qohelet, a feminine noun whose meaning and translation are disputed. It has traditionally been translated as Preacher, but recent translations offer renderings such as Speaker, Teacher, and Philosopher. The name Qohelet is derived from the noun *qahal*, "congregation" or "assembly"; but this provides no definitive clue about the meaning of Qohelet.

The book is traditionally regarded as the work of Solomon, because of the claim of 1:1 that the "teacher" was the son of David, king in Jerusalem. However, the way that the claim is put ("son of David, king in Jerusalem"; why not say Solomon?) alerts us to the fact that it is a literary device and not to be taken at face value. In fact, it is widely agreed that the book was written, not in the tenth century, but in the third century B.C.E. when Judah had become part of the Greek kingdom of Egypt ruled by the successors of Alexander the Great's general Ptolemy. This was a period of peace and prosperity for the rich in Judah, and the author of Ecclesiastes apparently belonged to the ruling or upper class, enjoying wealth and ease.

The outstanding feature of the book is the author's honesty. He is aware of the shortcomings of his society. He sees corruption: "in the place of justice, wickedness was there, and in the place of righteousness, wickedness was there as well" (3:16). He also sees oppression: "Look, the tears of the oppressed – with no one to comfort them! On the side of the oppressors there was power" (4:1). However, he does not know what he or anyone can do about these things. He has some hope in God as the final judge: "I said in my heart, God will judge the righteous and the wicked, for he has appointed a time for every matter and every work" (3:17). But he is also honest enough to see that this hope does not necessarily work out in practice, and he does not envisage an afterlife where justice will be done. Rather, it is death that is the great leveler. Death is God's way of reminding humans that they are also animals (3:18–21). It also brings rest to the oppressed.

What, then, of the achievements of human culture? That they are real is not denied (see 2:4–10); but the writer doubts whether they have any permanent value or meaning (2:18–23). They have certainly not brought him any sense of fulfillment. Indeed, even the belief in human creativity, which they may engender, is an illusion. In 3:1–8 there is a beautiful and remarkable poem in which, in each verse, two Hebrew words are contrasted with two other Hebrew words, for example,

| time to-be-born | time to-die |
| time to-kill | time to-heal |

This poem is often read as an affirmation of the beauty of the life that God has given to the human race. Nevertheless, in context the poem concerns the lack of freedom that humans have in their lives. We cannot control when we are born or die. The agricultural, mating, and even military seasons are dictated by external or natural constraints, as are times of mourning (after a death) and celebrating (at an agricultural festival).

Along with this lack of human freedom is the inability to discern a larger purpose. Nature and life are boringly repetitive (1:2–18), and a deeper purpose cannot be found (3:11). In this context, the wisdom teaching that found expression in Proverbs loses credibility, and it is probably the case that the writer deliberately parodies this type of teaching:

Dead flies make the perfumer's ointment give off a foul odor;
so a little folly outweighs wisdom and honor.   (10:1)

Whoever quarries stones will be hurt by them;
and whoever splits logs will be endangered by them.   (10:9)

We have here almost a disincentive to wisdom, honor, and hard work. The writer's attitude to religion is that it is better to be absolutely sincere in a small amount of observance than rash in a large amount (5:2–6).

It is easy to criticize the author's view of the world. If he saw corruption and injustice in his society, why did he not try to correct them (especially if he was a king or ruler)? Why did he apparently retreat into a general cynicism about the impossibility of improving society and see death as the great leveler that would in some way vindicate God? It is possible to contrast Ecclesiastes with those parts of the Old Testament that – because they relate the story of God's saving deeds – confess belief in a God who is intimately involved in the people's history, who is actively opposed to injustice and oppression, and who offers a vision of a renewed world and a kingdom of justice and peace.

The writer's apparent ignoring of these teachings in the Old Testament tradition raises questions about his location in the society of his day, which we cannot answer in the present state of our knowledge. But we can say two positive things at least. The first is that he could have been silent, and was not. If he was an active teacher, he was at least pointing out the shortcomings of materialism, indicating the transience of human life and achievements and condemning injustice. Perhaps he favored indirect, rather than direct, methods. Second, he wrote Ecclesiastes, and it was included in the Hebrew canon. Had this been otherwise, we should be immeasurably the poorer.

E.   SONG OF SONGS

This book is usually called the Song of Solomon because of the heading "Song of Songs which is Solomon's" (1:1). There are a number of references to Solomon in the text (e.g., 1:5, 3:7, 8:11) but nowhere does he speak, and although there is no scholarly agreement about the date or unity of authorship, or of how the book is to be divided into smaller or larger units, few, if any, experts would maintain Solomonic authorship.

Just as there is little agreement on matters of date, authorship, or literary structure, so there is no consensus about the book's purpose. It was once popular to see it as a dialogue between a bride and bridegroom, and the New English Bible, Revised English Bible, and New Jerusalem Bible translations actually add these headings, following the ancient Greek version in Codex Sinaiticus, a fourth-century C.E. codex. However, this is a very pre-emptive way of presenting the text to readers. A variation on the marriage interpretation has been to associate the book with a cultic liturgy, possibly one used when the king enacted a sacred marriage on behalf of a god. Today it is usually held that Song of Songs is a collection of love poetry, and it has been compared to Arabic love poetry and the love poetry of other ancient Near Eastern traditions. In what follows, the central themes of the poem will be explored as they are found in the final form of the book.

Two poems, strikingly similar, provide the central core of Song of Songs: 3:1–5 and 5:2–8. Both begin with a reference to sleep:

Upon my bed at night
I sought him whom my soul loves.   (3:1)

I slept but my heart was awake.   (5:2)

This introduces an element of uncertainty as to whether the female speaker is dreaming, fantasizing, or describing real events. This uncertainty enables the incidents to hover between dream and reality, so that we do not necessarily press the details. In the first poem the woman seeks her lover in the streets, has a neutral encounter with the sentinels of the streets, finds her beloved, and brings him to her mother's house.

In the second poem, there is a great deal of frustration. The woman hears her beloved knocking to be admitted, but by the time she has dressed and opened the door, he has gone. She searches for him in the streets and has a bad encounter with the sentinels, who beat, wound, and strip her. She does not find her beloved. Both poems end by bind-

LOVE POETRY IN THE ANCIENT NEAR EAST

THE SONG OF SONGS REPRE-
sents a unique genre in the
Hebrew Bible. However, love
poetry was common in ancient
Near Eastern culture. Biblical love
poetry shares features with both
religious literature from
Mesopotamia and secular traditions from Egypt.

Early in this century scholars
sought parallels to the Song of
Songs in Mesopotamian sacred
marriage liturgies. Sacred erotic
poetry from Mesopotamia was
used in the cult worship of Ishtar,
the goddess of fertility. According
to the Mesopotamian myth, each
year the god Tammuz (Dumuzi)
descended to the netherworld.
When his sister–consort, Ishtar
(Inanna), went to seek him, the
earth withered and died. When
Ishtar and Tammuz returned to
the land of the living, the earth
revived. These events were
played out, perhaps annually, in
ritual dramas. Some scholars
believe that during these cultic
celebrations the king and the
priestess of Ishtar took part in a
sacred marriage, representing the
god and goddess in sexual acts
which were designed to ensure
the land's fertility and abundance.
Several Sumerian songs have survived from this marriage liturgy
that are reminiscent of the Song
of Songs. They describe the
lovers' desire for one another and
praise their sexual attractions.
The poems share similar motifs:
natural beauty, an invitation to
the garden, praise of the beloved's

sweetness, the brother–sister
address.

Because scholars have been
unable to show that sacred marriage was a feature of Israelite
culture, the secular love poetry of
Egypt provides a more appropriate comparison for the Song of
Songs. Four major manuscripts
and some miscellaneous pieces of
Egyptian love poetry survive
from antiquity. These love songs
from Egypt date generally from
the Nineteenth and Twentieth
(Ramesside) Dynasties
(1305–1150 B.C.E.), a period
when Egyptian hegemony over
Palestine made Israelite contact
with Egyptian culture likely. Over
a thousand years elapsed between
the creation of these Egyptian
poems and the time when most
scholars think the Song of Songs
was written, and there are important differences between the two
traditions. Yet the similarities
between them are quite strong.
The Song of Songs probably represents the Israelite flowering of a
long-standing literary tradition
whose roots lie, at least partially,
in Egyptian love poetry.

Love poetry in Egypt did not
speak of great religious or national issues. Instead, this delightful
literature told of individual feelings and private concerns. Its
subject matter was sexual love
and the experiences of adolescent
lovers, their pleasures and their
frustrations. It sings of the joys,
desires, confusion, pain, and
hope of physical love. The Song
of Songs and the Egyptian love
poems share this subject matter.
They are also alike in their use of

dramatic presentation. Their
interest centers on the feelings,
personalities, and experiences of
dramatic characters rather than
on those of the poet. Their eroti-
cism is lush and delicate. The
poems accept premarital intercourse with restraint but rarely
with embarrassment or apology.
They are fascinated by love in its
infinite variety, and the world
they create is bright and happy.
The lovers' beauty is often projected onto the natural world.
Ancient Near Eastern love poetry
is an artistic exploration of
lovers' emotions, seldom focusing
on the larger issues of marriage,
reproduction, family alliances, or
national well-being.

Scholars have made several
suggestions about the function
and social setting of ancient Near
Eastern love poetry. Some have
suggested that the poems are
courting songs, or that they were
used in wedding celebrations.
Others have viewed this literature
as love magic or religious poetry.
More likely is the suggestion that
Egyptian (and Israelite) love poetry was meant primarily to entertain. Love songs have always
been popular in leisure time when
people are seeking diversion.
Love poetry was appropriate
entertainment when song, dance,
and merriment were in order. The
Song of Songs contains engaging
erotic allusions, sensual language,
and warm sentiments that would
have diverted audiences from
their everyday cares into the sensuous world of young lovers and
their sexual adventures.

ing the daughters of Jerusalem with an oath. In 3:5 it is that they should not "stir up or awaken love until it is ready," while in 5:8 it is that they should tell the man, if they find him, that his beloved is "faint with love."

These two central poems have echoes elsewhere. The refrain of 3:5 occurs also at 2:7 and 8:4. Indeed, 2:6–7 and 8:3–4 have in common not only the oath, but the verse

O that his left hand were under my head,
and that his right hand embraced me!   (2:6, 8:3)

Similar to the man's knocking on the door at 5:2 is his invitation to his beloved in 2:10–15 to come away with him. The phrase in 3:4

my mother's house,
. . . the chamber of her that conceived me,

is repeated in 8:2. Other poems amplify some of the sentiments of the core poems. Thus the man's call to the woman in 5:2, "Open to me. . . . my dove, my perfect one," is amplified in the description of the woman's beauty in 4:1–11, 6:4–10, and 7:1–9.

Taking the poems together, the following themes can be seen:

Innocence versus Convention   In 8:1 the woman exclaims:

O that you were like a brother to me,
who nursed at my mother's breast!
If I met you outside, I would kiss you,
and no one would despise me.

She laments the restraints placed upon innocent love by conventions that frustrate the natural desires. Something of this is also expressed in the two central poems, which is why it is important that we do not know whether the woman is actually searching for her lover at night in the streets, or whether she is dreaming or imagining that she is doing so.

Nature versus Culture   The frustration imposed by convention operates in the city, the place of culture. Here the woman is attacked by the sentinels; here the lover must come at night. In the wild, nothing of this applies. The lovers are free to express their feelings, in images drawn from nature.

The Garden   A haven for lovers is the garden that each possesses (4:13–15, 4:16–5:1, 6:2–3). This garden has been compared with that in Genesis 2–3, a garden in which disharmony arose between the man and the woman and between them and God. In Song of Songs there is no disharmony between the man and the woman. Away from the constraints imposed by the city and the culture it represents, they are equals, and their love is not sullied by shame or self-consciousness. Whether intended or not, Song of Songs stands in positive contrast to Genesis 3.

God is not mentioned in Song of Songs, but arguably, all that is celebrated in the poems in regard to the beauties of nature and the tenderness and devotion of love unspoiled by shame is a reflection of the divine nature. Song of Songs does not fear human love but affirms it. If there is any hesitancy in the poems, it comes from the restraints of convention, a convention understandably imposed because of the way in which human relationships can be, and are, abused. In the perhaps counterfactual way in which the poems describe love, we have a vision of the future comparable to those in the prophetic literature. Song of Songs is a remarkable testimony to the diversity of the literature that was admitted into the Hebrew canon.

F.   LAMENTATIONS

Lamentations consists of five poems that mourn the destruction of Jerusalem by the Babylonians in 587/6. Chapter 1 is divided into two equal parts: verses 1–11 and 12–22. In the first section, Jerusalem's plight is described and attributed to her sins, and in the second, the city speaks and acknowledges its faults and God's just judgment. In chapter 2, only some of the verses, such as 20–2, are Jerusalem's speech. The poem stresses the action of the zealous and all-powerful God against his people. In chapter 3, the speaker is an individual male (the New Revised Standard Version "I am the one . . ." is misleading here; the Hebrew has "I am the man . . ."). Precisely how he is to be identified is not easy to say; but what is important is that the poem is positive. God's anger will not last forever, his faithfulness is great, and he will restore his people. Chapter 4 returns to the themes of chapters 1–2, and chapter 5 is one of the most poignant descriptions of the plight of an oppressed people anywhere in the Bible.

Chapters 1–4 are different types of acrostic poem, that is, poems based upon the successive letters of the Hebrew alphabet. In chapters 1–2 and 4, each stanza (or verse in the way the text is set out in modern English translations of the Bible) begins with a successive letter of the alphabet, and thus these chapters have twenty-two verses, the Hebrew alphabet having twenty-two letters. Chapter 3 has sixty-six verses, verses 1–3 beginning with the first letter of the alphabet, verses 4–6 with the second letter, and so on. Chapter 5 is not an acrostic, but, it has twenty-two verses. The poems contain many examples of the lament (*qinah*) rhythm, in which three stressed syllables are followed by two. Indeed, it was the study of these poems in the nineteenth century that provided many suggestions about the importance of stressed syllables in Hebrew poetry.

Traditionally, the poems were ascribed to Jeremiah, and in English Bibles Lamentations follows the Book of Jeremiah. In the Hebrew canon, however, Lamentations is one of the five scrolls, (see p. 265) together with Ecclesiastes, Songs of Songs, Ruth, and Esther. It is not clear whether the five poems of Lamentations were written by one or more authors. Few, if any, experts today would argue that Jeremiah was the, or an author. At the same time, we cannot be sure about the place or date of composition.

The genre of a lament over the fall of a great city is well known from the ancient Near East, and a long and famous lament over the destruction of Sumer and Uris translated in *ANET* (pp. 611–19). It is not surprising that these laments (including the biblical Lamentations) have elements in common: allusions to the destruction, mention of enemies, mention of and appeal to gods, and descriptions of the plight of the survivors. It is likely that any similarities between the biblical Lamentations and those from ancient Mesopotamia derive from similar circumstances rather than from even indirect influence.

The striking thing about the poems is the way in which they gather together so much that can be found in poetry elsewhere in the Old Testament. This is not to say that they are conflations or lack originality. Rather, anyone familiar with Old Testament poetry will notice allusion after allusion to images and ways of expression found elsewhere, but which are brought together in Lamentations.

The poems are similar to psalms of lament, as well as to examples

ANCIENT NEAR EAST LAMENTS

DEATH, CALAMITY, AND BAD tidings were occasions that elicited rituals of mourning in the Hebrew Bible. Mourners wept and wailed, rent their clothes (Gen. 37:29), walked barefoot and covered their heads (2 Sam. 15:30), girded their loins with sackcloth (2 Sam. 3:31), and placed ashes on their heads (Isa. 61:3). The Levitical code prohibited traditional mourning rites like shaving one's hair or gashing the skin (Lev. 19:27–8), although in popular practice such customs seem to have been widespread in ancient Israel (cf. Jer. 16:6). Often professional mourners enhanced the atmosphere of grief (Jer. 9:17 ff.). They recited formal lamentations or elegies (Hebrew *ginot*), which were characterized by a stereotypical language of grief and a distinctive rhythmic pattern (see 2 Chron. 35:25).

Mourning extended beyond situations of individual loss to periods of national distress. Joshua grieved after the Israelites' defeat at Ai, as did Mordecai when he learned of Haman's plan to exterminate the Jews. In the Bible, Psalms 74 and 79 along with the Book of Lamentations are communal laments over the destruction of Jerusalem and the temple.

In many respects these Israelite customs are in line with long-standing traditional practices in the ancient Near East. Ninth-century B.C.E. reliefs from Assyria show women with one or both hands raised above their heads, a posture that indicates mourning or weeping. This gesture of sorrow belongs to an earlier iconographic tradition. Egyptian wall paintings depict women standing with upraised arms, weeping and tearing their hair in gestures of grief and mourning. An even more ancient tradition of lamentation comes from the Sumerian civilization, which thrived in the third millennium B.C.E. The conquest of Sumer, after its revival during the Third Dynasty of Ur, left a distressing and harrowing impression on the poets, who wrote lengthy laments for their lost cities. Sumerologists have translated documents that preserve the laments of various Sumerian city-states, including Akkad, Eridu, Lagash, Nippur, and Ur.

Some scholars of the Hebrew Bible have argued that the Book of Lamentations relies on these very early Sumerian texts for both its form and its general content. They contend that the Sumerian lamentations created a specific genre which evolved into a liturgical stereotype used by various civilizations for over two thousand years. Bitterness and sorrow and resignation to the divine will permeate both the Hebrew and the Sumerian compositions. Both sets of poems refer to hunger, famine, pestilence, social disintegration, the sacking of cities, the loss of valuables, and the captivity of inhabitants. However, the literary dependence of Lamentations on Sumerian materials is difficult to establish. Direct or indirect contact between Israel and Sumer is unlikely, and many of the alleged parallels between the two cultures' expressions of lament can be attributed to similar experiences and situations. The fate of most cities in the ancient Near East during siege and capture was usually quite the same.

elsewhere in the Bible of laments over fallen cities or peoples. Thus, Amos 5:1–7 has a lamentation that begins

> Fallen, no more to rise,
> is maiden Israel;
> forsaken on her land,
> with no one to raise her up.

It may or may not be significant than the term "wormwood" (a bitter-tasting plant) is used to express the perversion of justice in Amos 5:7 and the bitterness of collapse in Lam. 3:15, 19. Another passage that can be compared is Isa. 47:1–15, which begins

> Come down and sit in the dust,
> virgin daughter Babylon.

A disputed question is whether the poems in Lamentations were composed for communal use at a service of fasting and mourning or whether they are purely literary compositions. It is easy to imagine that communal gatherings to express corporate grief after the destruction of Jerusalem were socially valuable events; and it is not impossible that even purely literary compositions were used on such occasions. But all this is at the level of plausibility rather than probability. Whatever the original use and setting of the poems, they retain their power for modern readers.

G. RUTH

In English Bibles, Ruth follows the book of Judges because of its opening words: "In the day when the judges ruled" (Ruth 1:1). In the Hebrew canon, Ruth is one of the "five scrolls." The book has a simple and appealing story which, however, opens many possible lines of interpretation.

Because of famine a family from Bethlehem consisting of husband, wife, and two sons goes to live in Moab, east of the Jordan. The two sons die, leaving the wife, Naomi, with two widowed Moabite daughters-in-law. One of them, Ruth, determines to return with Naomi to Bethlehem (chap. 1).

On arrival in Bethlehem at the beginning of the barley harvest, Ruth gleans, with other young women, in a field belonging to Boaz, a relative of Naomi. Boaz treats Ruth kindly, having heard of her faithfulness to Naomi (chap. 2). Naomi now advises Ruth to indicate to Boaz her willingness to marry him by lying down at his feet on the threshing floor. Because of the provision of Hebrew law (Deut. 25:5–10), Boaz needs to ask a nearer relative of Naomi whether he is willing to do his duty by marrying Ruth in order to produce offspring for her dead husband (chap. 3). Boaz assembles the elders at the gate of the city and inquires of the nearer relative whether he will buy some land that Naomi must sell and whether he will also marry Ruth. The nearer relative refuses, as a result of which the duty of marrying Ruth passes legally to Boaz. A son is born to them who, according to the women, is reckoned to Naomi (4:17). He is named Obed and is, in fact, the grand-

MEGILLOT

Song of Songs, Ruth, Lamentations, Ecclesiastes, and Esther are the shortest books of the Hagiographa (one of the three main divisions of the Hebrew scriptures; also called the Writings) and together are known as the *ḥamesh megillot,* the "five scrolls." In ancient times, each book was written on a separate scroll for public reading at special seasons of the liturgical year. Today, many congregations merely recite the scrolls from a prayer book. The Book of Esther, however, is still read aloud from a separate scroll, which has come to be known as "the Megillah." Aside from their liturgical use, the five scrolls have very little in common. They represent sharp contrasts in genre, mood, and purpose.

The first scroll, Song of Songs, has been linked with Passover. It is read on the intermediate Sabbath of the Jewish holiday, which recalls Israel's miraculous escape from bondage in Egypt. According to the traditional interpretation, Song of Songs is an allegory of God's love for Israel and came to be associated with the spring festival (*ḥag ha-ʾabib*) because Passover is the springtime of that love. However, the religious and historical elements of Passover may not have been the original link between the festival and this scroll. Passover is a springtime holiday with parallels in the calendars of many peoples, a celebration of nature's rebirth and renewed fertility. Song of Songs – with its rich descriptions of natural beauty and sexual love

may have been associated early on with joyous celebrations of spring.

Ruth is read during the Feast of Weeks (*shavuʿot*), the annual celebration of the beginning of harvest, which comes seven weeks after Passover. Like the other major pilgrimage festivals (so called because they are celebrated in Jerusalem), the holiday has both historical and agricultural referents. According to rabbinic tradition, the children of Israel received the Torah on the sixth day of the month of Sivan (the first day of the Feast of Weeks). Thus, this holiday is also *zeman matan torah,* a remembrance of the giving of Torah. Ruth's association with the Feast of Weeks has several traditional explanations. The reference to "the beginning of the barley harvest" in Ruth 1:22 may explain why the book is traditionally read on the second day of the holiday. Another tradition suggests that the scroll is read at the first fall harvest festival because Ruth's acceptance of the Jewish faith parallels the experience of the people of Israel, who received the Torah on the first day of the Feast of Weeks. Another explanation suggests that the scroll's seasonal association comes from the Davidic genealogy that concludes the book; according to rabbinic tradition, King David was born and died during the Feast of Weeks (i.e., Pentecost).

Lamentations, the third scroll, plays an integral role in the synagogue liturgy for the Ninth of Ab. This scroll contains an extended dirge over the destruction of Jerusalem and the temple appro-

priate to the solemn fast which commemorates the saddest day of the Jewish calendar. According to rabbinic tradition, God ordained the ninth day of the month of Ab as an especially calamitous day for the Jewish people. Because the spies sent to Canaan brought back their discouraging report on that date (Num. 13–14), God made it an eternal day of mourning and ordained it as the date when the first and second temples would be destroyed.

The Sabbath of the Feast of Booths (*sukkot*) is the traditional time for the recitation of Ecclesiastes, the fourth scroll. Some commentators attribute this association to the duty of rejoicing during the Feast of Booths since Ecclesiastes also enjoins the pursuit of joy and pleasure. Eccles. 5:3–4 contains a warning not to neglect fulfilling vows, an injunction that some have thought appropriate to this holiday, which is the last festival of the annual cycle. Others argue that the reading of Ecclesiastes, with its somber and pessimistic outlook on life, was introduced to counteract the influence of the wild pagan celebrations that were common in autumn among ancient peoples.

Esther, "the scroll," is read during the festival of Purim. This strange book purports to explain the festival's origin. At both morning and evening services, the text is chanted to a special cantillation used only with the Book of Esther. The cantor chants from the scroll after it has been unrolled and folded to look like a

(*continued on p. 266*)

(*continued from p. 265*)

letter of dispatch. Tradition specifies certain emphases and phrasings for the reader, and it is customary for listeners to participate by making noise whenever the name of Haman (the story's villain) is mentioned.

The customary reading of the five scrolls originated in several historical periods. The scroll of

Esther seems to have been read already in the second temple period, and Talmudic literature mentions the reading of Lamentations. A post-Talmudic tractate records the use of Esther, Song of Songs, and Ruth (although in a different order from modern practice). Liturgical practice concerning the *megillot* probably did not reach its modern form until the medieval period.

father of King David. The book ends with a genealogy of David including Obed, who, however, is traced through Boaz's line, not Naomi's.

The story raises a number of difficult questions. Why, if Naomi possessed a field (4:3), was she so poor that Ruth had to glean to provide for them? Who had been looking after the field while she was in Moab? Why was the sale of the land connected with the marriage of Ruth? Why, if the purpose of Ruth's marriage to Boaz was to produce children for Naomi's dead husband and sons, was Boaz credited with being Obed's father in the genealogy of 4:18–22?

These questions are hard to answer. The Old Testament says that a man has the duty to marry his brother's widow if the marriage was childless, so that children can be reckoned to his dead brother (Deut.

JUSTICE IN THE GATE

THE HEBREW WORD *SHA'AR* refers to the entire gate complex of a walled city and the open area adjacent to it. Gates controlled access to the city. They shut out marauders and wild animals at night. As the weakest point in a city's defensive wall system, gates were often fortified with towers, equipped with multiple doors, secured with great bars of iron, and protected by guard rooms within the complex. But the gate served an important role in community life beyond its utility for protection and defense.

City gates were also the site of many social, administrative, and business transactions in the ancient world. Much like the Greek agora or Roman forum, the Near Eastern city's gate was the center of public discourse. All important issues were negotiated there. Abraham bargained at the Hittites' city gate for the cave at Machpelah (Gen. 23); the fugitive

requesting admission to a city of refuge was first interrogated by the community's leaders at the gate (Josh. 20:4). The gate served as the place where legal transactions took place (Ruth 4:1) as well as the site where some public punishments were administered (Deut. 17:5, 21:19). The square (oftentimes a threshing floor) inside the city gate was a natural place to congregate; it functioned as a central marketplace. By metonymy, the gate has the connotation of "community, assembly" (see Ruth 3:11, *kol sha'ar 'ammi*, "all my fellow countrymen" [lit., "people of the gates"]).

Especially in Canaanite cities, the gate was the seat of the community's elders. A text from Ugarit refers to the hero Dan'el, who "sits in front of the gate, by the dignitaries who are on the threshing floor" (2 Aqhat 5:6–7). Those who "go in at the gate" (Gen. 23:10, 18) are city fathers, all those who have an authoritative voice in the affairs of the

community. According to 1 Kings 22:10, Jehoshaphat, king of Judah, and the king of Israel also sat, "each on his throne, at the threshing floor at the entrance of the gate of Samaria."

From the gate, both kings and elders meted out justice to the people (Deut. 21:9, Josh. 20:4). The gate was the place of judicial decision making, analogous to a modern-day courtroom. Prophets often launched their invectives against official corruption from vantage points near the city gate, that is, near the site of the offense in the hearing of those being indicted. Prov. 22:22 warns against robbing the poor and crushing the afflicted at the gate. Amos lashes out against leaders who despise honest judgment. He says, "They hate him who reproves in the gate, and they abhor him who speaks the truth" (5:10). The prophet calls for his listeners to "hate evil, and love good, and establish justice in the gate" (5:15).

25:5–10). This was no doubt an important mechanism for ensuring that property was kept within the husband's family. There is also provision for a relative to buy a field if an Israelite is forced to sell it, for example, to pay off a debt (Lev. 25:25, cf. Jer. 32:1–15). However, these two provisions are not linked, as is done in Ruth. We do not know whether the author of the Book of Ruth knew institutions slightly different from those recorded in Leviticus and Deuteronomy or whether the author of Ruth misunderstood these institutions.

The book can be read in many ways and at many levels. Because women dominate the story, Ruth has received many treatments from feminist scholars. These have drawn attention to the strength of purpose and loyalty of the female characters in the story, notwithstanding the constraints of a patriarchal society, in which women gain justice and legitimacy only in relation to males. Another approach emphasizes the book's generous attitude to non-Israelites. Whereas Naomi's family was unwilling to take risks during the famine and the nearer relative was unwilling to take the risk of marrying Ruth, the heroine of the story is a Moabite woman who not only risked leaving her own country but whose loyalty to her mother-in-law produced a son who was an ancestor of David. Only in the Book of Jonah is there a comparably generous treatment of non-Israelites.

In Ruth, God is hardly mentioned; but it has been pointed out that the book is very much concerned with how God restored Naomi from utter hopelessness in chapter 1 to the point in 4:14 where the women say to Naomi, "Blessed be the LORD, who has not left you this day without next of kin; and may his name be renowned in Israel!" How has God restored Naomi? In various ways. There are the customs allowing the poor to glean in fields at harvest-time (cf. Lev. 19:9, Deut. 24:19) and specifying that relatives had to buy fields from their next of kin and marry childless widows of their brothers. In addition to these customs, there are the actions of the individual human characters, the loyalty of Ruth, the resourcefulness of Naomi, and the willingness of Boaz to take risks. These actions, in the context of the institutional structures of grace, enable God to bring hope to a hopeless situation. Here is a subtle, yet sincere, theology.

What, then, does the story of Ruth have to do with David? Does it function as an apology for David's possible foreign ancestry by exalting the loyalty of one of the representatives of that foreign strain? Or does it function as an apology for non-Israelites by appealing to the reverence with which David was regarded in Israel and by claiming that one of his ancestors was Moabite? The answer will depend on when we think the book was written. An apology for David would have been most necessary soon after his reign and thus would indicate a date in the tenth to eighth centuries B.C.E. An apology for non-Israelites would suggest a postexilic date, when the Jewish community was wrestling with problems of identity and relations with outsiders.

H. ESTHER

Like the Book of Ruth, Esther is a narrative about the workings of the unseen (and unmentioned!) God, whose purpose is achieved through the strength and resourcefulness of a woman. The Jewess Esther becomes the queen of the Persian king Ahasuerus (Xerxes, 485–465 B.C.E.) after the former queen, Vashti, has refused to obey her husband. Esther is chosen for her beauty from among many aspirants and is able to use her royal position to warn the king of a plot to assassinate him. Her informant is Mordecai, her cousin, who had adopted her on the death of her parents, and his part in saving the king is recorded in the annals. Because Mordecai refuses to bow down to the high official Haman, the latter decides to destroy Mordecai together with all the Jews. Using the lot (*pur*, a method of divination) he determines the thirteenth of the month of Adar as the date for carrying out his plan and, using the royal seal, sends letters to all the rulers of provinces ordering them to kill all Jews on that date.

Mordecai learns of the plot and tells Esther. While the Jews in the capital, Susa, fast, the queen arranges a banquet for Ahasuerus and Haman. Meanwhile, the king discovers that Mordecai was never properly rewarded for saving him from assassination, and publicly honors him. At the banquet, Esther reveals to Ahasuerus that Haman plans to kill all the Jews in the empire. The king is appalled, and Haman is executed on the very gallows that he had prepared for Mordecai. The danger for the Jews is not over, however, because of the letters that Haman had sent to all the provinces, and because the enemies of the Jews were looking forward to the coming slaughter. The king empowers Mordecai to reverse Haman's instructions and to authorize the Jews to attack their enemies and plunder their goods. Thus, on 13 Adar, the Jews attack their enemies, although they refrain from plundering them. In Susa the Jews kill three hundred persons; in the provinces they kill seventy-five thousand (Esther 9:15–16). In order to commemorate this deliverance, the Jews are commanded by Mordecai and Esther to observe the festival of Purim on 14 and 15 Adar. Mordecai becomes next in rank to the king himself (10:3).

The Book of Esther contains themes found elsewhere in the Old Testament. The advancement of a Jewish exile (Mordecai) to prominence at a foreign court can be compared with Joseph (Gen. 41:37–45), Nehemiah (Neh. 1:11), and Daniel (Dan. 1:3–21). Further, Esther shares with Daniel and his companions the distinction of being chosen from among many non-Jewish aspirants for their beauty. And Daniel (Dan. 6) and his companions (Dan. 3) are plotted against by their enemies at court, as is Mordecai. In addition there are allusions in the text to other parts of the Bible, although their implications are not easy to discern.

The genealogy of Mordecai in 2:5 describes him as son of Jair son of Shimei son of Kish, a Benjaminite. This links with Saul's genealogy at 1 Sam. 9:1, where Kish is one of Saul's ancestors, and with Saul's relative Shimei, who, at 2 Sam. 16:5, curses David during the latter's flight from Absalom. Another connection with the story of Saul is provided

PURIM

PURIM, ALONG WITH HAN-ukkah, has the status of a minor festival in the Jewish religious calendar. (Work is allowed on minor festivals.) Both festivals commemorate great deliverances of the Jewish people. Purim is celebrated on the fourteenth day of Adar (February–March). According to the Book of Esther (9:29), Mordecai and Esther declared the feast to celebrate the deliverance of the Jews from Haman's plot to kill them. The feast receives its name from the lots (Akkadian *puru;* Hebrew *purim*) which Haman used to determine the month when the slaughter was to take place.

Exactly when Purim was first observed remains something of a mystery. For various reasons, scholars have assigned the strange book of Esther a date much later than its purported Persian setting; Jewish literature lacks any reference to the festival before the first century B.C.E. In any case, the feast was firmly established in traditional practice by the second century of the common era, when a whole tractate (entitled *Megillah,* "scroll") of the Mishnah was devoted to the details of its observance.

The tractate *Megillah* is especially concerned with rules governing the reading of the scroll of Esther (*ha-megillah,* "the scroll"). The scroll is read at both evening and morning services. It is cus-tomary for the cantor to raise his voice at certain key points in the story, especially at the four so-called verses of redemption (*pesuqe ge'ulah,* 2:5, 8:15–16, 10:3). Also traditional is the recitation in one breath of the names of Haman's ten sons. This practice is said to signify that all of the sons died together, though some say this hasty recitation is a reminder not to gloat over the fate of one's enemies – even if they deserve it! Also ancient custom is children's noisemaking with special rattles (called grag-gers) whenever the name of the villain Haman is mentioned as the scroll is being read.

Mordecai's instructions to the Jewish communities of the Diaspora for the celebration of Purim have engendered several customs associated with the holiday. He called on the Jews to des-ignate and observe a day of feasting and gladness, to send food to one another, and to give gifts to the poor. The day is usually celebrated with a festive afternoon meal. The Babylonian rabbi Rava said of the celebrations, "A person should be so exhilarated [with drink] on Purim that he does not know the difference between "cursed be Haman," and "blessed be Mordecai" (b. *Meg.* 7b). Later authorities tried to cur-tail this permissive attitude toward imbibing on Purim, but the pleasures of strong drink are very much a part of Esther's story (see Esther 1:10, 2:18, 7:1–2). Families often exchange gifts of food on Purim. It was traditional for the poor to receive extra gen-erosity on Purim, and some con-gregations still collect a special offering in the synagogue vestibule.

Traditions from East European Jewry have enriched many mod-ern observances of Purim. Carnivals, costumes, and humor-ous songs are now a part of many Purim celebrations. *Hamantashen,* a three-cornered pastry filled with poppy seeds, is a frequent treat during Purim. In Hebrew the pastry is called *'ozne haman,* probably from the German *Haman Ohren* (Haman's ears). This tradition may have arisen from old illustrations which depict Haman wearing a three-cornered hat. In the modern State of Israel, Purim is celebrated as a national holiday.

Many families and communi-ties celebrate private Purims which commemorate their own special great deliverances. Purim is a celebration of hope and encouragement that has provided strength for Jews through the ages. The sages took literally Esther's promise that "these days of Purim will not disappear from among the Jews, nor the memory of them perish from their descen-dants" (9:28), and therefore wrote, "All the festivals will cease, but the days of Purim will not cease" (*Midrash Mishle* 9).

by Haman's genealogy. He is said to be an Agagite (3:1), which connects him with that incident in Saul's life when he fought against the Amalekite king Agag (1 Sam. 15:1–9, 32–3). In turn, this passage leads back to Exod. 17:8–14, where the Amalekites fought against the Israelites at Rephidim in the wilderness. Interesting as these allusions are, they are not immediately transparent, unless, for the author, Amalek is the archetypal enemy of the Jews and Saul is the archetypal deliverer. It is easier to appreciate the first of these symbols than the latter.

Research on the development of the narrative of the Book of Esther suggests that several independent stories have been woven together: the contest between Mordecai and Haman, the work of a Jewish woman in delivering her people under foreign rule, and the origin of the festival of Purim. Tracing this growth is helped by the fact that a Greek version of Esther (the so-called A text) exists that evidently represents a stage prior to the version in the traditional Hebrew text. We must also note that another Greek version (included in the Old Testament Apocrypha) adds letters, decrees, prayers, and conversations that expand parts of the story. They give the book as a whole a much more religious tenor than is the case with the Hebrew version, where the word "God" does not appear. Thus, the prayers attributed to Mordecai and Esther (Greek Esther chaps. 13–14, addition C) are utterances that recall God's saving deeds in the past and that pray for deliverance in the present.

If it is correct that the story of Esther developed from popular stories to its fullest form in the Greek version in the Apocrypha (it has also been argued that the Hebrew version is a *shortened* form of the book as found in the Greek apocryphal text), then we should not look for one particular date or setting except that it must have been later than the time of Xerxes (485–465 B.C.E.). The original stories expressed the universal human desire for good to triumph over evil, albeit in a national (Jewish) context. Actual danger to Jews in the Persian Empire ensured the popularity of the stories and their formation into a tale of national deliverance. Whether or not there was a national threat to the Jews as implied in Esther we do not know.

The origins of the festival of Purim, to which the story later became attached, are similarly unknown. Was this a pagan festival taken over by Jews from Babylonia or Persia, or does it commemorate a Jewish deliverance such as that during the Maccabean revolt of 167–164 B.C.E.? The account of Nicanor's defeat (1 Macc. 7:39–50) mentions a festival on the thirteenth of Adar to remember the occasion. Scholars do not agree. The additions to the Hebrew version show that after the Esther story was linked to the festival of Purim, the book was being used and adapted to the needs of a more specifically religious community and readership. Modern readers ought certainly to read not only the Hebrew version but also the full Greek version, as available in the New Revised Standard Version and Revised English Bible Apocryphas.

VI. THE WORLD OF APOCALYPTIC

A. THE SOCIOLOGY OF APOCALYPTIC COMMUNITIES

The title of this section makes an assumption: that there are such things as "apocalyptic communities" and that we can describe their sociology. This assumption needs to be challenged. In the Bible we possess literature that has been called "apocalyptic." It has been given this designation because the Greek word that underlies the word "apocalyptic" means "to uncover," "reveal," and because, in texts such as Dan. 8:15–26, the meaning of a vision or omen is explained to a human by a supernatural being. In the case of Dan. 8:15–26 Daniel's vision is explained by the angel Gabriel.

Apocalyptic literature has certain distinctive features, such as the interpretation of dreams, visions, and omens; an emphasis on supernatural beings, such as angels; a tendency to dualism between good and evil; and the dividing up of time into epochs or periods. This literature is also concerned with the future, as well as describing the past and present with the help of imagery and symbolism drawn from mythological literature. However, a difficulty arises when we try to put limits to establish exactly which features must be present in order

---

APOCALYPTIC

APOCALYPTIC (DERIVED from a Greek word meaning "to uncover," "reveal," "unveil") is a chief mode of discourse in the Jewish and Christian literature of the period 200 B.C.E. to 200 C.E. (see also pp. 271–280). The only fully developed example of apocalyptic literature in the Hebrew Bible is the second-century B.C.E. Book of Daniel, but other late biblical texts reflect the influence of early apocalypticism. For example, Isaiah 24–7 (a postexilic addition to the book) speaks of typically apocalyptic themes like the final judgment of the nations and the consummation of all things. Yahweh pronounces judgment on the earth, and the world is turned upside down (24:21). The sun and moon are darkened (24:23). The evil host of heaven are punished (24:21), and the righteous of all nations are invited

to a great feast after they are raised from the dead (25:6, 26:19; cf. Zech. 12:14, Joel 3:9–21). Many of the pseudepigraphic writings and the scrolls from Qumran take the form of apocalypses or at least share some of the characteristics of apocalyptic.

However, scholars have had great difficulty in defining clearly the literary genre, religious ideology, and social setting of this pervasive early Jewish phenomenon. In literary terms, apocalypses are usually cast in the form of visions about future events mediated to a seer through a superhuman being. These visions often employ strange mythological elements and bizarre cosmic imagery. They are generally esoteric and highly symbolic. Fantastic beasts and complicated numerologies are the codes in which this literature presents its message. Apocalyptic authors are pseudonymous.

The subject matter of apocalyptic literature usually involves the presentation of a systematic panorama of history that spans this age and the next. Apocalypses unveil the mystery of what is to come at the end of time. Apocalyptic conceives this mystery in terms of an essential ethical dualism throughout the universe, in which good (God and his angels) and evil (Satan and his demons) are engaged in a fierce battle for dominion in the world, and in the eyes of apocalypticists, evil seems in the present time to be winning. The two forces are presented in terms of their respective agents: highly developed angelology and demonology.

Apocalyptic holds a very pessimistic attitude toward the present world order. The world and most of its inhabitants are considered hopelessly corrupt.

---

for a text to be considered apocalyptic. If we have a strict view of what constitutes a piece of apocalyptic literature, certain texts will be excluded. If we broaden our view, the characteristic features will be added to and there will be more candidates for admission to the genre. In the case of the Old Testament this affects Isaiah 24–7 and Zechariah 9–14. Are these apocalypses? Isaiah 24–7 briefly mentions a mythological theme in the punishment of the fleeing serpent Leviathan (27:1) and it is concerned with God's future judgment of the world. There is even a possible reference to resurrection:

> Your dead shall live,
> their corpses shall rise.   (Isa. 26:19)

But do these features make it correct to call these chapters an apocalypse?

If it is not easy to delimit the genre, what hope is there in delineating the community? But there is another assumption that has to be questioned here, the assumption that we can infer the existence of social groups on the basis of literary genres. The viewpoint of traditional sociology has been that the history and sociology of groups could be reconstructed if there was tangible evidence available; and types of literature were considered to constitute such evidence. Recent sociological theory no longer accepts this. Communities are constituted by many factors – historical, economic, environmental, linguistic – and literature is only a small, and perhaps unrepresentative, product of a community.

Older scholarship looked for the origins of apocalyptic in Old Testament prophecy. In the period after the return from exile (540–150 B.C.E.), it was argued, prophecy declined and its place was taken by apocalyptic, which reflected the changed conditions of life in Judah of that period. The most important change was that before the exile, Judah and Israel had been independent nations, whereas after the exile, Judah alone remained and was part of the Persian Empire. Thus, whereas in prophecy Israel and Judah are often threatened with coming judgment at the hands of foreign nations, and whereas these nations can be both the instruments of God's judgment on Israel and themselves subject to divine judgment, apocalyptic represents foreign nations as almost demonic forces ranged against an innocent Jewish community, which can expect direct divine intervention to rescue it. Building on this approach, more recent scholarship tried to identify the authors of apocalyptic as antiestablishment groups in the Jewish community of this period.

The most satisfactory approach to the subject, however, is via mantic wisdom. Philip Davies defines manticism as "a name for a system of belief and practice in the discovery of heavenly secrets from earthly signs." Texts from the seventh century B.C.E. indicate that guilds of priests or diviners whose profession was to interpret many types of signs had long been established in Babylon. These enabled inquirers to know the will of the gods and to see into the future. The practice implied an understanding of reality in which the worlds of the gods and of humans were interlocked in such a way that inquiry by means of divination provided supernatural information for humans. However, we must not conclude that this understanding of reality was a *total* worldview. On the whole, humans depend on their own resources to cope with life, and they resort to practices such as divination only in extreme circumstances, when situations such as illness or war threaten their ability to survive.

In the Old Testament, divination is forbidden (Deut. 18:10–11), and the reliance of Babylon on enchantments and consultations is mocked (Isa. 47:12–15). Yet Daniel 1–2 tells of a Jewish exile in the Babylonian court in the sixth century B.C.E. who is doing precisely what the diviners were employed to do: interpret dreams. Daniel does this also in chapter 4, and in chapter 5 he interprets the famous omen or sign of "the writing on the wall." It is true that the biblical text emphasizes that Daniel's wisdom comes from God and is superior to Babylonian divination; but placing the Book of Daniel in the context of mantic wisdom helps us to understand the origin and setting of apocalyptic in postexilic Judaism, as well as features of the Book of Daniel.

The Babylonian mantic tradition spread throughout the Greco-Roman world so that by the third to second centuries B.C.E., when the first Jewish apocalypses were written, this tradition was part of the culture in which Judah found itself. It was not necessarily solely in the hands of priests but was also the province of scribes, who were the intellectuals engaged in teaching, administration, and writing. In the apocryphal Wisdom of Ben Sira (also called Ecclesiasticus), written about 200 B.C.E., there is a description of the scribe who

> seeks out the wisdom of all the ancients,
> and is concerned with prophecies;
> he preserves the sayings of the famous
> and penetrates the subtleties of parables;
> he seeks out the hidden meanings of proverbs
> and is at home with the obscurities of parables.   (Sir. 39:1–3)

In its list of famous figures from the past (Sir. 44–9), Ben Sira gives a prominent place to Enoch. It is now generally accepted that the earliest Jewish apocalypses are the First Book of Enoch, chapters 72–82 (the Astronomical Treatise), 1–36 (the Book of Watchers), 91–105 (the Epistle of Enoch), and 83–90 (the Book of Dreams), which date from 250 B.C.E. to 50 C.E.

Thus we can surmise that the Babylonian tradition of mantic wisdom as diffused through and mediated by the Greco-Roman world was known among the intellectual scribal classes of second temple Judah. They were interested in mythical traditions, astronomical and astrological calculations, history, and philosophy. Obviously, they adapted this non-Jewish tradition to their own religion. When the events of the early second century B.C.E. began to pose a threat to Judah's existence, the scribes produced the Book of Daniel, which drew upon the mantic tradition in order to interpret recent history and give assurance for the future. They did this, not as an anti-establishment group, but as a group intimately involved with the life – and survival – of the nation.

B. DANIEL

Even to the nonspecialist reader, the Book of Daniel presents an astonishing contrast between its first and second parts. The book begins with stories about Daniel and his three companions. Some of the stories are among the best known in the Bible: the three men in the fiery furnace, Belshazzar's feast at which appeared "the writing on the wall," and Daniel in the lions' den. These stories occupy chapters 1–6, after which there is an abrupt change. Daniel 7 is a vision seen by Daniel in which there is a battle between beasts whose description draws upon the mythic images of the chaos that preceded creation. Its climax is the coming of "one like a son of man," to whom dominion, glory, and kingship are given. Chapters 8–12 are different again. Although they record further visions and their interpretation, the mythic imagery is subdued, and the emphasis is on events concerning the nations that constitute Judah's neighbors.

Daniel is unique in the Old Testament in being composed in two languages (Ezra contains some letters in Aramaic). Daniel begins in Hebrew (1:1–2:4a) but soon has a long section in Aramaic (2:4b–7:28), which includes the well-known stories and the strikingly different chapter 7. The remainder of the book is in Hebrew.

These facts have made the unity of Daniel a long-running debate in scholarship. Were the stories of chapters 2–6 an originally independent book that was incorporated into a book composed of chapters 1 and 8–12? If this is so, where did chapter 7 come from, and why was it written in Aramaic? Why does the linguistic difference inconveniently extend from chapter 2 to chapter 7, instead of including the stories only? Why, if the book is the work of a single author, is it composed in two languages? In what follows, the sections will be discussed separately before an attempt is made to answer these questions.

1.   The Stories

That the stories in Daniel (chaps. 2–6) have their origin in stories that circulated widely in the ancient Near East is indicated by a fragmentary text discovered in 1952 in cave 4 at Qumram (part of the general discovery of the Dead Sea Scrolls). It concerns the Babylonian king Nabonidus, who had prayed to "gods of silver and gold . . . wood and stone and clay" and who had been healed by a Jew from an ulcer that had afflicted him for seven years in Teiman (Taima) (Vermes 1962, p. 229). There is an indication of historical accuracy to this text in that Nabonidus (556–539 B.C.E.) did indeed retreat to an oasis in the Arabian Desert, leaving Belshazzar in charge of the kingdom (*ANET*, p. 306).

The Nabonidus fragment reminds us of two of the stories in Daniel. The first is chapter 4, where Nebuchadnezzar is driven away from Babylon for "seven times," that is, for seven years (Dan. 4:16, 25), because of his pride; he lives with the wild animals until he comes to his senses and acknowledges that true sovereignty belongs to the

God of Daniel, who has forecast the event by interpreting Nebuchadnezzar's dream. The similarities with the Nabonidus fragment are the exile of the king from Babylon and the part played by a Jew in his restoration. In Daniel chapter 4 the name of the king has changed from the less well known Nabonidus to the more famous Nebuchadnezzar, while the unnamed Jewish healer has been identified as Daniel. Both of these processes (substituting a more famous person and supplying a name for an anonymous person) are well-established features of how stories change during oral transmission. The other similarity is with chapter 5, where Belshazzar and his guests praise the "gods of gold and silver, bronze, iron, wood, and stone" (Dan. 5:4; cf. the quotation from the Nabonidus fragment above).

Granted that we can be reasonably sure that some of the stories in Daniel 2–6 have their origins in stories that reflected events of sixth-century Babylon, we can explain their history and their development up to their incorporation into Daniel. Probably from the end of the sixth century there circulated among Jews who were exiled in Babylonia and elsewhere stories about how Jews had risen to prominence in the courts of foreign rulers, how rulers who had oppressed Jews had been punished by God, and how devout Jews who had maintained their faith had been delivered. These themes are found in the Book of Esther; and they have some foundation in figures such as Nehemiah (445–432 B.C.E.), who held an important office in the Persian court. Davies (1985) has argued that Daniel 2, with its story of the statue made of various metals, reflects the fall of the Babylonian Empire to Cyrus in 539. If this is correct, we have another of the stories whose origins go back to the sixth century.

In discussions of Daniel, scholars have been divided between those who held that Daniel 1–6 accurately described events that took place in Babylon in the sixth century and those who argued that the stories were freely composed in the second century B.C.E., when Daniel was written. The truth seems to be somewhere between these positions. Although they do not record events that happened in sixth-century Babylon, chapters 2–6 are based on stories that originated at that time, some of which have a historical core, but all of which have been shaped by retelling to express the themes noted above. These stories were popular in the Jewish Diaspora, and when the crisis occurred that precipitated the writing of Daniel, they were incorporated into Daniel because of their popularity and relevance. That crisis was the attack upon Judaism by the Hellenistic ruler of Syria Antiochus IV (175–164 B.C.E.) in 169–167; and Davies has argued that this crisis is implied in Daniel 5. This is the only one of the stories in which the king is punished with death for desecrating the sacred temple vessels, just as Antiochus desecrated the temple (Dan. 5:30, 1 Macc. 6:1–19). In the other cases, the king repents and acknowledges the power of the God of Israel. Thus, the stories have a long history of composition, retelling, and final use in the Book of Daniel.

Nothing has been said about Daniel himself so far. Ezek. 14:14 mentions three righteous men: Noah, Daniel, and Job. Ugaritic texts of the thirteenth century B.C.E. mention a hero called Dan'el. Thus, the name seems to be that of a popular heroic figure and was probably attached to the stories when they were being told among the Diaspora Jews.

2. The Vision in Chapter 7

Many scholars have commented on the strange imagery of Daniel 7 and its resemblance to the mythology of the ancient Near East. The chapter begins with the winds stirring up the sea, from

---

ANIMAL IMAGERY IN APOCALYPTIC AND DANIEL

THE LANGUAGE OF APOCA-lyptic is highly dramatic. With extravagant imagination the writers of apocalyptic embellish their message with fantastic – sometimes bizarre – imagery. Apocalyptic literature is filled with rich symbolism, which has its source in both the metaphors of the Hebrew Bible and the characters of ancient Near Eastern mythology. This strange imagery fosters the sense of secrecy and mystery characteristic of apocalyptic writings.

Particularly striking is the way that apocalypticists employed animal figures to symbolize the people and nations inhabiting their visionary portraits of history and beyond. Already in first and second temple times human characteristics are depicted in symbolic terms. The ram and the horn are symbols of power and dominion (Ezek. 34:17); the lion represents strength and ferocity (Hos. 5:14); oxen and lambs stand for domesticity and peace (Isa. 11:6–7). This tradition is quite marked in many apocalyptic writings. In the First Book of Enoch, the bull stands for the patriarchs from Adam to Isaac; the righteous Moses and Aaron are sheep;

Kings David and Solomon are rams; and Judah Maccabee is symbolized by a great horn. Wild beasts and birds of prey often symbolize the gentile nations. In the tradition of Ezekiel 39, apocalyptic literature describes the heathen under the figures of tigers, wolves, dogs, hyenas, boars, foxes, squirrels, swine, vultures, ravens, and reptiles. The Roman legions are depicted as eagles, and the Messiah, who redeems his people from them, is a mighty lion (2 Esd. 11:37; cf. Rev. 5:5).

Perhaps the most famous apocalyptic animal imagery comes from the night visions of Daniel. Daniel's four great beasts belong to no recognizable earthly species, suggesting that their origin is to be found in the world of ancient Near Eastern mythology. The general meaning of these strange creatures is more accessible than their source. The writer of Daniel uses this strange animal imagery to recount the progress of world history, depicting the four great empires: Babylonia, Media, Persia, and Greece. However, some parts of the symbolism are still lost in obscurity (e.g., the sea from which the beasts arise and the four winds which blow on it). The beasts in Revelation are similar in their origin and purpose (Rev. 12–14).

The great Leviathan also figures prominently in the animal imagery of apocalyptic writers. The beast is known variously as Behemoth, Rahab, the serpent, and the dragon. Its origins lie in the Babylonian account of creation where the creator god slays the sea monster Chaos and fashions the universe from the beast's carcass. This myth found its way (with significant modification) into the Hebrew tradition, and several biblical passages display reflections of it (Ps. 74:13, Job 40:15–24, Ezek. 29:3). However, the proto-apocalyptic section of Isaiah recasts God's defeat of the chaos monster from a past accomplishment to an event anticipated at the great and imminent Day of Yahweh (Isa. 27:1). In the apocalyptic tradition related to the First Book of Enoch, Behemoth and Leviathan become two distinct mythical monsters. Behemoth inhabits the land, and Leviathan dwells in the sea (cf. 1 En. 60:7–9, 2 Esd. 6:47–52). Some apocalyptic writings give these creatures an eschatological context and associate them with the appearance of the Messiah. According to 2 Baruch, Leviathan and Behemoth will be the food of the righteous at the Messianic Banquet, which inaugurates the kingdom of God.

---

which four great beasts emerge (Dan. 7:1–8). The fourth beast is the most terrifying; at first it has ten horns, and then another, little horn grows among them and displaces three of them. In the mythology of Babylonia the sea is the place of chaos; and it has been argued that even in the Old Testament there are allusions to a primal struggle between God and the sea (e.g., Isa. 51:9–10). The descriptions of the beasts recall the iconography of Babylonia with its strange monsters.

The use of this imagery indicates that the authors were well versed in the general literature and culture of their day and supports the view that we should place Daniel in the milieu of mantic wisdom (see above). The same consideration applies to the figure of "one like a son of man," who appears on the clouds of heaven in 7:13 and to whom is given dominion over the nations. Although it is not possible to discover an entirely convincing analogy to the son of man in ancient Near Eastern mythology (comparisons have been made with the Babylonian god Marduk; the Persian Gayomart, or first man; and the Canaanite god Baal, who "comes with the clouds of heaven" and whose father, El, is called "father of years" – cf. Dan. 7: 9, 13), such an origin cannot be ruled out and would have been known to the authors of Daniel. The matter of the *origin* of the son of man figure must not be confused with its use in Daniel 7, where it probably stands for the "holy ones of the Most High" (Dan. 7:27), who receive an everlasting kingdom and who are probably Jews who remained true to their faith during the persecutions initiated by Antiochus IV. The "little horn" that is judged and destroyed is Antiochus IV.

3.   The Visions in Chapters 8–12

The remainder of Daniel includes a number of visions and their interpretations. Chapter 8 is a vision whose interpretation (8:20–2) describes the defeat of the Medes and Persians by the Greeks (Alexander the Great, 356–323 B.C.E.) and the rise of four smaller kingdoms from the Greek kingdom. The vision (but not the interpretation) also implies the rise of Antiochus IV and his desecration of the temple (8:9–11).

Daniel 9 is a beautiful prayer that recalls other compositions such as 1 Kings 8. The people are in exile and Daniel requests God to look with favor on his desolated sanctuary and city (vv. 18–19). A strange passage concludes the chapter and foretells the "abomination that desolates" in the sanctuary (9:24–7). Chapters 10–11 continue the veiled references to the history of the fourth to third centuries B.C.E. in chapter 8, emphasizing the aftermath of the breakup of Alexander's kingdom and the struggle between his generals, especially that between the king of the south (the Egyptian Ptolemies) and the king of the north (the Syrian Seleucids). Daniel 12 is an epilogue that introduces us to the authors, the wise who "shall shine in the brightness of the sky." It contains one of the few explicit references in the Old Testament to resurrection:

SON OF MAN

THE ENIGMATIC PHRASE "son of man" underwent significant changes in meaning during the course of early Jewish history. In most of the Hebrew Bible, the words *ben 'adam* (Aramaic *bar 'enosh*) are simply Semitic expressions for humankind. Thus, the classic anthropological question posed in Ps. 8:4 places "son of man" in poetic parallelism with the notion of "person" (Hebrew *'enosh*). In the Book of Ezekiel, the phrase occurs eighty-seven times in reference to the prophet himself.

By the third century B.C.E., "son of man" may have taken on new connotations. Daniel 7:13 preserves a vision in which a glorious being "like a son of man" descends from the heavens to take up his dominion over the peoples of the earth. Scholars have long been divided on their interpretation of this enigmatic reference. Some believe that in this context, "son of man" merely designates the strange figure as a human being who symbolically represents the saints of God. This human figure stands in contrast to the strange beasts which also inhabit Daniel's dreams. Others understand the passage as a description of an angelic being whose *appearance* seems human. A few see in Daniel the beginning of an apocalyptic tradition that introduces the "son of man" as a key figure in the events that occur at the end of the age.

Apocalypticists either combined this terminology from Daniel 7 with Near Eastern mythological traditions or by their own imaginations vastly expanded its meaning. The apocalypses of Enoch and 2 Esdras clearly associate the phrase "son of man" with a superhuman – almost divine – redeemer figure. The picture of this figure developed in apocalyptic literature is quite striking. The son of man is a transcendent heavenly being with no prior human existence. Indeed, he is said to have existed before God created the world. He remains hidden until the time appointed by God, when he is revealed as an object of worship to the whole world. At the end of time, the son of man takes his seat to judge the mighty of the world. Especially in Enoch, the son of man comes to be identified with the Messiah ("God's Elect One," "the Lord's Anointed"), even though the two concepts had very different beginnings.

"Son of man" seems to have been the early Christian community's most frequent appellation for Jesus. Jesus himself apparently used the phrase as his own favorite self-designation. Sometimes the words are merely a circumlocution for "I" (e.g., Matt. 8:20). In other places, Jesus simply uses "son of man" as a traditional Semitic phrase that means "human being." However, the early church invested the title "son of man" with great theological significance. In line with the apocalyptic tradition, the Gospels portray Jesus as "son of man" as a transcendent heavenly figure, the exalted Lord who will come again in glory. Matthew also portrays the son of man as the righteous judge, enthroned with his angels in glory, who separates the righteous from the wicked like a shepherd divides the sheep from the goats.

But the New Testament son of man is also a suffering human figure who recalls the Servant of the Lord in Isaiah 53. The title figures prominently in Jesus' Passion predictions in Mark (e.g., Mark 8:31). It is the son of man who "came, not to be served, but to serve, and to give his life as a ransom for many" (Mark 10:45; cf. Matt. 20:28, Luke 22:27). Some scholars have argued that Jesus forged a new meaning for the traditional title "son of man" by combining and reformulating these conflicting traditions.

By the second century of the common era, "son of man" had lost much of its apocalyptic force. The early church fathers generally understood the phrase as biblical recognition of Jesus' human nature, in contrast to the title "Son of God," which pointed to the Savior's divinity.

> Many of those who sleep in the dust of the earth shall awake, some to everlasting life, and some to shame and everlasting contempt. (12:2)

The fate of those who are resurrected will, we presume, depend on whether or not they were faithful in the tribulations that caused the Book of Daniel to be written: Antiochus's assault on the temple and Jerusalem in 169–167 B.C.E.

RESURRECTION IN POSTEXILIC ISRAEL

MOST OF THE HEBREW Bible knows nothing of a resurrection of the dead; there is no developed concept of life after death. Preexilic Israelites viewed death as the severely diminished form of an individual's life, an enervated existence in the grave, where the "shades" (Hebrew *repha'im*) resided. For Israel, future hope was expressed in terms of the nation's ongoing corporate life (e.g., Ezek. 37:1–14), not with regard to individual destiny. Some poetic passages in the Hebrew canon seem to express a desire for a better form of life beyond the grave (e.g., Ps. 73:24, 1 Sam. 2:6, Job 19:19–27), but human existence beyond death is a generally bleak affair in most of the Hebrew Bible. Human beings were not obliterated when they died, but they existed in the abode of the dead (*she'ol*) as mere shadows of their former selves.

By the second century B.C.E., however, the idea began to arise that righteous individuals would live again in the world to come. This conception was normally cast in terms of a belief in the resurrection of the flesh, since Israelite traditions did not make a distinction between soul and body. Human beings were indivisibly spiritual and corporeal; unembodied life was a foreign notion. The doctrine of bodily resurrection appears suggestively in the pseudepigraphic work of 1 Enoch (22, 27). Opinions vary, but some scholars understand Isa. 26:19 as the first reference to resurrection in the Hebrew canon. Dan. 12:2–3, dating from the second century B.C.E., unambiguously preserves the belief that a general resurrection of the dead will take place at the last day.

Apocalyptic literature is divided over the exact nature of this resurrection. Some writings (1 En. 83–90 and Psalms of Solomon) suggest that only the righteous will be raised to everlasting life. Most apocalypses, however, speak of a universal resurrection of all persons – the just to eternal bliss and the unjust to eternal damnation. Jubilees uncharacteristically casts its doctrine of resurrection in the form of belief in the immortality of the soul.

The exact origin of these beliefs is a matter of continuing controversy. Some historians of ideas attribute the growing importance of life after death in Judaism to Greek influences. Others suggest that Persian Zoroastrianism, with its emphasis on the final judgment and its detailed system of reward and punishment, is the belief's ultimate source. Many scholars stress developments within Jewish political and intellectual history that led to the widespread acceptance of belief in the resurrection. A heightened sense of individualism characterized postexilic Israel, and there was growing dissatisfaction with the doctrine of corporate responsibility. Traditional beliefs that humans received proper recompense for their actions in this life came into question. Sometimes the wicked prosper and the righteous suffer. Since the present seemed inexplicable and unfair in light of divine justice, retribution was perhaps projected into the Hereafter, where both the wicked and the good would receive their just reward. The death of nationalist religious martyrs in the Maccabean revolts provided an important impulse for the Jewish belief in immortality and resurrection. Those who died defending the Torah would surely deserve a reward for their sacrifice. Since they did not receive it in this world, they would enjoy immortality in the next.

In the first century C.E., popular opinion was apparently still divided over belief in resurrection. According to Josephus and the Christian evangelists, the Sadducees dismissed the idea as having no foundation in the scriptures. However, belief in the bodily resurrection was a foundational tenet of the Pharisaic movement, and the covenanters at Qumran also seem to have looked forward to unending bodily life in the world to come. Resurrection went on to play a key role in classical Jewish and Christian doctrine. The rabbis included belief in the resurrection in the canonical liturgy, especially in the second of the Eighteen Benedictions (*shemoneh 'esreh*) in the Amidah (The Prayer). The tenth chapter of the Mishnaic tractate *Sanhedrin* begins, "All of Israel has a portion in the world to come, as it is said (Isa. 60:21), 'And thy people are all righteous, at the End they shall inherit the land . . .' and the following have no portion in the world to come: one who says, 'There is no resurrection of the dead.'" The doctrine of bodily resurrection formed a vital part of the early Christian faith, eventually becoming crystallized in the creeds declaring belief in the "resurrection of the dead and the life of the world to come."

4. Conclusion

Some of the questions posed at the outset have been answered. The Book of Daniel contains material that developed over several centuries before being put into its final form in the second century B.C.E. as a result of the attack on Judaism by Antiochus IV. Its disparate material – that is, its popular stories, its mythic imagery, and its detailed allusions to the history of Persia, Greece, and the Hellenistic kingdoms – is best explained by accepting that it was composed by "wise men" who were conversant with these types of literature and knowledge. The matter of the use of two languages is impossible to resolve.

What must not be overlooked is the theology of Daniel. Nowhere in the Old Testament do we have such striking and powerful assertions of the sovereignty of the God of Israel over the nations of the world, nor of the conviction that he will establish a kingdom that will endure forever. These hopes were expressed in the full knowledge that when it came to individuals faced by the threat of death, there was not likely to be the miraculous deliverance implied in some of the stories in chapters 1–6. We catch a hint of this realism in the reply of the three men who were about to be put in the fiery furnace:

> If our God whom we serve is able to deliver us from the furnace of blazing fire and out of your hand, O king, let him deliver us. But if not, be it known to you, O king, that we will not serve your gods. (3:17–18)

This same realism is also implied in the passage about resurrection, promising the faithful that they will not have died in vain.

Among the resources upon which the authors drew to express this hope were the past traditions of Israel, where it could be seen that, in all the ups and downs of their history, the people had been guided by a God who was ultimately more powerful than great empires, because he was the creator of the world. It says much for the creativity of Israelite religion that the authors of Daniel were able to write such a unique book from within their tradition in the face of a crisis that threatened their very existence. Further, their vision of hope, born out of suffering and centering on the faithful ones symbolized by "one like a son of man," produced narratives whose latent meaning gave confidence to later readers that God was with his people in the midst of persecution and suffering and that his purposes would ultimately triumph. That meaning would help Jesus of Nazareth shape and realize his mission.

BIBLIOGRAPHICAL AND BIOGRAPHICAL ESSAY

A. BIBLIOGRAPHY

1. Introductory Books on the Old Testament

Far and away the most popular text in America has been B. W. Anderson's *Understanding the Old Testament,* 4th. ed. (Englewood Cliffs, N.J.: Prentice-Hall, 1986). Anderson's treatment of the Hebrew Bible combines the best historical and archeological approach with a high standard of literary and theological analysis.

J. Rogerson, ed., *Beginning Old Testament Study* (London: SPCK, 1983), is designed to introduce readers to academic Old Testament study. It sketches the history of Old Testament study and then deals with specific issues such as methodology, the worldview of the ancient Israelites, Old Testament ethics and theology, the relation between the Old and New Testaments, and using the Old Testament in today's world. Although it is due for revision, it fulfills its purpose well. Co-contributors are John Barton, David Clines, and Paul Joyce.

R. Coggins, *Introducing the Old Testament* (Oxford: Oxford University Press, 1990), is also an excellent book for beginners, covering basic issues and approaches. *William Barclay Introduces the Bible* (London: Bible Reading Fellowship and International Bible Reading Association, 1992) has been a popular and much-appreciated introduction since it was first published in 1972. It explains how the biblical writings came into being and gained acceptance as Scripture, and how the Bible can be read and appreciated.

C. Westermann, *Handbook to the Old Testament* (London: SPCK, 1969), addresses the fact that the content of the Old Testament is unfamiliar to many readers today. It helps readers to become familiar with the Old Testament by summarizing each book, often with the help of diagrams, and by explaining briefly the date and purpose of each book and its sections.

J. Rogerson and P. Davies, *The Old Testament World* (Cambridge: Cambridge University Press, 1989), is a comprehensive introduction to the historical, social, and political backgrounds of the Old Testament as well as to its literature. Other more specialized introductions to aspects of the Old Testament include R. E. Clements, ed., *The World of Ancient Israel: Sociological, Anthropological and Political Perspectives* (Cambridge: Cambridge University Press, 1989); A. Mayes, *The Old Testament in Sociological Perspective* (London: Marshall Pickering, 1989), and L. Grabbe, *Judaism from Cyrus to Hadrian,* vol. 1, *The Persian and Greek Periods* (Minneapolis: Fortress Press, 1992).

Brevard S. Childs's *Introduction to the Old Testament as Scripture* (Philadelphia: Fortress Press, 1979), had an enormous impact on biblical studies in the 1980s in arguing for a new kind of "canonical criticism" based on the existing biblical text and the inner-biblical dialogue among the various components of the text. Norman K. Gottwald's *The Hebrew Bible: A Socio-literary Introduction* (Philadelphia: Fortress Press,

1985), had a similar impact on Old Testament study by applying sociological theory to the main periods of Israel's history and literary theory to the formation of the canon of Scripture. The book is best used as a reference work and supplement to biblical study. A collection of essays edited by Hershel Shanks, *Ancient Israel* (Washington: Biblical Archaeological Society, 1988), provides a very readable overview of recent trends in Old Testament historical study. There are excellent introductions to individual books of the Old Testament as well as to aspects of its history, sociology, geography, and archeology in *The Anchor Bible Dictionary*, ed. D. N. Freedman, 6 vols. (New York: Doubleday, 1992).

One of the important features of recent interpretation of the Old Testament has been the contribution made by writers committed to feminist or liberation approaches. Good introductions to these are A. L. Laffey, *An Introduction to the Old Testament: A Feminist Perspective* (Philadelphia: Fortress Press, 1988); N. K. Gottwald, ed., *The Bible and Liberation: Political and Social Hermeneutics* (Maryknoll: Orbis, 1983); and P. Tribble, *God and the Rhetoric of Sexuality* (Philadelphia: Fortress Press, 1978). C. L. Meyers's book *Discovering Eve* (New York: Oxford University Press, 1988) enables the student of the Old Testament to reread the all-important creation story in light of social-scientific and archeological materials. In this connection, Mark Smith's *The Early History of God* (New York: Harper-Collins, 1990) is invaluable since it offers a comprehensive study of Israel's concept of God in light of Northwest Semitic literature and archeology.

The recent book by A. G. Auld, *Kings without Privilege: David and Moses in the Story of the Bible's Kings* (Edinburgh: T. & T. Clark, 1994), proposes that Chronicles did not use Samuel and Kings as a source, but that the material common to Samuel and Kings, on the one hand, and Chronicles, on the other, represents a source used by both. This is not the same as the old theory that Samuel and Kings had used extensively, and Chronicles had used minimally, a common biographical source about the lives of David and Solomon. If Auld's theory, which is attractively argued, gains acceptance, this will require some modification of what is said in the present work about Samuel, Kings, and Chronicles.

The most helpful recent guide to biblical archeology is A. Mazar's *Archaeology of the Land of the Bible* (New York: Doubleday, Anchor Bible Reference Library, 1990). Mazar's treatment is by historical period and relates the material culture of each period to the known written sources of the period. Its greatest strength is the biblical period from ca. 1200 to 600 B.C.E.

2.   Texts from the Ancient Near East

A book referred to frequently in the present work with the abbreviation *ANET* is J. B. Pritchard, *Ancient Near Eastern Texts Relating to the Old Testament*, 3d ed. (Princeton: Princeton University Press, 1969). This is an invaluable collection of translations of texts from

Eyypt, Palestine, Syria, and Mesopotamia, covering history, law, myths, epics, wisdom literature, letters, and inscriptions.

3.   Atlases

A knowledge of the geography of the ancient world is important for understanding the Old Testament. *The Oxford Bible Atlas*, 3d ed., ed. J. Day (Oxford: Oxford University Press, 1984), is a handy, comprehensive, and reliable work. J. Rogerson, *Atlas of the Bible* (Oxford: Phaidon, 1989; New York: Facts on File, 1985), tries to break new ground by treating the subject geographically rather than historically, with emphasis on how the land looked in biblical, as opposed to modern times. Also recommended are M. Roaf, *Cultural Atlas of Mesopotamia and the Ancient Near East* (Oxford and New York: Facts on File, 1990); and J. Baines and J. Máalek, *Atlas of Ancient Egypt* (Oxford: Phaidon, 1980).

4.   Guides to Individual Books of the Old Testament

The series of inexpensive Old Testament Guides edited by R. N. Whybray and published by Sheffield Academic Press is strongly recommended to readers who wish to study particular books in greater depth. The series, which is almost complete, introduces readers to the main issues in the academic study of each book of the Old Testament and contains details for further reading.

5.   Books and Articles Referred to in the Text

Avigad, N. 1986. *Hebrew Bullae from the Time of Jeremiah: Remnants of a Burnt Archive.* Jerusalem: Israel Exploration Society.

Blum, E. 1984. *Die Komposition der Vätergeschichte.* Wissenschaftliche Monographien zum Alten und Neven Testament 57. Neukirchen: Neukirchener Verlag. A large and detailed work on the composition of the stories of Abraham, Isaac, and Jacob that argues that each set of traditions developed separately before being combined.

Calvin, J. 1975. *Genesis.* Trans. John King. Edinburgh: Banner of Truth Trust. A translation of the lectures of the famous reformer that shows that he held radical views on the purpose of the creation story in Genesis 1. It was not, according to Calvin, a scientific account of the creation of the universe but a description as it would have appeared to an ancient Israelite observer.

Clements, R. E., ed. 1989. *The World of Ancient Israel: Sociological, Anthropological, and Political Perspectives.* Cambridge: Cambridge University Press.

Davies, G. I. 1991. *Ancient Hebrew Inscriptions.* Cambridge: Cambridge University Press. A valuable collection of Hebrew inscriptions together with a concordance. For use by Hebraists only.

Davies, P. R. 1985. *Daniel.* Old Testament Guides. Sheffield: Sheffield Academic Press.

————. 1989. "The Social World of the Apocalyptic Writings," in Clements 1989, pp. 251–71.

————. 1992. *In Search of Ancient Israel.* Sheffield: JSOT Press. A stimulating and controversial book that forces readers to consider how they relate history, the Bible, and archeology in considering Israel's origins.

De Moor, J. C. 1990. *The Rise of Yahwism: The Roots of Israelite Monotheism.* Bibliotheca Ephemeridum Theologicarum Lovaniensium 91. Louvain: University Press and Peeters. An attempt to identify Moses and Israelite origins with the help of biblical and nonbiblical texts.

Finkelstein, I. 1988. *The Archaeology of the Israelite Settlement.* Jerusalem: Israel Exploration Society. An important account of ancient Israel's settlement in Canaan in the light of archeological surveys.

Fishbane, M. 1985. *Biblical Interpretation in Ancient Israel.* Oxford: Oxford University Press. Traces biblical interpretation within the books of the Bible. In the present work it is used for its discussion of the origin of Israel's legal traditions.

Gerstenberger, E. 1988. *Psalms: Part I, with an Introduction to Cultic Poetry.* Grand Rapids: Eerdmans. Dates the Psalms later (i.e., in the postexilic period) than the prevailing consensus.

Görg, M., and B. Lang, eds. 1988–. *Neues Bibel-Lexikon.* 10 vols. to date. Zurich: Benzinger. An excellent, authoritative, concise, and up-to-date reference work.

Heidel, A. 1963a. *The Babylonian Genesis.* 2d ed. Chicago: University of Chicago Press, Phoenix Books. This and the title that follows are standard translations and discussions of nonbiblical texts in their relation to the Old Testament.

————. 1963b. *The Gilgamesh Epic and Old Testament Parallels.* 2d ed. Chicago: University of Chicago Press, Phoenix Books.

Hopkins, D. C. 1985. *The Highlands of Canaan: Agricultural Life in the Early Iron Age.* Social World of Biblical Antiquity 3. Sheffield: Almond/JSOT Press. A pioneering discussion.

Houtman, C. 1986. *Exodus vertaaled en verklaard: Commentar op het Oude Testament.* Kampen: J. H. Kok. A massive commentary for specialists and readers of Dutch.

Jamieson-Drake, D. W. 1991. *Scribes and Schools in Monarchic Judah: A Socio-archaeological Approach.* Sheffield: JSOT Press. An important discussion of the centralization of administration in Judah based on statistical methods.

Keel, O., and C. Vehlinger. 1992. *Göttinnen, Götter, und Gottessymbole: Neue Erkentnisse zur Religionsgeschichte Kanaans und Israels aufgrund bislang unerschlossener ikonographischer Quellen.* Quaestiones Disputatae 134. Freiburg-im-Breisgau: Herder Verlag. This, and the title that follows, are important contributions to understanding "popular religion" in ancient Israel based on iconography.

Keel, O., et al. 1990. *Studien zu den Stempelsiegeln aus Palästina/Israel.* Vol. 3, *Die Frühe Eisenzeit: Ein Workshop.* Freiburg: Universitätsverlag Freiburg Schweiz; Göttingen: Vandenhoeck & Ruprecht.

Lang, B. 1981. *Ezechiel.* Darmstadt: Wissenschaftliche Buchgesellschaft.

Lohfink, N. 1983. "Die Schichten des Pentateuch und der Krieg." In N. Lohfink, ed., *Gewalt und Gewaltlosigkeit in Alten Testament,* pp. 51–110.

Quaestiones Disputatae 96. Freiburg-im-Breisgau: Herder Verlag. Considers how the different Pentateuchal sources deal with the question of war.

———. 1990a. "Bund." In M. Görg and B. Lang, eds., *Neues Bibel-Lexikon*. Lieferung 3. Zurich: Benzinger. A survey of the notion of covenant in the Old Testament.

———. 1990b. "Deuteronomium." In ibid.

———, ed. 1985. *Das Deuteronomium: Enstehung, Gestalt, and Botschaft*. Bibliotheca Ephemeridum Theologicarum Lovaniensium 68. Louvain: University Press and Peeters. A collection of papers on the origin and purpose of Deuteronomy.

Maurice, F. D. 1892. *The Patriarchs and Lawgivers of the Old Testament*. London: Macmillan. Collected sermons by a famous nineteenth-century theologian.

Mazar, A. 1990. *Archaeology of the Land of the Bible, 10,000–586 B.C.E.* New York: Doubleday, Anchor Bible Reference Library. A comprehensive survey of the material.

Mendenhall, G. E. 1962. "The Hebrew Conquest of Palestine." *Biblical Archaeology* 25, pp. 66–87.

Meyers, C. L., and E. M. Meyers. 1987. *Haggai–Zechariah 1–8*. Anchor Bible. New York: Doubleday.

———. 1993. *Zechariah 9–14, Malachi*. Anchor Bible. New York: Doubleday.

Müller, H.-P. 1982. "Die aramäische Inschrift von Deir ʾAlla und die älteren Bileamsprüche." *Zeitschrift für die alttestamentliche Wissenschaft* 94, pp. 214–44. Translation of and commentary on the Balaam inscription from Tell Deir Alla in the Jordan Valley.

———. 1985. "Das Motif für die Sintflut: Die hermeneutische Funktion des Mythos und seiner Analyse." *Zeitschrift für die altestamentliche Wissenschaft* 97, pp. 295–316. An important treatment of the Flood story in Genesis.

Riehm, E. 1890. *Einleitung in das Alte Testament*. Vol. 2. Halle: Eugen Stein. One of the major nineteenth-century introductions to the Old Testament.

Rogerson, J. W. 1978. *Anthropology and the Old Testament*. Oxford: Basil Blackwell. Reprint, 1984. Sheffield: JSOT Press. Discusses basic questions of method and approach.

———. 1984. *Old Testament Criticism in the Nineteenth Century: England and Germany*. London: SPCK. Examines how German biblical criticism developed and was received into England.

———. 1991. *Genesis 1–11*. Old Testament Guides. Sheffield: Sheffield Academic Press.

———. 1992. *W. M. L. de Wette, Founder of Modern Biblical Criticism: An Intellectual Biography*. Sheffield: JSOT Press.

Scholder, K. 1990. *The Birth of Modern Critical Theology: Origins and Problems of Biblical Criticism in the Seventeenth Century*. London: SCM Press.

Shiloh, Y. 1986. "A Group of Hebrew Bullae from the City of David." *Israel Exploration Journal* 36, pp. 16–38.

Staubli, T. 1991. *Das Image der Nomaden im alten Israel und in der Ikonographie seiner sesshaften Nachbarn*. Orbis Biblicis et Orientalis 107. Freiburg: Universitätsverlag Freiburg Schweiz; Göttingen: Vandenhoeck &

Ruprecht. A discussion of "nomads" in the ancient Near East on the basis of iconography.

Vermes, G. 1987. *The Dead Sea Scrolls in English*. Harmondsworth: Penguin, 3rd ed.

Weinfeld, M. 1972. *Deuteronomy and the Deuteronomic School*. Oxford: Clarendon Press. A classic study that links Deuteronomy with Israel's "wisdom" schools.

———. 1991. *Deuteronomy 1–11*. Anchor Bible. New York: Doubleday.

B. BIOGRAPHY

This section deals briefly with some of the scholars mentioned in the text. To avoid mention of such scholars in Old Testament study is to give a quite false impression of the discipline and how it has developed. However, the list here is necessarily very selective.

John William Colenso (1814–83) was Anglican bishop of the British colony of Natal, South Africa, and a great missionary to the Zulus. He was also a pioneering biblical critic, whose massive work in seven volumes, *The Pentateuch and Joshua* (1862–79), played an important part in the development of the view given classical expression by Wellhausen. Colenso was so far ahead of his generation in Britain that attempts were made to depose him from his bishopric on account of his radical views. However, his work was well known on the continent of Europe and he corresponded extensively with Abraham Kuenen.

Wilhelm Martin Leberecht de Wette (1780–1849) was one of the founders of modern biblical criticism. His doctoral dissertation, presented in 1804, argued that Deuteronomy must have been written no earlier than the seventh century B.C.E., and his *Beiträge zur Einleitung in das Alte Testament* of 1806–7 argued that, on the evidence of the Books of Judges, Samuel, and Kings, Moses did not institute a fully developed system of priesthood and sacrifice at a central sanctuary as implied in Exodus, Leviticus, Numbers, and Deuteronomy. These were much later developments. De Wette's writings opened up a completely new way of reconstructing the history of Israel's religion and system of sacrifice. He held posts in the Universities of Jena, Heidelberg, Berlin, and Basel.

Heinrich Ewald (1803–75) was born in Göttingen and taught there for most of his life except for a period in Tübingen, where he went when he resigned his Göttingen chair in protest at the suspension of the constitution of Hanover by the new elector of Hanover in 1837. He published commentaries on many books of the Bible, but his great contribution was that he wrote the first truly critical history of Israel (the first volume of which was published in 1843), based upon a critical study of the Bible and other relevant materials.

Hermann Gunkel (1862–1932) is best known for his commentaries on Genesis and the Psalms, in which he used the method of form criticism, that is, the classification of each short narrative or psalm according to a particular type or genre, which Gunkel then associated with a particular social setting. He was especially interested in oral traditions and folktales and published a small book entitled *The Folktale in the Old Testament* in 1917. He held posts in Halle, Berlin, and Giessen.

Abraham Kuenen (1828–91) was a professor in Leiden, the Netherlands, and one of the greatest of the biblical critics of the nineteenth century. He made a particularly important contribution to the theory that the priestly material in the books of Genesis to Numbers was a unity and was to be dated in its present form to the postexilic period. This helped to confirm de Wette's theory that the system of priesthood and sacrifice in Israel described in books such as Leviticus was a late development.

Hermann Samuel Reimarus (1694–1768) was a professor of oriental languages in Hamburg who wrote a number of radical articles, including pieces on aspects of the history of Israel and the New Testament. These were published after his death by G. E. Lessing between 1774 and 1778 and provoked considerable controversy in Germany.

Julius Wellhausen (1844–1918) is regarded as one of the major figures in the history of Old Testament study. His book *Geschichte Israels*, published in 1878, brought together his own researches and those of other scholars to present a radical view of the history of Israel's religion, which was integrated with the documentary hypothesis of the composition of the opening books of the Bible. According to this theory, the documents J and E, written in the ninth to eighth centuries B.C.E. reflected a period when there was no centralized priesthood or worship in Israel; the Book of Deuteronomy (D) was associated with Josiah's reform in 622 B.C.E. and was a move toward centralization; and the priestly document (P) was postexilic and reflected the time when priesthood and sacrifice were now centered in Jerusalem. Wellhausen was a professor at Greifswald, Halle, Marburg, and Göttingen.

PART TWO

JEWISH RESPONSES TO GRECO-ROMAN CULTURE, 332 B.C.E. TO 200 C.E.

Anthony J. Saldarini

I. JUDAISM ENCOUNTERS THE HELLENISTIC WORLD

A. ALEXANDER AND HELLENIZATION

The hellenization of the Near East began when Alexander the Great led his Macedonian troops through Asia Minor to Issus, on the border of Syria, where he defeated Darius the Persian in 333 B.C.E. and gained access to both Egypt and Mesopotamia. A year later Alexander had conquered the Mediterranean coast and Egypt with ease, except for sieges of Tyre and Gaza. During that year Jerusalem, along with all the other cities of the region, submitted. Alexander did not visit Jerusalem, despite the later rabbinic legend, but rushed off to battle the Persian king, Darius, for the last time. He conquered Mesopotamia, Persia, and surrounding territories as far as the Indus River (in present Pakistan). His untimely death in 323 left his unstable and scattered conquests in the hands of his generals, who quickly split up the empire and went to war with one another.

The hellenistic period extends from the time Alexander conquered the eastern Mediterranean area in 333–323 B.C.E. through the reigns of his successors from 323 down to the conquest of the area by the Romans between 200 and 31 B.C.E. During that time Greek practices and ways of thought influenced governmental and cultural institutions in the eastern Mediterranean area from Greece through Syria to Mesopotamia and down the coast to Egypt. Generally the native governing class adapted most comprehensively to hellenistic culture while the lower, farming class retained its traditional customs and beliefs with a thin veneer of Greek terms and practices. Cities were affected by hellenization more than rural areas, and international relations were more controlled than local politics.

One of Alexander's generals, Ptolemy, used the natural borders and wealth of Egypt to consolidate his rule there and finally had himself declared an independent king in 305 B.C.E. Another general, Seleucus, who ruled Mesopotamia from Babylon, had to fend off numerous attacks on his domains from native peoples and from Antigonus, the general ruling Asia Minor. After surviving exile from his own kingdom, Seleucus finally established his rule in 301 B.C.E. when he and a coalition of generals defeated Antigonus at Ipsus in western Asia Minor. Seleucus, who ruled until 281 B.C.E., and Ptolemy, who ruled until 285, established a pair of strong empires which dominated the eastern Mediterranean for well over a century and endured even longer in weakened form.

During the third century the Seleucids consolidated their power by building Greek cities and settling loyal veterans throughout eastern Asia Minor, Syria, Mesopotamia, and Persia. The Seleucid domains were constantly under pressure from native peoples and under attack from surrounding powers. Gradually Seleucus oriented the empire toward the Mediterranean by moving his capital first from Babylon to Seleucia, a new city on the Euphrates River, and then to another new city, Antioch, near the Mediterranean on the border between Syria and Asia Minor. Even so, the Ptolemaic Empire dominated the eastern Mediterranean region in the third century. The Ptolemies ruled from Alexandria, a Greek city founded by Alexander on the Mediterranean coast that became a preeminent cultural and governmental center for several centuries. Jews in Palestine were ruled first by the Ptolemies

EGYPTIAN AND SYRIAN RULERS	
Ptolemaic Kingdom	*Seleucid Kingdom*
Ptolemy I, 323–285	Seleucus I, 312–281
Ptolemy II, 285–246	Antiochus I, 281–261
	Antiochus II, 261–246
Ptolemy III, 246–221	Seleucus II, 246–226
	Seleucus III, 226–223
Ptolemy IV, 221–203	Antiochus III, 223–187
Ptolemy V, 203–180	Seleucus IV, 187–175
Ptolemy VI, 180–145	Antiochus IV, 175–164

Seleucid and Ptolemaic domains, c. 300 B.C.E.

Pella in Macedonia, Alexander's capital.

Anthony J. Saldarini.

Olive press in Bet She'an.

Anthony J. Saldarini.

and then by the Seleucids. Jewish cultural, political, and intellectual life was profoundly and permanently affected by Greek thought and practice.

1.   Palestine under the Ptolemies

During the third century Palestine and southern Syria were ruled directly from Alexandria. A cache of letters and documents found in the Fayum, a district in Lower Egypt, and written by Zenon, an employee of Apollonius, the Ptolemaic minister of finance, show that even the smallest towns were monitored by Egyptian officials. They testify that Palestine exported grain, wine, olive oil, smoked fish, cheese, meat, dried figs, fruit, honey, dates, and slaves. They also show that government monopolies and regulations provided for orderly transactions and maximum government revenue.

From the beginning the Seleucids contested the Ptolemaic claim to southern Syria and Palestine because of the strategic and profitable coastal cities there. During the third century B.C.E. these two dynasties fought five wars, which eventually led to Seleucid control of the coast and mountains. The first three wars changed the political status little but did stimulate political competition and unrest within Jerusalem. The high priest was normally the Jewish representative to the government and had enormous control and influence in political, social, and financial matters. After the death of Ptolemy II Philadelphus (285–246 B.C.E.), the high priest Onias II refused to send the taxes to the new Ptolemaic government, probably because he sided with the Seleucids in the third Syrian war (242 B.C.E.) in hope of achieving greater independence. His insubordination led to the appointment of the family of Tobias as official representatives of the Jewish people to the government.

2. The Tobiads

The family of Tobias seems to have been typical of many leading Jewish families who competed for power and influence during the hellenistic and Roman periods. It ruled over a large area east of the Jordan River from a fortified palace at 'Araq el-Emir. When Onias II resisted the power of Ptolemy III, Tobias seized the opportunity to have himself appointed chief representative of the Jewish people to the government. Tobias's son Joseph later had himself appointed chief tax collector by convincing Ptolemy that he could collect increased revenues if given centralized authority over tax collection and troops to enforce his will. Joseph brought the power of the Tobiads to its height by becoming an influential Ptolemaic official. He had close governmental contacts and a permanent financial agent in Alexandria in Egypt to manage his affairs. Joseph typified the native governing class, which was recruited to serve the empire with promises of continued power and wealth. In return, these native rulers adapted to hellenistic culture.

3. Hellenization

The ruling classes had to adapt greatly in order to preserve and enlarge their power and wealth. The Ptolemaic and Seleucid Empires assimilated local leaders who were willing to master Greek, adapt to Greek culture, and help maintain the empire. Wealthy landowners, high and low officials, military leaders, prosperous merchants, and their children benefited from a Greek education at a gymnasium or at least familiarity with Greek culture, which included athletics, Greek language, and some literature and philosophy. Greek cities, founded to provide islands of Greek culture and security in barbarian lands, helped hellenize the local leaders and keep the Greek and Macedonian residents true to their Greek heritage.

The majority of the population, who were uneducated farmers, continued to speak their native language, follow local customs, and worship their ancestral gods. Even when new temples were built to Greek gods, these gods were understood as oriental deities under another name, and traditional cults continued as usual. Intermarriage of native women with Greek settlers (mostly former soldiers) resulted in as much assimilation of the Greeks to local culture as the opposite. Everyone had to adapt to new government procedures, to foreign officials, and to modified taxation systems, but indigenous peoples had done this for centuries. In addition, local leaders and those engaged in commerce had to learn enough Greek to do business.

4. Palestine under the Seleucids

Though the first three wars against the Ptolemies in Egypt had not gained the Syrian Seleucids victory, the Seleucid ruler Antiochus III (223–187 B.C.E.) continued the assaults on the Ptolemies until he won Palestine. Finally, in 201–200, he conquered almost all of southern Syria, Palestine, and the coast and defeated Scopas and the Egyptian army at Paneas in northern Palestine. Two years later he had established permanent control over Palestine and the surrounding territories.

During these wars Jerusalem and other Jewish cities and towns changed hands numerous times. When Antiochus conquered Palestine, the pro-Ptolemaic party withdrew to Egypt, and the pro-Seleucids, led by Simon II, the high priest, were left in power. A decree of Antigonus notes that the Jerusalem leadership had furnished supplies for his army and aided the attack on the Ptolemaic garrison left in the citadel. The decree makes provision for the redemption of Jewish captives and for the repair of the destruction suffered by Jerusalem, including duty-free imports of timber to repair the temple. To give the residents of Jerusalem time to reestablish themselves, Antiochus freed them from taxes for three years. Antiochus also affirmed the Jews' right to live by their ancestral laws and left the high priest and council in place as the governing bodies in Judea.

During the second century the power of the Seleucids and Ptolemies steadily declined. Egypt spent the second century embroiled in a series of civil conflicts over dynastic succession and never again posed a serious threat to other Mediterranean powers. Antiochus III might have restored the Seleucid Empire to glory had he not been defeated by the Romans, who were expanding eastward. The Romans drove Antiochus III out of Greece and defeated him in the battle of Magnesia in western Asia Minor (190 B.C.E.). According to the subsequent peace of Apamea (188 B.C.E.), Antiochus had to withdraw entirely from Greece and Asia Minor and pay a huge indemnity to Rome.

LETTER OF ANTIOCHUS III CONCERNING JERUSALEM

KING ANTIOCHUS TO Ptolemy [the governor of Palestine], greeting. Inasmuch as the Jews, from the very moment when we entered their country, showed their eagerness to serve us, and, when we came to their city, gave us a splendid reception and met us with their senate and furnished us an abundance of provisions to our soldiers and elephants, and also helped us to expel the Egyptian garrison in the citadel, we have seen fit on our part to requite them for these acts and to restore their city which has been destroyed by the hazards of war, and to re-people it by bringing back to it those who have been dispersed abroad. In the first place we have decided, on account of their piety, to furnish them for their sacrifices an allowance of sacrificial animals, wine, oil and frankincense to the value of twenty thousand pieces of silver. . . . And it is my will that these things be made over to them as I have ordered, and that the work on the temple be completed, including the porticoes and any other part that it may be necessary to build. The timber, moreover, shall be brought from Judea itself and from other nations and Lebanon without the imposition of a toll-charge. . . . And all the members of the nation shall have a form of government in accordance with the laws of their country, and the senate, the priests, the scribes of the temple and the temple-singers shall be relieved from the poll-tax and the crown-tax and the salt-tax which they pay. And, in order that the city may be more quickly inhabited, I grant both to the present inhabitants and to those who may return before the month of Hyperberetaios exemption from taxes for three years. We shall also relieve them in the future from a third part of their tribute. (Josephus, *Antiquities* 12.3.3 [138–44])

The first of the terms cut him off from his supply of Greek and Macedonian settlers and soldiers, and the latter saddled his sons with a dire need for revenue, which adversely affected their ability to govern and expand their empire. A year after the peace of Apamea Antiochus was assassinated.

B. LITERARY RESPONSES TO HELLENISM BEFORE THE MACCABEAN REVOLT

During the hellenistic and Roman periods Jews in Palestine and the Diaspora produced an abundant literature in Hebrew and Greek. Many Hebrew works were translated into Greek, preeminently the Bible; in some cases only the Greek translation of Hebrew books has survived. Jewish authors revised traditional stories and materials and created new works based on both Greek and Jewish models. Though most of these works did not become part of the canonical Hebrew Bible, they influenced Judaism and early Christianity during the Greco-Roman period. In fact, several books found only in the Greek version of the Bible are recognized as canonical by Roman Catholics and Eastern Orthodox. Consequently, in this section on Jewish response to Greco-Roman culture a variety of Jewish works, some nonbiblical, will be treated so that the full story of post-biblical Judaism and its offspring, Christianity, may be understood.

Some of these Jewish books from the hellenistic and Roman periods were accepted by the early and medieval church as part of the Bible, and thus as authoritative and inspired, because they were found in the Greek biblical manuscripts. (See the sidebar with the list of Deuterocanonical books.) However, most of the Jewish community of the second to ninth centuries C.E. read the Bible in Hebrew and accepted only those books found in the Hebrew scrolls. During the Protestant Reformation in the sixteenth century the reformers sought to remove later accretions and return to the pristine simplicity of early Christianity. Thus they accepted only those books found in the Hebrew scriptures.

For Catholic and Orthodox Christians the Deuterocanonical books are part of the Bible. In the Protestant traditions they have often been approved as pious and edifying books. The other Jewish books from the hellenistic period, including the Dead Sea Scrolls, do not command the respect and assent from Christians and Jews that are accorded the Bible. For the interested reader, however, they are authentic writings of early Judaism and as such testify to the attitudes, teachings, beliefs, and conflicts found in the world of the late Old Testament and the New Testament. Thus these writings, many of which will be treated here, illuminate the religious, intellectual, and social development that fostered the growth of Christianity and rabbinic Judaism.

The most important Jewish document in Greek is the translation of the Bible. The Greek translation is often referred to as the Septuagint, from the Greek word for "seventy." The name (often identified simply by the Roman numeral seventy – LXX) alludes to the legend that seventy or seventy-two learned Jews were sent to Egypt at the request of

THE ROMAN EXPANSION TO THE EASTERN MEDITERRANEAN

IN THE LATE THIRD CENTURY B.C.E., Rome fought and won two wars to protect its colonists against the Illyrians across the Adriatic Sea, in what is today Yugoslavia. This began the expansion of its influence and power into the eastern Mediterranean. After gaining total control over their western competition, Carthage, in 201, the Romans defeated Philip V of Macedon in the second Macedonian War (200–196) and took control of Greek politics. Any resistance to Roman power was crushed. For example, Corinth, the capital of the Achaean League, was destroyed in 146. The Romans stopped the westward expansion of Seleucid power in Asia Minor by defeating Antiochus III (191–188). With the three heirs of Alexander the Great in Macedon, Syria, and Egypt in decline, Rome was free to expand its power during the next century and a half until it had total control of all the lands surrounding the Mediterranean.

DEUTEROCANONICAL BOOKS, APOCRYPHA, PSEUDEPIGRAPHA

NUMEROUS JEWISH BOOKS written in Hebrew, Aramaic, and Greek during the postexilic period have been imprecisely designated by the terms Apocrypha and Pseudepigrapha. The Apocrypha are books and parts of books found in the Septuagint (the Greek translations of the Bible) but not in the Hebrew. Some of these books are recognized as canonical by Roman Catholics and the Greek Orthodox. Since the term "apocryphal (= hidden) books" carries the connotation of "spurious" or "heretical," the term "Deuterocanonical" (= secondarily canonical), introduced by Sixtus of Siena, is to be preferred.

Different Septuagint manuscripts include various of the Deuterocanonical books in addition to the books of the Hebrew Bible. Roman Catholics recognize as canonical Tobit, Judith, Wisdom of Solomon, Ecclesiasticus (Sirach or Ben Sira), Baruch (including the Letter of Jeremiah), 1 and 2 Maccabees, and additions to the books of Esther and Daniel. The canon of the Greek Orthodox community includes those books plus 1 Esdras, the Prayer of Manasseh, Psalm 151, and 3 Maccabees, with 4 Maccabees as an appendix.

The term "pseudepigraphical (= written with false superscriptions) books" designates over sixty works written in the names of famous Jewish figures (Enoch, Baruch, Ezra, etc.) during the third century B.C.E. through the second century C.E. and in some cases beyond. These books, many of which are apocalypses, testaments, rewritings of the Bible, and psalms, reflect Jewish life and thought during the second temple and early Christian period.

King Ptolemy to translate the Jewish law (Torah, the Pentateuch) into Greek. (This story is found in the Letter of Aristeas, discussed pp. 294–5.) The term "Septuagint" does not designate a single translation of the whole Bible but is an umbrella term for different Greek translations of various books done over several centuries. The oldest version, the Old Greek, is a collection of translations of the various books from different hands and times. The translation of the Pentateuch probably came into existence in the third century, B.C.E., perhaps in Egypt. Other books were translated later and went through various revisions. Since there were multiple Hebrew manuscript traditions for the Bible, as shown by the Dead Sea Scrolls (see pp. 347–355), different editions of the Greek were based on discrete manuscript traditions. In addition, during the Roman period, further Greek translations of the Bible, as well as revisions and adaptations of books, were made to fit specific needs in the Jewish and Christian communities.

The Greek translations of the biblical books vary as to how literally they render the Hebrew and how much they modify the text through interpretation. The translators were forced to interpret the Hebrew text when it was obscure and often adapted it to their own culture or understanding of Judaism. For example, the Greek version of the Book of Job omits many, though not all, anthropomorphic references to God. "I have not departed from the commandment of his lips" becomes "I have not departed from his commandments" (Job 23:12). References to God's eyes are always paraphrased (e.g., Job 11:4, 34:21). On the other hand, the Septuagint Psalms retain references to God's bodily parts and emotions. In the Greek, Job's attacks on God are toned down to avoid the appearance of blasphemy and to present Job as a blameless martyr. Thus the Christian image of "patient Job" is derived from the Septuagint. For example, in the Hebrew, Job charges that God made him but hid his intention to oppress and despise him: "Yet these things you hid in your heart; I know that this was your purpose" (Job 10:13). In the Greek, Job's attack on God is turned into an affirmation of divine omnipotence: "Having all these things in yourself, I know that you can do everything; nothing is impossible for you." Job's hypothetical admission of sin in the Hebrew text, "And even if it were true that I erred, my error remains with me" (Job 19:4), might have suggested to some readers that Job sinned. The Greek protects his innocence by defining his hypothetical fault as a very minor failing, speaking in an unseemly way or out of season. In addition, though the Hebrew Book of Job does not manifest belief in an afterlife, the Greek introduces it into the text (Job 14:14) in order to conform Job to later Jewish theology.

1. Survival in the Diaspora

The destruction of Jerusalem and exile of its leadership in 587/6 B.C.E. stimulated a number of stories about Jewish survival in the Diaspora. These stories were revised, translated, and adapted for Jews spread throughout the hellenistic and Roman Empires and for Palestinian Jews living under foreign rulers, who faced the same problems as Diaspora Jews. The Greek version of the story of Esther (see p. 268) was later revised to meet new circumstances (see p. 295); the stories of Daniel were combined with visionary accounts as a response to the Maccabean persecution (see pp. 317–321) and later expanded in a Greek version in the face of Roman conquest (see p. 333). The Daniel stories counsel fidelity to God, cooperation with the empire, resistance to oppression, and courage in the face of death. Since God controls the fates of foreign empires and judges their kings, Jews who pray for help to God, trust in his care, and remain faithful to the Jewish way of life are promised divine guidance in facing the dilemmas of life in the Diaspora and divine protection against oppressive rulers.

The Book of Tobit was probably written during the third century

DIASPORA

IN JEWISH USAGE THE GREEK word *diaspora* (scattered abroad), sometimes translated as the "dispersion," is used to refer to Jews who lived outside the land of Israel after the destruction of the first temple in 586 B.C.E. and Babylonian exile. During the Greco-Roman period Jewish communities were found all over the empire, from Babylon to Spain, in Europe, North Africa, Asia Minor, Egypt, Syria, and Babylon. The communities in Alexandria and Babylon were the most prominent and fostered important Jewish literary activity.

Major centers of diaspora Judaism.

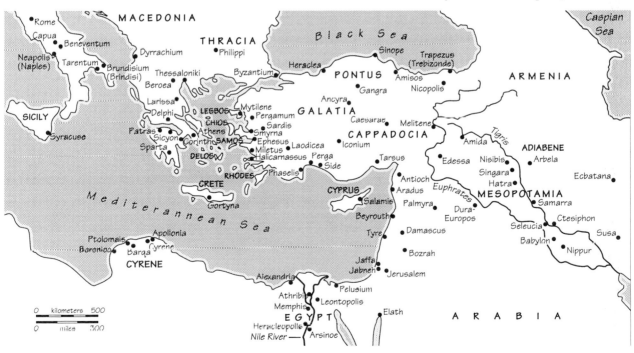

B.C.E. in Hebrew or Aramaic; its author is unknown. It was translated into Greek and went through several editions. The story, which appears in other cultures, is set in an international context; Tobit was taken into exile from the northern kingdom of Israel to Nineveh in northern Mesopotamia by the Assyrians. The plot revolves around the personal misfortunes that befall two exiled Jews: Tobit, who was accidentally blinded, and Sarah, a Jewish woman in Ecbatana, a city of Media (present northwestern Iran), whose seven successive husbands were killed by an evil spirit on their wedding night. To resolve these difficulties God sends the angel Raphael to guide and protect Tobias, Tobit's son, so that he can recover a deposit left in Media by Tobit, marry Sarah, exorcise the demon that kills her husbands, and return to Tobit with a cure for his blindness. Thus two faithful Jews, Tobit and Sarah, are saved from personal misfortune, and the future of their families (and, symbolically, of Judaism) is ensured by the marriage of Tobias and Sarah and the recovery of the family fortune.

Tobit is a model for Jews living under foreign powers because he resisted apostasy, tithed (Tob. 1:6), observed the dietary laws (1:10) and ritual purity (2:9), buried the dead even during persecutions, and practiced charity toward his fellow Jews (2:1–6). Tobit's advice to his son before he travels to reclaim the family fortune captures the piety, ethical code, and relationship with God necessary for Diaspora Judaism.

> Watch yourself, my son, in everything you do, and be disciplined in all your conduct. And what you hate, do not do to anyone. Do not drink wine to excess. . . . Give of your bread to the hungry, and of your clothing to the naked. Give all your surplus to charity, and do not let your eye begrudge the gift when you make it. Place your bread on the grave of the righteous, but give none to sinners. Seek advice from every wise man, and do not despise any useful counsel. Bless the Lord God on every occasion; ask him that your ways may be made straight and that all your paths and plans may prosper. For none of the nations has understanding; but the Lord himself gives all good things, and according to his will he humbles whomever he wishes. (Tob. 4:14–19 [New Revised Standard Version])

This practical advice is adapted from the Bible, especially the wisdom tradition. The confidence in God's control over history, manifested in prayers and instruction, is based on a sense of God's guidance and protection in the Diaspora situation, where foreign powers rule.

The main themes of the book show that God remains available and active on behalf of Jews wherever they are. Faithful Jews will receive divine guidance and protection because if they conform to the Jewish way of life and laws, their prayers will be heard by God. The paradigm for this relationship is God's response to the simultaneous prayers of Tobit and Sarah: "Raphael was sent to heal the two of them" (Tob. 3:17). The sorrows and uncertainties of life, emotionally portrayed in each of the trials faced by Tobit and his family, symbolize the difficulties faced by Jews living in a hostile world. Frequent exhortations to proper behavior give specific guidance concerning the proper response to these difficulties.

The fictional setting during the Assyrian captivity may have been used as a model for the Babylonian, Egyptian, or other Diaspora situations. Devotion to the temple and Jerusalem is prominent (Tob. 1:4, 13:9–18, 14:5–7). Both the return of the captives and the acknowledgment of God by the gentiles are expected. Though fidelity to Judaism is encouraged, sustained hostility toward the gentiles is absent. The Book of Tobit gives advice and encouragement to Jews who live under reasonably friendly foreign rulers and seek to preserve their Jewish identity.

Other prayers and exhortations from the hellenistic period warned against sin and encouraged trust and obedience toward God. Two typical works are Baruch and the Letter of Jeremiah, which are part of the Septuagint and are sometimes joined together as one book. The Greek version of Baruch is composed of several parts, some of which were translated from earlier Hebrew versions. The first two sections of the book (Bar. 1:15–2:5, 2:6–3:8) were translated into Greek along with the Letter of Jeremiah by the first century B.C.E. The latter two sections could be earlier or later and may have been written originally in Greek. Though the book claims to have been written by Baruch, Jeremiah's secretary in the seventh and sixth centuries B.C.E., several anonymous Jewish authors of the hellenistic period were responsible for its creation.

In the introduction (Bar. 1:1–14) Baruch, the secretary of Jeremiah, who is in Babylonian exile, reads his book to the exiles and arranges to send it, along with money for offerings in the temple, to the Jews in Jerusalem. The introduction establishes the purpose of the book: to promote cooperation with the empire and to encourage patience while awaiting the restoration of Jerusalem. The first two sections are a beautiful and detailed confession of Israel's sin (Bar. 1:15–2:5) and a prayer for God's help (2:6–3:8), both of which are suffused with Deuteronomistic theology (see pp. 88–95). God's justice is affirmed, and the sufferings of his people are attributed to their sins. God is asked to forgive the people's sins and restore them for his own sake. Repentance, obedience, and hope in God's mercy typify the attitudes suggested by this prayer.

The two poems in the second half of Baruch present solutions to Israel's dilemma. The first (Bar. 3:9–4:4) affirms God's gift of wisdom even though Israel is in exile.

> She [wisdom] is the book of the commandments of God and the law that endures for ever. All who hold fast to her will live, and those who forsake her will die. . . . Do not give your glory to another, or your advantages to an alien people. Happy are we, O Israel, for we know what is pleasing to God.

Thus, Israel's strength and hope are built on fidelity to the wisdom found in the biblical tradition. The final poem (Bar. 4:5–5:9), after rehearsing the sins that led to Israel's punishment, affirming God's love, and counseling courage in the face of suffering, promises the restoration of Jerusalem and the return of the exiles, using language drawn from Second Isaiah (Isa. 40–55).

The Book of Baruch shows that in the hellenistic period Jews con-

BARUCH

THE HISTORICAL FIGURE Baruch was a royal official from a highly placed Jerusalem family. He is associated with Jeremiah several times (Jer. 32, 36, 42, 43) and was instrumental in the preservation of Jeremiah's oracles. Several later Jewish works were associated with his name because of his authoritative position as a scribe, according to the Book of Jeremiah, and because his experience of the loss of the temple made him a fit spokesman for later authors grappling with the destruction of the first and then the second temple. The Book of 2 Baruch is a late-first-century C.E. apocalypse in which Baruch is a leader of the Jewish community, even more authoritative than Jeremiah. Along with 3 Baruch, from about the same time, it presents Baruch as the recipient of heavenly revelation meant to instruct and console the Jewish community, which has lost the temple.

Ezra the scribe, as depicted in the Dura Europos murals (Yale).

tinued to use the Babylonian exile as a paradigm for understanding their suffering and subordination to the nations, for affirming God's love, and for retaining their own identity. The experience of the exiles is proposed as a model for the behavior of the Jews remaining in Israel as well as of those in the Diaspora; both groups are encouraged to accept their gentile overlords and remain faithful to Judaism until they have suffered sufficiently for their sins and been freed by God.

The Letter of Jeremiah purports to be a communication from Jeremiah in Jerusalem to the new exiles in Babylon (597 B.C.E.), urging them to avoid idolatry. It is actually by an anonymous later author. Though it exists only in Greek (Greek manuscript fragments from the first century B.C.E. were found among the Dead Sea Scrolls), it was probably written originally in Hebrew. It is an attack on the impotence of idols and a mockery of pagan practices, using traditions found in Isaiah and Jeremiah. (See also the later Wisdom of Solomon 13–15, discussed on pp. 406–407) The purpose of this diatribe is to resist assimilation to pagan practices:

> Now in Babylon you will see gods made of silver and gold and wood, which are carried on men's shoulders and inspire fear in the heathen. So take care not to become at all like the foreigners or to let fear for these gods possess you when you see the multitude before and behind them worshiping them. But say in your heart, "It is you, O Lord, whom we must worship." (Let. Jer. 1:4–6)

Wherever the Letter of Jeremiah was written – in Babylon or somewhere else – idolatry was a strong temptation.

2. Greek Jewish Literature

Greek Jewish literature was written to enable Greek-speaking Jews to learn their traditions through Greek modes of expression and to show Jews that their traditions were the equal of those of the gentile Greeks. From the third century B.C.E. through the first century C.E., many Jewish authors wrote histories, stories, poems, philosophy, and apologetic works in order to defend Judaism against slander, encourage perseverance in the Jewish way of life, explain Jewish traditions to the gentiles, and express Jewish piety in ways familiar to Greek-speaking Jews. Alexandria in Egypt was the greatest center of Greek Jewish culture, but Jews in Palestine and Syria wrote significant works in Greek too. Many of these writings survive only in fragments. Some are very irenic, seeking to show that Jews can live together in mutual respect with Greeks and still remain Jews. Others reflect the hostility and oppression that sometimes broke out and the resentment felt by Jews against gentiles.

The Letter of Aristeas tells the story of how the Pentateuch was translated into Greek at the request of Ptolemy II Philadelphus (285–246 B.C.E.) of Egypt. Aristeas is supposedly an Alexandrian Jew writing to a certain Philocrates concerning the wise men from Jerusalem who created the Septuagint. Language, historical inconsistencies, and the legendary nature of the account of how the translation was made indicate that Aristeas is a third- or second-century B.C.E. Jewish apologetic work seeking to establish the dignity of Judaism in Greek circles and promote harmonious relationships with gentiles. The story that frames the work recounts that Ptolemy requested a Greek translation of the Jewish law for the library at Alexandria by sending an embassy to Jerusalem. The story of the embassy provides an opportunity for a detailed description of Jerusalem and the high priest and for speeches in which Ptolemy shows great respect for Jewish wisdom, scholars, and law. When the seventy-two translators arrive in Egypt, they are entertained by Ptolemy at seven banquets, during which they engage in long philosophical discussions concerning kingship and thus show that they are the equals of any hellenistic philosopher. Finally, the seventy-two translators produce the translation in seventy-two days and are sent home with great praise and gifts.

Aristeas is typical of the Jewish Greek literature that promoted adherence to the Jewish way of life and taught the compatibility of Judaism with hellenism. The central institutions of Judaism – law, Jerusalem, temple, high priest – are presented as ancient and laudable. Jewish law is reasonable and equal in dignity to Greek law and philosophy. The Jewish translators are scrupulous in keeping biblical dietary laws, and the high priest explains the seemingly strange details of Jewish laws as part of the natural law and essential to Judaism. Jewish laws are "unbroken palisades and iron walls to prevent our mixing with any of the peoples in any matter, thus being kept pure in body and soul, preserved from false beliefs, and worshiping the only God, omnipotent over all creation" (Aristeas 139). At the same time, the translators take part in a philosophical discussion of kingship, the content of which derives from Greek writings rather than Jewish tradition. They hold their own with their Greek equivalents so that they, along with their law and traditions, are honored by Ptolemy. Jewish law contains both the particular Jewish way of life and universal ethical principles. Thus the translation of the Bible into Greek provides an expression of the common foundation of Judaism and hellenism.

A number of Jewish writers who wrote in Greek and used Greek literary forms are known to us by name and from scanty fragments preserved most often by early Christian writers. Demetrius the Chronographer, Eupolemus, Artapanus, and Aristeas the Exegete wrote history or historical romance. Philo the Poet and Theodotus wrote epic verse, and Ezekiel the Tragedian wrote tragic drama. Aristobolus wrote philosophy and others wrote oracles and poems anonymously or pseudonymously in the names of known Greek writers. Nothing is known about these authors beyond their names. They responded to Greek culture by participating in it in order to defend Judaism against attack, to establish its standing in the hellenistic world, and to pass on its traditions in ways that fit the hellenized world of Judaism in Egypt, Palestine, and Syria. They were succeeded by numerous other authors who wrote works that have been preserved, such as 2–4 Maccabees, Joseph and Asenath, and the extensive writings of Philo and Josephus.

Philo the Poet wrote the epic poem About Jerusalem (third to sec-

ATTRACTION TO JUDAISM IN THE GRECO-ROMAN WORLD

THE GROWING INFLUENCE and impact of the Greco-Roman world upon Judaism, usually referred to as the *hellenization* of Judaism, has another side. That is, Judaism also had an impact and influence on the Greco-Roman world. It would seem that a significant number of people in the large Greek and Roman cities of the empire found certain aspects of Judaism attractive and were regularly drawn to the religion and to its gathering place, the synagogue, or house of prayer. For example, both Philo of Alexandria and the Acts of the Apostles speak of *proselytes*, or non-Jews who regularly participated in the worship and life of the synagogue. Similarly, the Acts of the Apostles refers to "God-Fearers," who were non-Jews, but who were nevertheless an important part of the life of the synagogue and the Jewish community throughout the Diaspora and cities of Asia Minor.

In *Satire* 14, the Roman author Juvenal speaks about a "sabbath-fearing" Roman father whose son, as a result of his father's interest in Judaism, converted to Judaism and was circumcised. The Jewish historian Josephus also talks about many Greeks who came to "respect and emulate" Judaism. Further, a number of prominent Diaspora communities show obvious signs of containing both Jews and Greeks. It is clear then that during the Roman period Judaism held a significant attraction for, and had an obvious influence upon many people in the Greco-Roman world.

ALEXANDRIA

THE CITY OF ALEXANDRIA, on the Mediterranean coast of Egypt, was founded by Alexander the Great and became, along with Athens, a major Greek cultural center. It was the capital of hellenistic Egypt and an industrial and commercial center. Even later, under the Roman Empire, Alexandrian citizens had special privileges. Under Ptolemy II and Ptolemy III it became a center of learning with a library famous for its comprehensiveness, a museum, a theater, and the other institutions characteristic of a Greek city. Alexandrian scholars collected, edited, and commented on Greek literature and grammar. An Alexandrian school of poetry flourished in the third century B.C.E., and succeeding generations continued to produce a variety of Greek literature. A large and creative Greek-speaking Jewish community flourished in Alexandria. The first-century C.E. author Philo was the most famous of many Greek Jewish authors. Persecutions in the first and second centuries brought an end to the power and literary productivity of the Alexandrian Jewish community.

ond century B.C.E.), in which he described and glorified the city and its history. The genre, an account and praise of a city, is hellenistic, and its use shows how Diaspora Jews expressed their high regard for Jerusalem through a hellenistic literary form. Theodotus (second to first century) wrote an epic poem on the Jews. Ezekiel the Tragedian (second century) wrote a play that recounted the Exodus, with stress on the Passover laws and Moses as the central hero. Aristeas the Exegete (third to second century) wrote a life of Job that enlarged on his patience and eliminated his questioning of God. The use of language found in persecution and martyrdom stories makes Job's life into an edifying example for Jews suffering oppression. In all cases these authors adapted and embellished the Bible, often using interpretive traditions known elsewhere in Jewish and hellenistic literature, to establish Judaism in the hellenistic world and encourage fidelity to Judaism within the community.

Aristobolus (mid–second century) was a Jewish philosopher who explicitly addressed larger hermeneutical questions and affirmed the antiquity and truth of Jewish traditions. The five extant fragments from his works explain biblical anthropomorphisms as symbolic of more elevated truths. The writer links the Passover festival and the Sabbath to astronomical and cosmic order and contends that Plato, Socrates, and Pythagoras knew parts of the Pentateuch from earlier Greek translations. Greek poems concerned with the heavens and the underworld are understood as dependent on Jewish teaching, as are Hesiod and Homer. Aristobolus summarizes his position and his desire to reconcile Judaism with hellenism succinctly:

> For it is agreed by all the philosophers that it is necessary to hold holy opinions concerning God, a point our philosophical school makes particularly well. And the whole constitution of our Law is arranged with reference to

The harbor in Alexandria, Egypt.
H. Keith Beebe

piety and justice and temperance and the rest of the things that are truly good. (Aristobolus, frag. 4:8)

The norms of piety, justice, and temperance are prominent in Greek Stoic philosophy.

Several Jewish historians retold biblical history for hellenistic audiences. Only the writings of Flavius Josephus, a first-century C.E. Jewish priest who wrote about the War against Rome and about previous Jewish history, have been completely preserved (see pp. 000–000). However, fragments of earlier historians, such as **Demetrius the Chronographer** and **Eupolemus,** testify to extensive Jewish participation in history writing, a popular hellenistic genre. The most striking Jewish account is a historical romance by **Artapanus** (third to second century). A long section on Moses claims that he was a leader and general in Egypt, was revered as Hermes, and founded much of the Egyptian administrative system, many of the cultural institutions, and even the worship of animals. This presentation of Moses owes much to hellenistic stories of legendary heroes, and the characteristics and deeds assigned him are designed to refute anti-Jewish polemical writings, especially those of Manetho, a third-century Egyptian priest and historian. Though Artapanus says that Egyptian religion was created by Moses, he shows that Egypt, its gods, and its culture are eventually made subordinate to the only real God when the Egyptian army is destroyed in the sea. Artapanus, more than other Jewish writers, entwined Moses and Abraham (both of whom are astrologers) with non-Jewish culture and, true to hellenistic taste, stressed the magical and miraculous in their lives.

3. Palestinian Responses to Hellenism

Judaism's response to the highly literate hellenistic culture was a stream of writings of every type. Palestinian Jewish writing was done in the three languages known by the educated classes: Hebrew, Aramaic, and Greek. Many works, like those of the Diaspora Greek writers, retold the biblical stories in expanded or edited forms, fashioned to meet the needs of a hellenistic, Jewish, Palestinian audience. Both the Genesis Apocryphon, an Aramaic work found among the Dead Sea Scrolls (first century B.C.E.), and the biblical Antiquities, probably a first-century Hebrew work now extant only in Latin, retell biblical history with an emphasis on details not found in the Bible, dramatic development of the events, elimination of contradictions, and inclusion of familiar elaborations of biblical stories, known in other sources as well. The Books of Enoch, the Book of Jubilees, the Testaments of the Twelve Patriarchs (all treated below), and 1 Esdras engage in a similar rewriting of the Bible for edification. Later laws and practices of Jewish groups were reconciled with the biblical text especially in the Book of Jubilees and the temple Scroll. The Jewish authors communicated their understanding of the biblical text, God, and Jewish life as one integral whole through fresh accounts of biblical laws and events.

ANCIENT ANTI-SEMITIC LITERATURE

A THIRD-CENTURY B.C.E. Egyptian priest named Manetho was the first to write an account of Egyptian religion, customs, and history in Greek. In it he attacked the ancient Hebrews as aggressors against Egypt. According to him, the "Shepherds" (= Hebrews) lived in a city named Auaris. They revolted and a priest of Hieropolis named Osarseph (Moses) took charge.

He made it a law that they should neither worship the gods nor refrain from any of the animals prescribed as especially sacred in Egypt, but should sacrifice and consume all alike. . . . After framing a great number of laws like these, completely opposed to Egyptian custom, he ordered them with their multitude of hands, to repair the walls of the city and make ready for war against King Amenophis. . . . Meanwhile the Solymites (Jerusalemites) . . . along with polluted Egyptians treated the people impiously and savagely . . . Not only did they set towns and villages on fire, pillaging the temples and mutilating the images of the gods without restraint, but they also made a practice of using the sanctuaries as kitchens to roast the sacred animals the people worshipped.

By the hellenistic period most of the books of the Bible were recognized by the Jewish community as authoritative and their texts were substantially fixed. Because rapid changes during the hellenistic period required the adaptation of existing traditions and the creation of new customs and more comprehensive viewpoints, the fixed texts of the Bible had to undergo constant and elaborate interpretations. Thus a fluid and varied interpretive tradition sprang up alongside the Bible. The Jewish literature of the hellenistic period testifies to the diverse and even conflicting viewpoints within the Jewish community. The struggles and disagreements of the period produced ever more sophisticated and elaborate strategies for understanding the Bible in a way consistent with the realities of Jewish life and the proclivities of various groups and movements in the midst of hellenistic culture.

The Wisdom of Ben Sira

In the early second century, before the Maccabean revolt of 167–164 B.C.E., a learned Jewish teacher wrote down his teachings in a book referred to as the **Wisdom of Ben Sira** (or Sirach; the book is also known as **Ecclesiasticus**). In the mode of Greek writers, he gives his name, which, though garbled in the manuscripts, is probably Yeshua [Jesus] ben Eleazar ben Sira (Sirach is the Greek for ben [son of] Sira). Late in the first century (about 132 or 117 B.C.E.) Ben Sira's grandson translated his book into Greek in Alexandria. In addition to the complete Greek text, some of the original Hebrew has survived. Though Ben Sira was never accepted into the Hebrew canon of scripture, it is often quoted as an authoritative book in the Talmud. Among early and medieval Christians and among Roman Catholic and Orthodox Christians today it is a canonical book and revered as the "ecclesiastical" (church's) book because of its copious ethical teaching and support of community life, authority, and worship.

Though Ben Sira's teachings are based almost wholly on the Bible, especially wisdom literature, nowhere does he quote it directly. Rather, like other authors of this period, he rewrites the biblical teaching into different literary forms and different modes of expression. For example, in Proverbs the dominant mode of expression is the proverb with two parallel, complementary or contrasting lines. Ben Sira treats traditional wisdom topics in medium-sized units of about six to twenty verses. Toward the end of his book, lengthy hymns and reflections predominate, and at the climax is a seven-chapter review of Israel's history.

Ben Sira gives us not only his name but also his view of his own role in Jewish society. His famous description of the ideal scribe (Sir. 38:24–39:11) testifies to the importance of the learned class of officials and teachers who created the abundant Jewish literature of the hellenistic period. Ben Sira notes that only one who has leisure can become wise (Sir. 38:24) and contrasts the scribal life with the physical difficulty of other jobs. He attributes to the ideal scribe all areas of knowledge, high government station, and lasting fame. The wisdom of the scribe is closely linked with and dependent on God because his main source of knowledge is the "law of the Most High," the study of which leads him to seek out "the wisdom of the ancients" and be "concerned with prophecies" (39:1). Both in the hymn to the scribe and elsewhere in Ben Sira the wise man is associated with the rulers and priests. The description of the scribe is so similar to the later descriptions of Israel's rulers, prophets, and priests in chapters 44–50 that Ben Sira implicitly includes himself and other scribes among Israel's leadership.

The room at Masada where part of a copy of the Wisdom of Ben Sira was found.

Anthony J. Saldarini.

Ben Sira allied himself with the leading priests and the temple, which he pictures as the center of Judaism. Because he was a teacher and had leisure to write a book and a literate audience to read it , he was likely from the upper classes and probably a dependent of wealthy patrons. He may have run a school in Jerusalem, if the concluding poem, which mentions a school (Sir. 51:23), can be taken as descriptive of his situation. Many topics of his teaching pertain to the wealthy and powerful, such as the danger of riches and of unscrupulous use of power as well as the obligation to give alms and instruction concerning proper etiquette at banquets.

Ben Sira's framework for understanding the traditional wisdom is more explicitly worked out than in the earlier tradition. Like the author of Proverbs, Ben Sira begins with a hymn to Wisdom, personified as a woman who was with God at creation. Frequently, he meditates on Wisdom, her attributes, and the struggle to gain her (Sir. 1:1–10, 4:11–19, 6:18–37, 14:20–15:10, 19:20–5, 24:1–29). Fear of the Lord is a key to wisdom and to all the other attitudes associated with right living (Sir. 1:11–2:18). Strikingly, for the first time in Jewish tradition, Ben Sira defines wisdom as Torah and thus links the wisdom tradition with the content of the Bible itself. Wisdom, formerly a possession of the international community of the Near East, is now preeminently tied to the Jewish people.

> Wisdom will praise herself and will glory in the midst of her people. In the assembly of the Most High she will open her mouth and in the presence of his host she will glory. . . . Then the creator of all things gave me a commandment, and the one who created me assigned a place for my tent. And he said, "Make your dwelling in Jacob, and in Israel receive your inheritance." . . . All this is the book of the covenant of the Most High God, the law which Moses commanded us as an inheritance for the congregations of Jacob. (Sir. 24:1–24)

In this hymn, wisdom is for the first time identified with the Bible and thus with the specifically Jewish way of life. The generically human wisdom common to Near Eastern culture and the hellenistic wisdom found in Greek philosophy and literature are implicitly subordinate and inferior to the Jewish wisdom and way of life. Israel's devotion to Torah involves a commitment to the biblical covenant and to the way of life demanded by it. Torah refers simultaneously to the Bible, God's will, Jewish law and custom, and all knowledge and practice consistent with God's will.

Wisdom for life is articulated in a myriad of teachings concerning virtues, vices, family, nation, God, and learning. Three hymns praising God's creation and the order of the universe (Sir. 16:24–17:14, 39:12–35, 42:15–43:33) undergird Ben Sira's interpretation of life and explain the problems of suffering and evil. Confidence in God's goodness and wisdom provide the context and motive for a good life. Though Ben Sira does not believe in an afterlife, a good life is rewarded by the survival of one's good name: "The mourning of men is about their bodies, but the evil *name* of sinners will be blotted out. Have regard for your *name*, since it will remain for you longer than a thousand great stores of gold. The days of a good life are numbered, but a good *name* endures forever" (Sir. 41:11–13).

The final major section of Ben Sira (chaps. 44–50) is a long account of famous leaders in Israelite history, culminating in the laudatory description of Simon, the high priest in Ben Sira's day. It is an epic-like presentation of Israel's heroes and provides a foundation for Ben Sira's understanding of Jewish society, centered on the temple and led by the high priest. Ben Sira stresses the offices held by each of the leaders and their contributions to Jewish society. Through this historical review he sketches an ideal picture of second temple Jewish society (515–180 B.C.E.) and its roots in Jewish history and ultimately in God's providence. The sins of the nation are blamed on the monarchy, and at the end of the poem the king is replaced by the high priest and sage. With the guidance of Wisdom and Israel's great leaders, Jewish society has been blessed by divine favor and has preserved its glory through fidelity to the covenant, worship at the temple, and virtuous action. The social disorder of the period, the conflicts between Ptolemaic and Seleucid parties, and the rivalries that would lead to Antiochus IV's persecution of Judaism are left aside in favor of a vision of social order based on wisdom. Unfortunately, Ben Sira's idealistic vision of Jewish society was soon shattered by conflict within the priesthood and assaults by the Seleucids.

1 Enoch

The First Book of Enoch is a collection of revelatory materials associated with the early biblical figure Enoch (Gen. 5:21–4). It is also called the Ethiopic Book of Enoch because a complete copy survives only in Ethiopic; it is cherished as scripture by the Ethiopic church. The book is actually a collection of materials written from the third century B.C.E. through the first century C.E. pseudonymously in the name of Enoch. Aramaic fragments of Enoch have been found among the Dead Sea Scrolls, and portions of a Greek translation exist also. The figure of Enoch was used as a source for this revelation because the biblical idiom for his death, "Enoch walked with God and he was not, for God took him" (Gen. 5:24), was later interpreted to mean that Enoch was taken up to heaven alive and thus was the recipient of divine revelation, a revelation which these books claim to communicate. Several parts of the book are apocalypses or apocalyptic in orientation (see pp. 332–344); they show the mystical, speculative, and cosmic side of Jewish thought. Two sections, the Book of Watchers (1 En. 1–36) and the Book of Luminaries (also called the Astronomical Treatise; (1 En. 72–82), have their origins in third-century B.C.E. Palestine.

The Book of Watchers is concerned with the origin of evil and its judgment by God. Gen. 6:1–4 has a truncated version of the fall of the angels, which is an alternative story of the origin of evil, and Enoch presents a full version. A group of angels called Watchers had intercourse with human women and produced the giants, who brought evil and destruction into the world (1 En. 6–11). Enoch is enlisted to pronounce doom on the angels and those who do evil on earth (1 En. 12–16). He receives his messages in dream visions and in chapter 14 has a vision of God similar to those described in later Jewish mysticism. Enoch's visionary experience, recounted in the text, provides authority for the worldview put forth by the author(s) of the book.

In the latter part of the Book of Watchers (1 En. 17–36), Enoch is taken on a journey to the remote parts of the world, where he sees the origin of humanity, the world, and evil; the workings of the natural universe; the unity of heaven and earth; the ultimate destiny of the world; and the final judgment, in which the good will be saved and the evil punished. Enoch's cosmic journey explains the larger workings of history and the meaning of life. It was written as an explanation and encouragement for oppressed Jews and is founded on the premise that the end, like the beginning, will be paradisal. The expectation of vindication for the just is coupled with speculation concerning the workings of the universe as a whole and God's providential care for all life.

The Book of Luminaries, or Astronomical Treatise (1 En. 72–82), is a long, complex, mathematical account of the movements of the stars, moon, and sun. Fragments of the book found among the Dead Sea Scrolls indicate that it was once longer than the abbreviated version found in the Ethiopic translation. The monotonous calculations of the movements of heavenly bodies assert that there is order to the universe and that moral and religious rectitude depends on a timely observance of Jewish seasons and festivals mandated by astronomical movements. Thus, nonobservance (sin) upsets both the moral and the cosmic order. The Book of Luminaries, along with the Book of Jubilees (see pp. 339–340) and various Qumran texts, advocates a 364-day solar calendar, rather than the traditional lunar calendar. Though the group or groups who proposed this calendar are unknown, they opposed the authorities, who ran the temple according to a lunar calendar. The new calendar was probably part of a larger critique of second temple Jewish life and linked to a reform movement seeking more regular and strict observance of Jewish festivals, laws, and customs based on a holistic understanding of the universe. In the change and uncertainty of the hellenistic world, many groups sought new ways of grasping and expressing the divine will and control over life.

LUNAR AND SOLAR CALENDARS

THE TRADITIONAL CALENDAR in the Near East was based on the monthly cycle of phases of the moon, which took about 29 and a half days. This system resulted in a year of 354 and a half days and required the addition (intercalation) of an extra month every two or three years. The Israelite lunar calendar began in the fall and the months were given numbers. Under Babylonian influence a spring New Year can also be found in the Bible, and gradually the Babylonian names for the months were accepted.

The Egyptians had at times used a solar calendar of 364 days, and a similar calendar is proposed by Jubilees, 1 Enoch, and some Qumran writings. Its attraction seems to have been its regularity: exactly 52 weeks, months of exactly 30 days, and seasons of 13 weeks. The first day of the year and of each season always fell on the same day of the week, as did all the major festivals. This regularity testified to the order of the universe and trust in divine control, typical of apocalyptic writings of this period.

II. ANTIOCHUS IV AND THE MACCABEAN CRISIS IN PALESTINE

A. THE HISTORICAL SETTING

The Jewish people's relatively peaceful relationship with the imperial authorities (first the Persians, then the Greeks) from the fifth through the third centuries B.C.E. came to a sudden and violent end in the first half of the second century B.C.E. in a series of conflicts with the Seleucid rulers Antiochus IV Epiphanes and his successors, who ruled Asia Minor, Syria, parts of Mesopotamia, the eastern Mediterranean seacoast, and the territory of ancient Israel and Transjordan. Antiochus IV (reigned from 175 to 164 B.C.E.) is notorious in Jewish history because he initiated the worship of gods other than Yahweh in the Jerusalem temple, compelled people in the villages to sacrifice to his gods, and forbade Jewish religious practices such as Sabbath observance, circumcision, and reading Torah. Hellenistic monarchs normally left native peoples to worship in peace and tried to entice only the ruling classes to adopt Greek ways. Antiochus's motives for persecuting the Jews have been hotly debated. Because Antiochus, who had been raised as a hostage in Rome, was eccentric and unpredictable in his personal behavior, the persecution has often been attributed to the quirks of his personality. However, since Antiochus pursued consistent political, military, fiscal, and social policies throughout his reign, he probably decided to persecute Jews in Judea for concrete reasons. In addition, intra-Jewish political conflicts may have been partly responsible for the persecution. Jewish sources give ample evidence of sharp divisions among Jews over how Judaism was to be lived, what constituted legitimate adaptation of hellenistic culture, and which factions would rule.

By the second century the Jewish province of Judea, with its capital city of Jerusalem, was thoroughly enmeshed in hellenistic culture. Like most peoples in the Seleucid Empire, the Jews lived by their own laws and customs and worshiped in their traditional manner. But the economy, language, arts, literature, and political institutions of the empire slowly changed the Jewish ways of thinking and acting, without destroying the unique ethnic and religious character of the people. The ruling classes were most affected by hellenism because they had to conform to the practices and demands of the empire and to compete for power and influence on the terms set by their foreign rulers. They constantly had to balance the internal needs of the people and the established ways of life against the external demands of their rulers and newer ways of living. Even the Maccabean revolt against the hellenistic Seleucids (167–164 B.C.E.) was powered by hellenistic political institutions and ways of thought. Though a sharp distinction is often drawn between Judaism and hellenism, these two cultures shared a broad, common field of activity and thought. It was within this gray area that disputes occurred among Jews concerning how Judaism was to be lived. Disagreements over the shape of developing Judaism were already visible in the time of Ezra and Nehemiah (fifth century B.C.E.)

NAMES FOR ISRAEL

IN BIBLICAL TIMES THE TERM "Israel" was used to refer to the people of Israel and their land. It also acquired a restricted usage, referring to the northern kingdom in contrast to the southern kingdom, Judea. After the exile, the Persians recognized the province of Judea, whence the name "Jew" was derived to designate its inhabitants. In the hellenistic period the Ptolemies referred to their possessions along the eastern Mediterranean coast as "Syria and Palestine." When the Seleucids, who already controlled the rest of Syria, gained control of the coast, the Lebanon, and Israel, they called the area Coele Syria and Phoenicia. Coele ("hollow") Syria refers most restrictedly to the valley between the Lebanon and Anti-Lebanon Mountains but in official usage included the area of Damascus across the Anti-Lebanon and of Israel to the south. The Romans referred to Israel as Palestine.

and continued for centuries until the dominance of Talmudic Judaism in the fifth and sixth centuries C.E.

The members of the Jewish governing class competed for power by trying to win the favor of various Seleucid officials and of Antiochus himself, on whom depended the appointment of the high priest and the attendant control of the nation. Their positions as traditional or hereditary leaders of the people and as the wealthy, landed aristocracy who dominated all aspects of society demanded maintenance of the status quo. The governing class learned hellenistic culture and adapted their way of life in order to promote a harmonious relationship with the sovereign and to keep peace at home. In addition, the leading families and individuals maneuvered to gain appointment to the highest offices, especially that of high priest.

1. Competition for Power in Jerusalem

The Book of 2 Maccabees recounts that during the reign of Seleucus IV (187–175 B.C.E.), while Apollonius was governor of Coele Syria and Phoenicia, Simon, the captain of the temple, had a disagreement with Onias III, the high priest, over the administration of the Jerusalem market. As a result he incited the governor and king to send Heliodorus to seize the temple treasures and then accused Onias of plotting against the king (2 Macc. 3:4–8, 4:1–6). These brief notices do not give a full description of the contest for power, but the interest of the Seleucids in obtaining money from Judea and the willingness of high Jewish officials to trade it for power stand out.

When Antiochus IV acceded to the throne on the death of his brother (175 B.C.E.) by displacing his brother's son, he had the usual need for funds. Jason, the brother of High Priest Onias, persuaded Antiochus to appoint him high priest by promising the king that he would use his new office to collect huge revenues. Jason promised additional revenue from enrolling the upper class as "citizens of Antioch" and establishing key Greek institutions, including a gymnasium where Greek culture and sports would be taught, an arena, and an "ephebate," that is, an official body of youth trained in Greek ways. Though the pious author of 2 Maccabees decries these innovations as the abandonment of Jewish life, Jason was merely trying to please his overlord by producing more revenue while consolidating his power by creating a core of well-trained and loyal leaders acculturated to both the Greek and the Jewish worlds.

The exact nature of the group of "citizens of Antioch" in Jerusalem, founded by Jason, has been a subject of controversy. Jason may have reorganized the city government and society to conform to that of an independent Greek city, or he may have merely organized the leading citizens into a political organization whose members were recognized as citizens of the king's capital, Antioch. (It was common practice for leading citizens in many parts of the Roman Empire to be made citizens of Rome.) In neither case would the status of ordinary citizens have been affected, because only the upper classes who ruled the city through high offices and a council would have become citizens, not the

GREEK CITIES

AFTER THE CONQUESTS OF Alexander the Great, numerous independently governed cities were founded or recognized. These cities acknowledged the sovereignty of the emperor and paid taxes but controlled their own internal affairs. A city usually included both a walled central city and the surrounding villages and towns (often numerous) on which it depended for food. The rights of cities varied; for example, some were exempt from certain taxes, and others were authorized to mint coins.

Citizenship was restricted to a portion of the population. Typically, a council (*boule*) of up to several hundred members ruled the city and was aided by various officials and judges charged with specific tasks.

A Greek city usually had a number of Greek cultural institutions to train the young and maintain Greek traditions. A stadium for races, a theater for drama and other entertainment, a gymnasium for training youth in mind and body, and the organization of youth into an ephebate were common in Greek cities. Ephebes, Greek youth in their

mid-teens, were originally subjected to rigorous physical and military training. They wore distinctive dress and engaged in communal activities. In the hellenistic period the ephebate gave equal or greater emphasis to training in literature and philosophy. The gymnasia were public institutions for physical training and sport open to all citizens and especially used by the ephebes, who were taught by schoolmasters. Gymnasia were often associated with sacred groves and included baths, dressing rooms, storage rooms, and some athletic buildings.

uneducated mass of inhabitants. The hellenization of the governing class, which so horrified the author of 2 Maccabees, provided Jason with a solid core of committed officials and supporters and winnowed out more traditional leading citizens who were hostile to him. Whether these leaders worked through the existing council in Jerusalem or established a specifically Greek council (*boule*), they moved the Jewish way of life closer to hellenism.

Though 2 Maccabees presents Jason and his party as radical hellenizers and traitors who sought to destroy Judaism, Jason did not seek to suppress traditional Judaism, impose Greek culture on the people, or overturn the laws and customs of the Jews that had been confirmed by previous monarchs and on which his won rule was based. Jason was seeking to consolidate his power with his followers and to extract heavy taxes for the Seleucid officials, on whose good will and patronage his own rule depended.

Three years after Jason secured the high priesthood from Antiochus IV by promising him increased revenues from Judea, he was outbid for the post. Menelaus, his envoy presenting the yearly tribute, promised 50 percent more tribute to Antiochus and was promptly appointed high priest in place of Jason in 172 B.C.E. (2 Macc. 4:23 ff.). In 2 Maccabees, Menelaus is depicted as tyrannical, cruel, and totally unfit for the high priesthood (2 Macc. 4:25). Jason fled to Transjordan to plot his return to power. The financial importance of Judean revenues became apparent within a couple of years when Menelaus, unable to pay the taxes he had promised to the king, was summoned to Antioch. To pay what he owed and thereby preserve his position, Menelaus took some of the gold implements from the temple, sold some to Tyre and other cities, and gave others to Andronicus, the king's viceroy, presumably as a bribe. (The king himself was attending to major political matters, suppressing two rebellious cities in Asia Minor.) Onias III, the high priest who had been ousted by Jason, exposed Menelaus's sacri-

Greek philosopher. Found in Sebaste in Samaria. Roman copy of an earlier Hellenistic model.

Harvard Semitic Museum.

HELLENISTIC AND ROMAN TAXES

TAXES AND TAX COLLECTION systems varied widely by locale and period within the hellenistic and Roman Empires. The most important tax was collected from the owners of agricultural land, who in turn collected a percentage of the crop (often 30–70 percent) from those renting the land. The other most common tax was the poll, or head, tax, either a percentage of one's worth or a flat rate for each person in a social class. Duties were collected on goods in transit and in marketplaces by local publicans who paid a flat rate for the right to collect these taxes. For example, Levi (Mark 2:14) and Zacchaeus (Luke 19:1) collected customs in Capernaum and Jericho, two medium-sized towns on trade routes. Special taxes could be levied as needed. In addition, each Jew paid a traditional half-shekel tax to the temple, as well as other tithes. After the temple was destroyed in 70 C.E., the half-shekel tax (now two drachmas and called the *fiscus judaicus,* the "Jewish tax") was paid directly to the temple of Jupiter in Rome as a punishment for revolt.

Land and poll taxes were collected by either the local authorities or imperial authorities or publicans. Under the Ptolemies in the third century, taxes were first paid in a lump sum by the high priest, who collected them from the people. Later, the right to collect them was sold to publicans, notably the Tobiads. As Judea became independent of the Seleucids in the second century, the tribute was paid by the high priests Jonathan and Simon until they were "released" from this obligation, a sign that the Seleucids had lost control over Judea. During the Roman period independent cities and client kings, such as Herod and Herod Antipas, collected taxes as they wished and paid a fixed tribute to Rome. For example, Herod instituted a market tax in Jerusalem. Herod's reign was notable for heavy taxation to finance his military ventures, extensive building projects, and generous donations to his imperial patrons. In the first century, the prefect or procurator who ruled Judea and Samaria collected the land and poll taxes directly for Rome, while Herod Antipas, the Jewish client king who ruled Galilee, collected taxes there and paid tribute to Rome.

legious behavior and threatened his position, so Menelaus convinced Andronicus to have Onias murdered. Subsequently, the king responded to protests concerning this murder, as well as others, by executing Andronicus. However, the king continued to support Menelaus, his valued ally and financial supporter in Jerusalem, to the extent of executing Jewish representatives from Jerusalem sent to protest what Menelaus had been doing.

The next threat to Menelaus came while Antiochus IV was campaigning in Egypt. In 169, while Rome was fighting in Macedonia, Antiochus IV attacked and conquered most of Egypt and had himself briefly proclaimed pharaoh. While Antiochus was engaged in his Egyptian campaign, Jason attacked Jerusalem, took the city, and besieged Menelaus and his supporters in the citadel. For Antiochus, Jason's action was rebellion at his rear flank, so, as he was returning from Egypt, he went to

Greek theater in Bet She'an.
Anthony J. Saldarini.

GREEK GAMES

FROM ANTIQUITY THE Greeks had celebrated festivals, leaders' deaths, and other major events with athletic contests. In these contexts, of which the Olympic Games are the best known, individual events predominated, including foot races, throwing the javelin and discus, long jumping, wrestling, boxing, and horse races. The construction of an amphitheater and sponsorship of such games were characteristic of Greek cities in the eastern Mediterranean. During the Roman period gladiatorial contests were also common. The Greek custom of competing naked in some events and the association of the games with the worship of the gods made these games repugnant to Jews. Even so, Herod sponsored games in various non-Jewish cities to win favor in the empire.

Jerusalem, drove Jason out, reestablished Menelaus's authority and took huge sums of money and golden vessels from the temple (1 Macc. 1:20–4, 2 Macc. 5:1–23).

Threats to Menelaus did not cease and prompted further and decisive Seleucid intervention. In 167, Apollonius, a tax collector, deceitfully attacked Jerusalem, causing great damage to the city, and established a Syrian-controlled citadel near the temple mount (1 Macc. 1:29–32, 2 Macc. 5:24–6). No clear reason for his intervention at Jerusalem is given, but the probable causes were tax resistance and civil unrest, which threatened Antiochus's surrogate, Menelaus. The founding of the Syrian citadel, called the Akra, was designed to keep Jerusalem firmly in Seleucid hands. It withstood all attempts at seizure for over twenty-five years, even after the Hasmonean family had control of Jerusalem and the government. Only when the citadel was finally conquered by Simon Maccabee in 141 B.C.E. were Judea and Jerusalem truly independent of effective Syrian control.

2. Prohibition of Jewish Practice

In 167 Antiochus modified the worship in the temple and forbade conformity to the Jewish laws, including observance of the Sabbath and circumcision, and destroyed all the copies of the Torah that could be found. The exact nature of the changed temple worship and the causes for the suppression of Judaism have been much disputed. The government erected an "abomination of desolation upon the altar of burnt offerings" (1 Macc. 1:54). In Hebrew "abomination" is a pejorative term used instead of the name of the most popular Canaanite god, Baal. "Desolation" is similar in sound to the Hebrew phrase "of the Heavens," the epithet most commonly connected to Baal. Thus, even though 2 Macc. 6:2 says that the temple was dedicated to a Greek god, Olympian Zeus, it is likely that traditional Canaanite worship of Baal of the Heavens was introduced into the temple and that Baal was identified with the chief Greek god, Zeus.

Other gods were probably worshiped in the temple as well, including Dionysus (2 Macc. 6:7) and the goddess Anath, a consort of Baal, whose presence is suggested by the practice of prostitution in the temple (2 Macc. 6:4). Though some have imagined a statue of Zeus in the temple, it is likely that stone pillars, the traditional symbols for gods in Canaanite high places of worship (cf. Old Testament *maṣṣebot*), were placed on the altar and sacrifice offered on them (see 1 Macc. 1:59, which refers to a "pagan altar" placed *on* the legitimate altar of sacri-

ANTIOCH

ANTIOCH (MODERN-DAY Antakya) was established by Seleucus I, the founder of the Seleucid dynasty, on the bank of the Orontes River fifteen miles from the Mediterranean Sea. Because it was situated at the juncture of Asia Minor and Syria–Mesopotamia, it became the capital of the Seleucid Empire. Its strategic location on caravan routes and its port at the mouth of the Orontes, on the

Mediterranean, made it a major commercial center. The extensive plain which lay before it ensured its prosperity by providing food for its large population and exports of wine and oil. It was one of the largest cities of the East and played a major role in the later Seleucid dynastic struggles. Under the Roman Empire it was the capital of the senatorial province of Syria and later became a center for Christian monasticism and theological inquiry.

fice). Thus, when the temple was purified and rededicated, the priests "cleaned the sanctuary and removed the defiled *stone* to an unclean place" (1 Macc. 4:43) and then took apart the Jewish altar itself and stored its stones until a prophet should tell them what to do with them.

The suppression of the Jewish cult was widespread. Many other altars and shrines were set up in Jerusalem, and the surrounding cities and towns and people burned incense at the doors of their houses. People were forced to take part in non-Jewish cultic practices and were executed for having their children circumcised, for possessing a copy of the Torah, or for in any way keeping Jewish laws. The highly partisan accounts in 1 and 2 Maccabees do not make clear how many complied with the imperial decrees and how many resisted. The writers' stress on the extraordinary courage of those martyred (2 Macc.) and the popular resistance by flight into the wilderness (1 Macc.) suggests

THE AKRA

THE GREEK WORD *AKRA* refers to a fortress built on high ground, dominating a city. The Jewish supporters of the Seleucids built a stronghold in the City of David which dominated the temple (1 Macc. 1:33–40). The "City of David" often designates the hill south of and lower than the temple, an impossible location for a fortress dominating the temple mount. Consequently, the location of the Akra has been disputed. To dominate the temple such a fort must have been to the north of the temple where the ground rose above it. Here the lack of steep slopes required extra fortification.

The term "City of David" thus includes the whole walled area on the eastern hill of Jerusalem, including the temple and any installations north of it, not just the low hill south of the temple (see 1 Kings 11:27; Isa. 22:9). The garrison in the Akra was probably composed mostly of Jews sympathetic to the Seleucids and some non-Jewish Seleucid soldiers.

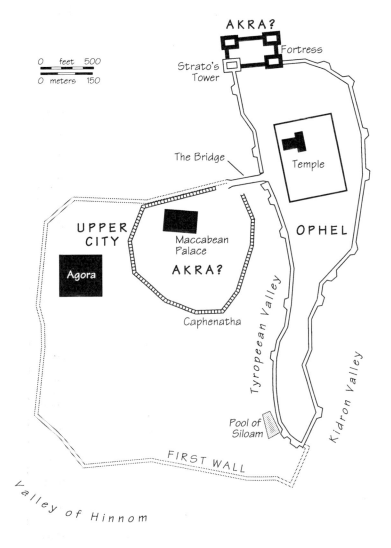

Jerusalem in the hellenistic period, with possible locations of Akra.

EASTERN MEDITERRANEAN DEITIES

THE DIVINITIES OF DIVERSE ethnic groups in Asia Minor, Syria, and Mesopotamia had many similarities with one another, as did the Greek and Roman pantheons farther to the west. During the hellenistic and Roman periods many of these gods were identified with one another. The worship of ethnic gods spread to other peoples, and mythic and symbolic patterns crossed cultures. Usually there was a chief heavenly god: in ancient Syria and Canaan he was El, the plural form of which is translated from Hebrew as "God." In Greece the chief god was Zeus, and in Rome Jupiter. In Canaanite and Syrian religions during the biblical and Greco-Roman periods the younger, more vigorous storm god, Baal, was the chief god. All these chief gods were identified with one another during the Greco-Roman period.

The consort and sister of the high god was Anath or Asherah, the Queen of Heaven (Jer. 7:18, 44:15–25). She was often identified with Athena, Zeus's daughter, the warlike and wise patroness of Athens, rather than with Zeus's consort, Hera. The Greek Aphrodite, Semitic Astarte, and Egyptian Isis often achieved eminence as patronesses. Also common was a younger god associated with wine or ecstatic experience and with dying and rising. The Greek Bacchus, Roman Dionysus, Egyptian Osiris, Phoenician and Antiochene Adonis, Phrygian Attis, Mesopotamian Tammuz, and Tyrian Melqart often fill this role. In addition, a plethora of local gods fulfilled the various hellenistic yearnings for contact with the divine in a changing world.

Head of Dionysus, from Thessalonica in Greece.

Koester-Harvard Archaeological Resources for New Testament Study.

that only a minority of Jews resisted the imperial decrees, but the majority complied. Accordingly, when the Hasmonean family began active resistance to the government, they forcibly circumcised any Jewish children they found (1 Macc. 2:45–6) and killed "sinners" and "lawless men," meaning Jews who had collaborated with the authorities (1 Macc. 3:5–8). It is likely that most people were greatly confused and pressured and so adhered to no common policy or viewpoint. Rather, as the literature of the period will show, great effort was put forth by numerous groups to take control of the situation and to define the norms for Jewish identity.

The imperial decrees prohibiting the Jewish way of life have long puzzled scholars. Normally, the hellenistic authorities encouraged the

Zeus statue from Mount Gerizim, Samaria.

Howard C. Kee.

ruling classes to adopt Greek cultural ways, including religious practices, but left the common people free to worship their gods in the traditional manner. The attempt to suppress Jewish worship and other practices was very unusual. Though 1 and 2 Maccabees attribute the persecution to the malevolence of Antiochus IV and some ancient sources describe Antiochus as unstable and strange in certain ways, the persecution stemmed from a hardheaded policy decision in response to a special situation. Given the long and firm collaboration of Menelaus and Antiochus and their mutual need to preserve control and extract revenue from Judea, the decision to modify Jewish religious practices and suppress all opposition was probably taken to regain social control over a troubled province. If Antiochus and Menelaus, whose position in Jerusalem depended on the successful implementation of Antiochus's policies, wished to gain political, military, and financial control of Judea through structural changes in Jewish society, those changes had to include changes in local law, customs, officials, religious practices, and institutions. What better way to achieve this goal than by suppressing the traditional leaders, institutions, and customs, including the very strong religious practices that served as a symbolic center for the culture?

The reforms that Antiochus and Menelaus tried to impose on Judea in order to salvage their failed Judean political and social policy were not completely strange. Since they wanted a pliant population reconciled to the new Greek ways, heavy taxation, and Seleucid rule, they sought to institute the worship that was normal in Greek cities of the eastern Mediterranean and that would be considered reasonable by any inhabitant of the empire. Such a reform would fit Antiochus's predisposition to foster hellenistic culture and ways of life. They knew that the effort would involve violence and struggle, but they miscalculated the intensity of the resistance; thus their policy failed.

THE NAMES "MACCABEE" AND "HASMONEAN"

THE WORD "MACCABEE" probably derives from the Hebrew/Aramaic *mqby* and may mean "hammerlike" and was a nickname given to Judas, the son of Mattathias. Nicknames were often given to differentiate people with common names, such as Judas or Simon. Because Judas was the original military leader of the family, his nickname was given to the books concerning their resistance to Syrian persecution and domination. According to Josephus and other sources, the family was called the Hasmoneans (from the Hebrew *hashmonay*), a designation that was either the name of an obscure ancestor or an earlier nickname which had stuck to the family. The rulers in succeeding generations of this family are known as the Hasmoneans.

Modern Jerusalem.
Anthony J. Saldarini.

THE HASIDEANS

THE WORD "HASIDEANS" (Hebrew *ḥasidim*, "pious ones") seems to designate people who faithfully kept Jewish law and wished to protect the Jewish way of life in the face of persecution (1 Macc. 2:42, 7:14). During the persecution of Antiochus IV they joined the Maccabean resistance for a time but later broke away. A number of scholars have theorized that the "pious ones" were a clearly defined and organized group which exercised influence on Jewish society in the mid–second century B.C.E. Others speculate that during the Hasmonean rule they split into the Essenes and Pharisees. Others use rabbinic references to the term "pious ones" to elaborate the history and nature of this group. However, little evidence supports these hypotheses. The term "Hasideans" is a generic designation for various types and groups of Jews notable for their faithful adherence to the law.

3.   Popular Resistance to Antiochus's Policy

Those who rejected the government decrees against the Jewish way of life did as resisters had always done in Palestine. They left their homes and villages and lived in the wilderness, the uninhabited hill country, which afforded them some protection from pursuit and a meager existence (1 Macc. 2:27 | ff., 2 Macc. 5:29). Various groups gradually formed a coalition that included the priestly Hasmoneans, a group of Hasideans ("pious ones," who wanted to fight for the Jewish law and way of life), and many other refugees. They formed an organized fighting force and began to re-Judaize the countryside, killing collaborators, tearing down altars, and circumcising children (1 Macc. 2:42–8, 3:5–8). Though the majority of the Jewish people had passively accepted the changes, they were sympathetic to those who resisted the government and helped them live off the land (2 Macc. 8:1–7).

In Judea a priestly family, the Hasmoneans, led the resistance to the Seleucid policy and aroused armed opposition to the governing forces from Syria and to those Jews who supported the Seleucid policy. Judas Maccabee (Maccabeus), one of five brothers, led the revolt against Antiochus IV. After his death, two other brothers in succession led the resistance until Judea freed itself from the Seleucid Empire. As a popular leader, Judas Maccabee could rally some ill-equipped forces and win battles on his own mountainous terrain, but he could not stand against the full might of the imperial army. During his lifetime he was able to gain only temporary victory over the Seleucids and abrogation of the decrees against the Jewish law and way of life. During the subsequent twenty-five years of resistance to the Seleucids, the Hasmonean family became the accepted leaders of Judea and, due to internal weaknesses in the empire, were able to gain concessions from the Seleucids and eventually independence from them.

Wilderness of Judea.
Anthony J. Saldarini.

Pass at Beth-horon.
Anthony J. Saldarini.

The complex series of battles fought by Judas Maccabee and his brothers Jonathan and Simon cannot be recounted here. A sketch of a few important events will provide sufficient background to understand the literature of the period. The first Syrian response to Judas's military operations was mounted by the local governor, Apollonius, using indigenous militia who were probably not professional troops. They were easily defeated (1 Macc. 3:10–12). The second response was a stronger army with professional soldiers led by Seron, a Syrian military commander (1 Macc. 3:13|ff.). Judas and his small company ambushed and routed the larger force in a mountain pass near Beth-horon, a dozen miles northwest of Jerusalem. Finally, a large force led by three experienced courtiers ("friends" of the king) was assembled and sent by Antiochus IV's regent, Lysias (1 Macc. 3:27 ff.). The king himself was campaigning in Persia to collect much needed revenue, so he left lesser problems, like Judea, in the hands of his subordinates. The Syrian army encamped on the plain below Jerusalem and sent a detachment of six thousand into the mountains to launch a surprise attack on Judas's camp. Judas evaded the trap and launched a surprise attack on the Syrian camp; he routed the main force and then the returning strike force (1 Macc. 4:1–25). All these battles took place in the mountains, away from the flat plain, which favored the deployment of large forces, or were guerilla raids and ambushes. In all these battles Judas was following the classic tactics used by guerilla forces and by popular bandits (landless peasants) who have the support of the people in their protest against the government.

Eventually, in 164 B.C.E. Judas gained control of the temple mount, except for the citadel (the Akra), whose garrison protected Menelaus

Battles of Judas Maccabee.

and his partisans. While Judas was besieging the citadel, he ordered the temple to be purified from non-Jewish sacrifices and rededicated to the worship of the single Jewish God. The resumption of worship was celebrated with an eight-day festival, the length of many of the major biblical festivals (1 Macc. 4:36–61, 2 Macc. 10:1–8).

> At the very season and on the very day that the gentiles had profaned it [the altar], it was dedicated with songs and harps and lutes and cymbals. All the people fell on their faces and worshiped and blessed Heaven, who had prospered them. So they celebrated the dedication of the altar for eight days and offered burnt offerings with gladness; they offered a sacrifice of deliverance and praise. (1 Macc. 4:54–6)

Hanukkah memorializes this event. Judas fortified the temple mount and Beth-zur in the south to provide security against the Syrian army. The Seleucid attempt to suppress traditional Judaism had failed, but Menelaus and his associates still held out in the citadel.

About the time of the rededication of the temple (164 B.C.E.), Antiochus IV died in the East, and two of his generals, Lysias and Philip, competed for control of the regency of Antiochus's young son, Antiochus V Eupator, who reigned only two years (164–162) before

SIEGES

ANCIENT COMPLEX MILITARY tactics were centered on well-engineered fortified cities and siege machines capable of breaking down those fortifications. Ideally, fortified cities were built on high ground with steep approaches and a water source within and were supplied with ample food and sufficient defenders. The simplest siege starved the inhabitants by blocking access to the city until food ran out and they could no longer defend the city. However, a wealthy city with ample supplies could hold out for years and sap the resources of the besieging army. Consequently, attack was preferable. The wealthier cities had thicker and higher walls and towers, stronger gate buildings, and more ditches, outer defenses, catapults, and so on. To overcome these defenses Greek and Roman engineers developed a variety of siege machines and engineering techniques. Catapults and bolt shooters could attack the walls from afar. Mobile siege towers several stories high carried catapults and battering rams up to the walls. Mobile sheds protected soldiers as they filled ditches, dug under the walls, or brought up battering rams, hooks, borers, and other weaponry. Engineers built timbered tunnels under the walls and then collapsed the tunnels and walls above by burning the support timbers. Though cities with multiple walls, ditch systems, and artillery could resist attack, few could hold out against such tactics forever.

being killed by his regent. During the disorder in Syria, Judas engaged in various campaigns to help Jewish communities in surrounding territories (1 Macc. 5). Judas and his brothers Jonathan and Simon besieged and destroyed cities in Transjordan and defeated gentile forces in Galilee. These campaigns did not result in permanent conquest but in relief of Jewish communities under attack. Both Judas and Simon brought oppressed Jews back to Judea, where they could be protected. Permanent control of these areas awaited the development of greater strength by the Maccabees.

Subsequent Syrian campaigns resulted in Judas's defeat and death (1 Macc. 6:28 ff., 9:1–22). After further conflict, the Seleucid general Bacchides made peace with Judas's brother Jonathan. The pro-Seleucid forces remained in control of the government in Jerusalem, but Jonathan increased his control in the countryside from a base at Michmash, several miles north of Jerusalem. Ten years of conflict had settled nothing. Jewish society was still divided, the Seleucid government and its Jewish appointees were still in charge, and the Hasmoneans' power was still limited by the threat of Syrian military might. Though 1 Maccabees is very pro-Hasmonean and treats the Maccabees as the heroes of the struggle against the Seleucids, it is clear from 2 Maccabees and even from 1 Maccabees that the Jewish community was deeply divided on how Judaism was to be lived and what response should be given to the empire. These divisions are reflected in the literature of the period, some of which is deeply hostile to the Hasmoneans, especially after they gained the high priesthood and effective control over Jewish society.

4. The Foundation of the Hasmonean Dynasty

In the twenty years following the death of Judas Maccabee, his brothers Jonathan and Simon took advantage of constant civil war between rival claimants to the Seleucid throne to gain for themselves the high priesthood and leadership of Jewish society, the expansion of

Mosaic in a public bath at Bet She'an.
Anthony J. Saldarini

THE ORIGINS OF THE QUMRAN COMMUNITY

BOTH THE ARCHEOLOGY OF Qumran and allusions to the community's history in its literature suggest that the site was settled in the middle of the second century B.C.E. This date does not preclude the previous existence of the group, nor does it identify the nature of the group or the causes of its formation. The most widely accepted theory suggests that this priestly-oriented community rejected the Hasmonean high priesthood and control of the temple and left Jerusalem in protest to live a sectarian existence near the Dead Sea. Since much of what is learned of this group from Qumran literature matches the descriptions of the Essenes in Josephus and Philo, the group is usually identified as Essene. Essenes lived in cities and towns as well as in separate communities like Qumran, according to Josephus and Philo.

Since some of the literature found in the Qumran collection comes from before the Maccabean revolt, certain scholars suggest that a dissident priestly group pre-existed the revolt. One suggestion has a group of priests returning from Babylon. Another places the rise of the Teacher of Righteousness, the leader of the community, in the very early second century and the conflict with the Wicked Priest (Jonathan Maccabee) after 152 B.C.E. at the end of the Teacher's career. Allusions to the history of the sect are so vague and the data so sparse that no certain conclusion can be reached.

Qumran seen from the top of the cliff.
Anthony J. Saldarini.

their territory beyond Judea, the fortification of their country, exemption from paying tribute to the Seleucids, and finally control of the Akra, the Syrian fortress in Jerusalem. In gathering power to themselves, the Hasmoneans built upon their popular leadership during the war with Syria and displaced the families who had previously controlled the high priesthood and other major government offices. Menelaus, Alcimus, and their allies were gone or discredited, and Onias IV, the son of the murdered, legitimate high priest Onias III, had founded a Jewish temple at Leontopolis in Egypt. Because the Maccabees were not from a traditional high priestly family or from the royal line of Judah and because they and their followers displaced many previously powerful families and groups, they met with significant opposition, which is attested in Jewish literature, especially Qumran literature (see pp. 347–355).

The importance of two events during the reigns of Jonathan and Simon, the accession to the high priesthood and the cessation of tribute, must be emphasized. In 152 B.C.E. the Seleucid ruler in Antioch, Alexander Balas, appointed Jonathan high priest (and therefore ruler of Judea) in return for his support in a civil war against a rival claimant to the throne. Ironically, the Maccabean popular leadership in Judea received recognition from the Seleucids, whereas the pro-Seleucid Jewish party went into decline. During ensuing Seleucid dynastic struggles Jonathan enlarged his power until finally, alarmed by the growing independence of Judea, Trypho, who had gained the Seleucid throne, captured Jonathan by a ruse and executed him (143–42 B.C.E.). His brother Simon immediately switched his allegiance from Trypho back to his dynastic opponent, Demetrius II, who relieved Judea from any tax obligations in 141 B.C.E. Though Demetrius was in no position to impose tribute on Simon anyway, this was the final and official release of Judea and Jerusalem from foreign tax obligations.

Simon quickly conquered Joppa, Gazara (ancient Gezer), and Beth-zur and then, more significantly, removed the final vestige of Seleucid control by starving out the garrison in the Akra (1 Macc. 13:49–52). According to 1 Maccabees, in 140 B.C.E. Simon was approved by the assembly of priests, people, rulers, and elders to be their high priest and leader, an office he had previously held by Seleucid appointment (1 Macc. 14:25–49). Thus the Hasmonean dynasty, which was to endure for about one hundred years, was officially established.

Though the Hasmoneans dominated Jewish society, they did not meet with universal approval. The Essenes of Qumran had broken with Jerusalem, probably over the accession of Jonathan and Simon to

Alexander Jannaeus' kingdom, 103 – 76 B.C.E.

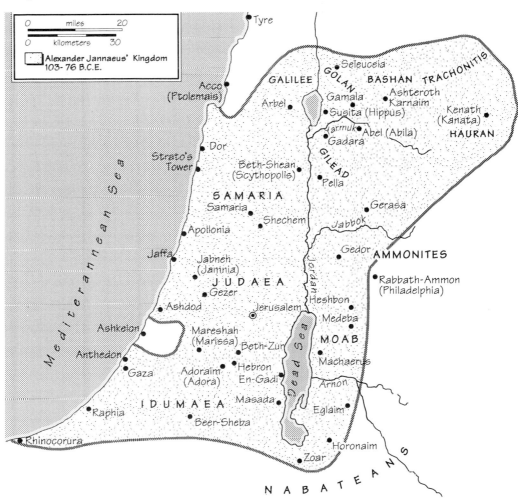

THE HASMONEAN RULERS

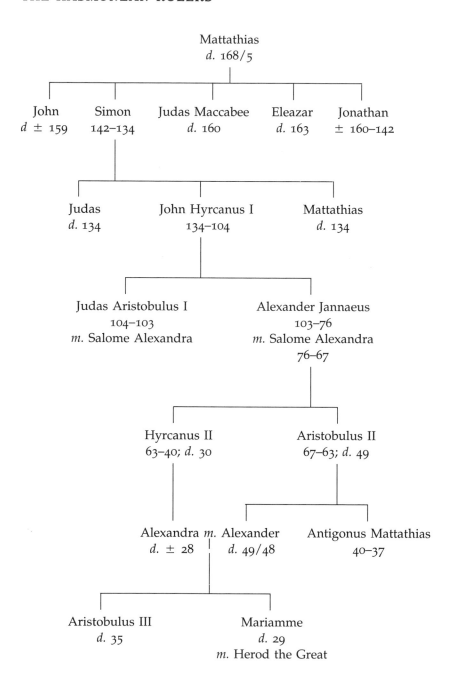

d. = died
m. = married

the high priesthood. Various other parties, such as the Pharisees and Sadducees, also arose with the object of influencing or controlling Jewish society. Disagreements over how Jews were to live and over the appropriateness of governmental policies and decisions as well as rivalries over who was to rule continued through the succeeding decades until the Romans took over in 63 B.C.E. (see pp. 355–358).

B. LITERARY RESPONSES TO THE REVOLT AND THE MACCABEES

Accounts of the historical and social events of the Maccabean crisis appear in two ancient books, 1 and 2 Maccabees. Both are very partisan interpretations of these events, and each has its own heroes and villains. Both construct their accounts under the influence of biblical parallels and are filled with the echoes of divine providence and judgment. Both books were written years after the Maccabean persecution and war were over, but they still breathe some of the passion and pain felt by Judean Jews during the horrors of oppression and the convulsion of civil war. The authors of 1 and 2 Maccabees disagree strongly in their interpretations of the crisis. The author of 1 Maccabees strongly supports the activities of Judas Maccabee and his brothers and celebrates their accession to power. The author of 2 Maccabees praises Judas Maccabee with restraint, ignores his brothers, and attributes the defeat of Antiochus IV and the salvation of Israel to the fortitude of the Jewish martyrs and to divine intervention. Other documents of the period, especially some of the apocalypses, testify to the diversity of Jewish responses to crises and the strength of their loyalty to their God and way of life. None of these books is an "objective history" by modern standards. Each in its own way sees the sufferings and victory of the Jewish people as part of God's plan rather than as the result of the normal course of imperial politics and military policy. The ambiguities and complex motives of the conflict are reduced to sharp contrasts between Jewish heroes and sinners, between righteous Jews and arrogant foreigners. Thus 1 and 2 Maccabees each have differing interpretations of what went wrong and competing visions of how Jewish society must operate if it is to know peace in harmony with God.

1.   1 Maccabees

The author of 1 Maccabees wrote his account of the Jewish conflict with Syria in order to justify and legitimate the rule of the Maccabees and the establishment of their dynasty. The book begins with an unprovoked Syrian attack on Judaism and ends with the reign of Simon Maccabee, in which Syrian control has been thrown off and the people have accepted Simon and his heirs as their kings (1 Macc. 14:41; see 2:65). Although God does not directly intervene in human affairs in this account, the Maccabees are God's chosen instruments to deliver the people from persecution, reestablish the rule of Jewish law, and bring about peace and independence (1 Macc. 5:61–2, 13:2–6,

14:26). The poem in honor of Simon (1 Macc. 14:4–15) presents an ideal description of peaceful life in Israel as the climax of the Maccabean leadership and as a sign of God's favor and approval of the emerging Hasmonean dynasty:

> The land had rest all the days of Simon.
> He sought the good of his nation;
> his rule was pleasing to them,
> as was the honor shown him, all his days.
>
> ·
>
> He extended the borders of his nation
> and gained full control of the country.
>
> ·
>
> They tilled the land in peace;
> the ground gave its increase,
> and the trees of the plains their fruit.
> Old men sat in the streets;
> they all talked together of good things.
>
> ·
>
> He established peace in the land
> and Israel rejoiced with great joy.   (1 Macc. 14:4–11)

The praise of Simon is followed by the formal acceptance of Simon's rule by the people:

> In the great assembly of the priests and the people and the rulers of the nation and the elders of the country, the following was proclaimed. . . . The Jews and their priests decided that Simon should be their leader and high priest forever, until a trustworthy prophet should arise, and that he should be governor over them and that he should take charge of the sanctuary and appointment over its tasks and over the country and the weapons and the strongholds, and that he should take charge of the sanctuary, and that he should be obeyed by all, and that all contracts in the country should be written in his name, and that he should be clothed in purple and wear gold. (1 Macc. 14:28, 41–3)

In recounting the complex events of the mid–second century to the best advantage of the Maccabees, the author simplifies the diverse social realities sketched in the previous section. The Jerusalem leadership who were balancing the preservation of Jewish life with adaptation to the empire are treated as lawless sinners (1 Macc. 1:11–15) and as a distinct minority who caused suffering for the majority. The attacks on Judea and Jerusalem by the Syrians are presented as completely unprovoked initiatives caused by the malevolence of Antiochus IV, who finally was punished by God through a horrible death (1 Macc. 1:20, 29, 41; 6:1 ff.). No mention is made of the Jewish support for a more hellenized way of life or of Jewish civil strife and resistance to the empire as causes for the Seleucid attacks. The solution to the Syrian persecution, against which the people are helpless victims, is neither diplomacy nor compromise but military resistance led by the Maccabees.

Maccabean leadership is personified in Judas Maccabee, whose career is introduced by a hymn of praise (1 Macc. 3:3–9) and whose death is noted with the biblical formula for the death of a king (1 Macc. 9:22).

> He extended the glory of his people. Like a giant he put on his breastplate; he girded on his armor of war and waged battles, protecting the host by his sword. He was like a lion in his deeds, like a lion's cub roaring for prey. He searched out and pursued the lawless. (1 Macc. 3:3–5)

Throughout 1 Maccabees Judas is compared to a mighty biblical warrior who can call on God for help as he fights holy war for the sake of God's law and people. The Hasmonean family, to which Judah belonged, had hereditary right neither to the high priesthood nor to the monarchy. Their accession to the high priesthood and authority in Israel is justified by reference to their service in preserving Judaism and their charismatic biblical leadership. The zeal of Judas's father, Mattathias, in beginning the resistance is compared to that of Phinehas (1 Macc. 2:26; Num. 25:6–15). Judas is like numerous mighty warriors of the Old Testament, fighting God's battles. For example, he is similar to Joshua in 1 Macc. 5, to David in 1 Macc. 11:60–74, and to biblical judges in 1 Macc. 3:30 and 9:73. Numerous allusions to biblical prophecies suggest that the author saw the Maccabees and their dynasty as bringing once again to fulfillment the biblical promises to Israel.

The author of 1 Maccabees wrote long after the battles that brought the Hasmonean house to power in Judea and Jerusalem. He ends with the death of Simon in 134 B.C.E. and alludes to the chronicles of John Hyrcanus's deeds as high priest (1 Macc. 16:23–4). Thus he probably wrote at the end of John's reign (134–104 B.C.E.) or, after John's death, during the reign of Alexander Jannaeus (103–76 B.C.E.). His positive attitude toward the Romans indicates that the Romans had not yet conquered Jerusalem (in 63 B.C.E.). His account is a late, "establishment" view of the foundation of the Hasmonean dynasty that eliminates the negative and stresses the glory and legitimacy of the Hasmoneans. The book was written originally in Hebrew, probably to counteract the criticism and resistance to the Hasmoneans that grew up during the reign of John Hyrcanus and Alexander Jannaeus. The anonymous author was a supporter of the Hasmonean rulers of Israel and perhaps had them as his patron. He was probably responding to criticism that the kingdom that had been established to preserve Judaism from destruction in the face of hellenism had become all too hellenized.

2.   2 Maccabees

The author of 2 Maccabees abbreviated a five-volume history of the Maccabean revolt written by a Greek-speaking Diaspora Jew, Jason of Cyrene. The absence of any account of the consolidation of power under Jonathan and Simon and lack of mention of the independence of Judea make it likely that Jason wrote before these events transpired. In addition, Jason refers to Eupolemus (2 Macc. 4:11), a mid-second-century Jewish hellenistic writer, as a contemporary. (An alternative interpretation places Jason at about 100 B.C.E., attributing to him the use of numerous sources and government records, and thus moves the date of 2 Maccabees into the first century.) Jason's account of the revolt served the needs of the author of 2 Maccabees, who abbreviated it and arranged its materials to argue for the centrality of the temple and the importance of obedience to God. That he wrote in Greek suggests an audience of bilingual ruling-class Jews and Diaspora Jews.

Establishing the date and audience of 2 Maccabees is complicated by the two letters which preface it. The first (2 Macc. 1:1–9) purports to be addressed by Jews in Jerusalem and Judea to Egyptian Jews and is dated to the year 124 B.C.E. (2 Macc. 1:9). It refers to a previous communication on the death of Jonathan Maccabee (2 Macc. 1:7) and urges that the feast of the rededication of the temple (Hanukkah) be observed by Egyptian Jews. This letter is probably genuine but may have been appended to 2 Maccabees after the book was written. The second letter (2 Macc. 1:10–2:18) has an account of Antiochus's death that is at variance with the account in the main body of the work. Though the letter claims to have been written in 164 B.C.E., the year of Antiochus's death, most scholars date it later, to the first century C.E. Both letters were appended to 2 Maccabees, probably by the author. Though the author is anonymous, he defends a type of temple-oriented Judaism which was resisting the dominant ideology of the Hasmoneans.

According to the 2 Maccabees, the temple and the fidelity of the people to God, not the Hasmonean dynasty, are crucial to Judaism's survival. Using the understanding of divine retribution found in Deuteronomy (see pp. 93–95), the author shows that arrogant leaders who attack the temple will succeed only if the people are sinful. The temple of a faithful, pious people who call for divine help will be defended by God. In addition, the pious who suffer because of the nation's sins will be rewarded through resurrection, and sinners will receive just retribution (typified by Antiochus's horrible death). The narrative is divided into accounts of three great defeats of arrogant gentiles who sought to harm the temple and its people: Heliodorus, Antiochus IV, and Nicanor. The defeats of the last two are commemorated by festival days, the Rededication (Hanukkah) and Nicanor's Day.

In the first conflict, paradigmatic for the whole book, God directly intervenes to preserve the integrity of the temple. Heliodorus, the agent of Antiochus who tried to enter and plunder the temple, is punished by angels (2 Macc. 3). The piety of High Priest Onias III and the people, who mourn the threat of the temple and pray to God for help, keeps the temple from harm and brings divine help immediately to the scene. Angels accost Heliodorus before he enters the temple and beat him to the point of death.

The account of the conflict with Antiochus and the consequent persecution (2 Macc. 4–9) forms the center of the book and differs from that in 1 Maccabees. The responsibility for the sufferings of the Jewish people and the desecration of the temple is shared by the people and Antiochus. Because many of the people (especially the leaders) sinned by deserting Jewish law for Greek ways, God brought punishment to

THE FEAST OF HANUKKAH

SINCE THE SECOND CENTURY B.C.E. Jews have celebrated the rededication (*hanukkah*) of the temple by the Maccabees for eight days during December (1 Macc. 4:42 ff.; 2 Macc. 10:1 ff.). In rabbinic literature this celebration is called the Feast of Lights because the lighting of one additional candle in an eight-branched menorah each evening is the characteristic practice of this feast. The Talmud connects this practice with a legend that at the rededication of the temple the single, undefiled container of oil left in the temple burned for all eight days rather than for only one (b. *Shabbat* 21b). Joy along with light characterizes the feast; special prayers of thanksgiving are recited and the Hallel (Pss. 113–18) is sung.

RESURRECTION

THE FIRST EVIDENCE FOR belief in an afterlife among the Jews comes from Daniel 12:1–3 during the Maccabean revolt. The just are to be exalted like the stars in heaven and vindicated for their fidelity and martyrdom. Though the passage is obscure, the belief in an afterlife seems to involve living in the heavens like the angels, who were conceived of as stars and other heavenly bodies. Two other types of afterlife are common in Jewish literature in the hellenistic period. One is a return to life with God through resurrection of the body, found in 2 Maccabees and the New Testament. Native Jewish thought conceived of body and spirit as one integral whole, and so the resurrection of the whole person is to be expected. In addition, the martyrs, who suffered extreme physical pain and mutilation, culminating in the loss of physical life, were fittingly rewarded by the restoration of their bodily integrity. At the same time, under the influence of Greek thought, some Jewish works, like the Wisdom of Solomon, affirmed the immortality of the soul, the Greek inner principle of life, thought, and will. In all cases, afterlife leads to divine judgment of good and evil and subsequent reward or punishment.

Jerusalem for a time. Thus 2 Maccabees gives more attention than 1 Maccabees to the inner Jewish conflicts that tore the society apart and to the resistance to the Seleucids that gradually arose in society before the advent of the Maccabees.

The author of 2 Maccabees valued martyrdom at least as much as military resistance and recounted the stories of the martyrs with great emotion, both to praise their sacrifice and to encourage his listeners to be equally faithful. A leader, Eleazar the scribe (2 Macc. 6), and a woman and her seven sons (2 Macc. ch. 7) are tortured and killed. The tortures are described in great detail and include the rack, dismemberment, and fire. The martyrs give speeches expressing their fidelity to God's law, confidence in resurrection from the dead to replace their mutilated bodies, and desire to set a good example. Eleazar summarizes his responsibility and the author's view: "By manfully giving up my life now, I will show myself worthy of my old age and leave to the young a noble example of how to die a good death willingly and nobly for the revered and holy laws" (2 Macc. 6:27–8). Only after the martyrs have died does Judas Maccabee organize his army and defeat the Seleucid general Nicanor (2 Macc. 8), and only after God has brought a horrible death on Antiochus (2 Macc. 9) does Judas rededicate the temple (2 Macc. 10). God's power, not military action, is emphasized.

MARTYRDOM

THE VALUE OF THE SUFFERings of the just in the face of attacks on their religious beliefs and practices is first affirmed during the hellenistic period. The Books of 2, 3, and 4 Maccabees, the Testament of Moses, the Book of Daniel, the works of Philo and Josephus, and other Jewish writings as well as the New Testament testify to this new view of suffering and death under oppression. Passive resistance to evil was not a sign of impotence but part of the eschatological process that would lead to the judgment of the wicked and the vindication of the just. Virtuous suffering under oppression became a prime mode of testimony in both Judaism and early Christianity during the Roman period. It can be seen in the story of Jesus' crucifixion, in the Acts of the Apostles, in Paul's accounts of his own sufferings, in the exhortations to fidelity in many New Testament documents, in Jewish and Christian collections of the Acts of Martyrs, in Talmudic stories of martyrdom, and in patristic treatises on the subject.

THE GREEK HERO FIGURE

WITHIN GREEK LITERATURE there is ample evidence of the development of a hero figure or ideal wise man. The stories about these men instructed and inspired others. For example, Plato's treatments of Socrates in the *Apology* and the *Phaedo* helped shape the heroic persona of Socrates. Wise statesmen are seen as divinely inspired men in the *Republic* and the *Laws*. In Greek literature heroic men served as models of wisdom, divine inspiration, and perfection. Epicurus, the Stoic wise man, and Hercules, a favorite of the Cynics and Stoics, are other examples of this figure.

As Judaism engaged the broader Greco-Roman world, the important figures of their history took on some of the traits of these Greek figures of wisdom and virtue. This is seen clearly in the portrayals of Moses by Philo and Josephus. Moses emerges as familiar with natural law and with some of the essential Stoic doctrines, so that he is a figure filled with wisdom and virtue like the Greek hero figure. In Christian literature the same impact of the Greco-Roman world and the Greek hero figure can be seen in Luke's portrayal of Paul as a person acquainted with Stoic philosophy, Roman law, as well as Torah. The Pauline epistles contain some of the same Greek Stoic and Cynic influence, and Paul himself takes on some of these heroic qualities. The Greek hero figure's impact on Jewish and Christian literature is an example of the way in which both bodies adapted and shaped the conventions of the wider culture to express their message and beliefs.

Judas Maccabee plays a major role in 2 Maccabees, but less so than in 1 Maccabees. Judas is assimilated to the pious Jews who resisted Antiochus IV rather than contrasted with them as in 1 Macc. 7:12–25. In 2 Maccabees Judas does not fight on the sabbath (2 Macc. 12:38, 15:1; contrast 1 Macc. 2:39–41). He is the leader of the "pious" (2 Macc. 14:6) rather than being joined by them (1 Macc. 2:42). He believes in resurrection of the dead, an idea not mentioned in 1 Maccabees, and offers sacrifices for those killed in battle (2 Macc. 12:43–5). The author's refutation of objections to Judas's belief in resurrection (2 Macc. 12:44–5) suggests that Judas was "recruited" by the author to serve as a contrast to the later Hasmoneans. The author's anti-Hasmonean stance can be seen in his omission of the activities of Judas's brothers Jonathan and Simon (who eventually became high priests and rulers) and in the negative notice given to Simon (2 Macc. 10:20, 14:15–18). Even Judas himself is of secondary interest. He is assimilated to earlier biblical heroes. When he has fulfilled his task, to make the temple safe, the book ends with no further notice of his subsequent battles or death.

In the final sequence of events (2 Macc. 10:10–15:36), Nicanor, the Seleucid governor, arrogantly demands that Judas be handed over to him.

> [Nicanor] stretched out his right hand toward the sanctuary and swore this oath: "If you do not hand Judas over to me as a prisoner, I will level this precinct of God to the ground and tear down the altar, and I will build here a splendid temple to Dionysus. (2 Macc. 15:33)

In threatening the temple he equates himself with and challenges God. The people and Judas respond as they should: they pray for divine help and defeat Nicanor in battle: "Judas and his men met the enemy in battle with the invocation to God and prayers. So, fighting with their hands and praying to God with their hearts" (15:26–7), they defeated Nicanor and cut off the arms, tongue, and head of the man who had used them to threaten the temple. In this final scene things happen as they should and as the author hopes they will remain ("And from that time the city has been in the possession of the Hebrews" [15:37]). God works through the purified and holy people to protect his city and temple from an arrogant, foreign attacker.

2 Maccabees is written in a very literate Greek style and follows popular Greek historical conventions by creating dramatic scenes and rhetorical speeches. Thus it was originally written in Greek. The lurid descriptions of the suffering of the martyrs, the high emotion of the confrontations between Jews and their opponents, and the improbable repentance of Antiochus all serve to involve the hearers and readers and arouse their emotions. Rather than defending the present leadership of Judaism, the author sought to foster a deeply felt commitment to the covenant, loyalty to the law, dependence on God, and respect for the temple. The book comes from the pietistic circles that participated in the resistance to the Seleucids but did not fully support the new political and social order brought about by the Maccabees. The group from which the anonymous author sprang, along with other groups

such as the Pharisees and Essenes, would continue to influence Palestinian Jewish society right up until the destruction of the temple in 70 C.E.

3. Judith

The Book of Judith indirectly comments on the Maccabean wars by speaking of a threat to Jerusalem and the temple in times gone by. It affirms God's protection for Israel against foreign invaders and the necessity of trust, obedience, and courage in the face of danger. Historical events and persons from the Assyrian and Babylonian period are combined to produce a dramatic narrative in which a faithful, courageous Jewess rescues her people and city. The name "Judith" means literally "a woman from Judea" and, in its wider extension, "a Jewish woman." Judith symbolizes the Jewish people at their best, observant of the law, properly dependent on God, courageous, resourceful, and wise. The first verse, which refers to Nebuchadnezzar as king of the *Assyrians*, contradicts what every Jew would have known from 2 Kings 24–5: that Nebuchadnezzar, who destroyed the temple in 587/6, was the king of *Babylon*. Thus, the narrative is clearly imaginary and meant to symbolize any threat against Israel. The reference to Assyria, Israel's ancient historical enemy, may include a covert reference to Syria, that is, the Seleucid Empire of the third and second centuries B.C.E. Holofernes' threat against the temple and Jerusalem, which is said (unhistorically) to have been recently consecrated after the return from captivity (Jth. 4:2–3), alludes to Antiochus IV and the profanation of the temple in 167 B.C.E. Though Judith lives in an imaginary city, Bethulia, located in northern Samaria near the Esdraelon Plain, the story is focused on Jerusalem and Judea, with Samaria seen as part of a unified Jewish homeland. The view of Samaria as part of a unified Jewish territory with Jerusalem as its capital and the stress on territorial integrity and freedom from foreign empires make it likely that the present Greek version of Judith was written during the Hasmonean period, perhaps after John Hyrcanus had conquered Samaria in 107 B.C.E. and Jerusalem was free of any significant foreign domination and threat. The author of Judith is unknown. Many scholars theorize that the Greek version of Judith derives from a lost Hebrew original, but no convincing proof for this position exists at present.

The story is simple in out-line but complex in its literary artistry. When Judea, Samaria, and other provinces in the western empire

Colonnaded street in Sebaste, Samaria. Harvard Semitic Museum.

refuse an order to send troops for a war in the east, the emperor Nebuchadnezzar sends his general Holofernes to punish them (Jth. 1–3). The people respond by prayer and repentance, acknowledging their weakness and dependence on God, and by making military preparations. Holofernes besieges Bethulia to the point of capitulation. Within the town Judith gives a speech to the elders opposing a proposed surrender and promises to save the city (8:11–27). She prays to God for help in carrying out her plan (chap. 8), beautifies herself, and goes to Holofernes. After giving him false advice concerning when to attack, she is invited to a banquet in order to be seduced. When Holofernes is drunk, Judith decapitates him and returns to Bethulia with his head (chaps. 10–13). When Holofernes' corpse is discovered, his army flees, and the Israelites slaughter many, plunder the camp, and hold a great celebration in Jerusalem (chaps. 14–16).

Judith's success is based upon Deuteronomistic theology: if Israel obeys the law, it will be safe; if not, it will be conquered. The reality of this theological scheme is established by having a gentile, Achior the Ammonite, explain it to Holofernes (Jth. 5) and by having Holofernes trust Judith when she offers to tell him when Israel has sinned so he can safely attack (chaps. 11–12). In recounting Israel's history, Achior says:

> As long as they did not sin against their God, they prospered, for the God who hates iniquity is with them. But when they departed from the way which he had appointed for them, they were utterly defeated in many battles and were led away captive to a foreign country; the temple of their God was razed to the ground, and their cities were captured by their enemies. (Jth. 5:17–18)

He then draws the obvious conclusion for Holofernes and prepares for Judith's deception:

> If there is any unwitting error in this people and they sin against their God and we find out their offense, then we will go up and defeat them. But if there is no transgression in their nation, then let my lord pass them by; for their Lord will defend them, and we shall be put to shame before the whole world. (Jth. 5:20–1)

In fact there is no sin and Holofernes is doomed to destruction. The people are pictured as faithful and obedient Jews who tithe and offer first fruits (Jth. 11:13). Judith especially observes sabbaths and new moons, mourning, and dietary customs (8:6, 11:2–4) and perhaps ritual purity (11:7). The absence of the major biblical sin, idolatry, is specifically noted (8:18). By contrast, Holofernes declares that Nebuchadnezzar is the only God (6:2) and seeks to impose worship of him (3:8). This sets up a classic test of strength between God and one who seeks to usurp his place. In the numerous prayers offered by the people, officials, and Judith, God's strength and fidelity to Israel and Israel's weakness and need are acknowledged (chaps. 4, 7, 9, 15–16). The truth of Deuteronomistic theology and the reliability of God are borne out by the death of Holofernes at the hands of one Israelite, a woman (9:10, 13:15, 14:18, 16:6–7), and by the preservation of the nation in the face of overwhelming military force.

The author's view of Israel's relation to God is conveyed by the narrative. God does not directly intervene but works through reliable and faithful leaders. When the high priest and city elders failed to take effective action, Judith acted. Though she did not receive direct divine revelation or approbation, her piety, prayers, support from the people, and success leave little doubt that God raised up Judith. Judith stands in the line of biblical women such as Miriam (Exod. 15:20–1), Deborah (Judg. 5), and Jael (Judg. 4:17–22), as well as judges and leaders of old (and the Maccabees). Judith as a literary figure breaks many stereotypes of Jewish women. She begins and ends as a childless widow who refuses offers of marriage (Jth. 16:22). Ordinarily women are expected to be wives and mothers, and the lack of husband or children is traditionally lamentable and a sign of divine disapproval. But Judith's atypical social status frees her for her other roles and is a sign of her special election by God. She successively challenges the male elders of Bethulia for leadership in the crisis, plays the part of a loose woman who seduces Holofernes, kills her enemy, and gives orders for the attack like a soldier and leads Israel in giving thanks to God as a cultic leader.

The story ends with an ideal of peace and security from foreign enemies which best fits hopes and goals of the Hasmonean period. In 141 B.C.E. Israel became free of foreign domination, a freedom won by force of arms and astute statesmanship. The reputation of Israel as depending on the terrain for military success and as strong defenders of their mountainous homeland (Jth. 7:10–11) fits the Maccabean experience. Unlike 1 Maccabees, the Book of Judith does not praise the official leaders of the community but the woman (= the people?) who rose up to defend Israel and lived piously and faithfully according to the law

---

WOMEN IN JEWISH SOCIETY

INFORMATION ABOUT THE role of women in ancient Judaism is difficult to uncover. In the rabbinic period one can observe the relegation of women to the domestic or private sphere for purposes of childbearing and housework. Women were a source of impurity due to menstruation and seem to have had little role in the hierarchy of rabbinic Judaism.

This is not to say however that women could not acquire some sort of *de facto* authority.

Mishnah Ketuboth speaks about women who possess wealth as a result of a husband's death or termination of a marriage. Some inscriptions testify that at least certain women did possess both wealth and power. The heroine of the first-century B.C.E. Book of Judith might be just such an example, though such women are admittedly rare.

It has been suggested that the earlier Jewish wisdom tradition may have afforded a more prominent place for women within the communities behind such documents as Judith, Proverbs, and Ben Sira. The New Testament provides

some information about the role of women within Judaism. Women were a part of the early Jesus movement and may have played a prominent role (Mark 14:9, Luke 24:10). Women were witnesses to the resurrection but were not apostles. Romans 16 speaks of women who were "deacons and saints," and who hosted churchs in their homes. It is striking, however, that soon women were closed out from roles of authority or influence (Eph. 5:22, Col. 3:18). Within Judaism women were not given a large role and shared the social limitations common to other women in antiquity.

of God. Unlike 2 Maccabees, Judith does not value martyrdom or speak of resurrection. Control of earthly events is left in human hands, which receive their strength from God.

4. The Qumran Commentary on Habakkuk

Among the Dead Sea Scrolls discovered near Qumran (see pp. 347–349) was a commentary on the Book of Habakkuk. The anonymous author of this commentary on a late-seventh-century biblical prophet uses the commentary as an occasion for interpreting the historical events and people relevant to the origins of the Qumran community in the second century B.C.E. and its subsequent history in the next two centuries. The manuscript of this commentary dates from the last half of the first century B.C.E. It uses the Hebrew word *pesher* (meaning "interpretation") to introduce its interpretive comments, and so it is often referred to as the Habakkuk Pesher. The comments refer frequently to the coming of the Romans (called Kittim) as a sign of the end of days and of the final punishment of the wicked by God (see p. 363). But many sections refer to the founder of the Qumran community (or its earliest guide), the Teacher of Righteousness (perhaps best translated "The One Who Teaches Rightly"), and his opponent, the Wicked Priest. The charges made against the Wicked Priest's misuse of power, avarice, pollution of the temple, and so on, the rejection of temple worship as presently practiced, and the formation of a community in the wilderness near the Dead Sea suggest that the Teacher of Righteousness, who was a priest, resisted the accession to the high priesthood of either Jonathan (152 B.C.E.) or Simon (142). According to the Habakkuk Pesher (abbreviated as 1QpHab), the Wicked Priest was originally a legitimate leader but later became corrupt:

> The Wicked Priest . . . was called by the true name at the beginning of his course, but when he ruled in Israel, he became arrogant, abandoned God, and betrayed the statutes for the sake of wealth. He stole and amassed the wealth of the men of violence who had rebelled against God, and he took the wealth of peoples to add to himself guilty sin. (1QpHab 8:8–12)

He is also charged with impurity, presumably concerning the conduct of temple ritual. Some passages in the Habakkuk Pesher suggest that the Wicked Priest defeated the Teacher of Righteousness, who seems to have been a high-ranking priest, in a battle for power in the council. The "House of Absalom" – either the family of Absalom which supported the Maccabees (2 Macc. 11:17; 1 Macc. 11:70, 13:11) or a party given the pejorative epithet Absalom after David's traitorous son – is accused of abandoning the Teacher of Righteousness: "The House of Absalom and their partisans . . . were silent at the rebuke of the Teacher of Righteousness and did not support him against the Man of the Lie – who rejected the Law in the midst of all their council" (1QpHab 5:8–12).

After the Teacher had left Jerusalem, the conflict continued. The Qumran scrolls show that the community followed a solar calendar, which differed from the lunar calender traditional in Jerusalem. Thus

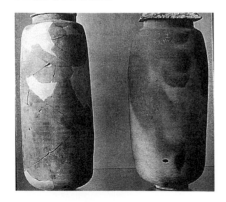

Jars from Qumran in which Dead Sea Scrolls were found.

Dead Sea Scroll fragments.
Palestine Archaeological Museum.

the community would have celebrated the Day of Atonement on a different day from Jerusalem. This gave the high priest in Jerusalem an excuse to harass the Teacher and perhaps subject him to armed attack. "The Wicked Priest . . . pursued the Teacher of Righteousness – to swallow him up with his poisonous vexation – to his place of exile. And at the end of the feast, (during) the repose of the Day of Atonement, he appeared to them [the Qumran community] to swallow them up and to make them stumble on the fast day, their restful Sabbath" (1QpHab 11:4–8). As punishment for these offenses God gave the Wicked Priest "into the hand of his enemies to humble him with disease for annihilation in despair" (1QpHab 9:9–10). Perhaps this is a covert reference to Jonathan Maccabee, who was killed by Trypho, or to Simon his brother, who was assassinated by a family member. The interpretation is vague enough to refer to many kinds of misfortune and suffering.

The allusions to the Qumran community's origins best fit the Maccabean period and show some of the opposition the Maccabees faced on their way to a reorganization of Jewish government and polity and the establishment of their dynasty. Political, social, religious, and economic conflicts affecting all the population, and especially the ruling classes, had to be fought out and solved. The literary responses to the Maccabean crisis show that even years later writers disagreed concerning how Judea and Jerusalem had achieved independence, whether through the efforts of the Maccabees, the fidelity of pious Jews, or divine intervention. They also disagreed in their evaluation of the Maccabean reform of Judaism and the changes it brought. Though Judas's fight against persecution was widely admired, his family's accession to power met substantial opposition. Judas's military resistance to the Seleucids, which met with only partial success at best, was followed by a series of political, diplomatic, and military maneuvers by his brothers and other forces in Jewish society. Freedom was won from the Seleucid rulers in Syria at the expense of establishing a petty hellenistic monarchy, with the new Hasmonean high priest displacing previously powerful families, thwarting the ambitions of many leaders, and frustrating reform programs promoted by other movements and groups.

C.   APOCALYPTICISM

At about the time of the Maccabean revolution (167–164 B.C.E.), Jewish groups began producing apocalypses. Using mythic, historical, and prophetic traditions from the Bible, various authors reported visions of the heavenly world and future judgment as responses to the political deficiencies of the world empires of their times, as protests against the oppression of Israel, and as reaffirmations of the reality and power of the heavenly world. Apocalyptic imagery, the emerging belief in life after death, and traditional eschatological confidence in the triumph of God's justice influenced a wide range of Palestinian and Diaspora literature, indicating that the apocalyptic viewpoint had deeply penetrated Jewish culture. Apocalyptic imagery, which includes mythological beasts, angels, otherworldly battles, tours of the heavens, and the judgment of world empires, has often been viewed as escapism, psychological pathology, or just strange and outdated nonsense. However, apocalypses were passionate political protests against the ruling powers and prompted resistance as often as withdrawal. In the face of overwhelming oppression, apocalypses reaffirmed traditional views of God's power and justice. Their sharply dualistic view of good and evil, God and Satan, was a prelude to affirming the dominance of the heavenly world over the evil earthly world. The eventual triumph of God and the heavenly world was put to work encouraging the faithful to active or passive resistance. The kingdom of God promised in apocalyptic works was never a vapid, internal, and individual state of soul but was to be a public manifestation of God's power over evil both on earth and in heaven.

In most apocalypses a human

Inkwells from Qumran.

Howard C. Kee – Palestinian Museum.

holy man is instructed by a vision, message, or heavenly journey that is mediated or interpreted by an angel. The content of the message concerns the ultimate destiny of humanity, including the history of good and evil, the events of the end time, and accounts of judgment and punishment. Equally important are descriptions of heaven and hell, angels, and the workings of the cosmos, stars, and weather. All these future events, heavenly places, fantastic figures, and even the esoteric knowledge of the universe (see pp. 335–339, on Enoch) engendered confidence in the larger divine universe beyond the immediately perceptible world, and especially in the divine will to enforce justice on behalf of the faithful.

1.   Daniel

The Book of Daniel was written in its final form during the persecution of Antiochus IV Epiphanes, when proper temple worship was violated and those faithful to the law were being killed. In Daniel 1–6 the anonymous author used earlier stories about life in exile under an oppressive regime to instruct his audience in trust and fortitude (see pp. 274–275). The traditional wise man, Daniel, is used as the hero of these stories and the recipient of subsequent revelation. The author of chapters 7–12 wrote in 167–165 B.C.E., before the rededication of the temple and the death of Antiochus, because in his detailed review of Antiochus's reign, the author incorrectly predicted Antiochus's final battle and place of death (Dan. 11:40–5). Revised dates for the coming of God's victory and judgment in the penultimate verse (Dan. 12:12) indicate that the author wrote amid the turmoil and uncertainty of the persecution and had to adjust his predictions to fit unfolding events. The author does not value or acknowledge (other than in 11:34?) the military efforts of the Maccabees and looks for direct divine intervention to save those who endure persecution faithfully.

The central, thematic visions of chapters 2 and 7 speak of the destruction of four great world empires. The last and worst is the hellenistic empire established by Alexander the Great and brought to its evil climax by Antiochus IV. Against the overwhelming and malevolent power of this empire the author of Daniel sets God's heavenly kingdom, established and protected by God's divine power. The earthly kingdoms, symbolized by a great statue, are destroyed by a "stone [which] was cut by no human hand" (Dan. 2:34), that is, by divine power. In the later judgment scene, when "the Ancient of Days" (God) appears, the fourth and most terrible beast, which causes great suffering, is summarily "slain, and its body destroyed and given over to be burned with fire" (Dan. 7:11).

The scheme of the fall of four empires, found in chapters 2 and 7, was common in oriental political protest literature and was used in a variety of contexts. The author of Daniel applied this scheme to his view of Jewish history in order to make sense out of the crisis caused by Antiochus's persecution. The wise and faithful Jewish heroes of the Diaspora stories had remained obedient to God's law and trusted in divine revelation and wisdom to guide them out of political danger. God intervened in

THE FOUR EMPIRES

Daniel 7 describes four beasts, which arise from the sea, as symbols for the four world empires: the Babylonian, Median, Persian, and Greek. Daniel 2 describes a huge statue with parts made of gold, silver, bronze, and iron to symbolize the same empires. The scheme of four empires was part of Near Eastern political propaganda which reacted to a decline in vitality and an increase in cruelty and oppression by these empires. Both the four empires and the four metals are found in a Persian document (the Zand-i Vohuman Yasn), and the mention of a Median kingdom, which ruled briefly in Persia only, makes a Persian origin for this scheme likely. This scheme spread to the West and is found in a second-century B.C.E. Roman historian (Aemilius Sura) and in an early Greek oracle contained in the first-century C.E. Fourth Sibylline Oracle (ll. 49–101). In this final text the Roman Empire has been added as a fifth member of the scheme (ll. 102–51).

JEREMIAH'S SEVENTY YEARS

ABOUT 605 B.C.E. THE prophet Jeremiah correctly predicted that Babylon would conquer Judea and taught that God was using Babylon as an instrument to punish Israel. He also prophesied that after seventy years Babylon would be punished and Israel restored (25:11–12, 29:10). Seventy, like seven, is a favorite biblical number, and seventy years is almost two generations (forty years to a generation). During the Maccabean crisis (ca. 165 B.C.E.) the author of Daniel 7–12 reinterpreted Jeremiah's seventy-year prophecy in order to apply it to his own generation and the Seleucid persecution. The seventy years were understood as seventy weeks of years, that is, 490 years, roughly equivalent to the number of years between Jeremiah and the Maccabean period. (Ancient chronology was an approximate science at best.) The author of Daniel thought that sixty-nine weeks of years had passed before the persecution began and that one week of years of persecution would precede God's intervention (9:24–7).

human reality through dreams, miracles, and the manipulation of historical events in order to save the faithful. But the persecution of Antiochus IV threatened the center of Judaism itself. Consequently, the author envisioned God's punishment of the empire and protection of his wise and faithful people as more direct and massive. The harm that came to those who persevered and trusted in God could now be vindicated only by divine intervention, judgment, and afterlife for the martyred.

In chapters 7–12 Daniel receives a series of visions, mediated or interpreted by angels, some of whom are national guardian angels and directly involved in earthly events. These visions were actually written in 167–165 B.C.E. during the war against Antiochus IV. However, in the text Daniel is presented as a faithful wise man during the sixth century B.C.E. who has visions about the awful events of the second century B.C.E. His God-given "mantic" wisdom (the ability to interpret dreams, visions, and oracles), which played a prominent part in the stories in chapters 1–6, becomes the vehicle for understanding the Maccabean crisis. In each vision (chaps. 7–8, 10–12) and in the reinterpretation of Jeremiah's prophecy of seventy years (Jer. 25:11–12, 29:10) into seventy weeks of years (chap. 9), evil reaches its climax in the reign of Antiochus, who violated the temple and threatened to suppress the Jewish way of life entirely and is met by divine justice, which destroys the wicked and vindicates the faithful. The allegorical and allusive reviews of Jewish history, especially during the hellenistic period, indicate the author's detailed knowledge of and passionate interest in political events that affected the welfare of the Jewish community.

The Book of Daniel's interpretation of Jewish society can be seen in its account of Antiochus's persecution (Dan. 11:30–9). Antiochus is allied with "those who forsake the holy covenant" (11:30), whom he seduces with flattery ("smooth things"). Opposed to those traitors are the members of the author's group, who are wise and understanding: "The people who know their God will stand firm and take action. And those among the people who are wise will make many understand, though they will fall by the sword and flame, by captivity and plunder, for some days" (11:33). Those who understand – that is, the author and his community – are to instruct and also suffer for the many. They do not envision themselves fighting the Seleucids and their hellenizing Jewish allies, as the Maccabeans and Hasideans (the Hebrew term for "pious ones") did (1 Macc. 2:42). They are committed to active, non-militant resistance, which includes suffering and teaching the people, and they hope for eventual divine intervention.

The Book of Daniel embraces suffering and persecution in a way similar to the martyrdom stories in 2 Maccabees and the Testament of Moses. Like Daniel and his companions in exile (Dan. 1:4), the members of this group are wise in the ways of God and the interpretation of divine purposes. Because of their knowledge of the heavenly world revealed in the visions and their confidence in final exaltation with God, they can endure suffering and remain faithful to God. They endure martyrdom not just to defy the Seleucids but to purify themselves for union with God and his angels: "Many will purify themselves, and make themselves white, and be refined; but the wicked will do wickedly; and none of the wicked will understand; but those who are wise will understand" (Dan. 12:10). Their ultimate fate is described in the only passage in the Hebrew Bible that refers unambiguously to life after death:

> At that time [during the final trouble] your people will be delivered, everyone whose name will be found written in the book. And many of those who sleep in the dust of the earth will awake, some to everlasting life and some to shame and everlasting contempt. And those who are wise will shine like the brightness of the firmament; and those who turn the many to righteousness, like the stars forever and ever. (Dan. 12:1–3)

The wise, who gave their lives for Judaism because they received revelation through the apocalyptic visions and thus knew how to face persecution, will live in the heavens with the other divine beings who serve God. (The image of the just as stars is common in apocalyptic literature, e.g., 1 En. 104.) No earthly restoration is envisioned, in contrast to the Apocalypse of Weeks in 1 En. 91:13, where the just acquire houses, and to 2 Maccabees, which rejoices in a restored temple.

The broad knowledge of the Jewish tradition and of hellenistic history shown in the Book of Daniel, and the intense involvement with the political events of Antiochus's period, suggest that the author and his core group were learned Jews who, subject to foreign persecution in their own country, identified with Daniel and his companions in Babylonian exile. They drew upon prophetic and wisdom traditions as well as traditional mythic patterns, especially that of God as divine warrior, in order to meet the challenges posed by the suppression of Judaism in its home territory and temple. Due to the military superiority of the Seleucids and the long foreign domination of Judea and Jerusalem, the apocalyptic group envisioned, not a military solution, but rather divine intervention. They conceived of their role as that of purifying the people through their suffering (see the Suffering Servant in Isa. 53) and instructing them so that they too might embrace the group's vision of God and the destruction of evil and thus acquire the confidence to endure persecution. Their ultimate goal was to inherit the kingdom promised to "the people of the Saints of the Most High" (Dan. 7:27).

2. The First Book of Enoch

The First (or Ethiopic) Book of Enoch (abbreviated as 1 En.) is a collection of materials from different periods (see pp. 272–273). It contains two or three sections that derive from the Maccabean period: the Animal Apocalypse, the Apocalypse of Weeks, and perhaps the Epistle of Enoch. All three sharply distinguish the just from sinners, await God's judgment to bring justice to the world, and look forward to life after death. The first two divide history into periods that end with the reign of God, a scheme that affirms order in the universe and promotes confidence in God and a sense of ultimacy in the audience.

The structure of 1 Enoch. 1 Enoch, which is preserved in its entirety in Ethiopic, has been compiled from several earlier books from different centuries.

Chapters	Name	Century
1–36	Book of Watchers	3–2 cen. B.C.E.
	1–5 Introduction	2–1 cen. B.C.E.
	6–11 Rebellion of the Angels	3 cen. B.C.E.
37–71	Similitudes of Enoch	1 cen. C.E.
72–82	Astronomical Book	3 cen. B.C.E.
83–90	Dream Visions	2 cen. B.C.E.
	83–84 Vision of the Deluge	2 cen. B.C.E.
	85–90 Animal Apocalypse	2 cen. B.C.E.
91–108	Epistle (Letter) of Enoch	2–1 cen. B.C.E.
	93:1–10; 91:12–17 Apocalypse of Weeks	2 cen. B.C.E.

The Animal Apocalypse (1 En. 85–90) is the second and longer of two dreams that make up the Book of Dreams (1 En. 83–90) in 1 Enoch. In the Animal Apocalypse the history of the world is narrated allegorically from Adam to Judas Maccabee, with animals standing for humans and human figures used for angels. The house in the vision represents Jerusalem, and the temple is symbolized by a tower. The author judges Judaism in the postexilic period very negatively. The rebuilt temple was always polluted and the people associated with it were blind (1 En. 89:73–4). When judgment has been completed, the old Jerusalem (symbolized by a house) will be dismantled and a new one built. The disorder, strife, and suffering of the postexilic period, especially the rule of gentile nations over Israel, are explained by the seventy shepherds. Because of its sins, God relinquished direct rule over and care for Israel and gave it to seventy shepherds who are the guardian angels (and sometimes kings) of the gentile nations, traditionally seventy in number (89:59 ff.). According to 1 Enoch, justice would eventually be done because the misdeeds and excessive oppression of Israel sanctioned by these shepherds have been recorded for use at the judgment (90:22). After the (present) evil period of the seventy shepherds, God will rule over a new Jerusalem and a transformed people (90:28 ff.), including the risen martyrs.

Since the last event in the historical account is the climactic struggle of Judas Maccabee (the "great horn of one of the sheep") against the gentiles, the Animal Apocalypse was written during the Maccabean revolt (167–164 B.C.E.), which is also the time when the Book of Daniel was compiled. The author does not lament the desecration of the temple by Antiochus, because he considered it already polluted. He continually attacks the blind sheep, that is, Jews who reject the message of the author and accommodate themselves to the gentile way of life. Thus, the group that produced the Animal Apocalypse, like the Essenes and other groups, sought to reform or replace Palestinian Jewish leadership and the administration of the temple. One passage (1 En. 89:7–8) suggests that the author was a supporter of Onias III (early second century). The rejection of the Jerusalem leadership and sharp division of Jews into the blind and the sighted are typical of the Jewish literature of this period.

ENOCH

ENOCH IS AN ANCIENT wisdom figure found in much Near Eastern literature, including the Bible. In Gen. 5:21–4 he is in the seventh generation after Adam; at the end of his life he "walked with God and was no more." To later generations, that Enoch "walked with God" meant that he was still alive and therefore available to reveal hidden, heavenly wisdom to humans.

In the Sumerian King List, the seventh king, Enmeduranki, king of Sippar, is similar to Enoch. He is brought into the assembly of the gods and shown how to predict the future through divination. The biblical author may have drawn on these and other Babylonian traditions for the figure of Enoch.

In Jewish apocalyptic literature Enoch was an intermediary who received revelation from God concerning the future and communicated it to the people. Besides the five originally independent works that make up 1 Enoch, a late-first-century B.C.E. work called 2 Enoch (extant only in Slavonic) recounts primeval times and Enoch's journey to the seven heavens, where he learns about creation, the workings of the cosmos, the course of history, the wonders of heaven, and the punishments of the wicked from God. The work designated 3 Enoch, the Hebrew Apocalypse of Enoch (fifth to sixth centuries C.E., with earlier material included), shows that the Enoch traditions continued into the rabbinic period. It offers an account by Rabbi Ishmael of how he journeyed to heaven, saw God's throne and chariot (the traditional objects of rabbinic mystical contemplation), received revelation from the archangel Metatron, and saw the wonders of the heavenly world.

The Apocalypse of Weeks is briefer and less detailed than the Animal Apocalypse. It comes near the beginning of the Epistle of Enoch (the final section of 1 Enoch), which is a long exhortation stressing the judgment of the wicked. The Apocalypse of Weeks, part of which is dislocated in the Ethiopic text (1 En. 91:12–17 belongs after 93:1–10), divides world history into ten weeks. Enoch was born in the first week, which was a righteous period. At the close of the fifth week, "the house of glory and dominion shall be built forever" (1 En. 93:7). Thus the author envisioned the temple as enduring eternally in some form, contrary to the author of the Animal Apocalypse. The sixth week is the period of the divided monarchy (1–2 Kings), in which "all who live in it will be blinded, and the hearts of all of them will godlessly forsake wisdom" (1 En. 93:8). This period ended with the destruction of the temple.

The postexilic period, the seventh week, receives as negative a judgment as it does in the Animal Apocalypse, for it is an apostate generation (1 En. 93:9). However, at the end of this period the author's group arises: "At its close will be elected the elect righteous of the eternal plant of righteousness, to receive sevenfold instruction concerning all his creation. And they will have rooted out the foundations of violence and the structure of falsehood therein, to execute [judgment]" (1 En. 93:10 [Ethiopic]; 93:11 [Aramaic]). As in the Animal Apocalypse and Daniel the righteous group is characterized by special knowledge and confronts opposition groups. The author seems to refer to the hellenizing Jews at the time of the Maccabean revolt as the apostates. Because the Apocalypse of Weeks does not clearly refer to the events of the Maccabean revolt, it may come from just before the revolt. An exact dating is impossible since we do not know the group to which the author belonged.

Though the events of the eighth week (1 En. 91:12–13) have sometimes been understood as referring to the activities of Judas Maccabee, they really describe God's kingdom (without a messiah) before the final judgment and destruction of the earth. It is a time when a sword will be given to the righteous to execute judgment on the wicked and then houses (in the Aramaic text: riches) will be given to the righteous and a new temple built for God. In the ninth week, earth and its evil will be judged and destroyed; in the tenth, the angels will be judged, a new heaven will replace the old heaven, and goodness and righteousness will endure for weeks without number (1 En. 93:14–17).

The divisions within the Jewish community and the conflict over acceptable ways of living Judaism in the hellenistic period, alluded to in the Animal Apocalypse and Apocalypse of Weeks, appear in great detail in the Epistle of Enoch (1 En. 91–108). The Epistle, written as Enoch's final testament to his sons (91:1), contains many exhortations to future generations (92:1). Drawing on both prophetic and wisdom traditions, the author condemns a number of social ills, including oppression of the poor by the rich and of the weak by the powerful, lying, theft, doing evil to fellow countrymen, self-indulgence, and idolatry (see especially 1 En. 94–5, 99). The righteous are promised vindication and reward, in contrast to the punishment visited on sinners in the climactic judgment scene (102–5).

The Epistle of Enoch contains little information to help date it. It may describe social ills in Judea before the Maccabean revolt or later in the second century, after the Hasmoneans were ruling. It testifies to the rifts and struggles that characterized second-century Judaism and to the sharp divisions that some groups saw between themselves and the governing class. The audiences to whom the Animal Apocalypse, the Apocalypse of Weeks, and Epistle of Enoch were addressed had similar outlooks and expectations. Rather than picture these people as a single group or an organized social movement, we should understand the groups whose traditions are presented in the Enoch collection as part of a broad tendency in Jewish society (reflected in Enoch, Jubilees, and some Dead Sea Scrolls) to criticize the temple leadership, the conduct of worship in the temple, the official calendar, excessive hellenization, accommodation to the gentiles, oppression of the poor, and other social ills. Regrettably, these groups remain nameless, and our knowledge of the Jewish society is too scanty to give more than a glimpse of the ferment that produced Daniel, the Enoch traditions, and the literature that followed.

3. The Influence of Apocalyptic Thought

Several other second-century B.C.E. Jewish writings have a strongly apocalyptic outlook and content fused with other literary forms. The Book of Jubilees focuses on a reform of Jewish law, the Testaments of the Twelve Patriarchs on moral exhortation to virtue, and the Sibylline Oracles on political protest. Apocalyptic imagery and restricted apocalyptic sections of these works provide the horizon against which the protests and rhetoric of these documents stand and the ultimate sanction which gives them meaning. All claim to be revelations or authoritative judgments of the present and future and buttress their claim with apocalyptic imagery of heaven and judgment.

Jubilees

The Book of Jubilees is an extensive elaboration of Genesis and the first part of Exodus. It often recasts the biblical narrative with interpretive expansions, revisions of pentateuchal law, indirect comments on contemporary events, and omission of offensive or "unimportant" material. The author concentrates on a reform of inner Jewish life and stresses keeping the Sabbath (chaps. 2 and 50, the beginning and end of the book), not fighting on the Sabbath (50:12), practicing circumcision, observing proper sacrificial and dietary laws, keeping the festivals, and avoiding illicit sexual practices and injustice. Great hostility to the gentiles appears in many places (22:16 ff.), especially concerning their practices of nudity when exercising (3:31), idolatry, and intermarriage (30:10). In addition, some specific practices championed by Jubilees are not found in the Bible and testify to the special nature of the group from which it emerged.

The author argues for his version of the Jewish way of life on the basis of heavenly revelation, the practice of the patriarchs, and a new calendar. Moses is said to have received the revelation in Jubilees from an angel on Sinai; the laws revealed to him (biblical and nonbiblical), as well as the events predicted, are said to be written on heavenly tablets (Jub. 3:10, 31:32; 32:10). Like the visions in apocalypses, the teachings in Jubilees are based on a divine revelation that is connected to, but goes beyond, the biblical text. In his retelling of the biblical stories of the patriarchs from Genesis, the author has the patriarchs keeping the laws and festivals that were only later revealed to Moses in Exodus and exhorting their sons to the same virtues and practices of Judaism that Jubilees recommends to Jews in its day. Finally, the author connects all events and festivals to a 364-day solar calendar and thus roots all Jewish practice and history in his version of the order of the universe. In promoting a solar calendar, against the traditional lunar calendar used at the temple then (and by Jews to this day), Jubilees reveals that it is associated with a third- and second-century B.C.E. reform movement of some type, since this calendar is found in the Astronomical Treatise of 1 Enoch (chaps. 72–82; see p. 336) and in many Dead Sea Scrolls.

Though Jubilees apparently speaks only about early biblical events, it in fact alludes to the Maccabean situation in the second century before the death of Judas Maccabee. The apocalyptic review of history in Jubilees 23 seems to describe the oppression and apostasy of the Maccabean period (Jub. 16–25), the rise of the faithful group to whom Jubilees is written (Jub. 26), and then God's direct, apocalyptic intervention in history (Jub. 27–31). In addition, the battles against the Amorites (Jub. 34) and the Edomites (Jub. 37–8) – neither of which is reported in the Bible – allude to Judas Maccabee's battles against Nicanor (1 Macc. 7:39–50) and against the Edomites. Jubilees was found among the Dead Sea Scrolls but is not a sectarian text. It proba-

THE BIBLE REWRITTEN

A NUMBER OF JEWISH works from the second temple period retell the biblical narrative in order to clarify it and make it more relevant and attractive for their readers. Such works are not commentaries, which explicitly cite the text (such as the Qumran *pesharim*), or books that merely utilize a biblical framework (4 Ezra, 2 Bar; see pp. 424–426). They cover the same ground as the biblical books through paraphrase, addition, omission, etc. Jubilees retells stories in Genesis and Exodus with a focus on a renewed understanding of many feasts and the legitimation of later laws and a solar calendar. The Qumran Temple Scroll describes an ideal temple and the regulations concerning it and then reorganizes some of the laws in Deuteronomy 12–26. Pseudo-Philo's Biblical Antiquities interweaves biblical and legendary accounts from Genesis to 2 Samuel to stress Israel's chosenness and the necessity of good leaders. The Qumran Genesis Apocryphon reworks stories of Noah and Abraham to make them more dramatic and detailed, as well as explain geographical terms and remove interpretive difficulties. Josephus's *Antiquities of the Jews* retells biblical history for the Greco-Roman world, using interpretations from the Jewish tradition and stressing God's providence, the necessity of morality, and the respectability of Judaism.

bly antedates the foundation of the Qumran community in the mid–second century and so was written between 160 and 140 B.C.E..

The group from which the author of Jubilees arose is unknown. Similarities shared with parts of the Enoch tradition, parts of Daniel, the Genesis Apocryphon, and Qumran literature suggest that these circles of apocalyptically oriented Jews had much in common. Since Levi (the priesthood) is given priority over Judah (the monarchy) (Jub. 31:12) and made custodian of the books and traditions of Israel (Jub. 45:15) and since great emphasis is placed on the cultic life of Israel, the author was probably a priest. Jubilees argues against the view of hellenizing Jews that the laws and practices of Judaism were no longer relevant or could be changed. It polemicizes against apostasy and insists that the laws, which came from the earliest patriarchal period and are inscribed on heavenly tablets (Jub. 3:10, 31, etc.), remain eternally valid and must not change (Jub. 30:10, 32:10). The author's zeal for fidelity to Israel and his rejection of the gentiles are based on his interpretation of Genesis 34, in which Levi rejected the gentile Shechem's offer to marry Levi's sister after her rape and then slaughtered the inhabitants of Shechem. For this, according to Jubilees, Levi received the priesthood (Jub. 30:18–20). The author of Jubilees sees his vocation, like Levi's, to be the protection of Israel from intermarriage and other gentile practices.

The Testaments

During the second century B.C.E. through the first century C.E., when apocalypses were being written, an allied literary genre, the testament, became popular. Testaments are the purported last words of a famous figure to his sons or followers. Testaments have survived in the names of the patriarchs, Moses, Job, and others. In a testament the historical figure usually tells something about his life, exhorts his descendants to virtue, and predicts their future. In many testaments the prediction of the future takes the form of an apocalypse concerning the last days and the ultimate destiny of Israel and the world. The hortatory sections are similar to the wisdom literature. Parts of Aramaic testaments of Levi, Judah, and Naphtali have been found among the Dead Sea Scrolls and other manuscripts, and are evidence of the vitality of this genre of instruction and exhortation.

The Testaments of the Twelve Patriarchs   The most extensive collection of second-century B.C.E. testaments is the work known as the Testaments of the Twelve Patriarchs. These twelve testaments, in the names of the twelve sons of Jacob and tribes of Israel, are not translations of earlier Hebrew and Aramaic testaments but a free Greek Jewish composition loosely based on earlier models. A few Christian passages are scattered through the Testaments of the Twelve Patriarchs, but they were probably added later by a Christian copyist. There are few clues to the date and place of composition. The author may have been a learned Palestinian Jew, especially given the emphasis on the dominance of Levi and the priesthood. However, lack of accuracy concerning place-names, the use of hellenistic ethical exhor-

---

BIBLICAL LAST BLESSINGS

THE TESTAMENTS OF THE second temple period were modeled on the last blessings given by Jacob to his twelve sons (Gen. 49) and by Moses to the people of Israel (Deut. 33). The biblical blessings reflect events in biblical history, just as the later testaments reflect the history of their own times. For example, Jacob's blessing of Judah, the tribe of the Davidic royal line, predicts: "Judah is a lion's [symbol of royalty] whelp. . . .The scepter shall not depart from Judah, nor the ruler's staff from between his feet, until he comes to whom it belongs" (Gen. 49:9–10). Simeon and Levi, who led the attack on Shechem (Gen. 34), are cursed and condemned to be divided in Israel (49:5–7), a reflection of the fact that the tribe of Simeon was later absorbed into Judah and the tribe of Levi became a landless priestly class. The final blessing of Moses reflects other realities of Israelite history. The tribe of Levi is praised as faithful priests: "Give to Levi your Thummim, and your Urim to the godly one, whom you tested at Massah. . . . For they observed your word and kept your covenant. They shall teach Jacob your ordinances and Israel your law" (Deut. 33:8–10). Joseph, the progenitor of Ephraim and Manasseh, the two powerful tribes who held the rich central hill country, is praised extensively and called prince among his brothers (33:13–17), a reflection of anti-Davidic sentiment.

tation, which has no analogue in Semitic Jewish literature, and the fact that the sequence of world empires given ends with the reign of the Seleucids in Syria (Test. Naphtali 5:8) suggests that the author may have been living under Seleucid rule in Syria. Others have looked for the place of origin of this work in the well-established and literate Jewish community in Egypt because of the strong emphasis on Joseph as a model of virtue in several of the testaments (Test. Reuben 4:8–10; Test. Benjamin 3; Test. Judah 25:1) and because the Testament of Joseph is very elaborate. If the Testaments of the Twelve Patriarchs derives from the Diaspora, it shows that apocalyptic thought and hopes were powerful beyond the borders of Palestine.

The date of the work is disputed. If the combination of the prophetic, priestly, and kingly roles in the Levitic Messiah (Test. Levi 18) was prompted by the reign of John Hyrcanus (134–104 B.C.E.), then the Testaments of the Twelve Patriarchs probably dates from the same period. If, as is more likely, this figure developed in a number of works in the Maccabean period, the collection may have been written soon after the Maccabean crisis. This would accord with the connections between the Testaments of the Twelve Patriarchs and the Dead Sea Scrolls and its frequent mention of the Book of Enoch.

All the testaments in the Testaments of the Twelve Patriarchs, except that of Levi, contain a narrative from the patriarch's life which is used as an example of virtue or vice. This is followed by an ethical exhortation to copy the virtue in question and by a prediction of the future of the tribe (or all Israel). After a brief final moral appeal, the patriarch dies and is buried. The testaments attack vices such as sexual licentiousness, deceit, envy, avarice, anger, and hate and promote virtues such as integrity, self-control, courage, brotherly love, and mercy. Though obedience to God and his laws is mentioned often, specific Jewish laws and practices are not, which stands in sharp contrast to Jubilees. To characterize the good Jew the author uses hellenistic terms for ethics, virtue, and piety.

In the Testaments of the Twelve Patriarchs, the larger world within which the struggle between virtue and vice takes place resembles that found in the apocalypses. There are two spirits, of good and evil, which move humans in opposite directions. The reign of evil is under the sovereignty of Beliar, an evil spirit found in much of the literature from this period. The final victory of God over evil is depicted with a variety of apocalyptic images and scenarios, including resurrection (Test. Judah 25:1–4; Test. Zebulun 10:2), a new Jerusalem, and paradise.

The author's solution to the political woes and disorder in the community is communicated through frequent exhortation to obey Levi and Judah, that is, the priesthood and the monarchy. Since in the author's day the monarchy was dead, Levi and the priesthood are dominant, and the monarchy is said to be subordinate to the priesthood (Test. Judah 21:1–4). The Testament of Levi differs from the others by being an apologetic tract to legitimate the authority of the priests. Levi is taken on a journey to heaven (Test. Levi 2–5) and given a sword to avenge his sister's rape (Test. Levi 5:3; cf. Gen. 34). Because of his zeal in avenging his sister, he is given all power through the

COVENANT

ACCORDING TO JEWISH literature from the Maccabean revolt to the editing of the Mishnah, salvation was obtained through membership in the covenant people. That is to say, it was believed that by membership in the community constituting God's chosen people (the people to whom God had given the promise of salvation and vindication), salvation was secured. The connection between the covenant and salvation is constant. With very few exceptions, the documents from this period reveal the belief that despite the persecution and suffering of his people, God would be true to his promise and would remember his true people, namely, the chosen community. The Books of Jubilees and 2 Baruch, the hellenistic Jewish book Joseph and Aseneth, and the works of Philo of Alexandria and many others stress that salvation and vindication are wrapped up with the notion of membership in God's covenant, or chosen, people.

This insight suggests two important things. First, it stresses the corporate nature of salvation as it was understood by these ancients. Salvation was found not individually but collectively, through membership in the community. Second, it highlights the central place in the thinking and self-understanding of most Jewish groups of the particular, select place they held in the plan and will of God. Naturally, conflict between the various defined "true and chosen" communities would and did erupt. But it is important to note how central was the belief that they alone constituted God's *covenant people.*

HELLENISTIC VIRTUES

THE TESTAMENTS ENCOURage the practice of universal virtues, in the hellenistic mode, rather than obedience to particular Jewish laws. Of course, obedience to the Law is one of the virtues, as well as piety, uprightness, generosity, honesty, compassion, integrity, hard work, and self-control. Appeal is made to another Greek idea, conscience (the universal potential for responding to the natural law). Even sexual misdeeds are to be avoided through temperance, not by adherence to specifically biblical commandments. Homosexuality and idolatry are condemned because they are contrary, not to biblical law, but to the law of nature. The influence of this ethical approach can be seen in Paul the Apostle, who appeals to conscience (Rom. 2:15) and lists virtues to be acquired and vices to be avoided (Gal. 5:19–23).

priesthood and is associated with kingly rule. In promoting the leadership of the priests, the Testaments of the Twelve Patriarchs is similar to the Qumran writings and other literature from this period, and even to the hopes Ben Sira placed in the legitimate and virtuous high priest Simon II (Sir. 50).

In the Testament of Levi, Levi and the priestly Messiah (Test. Levi 18) dominate the eschatological future and overshadow the Davidic Messiah (i.e., the anointed leader from the tribe of Judah and dynasty of David sent by God; Test. Judah 24–5) and the eschatological prophet promised in scripture (Deut. 18:15–19; see Test. Benjamin 9:1–2).

> The Lord will raise up a new priest to whom all the words of the Lord will be revealed. He will effect the judgment of truth over the earth for many days. And his star will rise in heaven like a king. . . . And the spirit of sanctification will rest upon him . . . and there will be no successor for him from generation to generation forever. . . . And in his priesthood sin will cease . . . and righteous men will find rest in him. And he will open the gates of paradise; he will remove the sword that has threatened since Adam, and he will grant the saints to eat of the Tree of Life. (Test. Levi 18)

Clearly the author sees the priesthood as the legitimate and only hope for Judaism and envisions it as ultimately triumphant at the end. Both the biblical figure Judah and the Levitic Messiah are military leaders (Test. Levi 18:12) as well as cultic functionaries. Their authority and responsibilities cover all areas and they replace the Davidic Messiah and the monarchy as the ruling and guiding force in Judaism.

Sibylline Oracles

Among Jews in the Diaspora, especially in Egypt, apocalyptic prophecies of the future and political protest against the ruling empires utilized the Greco-Roman form of the Sibylline Oracles. In that tradition the Sibyl was an aged prophetess, given long life and the power of prophecy by the gods. Various locales claimed oracles (Michelangelo put five of them in the Sistine Chapel with the prophets). Generally, the written oracles which have survived are filled with predictions of disaster for specific cities and countries. Many contained political protests and propaganda of eastern countries against their Greek and Roman conquerors. They often envisioned the return to a golden age under an ideal king, such as that described in Vergil's Fourth Eclogue and associated there with the Sibyl in Cumae (near Naples). Their subversive nature caused Augustus to order copies of many oracles in Rome destroyed.

The surviving collection of Sibylline Oracles derives from Jewish

VERGIL'S FOURTH ECLOGUE

VERGIL (ALSO SPELLED Virgil; first century B.C.E.) was one of the greatest Latin poets, most famous for his epic the *Aeneid.* During his life, political upheaval changed Rome from a republic to an empire. Vergil voiced the aspirations of Rome in one of his eclogues (poems with a pastoral setting) in which he praised the birth of a special child and anticipated a new, golden age. The poem sounded so messianic that some later Christian writers took it as an anticipation of the coming of Jesus Christ. In reality it is similar to the political oracles common in the Greco-Roman world (the Sibyl of Cumae is referred to), only it is propaganda for, rather than protest against, Roman rule.

> Now the Virgin returns, the reign
> of Saturn returns;
> now a new generation descends
> from heaven on high.
> . . . .
> Smile on the birth of the child,
> under whom the iron brood
> shall first cease,
> and a golden race spring up
> throughout the world
> . . . .
> For you, child, shall the earth
> untilled pour forth
> . . . .
> Uncalled, the goats shall bring
> home their udders
> swollen with milk
> and the herds shall fear not
> huge lions
> . . . .
> The serpent, too, shall perish.

> When the strength of years has
> made you a man,
> even the trader shall quit the
> sea,
> nor shall the ship of pine
> exchange wares;
> every land shall bear all fruits.
> The earth shall not feel the harrow,
> nor the vine the pruning-hook;
> the sturdy ploughman, too,
> shall now
> loose his oxen from the yoke.
> . . . .
> Enter on your high honor – the
> hour will soon be here –
> O dear offspring of the gods,
> mighty seed of a Jupiter to be.
> Behold the world bowing with its
> massive dome,
> earth and expanse of sea and
> heaven's depth.
> Behold, how all things exult in the
> age that is at hand.

and Christian circles. Most oracles are composites of smaller units and modified by additions to bring them up to date. They are characterized by predictions of doom for various nations, the hope of judgment, and the coming of an ideal kingdom, as well as moral exhortations which condemn especially idolatry, adultery, and homosexuality. (Parts of the Oracles are discussed on pp. 427–428, below.)

A major part of the Third Sibylline Oracle (ll. 97–349, 489–829) comes from mid-second-century B.C.E. Egypt, when good relations between the Jews and Ptolemy VI Philometor (163–145) encouraged some Egyptian Jews to hope for an ideal kingdom under a "seventh king" (3 Sib. Or. 193, 318, 608). No reference is made to the Maccabees or the wars in Judea. Rather, the author uses a traditional scheme of ten ages or empires, of which the last two are the Greek and Roman Empires (the latter an increasingly menacing presence in the eastern Mediterranean in the second century). Two lists of empires (3 Sib. Or. 156–61, 165–95) end with the Romans, and the second predicts their overthrow by the seventh Egyptian king (3 Sib. Or. 191–5).

The Jewish author treats the Egyptian king, designated by the traditional title "the king from the sun," as an eschatological figure who will be the final ruler to precede the cosmic judgment and God's kingdom:

> And then God will send a king from the sun who will stop the entire world from evil war, killing some, imposing oaths of loyalty on others; and he will not do all these things by his private plans but in obedience to the noble teachings of the great God. (3 Sib. Or. 652–6)

Cybele, seated.
Koester-Harvard Archaeological
Resources for New Testament Study.

The place given the Egyptian king in God's plans is like that given Cyrus by the exilic author of Second Isaiah (Isa. 44:28, 45:1 ff.). In both cases Diaspora authors adapted Jewish expectations to local culture. The Egyptian Jewish author of the Third Sibylline Oracle did not look to Palestine or its leadership but supported his local monarch, hoping that God would work through him to bring about justice. The apocalyptic expectations of war and suffering followed by judgment and a divine kingdom, which fill the latter part of the oracle (3 Sib. Or. 601–808), were used to encourage loyal adherence to a good Egyptian king against invaders (such as Antiochus IV or the Romans). The author's attitude toward his gentile rulers contrasts starkly with the hostile attitudes of many Palestinian groups and with later Egyptian Jewish conflict with the authorities.

Though the Third Sibylline Oracle alludes to neither the Maccabees nor Palestinian Judaism, it puts great emphasis on the sanctity and centrality of the temple and its holy city (3 Sib. Or. 286–94, 564–7, 657–68, 715–40, 772–5). Warnings are given not to attack it. Through it, the gentiles will attain peace, and in the end they will offer sacrifice there only. The support for the temple of the one God is consistent with the author's urgent condemnation of idolatry. Both idolatry and sexual license were traditionally seen as the characteristic sins of the gentiles, so the Third Sibylline Oracle combats them strongly and envisions their eradication through the triumph of God and the Jewish way of life, with the temple as the center of worship.

The prominence of apocalyptic imagery within other literary genres such as testaments and oracles, even in the Diaspora, testifies to the wide attraction of this mode of thought. All over the eastern Mediterranean, Jews and other groups were deeply dissatisfied with the oppression, disorder, and uncertainty of the failing hellenistic empires. Apocalypses offered an explanation of the larger workings of the universe and history as well as hope for order and justice, based on confidence in a divine power to whom empires, no matter how powerful and evil, were subordinate. Numerous groups used the imagery, mythology, and cosmic vision of apocalyptic literature to consolidate their identity and to mark boundaries between their just community and the evil world around them.

D.   CHANGES IN JEWISH SOCIETY

The family of Simon Maccabee ruled for about seventy years after his death. His son John Hyrcanus (134–104 B.C.E.) was succeeded by two of John's sons, Aristobulus I (104–103) and Alexander Jannaeus (103–76). The rule then went to Alexander's wife, Salome Alexandra (76–67). Independent rule ceased when civil war between two of her sons, Aristobulus II and Hyrcanus II, led to the Roman annexation of Palestine in 63 B.C.E. The early years of the dynasty were generally successful. After the death of Simon in 134, his successors quickly enlarged Israel's borders so that it became a petty hellenistic monarchy, like many others in the eastern Mediterranean, competing for territory, revenues, and influence. Aristobulus I and Alexander Jannaeus even took the long-unused title "king" along with that of high priest. Like other hellenistic monarchs, they hired mercenaries to carry out their military policies and maintain internal security.

After Simon's assassination, his son John Hyrcanus gained control of Jerusalem and defeated Ptolemy, the assassin, who aspired to the throne. In John's first year of rule (134) the newly resurgent Seleucid monarch Antiochus VII Sidetes besieged Jerusalem and forced John to pay tribute, to demolish the city's fortifications, and to turn over his army's weapons. This final gasp of Seleucid power ended in 129 with the death of Antiochus; a series of dynastic struggles in succeeding decades left Palestine free to conquer the southern region of the Seleucid Empire.

John Hyrcanus conquered part of the seacoast in the west, Samaria in the north, part of Transjordan in the east, and Idumea in the south. He destroyed the Samaritan temple on Mount Gerizim and razed the city of Samaria to the ground, causing a final, hostile break between Jerusalem and Samaria. He forcibly converted the Idumeans to Judaism in order to keep the country Jewish. (Ironically, certain Idumeans – Antipas, his son Herod, and their dynasty – eventually ruled Palestine.) After John Hyrcanus, Aristobulus, though sick and king for only a year (104–103), ordered the conquest of upper Galilee by his brother Antigonus. His successor, Alexander Jannaeus (103–76), engaged in constant warfare, only some of which was successful. He conquered most of the coast, the northern part of Transjordan, and areas to the north of it, including Golan, Bashan, Trachonitis, and Hauran, as well as the territory east and south of the Dead Sea. Alexander Jannaeus brought to fruition the policy of his house, the Hasmoneans, who had sought to break the power of the independent Greek cities that had been set up by the Seleucids and Ptolemies, to Judaize much of the country, and to secure an economic base for their rule by collecting taxes on the extensive commerce that flowed through the region. This Hasmonean expansion was contained only by the growing power of the Nabatean Arabs in the east and south and by the remnants of Seleucid power in the north. The new independence and prosperity of the Jewish kingdom, like those of many other principalities in the eastern Mediterranean, were soon destroyed by the advancing Roman armies in 63 B.C.E.

Though Jewish society prospered economically under the Hasmoneans and achieved a measure of security, the constant wars brought periodic invasions by the Seleucids, Ptolemies, and Nabateans. As late as 83 B.C.E. Alexander Jannaeus had to negotiate peace with a Nabatean army that invaded Judea. Hasmonean dynastic intrigues were frequent. John Hyrcanus barely escaped his father's assassin; Aristobulus I imprisoned and starved to death his mother to keep her from taking power. He then executed his brother Antigonus, whom he falsely suspected of plotting against him. Two of Alexander Jannaeus's sons, Hyrcanus II and Aristobulus II, engaged in constant civil strife from 67 until 63, when the war-weary community leaders requested the Romans to intervene.

1.   Jewish Voluntary Associations

Struggles for political power were frequent, and many factions, coalitions, and interest groups emerged during the hellenistic period. The internal strife among competing priestly and aristocratic families, as well as popular social movements, included the activities of the three groups described by Flavius Josephus, the first-century C.E. Jewish historian: the Pharisees, Sadducees, and Essenes. Though the three groups are often called sects, philosophies, or schools of thought, the Greek word used to describe them most often in Josephus is *hairesis* (lit., "a choice"). The Greek term denotes a choice of a way of life and can refer to a philosophy or a school of thought, including its customs, dress, and activities. These "choices," or voluntary associations, may have sectlike characteristics but need not be sectarian in the classic sense, that is, a subordinate group reacting in protest against the dominant group and claiming for itself the only legitimate interpretation of the tradition.

According to Josephus, the Pharisees and Sadducees behaved like political interest groups, seeking to influence the governing class and ultimately seeking direct power over social laws and policies. (The Essenes, who lived both in the towns and in isolated centers in the wilderness, will be treated in conjunction with the Dead Sea Scrolls below.) Under John Hyrcanus (134–104) they competed for influence so that their interpretations of Jewish law would govern the state. Initially, the Pharisees had the ear of their ruler, but court intrigue and a trap set by the Sadducees resulted in the Pharisees' falling out of favor with John and the Sadducees' convincing him to follow their laws (Josephus, *Antiquities of the Jews* 13.288–98). Later, under Alexander Jannaeus (103–76) the Pharisees gained a large following among people protesting the policies and authoritarianism of Alexander Jannaeus, so much so that when Jannaeus was dying, he advised his wife, Alexandra, to make an alliance with the Pharisees in order to secure her own position as ruler (13.399–417). She did so and under Alexandra the Pharisees attained real and direct power over domestic policy and proceeded to punish their enemies and implement their policies. Their dominance did not survive Alexandra's reign (76–67), but they remained active in Palestinian politics through Herodian and Roman rule and into the revolt in 66–70 C.E.

Since the Sadducees were members of the governing class (Josephus, *Antiquities* 18.17), they had more direct access to power. However, not all the chief priests and aristocrats were Sadducees. Their nature and program are unclear. They supported the traditional interpretations of Jewish life and resisted reforms and innovations that threatened the power of the ruling classes. Perhaps they were a reform group that resisted excessive hellenization or venal abuses of power.

The Pharisees and Sadducees had different interpretations of Jewish law and life. Josephus treats them as Greek philosophies, stressing that the Pharisees believed in life after death and the Sadducees adhered to the older position that there was no life after death. He attributes to the

Sadducees a belief in human responsibility without divine judgment and to the Pharisees a balanced view of fate and human responsibility. The Pharisees are described as urban and pleasant and the Sadducees as rude and boorish. The Pharisees, who were a new group seeking influence, proposed interpretations of Jewish law and life that were attractive to the people. The Sadducees adhered closely to the traditional ways of life that had been promoted by their fellow leaders for generations. Allowing for Josephus's biases and stereotypes, these descriptions generally fit the social station of each group. The Sadducees were from the governing class and the Pharisees were subordinate to them. Thus the Pharisees had to seek influence and power actively and propose new interpretations of laws consistent with their program, whereas the Sadducees held on to traditional teachings and customs, which supported their dominant station in society.

2. The Essenes and the Dead Sea Scrolls

Josephus presented the Essenes as an ideal ascetic group because his Greek and Roman readers found such eastern movements fascinating. According to Josephus, the Essenes emphasized God's activity in life rather than human freedom, believed in the immortality of the soul, refused to participate directly in temple worship because they disagreed with purity rites, cultivated virtue, and lived simply. Josephus's description of the Essenes was validated by the discovery, in 1947, of several complete manuscripts and thousands of fragments in eleven caves near Qumran, on the northwest shore of the Dead Sea. These Dead Sea Scrolls were written in Hebrew, Aramaic, and Greek, the common languages of Palestine. They contained a variety of Jewish literature, including Hebrew and Greek copies of the Bible (often with significantly different readings); non-biblical, pseudepigraphical, and anonymous Jewish literature known from elsewhere; writings peculiar to the Essene community; biblical commentaries (called *pesharim*) which connected the history of the sect to biblical prophecy; hymns and psalms; and a variety of astronomical, esoteric, apocalyptic, and mystical texts. The Qumran library has contributed greatly to our understanding of Judaism from the time of the Hasmoneans (164–63 B.C.E.) through the early Roman period (63 B.C.E.–70 C.E.), a period that includes the beginning of Christianity. The many connections between these sectarian documents and New Testament practice and thought have shown concretely how deeply rooted the early Christian community was in Judaism. New Testament communities shared characteristics with the Qumran community, including the office of overseer (= the New Testament Greek word *episcopos*, usually translated "bishop"), voluntary poverty (like the Jerusalem community in Acts 2:44–5), lively apocalyptic and messianic expectations, and the use of biblical interpretation to establish the legitimacy of the community as the true Israel.

The scrolls belonged to a community centered in a settlement built on the cliffs at Qumran. The settlement was walled and included a

MAJOR DEAD SEA SCROLLS

HUNDREDS OF FRAGMENTS of scrolls were found in eleven caves near Qumran and in other caves further south. Some fragments are very difficult to interpret, but many have added immeasurably to our understanding of second temple Judaism. A list by caves of some of these scrolls, using their most popular names, follows:

Cave 1:
Isaiah Scroll
Commentary on Habakkuk
Manual of Discipline, or Rule of the Community
Covenant of Damascus, or Damascus Document
Genesis Apocryphon
War Scroll
Hymn Scroll, or Thanksgiving Hymns

Cave 4:
Angelic Liturgy
Commentary on Nahum
Commentary on Isaiah
Commentary on Psalm 37
Messianic Florilegium
Messianic Testimonium

Cave 11:
Psalms Scroll
Targum of Job
Melchizedek Text
Temple Scroll

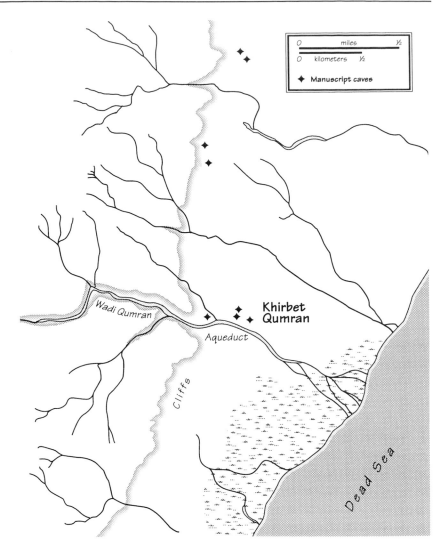

Dead Sea area.

tower, elaborate aqueducts and cisterns to collect water in the arid wilderness, and numerous installations, such as a kitchen, stables, courtyards, potters shops, and ritual baths. They also had a scriptorium, where scrolls were copied, and an assembly hall for meetings and meals. The community rules and teachings indicate that the Qumran community was part of the Essene movement. Qumran was probably occupied by a small group of dissidents from Jerusalem in the mid–second century B.C.E.; during the next hundred years the community grew much larger. Two springs several miles to the south at Ein el-Ghuweir and Ein Feshka also show evidence of Essene occupation.

The Nahum Pesher refers explicitly to events in Alexander Jannaeus's reign, specifically, Demetrius III's attack on Judea and the crucifixion of those who conspired with him (the "Seekers-after-Smooth-Things") by Alexander Jannaeus (the "Lion of Wrath"):

"Where the lion went to enter, there (is) the lion's cub and no one disturbs (it)." (Nah. 2:11) The interpretation (*pesher*) of it concerns Demetrius, king of Greece, who sought to enter Jerusalem on the advice of the Seekers-after-Smooth-Things, [but God did not give Jerusalem] into the power of the kings of Greece from Antiochus until the rise of the rulers of the Kittim; but afterward she (the city) will be trampled [and will be given into the hand of the rulers of Kittim. . . .] "The Lion tears enough for his cubs and strangles prey for his lionesses" (Nah. 2:12). [The interpretation of it concerns Demetrius, who made war] against the Lion of Wrath (Alexander Jannaeus), who would strike with his great ones and his partisans, [but they] fled before him (Demetrius). "And it fills up] its cave [with prey,] and its den with torn flesh" (Nah. 2:12). The interpretation of it concerns the Lion of Wrath, [who has found a crime punishable by] death in the Seekers-after-Smooth-Things, whom he hangs up as living men [upon the tree, as it was thus done] in Israel from of old, for regarding one hanged alive upon the tree [it] (scripture) reads, "Behold I am against you, says[s Yahweh of Hosts]" (Nah. 2:13). (Nahum Pesher 3–4.i.1–9)

The mention of Demetrius's name and the explicit references to the events of the revolt against Alexander Jannaeus in 90–85 B.C.E. provide a sure historical context. The punishment of the rebels by crucifixion seems to be recounted with approval, and a passage in the Qumran Temple Scroll (64:6–13) indicates that the Essenes approved of crucifixion as a means of execution for treason or for violation of the covenant as they perceived it.

The Seekers-after-Smooth-Things (also called "Ephraim"), who are opponents of both Alexander Jannaeus and the Essenes, have often been identified with the Pharisees. Since this identification is not certain, the Seekers-after-Smooth-Things could have been any established group or a series of groups whom the Essenes rejected. The Seekers-after-Smooth-Things are attacked for deceit, false teaching, and leading the people astray and are condemned to punishment by war, exile, and death. Because they deceived Israel, their

> wicked deeds will be revealed to all Israel at the end of time, and many will discern their sin, will hate them, and consider them repulsive (?) on account of their guilty insolence. But when the glory of Judah is [re]vealed, the simple ones of Ephraim will flee from the midst of their assembly. They will abandon those who led them astray and will join Israel. (3–4.iii.3–5)

The condemnation called down on these leaders is typical for apocalyptic groups such as the Qumran community. For the Qumran Essenes withdrawal was the proper response to what they saw as a corrupt government, priesthood, and temple; any accommodation or compromise implicated a person in the evil system, which stood under apocalyptic judgment. In their polemics against their enemies, the Essenes of Qumran reveal themselves as an apocalyptic sect which has withdrawn from the main body of Israel, whom they judged to be evil and unfaithful. They claimed to be the true Israel and awaited the final

Cistern at Qumran cracked by the earthquake in 31 B.C.E.

Anthony J. Saldarini.

intervention of God, who would punish their enemies and vindicate their faithful adherence to the covenant.

Two foundation documents that give the goals, origins, and constitution of the Qumran community are the Rule of the Community (also known as the Manual of Discipline) and the Covenant of Damascus (also known as the Damascus Document and the Zadokite Document). They contain the rationale for the Essene way of life, fundamental rules governing their life, and allusions to their early history. Both documents are composites which developed over two centuries. Neither indicates who wrote it. The earliest section of the Rule of the Community (abbreviated 1QS) is a manifesto calling for true Israelites to found

> a House of Perfection and Truth in Israel that they may establish a Covenant according to the everlasting precepts. And they shall be an agreeable offering, atoning for the Land and determining the judgment of wickedness, and there shall be no more iniquity. (1QS 8)

When they have formed the community, they are ordered to

> separate from the habitation of ungodly men and go into the wilderness to prepare the way of Him; as it is written, "Prepare in the wilderness the way of . . . make straight in the desert a path for our God" (Isa. 40:3). This (path) is the study of the law which he commanded by the hand of Moses. (1QS 8)

The Essene group sought to establish a holy and pure Israel, faithful to the covenant, separate from the nations who had come to dominate Israel through hellenization, and living according to their own strict interpretations of biblical law.

The Covenant of Damascus envisions members of the community living both in cities and in camps (probably isolated communities like Qumran). Josephus testifies to this dual way of life, with some Essenes living in the cities and towns of Judea and others in separate communities in the wilderness. Some obscure references to conflict within the community suggest that over time the Essenes may have divided into distinct branches. The Rule of the Community is written for a community living apart from the larger society and presumably was the rule in effect at the Qumran community. Thus the Qumran community was a sect that withdrew from society in response to the corruption it saw there, whereas the groups governed by the Covenant of Damascus were a sect or voluntary association that remained within society but lived a distinct way of life.

Both the Rule of the Community and the Covenant of Damascus contain detailed regulations governing community organization and life, as well as particular interpretations of biblical law. The community was divided into hereditary priests and laypeople. The members of the community were male and probably were committed to celibacy. The priests had precedence in ritual and governance, but an assembly of all the members had great power. Members were admitted to the community only after a probationary period during which they were tested and their behavior was carefully watched. They had to follow the community's interpretation of biblical law meticulously and

ESSENE AND CHRISTIAN USES OF THE BIBLE

BOTH THE NEW TESTAMENT and the Qumran Rule of the Community cite Isaiah, chapters 28 and 40, but for very different purposes. In Isa. 28:16 God says: "Behold, I am laying in Zion for a foundation a stone, a tested stone, a precious cornerstone, of a sure foundation" In Isa. 40:3 the end of the exile is signaled by a voice crying, "In the wilderness prepare the way of the Lord, make straight in the desert a highway for our God."

The Qumran Rule of the Community applies Isa. 28:16 (paraphrased) and 40:3 to the Council of the Community, which refers to a leadership group that perhaps was the founding institution of the Qumran community, and also to the community at large. According to the Rule of the Community (col. 8), the Council of the Community shall be

> witnesses to the truth at the judgment, and shall be the elect of goodwill who shall atone for

the Land and pay to the wicked their reward. It shall be that tried wall, that "precious cornerstone," whose foundations shall neither rock nor sway in their place (Isa. 28:16).

When the Council of the Community (probably meaning the community members at large) have become secure members according to the rules,

> they shall separate from the habitation of ungodly men and shall go into the wilderness to prepare the way of Him [God]; as it is written, "Prepare in the wilderness the way of . . . make straight in the desert a path for our God" (Isa. 40:3). This (path) is the study of the Law which He commanded by the hand of Moses, that they may do according to all that has been revealed from age to age, and as the Prophets have revealed by His Holy Spirit.

The Qumran community and study of the law are the focus of the Rule of the Community. In contrast, the New Testament, seeking an equally thorough reform of Judaism, looks to Jesus as the rock and new Exodus.

The Gospel of Mark begins with a composite quotation from Mal. 3:1 and Isa. 40:3 which it applies to John the Baptist and Jesus: "Behold I send my messenger before your face, who shall prepare your way; the voice of one crying in the wilderness: Prepare the way of the Lord, make his paths straight."

In Rom. 9:33 Paul changes the point of Isa. 28:16 concerning a secure foundation and cornerstone for Zion by combining it with Ps. 118:22 concerning a stumbling stone: "Behold I am laying in Zion a stone that will make men stumble, a rock that will make them fall; and he who believes in it/him [Jesus] will not be put to shame." Isa. 28:16 and Ps. 118:22 are also combined in 1 Pet. 2:4–8. The stumbling stone is Jesus and the metaphor is used to explain Jesus' rejection by Israel. Ps. 118 is also used in the synoptic Gospels (Mark 12:10, Matt. 21:42, Luke 9:22) and Acts 4:11, in all cases in an apologetic explanation of the rejection of Jesus' teaching by Israel.

observe ritual purity carefully. At Qumran all or a majority of the members were unmarried and had to separate themselves from contact with gentiles and nonmember Israelites. During the second year of probation a new member gave up his private property to the community.

The community was presided over by a variety of officers and councils, of whom the priest, the "overseer" (a Levite), and the Council of the Community were most important. The priest presided at solemn meals and worship; the overseer taught the community and maintained community discipline. The Council of the Community, which consisted of either all the fully initiated members or a group of the senior members, met nightly to study and pray. It also gathered for the formal community meals presided over by the priest. At meetings of the community, members sat and spoke according to rank, which was presumably based on their stage of initiation, seniority, and office. The presiding officials and another community council were responsible for investigating the conduct of new members and imposing penalties for infractions of the rules by members.

The community rules governed all aspects of life, including fraternal relations, ritual purity, relations with outsiders, and worship. Infractions of the rules were punished by fasting and penance for periods of a few days to two years and ultimately by expulsion. The community organization and rules, with their underlying zeal for a renewed covenant with God and faithful adherence to God's will, attest to the community's goal of forming an ideal Jewish society. Fully conscious of the (to them) corruption and infidelity of Jewish society in general and of the temple worship in particular, the community sought to atone for Israel's sins and re-create a perfect society through their faithful observance and worship. They expected vindication of their way of life through the coming of God in power at the end of the present age, when he would effect the final purification of Jewish society and institute the rule of the priestly and Davidic messiahs.

The community's activity was also influenced by one other collection of rules, the Temple Scroll, which reorganized and modified many regulations found in the Bible in order to articulate the shape of a reformed and just society. Regulations in the Temple Scroll cover sacrifices and festivals, the plan of the perfect temple, the sanctity of Jerusalem, ritual purity, the judicial system, cult laws, idolatry, kingship, governmental institutions, and war.

The worldview expressed in the Dead Sea Scrolls has many similarities to that found in other contemporary Jewish documents and early Christian literature. True to their Jewish heritage the Essenes experienced God as active in history, as just toward humans, and as merciful to those who repented and obeyed him. Salvation came from God's grace, that is, his mercy and care for sinful humans. Joined with this confidence in God is a robust sense of human sinfulness and helplessness in the face of evil. The Hymn Scroll (abbreviated 1QH) contains many personal and communal expressions of the Qumran community's view of God and humanity. Though some have suggested that the early guide of the community, the Teacher of Righteousness, wrote these hymns, it is more likely that these hymns, along with many others, gradually evolved as an expression of the community's attitudes and aspiration in prayer. The more than two dozen hymns in this scroll express human weakness and need for divine help, describe the struggle with evil, and proclaim confidence in divine intervention and the triumph of justice.

As for me, shaking and trembling seize me and all my bones are broken; my heart dissolves like wax before fire. . . . For I remember my sins and the unfaithfulness of my fathers. When the wicked rose against your covenant and the damned against your word, I said in my sinfulness, "I am forsaken by your covenant." But calling to mind the might of your hand and the greatness of your compassion, I rose and stood, and my spirit was established in the face of the scourge. I lean upon your grace and on the multitude of your mercies, for you will pardon iniquities and through your right-eousness [you will purify man] of his sin. (1QH 4)

The Dead Sea Scrolls distinguish sharply between good and evil, light and dark, the elect and the condemned, the good spirit and the evil spirit. Without denying free will or reducing the responsibility of community members to turn to God and obey him, the hymns stress the de facto division between good and evil and God's role in this mysterious conflict (e.g., 1QH 15). The scroll's stark reverence for divine control and predestination is founded on the certainty of apocalyptic divine intervention to end evil and bring justice. As may be seen in the War Scroll (see below, p. 363), the community expected to fight with the angelic armies of God in a final victory over the Romans and their sinful Jewish allies. In the meantime, the overwhelming force of human evil was explained not only by malevolent human choice but also by the activities of good and evil spirits which fought for control of humans.

> (God) has created man to govern the world, and has appointed for him two spirits in which to walk until the time of his visitation: the spirits of truth and falsehood. Those born of truth spring from a fountain of light, but those born of falsehood from a source of darkness. All the children of righteousness are ruled by the Prince of Light and walk in the ways of light, but all the children of falsehood are ruled by the Angel of Darkness and walk in the ways of darkness. (1QS 3)

This division of humans and their ways of life into children of light and children of darkness carries on into the final battle between good and evil, when Melchizedek, here the angelic leader of the sons of light, will judge the good and evil humans and destroy Satan. The Melchizedek text (11QMelch) envisions a heavenly figure named Melchizedek who will judge the evil spirits serving under Beliar.

The final, apocalyptic resolution of history and the struggle between good and evil mirrors the community's structure and its interpretation of God's law and will. The kingdom of God will be presided over by two messiahs, a priestly messiah and a messiah of Israel (or royal political messiah from the House of David), who correspond to the priestly and lay sections of the community. A supplement to the Rule of the Community describes the so-called Messianic Banquet, during which the priest messiah sits at the head of the priests and blesses the food, which is then blessed by the messiah of Israel at the head of the chiefs of the clans of Israel. Another text describes the measurements of an ideal Jerusalem, in which the faithful will live. Many other descriptions of the end, collections of scriptural passages, recitations of the final apocalyptic battles, and prayers testify to the community's strong apocalyptic expectations.

The Dead Sea Scrolls place a great stress on revealed knowledge as essential to salvation. In order to understand fully God's plan and will and in order to separate oneself from the ordinary, sinful mode of living Judaism, a person needs special insight into scripture. The writings of the Teacher of Righteousness, who helped found the community,

PSALM 151 (GREEK VERSION)

I was small among my
  brothers,
and youngest in my father's
  house;
I tended my father's sheep.

My hands made a harp,
my fingers fashioned a lyre.

And who will declare it to my
  Lord?
The Lord himself; it is he who
  hears.

It was he who sent his messenger
and took me from my father's
  sheep,
and anointed me with his anointing oil.

My brothers were handsome and
  tall,
but the Lord was not pleased
  with them.

I went out to meet the Philistine,
and he cursed me by his idols.

But I drew his own sword;
I beheaded him, and removed
  reproach from the people of
  Israel.

and the other teachings of the community are accorded a very high status as the only true interpretations of scripture and the Jewish way of life. The Habakkuk Pesher, which contains the community's own version of its foundations, claims that "God told Habakkuk to write down the things that are going to come upon the last generation" but did not make known to him the time of the end. It was the "Teacher of Righteousness to whom God made known all the mysteries of the words of his servants the prophets" (1QpHab 7). The community studied scripture daily, and new members were allowed to learn the community's teachings only after a period of probation. The mysteries that the community contemplated included the apocalyptic end of the world, as planned by God, and the particular Jewish way of life needed to participate in God's victory. The stress on knowledge and revelation came from the biblical wisdom and apocalyptic traditions and is found in many other Jewish documents of the period.

Perhaps the best metaphor for summing up the life and worldview of the Qumran community is worship. Many texts found there contain hymns, poems, and prayers. The community sought to keep itself free from sin, maintain ritual purity, and commit itself firmly to God so that it could worship God as the angels did. Because the community rejected the way worship was carried out by the Hasmoneans in the temple, they turned to the angelic worship in heaven and saw the community as a kind of temple. A set of Sabbath hymns, often called the Angelic Liturgy, involve the community with angelic worship in heaven and describe the heavens in the manner of Jewish mysticism. Praise of God occupies most of the hymns:

> Song of the sacrifice of the seventh Sabbath on the sixteenth of the month. Praise the God of the lofty heights, O you lofty one among all the "gods" of knowledge. Let the holiest of the godlike ones sanctify the King of glory who sanctifies by holiness all His holy ones. O you chiefs of the praises of all the godlike beings, praise the splendidly [pr]aiseworthy God. For in the splendor of praise is the glory of His realm. (4QShirShab, trans. C. Newsom, p. 211)

Other hymns describe the heavenly realm and put the worshipers there in spirit:

JEWISH MYSTICISM

Surviving Jewish mystical texts come mostly from the Talmudic period (the third century C.E. on), but the Angelic Liturgy at Qumran, apocalyptic visionary experiences and heavenly journeys, and hints in other early documents suggest that a limited but active interest in mystical topics extended back into the second temple period. Visionary experience concerning God was based on the vision of the divine chariot (*merkavah*) in Ezekiel 1 and is referred to as Merkavah mysticism. Speculation on creation and cosmogony was centered on the creation account in Genesis 1 and is referred to as the Story of Creation (*ma'ase bereshit*). Texts which speak of the heavens and God's palaces (*hekhalot*) are designated Hekhalot mysticism. Rabbinic mystical teaching stressed the dangers to the mystic and was restricted to private discussion between mature scholars. The nature of the heavens and its angelic inhabitants, the course of history with its eschatological resolution, the workings of the cosmos, and the vision of God were all topics taken up in mystical works.

[And the liken]ess of living divine beings is engraved in the vestibules where the King enters, figures of luminous spirits, [. . . K]ing, figures of glorious li[ght, wondrous] spirits; [in] the midst of the spirits of splendor (is) a work of wondrous colors, figures of the living divine beings. (4QShirShab, trans. C. Newsom, p. 280)

Later Jewish mystical texts continue the tradition found in the Angelic Liturgy.

Many nonbiblical psalms have also been found at Qumran. One scroll contains about thirty-five canonical psalms along with several noncanonical psalms. One psalm, known in the Septuagint as Psalm 151 and accepted as canonical by the Eastern Orthodox churches, appears at Qumran in a longer version. In both versions David celebrates his choice by God to be king, though he was smaller and less handsome than his brothers. In the shorter Greek version he celebrates his victory over Goliath; in the longer Hebrew version he praises God at greater length and focuses on his choice as leader in Israel. The presence of this psalm in the Greek Bible and among the Qumran manuscripts and the presence of another psalm both at Qumran and in the Wisdom of Ben Sira testify to the variety of psalms being written, revised, and used in different contexts by second temple Judaism.

III. ROMAN INVASION AND JEWISH RESPONSE

A. HISTORICAL AND SOCIAL DEVELOPMENTS

For a century and a half before the Romans conquered Palestine and Jerusalem (63 B.C.E.) they had gradually spread their power and influence over Macedonia, Greece, and Asia Minor (modern Turkey) by military conquest, political domination, and annexation. The very threat of the Roman legions, who had prevailed in many crucial battles and through several long and stubborn wars, kept most cities and territories cooperative or passive in international affairs but left them autonomous internally. Despite this dominant pattern of political and social life in the East, social and political relations constantly changed. The struggle for control in Rome during the first century B.C.E. and the conflicts among powers in the East produced a series of crises and wars that finally led to the consolidation of the Roman Empire in the East and relative peace under Caesar Augustus (31 B.C.E.–14 C.E.).

The three powers that threatened Roman influence in the East during the first century B.C.E. were Pontus (in Asia Minor), Armenia, and Persia. Mithradates of Pontus attacked the Roman provinces of Asia and Greece, but the Roman general Sulla defeated him and halted his imperialistic expansion (88–83 B.C.E.). Later, both Mithradates and Tigranes of Armenia sought to establish control over Asia Minor and Syria but were driven off by Roman armies again (74–66 B.C.E.). During this period Alexandra, queen of Judea, submitted to Tigranes while he was besieging Ptolemaïs (Acre) by sending gifts and making treaties (Josephus, *History of the Jewish War* 1.5.3 [116]).

Both Mithradates and Tigranes remained potent threats to other

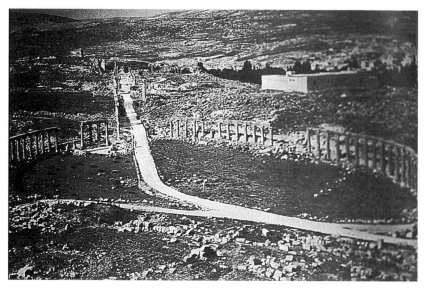

Forum in Gerasa, a city of the Decapolis.

C. Kraeling, Gerasa (American Schools of Oriental Research, 1938) Plate XXXII.

regional rulers until Pompey came east in the sixties B.C.E. to establish Roman control. Pompey acquired a mandate to pacify and rule the Mediterranean because of his immense domestic popularity and the Roman frustration at having previously failed to establish decisive control over the eastern Mediterranean. He conquered the Mediterranean pirates and swept away Mithradates, Tigranes, and the remnants of the Seleucid dynasty in Syria. He also stopped the civil war in Jerusalem and established the initial Roman control over Judea and Galilee, which culminated in the reign of Herod thirty years later.

The unrest caused by the political, military, and economic dominance of the Romans, which affected all eastern peoples, had a major impact on Jews in Judea and Galilee from 63 B.C.E. right through their two wars with Rome: the Great War against Rome (66–70 C.E.), in which the temple was destroyed, and the Bar Kosiba War (132–5 C.E.), following which the city was given a pagan name and the temple replaced by a pagan shrine. The strong and expansionary reign of Alexander Jannaeus (103–76 B.C.E.) and the relatively stable rule of his wife, Alexandra (76–67), dissolved amid previously suppressed, inter-

THE FIRST TRIUMVIRATE

IN THE ROMAN REPUBLIC, boards of three men (*tresviri;* popularly in English, "triumvirate") were often appointed to govern or administer public matters. The so-called first triumvirate of Pompey, Julius Caesar, and Crassus was really a political coalition formed in 60 B.C.E. and not a legal triumvirate. From 130 B.C.E. on, the traditional artistocratic senatorial class in Rome had been struggling to keep control in the face of a loose coalition of popular forces and leaders. The popular forces wanted political power, administrative reforms in the face of corruption, and increased economic benefits. The senatorial party could neither satisfy the people of Italy nor successfully manage Rome's colonies and frequent wars. A series of civil wars and revolutions caused enormous bloodshed, civil unrest, and disorder.

In the sixties Pompey, a member of the senatorial party, gained a mandate to bring order to the eastern Mediterranean and in the process conquered Palestine. In Rome Julius Caesar, a high-born noble, and Marcus Licinius Crassus, who had been a consul with Pompey, dominated Roman politics and succeeded in placating all sides. Pompey entered into an informal coalition with them and for a few years they shared power peacefully. Caesar conquered Gaul (present France) during the fifties and Crassus was killed fighting the Parthians in the east in 53. Meanwhile, Pompey had mismanaged the government of Rome and used the resulting chaos to acquire dictatorial powers. Caesar's faction under Mark Antony fled north from Rome to join Caesar and his army in 49. Caesar marched on Rome and Pompey fled to Greece, where he was defeated in battle. Pompey was murdered in Egypt. Caesar became the most powerful leader, but not officially emperor. He was assassinated in 44 and replaced by the second triumvirate (see p. 369).

nal tensions. Two of their sons, the energetic Aristobulus and the ineffective high priest Hyrcanus, fought for control. Hyrcanus was aided by the ambitious, non-Jewish Antipater, who had been appointed governor of Idumea by Alexander Jannaeus and who, along with his sons Herod and Phasael, had continually accumulated power. Antipater recruited Aretas, the Arab king of Nabatea (across the Jordan River), to besiege Aristobulus in Jerusalem. The Roman general Scaurus, who had been sent to Damascus by Pompey, ordered the siege lifted, but Antipater continued the conflict by appealing to Pompey. After much political intrigue over who would rule – Aristobulus or Hyrcanus – Aristobulus fled Pompey's camp to Jerusalem in a bid to take control of the situation. Eventually Pompey, whom the people allowed into the city in 63 B.C.E., captured Aristobulus and besieged his supporters on the temple mount for three months with a great loss of life. Aristobulus and his family were sent to Rome, the walls were breached, and Pompey sacrilegiously entered the Holy of Holies. Any semblance of Jewish independence in the ancient world permanently ended as Galilee and Judea once again became part of the dominant empire in the Near East. However, Pompey did not plunder or destroy the temple or dismantle the Jewish leadership in Jerusalem. He reduced the power of the Jewish state by separating the cities and territories of the Mediterranean coast, Samaria, and Transjordan from Jewish rule and left only the Jewish areas – Jerusalem, Judea, Idumea, and Galilee – under the control of the last Hasmonean high priest, Hyrcanus, with Antipater as the real power behind the throne. The existence of a Roman colony in Jerusalem prevented the rebuilding of the walls and discouraged revolt. This fulfilled the policy of both the Romans and the sympathetic Greek city-states surrounding Judea, who sought stability and the end of a strong Jewish state which could threaten the regional peace and take independent action.

The Roman invasion and Pompey's entry into the Holy of Holies in the temple put a terrible strain on Jewish society and exacerbated the tensions which had already become manifest in the civil wars after Alexandra's death. Both the political conflicts and the literature of the period reveal many factions and political interest groups competing for power and moved by different visions of what a Jewish state should be. The desire to be independent and the popularity of the Hasmoneans did not end immediately. Some of the Jews supported Hyrcanus; some, Aristobulus and his sons; others wanted a theocracy and an end to Hasmonean rule, which they considered illegitimate. A few years after Pompey had set up the new order, Aristobulus and his sons, Alexander and Antigonus, who had escaped Roman custody, led several insurrections against the Romans but were defeated and recaptured (57–55 B.C.E.). At this time Gabinius, the Roman governor in Syria, completed the dismantling of Hasmonean power and the Jewish nation. He removed all political power from Hyrcanus by restricting him to high priestly duties in the temple, and he established five districts, each with a local council charged with keeping order and collecting tribute. This more direct Roman rule resulted in further oppression and conflict. Crassus, the new Roman governor, took the temple

ADMINISTRATIVE REORGANIZATION OF PALESTINE

FOLLOWING POMPEY'S domination of Coele-Syria ca. 66 B.C.E., Judea and indeed much of the Roman east were reorganized – an arrangement of Asia Minor and Judea that was still in force in the third century C.E. according to Dio Cassius. Pliny's letters from the second century C.E. also reveal some of the provisions of the *Lex Pompeia*. Palestine was reorganized ca. 55 B.C.E. by one of Pompey's generals, Gabinius. Gabinius divided Palestine into five administrative districts, each with a capital city and *synedrion*, composed of local nobles. This deprived the Hasmonean lords of any *de jure* authority and placed it instead in the hands of the people selected or approved by Gabinius. Many cities and villages had been destroyed during the fighting and sieges of 65–63. It was Gabinius who a few years later began in earnest the real work of restoration in Palestine.

Galilee was one of the administrative districts, with Sepphoris as its capital. Judea proper was another, with Jerusalem as its capital. Jericho, Gadara, and Amathus were three other cities along the Jordan Valley that were administrative capitals. Scythopolis was an important center for Pompey and Gabinius and was the largest member and the capital city of the Decapolis league of Greek cities (see the discussion in Josephus, *Antiquities* 14.4.4 and *Jewish War* 1.7.7). This reorganization imposed an order and administrative structure on Palestine that would endure for several centuries.

IMPORTANCE OF PALESTINE IN THE ROMAN EMPIRE

PALESTINE EMERGED AS A very important region within the Roman Empire in the time of Pompey. This was so for several reasons. (1) Palestine held significant strategic importance because of the ongoing struggle along the eastern border of the empire with the Parthians. Palestine and the region immediately east of it were essential military sites for Roman legions and defense. Sepphoris, Scythopolis, and Legio are examples of important Roman military sites during this period.

(2) Palestine, and Galilee in particular, were centers of trade. The Roman road system from this time reflects the large amount of goods that came through Palestine from the east, from the Decapolis, and from Arabia, and headed to the Mediterranean and on to Rome. Wine, grapes, balsam, and olive oil were a few of the exports from Palestine valued throughout the empire. During this period western Palestine and Galilee were among the most densely populated regions of the entire empire.

(3) The tremendous building programs and the founding of cities in Palestine initiated by Herod the Great and others in places like Sepphoris, Tiberias, and Caesarea, and of course the Jerusalem temple, stand even today as monuments to the importance and vitality of Palestine within the Roman Empire during this period.

treasure to finance his campaign against the Parthians in the east (54 B.C.E.), and in succeeding years the country needed constant "pacification."

The war between Julius Caesar and Pompey for control of Rome ended with the defeat of Pompey at Pharsalus in eastern Greece (49 B.C.E.) and his subsequent murder in Egypt. When Caesar had gained control of the empire, he confirmed Hyrcanus as high priest and made him "ethnarch" (i.e., leader of a nation or ethnic group), thus restoring the governing powers Gabinius had taken away from him. Antipater was appointed custodian (*epitropos*) of Judea, with responsibility for collecting the Roman tribute. Judea was enlarged to include Jaffa and some villages in the Esdraelon Plain in the north. In fact, Antipater ruled Judea, and his son Phasael was governor (*strategos*) in Jerusalem. Herod (often called Herod the Great to distinguish him from other family members with the same name) was governor in Galilee and later in Coele Syria to the north and Samaria to the south. During this time Herod killed the bandits who were causing disruption in Galilee and defied the Jerusalem council, which wished to exercise control over him and bring him to account for exceeding his authority (Josephus, *Antiquities* 14:163–84). Thus, during the gradual extension of Roman authority, the dissolution of the Hasmonean rule in Palestine, and the disorder and civil war among Rome's rulers, the family of the Idumean Antipater continued to gain power and to erode the influence of the traditional rulers of Judaism – the priests, wealthy families, and respected officials and elders. A myriad of reform and protest movements, including the Jesus movement, filled the leadership gap left by the weakened traditional patterns of community organization and produced many social conflicts, the greatest of which was the war with Rome in 66 C.E.

B. LITERARY RESPONSES TO ROMAN AND HELLENISTIC CULTURE

The Roman dominance in the eastern Mediterranean was so absolute and their presence so pervasive that political protest literature was common. Many Jewish works adapted biblical and adopted hellenistic forms of expression in order to deplore the Roman conquest, to protest the rule of the nations over Israel, and to envision the triumph of God and his people. The anger and resistance to the Romans and the divisions in Jewish society caused by different responses to altered circumstances were similar to those of the hellenistic period (whose cultural legacy the Romans adopted) and continued through the lifetime of Jesus and into the second century. Jewish literature from the Roman period, much of it from unknown authors or groups, shows the depth of Jewish feeling and explains the revolts against the Romans as well as the thirst for reform and renewal that nurtured many Jewish movements, including the Jesus movement. Some Jews cooperated with the Romans out of fear of their awesome power (e.g., Herod, Josephus), some tried to live quietly with as little contact as possible, some with-

DIVISIONS WITHIN JEWISH SOCIETY

THE FIRST CENTURY B.C.E. was a period characterized by factionalism and splinter groups within Jewish society. This was a period of military struggle and expansion, as well as shifting political loyalties and power. Alliances and reactionary groups were formed in response to the various groups in power. The literature of these factions reflects the animosity and deep divisions typifying this period in Jewish history.

For example, the scrolls from the Dead Sea community reflect a disdain for the "false" priests occupying the Jerusalem temple. They are corrupt leaders who have betrayed God. The Psalms of Solomon, from the mid–first century B.C.E., clearly reflect another community rejecting those in power and seeing itself as the true carrier of God's word and will. The First Book of Enoch 93ff. may date to the period of the Maccabean revolt, but it also captures the later division and conflict between various groups within Jewish society.

These internal struggles and divisions should not be underestimated in terms of their impact on the communities and documents from this period. These documents played a crucial role in defining each respective group, in legitimating each group's position and beliefs and contrasting them with those of their opponents, and in instructing group members about the "true" understanding of God's law and will for God's people. The documents from this period reflect the divisions within Jewish society and the subsequent struggle and competition among these groups.

drew from full social life, some protested in word or deed, and some sought amelioration of social conditions through reform.

1. The Psalms of Solomon

The Psalms of Solomon, a collection of eighteen psalms, are a response to the Roman invasion of Jerusalem in 63 B.C.E. and events in subsequent decades:

> Arrogantly the sinner broke down the strong walls with a battering
> ram and you did not interfere.
> gentile foreigners went up to your place of sacrifice; they arrogantly
> trampled (it) with their sandals. . . .
> For the gentiles insulted Jerusalem, trampling (her) down; he dragged
> her beauty down from the throne of glory.   (Pss. Sol. 2:1–2, 19)

This coded reference to Pompey's capture of Jerusalem (described also in Pss. Sol. 8 and 17) is closely linked with condemnation of the sins of the Jerusalem leaders, which caused the temple to be defiled and the people to suffer:

> They stole from the sanctuary of God as if there were no redeeming
> heir.
> They walked on the place of sacrifice of the Lord, (coming) from all
> kinds of uncleanness;
> And (coming) with menstrual blood (on them), they defiled the sacri-
> fices as if they were common meat.
> There was no sin they left undone in which they did not surpass the
> gentiles.   (Pss. Sol. 8:11–13)

The author understands the shocking loss of control over the temple and government as well as the profanation of the temple as just pun-

Roman theater at Bet She'an.
J. Andrew Overman.

ishment for the failures of the priests and other leaders. In reality the actions of Pompey and those of the warring Jewish leaders who appealed to him to settle their disputes were the same. Both the Jewish leaders and Pompey treated the people violently, stole from them, and failed to preserve the ritual purity and holiness of God's temple.

The purpose of the psalms is to affirm the justice of God and ask God to save Israel from gentile control, oppression, and injustice. The psalms were written in the decades following the conquest of Jerusalem (Pss. Sol. 2:27–9 refers to the murder of Pompey in 48 B.C.E.). They reflect the pain of the Jewish community under Roman occupation, the crisis of confidence in God, who allowed a century of independence to end with gentile control, and the complex political and religious conflicts among various Jewish groups over how the community should adapt and survive. Though neither the author's community nor the wicked Jews he opposes are identified explicitly, those singled out for condemnation had public power and were probably rich and influential citizens who cooperated with the Romans, who compromised the Jewish way of life (as understood by Pss. Sol.), and who oppressed faithful Jews in various ways:

> The words of the wicked man's tongue (are) twisted so many ways. . . .
> His visit fills homes with a false tongue, cuts down trees of joy, inflaming criminals; by slander he incites homes to fighting. . . .
> May the Lord protect the quiet person who hates injustice; may the Lord guide the person who lives peacefully at home. . . .
> And may the Lord's devout inherit the Lord's promises.
>
> (Pss. Sol. 12:2–3, 5–6)

> And the children of the covenant (living) among the gentile rabble adopted these (idolatrous practices).

No one among them in Jerusalem acted (with) mercy or truth.
Those who loved the assemblies of the devout fled from them as sparrows flee from their nest.   (Pss. Sol. 17:15–16)

Numerous parallels in phrase and thought between the Psalms of Solomon and the biblical Psalms and prophets indicate that the author drew inspiration from the Bible and articulated the community's needs by adapting traditional literary modes of expression. The Psalms of Solomon's prayer for God's mercy on faithful Israelites is coupled with confidence that God will judge and punish evil Jews and gentiles (Pss. Sol. 9–10, 13–15). The responsibility of individual Jews to resist temptation and remain faithful to God's way of life under duress depends on God's mercy (Pss. Sol. 16), but those who reject God will be destroyed.

The power of the Romans was so great and the plight of the faithful so desperate ("When a person is tried by his mortality, your testing is in his flesh, and in the difficulty of poverty"; Pss. Sol. 16:14) that the author anticipates, not a military victory over the Romans or political reform, but the coming of a messiah (anointed one) like David to reinstitute God's just rule, to drive out evil gentiles and Jewish sinners, to purge Jerusalem and make it holy, and to rule over just Israelites and all the nations:

He will gather a holy people whom he will lead in righteousness;
and he will judge the tribes of the people that have been made holy by
    the Lord their God.
He will not tolerate unrighteousness (even) to pause among them.
For he shall know them that they are all children of their God. . . .
the alien and foreigner will no longer live near them.
He will judge peoples and nations in the wisdom of his righteousness. . . .

Kidron Valley and tomb of Absalom from Jerusalem's walls.
Anthony J. Saldarini.

And he will purge Jerusalem (and make it) holy as it was even from
   the beginning. . . .
There will be no unrighteousness among them in his days,
for all will be holy, and their king shall be the Lord Messiah.

(Pss. Sol. 17:26–32)

Psalms of Solomon 17 envisions divine intervention in Israel and Jerusalem through a leader anointed by God so that Israel may live a secure and just life as promised in the Bible. The author, using apocalyptic themes and images, can imagine the overthrow of the Romans and the rectification of Israelite social and political life only through extraordinary leadership, beyond that of the Hasmonean high priests or any other traditional forces in Jewish society.

Both the antipathy to the Romans and the apocalyptic hopes for a messiah and justice found in the Psalms of Solomon are typical of Jewish and early Christian works during the Roman period. Jewish society was characterized by diverse political and social policies and hopes for the future based on differing interpretations of Jewish life and responses to external oppression. The major themes of the Psalms of Solomon were common to many groups, parties, and movements, whose names we lack. The author and community which produced this particular configuration of traditional themes felt oppressed by both the Romans and the Jewish authorities, disapproved of many Jewish practices, which they viewed as assimilationist, and hoped for God-given justice in the future. Since condemnation of the temple and its priests is implied by these charges of impurity and theft in the temple, the author and audience probably did not belong to the governing classes.

The polemics against fellow Jews in the Psalms of Solomon resemble the polemics between Jews and Christians found in the New Testament. Conflicts over purity, relations with the gentile government, and social relations continued from the time of the Psalms of Solomon until Jesus and the time of the early Christian community. Hope for God's justice, brought by a powerful emissary, was transmuted by the early Christian community into faith in Jesus as the Messiah. These traditional modes of expression and

MESSIAH

"MESSIAH" IS AN ANGLIcized form of the Hebrew word *mashiah*, meaning "anointed one." The Greek translation of this term is *christos* (English "Christ"). Even by the time of Paul in the 50s the messianic title had become so closely associated with Jesus that "Christ" had become part of his name (e.g., 1 Cor. 1:1–4). Because Christians saw Jesus the Messiah as so important for faith, salvation, and eschatology, they assumed that the expectation of a messiah was central and clear in Judaism. This, however, is not the case.

In the Bible the "anointed ones" – that is, those officials anointed as a sign of their being chosen for, and initiated into, office – are the king and high priest. The figure of a suprahuman and ideal anointed leader gradually appeared in *some* second temple Jewish literature; more often God was the savior and ruler of Israel without the presence of an anointed one. In some texts the transcendent leader is called by other titles, such as son of man, the Elect One, or a "prophet like Moses." Where a Messiah or messianic figure appears, he has varied characteristics. In some texts he fights against the forces of evil; in others he arrives at the end time to rule over God's kingdom; and in still others he rules over an interim kingdom and then gives the rule to God (see this tradition in Rev. 20). In some Dead Sea Scrolls two Messiahs are expected, corresponding to the two categories of membership in the community: a priestly Messiah and a Davidic (lay) Messiah. At no time during the Greco-Roman period did any single, unified messianic expectation dominate and motivate Jewish society.

the hopes associated with them were drawn from the literature of the Maccabean period and its antecedents. The contrast between the devout and sinners in Judaism is found in 2 Maccabees and many other works, while the concern for the poor and weak with concomitant condemnation of the strong and corrupt has a pedigree stretching back to the Israelite prophets.

2.   The War Scroll

The conflicts within Jewish society and with the empires are clearest in the Dead Sea Scrolls, which refer to the Romans under the symbolic name "Kittim" (Num. 24:24). The Habakkuk Pesher, which recounts the community's history from the mid–second century on, alludes to a fearful, warrior people from the islands of the sea who will cruelly dominate Israel (1QpHab 3–4, 6:1–2) and will be used by God to punish the "last priests" of Jerusalem. The subjection of Jerusalem, the trials of the Hasmonean high priestly family in its last decades, and the continual conflicts with Roman authority seem to be the focus of the author's reflection. The description of the Roman weight on Jewish society fits the power struggles and disorder that followed Pompey's conquest and that received an unattractive resolution in Herod's authoritarian rule in the latter part of the century.

The War Scroll ("The War of the Sons of Light with the Sons of Darkness") is one of the Dead Sea Scrolls that depicts a final, eschatological battle that ranges Michael and the forces of good (angelic forces and the Qumran community) against Beliar and the forces of evil, which include the Kittim, other nations, and apostate Jews. The author imagines the battle as a holy war in which ritual purity is observed, highly symbolic banners are carried, appropriate prayers and hymns are recited, curses hurled, and battle formations maintained. The course of the battle is rehearsed in great detail, with the forces of good suffering reverses before divine intervention produces a final victory. The details of weapons and tactics fit those of the Roman army and suggest that the War Scroll, which is a composite document, was written when Roman military might had been felt in the Near East and probably after the Roman conquest. The War Scroll assumes a complete and utter rejection of the Romans and all other unjust peoples but cannot envision overcoming them through ordinary political means. Only apocalyptic imagery for divine power can depict the force needed to overcome the Romans. The author's sense of helplessness before the Roman might is ironically conveyed in the use of Roman tactics and weapons by the angelic armies against the Romans themselves. The detailed military descriptions bespeak the author's vivid awareness of Roman military power, frustration with its oppressive rule, and fervent hope for its eventual destruction.

C.   ALEXANDRIA

1.   3 Maccabees

Jewish writings from communities outside Palestine reflect fear of the power and arrogance of the gentiles, yet accept the gentile world and hope for a secure place in it. The Book of 3 Maccabees is a Jewish story of the first century B.C.E. written in Alexandria in Egypt. The language is florid and emotional and the plot dramatic in the style of a hellenistic romance. The author affirms the loyalty of the Jewish community to the Egyptian government even while assailing the injustice of the king's actions; in the end the Jewish community returns to its honored place in Egyptian society. The author supports fidelity to traditional Jewish customs, including the food laws and modes of worship, and is devoted to the temple in Jerusalem. Egyptian Jews are pictured as reasonable and valuable citizens whose elders restrain the younger community members who wish to "die courageously for the ancestral law" (3 Macc. 1:22–3), a position that contrasts sharply with that of the Palestinian community, which encouraged its people to fight for the law and independence (1 Macc. 2:40–1; 3:21, 13:3–4; 2 Macc. 8:21). The uncertainty of Jewish life in Egypt, the prejudice and cruelty of gentiles, and the suffering of the community make up the bulk of the story, but the arrogance and power of the gentiles is offset by the holiness and mercy of God, to which the Jewish community appeals. The gentile persecutions of the Jews have many patterns and traditions in common with 2 Maccabees, though the setting is different because Egyptian Jews, as a minority, cannot envision revolt and independence.

The main character in the story of 3 Maccabees is the Egyptian king Ptolemy IV Philopater (221–205 B.C.E.), who acts arrogantly against God, is rendered insane by God, and finally repents of his hostility to the Jews. The king is not admirable, but his is the controlling power with which the Jews must deal, so in the end he is rehabilitated as a supporter of the Jewish community. According to the narrative, during Ptolemy's triumphant tour after his defeat of the Seleucid king Antiochus III at Raphia in 217 B.C.E., he visited the temple of his Jewish allies in Jerusalem and wished to inspect the whole temple, including the Holy of Holies. Neither emotional outbursts from the people nor the prayer of the high priest, Onias II (219–196 B.C.E.), changed his mind. Only the intervention of an angel stopped the king from entering the Holy of Holies. (see 2 Macc. 3 for a similar story.) Because the king's arrogance and determination were thwarted by the Jewish God, he returned to Egypt determined to punish the Jewish community. He offered the Jews the choice of sacrificing to Egyptian gods or being registered as slaves, taxed, and branded (3 Macc. 2:25–30). The author notes that the deep hostility of the gentiles was aroused by the king's anger, which sought the destruction of the Jews (3 Macc. 4:1, 16). The author maintains that Jews are good citizens and never envisions Jewish attacks on gentiles (contrary to Esther, 1–2 Macc., etc.). At the end, apostate Jews – "those who transgressed the law of God" – not hostile gentiles, are killed by the newly enfranchised Jewish community in order to maintain internal discipline and fidelity to God and Crown (3 Macc. 2:31, 7:10–15). According to the author, gentile hostility is based on misunderstanding of Jewish dietary and worship laws (3 Macc. 3:4–7), and Jews are really loyal subjects (3 Macc. 3:8, 7:11).

The body of the story recounts with great emotion, exaggeration, and slapstick humor how Jews were gathered from the whole country, how they were too numerous to count, how God caused mental confusion in the king so he forgot that he meant to have them trampled to death by drugged elephants, and finally how the drugged elephants turned on the king's troops. As in Esther and Daniel, the disaster that threatens the community is averted by trust in God, prayer, and divine intervention so that the community may maintain both its fidelity to God's law and its loyalty to the Crown. Though the story is replete with Exodus themes, including persecution, deliverance, divine manipulation of the king, and liturgical remembrance (3 Macc. 6:30–6 refers to an Alexandrian festival commemorating a deliverance), the gentile king is not destroyed nor is Israel liberated. Like other Diaspora stories, 3 Maccabees seeks the patronage of the king and good relations with the gentile majority, rather than revolt, independence, or Jewish dominance. Consequently, though Ptolemy has been portrayed as arrogant, unstable, and vindictive, he cannot be removed but must be rehabilitated by a very imperfect repentance when frightened by two angels (3 Macc. 6:18–23). Peaceful relations with the established powers, however fragile and grudging, must be maintained.

2.   Additions to Esther

The Hebrew story of Esther (see above, pp. 268–270) is similar to 3 Maccabees in narrative patterns and underlying attitudes. Gentile hostility to Jews because of their customs, the threat of total destruction, the battle for the king's mind, and the royal change of heart are all present, but in a greatly different context. The Book of Esther has no direct divine intervention and does not even mention God's name directly. Court intrigue and competition between Jews and gentiles is more prominent, and Esther keeps her nationality secret so that she may marry the king. In the end the gentile enemies of the Jews, but not the king, are destroyed.

During the hellenistic period additions were made to the Book of Esther. Some may have been added to the Hebrew Book of Esther and then translated into Greek, and others (or perhaps all) were written in Greek. They have survived only in the Greek translation of Esther and date from either 114 or 77 B.C.E. according to a translator's note preserved at the end of Greek Esther. Several verbal similarities with 3 Maccabees suggest a literary relationship. The revised Book of Esther functioned like 3 Maccabees in the Alexandrian community as a guide and encouragement to Jews seeking to survive and remain loyal in an indifferent or hostile gentile world. The revised Esther, like other rewritten biblical texts, encouraged and guided Jews to be loyal to their traditions and trust in God during times of distress.

The additions to the Book of Esther make God's activity in the story explicit and the narrative more dramatic and emotional, in the hellenistic mode. Mordecai, the Jewish protagonist, has a symbolic dream depicting his struggle with Haman, the Persian opponent of the Jews. This dream makes the danger to the Jewish community patent and serves as an introduction to the story. An interpretation of the dream ends the book, so that the dream functions as a summary of the story and, as in Daniel and other works, as a witness to God's power and providence in history. In another of the additions, Esther prays at length to God that she will succeed in convincing the king to void the decree of destruction against the Jews. The prayer makes clear Esther's commitment to and submission to God as well as God's influence on the events of history. Esther's audience with the king is expanded into a dramatic and emotional confrontation similar to those found in Greek romances. Both the prayer and the audience with the king reveal the inner attitudes and emotions of the leading characters, a dimension of the story missing in the semitic original but literarily necessary in the hellenistic world. The Greek audience's assent to the story is sought in two extensive royal decrees, written in florid and rhetorical Greek, in which the king condemns and then exonerates the Jews. The decrees make the story more believable and authoritative for hellenistic Jews and allow a review of the typical anti-Jewish propaganda, which charged Jews with being hostile to the kingdom's laws and unity because of their exclusive customs. In response to these charges in the first decree of destruction, the second decree, which rehabilitates the Jews, makes clear that they are loyal and good citizens. Relations between Jews and the gentile majority (Persians in the narrative; Greeks in the actual social setting of the book's audience) remain tense and unresolved. Esther's cloaking of her nationality and her marriage to the king did not fit the hellenistic Jewish pattern, nor was her fidelity to Jewish law patent to hellenistic readers. The author of the Greek additions has Esther explain in her prayer that she keeps the dietary laws and submits to sexual relations with the king only out of duty (14:15–18). The author also reveals his resentment against his Greek overlords when he has the king identify Haman as a Macedonian (Greek) rather than as an "Agagite" (as the Hebrew has it in Esther 10:24). The author also emphasizes the original story's plot, in which the Jews avenge themselves on their gentile enemies (16:10–20).

3. Joseph and Aseneth

Egyptian Jews had a variety of responses to the surrounding gentile culture. The story of Joseph and Aseneth, an expansion of the biblical story of Joseph the son of Jacob in Genesis 37–50, resolves the tensions with the gentile world by the conversion of the gentiles and the triumph of monotheism and Jewish laws over gentile practices. The Bible simply states that Joseph married "Asenath," the daughter of an Egyptian priest (Gen. 41:45), without explaining the rationale for a mixed marriage. But in the story of Joseph and Aseneth, a Greek tale replete with the high drama and intense emotion characteristic of Greek romances, Aseneth is converted to Judaism. Her conversion is explained in such a way that the superiority of monotheism, Jewish dietary customs, and ethical norms is made manifest and the boundaries between Jews and gentiles are clearly maintained. This work was probably written in the first century B.C.E. or C.E. in Alexandria. Aseneth's name, which connects her with the Egyptian goddess Neith, the sun imagery used in the description of Joseph, the heavenly honeycomb that Aseneth eats, and many other symbolic features of the text allude to the clash between Jewish and Egyptian religion. Before they meet, the Egyptian Aseneth is hostile to Joseph. When she falls in love with him, many of her Egyptian practices and beliefs must be changed. Aseneth's prayers and practices leading to repentance and Joseph's dialogues with her make clear the inferiority of idolatry in the face of monotheism, the importance of sexual and dietary purity according to the Jewish laws that separate Jews and gentiles, the socially just and benevolent ethics of the Jewish community, and the ultimate promise of immortality that awaits the faithful. This work assumes close contacts between Jews and gentiles and promotes firm boundaries to preserve Jewish identity. The relations between Jews and gentiles are peaceful; Joseph is a high Egyptian official, and in the only hostilities depicted in the book, between Joseph and some of his brothers in the last section (chaps. 22–9), Jews and gentiles are found on each side of the struggle.

Both Joseph and Aseneth are exaggerated as ideal types. Aseneth is a highborn, wealthy, and beautiful Egyptian who has carefully preserved her virginity and proudly rejected all suitors. Her only vice is an arrogant attachment to Egyptian idols and ways of life. Joseph, the pharoah's regent, meets Aseneth while gathering crops for the approaching famine. Aseneth resists her parents' desire for her to marry Joseph until she sees him and is smitten. Aseneth, the best Egypt has to offer, becomes subordinate to Joseph. When she desires to kiss Joseph, a symbol of the union of the two cultures, he refuses her because she, though an upright virgin, is impure in her worship and dictary habits. The course of Aseneth's conversion includes fasting, sackcloth, visions, giving alms, rejection of luxury, giving up of certain food and other impure items, the destruction of her idols, and an angelic appearance during which she is fed a heavenly honeycomb which symbolizes pure bread, wine, and oil as well as immortality. Her new name, "City of Refuge" and her marriage to Joseph, sanctioned by pharaoh, suggest a political and communal stability that can only be reached through gentile understanding and acceptance of Judaism. The final incident, in which pharaoh's son and four of Joseph's brothers attack Aseneth and are defeated by the other brothers and by divine intervention, suggests both opposition to the author's vision in the Jewish and gentile communities and his confidence in divine favor.

Unlike 3 Maccabees and the additions to Esther, Joseph and Aseneth does not focus on the threat of persecution but on the dangers and opportunities presented by contact between Jews and gentiles. Jewish superiority to gentiles is asserted in such a way that Jewish influence,

THE GREEK NOVEL (ROMANCE) AND POLITICAL APOLOGETIC

A NUMBER OF LONG compositions in rhetorical prose that contain elements of storytelling, history, mythology, legend, and oratory are called novels or romances. Many other narratives are associated with this very loose "genre." Some aspects of the narratives concern divine–human relations and thus are related to myths; others concern social and political affairs and are thus similar to historical and political writings. Some of the heroic and tragic stories in 2–4 Maccabees, Joseph and Aseneth, as well as the writings of some Jewish hellenistic writers used story and rhetoric to glorify their tradition, defend it in the face of hellenistic culture, and render it attractive to its adherents.

rather than Jewish military strength or independence from gentile control, gives the community stability and confidence in an alien world. In all these works great stress is put on faithfulness to the Jewish way of life and on prayer for God's aid, which is granted either directly or in the course of events.

4.   The Prayer of Manasseh

The Book of 3 Maccabees, the additions to Esther, and Joseph and Aseneth are all notable for the long and emotional prayers of repentance addressed to God in times of stress. The Prayer of Manasseh is found in the Septuagint, the Greek translation of the Bible made by Jews in the Diaspora, and is recognized as canonical in the Orthodox churches. Though the Hebrew Bible excoriates Manasseh for his idolatry and blames the eventual destruction of Jerusalem on him (2 Kings 21), Chronicles says that he was taken by the Assyrians into exile in Babylon, repented of his sins, and was returned to Jerusalem (2 Chron. 33:18–19). The Hebrew text refers to a prayer of Manasseh and says that it is recorded elsewhere; the Greek Prayer of Manasseh provides an appropriate prayer to supplement the text of Chronicles. The prayer is a simple invocation of God in his power, an appeal to his mercy toward sinners who repent, a confession of many sins, a cry for forgiveness, and a promise to praise God. This prayer, as well as numerous prayers in other Diaspora and Palestinian works, reflects the fundamental relationship of Jews to their God, even in times of personal, community, or national trouble. No matter how grave the sin or how perilous the situation, God remains near his people and will respond to the repentant sinner, such as Manasseh or Aseneth, and to the faithful community, such as that depicted in Psalms of Solomon or 3 Maccabees. This prayer shares the common hellenistic and biblical heritage of Jews and Christians, repentant and trusting before their God.

IV.   HEROD

Herod's rise to power coincided with the end of the Hasmonean dynasty, the defeat of invading Parthians (Rome's competing empire in Mesopotamia), and the emergence of a single emperor in Rome. His continuance in power depended on his ability to bring stability to Palestine and to placate a succession of powerful Roman rulers. Herod, who was at times a decadent and arbitrary tyrant, was also an energetic and brave military commander, a ruthless and effective political leader, and an efficient economic and social administrator. He was supported by the Romans because he was able to collect taxes, keep the peace, and provide military support at the border of the empire. He remained loyal to the Romans because he had sense enough to know that he could not successfully revolt against Rome. At the same time he was a typical hellenistic despot who killed his opponents. Culturally he was a Roman more than a Jew, and he was of mixed Idumean and Jewish parentage. He succeeded in carving out relative security and independence for his people within the empire, a task that the next two Jewish generations failed to accomplish, with catastrophic results for the Jewish nation, Jerusalem, and the temple.

In 44 B.C.E., Julius Caesar was murdered in Rome. Cassius controlled the eastern empire. Herod, with his father and brother, helped Cassius by collecting taxes to support his army. During this period of Roman civil strife, when Roman control in the East weakened, Herod's father, Antipater, was assassinated, and the Hasmonean Antigonus son of Aristobulus invaded Galilee from Chalcis in the north. However, Herod defeated Antigonus and retained control of his Galilean territory. In 42 B.C.E. Mark Antony, a member of the second triumvirate, defeated Brutus and Cassius at Philippi and demanded a heavy indemnity from their supporters in the East. Herod and his brother Phasael paid the tax and kept their governorships in Palestine but incurred great resentment from the people from whom they exacted the money. When the Parthians took advantage of Roman weakness and disorganization on their eastern border and invaded Syria, Palestine, and the coast in 40 B.C.E., the people revolted against Herod and the other authorities. Phasael was captured and committed suicide, and Hyrcanus, the high priest, the nominal leader of Judaism, was mutilated so he could no longer serve as high priest. Herod escaped to Petra across the Jordan, and Antigonus was made king in Jerusalem by the Parthians (40–37 B.C.E.).

While the Parthians controlled Palestine, Herod went to Rome and was appointed king of Judea, Idumea, Galilee, and Perea in 40 B.C.E. But first he had to recover his kingdom. In 39 the Roman legions drove off the Parthians and Herod returned to Palestine. First Herod cleaned out the bandits in the caves of Galilee, showing great personal bravery in the campaign. Herod began his reign as king in fact in 37, when Antony sent the general Sosius with an army from Syria to take

THE SECOND TRIUMVIRATE

AFTER JULIUS CAESAR'S assassination by the Senate in 44 B.C., Mark Antony, his protégé, and Gaius Octavius (Octavian), his adopted son and heir, formed an alliance to gain control of Rome. Along with Lepidus, the governor of Gaul and Spain, they were given absolute power. They killed over two thousand members of the Republican faction, which had opposed Julius Caesar, and pursued his assassins to the eastern Mediterranean. Octavian ruled Italy and surrounding areas, and Mark Antony ruled the eastern Mediterranean, where he entered into his famous liaison with Cleopatra, the ruler of Egypt. In 36 Octavian forced the retirement of Lepidus, and in 31 he defeated Antony in a sea battle at Actium and thus centralized all power in himself. He was recognized as emperor, taking the name Caesar Augustus, and thoroughly reorganized the Roman Empire.

The harbor at Caesarea Maritima.

H. Keith Beebe.

THE ROMANS AND THE PARTHIANS

WHEN POMPEY CONquered the remnants of the Seleucid Empire and incorporated Syria into the Roman Empire as its eastern border, Rome began a series of clashes with the expanding empire of the Parthians, who controlled the northern Iranian plateau and Mesopotamia. In the mid–third century B.C.E., the nomadic Parni tribe migrated from the steppes of Russia, through the mountains between the Caspian and Aral Seas, and into the Seleucid satrapy of Parthia (Parthava). There they assimilated some hellenistic culture and wavered between independence and incorporation into the Seleucid Empire. Antiochus III fought and defeated them in 210 but had to settle for an alliance with the Parthian king as a vassal. Seleucid control over the eastern end of Alexander's empire was tenuous and perfunctory; the vassal kingdoms there were constantly threatened by nomadic invaders from the north. Under Mithradates I and his successors (from 171 on) the Parthians gradually gained control of most of the territory from the Euphrates to the Indus and kept probing westward toward Syria and Asia Minor. In 53 B.C.E. they destroyed a Roman army led by Crassus at Carrhae. In 40, during the confusion after the assassination of Julius Caesar, they briefly invaded Syria and Palestine. They, and their Persian Sassanian successors in the third century C.E., remained a permanent threat to the eastern border of the Roman Empire. Consequently, the Roman province of Syria, to which Palestine was subordinate, was a senatorial province with a former consul as governor and a garrison of several legions. The security of Syria and Palestine was of the utmost importance to the Roman Empire. Mark Antony, Octavian, Tiberius, Nero, Trajan, and Septimius Severus all fought wars against the Parthians. Finally weakened in the third century, they succumbed to the rulers of the province of Persis, the Sassanians, who formed a new empire, which lasted until the Moslem conquest.

Jerusalem. Herod spent the rest of the decade putting down resistance to his rule in Palestine and neutralizing the political intrigues of Antony's Egyptian consort, Cleopatra, and the remnants of the Hasmonean family, both of whom sought to control Palestine. A Roman legion stationed in Jerusalem supported Herod's rule with force, while Herod sought to legitimize his rule by marrying the granddaughter of Hyrcanus and ransoming Hyrcanus from the Parthians. He controlled the high priesthood by appointing a non-Palestinian priest from Babylon who was totally dependent on him. After intense political pressure, he appointed Aristobulus III, a teenage grandson of Hyrcanus, as high priest, but so feared his popularity that he had him murdered in a year.

In 31 Herod overcame several crises that threatened his position and from then on ruled securely until the civil unrest of his final years. When the Nabatean kingdom across the Jordan, from whom Herod collected Roman taxes, withheld payment, Herod went to war with them and succeeded in subduing them only after the loss of a crucial battle and a hard-won victory in another. In this war he proved his ability as a general and reaffirmed his personal valor in battle. In the same year a disastrous earthquake destroyed the economic base in many of his cities and towns and disrupted the collection of taxes. Most critically, Herod's Roman patron in the East, Mark Antony, was defeated by Octavian at Actium in Greece (31 B.C.E.) and the empire was united under the new Caesar Augustus. The change in leadership put Herod's position as king in grave jeopardy, but Herod was able to confirm his position. First, he removed one possible rival by executing the aged Hyrcanus. Then he met the new emperor, Octavian, on

THE NABATEANS

THE NABATEANS WERE A nomadic Arab tribe participating in trade over the caravan routes running through Syria to the Gulf of Aqaba, Arabia, the Sinai, and the Red Sea. They gradually settled in outposts along the caravan routes, established relationships with the Ptolemies and Seleucids, and constructed a central stronghold in Petra, halfway between the Dead Sea and the Gulf of Aqaba. Their first king, Aretas I, dates from 169 B.C.E. Their inscriptions are in their own dialect of Aramaic, the lingua franca of the Near East, and in Greek; their art shows hellenistic influence. As the Seleucid dynasty broke up in the early first century B.C.E., the Nabateans gained more control in Transjordan, clashing frequently with the Hasmonean dynasty. In 85 B.C.E. Aretas III became ruler of Damascus. (The rule of one of his successors over Damascus is mentioned by Paul in 2 Cor. 11:32.) Subsequently, the Nabateans clashed with Rome and Herod. Nabatea was incorporated into the Roman province of Arabia under Trajan (106–7 C.E.) and gradually lost power as the trade routes shifted north.

Herod's kingdom and its stages of growth.

Colonnaded street at Petra.
H. Keith Beebe.

Rhodes and convinced him that he would continue to be loyal and efficient in governing Judea on behalf of Rome. Octavian was pleased to have Herod in control of this crucial land bridge between Syria and Egypt and confirmed him in his office.

Like other dependent native rulers, Herod was expected to collect taxes, to provide military supplies and troops as needed, but to leave all initiative in foreign policy to the Romans. Luckily no further major wars or disruptions took place in the East, so Herod was free to consolidate his power. Since his position in Palestine was totally dependent on the goodwill of Caesar Augustus, Herod cultivated close personal relations with the emperor and his major deputies, such as Agrippa. Herod built Greek cities with temples, arenas, and baths in honor of the emperor, most notably Caesarea on the coast and Sebaste in Samaria, as well as temples and other public facilities in other coastal cities. In a variety of Greek cities he gave frequent gifts, sponsored the construction of public baths and temples, supported the Olympics, and sponsored games every four years at Caesarea. His court was made up of many gentiles and hellenized Jews from the Diaspora, and he patronized the Greek arts and literature. In all this Herod acted like any other Greco-Roman leader and was respected and accepted by the Roman Empire as part of its governing class. He began to lose the emperor's support only late in his life, when he initiated a conflict against the Nabatean Arabs without Caesar's permission. In addition, as his health weakened, he lost control of his family and followers. Many family members and factions plotted to take power and were jailed by him or executed.

As might be expected, Herod, the successful hellenistic ruler, was far less than a proper Jewish ruler. He imposed burdensome taxes to support the grandiose lifestyle and policies demanded by his high status in the empire. He preserved a stable power base by savage and constant repression of any serious opposition. In his domestic policy Herod and his ruling clientele were no different from other gentile governing classes of that era. They supported the workings of empire and state by heavy taxes (often 50 percent or more) on the farmers, who made up the bulk of the population. Herod's kingdom was prosperous and peaceful, especially in contrast with the chaotic civil unrest in the last years of Hasmonean rule. The majority of the population, although not enthusiastic supporters of Herod, submitted to his rule out of fear and convenience.

During his lifetime Herod controlled political affairs by appointing the high priest, subordinating the *synedrion* (the ruling regional council) to his wishes, and appointing family members and relatives by marriage to all high posts. For many years his father-in-law, Simon son of Boethus from Alexandria, was the high priest. Pheroras, his younger brother, was appointed tetrarch of Perea by Caesar Augustus, and other districts were governed by relatives. The independent cities in his reign were attached to various districts and closely monitored. His army could be counted upon to control the Jewish population because it was drawn mostly from gentile settlers whom he had established in new cities, such as Sebaste, and from other Greek areas, which supported his fundamentally non-Jewish policies. Herod's gentile settlements greatly weakened Jewish control of their homeland and led to later conflicts and eventual loss of independence.

To secure his reign Herod built many fortresses and palaces in a variety of cities. Herodium (east of Jerusalem) and Masada (on the western shore of the Dead Sea) are the most famous and contained splendid palaces for Herod's enjoyment as well as serving as refuges in times of trouble. His palace in Jerusalem had three great towers and the one in Jericho featured beautiful decorations, baths, and pools. He supported the elaborate machinery of state by developing and settling

Herodium.

Anthony J. Saldarini.

BANDITRY

IMPRECISE ENGLISH USAGE associates banditry with some kind of theft. However, social banditry in peasant societies was a form of pre-political rebellion. Bandits or brigands became numerous in the Roman period and were one of the social forces leading to the revolution against Rome in 66 C.E. Peasants forced off the land by harsh economic conditions, politically inefficient governments, and military oppression typically banded together in order to take food and other necessities from the upper classes. They usually had the support of the peasants, who were also threatened, and were sometimes popular heroes (like Robin Hood) who rectified injustices and provided a measure of security to those still on the land. Banditry is pre-political because no attempt is made to overthrow the existing government or replace it with an alternative. Rather, it is a form of social resistance.

Since bandits threatened civic order and the social hold of the governing class, great efforts were made to suppress them. Herod the Great made his military reputation rooting out bandits; bandits finally seized control of the Jewish revolt and killed many of the governing class in Jerusalem. Jesus was crucified between two bandits (Mark 15:27), and he rebuked the arresting officers for treating him like a bandit (Mark 14:48).

new agricultural lands, especially in northern Transjordan, by confiscating the estates of his enemies in order to gain their great revenue, and especially by agricultural taxes, sales and purchase taxes, and a variety of customs duties.

The dissatisfaction of the people erupted in periodic insurrections and unrest, usually involving small numbers. Many felt a continuing affection for the Hasmonean House, which manifested itself in their support of Herod's sons Alexander and Aristobulus, born of the Hasmonean Mariamne. The quality of Herod's rule explains the nature of the resentment against it. Herod was an Idumean, a people who, ironically, had been forcibly converted to Judaism by John Hyrcanus, and who were not considered wholly Jewish, a view that was strengthened by Herod's very un-Jewish behavior as a Roman-appointed allied king. The profusion of prophets, messiahs, and other religious leaders who arose during and after Herod's reign and the abiding enthusiasm for the Hasmonean family, who had liberated Israel a hundred years earlier, point to a strong, popular desire for a traditional Jewish leader to reorder society and end the rule of the Romans. The constant problems with bandits (i.e., dispossessed peasants who had been driven out of the agricultural economic system by taxation and debt and were supported by the people) and the periodic threats of riot testify to the unbearable economic burden Herod and the empire placed on Palestine. The final result was civil disorder when the fear that kept most of the population passive exploded into anger after Herod's death and was transmuted into violence, which later had to be suppressed by Roman legions.

As Herod aged and his health failed, his family and followers began to plot against one another in a bid to succeed him. Herod had married nine wives. In the last decade of his life, 14–4 B.C.E., as factions fought for influence and control both in Jerusalem and in Rome, Herod condemned his three most prominent sons to death. The plotters against him included his brother Pheroras's wife, a group of Pharisees supporting her, and other family members, all of whom were executed after Pheroras died. His final will divided his kingdom among three sons, subject to the approval of the emperor.

Herod's death was followed by social and political chaos. To eliminate any rival during his lifetime, Herod had killed, impoverished, or otherwise neutralized the Hasmonean governing class. Herod had depended for governance and support on his family, on Diaspora Jews, and on emerging families who owed their status to him, and he had suppressed or controlled the traditional leadership, which had considerable influence among the people. The removal of the traditional leadership left the populace difficult to control at Herod's death. Although the high priests appointed by Herod came from leading priestly families, they were new in this office. The gap between the people and the leadership personally dependent on Herod was filled by popular leaders who arose from traditional village society, from reform movements that sought to respond to the influence of hellenism, from revival movements that sought to deepen the roots of the covenant among the people, and from revolutionary movements that sought immediate political change. The popular leaders were strongly inclined to oppose the government and empire and thus caused frequent unrest.

V. HEROD'S HEIRS

Herod divided his kingdom among three of his sons. Archelaus was to rule Judea, Samaria, and Idumea; Herod Antipas, who was tetrarch in Galilee during Jesus' life, received two territories, Galilee and Perea (the latter was a district east of the Jordan River), which were separated by the Decapolis (a league of ten independent, hellenistic, gentile cities; see p. 372); and Philip (Mark 6:17, 8:27) was willed the areas north and east of the Sea of Galilee. Herod's wish that Archelaus be appointed king so that some semblance of unity could be maintained in his kingdom was never ratified by Caesar Augustus. The uncertainty during the transition from Herod to his heirs allowed

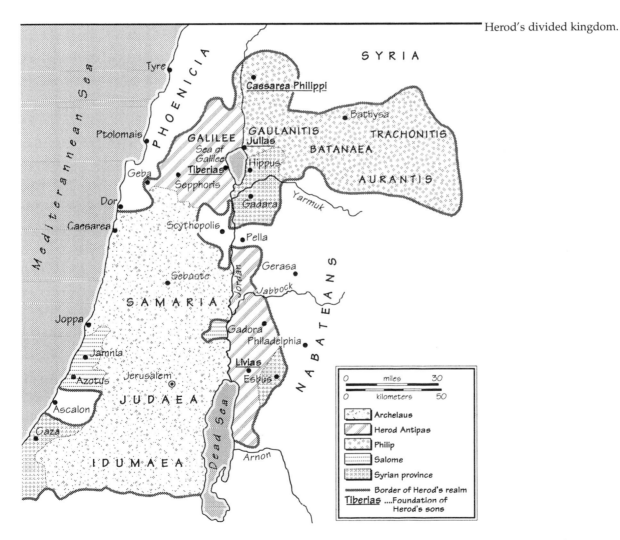

Herod's divided kingdom.

the people to vent their anger and frustration in violent insurrections which were put down with great difficulty by the Roman legions.

When Archelaus returned to Jerusalem from Jericho, where Herod had died, the crowds gathered for Passover cheered him but immediately sought relief from Herodian oppression through a reduction in taxes and the release of prisoners. Archelaus rejected these demands and put down the unruly mobs by having loyal soldiers massacre them. Resentment against the Herodians was so great that new riots broke out all over the country while Herod's heirs were in Rome seeking Caesar Augustus's approbation as rulers. Varus, the Roman governor of Syria, put down the first wave of violence and left a legion to garrison Jerusalem. When Sabinus, Varus's procurator, imprudently tried to seize Herod's treasure, the crowds at the Feast of Booths along with some of Herod's troops revolted and besieged the Romans in the Tower Phasael of Herod's palace.

A series of peasant revolts sprang up in different parts of the country led by popular leaders who gained the support of the people and some of whom claimed to be kings anointed by God. The revolts were not coordinated but were spontaneous expressions of frustration and desperation by peasants who had suffered constant and severe hardship and who were taxed off their land or threatened with ruin. Athronges, a shepherd, and his brothers won a series of battles in Judea and wiped out a Roman detachment at Emmaus. In Transjordan Simon, one of Herod's slaves, led attacks on royal property, including the palace at Jericho. Another group of rebels burned down the palace in Ammathus. In Galilee, Judas, the son of the bandit leader Ezekias, who had been killed by Herod, captured Sepphoris, the capi-

---

FEAST OF BOOTHS (OR TABERNACLES)

THE FEAST OF BOOTHS (OR tabernacles) is a fall agricultural festival celebrating the end of the harvest. In the rural areas the people danced and rejoiced in the vineyards and fields and lived in roughly made huts during the festival. The name of the feast in Hebrew (*sukkot*) is usually translated inadequately as "booths" or "tabernacles." The term actually designates huts made of branches and leaves; it referred specifically to the huts erected by the harvesters in the fields and vineyards to provide shelter at midday and sometimes at night. The Feast of Booths was designated one of the three feasts of pilgrimage to the Jerusalem temple and was associated with the wandering in the desert when Israel lived in tents. Some biblical texts suggest that it was the most solemn of the three pilgrimage festivals (Ezek. 45:25, Lev. 23:39, Zech. 14:16), but because it was not adopted into the Christian liturgical calendar, as Passover and Pentecost were, it is less well known to Christians.

The feast lasted for seven days, followed by a solemn eighth day; work was forbidden on the first and eighth days. Many special sacrifices were offered (Num. 29:12–34). Later customs included carrying around branches and fruit in procession (Lev. 23:40–1). This festival was celebrated in the Diaspora by the building of huts, prayer, and joyful processions. Music, trumpet blasts, dancing, and pouring of water libations are prominently mentioned. The Mishnah specifies that participants must carry around a palm branch (*lulav*) and a citron ('*etrog*), a custom followed in synagogues today.

Feasts were often an occasion for public unrest and rebellion because so many Jews gathered in Jerusalem with religious and national feelings running high. Josephus tells of numerous disturbances, especially on Passover (*Antiquities* 17.213; 18:29, 90; 20:106), and the gospels are also aware of this problem (Luke 13:1–2, Matt. 26:3–5).

tal, and in further campaigns used the weapons acquired there.

The leaders of the uprisings were from the lower classes, which had been taxed and repressed by Herod; they claimed legitimate royal authority in the face of the illegitimate exercise of power by Herod, the Romans, and their Jewish allies. They appealed to the royal covenant traditions of the Bible and perhaps to apocalyptic expectations of divine intervention. This type of independent brigandage by discrete bands of landless peasants had arisen during the transition from Hasmonean to Herodian rule, survived at the fringes during Herod's strong reign, and exploded in the chaos following his death. All through the first century peasant unrest broke out sporadically, culminating in the peasant revolt in Jerusalem during the Great War against Rome.

To put down the unrest in Herod's territory after his death in 4 B.C.E., Varus invaded with two of his three legions stationed in Syria and with an army of Nabatean allies from Transjordan. The population of Sepphoris was enslaved, and both Sepphoris and Emmaus were burned to the ground. Over two thousand Jews were crucified, and the Nabateans looted many towns. After order was restored, Archelaus tried to imitate Herod's grand and cruel manner of rule, but he lacked Herod's skill as a politician. After ten years he was removed and exiled by the emperor because of persistent protests from both Judeans and Samaritans. Though Archelaus's brothers Antipas and Philip continued to rule Jewish areas in the north, for the first time since the Persian period Jerusalem and Judea, the heart of Judaism, were ruled directly by a succession of foreign (Roman) governors. The Romans left day-to-day governance and the administration of the temple to the high priests and their council (*synedrion*). But the high priest and wealthy Jewish leaders in Jerusalem were responsible to the Romans for collecting taxes and maintaining public order; they were subject to the local governor's wishes and so had far less independence than at any

Roman theater at Sepphoris.
J. Andrew Overman.

Herodian cistern north of the temple mount.

Anthony J. Saldarini.

time previously. High priests were replaced regularly by the Roman governors, though several came from the family of Annas (John 18:13). Rather than suppressing opposition with craft and consistency like Herod, the Roman governors inflamed the people by theft on a grand scale and by insults to their religious traditions and insensitivity to their needs. It was into this chaotic and dissatisfied society that Jesus was born, and to it he addressed his message of reform and renewal. Though Galilee, under the rule of Antipas, was more peaceful than Jerusalem, the weight of taxation, the numbers of landless peasants (Joseph of Nazareth, the carpenter, was probably one of them), and the pressures of Greco-Roman culture stimulated a search for national identity and new ways of Jewish life.

A. LITERARY RESPONSES TO ROMAN RULE

1. The Testament of Moses

The Testament of Moses (sometimes called the Assumption of Moses) communicates the Jewish confidence in God and rejection of unjust domestic and foreign rule that marked the Roman period (see p. 000, above). Its author and place of composition are unknown, though Palestine is a likely location. In the narrative Moses gives his final advice and encouragement to Joshua, who fears the worst for Israel after Moses has left (Test. Moses 1–2, 11–12). The core of the book dates from the Maccabean period, but it was revised to allude to the reign of Herod and to Varus's suppression of unrest after Herod died. Like some other apocalyptic writings, the Testament of Moses reviews Israel's history as a record of sin and punishment culminating in the salvation of a repentant remnant through the intervention of God, who establishes his just kingdom. The troubles of the Herodian period and Roman invasions are viewed as merely another painful chapter in misrule to be followed by more intense persecution and decisively rectified by the appearance of God and his kingdom.

The Testament of Moses criticizes all Jewish leaders associated with the temple during the second and first centuries and is another witness to the Jewish desire for renewal, reform, or revolution. Concerning the pre-Maccabean high priests, the author has Moses predict: "They will pollute the house of worship with the customs of the nations; and they will play the harlot after foreign gods" (Test. Moses 5:3). "Those who are the leaders, their teachers, in those times will become admirers of avaricious persons, accepting [polluted] offerings, and they will sell justice by accepting bribes" (5:5). The hundred-year rule of the Hasmoneans and their forging of an independent principality are dismissed in one line: "Then powerful kings will rise over them, and they will be called priests of the Most High God. They will perform impiety in the Holy of Holies" (6:1). Since the Maccabees were not from legitimate high priestly families, had disenfranchised the previous governing class of Judaism, and had acted like independent hellenistic kings, the author dismisses their achievements as destructive of Judaism. Herod receives little more attention:

And a wanton king, who will not be of a priestly family, will follow them. He will be a man rash and perverse, and he will judge them as they deserve. . . .

He will kill both old and young, showing mercy to no one. Then fear of him will be heaped upon them in their land . . . and he will punish them. (Test. Moses 6:2–7)

His disastrous reign is concluded by the invasion of Varus to put down unrest: "After his death there will come into their land a powerful king of the West who will subdue them; and he will take away captives, and a part of their temple he will burn with fire. He will crucify some of them around their city" (6:8–9). Each of the details matches Josephus's account of Varus's punitive expedition into Israel.

The Jewish leaders who followed Herod and his son Archelaus are attacked as avaricious, deceitful, godless men who pollute the temple and "consume the goods of the [poor], saying their acts are according to justice" (Test. Moses 7:6). Their hypocrisy and destructive leadership bring a final punishment upon the nation (Test. Moses 8). The description of the tortures, forced worship of other gods, and prohibition of circumcision may have derived from the time of Antiochus IV, but it is offered here as an account of the final trials of Israel. The experience of waiting faithfully for God amid persecution is revealed in the story of Taxo (chap. 9), a strange figure who retreats to a cave to die with his sons rather than remain in society and disobey God's commands. The fidelity of Taxo, symbolic of the author's faithful community and similar to the martyrs in 1–4 Maccabees, is the climax of the righteous suffering in the history of Israel and introduces the reign of God.

The economic burdens and political upheavals of the Roman period, which caused many uprisings, untold suffering, and eventually an

Stairs up to the double gate (now closed) leading to the temple platform from south of the temple mount.

Anthony J. Saldarini.

The problem of debt in first century Palestine

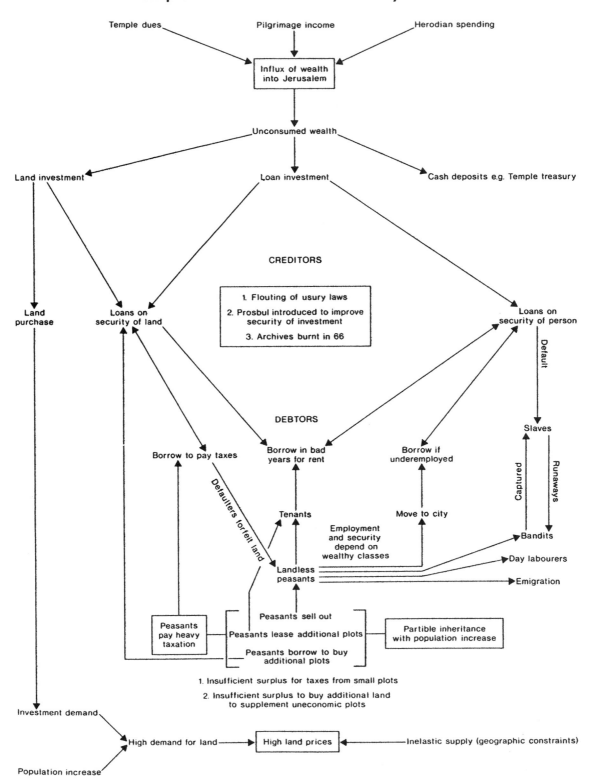

all-out war with Rome, are placed by the Testament of Moses in a historical perspective that gives full weight to these negative events but promises the restoration of Israel as it should be and the submission of the most powerful empire of the ancient world:

> Then his kingdom will appear throughout his whole creation. Then the devil will have an end. Yea, sorrow will be led away with him.
>
> Then will be filled the hands of the messenger, who is in the highest place appointed. Yea, he will at once avenge them of their enemies.
>
> For the Heavenly One will arise from his kingly throne. Yea, he will go forth from his holy habitation with indignation and wrath on behalf of his sons. (Test. Moses 10:1–3)

The messenger (angel) is a messianic figure sent by God. The expression "whose hands are filled" suggests priestly appointment, an idea consistent with warlike activities in this literature. After the intervention by the angelic messenger and God, the earth will be shaken and the sun and moon will cease to give light and the waters will fail, the nations will be punished and destroyed, and Israel will be happy and will trample the necks and eagle's wings (probably a reference to Rome) and finally be raised to the heavens (Test. Moses 10). The description of the end is typical for apocalyptic literature and similar to that found in the gospels (cf. Mark 13). The compressing of the activities of the dominant political power, Rome, into a single event in the larger scheme of Jewish history affirms the ultimate power and rule of God, to which the author witnesses in the midst of persecution. The vision of the kingdom expresses the author's faith in God and summarizes God's promises of a just society to Israel, a vision common to much of Jewish literature and fundamental to the teachings of Jesus and other Jewish reformers.

2. The Revised Third Sibylline Oracle

The Third Sibylline Oracle, a Jewish political protest tract from second-century Egypt (see pp. 343–344), was revised and updated around the time that Antony and Cleopatra ruled the East and then were defeated at the battle of Actium in 31 B.C.E. The author of the oracle and its reviser are not known, but such oracles were numerous in the Greco-Roman world and were used as a form of political protest. In the section where the punishment of various nations is predicted, an oracle on the Romans was added (3 Sib. Or. 350–80), with the prediction that Asia (meaning Egypt) would exact three times as much tribute from Rome as Rome had from Asia. The oracle lacks the historical and cosmic range of the Testament of Moses and its subtlety. It is a political protest tract in which the identity of Rome is clear, the punishments to be visited on Rome are specific, and the agent of humiliation is a human, Cleopatra:

> Whatever number from Asia served the house of Italians, twenty times that number of Italians will be serfs in Asia, in poverty, and they will be liable

PRAISES TO ISIS

Dᴜʀɪɴɢ THE HELLENISTIC period the Egyptian goddess Isis became hellenized and her worship spread throughout the Mediterranean world. Geographical mobility and political upheaval separated many people from their religious roots and shook their confidence in the traditional gods. For these people Isis and similar gods were patrons in the face of an unfamiliar and threatening world. In his *Metamorphoses*, Book 11, Lucius Apuleius Africanus recounts his wandering and trials (including being turned into an ass), his salvation by Isis, and his mystic experience of conversion during his initiation into the mysteries of Isis. He ends his account with a prayer to Isis that has much in common with Jewish and Christian prayers of the Greco-Roman period:

O holy and blessed dame,
    the perpetual comfort of human
    kind,

who by your bounty and grace
    nourishes all the world
and bears a great affection to the
    adversities of the miserable as
    a loving mother,
you take no rest night or day,
neither are you idle at any time
    in giving benefits and succour-
    ing all men as well on land as
    sea;
you are she that puts away all
    storms and dangers from men's
    life by stretching forth your
    right hand,
whereby likewise you unweave
    even the inextricable and
    entangled web of fate

and appease the great tempest of
    fortune,
and keep back the harmful
    course of the stars.
The gods supernal honor you;
the gods infernal have you in
    reverence;
you make all the earth turn, give
    light to the sun,
govern the world, tread down the
    power of hell.
By your power the stars give
    answer,

the seasons return, the gods
    rejoice, the elements serve.
At your command the winds
    blow,
the clouds nourish the earth, the
    seeds prosper, and the fruits
    grow.
The birds of the air, the beasts of
    the hill,
the serpents of the den, and the
    fishes of the sea tremble at
    your majesty.
But my spirit is not able to give
    you sufficient praise,
my patrimony is unable to satisfy
    your sacrifices;
my voice has no power to utter
    that which I think of your
    majesty,
no, not if I had a thousand
    mouths and so many tongues
    and were able to continue fo-
    rever.
Howbeit as a good religious per-
    son, and according to my poor
    estate, I will do what I may:
I will always keep your divine
    appearance in remembrance
and close the imagination of your
    most holy godhead within my
    breast.

to pay ten-thousandfold. . . . Often the mistress [Cleopatra] will cut your delicate hair and, dispensing justice, will cast you from heaven to earth. (3 Sib. Or. 353–60)

The references to slavery and forced labor show how much Rome relied on coercion of its subjects and how greatly this was resented. Even so, Rome will not be destroyed but will be raised up again. After other cities are punished, Asia will rule in a peaceful and prosperous society:

Serene peace will return to the Asian land, and Europe will then be blessed. The air will be good for pasture for many years, bracing, free from storms and hail, producing everything. . . . For all good order and righteous deal- ing will come upon men from starry heaven and with it temperate accord. . . . Bad government, blame, envy, anger, folly, and poverty will flee from men and constraint will flee. (3 Sib. Or. 367–78)

The utopian society pictured here and the figure of Cleopatra ruling Rome and the Mediterranean are based on prayers and praises of the Egyptian goddess Isis. The Egyptian Jew who wrote this, before

Antony and Cleopatra were defeated by Octavian, put his trust in non-Jewish human agencies to bring about better times.

How fragile that hope was can be seen by additions near the beginning of the Third Sibylline Oracle that were made after the battle of Actium. Here the author, faced with the defeat and death of Antony, sees the rule of the world by a widow (Cleopatra, after the death of Antony) as an introduction to divine judgment and destruction of the world (3 Sib. Or. 75–92). Later, with Rome fully in charge in Egypt he predicts that "the most great kingdom of the immortal king will become manifest over men" and "a holy prince will come to gain sway over the scepters of the earth forever, as time presses on. Then also implacable wrath will fall upon Latin men" (3 Sib. Or. 47–51). The author drew on Jewish apocalyptic themes of divine intervention, judgment, and punishment, but he did not envision a completely renewed world ruled by God in the Palestinian mode. Like the Sibylline Oracle he edited, this Egyptian Jew still hoped for political independence for his country and a better life on earth through an enlightened ruler (see also the discussion of Joseph and Aseneth on pp. 366–368). Egyptian Jews had not yet suffered the political and cultural oppression that motivated the apocalyptic response of Palestinian Judaism in the Seleucid and Roman periods.

VI. THE WORLD OF JESUS

After the exile of Herod's son Archelaus in 6 C.E., political, military, and judicial power in Judea and Samaria was vested in a Roman governor appointed by the emperor rather than in a Jewish leader subordinate to Roman authority. This was the first time an empire controlling Palestine had failed to appoint a Jew as proxy and mediator between the foreign authorities and the people. The misunderstandings, hostilities, and conflicts created by this arrangement increasingly poisoned the atmosphere in Judea and contributed to the war with Rome sixty years later. Provincial governors, who were expected to enrich themselves with excess tax collections, often engaged in even less ethical practices, such as soliciting bribes and expropriating private property. Provinces where governors changed frequently could easily be bled dry as each new governor enriched himself.

The Roman governor of Palestine was first a prefect (a military commander) and later a procurator (a civil administrator). The governors of Palestine came from the second rank of Roman society, the equestrian order, from whom were drawn many second-level officials of the empire. The Palestinian governor was under the supervision of the legate of Syria, who was of the highest order in Roman society, the senatorial order. Because the Syrian governor was responsible for the security of the eastern border of the empire and had four legions under his control, he was not only a member of the Roman Senate but also an ex-consul (the highest military and civil magistrate in Rome). The governor of Palestine, who was much less important, ruled Judea, Samaria, the coast, and Idumea from his capital at Caesarea on the coast and had at his disposal non-Jewish auxiliary troops drawn from

ROMAN GOVERNORS IN PALESTINE

FROM THE END OF Archelaus's reign in 6 C.E. until the interruption of Roman rule at the inception of the revolt in 66 C.E., Judea and Samaria were ruled by Roman governors, except for the reign of the Jewish king Agrippa (41–4). Most Roman provinces were administered by governors drawn from the senatorial order, that is, the leading Roman families who had a member in the Roman Senate. Syria, which was a crucial border province, had as governor a senator who had held the consulship, the highest office. A few smaller provinces, like Judea, were governed by members of the lower, equestrian order. Equestrians were drawn from a wide range of people, many of whom were financially successful. Under Augustus and his successors the equestrians became more important as officials in the empire.

From 6 to 41 the governors were designated *prefects,* originally a military title. From 44 on, they were titled *procurators,* originally a financial officer representing the emperor on an estate or in a senatorial province. As time went on, the differences between the offices disappeared and the terms became confused, even by the Roman historian Tacitus, who calls Pontius Pilate a procurator, though he was actually a prefect. In the New Testament he is most often called *hegemon,* Latin *praeses,* a title most properly used for a senatorial governor. In any case, the governor had military command of auxiliary units, financial responsibility for the province, and ultimate judicial power. The Roman governors of Palestine were:

Coponius	6–9
Ambibulus	9–12
Rufus	12–15
Valerius Gratus	15–26
Pontius Pilate	26–36
Marcellus	36
Marullus	36–41
Cuspius Fadus	44–6
Tiberius Julius Alexander	46–8
Ventidius Cumanus	48–52
Felix	52–60?
Porcius Festus	60–2
Albinus	62–4
Gessius Florus	64–6

FIRST-CENTURY HIGH PRIESTS

DURING THE REIGNS OF Herod, Archelaus his son, and the Roman governors, the high priest, who had been the supreme authority during the Hasmonean period, lost his direct political power. He remained the highest ranking and symbolic head of Judaism, however, and had to be controlled by the governing authority. Thus, high priests were appointed at government discretion rather than being chosen for life. First, Herod, Archelaus, and the Roman prefects appointed the high priests. Then, from the mid–first century, the Jewish kings Agrippa I and Agrippa II appointed the high priests. A list of the high priests through the first third of the first century C.E. (drawn mostly from Josephus, with problems of dating noted) shows the political turnover in the high priesthood.

Ananel, a Babylonian	37–36 B.C.E.
Aristobulus III, the last Hasmonean	35
Ananel (again)	34–?
Jesus son of Phiabi	?
Simon son of Boethus or Boethus	?–5
Matthias son of Theophilus	5–4
Joseph son of Ellem	?
Joazar son of Boethus	4
Eleazar son of Boethus	4 B.C.E.–?
Jesus son of See	?
Joazar (again)	?
Ananus or Annas son of Sethi	6–16 C.E.
Ismael son of Phiabi	15–16
Eleazar son of Ananus	16–17
Simon son of Camithus	17–18
Joseph Caiaphas	18–36
Jonathan son of Ananus	36–7
Theophilus son of Ananus	37–?

By the middle of the War against Rome, twelve more high priests had been appointed. Note that the family of Ananus (Annas) is very prominent and that Ananus was the father-in-law of Joseph Caiaphas (18–36); both are mentioned in John 18:13.

the area, including an especially loyal contingent from Sebaste in Samaria. He was responsible for keeping order, supervising tax collection, and judging major cases concerned with security.

Roman prefects left the local administration of justice to the traditional town and national authorities, who were usually the wealthy and hereditary community leaders. Because their social position and prosperity were subject to Roman power and dependent on an orderly society, the elites of all the provinces were co-opted by the Romans to keep the peace and collect taxes. The highest authorities in Jerusalem were the high priest; the leading high priestly families of Phiabi, Boethus, Camith, and Ananus (John 18:13); and other wealthy and established, but nonpriestly families who had survived the reigns of the Hasmoneans and Herod. They exercised control through a supreme council in Jerusalem, local councils, major administrative offices, and a variety of lower officials, guards, courts, and other institutions.

Since national identity, laws, customs, and religious practices were one unified whole, the administration of the temple, the legislation of new law, the judging of any offense against the laws, and the formation of national policy toward the Romans were all carried out by the same agencies. The Jerusalem leaders dealt with Roman relations, temple activities, and civil unrest as one since these matters were inextricably intertwined. At lower levels of government and in the towns, however, scribes, some Pharisees, and the traditional leading citizens administered the law and settled disputes through local councils and courts. The Romans exercised oversight but interfered only when their interests required it. Thus, Pilate's attempt to have the Jewish authorities deal with Jesus fit the first-century situation perfectly, as does his eventual condemnation of Jesus on political charges.

A.   THE COUNCIL (SANHEDRIN)

The supreme legislative, executive, and judicial council in Judea met in the temple compound. It is often called by the Hebraized form of the Greek word for council, "Sanhedrin," first found in the Mishnah (200 C.E.; see p. 429). The powers and membership of the Jerusalem council and of other subordinate bodies varied according to the strength of the domestic or foreign ruler, and so neither the *synedrion* nor any other institution can be treated as unchanging and continuous. For example, under Herod the *synedrion* was an advisory council of his family and friends; under the Romans it was the major indigenous power in Judea, firmly subordinated to Roman policy and the Roman governor. Differing accounts of this body in the New Testament, rabbinic literature, and the works of the Jewish historian Josephus reflect this change over time. The Jewish council, like other municipal and ethnic councils, assemblies, and courts in the Greco-Roman world, was composed of the traditional leaders of society and of those who had gained power at any given time. In Jerusalem the hereditary chief priests, led by the high priest, dominated most of the time and were assisted by the heads of highborn and wealthy Jewish families as well as by learned officials and the leaders of other socially influential groups (e.g., Josephus, *Antiquities* 14.168–76), such as the Pharisees and Sadducees. The council's duties included anything pertaining to the overall welfare of the state, especially political affairs, international relations, religious conflicts, the maintenance and administration of the temple, the collection of taxes, the adjudication of important legal cases, and the interpretation of local law and Jewish custom. Since religious law and practice were thoroughly integrated into political and economic society in antiquity, any attempt to separate the council's religious from its secular authority is misguided (as is positing two councils, one religious and the other secular).

We do not know the exact constitution of the Jerusalem council during the first century. The gospels testify that the high priest, elders, and scribes (lower-ranking officials) were members. Since these parties are the same mentioned in the Letter of Antiochus III in the early second century B.C.E. as the leaders of Judaism (Josephus, *Antiquities* 12.142), the gospel tradition is probably accurate. The functions the council exercised in relation to Jesus – investigating his activities; arresting, interrogating, and trying him; and finally recommending to the Roman governor that action be taken to keep the peace – are entirely in keeping with the ordinary activities of such councils. The lack of evidence concerning the council in the first century has raised a number of disputes concerning several gospel traditions: whether it really

---

TERMS FOR THE COUNCIL (*SANHEDRIN*)

SANHEDRIN, THE TERM MOST commonly used for the Jerusalem supreme council, is a Hebraized form of the Greek word *synedrion*, which refers to a council of leaders – political, military, or organizational. The Jewish historian Josephus uses *synedrion* for various civil bodies, including the Jerusalem council. The Gospels and Acts use it in the same way. The Greek term *synedrion*, literally, a "sitting down with," probably came into use for the Jewish council in the Roman period because the Romans favored putting local affairs and tax collection into the hands of regional assemblies called *synedria*. Traditionally in Greek cities the supreme legislative body had been a senate

called a *boule* (from the word for "counsel," "plan") or a *gerousia* (from the root for "elders"). The usage of these words overlaps in Greek literature, including Josephus and the New Testament (Luke 23:50, Acts 5:21).

Because different functions and a different composition are given to the Jerusalem council in Josephus, the New Testament, and rabbinic literature, it is likely that no single, continuous institution with a stable membership ruled Judea. The theories that the council was solely political or solely religious or that there were two councils are unnecessary and incoherent. Religious matters were embedded in the political, social fabric of the nation, and whoever was powerful and influential sought to control the entirety. Some postulate that the Pharisees had their own council;

if, as is likely, they were a structured voluntary organization, they probably had a council, as the Qumran community did, but this council should not be confused with the supreme national council in Jerusalem (on which Pharisees sat at times).

The Hebraized Greek term "Sanhedrin" is used sparingly in rabbinic literature to refer to the bodies of elders and leaders who functioned as both legislative councils and judicial courts; perhaps the Mishnah seeks to legitimate its own institutions by connecting them with the Greco-Roman *synedrion*. The indigenous and more frequent Hebrew term found in the Mishnah is *bet din*, literally, "house of judgment." The great council in Jerusalem is called the *bet din ha-gadol*, "the great house of judgment."

lacked the power to impose capital punishment; whether a formal Jewish trial of Jesus was held; and whether action against Jesus was really initiated by Jewish or by Roman authorities. In a certain sense, however, the council and the Roman governor form a continuous whole within the empire.

B. THE TEMPLE

The major institutions with which Jews came into contact were the temple and the courts. The temple in Jerusalem was the symbolic center of Judaism, even for Jews who had never seen it. It was mandated, described, and glorified in many biblical books and served as the focus of God's presence in Israel and as a guarantee of God's choice of and love for Israel as his own people. The morning and evening sacrifices offered for the nation and the special festival ceremonies were part of the divinely given order of Judaism and of the universe itself, according to the Jewish worldview. Many sacrifices in thanksgiving for God's favor or in reparation for sin are prescribed in the Bible and frequently offered. Three times a year Jewish males in Palestine were expected to travel to the temple to celebrate the ancient agricultural festivals of Passover, Weeks (Pentecost), and Booths (in the fall). At these times thousands of Jewish pilgrims filled the city, and if civil unrest were threatening, festival time was a likely occasion for it to break out.

Public prayer and sacrifice in the temple required the labor of numerous priests and Levites. During this period Levites were a lower class of priest entrusted with keeping order in the temple, providing for physical necessities, and leading the singing with voice and instrument. Central moments in temple worship were announced by trumpet blasts, and the daily sacrifices were accompanied by music and the singing of psalms. During the day private sacrifices were brought by the people and offered by the priests. When animals were offered, the fat of the animal and certain inner parts were burned on the altar, the hind quarter and breast went to feed the priests, and the rest of the animal went to the worshipers in a sacred meal eaten on the temple property. The blood of the animals was thrown against the base of the altar because blood was considered a holy source of life. Various grains and vegetables were also offered, with a small portion burned on the altar and the balance dedicated to the support of the priests. In some sacrifices wine was poured out at the base of the altar.

The temple compound was a huge open space with the sacred temple building in the center, surrounded by storage and utility buildings. Around the perimeter of the temple mount were colonnades and other buildings, surrounded by a massive wall with several strong gates. Thus the temple was the last redoubt in the fortifications of Jerusalem as well as the administrative and judicial center of Judaism. In various chambers the wealth of the nation and deposits left by rich individuals were stored. The temple equipment, much of it made of gold and other precious substances, was stored there along with a variety of foods to feed the priests. Weapons for the defense of the temple and

Herodian wall in the Jerusalem Citadel.

Anthony J. Saldarini.

city and other paraphernalia of government filled buildings and underground storerooms. Councils and courts met in various chambers of the temple, and the leaders of the nation often conferred there, especially after the Romans took control of Herod's palace and the Fortress Antonia (located at the northwest corner of the temple compound) in the first century. The temple was a military, civic, and economic, as well as religious, institution.

C.   TAXES

The temple and priesthood were supported by agricultural tithes mandated by the Bible on produce of the land of Israel and by a half-shekel tax collected from every Jew in Israel and the Diaspora. The tithes (one-tenth of the produce of a field, of new fruit, wine, etc.) mandated by the Bible were complex and changed over time. Complaints about nonpayment of tithes testify to the natural human resistance to taxation. Ideally, the first fruits of trees were brought to the temple and the firstborn of animals were redeemed by money paid to the temple. The agricultural tax was to be divided among the various levels of priests and Levites. Priests were further supported by the portions of sacrifices brought to the temple which were reserved for them, and the temple benefited from benefactions regularly bestowed upon it by Jewish and foreign rulers. In summary, the temple was a governmental institution in Israel and was supported by the taxation system, which gathered economic resources for the Jewish state and, when necessary, for the ruling foreign power. Taxes demanded and collected probably varied considerably with changing rulers and the effectiveness of central government.

D.   RESISTANCE TO ROMAN RULE

Under Roman rule, the Jerusalem leadership, led by the high priest, was responsible for collecting the yearly tribute and keeping social order. The usual Roman requirement that each temple in any part of the empire offer sacrifice to the emperor or to Roman gods as a sign of loyalty was adjusted in favor of a daily sacrifice offered for the welfare of the emperor and empire. In order to keep the priesthood compliant and to assert its power, the Roman governor kept custody of the high priestly robes worn on the three pilgrimage festivals and the Day of Atonement and released them yearly to the high priest. Only in 36 C.E. did the Roman governor of Syria, Vitellius, return the robes to Jewish custody in order to win popular approval. Given the constant irritants in the Roman–Jewish relationship, great effort and compromise by the high priest and other leaders were required to prevent serious conflict and misunderstanding. Even with their efforts, the tolerance of the people for Roman rule and for their own leaders gradually dissipated and led to an all-out confrontation between Jerusalem and Rome in the Great War of 66–70 C.E.

The escalating problems of the first century could be seen at the inception of direct Roman rule in 6 C.E. Even though local Jewish authorities handled daily matters, the presence of Roman garrisons in large cities, the constraints placed on Jewish society by Roman policy, the need to satisfy the Roman administration, and the burden of taxes put a severe and constant strain on Jewish society. Offensive Roman administrative practices and tactless governors frequently aggravated the situation. For example, when Judea became a Roman province in 6 C.E., the new Roman governor in Syria, Quirinius, and the new governor of Judea, Coponius, immediately conducted a census and registration of property in order to establish a tax base. This census was wide-

Beth Natofa Valley, north of Sepphoris, a west–east trade route.

J. Andrew Overman.

ZEALOTS AND REBEL MOVEMENTS

FIRST-CENTURY PALESTINE was rife with royal pretenders, messianic movements, prophetic figures, and rebellious brigands, many of whom are mentioned in Josephus. Besides the longing for an anointed leader which appears in some Jewish literature, the old Israelite tradition of popular, anointed kingship arose once more during the Roman period. A shepherd named Athronges and a servant of Herod named Simon both claimed to be king and led armed groups of bandits until finally defeated and captured (*Antiquities* 17. 273–85). Note that the official charge against Jesus was that he claimed to be "King of the Jews." In the first century a prophet named Theudas (*Antiquities* 20. 97–8; Acts 5:36) led followers toward the Jordan River but Roman cavalry killed him and many of his followers. In such an atmosphere the Roman and Jewish authorities who wished to keep civil order could easily see the leader of a popular movement, such as Jesus, as a threat and take steps to neutralize the threat.

Though many attribute the first-century unrest to a group called the "Zealots" and locate their origins in the late-first-century B.C.E., this term, as used by Josephus, really refers to a coalition of popular resistance movements at the time of the revolt in 66 C.E. This coalition wrested control of Jerusalem from the traditional aristocratic and priestly elders and promoted radical and uncompromising resistance to Rome. These Zealot groups were made up of peasants who had been driven off the land into Jerusalem by the war. The Zealot coalition led a popular peasant revolt which ultimately failed and resulted in the destruction of Jerusalem.

SCHOOL OF THOUGHT (*HAIRESIS*)

THE PHARISEES, SADDUCEES, Essenes, and fourth (revolutionary) philosophy were called by Josephus *haireseis*. This word is usually translated as "sect" or "school of thought." A *hairesis*, literally, "choice," was a coherent and principled choice of a way of life. This choice included both an understanding of life and a recognizable way of living out that understanding. Philosophy was not just an academic subject in antiquity. People who were committed to one of the Greek schools of philosophy lived according to a recognizable code of conduct. The term "sect" sometimes fits such a group, especially if used in a loose sense. "School of thought" is a reasonable translation as long as it is understood that the thought was not only academic or theoretical but put into practice.

ly opposed, and only the mediation of High Priest Joazar, son of Boethus, prevented violence. Though peasants often paid 30–70 percent of their crop to someone else – the landowner, local governor, or empire – the payments to the Romans without the mediation of a Jewish king were particularly galling.

Josephus saw the advent of direct Roman rule as a crucial turning point in the nation's history that led to war and the destruction of the temple and Jerusalem. In response to the census and new taxes in 6 C.E., a Galilean named Judas led a revolt in which he encouraged his countrymen to refuse to pay tribute to Rome and to acknowledge only God as their ruler (*despotes*). This rebel was different because he was "a teacher [*sophistes*] of his own school [*hairesis*]" (Josephus, *Jewish War* 2.118), which was a fourth philosophy in addition to those of the Pharisees, Sadducees, and Essenes. With the aid of Saddok, a Pharisee, Judas aroused rebellious feelings in many people and provided the theoretical basis for later unrest. (See *Jewish War* 2.119–66 and *Antiquities* 18.11–25.)

The revolutionary movement, of which Josephus disapproves, is designated by him pejoratively as a "fourth philosophy." The three traditional philosophies of Judaism, according to Josephus, were those of the Pharisees, Essenes, and Sadducees. Because they were centuries old, nonrevolutionary, and respectable, Josephus recommended them to his Greco-Roman audience and contrasted them with this illegitimate innovation, the revolutionary philosophy. This philosophy was the same as the Pharisaic philosophy, according to Josephus, except for its passion for liberty, for its acceptance of God alone as ruler, and for its revolutionary aims. Though Judas incited his countrymen to resist the Romans, he seems not to have led a large insurrection in Galilee but to have fostered a negative attitude toward the Romans which led to further problems. Because of the disorder and suffering it caused,

Josephus branded this philosophy novel and intrusive. However, the adherents of the philosophy resemble the martyrs described in the Books of the Maccabees. Their willingness to undergo great suffering in resisting the Romans rather than to engage in military exploits is emphasized. Though Josephus disapproved strongly of resistance to the Romans, his account of Judas and his followers testifies to the uninterrupted tradition of fidelity to God and resistance to gentile powers during the Greco-Roman period.

E. SADDUCEES AND PHARISEES

In contrast to his description of the new fourth philosophy, Josephus describes the three traditional, ancient, and legitimate philosophies as a respectable and permanent part of Judaism in order to establish Judaism's dignity in the eyes of his gentile readers. The Pharisees, Sadducees, and Essenes, along with many other groups, were active in Palestinian society during the first century. The Essenes (see pp. 347–355) were relatively separate from the political life of Jewish society. The Sadducees, about whom little is known, were mainly drawn from the governing class and had a small following among the people. Since the governing class acted according to Roman wishes and had great economic and political power over the people, their natural separation from the lower classes was intensified. Though many scholars have assumed that all the high priests and aristocrats were Sadducees, Josephus says only that the Sadducees were drawn from the upper classes. These very diverse groups such as the Pharisees and Sadducees were themselves split by factions and internal power struggles.

If Josephus is correct in presenting the Sadducees as a school of thought or philosophy, then they were probably a small group within the governing class with particular ideas about how Jewish life should be lived and the nation guided. Their view of God as wholly transcendent and not involved in human affairs may have derived from loss of confidence in the biblical promises of an active God providing security for the nation and an eternal dynasty. Continual invasion and subjugation of the governing class may have turned them from overt reliance on divine aid to dependence on human efforts in conducting human affairs, although in accordance with divine law. Such an outlook would fit their task of governing the nation in difficult times without prophetic or other divine guidance. Their denial of resurrection and of the coming of God's kingdom is consistent with the governing

Nazareth. This small village, founded in the third century B.C.E., was for centuries devoted wholly to agriculture. Archaeological investigation indicates that in the first century C.E. it occupied just over 50 acres and had a probable population of less than 400. Located a few miles from Sepphoris, the Greco-Roman city which was for a time during Roman rule the governmental center of Galilee, Nazareth is not mentioned in the Jewish scriptures or by Josephus. Caves and meeting rooms with Christian symbols date back to the fourth century C.E. Only in the fifth century C.E. were a large church and monastery built there; it became a Christian city of modest size.

Anthony J. Saldarini

Robinson's arch in the wall of the temple mount.

Anthony J. Saldarini.

class's emphasis on preserving the status quo in which they are in control and would explain their aversion to the apocalyptic resolution of history. Perhaps they also supported a special fidelity to Israel's ancient traditions in reaction against overly hellenized and assimilationist members of the governing class. The balance between accommodating a foreign power and protecting a cultural tradition is difficult if not impossible to maintain, and it is likely that disagreements within the governing class would have spawned groups and movements, such as the Sadducees, with different understandings of Judaism.

The Pharisees had been an active political interest group from the mid–second century B.C.E. (see p. 346) and continued to seek power and exercise their influence during Herodian times. They encouraged the tithing of agricultural products by all Jews, observed biblical laws of ritual purity formerly restricted to the priests in the temple, and kept the Sabbath especially holy as a way of living out their Judaism zealously. Their program required an intense commitment, which appealed to many. They had influenced John Hyrcanus's laws for a time in the second century B.C.E. and had had great domestic political power during the reign of Alexandra in the first century B.C.E. Like every other influential group, the Pharisees lost ground during the reign of Herod, though early on, certain Pharisaic leaders were patronized by, and to some extent supported, Herod. Late in Herod's reign many Pharisees were executed when caught conspiring with Herod's sister-in-law to control the royal succession.

Most Pharisees were probably literate officials working for and seeking to influence the governing class of Judea. As such they would have been educators, lower-level officials and judges, and in a few cases members of the governing class itself. The advent of direct Roman rule left less room for political maneuvering, so Josephus is

Cardo (ancient main street) in Jerusalem.

J. Andrew Overman.

silent about the Pharisees' activities in Jerusalem until the war in 66 C.E., when several appear in various leadership capacities. Acts of the Apostles (23:6), a late-first-century work, places Pharisees in the Jerusalem *synedrion*. In the synoptic Gospels (see Part III) the Pharisees appear mainly in Galilee as lower-level community authorities and officials. They would logically have been the ones to come in contact with Jesus, and it is their influence that he threatened. Only in Jerusalem when Jesus was perceived as a danger by the highest authorities did the chief priests and the rest of the governing class notice, oppose, and arrest him.

F. GOVERNANCE

While Jesus was active in Galilee, Herod Antipas ruled there, Pontius Pilate was governor in Judea and Samaria, and the reclusive Tiberius was emperor of Rome. After the death of Caesar Augustus in 14 C.E., his successor as emperor was Tiberius, his stepson, who had been exiled earlier and was made heir only after Augustus's earlier heirs had died. He stabilized the borders of the empire and established it on a sound fiscal footing. Tiberius's earlier struggles with rival heirs had left him so suspicious that he executed many of the Roman governing class. He spent the latter half of his reign as a recluse on the island of Capri and gave Sejanus, an equestrian, great power in Rome. Sejanus was an unscrupulous ruler until his execution in 31 C.E. Pilate, a protégé of Sejanus, obtained his position as governor of Palestine through his patron and was protected by him in the early years of his term of office.

Pilate was a typical governor and used his power cruelly to preserve Roman rule. He often acted arbitrarily, without sensitivity to Jewish customs and laws; eventually the complaints against him resulted in his recall to Rome in 36 C.E. During his first year as governor, he sent his troops from Caesarea to Jerusalem for the winter and allowed them to bring military standards with a bust of Caesar on them into the military compound in the heavily fortified Herodian palace. Because images were forbidden in Jerusalem, especially images that were part of emperor worship, Roman governors had previously used standards without images. For several days a large number of Jews from Jerusalem protested this action in Caesarea. When Pilate surrounded the crowd with soldiers in the stadium, they offered to be killed rather than accept the images in Jerusalem. This obstinate zeal caused Pilate to remove the images from Jerusalem.

In a more serious financial matter, however, Pilate did not yield. He took money given to the temple for sacrifices and used it to build an aqueduct to bring water to Jerusalem. Though the municipal planning was sound, the financing was blasphemous. When people thronged around Pilate's tribunal in protest, his soldiers, dressed as civilians among the crowd, beat the crowd into submission, killing many. Since Sejanus, Pilate's patron and the active power in Rome, was anti-Jewish, Pilate's challenges to Jewish customs may have been calculated insults to please his sponsor; or they may have been typical colonial policies perfectly reasonable to an arrogant governor who looked down on and dominated his "barbaric" subjects. Conflicts such as these, the crisis over Emperor Gaius's attempt to place a statue of himself in the temple in 41 C.E. (see p. 399), and continuing tension over taxation led eventually to the Great War against Rome. Though Jesus spent most of his life in Galilee under the nominally Jewish ruler Herod Antipas, all Jewish areas were affected by events in Jerusalem and the actions of the Roman governor of the central city.

G.   GALILEE

Antipas, the son of Herod, successfully ruled Galilee until he was removed from office in 39 C.E. Though he had no direct control over Jerusalem, as the senior Jewish ruler in the region he had some influence on temple affairs and sometimes mediated disputes with the Romans. He ruled Galilee in the north and Perea, the district east of the Jordan River. Both areas were predominantly Jewish and were separated geographically from one another by the Decapolis, a league of ten independent Greek cities with mostly non-Jewish populations. Like his father, he engaged in many building projects, including some that benefited the non-Jewish population. Most significant was his rebuilding of Sepphoris as the capital of Galilee and his resettlement of the city with both Jews and non-Jews. The people of Sepphoris were thoroughly hellenized and loyal to Antipas, so that they later refused to join the rebellion against Rome. Antipas subsequently built himself a new capital, Tiberias, on the shore of the Sea of Galilee and settled it by force with foreigners and landless poor. Its mixed population, its site on a graveyard, and its hellenistic public buildings, complete with images, made the city offensive to many Jews.

Both Sepphoris and Tiberias were relatively large cities of many thousands and were extremely cosmopolitan and involved in the governance of the province. Their populations were a mixture of Jews and many other ethnic groups and languages, and for this reason Jesus is never connected to either city, even though Sepphoris is only about three miles from Nazareth. He is associated with medium-sized cities, such as Capernaum and Bethsaida, which were predominantly Jewish. In these cities he met knowledgeable, wealthy Jewish leaders such as the Pharisees, the Herodians (officials and supporters of Herod Antipas in Mark 3:6, etc.), and Jewish elders such as Jairus, the ruler of the synagogue (Mark 5:22), as well as lower-level Roman officials such as the centurion in Capernaum (Matt. 8:5). Jesus concentrated his efforts on reforming the population of the place where he grew up: lower Galilee, the hills around it, and the northern and western shore of the Sea of Galilee. There the villages were close together, often within sight of one another, and everything was within one or two hours' walking distance.

Life in Galilee centered on agriculture and on fishing in the Sea of Galilee. Probably only a small percentage of the population was literate and had immediate interests beyond the village or town. However, Galilee was not a rural backwater, unaffected by Greco-Roman culture.

Synagogue at Capernaum.

J. Andrew Overman.

The great Esdraelon Plain running through lower Galilee was a major trade route between the coast and Syria, and the Jewish villages of Galilee were within a day's walk of many local Greek cities and the great coastal trade cities. The physical evidence recovered by archeologists shows that trade with the rest of the empire was lively and constant. Galilee exported wine and olive oil to other parts of the empire and imported luxury goods for the rich.

The leaders of Galilee, especially Herod Antipas, were members of the governing class of the empire, who traveled frequently, maintained

SYNAGOGUE

THE GREEK TERM *synagoge* ("assembly of people or gathering of things") became the technical term for both the Jewish assembly and the building in which it met. "Synagogue" is used in Josephus and the New Testament, both first-century sources. Philo, Josephus, and Acts (16:3, 6) also use the term "house of prayer" (*proseuche*) for Jewish assemblies. The synagogue probably began as a voluntary gathering for prayer, education, and the fostering of community life. Such gatherings probably met in private homes or public buildings used for many purposes. In Palestinian villages with a large plurality of Jews it is likely that the town assembly for business and celebration was coextensive with the assembly for prayer on Sabbaths and feasts. It probably met in the town square, in the courtyard or a room of a large house, or in the town assembly building. It is doubtful that small, poor villages had their own Torah scroll or a teacher learned in the law. The same prominent and (more or less) learned leaders who directed the community probably led the synagogue, since political and religious society were one integral whole.

Synagogue buildings have been found in abundance from the third century C.E. on, both in Palestine and in the Diaspora. Alleged first-century synagogues in the fortresses at Masada and Herodium and on the island of Delos are assembly halls but lack the distinctive architectural and decorative features associated with later synagogues dedicated solely to worship and study. The rabbis gained power as synagogue leaders only during and after the Talmudic period (third to sixth centuries). Synagogue inscriptions from the third century on list as the most common officials "head of the synagogue" (*archisynagogos*), "leader" (*archon*), and "scribe."

complex political and personal relations with the emperor and his court, and lived lives different from those of the peasants. The Herodians mentioned in the Gospels (Mark 3:6, 12:13) were the officials and upper-class supporters of Herod Antipas, and appropriately enough, they engaged in political conspiracies with the Pharisees against Jesus, whom they saw as a rising social force and political threat to their control and influence. According to Luke, the wife of one of these officials was a follower of Jesus (Luke 9:9).

Herod Antipas himself is mentioned a number of times in the Gospels. He was apprehensive about the growing reputation of Jesus and associated him with the movement of John the Baptist, whom he had executed (Mark 6:14). According to Luke, Herod wished to exe-

Galilee in the first century.

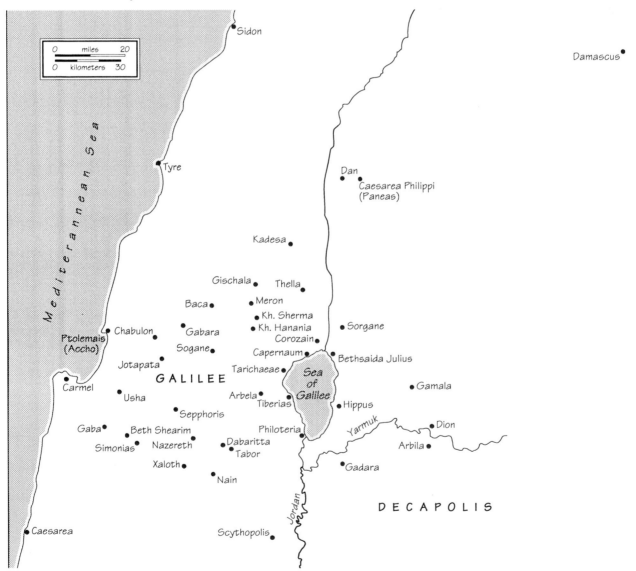

cute Jesus also (13:31) and finally met him when he was arrested in Jerusalem (23:7–12). Though the historical reliability of Luke's accounts is disputed, the report of Herod's concern about Jesus as a potential threat to the civic peace is wholly plausible.

Herod Antipas is notorious in the gospels for marrying his brother's wife, Herodias, and for executing John the Baptist, who criticized him for it. According to Josephus, on a journey to Rome Herod Antipas visited his brother Herod, son of Mariamne, and fell in love with that Herod's wife, Herodias, who was their first cousin. (In Mark 6:17 Herod the husband of Herodias is incorrectly identified as Herod Philip, the ruler of the areas to the northeast of the Sea of Galilee.) Antipas and Herodias agreed to marry when he returned from Rome, a pact that caused Antipas's wife, the daughter of the Nabatean Arab king Aretas, to return to her father. The ill will from this incident prompted Aretas to take some boundary territory from Antipas in 36 C.E., when Aretas defeated Antipas's troops decisively. The emperor Tiberius ordered the Syrian governor, Vitellius, to punish Aretas, a task he reluctantly undertook and quickly dropped when Tiberius died in 37 C.E. Herod Antipas's end as ruler came when his wife urged him to request the new emperor, Gaius Caligula, to promote him from tetrarch to king. Rivals cast doubt on his loyalty to the emperor and he was exiled to Gaul.

In the conduct of his personal and public affairs Antipas acted like a good native leader who had been recruited into the Roman governing class. He was descended from a successful ruler, engaged in large building projects, cultivated patrons in Rome, visited there frequently, and sought to enlarge his power. He divorced his wife and married his niece with the ease of an upper-class Roman. He also kept a firm hand on any people or movements that might threaten the security of his territory. He imprisoned John the Baptist in his beautiful palace fortress at Machaerus in Perea, one of the districts where John had been preaching. John's reform movement and criticism of Antipas's non-Jewish lifestyle promoted political unrest. The gospel story that he executed John in response to the request of his wife's daughter, Salome, is possible, but a simple political execution is more likely. He also kept an eye on Jesus and any other popular reformers. Because Antipas was not just a Jewish king but a Roman official who implemented pro-Roman policies, he had an ambiguous relationship with his Jewish subjects.

H.   THE JESUS MOVEMENT

The reform movement begun by Jesus flourished in Antipas's Galilee (see pp. 394–397). The tenor of the teachings preserved in the gospels suggests, with allowance made for late-first-century editing, that Jesus promoted a renewed commitment to the covenant and traditions of Israel. He envisioned an Israel ruled by God, both in the present and in the future, when the son of man was to come. The norms governing this renewed Israel stressed care for the poor and needy, reliance on God, reconciliation in social relations, and de-emphasis on

JESUS AND JOHN THE BAPTIST IN JOSEPHUS

JOSEPHUS MENTIONS JESUS' life and activity once. Since Josephus often mentioned popular leaders who caused social unrest and were executed, his reference to Jesus is not unexpected. However, since the passage acknowledges that Jesus was the Messiah, hints at his divinity, and accepts the Resurrection, it was either inserted by a Christian copyist or thoroughly revised by one. The passage reads:

At about this time lived Jesus, a wise man, if indeed one might call him a man. For he was one who accomplished surprising feats and was a teacher of such people as accept the truth with pleasure. He won over many Jews and many of the Greeks. He was the Messiah. When Pilate, upon an indictment brought by the principal men among us, condemned him to the cross, those who had loved him from the very first did not cease to be attached to him. On the third day he appeared to them restored to life, for the holy prophets had foretold this and myriads of other marvels concerning him. And the tribe of the Christians, so called after him, has to this day still not disappeared. (*Antiquities* 18.3.3 [63–4])

Josephus also mentions John the Baptist and stresses the political unrest he caused as the reason for his execution by Herod Antipas. Josephus's praise of John's message fits his concern to present Judaism as a virtuous way of life. His lack of personal condemnation of the execution of John is consistent with his opposition to anyone who might disturb civil order.

Herod put [John] to death, though he was a good man and had exhorted the Jews to lead righteous lives, to practice justice towards their fellows and piety towards God, and so doing to join in baptism. In his view this was a necessary preliminary if baptism was to be acceptable to God. They must not employ it to gain pardon for whatever sins they committed, but as a consecration of the body implying that the soul was already thoroughly cleansed by right behavior. When others too joined the crowds about him, because they were aroused (variant: *overjoyed*) to the highest degree by hearing his words, Herod became alarmed. Eloquence that had so great an effect on mankind might lead to some form of sedition (variant: *revolt*), for it looked as if they would be guided by John in everything that they did. Herod decided therefore that it would be much better to strike first and be rid of him before his work led to an uprising, than to wait for an upheaval, get involved in a difficult situation and see his mistake. Though John, because of Herod's suspicions, was brought in chains to Machaerus, the stronghold that we have previously mentioned, and there was put to death, yet the verdict of the Jews was that the destruction visited upon Herod's army [by Aretas, the Arab king] was a vindication of John, since God saw fit to inflict such a blow on Herod. (*Antiquities* 18.5.2 [116–19])

human authority, honor, and accomplishment. Jesus' program offered healing for the sinfulness and weakness of humans and hope for the impoverished Galilean peasants, who had no control over their government or lives. His program was based on faith in God's active presence as protector of Israel.

Though such a program can be couched in apparently innocuous biblical and spiritual terminology, in ancient society a claim that God ruled implied that the current human rulers were illegitimate or seriously deficient. A program for religious reform involved major changes in social relations, changes that threatened the wealth, power, and influence of the governing class and the stable traditions that legitimated their position in society. For these reasons Herod Antipas, the chief priests, and the scribes (who were educational, bureaucratic, and religious functionaries in society) correctly viewed Jesus as a threat to their Roman-supported state and opposed him. The Pharisees, who promoted an older program for the reform of Jewish life and the reinvigoration of the covenant in society, disputed Jesus' rival interpretation, which threatened their influence and reforms. The Pharisees sought to establish and protect Israel as a people holy to God through faithful observance of the ritual purity regulations reserved by the Bible for the priests in the temple. They also stressed tithing as an expression of covenant fidelity. Jesus' program for the renewal of society through a reinvigorated commitment of God's kingdom and renewed bonds among humans appealed strongly to the outcasts, poor, and powerless, who were not incorporated fully into the social and sacred system of Judaism. Jesus' popularity with the crowds, their eagerness to hear him and experience his power, and the opposition of the authorities all fit within the context of Galilean Jews who had been conquered by Rome, were sternly ruled by a Jewish proxy of Rome, and suffered heavy taxes with no avenue of appeal or control over their own society.

VII. MID-FIRST-CENTURY CRISES

After the governorship of Pontius Pilate ended in 36 C.E., tensions with Rome continued to increase over economic, political, and religious issues. Even the rural population whom Jesus had addressed was affected by hellenistic cultural currents flowing through Galilee and by the actions of the faraway government in Rome. It was in this Palestinian Jewish world of dissatisfaction and resentment that the earliest followers of Jesus became organized into communities. The first followers of Jesus had been born Jewish, identified themselves as Jews, and continued to live according to what they regarded as the central laws of Judaism. They were one of many Jewish groups aspiring to renovate or reform Judaism, each through its unique understanding of and emphasis on certain crucial elements of the Jewish tradition.

The most serious crisis was caused by the Roman emperor who replaced Tiberius, Gaius Caligula (37–41 C.E.). Gaius took emperor worship seriously, and when Jews in Jamnia, near the Palestinian coast, tore down an altar to the emperor, he ordered a statue of himself placed in the temple of Jerusalem in reprisal. All responsible officials – including Agrippa I (a grandson of Herod the Great), who was in Rome at the time of the crisis; Petronius, the Roman governor in Syria; the Alexandrian Jewish community; and the Jerusalem leadership – knew that transporting the statue to Jerusalem would produce an all-out revolt with unimaginable slaughter. Eventually Agrippa convinced Gaius to revoke his order to place a statue in the temple, but the emperor's edict allowed the erection of statues to himself anywhere outside Jerusalem, a practice almost as abhorrent to the Jewish community. Actually, Gaius secretly planned to bring a statue to the temple when he visited Palestine. His plans concerning the statue were annulled only by his death.

Gaius's contempt for the Jews became manifest also in his dealings with the Alexandrian Jewish community. Perhaps at the instigation of the emperor, Alexandrian crowds responded to a visit of Agrippa I in 38 C.E. with insults and bullied the governor, Flaccus, into placing statues of the emperor in Jewish houses of prayer, curtailing Jewish rights,

PHILO'S *EMBASSY TO GAIUS*

THE ALEXANDRIAN JEWISH philosopher and biblical interpreter Philo was a member of the legation sent to Emperor Gaius Caligula to present the grievances of the Alexandrian Jews. Gaius treated the ambassadors poorly and postponed meeting them. While waiting, they were informed of Gaius's plan to place a statue of himself as a god in the temple at Jerusalem. Later, he surprised the Jewish king, Agrippa I, with the news. The ambassadors' reactions reveal how abhorent this sacrilege was to them. The person bringing the news to the embassy asked,

> "Have you heard the new tidings?" and when he was going to report it, he was brought up short, as a flood of tears streamed from his eyes. He began again and the second time stopped short and so too a third time. . . . He managed with difficulty while sobbing and breathing spasmodically to say, "Our

temple is lost, Gaius has ordered a colossal statue to be set up within the inner sanctuary dedicated to himself under the name of Zeus." As we marvelled at his words and, petrified by consternation, could not get any further, since we stood there speechless and turned to water, others appeared bringing the same woeful tale. (186–9)

Gaius's motive for ordering the statue placed in the temple is revealed in his conversation with King Agrippa, who was his client and friend:

> [Gaius] said "Your excellent and worthy fellow-citizens, who alone of every race of men do not acknowledge Gaius as a god, appear to be courting even death by their recalcitrance. When I ordered a statue of Zeus to be set up in the temple they marshalled their whole population and issued forth from the city and country nominally to make a petition but actually to counteract my orders." He was about to add further charges when Agrippa in deep distress turned every kind

of color, blood-red, dead pale and livid all in a moment. And by now from the crown of his head to his feet he was mastered by a fit of shuddering, every part and every limb convulsed with trembling and palpitation. With his nervous system relaxed and unbraced he was in a state of utter collapse, and finally thus paralysed was on the point of falling. But some of the bystanders caught him and . . . took him home on a stretcher, quite unconscious in his coma of the mass of troubles which had fallen upon him. Gaius indeed was still more exasperated and pushed his hatred of the nation still further. "If Agrippa," he said, "who is my dearest and most familiar friend and bound to me by so many benefactions, is so under the dominion of its customs that he cannot even bear to hear a word against them and is prostrated almost to the point of death, what must we expect of the others who are not under the influence of any counter-acting force?" (265–8)

and sanctioning a general persecution in which Jews were robbed, forced to break their laws, and killed in great numbers. Thirty-eight members of the Jewish council of elders, who were leading citizens, were publicly flogged in the theater. Philo, the great Alexandrian Jewish writer, wrote extensive protests against this outrage. Flaccus, who was not in good graces with Gaius, was soon exiled and replaced by Pollio. How fiercely the Jews were oppressed in the next two years is not clear, but in 40 C.E. the Alexandrian Jewish community and government sent embassies to present their cases to the emperor in Rome. After long delays and poor treatment by the emperor, the Jewish delegation was dismissed. Only after Claudius, the new emperor, succeeded Gaius in 41 C.E. was the situation resolved by the reinstatement of traditional Jewish privileges and by the execution of the Alexandrian officials who had instigated the strife.

Claudius appointed Agrippa I king over Judea and Samaria. He had already been appointed ruler of Galilee and areas to the north by the previous emperor, Gaius Caligula. Though Agrippa had been constantly in debt from dissolute and luxurious living and had gotten into various political troubles, in Palestine he observed Jewish law, governed tactfully, and is therefore remembered as a good ruler. Outside Palestine he continued the practice of giving donations to hellenistic temples and games. Unfortunately, death ended his reign after only three years.

After Agrippa's death in 44 C.E. a succession of Roman procurators resumed direct control over all of Palestine. Many of these procurators were bad governors who treated the people unjustly and inflamed their passions with culturally repugnant acts. During the period both banditry and armed insurrection increased in Judea as well as in Galilee. Bandits, who were landless peasants living off exactions from the rich, had the support of the common people, who gave them shelter and protected them from capture. Roman officials were attacked and robbed, leaders were killed, and organized bands occasionally protested the governmental and social system. For example, an Egyptian claimed to be a prophet and led a large group into the desert with the promise that upon their return to the Mount of Olives, the walls of Jerusalem would collapse and the Roman garrison go down to defeat. (Acts 21:38 mentions this leader, and the complete story is told in Josephus.)

Josephus has numerous stories of the Roman governors' ill-advised behavior which contributed to the outbreak of war in 66 C.E. Felix (52–60? C.E.) is typical. He was a freedman (a former slave, legally free but still serving his former master) of the imperial household whose brother, Pallas, was a high official. In his personal and public life he was arrogant and self-seeking. Corruption and insensitivity to Jewish feeling were characteristic of his rule, and as a consequence, banditry, protest, and rebellion became a normal part of social relationships. The Sicarii, a group of terrorist assassins, became active during this period. Felix married a Jewish princess, Drusilla, who was a daughter of Agrippa I and sister of Agrippa II, who ruled over part of Galilee and areas to the north. Agrippa II is noted for a possibly incestuous relationship with his sister Bernice. Felix, Drusilla, Agrippa, and Bernice appear in Acts 23–6 as the judges of Paul, who had been arrested by the Roman Jerusalem garrison and accused by the temple authorities of fomenting unrest. Felix left Paul in jail for two years to avoid trouble. The next procurator, Festus, sent Paul to Rome for trial after consulting with Agrippa II. Acts and Josephus agree in presenting both the nominally Jewish and the non-Jewish leaders of Palestine in the mid–first century as cultural foreigners to Judaism and as ineffective and unjust rulers.

A. LITERARY RESPONSES TO ROMAN OPPRESSION IN THE FIRST CENTURY

The increasing hostility toward Rome, social unrest in the face of an unjust government, and cultural frustration with corrosive hellenistic practices probably fostered the mood of apocalyptic expectation in early gospel traditions and in Paul's letters, as well as nourishing those traditions in Jewish literature. Apocalyptic literature looks for a solution to the massive evils of the present by direct divine inter-

KING AGRIPPA I

AGRIPPA I WAS A GRANDSON of Herod the Great. He was sent to Rome to be educated with the highest echelon of Roman society. He was a close friend of the future emperor, Gaius Caligula. As a young man he was a spendthrift, constantly in debt and even jailed briefly by Tiberius. When Gaius became emperor, he gave Agrippa wealth and the rule of Galilee and areas to the north. When Claudius replaced Gaius (41 C.E.), he added Samaria and Judea to Agrippa's rule. Agrippa ruled well in accordance with Jewish law for three years but died suddenly. According to Acts 12, he beheaded James the son of Zebedee and imprisoned Peter.

vention in the near future and by a radical and comprehensive reform or revolution in social relationships. These aspirations can be felt in a section of 1 Enoch (the Ethiopic Book of Enoch), the Similitudes of Enoch (chaps. 37–71), which probably dates from the first half of the first century. Its author is unknown, but he drew upon other parts of 1 Enoch in order to comment on events in his own day. A clear reference to the Parthian invasion in 40 B.C.E. (Simil. En. 56:5–8) puts the Similitudes of Enoch after the middle of the first century B.C.E. Its obsession with the powerful rulers of the earth fits well into the mid–first century C.E. and its experience of conflict with the Roman government.

The Similitudes of Enoch present three visions of the triumph of the righteous over the powerful leaders of the earth through divine judgment by the son of man and the establishment of God's just kingdom on this earth. In the face of Roman military might and undisputed sovereignty, the author turns to divine revelation of the future, derived from Enoch's journey to heaven, and secret knowledge of the universe, given by heavenly mediators. The three similitudes (or parables) that convey this revelation provide analogies and models for understanding the workings of the universe and human history. For example, references to the punishment of angels and Noah's flood (Simil. En. 39, 54) foreshadow the punishment of the powerful earthly leaders and the overthrow of evil. The narrative transforms the present ills of society into minor events in a triumphant cosmic history.

The Similitudes of Enoch provides hope to a society suffering continuing oppression and powerlessness. The faithful believers who were enduring economic and political evils were assured of a secure special destiny in a divinely founded society. The first parable begins with the main themes of the work:

> When the congregation of the righteous shall appear,
> And sinners shall be judged for their sins,
> And shall be driven from the face of the earth;
> And when the Righteous One shall appear before the eyes of the righteous,
> Whose works hang upon the Lord of Spirits,
> And light shall appear to the righteous and the elect who dwell on the earth,
> Where then will be the dwelling of the sinners,
> And where the resting place of those who have denied the Lord of Spirits?
> It had been good for them if they had not been born.
> When the secrets of the righteous shall be revealed and the sinners judged,
> And the godless driven from the presence of the righteous and elect,
> From that time those that possess the earth shall no longer be powerful and exalted;
> And they shall not be able to behold the face of the holy,
> For the Lord of Spirits has caused his light to appear

On the face of the holy, righteous, and elect.
Then shall the kings and the mighty perish
And be given into the hands of the righteous and holy.

(Simil. En. 38:1–5)

This view of society continues through the Similitudes of Enoch and is fundamental to its understanding of the cosmos. The world is divided between a group of chosen, faithful, good people and the majority, who are evil people led by the powerful of society. It is unclear whether all Israel or only a faithful part is righteous. The main accusation against the opponents of the righteous, that they have denied the Lord of Spirits (a frequent title for God in the Similitudes of Enoch), could pertain to non-Jews and assimilationist Jewish leaders. The solution to the present unjust political order will be an appearance of God to judge evil people and to effect the destruction of the kings and mighty rulers of this world so that the good may possess a renewed earth in peace.

These themes are elaborated in many polemics against the mighty rulers of the world (e.g., Simil. En. 46, 48), in promises of vindication for the righteous (e.g., Simil. En. 50–1), and in judgment scenes in which both angels and humans are punished (Simil. En. 53–4). In the climactic scene, reminiscent of the gospel parable of the sheep and goats (Matt. 25:31 ff.), the son of man judges the world, rewarding the just and punishing the evil kings. The author envisions a resurrection of the just from the dead (Simil. En. 61:5) and the renewal of the earth under God's just rule (Simil. En. 51:4–5) as a solution for the profound political and social evils and dislocation of his day. The roots of his outlook run back into Israel's past and include myths about the origins of the cosmos and evil. The Similitudes of Enoch draws upon many older stories of the fall of the angels, the heavenly battle between good and

THE "RIGHTEOUS" AND JEWISH FACTIONS

THE PERIOD OF JEWISH history from ca. 165 B.C.E. to 135 C.E. can be characterized as a period of sectarianism within Judaism. There were a number of competing factions, which often viewed one another with suspicion, if not contempt. The struggle between these competing factions is evidenced by the harsh language the documents from this period utilize when describing their opponents. The Dead Sea Scrolls, 1 Enoch, the Psalms of Solomon, and the late-first-century C.E. documents of 2 Baruch, 4 Ezra, and the Gospel of Matthew are just a few of the documents from this period of history that contain this strident language.

Terms like "lawless," "hypocrites," "corrupt," and "godless" are just a few of the epithets regularly used to describe the enemies of the sect or group. The group being attacked usually is the one in control and is depicted as oppressing the sect. Conversely the group employing the harsh language thinks of itself as the "righteous," the "faithful and lawful," "a remnant," and "God's true people." The use of "righteous" and other similar terms reflects the belief on the part of the community that they constitute God's true people, to the exclusion of other groups, particularly those in power. Judaism had a number of competing groups during this period, each of which portrayed itself as "God's true people" and the "righteous." The use of such exclusive or harsh language provides an insight into the self-definition of the community in question, as well as into the volatile and highly charged atmosphere of this period in history.

evil, the origin of humans, and the structure of heaven to make its case. The overwhelming might of Rome and the intractable political repression of Israel are met by the divine forces of the cosmos and the inevitable justice of God's judgment.

B.   DIASPORA RESPONSES TO ROMAN RULE

1.   The Fourth Book of Maccabees

Hostility to the Romans and conflict with hellenistic culture were not limited to Jews in Palestine. Jews living in other parts of the Roman Empire faced occasional persecution and constant pressure to assimilate. Several works from the first century show the difficulty of living as a Jew in other countries even as they seek to adapt hellenistic modes of thought and life to support Judaism. The Fourth Book of Maccabees is a philosophical exhortation to religious reason that uses martyr stories found in 2 Maccabees as points of illustration. The Fourth Book of Maccabees was probably written in Syria, perhaps in the major cultural center, Antioch, in the first century and may have been recited at a yearly festival in honor of Jewish martyrs (4 Macc. 1:10). The author is unknown. The use of the martyrdom of Eleazar and of the mother and her seven sons from 2 Maccabees two centuries earlier reflects continuing Jewish uneasiness with the surrounding culture and lively awareness of proximate hostility. The highly detailed and rhetorically flamboyant descriptions of the tortures inflicted on the martyrs and the numerous exhortations and apologetic speeches exchanged among the characters create an intense emotional atmosphere charged with danger and promise.

The thesis of 4 Maccabees, that the passions must be ruled by reason, derives from Platonism and Stoicism and was part of popular Greek philosophy in the East. According to this scheme, reason is governed by the virtue of prudence, which in turn governs the passions through justice, temperance, and courage. The Jewish author of 4 Maccabees argues for the reasonableness of Jewish laws, including the dietary laws and other customs that kept Greeks and Jews apart. Thus the Jewish martyrs argue that fidelity to the law accords with reason, and they refute rational arguments that urge them to abandon the Jewish way of life (4 Macc. 5:7 ff., 8:16 ff.). To Antiochus's charge that Eleazar's refusal to eat non-kosher meat is irrational, Eleazar answers:

> Do not suppose that it would be a petty sin if we were to eat defiling food; to transgress the law in matters either small or great is of equal seriousness, for in either case the law is equally despised. You scoff at our philosophy as though living by it were irrational, but it teaches us self-control, so that we master all pleasures and desires, and it also trains us in courage, so that we endure any suffering willingly; it instructs us in justice, so that in all our dealings we act impartially, and it teaches us piety, so that with proper reverence we worship the only real God. (4 Macc. 5:19–24)

Synagogue on the island of Delos.
J. Andrew Overman.

The presentation of Jewish law as philosophy and the argument that commitment to Jewish law is an exercise of the key Stoic virtues of self-control, courage, and justice are an attempt to make the Jewish way of life comprehensible and acceptable to hellenized Jews pressured by an alien environment. Even the final reward of the martyrs, immortality (4 Macc. 14:5–6), is drawn from Greek thought. In a more distinctively Jewish vein the author also notes that the martyrs atone for Israel's sins by their blood (6:27) and that the persecuting king, Antiochus IV, will be punished (12:12). Though the author makes use of Stoic and Platonic ideas, his fundamental values are Jewish and founded upon adherence to biblical law. Many particulars of his teaching remain Jewish – for example, his insistence that the passions are naturally good and to be controlled (2:22), contrary to the Stoic doctrine that they are to be eradicated.

The author's attitude toward hellenistic civilization is complex. Though the stories of martyrdom bespeak hostility and estrangement between Greco-Roman and Jewish culture, the author envisions only the punishment of the offending king, not the destruction of hellenistic society or the apocalyptic rule of Israel over the world. According to the author, the persecutions were preceded by a period of friendly relations between Jews and Greeks (4 Macc. 3:19–21), and a return to that state is desired. So friendly are Jews with Greeks that the major Jewish characters in the drama speak to their fellow Jews against assimilation, an ever present danger. Most striking, the author defends Judaism against Greco-Roman culture and political power by writing a Greek diatribe which unites Greek philosophy and Jewish traditions into a Greek rhetorical exhortation whose purpose is to preserve Jewish identity from assimilation to Greek culture.

2. The Wisdom of Solomon

Jewish wisdom is more directly praised at the expense of gentile persecution and idolatry in the Wisdom of Solomon, which was written in Alexandria in the later first century B.C.E. or the early first century C.E. (A recent study has argued that the Greek vocabulary belongs to the first century C.E. and that the intensity of the persecution reflected in chap. 5 may reflect the Alexandrian persecutions of 38–41 C.E.) The Wisdom of Solomon was written in excellent Greek by an anonymous, well-educated author as an exhortation for the Jewish community of Alexandria, using the biblical wisdom tradition as its central theme and many other biblical traditions as examples in its argument and exposition. It opens with an appeal to the rulers of the earth to love righteousness and with a description of Wisdom (rather than the son of man, as in the Similitudes of Enoch) as the judge of evil. The first five chapters draw on apocalyptic traditions to portray the fate of the innocent sufferer who is persecuted by unjust and powerful men. Eventually "the righteous man will stand with great confidence in the presence of those who have afflicted him. . . . When they see him they will be shaken with dreadful fear and they will be amazed at his unexpected salvation" (Wisd. of Sol. 5:1–2). The judgment of the evil and the vindication of the righteous lead to reward and immortality: "The righteous live forever and their reward is with the Lord" (5:15).

In the description and praise of Wisdom in chapters 6–9 the author links obedience to Wisdom's laws with attaining immortality: "Giving heed to [Wisdom's] laws is assurance of immortality, and immortality brings one near to God" (6:19; see also 2:23). Immortality is a Greek conception of life after death which envisions the survival of the soul but not the body. It was used as an alternative to resurrection of the body and exaltation of the blessed in some Jewish writings, such as 2 and 4 Maccabees. The author's discourse about Wisdom and faithfulness to Judaism is a standard Greek exhortation that makes use of Greek philosophical terminology and Greek rhetorical strategies. After a description of Wisdom and her invitation to humans, drawn mainly from biblical models, the author describes Wisdom in Greek categories:

> For in her [Wisdom] there is a spirit that is intelligent, holy, unique, manifold, subtle, mobile, clear, unpolluted, distinct, invulnerable, loving the good, keen, irresistible, beneficent, humane, steadfast, sure, free from anxiety, all-powerful, overseeing all, and penetrating through all spirits that are intelligent and pure and most subtle. For Wisdom is more mobile than any motion; because of her pureness she pervades and penetrates all things. For she is a breath of the power of God, and a pure emanation of the glory of the Almighty; therefore nothing defiled gains entrance into her. For she is a reflection of eternal light, a spotless mirror of the working of God, and an image of his goodness. (Wisd. of Sol. 7:22–6)

In this document the Platonic philosophy of emanations and of type and archetype as well as a variety of Greek metaphors have been applied to Wisdom in order to make her the Jewish equivalent of Greek philosophical wisdom.

In the last half of the book (chaps. 10–19) the author interprets history as Wisdom's activity among humans. He consoles his fellow Jews with examples of God's mercy to Israel in contrast to his punishment of the Egyptians in the Book of Exodus. The sin of the Egyptians is dramatized by a long polemic against idolatry (13:1–15:17) which reflects the fundamental Jewish rejection of the surrounding culture even while the author uses Greek language, rhetoric, and argument to uphold the Jewish traditions on which his book is based.

In praising Wisdom and attributing God's activity in history to her, the author advocates the superiority of the Jewish tradition over the dominant hellenistic Egyptian tradition. Against the attractions of hellenism he encourages faithfulness to Judaism through a skillful blend of Jewish and hellenistic ideas and traditions. The sophistication and integrity of the Wisdom of Solomon's exhortation manifests how inextricably – but uneasily – Judaism had joined the Greek and Roman cultures.

3. Philo of Alexandria

Finally, Philo of Alexandria typifies the creative tensions that beset Judaism in the Roman Empire. The little we know of Philo's life and family mirror his writings. His family was prominent and wealthy. His brother, Alexander, was a high official in charge of customs collection, and Alexander's son, Tiberius Julius Alexander, apostatized from Judaism, became a high Roman official, and even assisted in the siege of Jerusalem. In his old age, Philo was part of the delegation sent by the Alexandrian Jewish community to Gaius Caligula in 40 C.E. to seek relief from persecution. The Jewish community to which he belonged in Alexandria was very large, with numerous houses of prayer and great influence. It was concentrated in its own Jewish quarter of the city, but many Jews lived elsewhere in the city as well. Though Jews were not full citizens of Alexandria, the Jewish community was a recognized political entity with legal rights, an organized leadership, and substantial internal control.

Philo's voluminous writings are typical of the Alexandrian modes of philosophical thought and textual interpretation. Philo sought a philosophical interpretation for the Bible and Jewish traditions. In commentary after commentary Philo used allegory to harmonize biblical traditions with Greek philosophy and to show the superiority of the Jewish tradition. His interpretation of biblical stories as allegories for philosophical and ethical truths depended on Platonic philosophy. His philosophical treaties integrated biblical and philosophical principles, especially those of the middle Platonists and Stoics. In his apologetic writings Philo defended Judaism against anti-Semitic attacks, misunderstandings common in the Roman world, and political attacks against Jewish status in Alexandria.

Philo's transposition of the biblical tradition into Greek philosophy

PLATONIC PHILOSOPHY

IN THE EARLY FOURTH century B.C.E. the philosopher Plato, who was a disciple of Socrates, began a school in Athens, the Platonic Academy, which survived until the sixth century C.E. Platonic philosophy was one of the most influential schools of thought in the ancient world. It underwent an evolution from early Platonism, through the middle Platonism of the first centuries B.C.E. and C.E., to Neo-Platonism in the third and fourth centuries C.E.

Platonic philosophy affirmed a non-material basis for material reality and stressed the changeability, corruptibility, and imperfection of the perceptible world. The philosopher's task was to understand and to be guided by the models, or the immaterial forms, of that which exists materially. Each aspect of creation as we know it was conceived of as a copy or model based on an original, eternal, immaterial form (or type–archetype). Middle Platonism took a religious and ethical turn. It identified the earlier Platonic forms with the divine mind and posited a relation between this divine mind and human minds. Physical reality was something which emanated from the immaterial and owed its existence and nature to that primordial immaterial reality. The human mind had to purify itself of the material to reach knowledge of the transcendent and immaterial world, which was fully real.

goes deeper than the moral exhortation of 4 Maccabees, yet it also promotes fidelity to biblical law and the Jewish way of life. The simple statement that "Abraham went [to the Promised Land] as the Lord commanded him" (Gen. 12:4) becomes for Philo the adoption of a philosophical way of life:

> "Abraham went as the Lord commanded him." And this is the end which is celebrated among those who study philosophy in the best manner, namely, to live in accordance with nature. And this takes place when the mind, entering into the path of virtue, treads in the steps of right reason, and follows God, remembering his commandments, and at all times and in all places confirming them both by word and deed; for "he went as the Lord commanded him." And the meaning of this is, as God commands (and he commands in a beautiful and praiseworthy manner), in that very manner does the virtuous man act, guiding the path of his life in a blameless way, so that the actions of the wise man are in no respect different from the divine commands. (*On the Migration of Abraham* 23:127–9)

Philo's exegesis of a simple statement that Abraham went to the land of Israel as God commanded is not arbitrary or unreasonable. It is based on a Platonic epistemology which searches through mystical knowledge for the unseen and inner basis of visible reality. In response to God's call and blessing (Gen. 12:1–3), Abraham took up a new way of life by leaving Haran, where he had been living, and transporting his family to a new and alien land. In so doing he initiated a new people and a new way of life and affirmed two basic principles of Judaism: faith in God and obedience to divine commands. Implicit in Abraham's obedience is the reception of new knowledge about God and how to live, knowledge that was revealed subsequently to Moses. Thus, from Philo's perspective, Abraham's act is symbolic of the commitment to a philosophical way of life.

Like the author of 4 Maccabees, Philo uses Greek philosophy to expound and defend Jewish tradition. He associates God's wisdom and activity with *logos*, a key Greek philosophical concept which suggests reason, understanding, and the rational order of the universe. Abraham becomes an example of right reason in action. Philo's description of the persecutions that came upon the Alexandrian community testifies to his personal experience of these atrocities and rivals 3–4 Maccabees in rhetorical intensity and descriptive detail. His concentration on the reward of virtue and the punishment to be visited on Flaccus, the Roman governor who conducted the persecutions, also shows thought patterns similar to those of 4 Maccabees.

VIII. THE JEWISH WORLD AFTER THE FALL OF JERUSALEM

A. THE WARS AGAINST ROME

The last third of the first century C.E. and the first third of the second saw Palestinian and Diaspora Jews engaged in a series of military conflicts with the Roman government. For the Romans such peri-

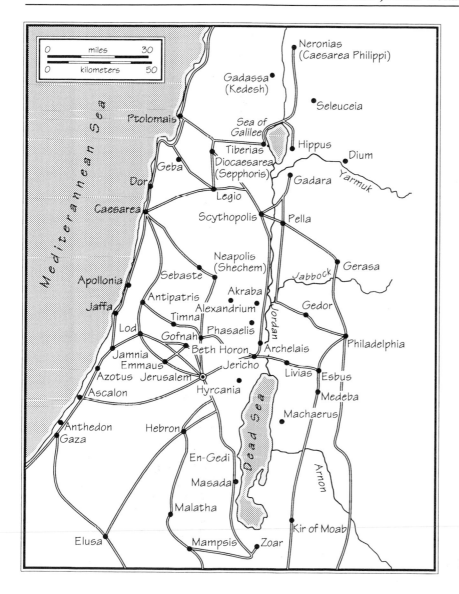

Roman road system.

odic wars were expected crises in imperial administration, and the
Jewish rebellions, like others, were put down with military might and
calculated destruction. In the first war with Rome (66–70 C.E.)
Jerusalem and the temple were destroyed and Judaism lost its traditional center and any vestige of priestly self-government. That this loss
and subjection to the Roman Empire were not meekly accepted is
shown by the widespread uprising of Diaspora Jewish communities in
the eastern Mediterranean (115–17 C.E.) and the second Palestinian war
against the Romans, the Bar Kosiba War (or Bar Kokhba War) (132–5
C.E.), which so devastated Judea that the center of Palestinian Judaism
moved to Galilee.

The wars killed many of the traditional leaders of Palestinian
Judaism and destroyed the institutional structure of the national community. Those Jewish groups that survived the wars cherished the bib-

THE FORTRESS ANTONIA

THE TOWER, OR FORTRESS Antonia, was built at the northwest corner of the wall enclosing the temple mount. The Hasmoneans had built the original fort there (the Baris) because the land leading up to the walls was level and needed stronger defenses. Herod luxuriously rebuilt it and named it for his patron, Mark Anthony. In the first century C.E. the Antonia was a key Roman military installation. It overlooked the temple compound and was connected to the temple enclosure by a bridge. Thus, the Romans could observe what went on in Jerusalem's strongest fortification, the temple enclosure, and send in troops if necessary. For Jews the Antonia was an irritating symbol of Roman domination, especially since the high priest's vestments were kept there by the Romans between festivals as another measure of control. At the beginning of the revolt against Rome in 66 the bridge between the Antonia and temple mount was destroyed and the Roman garrison besieged. Some scholars hold that Jesus was tried there by Pilate, but it is perhaps more likely that Pilate had his Jerusalem headquarters in Herod's palace on the western hill (at the contemporary Jaffa Gate). During the siege of Jerusalem the Antonia was destroyed along with the rest of Jerusalem.

lical tradition and continued to live in the traditional way in both Palestinian villages and Diaspora cities. Between the wars apocalyptic works contributed to the expectation of divine aid, which helped set the stage for the second war. After a second crushing defeat, the people did not revolt again and apocalypses ceased to be written, though the tradition continued to influence Jewish belief and thought. The torrent of Jewish literature during the hellenistic and Roman period dried up with the destruction of Jerusalem and its learned leaders. Only with the formation of a new learned group – the sages, or rabbis – did Palestinian Judaism produce a major corpus of religious literature, the Mishnah (ca. 200 C.E.). Gradually, during the following several centuries, a new form of Judaism, rabbinic Judaism, took shape and then gained acceptance and dominance within the Jewish community. In seeking to legitimate these developments, the rabbis claimed roots and antecedents going back to Moses through an alleged oral tradition.

Christianity took its more mature and definitive shape against this background of severe disruption and change in the Jewish community. In the late first century, after the destruction of the temple, Matthew, Luke–Acts, and John were written. The mother church of Christianity, the Jerusalem community, was destroyed in the sack of Jerusalem, so power shifted definitively to the gentile communities around the Mediterranean. Followers of Jesus continued to interpret the Bible to match their evolving understanding of Jesus and new communal circumstances.

1. The Great War

During the venal rule of the Roman procurator Felix (52–60? C.E.) resistance to Roman government and popular resentment intensified. Felix's successor, Festus, was ineffective and was followed by Albinus (62–4), who, like Felix, was notable for his greed and unjust administration. The Sicarii ('dagger men') flourished under these last procurators, assassinating their Roman and Jewish opponents in order to destabilize society and encourage rebellion. Under Albinus they took prominent Roman and Jewish hostages to exchange them for ransom and their own captured members. Albinus conspired with both the Sicarii and the chief priests in order to collect the maximum amount of bribes. Albinus's successor, Florus (64–6 C.E.), plundered cities and rich individuals more openly than previous procurators and made no pretense of administering justice.

The high priests conspired with the Romans and competed among themselves for power and wealth. In the interregnum between Festus and Albinus, High Priest Ananus executed numerous opponents, including James, who was the brother of Jesus and the leader of the Jerusalem Christian community. His successor, Ananias, stole the tithes due other priests and had his armed guards collect these tithes on the threshing floors. On another occasion the supporters of a deposed high priest and of his appointed successor battled for control on the streets of Jerusalem. Because of the governors' and high priests' interest in their own self-aggrandizement, anti-Roman sentiment among the people grew strong and eventually exploded beyond control.

In April–May 66 C.E. Florus took seventeen talents of gold from the temple treasury. (A talent was a Hebrew measure of weight equal to about seventy-five pounds and when made of precious metal became a monetary unit.) This blasphemous act goaded the people to riot, so Florus had his troops put down the disorder and sacked part of the city. Florus then insisted that the people give a ceremonial welcome to his troops, but the people shouted insults and Florus again attacked them. In the battle that followed the people gained control of the temple mount and cut the bridge to the Roman fortress, Antonia. Outmaneuvered, Florus withdrew to Caesarea.

Agrippa II, son of Agrippa I (d. 44 B.C.E.) and great-grandson of Herod the Great, was the ruler of Batanaea, Gaulanitis, and other areas north and east of Galilee. He was also a natural mediator between Jerusalem and the Romans. Informed by a messenger about the crisis, he returned to Jerusalem from Alexandria, where he was visiting. However, he was unable to convince the people to rebuild the connection to the Roman fortress and to pay their back taxes. Further attempts by the chief priests to take control of the city, using troops supplied by Agrippa, also failed, and in a series of battles lasting until September, the palaces of the high priest and Agrippa were burned, all of the city fell to the rebels, and High Priest Ananias as well as the Roman garrison were murdered. Though the majority of the governing class opposed the revolt and feared Roman military might, Eleazar, the son of Ananias, was a leader of the insurrection. Thus conflicts within the ruling classes, along with lower-class dissatisfaction, contributed to the social disorder. In addition, fighting between Jews and gentiles erupted in many cities near Judea and resulted in slaughter on both sides.

Cestius Gallus, the Roman governor of Syria, who had ultimate responsibility for peace in the East, made the first attempt to put down the revolt. Though he subdued the villages in the vicinity of Jerusalem, his force was not strong enough to take Jerusalem. As he withdrew, his troops were ambushed and routed in the pass at Beth-horon, as the Seleucid forces had been over two centuries earlier.

During the winter of 67–8 the governing classes regained control of Jewish society by agreeing to supervise preparations for war with Rome. High-ranking priests and aristocrats divided up responsibility for fortifying numerous cities and towns, gathering supplies and recruiting fighting forces. For example, Josephus, the Jewish historian, had responsibility for Galilee. Military preparations were hampered by rifts in society, however. Josephus, in his *Life*, tells the story of intrigue and conflict with a Galilean leader, John of Gischala. Their struggle for power was complicated by the fact that not all of the population of Galilee was for war. When the Roman army, under Vespasian, arrived in the spring of 67, Sepphoris, one of the two major cities of Galilee, immediately submitted and accepted a Roman garrison. Later, Tiberias, Gischala, and other towns submitted without a siege. Others, like Jotapata and Gamala, across the Sea of Galilee, were

AGRIPPA II

AGRIPPA II WAS THE SON of Agrippa I. He was educated in Rome and resided there until about 52. Because he was only seventeen when his father died, he did not succeed him in the rule of Palestine. For a couple of years he ruled the small kingdom of Chalcis in Lebanon and then was given the areas north and east of Galilee. Later, in the sixties Nero gave him parts of Galilee as well. He was also given supervision of the temple and the right to appoint high priests. Agrippa totally subordinated himself to Rome but supported Jewish causes and customs when it suited him. In Acts 25–6 he is pictured as advising the Roman procurator Festus and interviewing the prisoner Paul. An allegedly incestuous relationship with his sister Bernice tinged his personal life with scandal. (After the destruction of Jerusalem, Bernice engaged in a love affair with Titus, the conqueror of Jerusalem, until social disapproval in Rome forced him to send her away.)

When the revolt against Rome broke out in 66, Agrippa rushed back from Egypt to Jerusalem and tried to quiet the people. After he failed and his palace was burned, he aided the Romans in their war effort. He and Bernice supported Vespasian when he became emperor in 68. After the war Agrippa's territory was greatly increased; he died in the early nineties, the last of the Jewish kings.

Hoard of coins from the revolt against Rome.

conquered only after stiff resistance. By the winter of 67–68 all Galilee was in Roman hands.

In the spring and summer of 68 Vespasian captured the cities surrounding Jerusalem and was preparing his attack on Jerusalem when the emperor, Nero, died. During the next two years three generals were proclaimed emperor by the armies, but each was subsequently assassinated. Finally, in late 69 Vespasian, who had previously been proclaimed emperor by the armies in the East, was accepted by the whole empire. During the two years of civil strife over succession, Vespasian did not mount a siege of Jerusalem, though he did subdue all of Judea except for the Herodian fortresses. Not until the spring of 70 did Vespasian's son Titus begin the siege of Jerusalem.

The two-year respite from Roman attack did not improve Jerusalem's chance for survival, because civil war among classes and

Jerusalem at the time of the revolt.

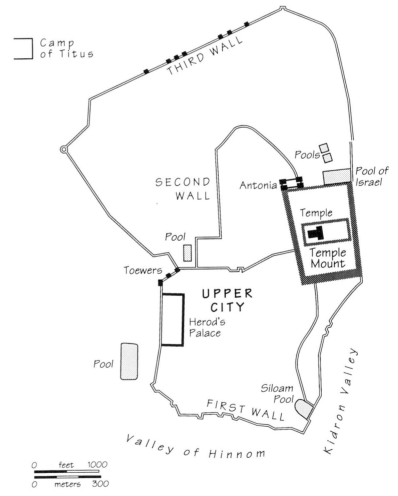

factions within Jerusalem divided the city, destroyed its food supplies, decimated its leadership, killed many of its inhabitants, and weakened its defenses. A coalition of those who strongly favored revolution, the Zealots, formed around John of Gischala, who had escaped from Galilee with his forces. Other revolutionaries from the countryside fled to Jerusalem and joined John or other factions there. The Zealots killed many of the pro-Roman governing class and replaced the high priest with a priest from the lower orders. Aided by an Idumean force, the Zealots fought the traditional leaders and killed most of them. Subsequently, an army of dispossessed peasants, who had controlled southern Judea, were driven into Jerusalem by the Roman armies. This group, led by Simon bar Giora, fought John of Gischala's Zealots, so that the city was terrorized by two groups.

Just before the arrival of the Romans, part of John's faction broke off under the leadership of Simon Bar Giora's son, Eleazar, and then there were three Jewish armies in Jerusalem locked in civil war. Eleazar held the inner forecourt of the temple, John the temple mount, and Simon the upper city and a large part of the lower city. They depleted the city's defenses and population and burned much of its food to keep it from opposing factions. Even after the Roman siege had begun, John of Gischala smuggled armed men into the temple forecourt during the Passover festival and killed Eleazar and his supporters. The fight in Jerusalem was for control of Jewish society against both the Romans and other Jewish factions and coalitions.

The Roman assault on Jerusalem, which followed classic form, began to the north where the land was flat. The Romans built several ramparts up to the walls and brought battering rams to bear. The defenders, who finally united, fought back by strengthening the walls, sallying out against the attackers, and burning or undermining the siege works. The first wall fell in fifteen days, the second nine days after that, but the fortress Antonia and the temple mount took over three months to be seized and the upper city a little longer. When the Romans finally took the temple mount in 70 C.E., they burned the temple and slaughtered the defenders. The historian Josephus's claim that Titus, the Roman general, tried to save the temple is unlikely and probably part of Josephus's attempt to flatter Titus, who was his patron, and to exculpate him so that Jews might more easily accept Roman rule.

During this extended siege, the people of Jerusalem and their leaders suffered grievously. The city ran out of food and those who tried to leave were driven back in or crucified by the Romans. During the battle many died and after the Roman conquest the soldiers plundered and burned the city for several days. Those who survived were sold into slavery or sent to the mines. Only Herod's three towers and a part of the wall were left standing to be used by the Roman camp occupying the site. Titus departed in triumph for Rome. Jerusalem was left uninhabitable, and Judean society, until then the center of Judaism, was shattered. The top level of the governing class had been stripped off, and all the officials, political groups and dissidents who gave Judaism its shape were no more. The Pharisees, Sadducees, Essenes,

THE FLAVIANS, VESPASIAN AND TITUS

AFTER NERO'S DEATH IN 68, three Roman generals held brief tenure as emperor during 68–9, until each was assassinated. Finally, the eastern legions recognized as emperor Vespasian, who was conducting the campaign against Palestine and Jerusalem. When the Danubian armies quickly ratified this choice, Vespasian's position was ensured. After he became emperor, his son Titus completed the conquest of Jerusalem. In Rome Vespasian instituted fiscal reforms to erase the deficit incurred by Nero, and with Titus, he reorganized the army to prevent further civil war and built a loyal party to support his rule. Since he came from an undistinguished family, he and his sons, Titus and Domitian, accumulated numerous offices and honors to legitimate their rule and to ensure that the dynastic principle would apply to their family. Vespasian restored the capital, built a forum and the Temple of Peace and began the Colosseum, which Titus completed.

Titus succeeded Vespasian in 79 but died in 81. He had shared much power with Vespasian, especially in suppressing dissent and rival factions. His own short reign, however, was relatively peaceful. His brother, Domitian, who ruled from 81 to 96, improved public administration, broke the power of the Senate, but faced military and financial difficulties. The last years of his reign were marked by many conspiracies and executions, until finally Domitian was assassinated and the Flavian line ended.

THE IMPERIAL TRIUMPH AFTER THE FIRST JEWISH WAR

TRADITIONALLY, SUCCESSFUL Roman generals were awarded a triumph by the Senate. In the imperial period triumphs were often reserved for or shared with the emperor. When Titus returned from the conquest of Jerusalem, he and his father, the emperor Vespasian, shared a triumph. Seven hundred handsome prisoners and the leaders Simon bar Giora and John of Gischala were brought to Rome along with the spoils of the conquest to be displayed in a parade. The seven-branched candlestick and the table of showbread from the temple, a copy of the law, and many other items were carried in procession and deposited in the temple of the goddess Peace. The booty from the victory was followed by images of the victory and the chariots carrying Vespasian and Titus. Scenes from this triumph are sculpted on the Arch of Titus in Rome.

During the procession, Simon bar Giora was taken, according to Roman custom, outside the forum and executed. The triumphal procession ended at the temple of Jupiter Capitolinus, where sacrifices were offered. The ceremonies were followed by feasting and celebration of the victory.

Zealots, Jerusalem scribes, and the Jerusalem (Jewish-) Christian community were swept away.

Even before the Roman siege started, Jewish society had begun to dissolve as a result of its inner tensions. Previously, as Jewish society had strengthened and developed new confidence in the hellenistic period, it had successfully revolted under the leadership of a priestly family which deposed the traditional ruling families. The usurpers, the Hasmoneans, had enjoyed wide popular support, but they gradually squandered it until they in turn lost their exclusive grip on Jewish society during the Roman period. Remnants of the Hasmoneans, the Herodians, high priestly families, and other wealthy families retained some power and cooperated with the Romans in order to preserve their privileged position and to avoid military confrontation with a superior force. In the late 60s many of the people and some of the ruling classes rejected this compromise in favor of an all or nothing confrontation with the empire. The bulk of the people who came to Jerusalem from the country were dispossessed peasants led by disaffected members of the governing classes. The revolt was not a struggle for power among the upper classes but a true peasant revolt. Significant sections of society rejected both the Romans and their own traditional leaders. Win or lose, Judaism was bound to change. Thus the centuries following military defeat at the hands of the Romans saw many conflicts over how the destruction was to be understood and what new patterns were to be tried in Jewish life.

2. Between the Wars

After the war the chief priests and other leading families in Jerusalem, as well as lower officials, leaders of the revolt, and many others who had led Judaism, had been killed, leaving a gap at the top of Jewish society. Because the temple had been destroyed, the remaining priests had no function, the central council and the courts associated with the temple could not be reestablished, and taxes, in the form of tithes and sacrificial animals, could not be collected. Judaism in Palestine had permanently lost its national, political leadership, and Jerusalem had become a Roman army camp.

Rome made Palestine into a separate senatorial province with a higher-ranked governor than previously and a legion of its own to keep order. The new province of Judea included Samaria, most of Galilee, and the coast. The Roman governor ruled, as before, from Caesarea on the coast, aided by Roman garrisons and officials scattered throughout the country to keep order. King Agrippa II, who had remained loyal to Rome, ruled part of Galilee and areas to the north and east until his removal or death in the 80s or 90s.

Jewish life in the rest of Palestine continued normally. The majority of the people lived in villages or small cities. All had been touched by the war, but most had not been destroyed. The Jewish way of life (including its religious customs and laws) was presided over by the traditional village notables, that is, the landed, wealthy families. Political activity and resentment against Rome must have continued because about sixty years later another war with Rome broke out. In resenting and resisting Rome, Palestinian Jews were like Diaspora Jews and many other peoples throughout the empire. Roman armies continually suppressed ethnic groups which resisted Roman authority and taxation.

The so-called War of Trajan (115–17) was a widespread revolt of Diaspora Jews in the eastern Mediterranean. While Trajan was fighting in Mesopotamia, Jews in Egypt and Cyrene (modern Libya) revolted against Roman authority and their non-Jewish countrymen. The Roman governor of Egypt lost a number of battles with Jewish forces in the

Arch of Titus in Rome, erected to celebrate the conquest of Jerusalem.

Anthony J. Saldarini

countryside, though in Alexandria the citizenry prevailed and slaughtered the Jewish community. In Cyrene the Jewish community proclaimed as king their leader, Lucuas. An ancient historian gives a lurid and exaggerated depiction of the killing and destruction. However, the attention given to the rebellion, archeological evidence of destroyed temples, and an inscription concerning repopulation of the province all testify to its seriousness. Marcus Turbo, one of Trajan's best generals, quelled the revolt in a long series of battles which led to the death of thousands of Jews who had allied themselves with their king, Lucuas.

On Cyprus the Jewish communities rose up and killed so many thousands of non-Jewish islanders that after the revolt was suppressed, no Jews were allowed on the island. In Mesopotamia, too, Jews began to revolt at the rear of Trajan's army, which had advanced into Parthia. The unrest may also have extended to Syria and Palestine. General Lucius Quietus put down the insurrection with great loss of life. It is striking that Jews in the Diaspora felt alienated from the Roman Empire enough to attack not only the Roman authorities proper but also other ethnic groups which, like the Jews, had been conquered by Rome. The sparse historical information does not provide us the reasons for the revolt, but resentment against Rome, tensions over the "odd" Jewish way of life, and a desire for freedom and the restoration of Israel are likely causes.

3. The Bar Kosiba War

The Bar Kosiba War (132–5 C.E.) was more extensive and costly for both Jews and Romans than the Great War in 66–70 and the War of Trajan. (The first war is stressed more by modern historians because during it the temple was destroyed and after it Josephus wrote its his-

THE NAME "BAR KOSIBA"

THE LEADER OF THE JEWISH rebellion in 132–5 is often referred to by a laudatory or pejorative nickname. The most common Aramaic form of his name, Bar Cochba (or Kocheba), meaning "son of the star," derives from Christian writings and refers to his messianic claims. Rabbinic literature, which opposed his messianic status, usually refers to him as Bar Koziba (Hebrew Ben Koziba), a play on words which means "son of the lie" (liar). Recently discovered Hebrew, Aramaic, and Greek documents from the time of the revolt record his correct name as Simon bar/ben Kosiba.

tory.) The prelude to and causes of the Bar Kosiba War are uncertain. Jewish restiveness after the conflicts under Trajan evidently continued unabated. Roman government and taxes were never light, and the memory of having stood up to the Romans may have offered many disadvantaged people some hope of succeeding through military activity. The length and severity of the war suggest that it was not a sudden, popular outburst but prepared in advance and founded on mature determination. Roman troop movements and the presence of two legions in Palestine before the war indicate that the Romans judged the situation to be insecure.

Two proximate causes of the revolt under Bar Kosiba were mentioned by Roman historians: the Roman emperor Hadrian's decisions to ban circumcision and to build a Roman city on the site of the destroyed temple. Hadrian at some point forbade castration, which was probably understood to include circumcision, in order to rid the empire of "barbaric" practices which were repugnant to the Romans. It is not certain he did this before the revolt, however. Hadrian also constructed buildings, conducted games, and founded cities on a grand scale when he toured the eastern empire in 129–31. The ruins of Jerusalem provided him with a perfect opportunity to restore its once great magnificence as Aelia Capitolina, with a temple to Zeus at its center. This act of largesse could easily have been seen by Jews as an attack on their holy places and way of life.

The war began in the spring of 132 and lasted three and a half years, until the late summer of 135. The Jewish revolutionaries were led by Simon bar Kosiba, who claimed the traditional title *nasi* (prince or leader) of Israel and was proclaimed Messiah by some. He took and held the southern Judean desert and its towns for three years, though the lack of an account like Josephus's *History of the Jewish War* leaves only fragments of evidence from which to reconstruct the story. Documents and coins from the period testify that the revolutionaries set up a complete administration for Israel (Judea) and considered that a new era had begun. The new era is designated in documents as "The redemption of Israel by Simon bar Kosiba, *nasi* of Israel," and the coins struck, which contain shortened forms of this slogan, are numbered according to the first three years of the revolt.

A full roster of officials were appointed for various districts, refugees were cared for, supplies transported, and order maintained. Leases and contracts were written and dated according to the new era, with Bar Kosiba designated as leader. Bar Kosiba and his men showed their zeal and commitment by referring to each other as brothers, by not moving caravans on Sabbath, and by laying in supplies for celebrating Jewish festivals. But not all were loyal and enthusiastic supporters of the revolt. Letters from late in the war refer to punishments for people who profiteer, mistreat refugees, refuse to contribute supplies, or malinger. Letters from the end of the war reveal that travel became impossible, supplies ran out, and the Roman forces were closing in.

Roman documents and inscriptions indicate that the threat to Roman rule from Bar Kosiba was greater than that of the first revolt.

The forum of Aelia Capitolina,
Hadrian's city at Jerusalem (often identified as the Lithostratos of
the Gospels).

Anthony J. Saldarini.

The Romans deployed massive forces against Judea. Several legions
and detachments of auxiliary troops were called in from all over the
empire, and Julius Severus, the best of Hadrian's generals, was
recalled from Britain at the other end of the empire to direct operations. Casualties were high, though the frequently repeated claim that
a whole legion was wiped out, lacks real support. When the war
ended, there was no triumph in Rome and when Hadrian reported to
the Senate, he omitted the customary opening formula that he and the
legions were well.

Since small guerilla actions predominated during the war, destruction was widespread. One historian says that the Romans destroyed 50
forts and 985 villages. Even if this is exaggerated, it shows that the
Romans defeated the Jewish forces the hard way: piece by piece. Near
the Dead Sea the remains of forty partisans were found in their cliffside cave, where they had been starved to death by the Romans. Bar
Kosiba made his last stand at the fort of Bethar, seven miles southwest
of Jerusalem. Amid siege and starvation he and his forces fought to the
end. When the war was over, thousands had been killed, all settlements in Judea had been devastated, and so many Jews had been sold
into slavery that the slave markets were glutted.

After the defeat of Bar Kosiba, Judea ceased to be the center of
Jewish life. Hadrian built his Roman city on the site of Jerusalem and
forbade Jews to go there to mourn the loss of the temple. The areas surrounding the new city, Aelia Capitolina, were annexed and the
province was renamed Syria Palestina in order to remove the Jewish
name, Judea. The Romans put their stamp on the province by building
new temples, installations, and cities. Roman roads were constructed
to speed military movements in case of trouble, and two legions with
supporting units were permanently stationed in Palestine. Hadrian
made sure that security would be so firmly established and the home-

THE BAR KOSIBA DOCUMENTS

A NUMBER OF CLIFFSIDE caves in valleys south of Qumran and southeast of Jerusalem have yielded documents from the period of Bar Kosiba. One cache contains the legal papers of a Jewish woman, "Barbata, daughter of Simon," including her marriage contract, a tax return sworn before a Roman magistrate, and property deeds. Other documents are letters to and from Bar Kosiba and his officials, mandating a fair distribution of resources and adherence to Sabbath observance, tithing, and the Sabbath year. These documents are written in the three most common languages of Palestine – Hebrew, Aramaic, and Greek – as well as in Nabatean, the language of Arabia, across the Dead Sea. They reveal some of the workings of the Roman Empire and how integral it was to Jewish life before the revolt. The documents from 132–5 show that Bar Kosiba organized the territory he controlled into districts, appointed officials, collected taxes and supplies, and instituted a new calendar beginning with the first year of freedom from the Romans.

land of the Jews so thoroughly transformed that there would not be a third Jewish war.

After the war Judaism was widely persecuted and proscribed in Palestine. Talmudic stories from the period treat it as a time of desperate danger in which many were executed or fled. Hadrian is more frequently and severely cursed than Titus, the destroyer of Jerusalem. Though the historical worth of these accounts is hard to judge, they certainly reflect Roman oppression and hostility after the Bar Kosiba War. Rabbinic tradition says that circumcision, Sabbath observance, ordination of rabbis, and study of Torah were forbidden. The law against circumcision was probably a continuation of a prewar policy, and the prohibition against Sabbath observance may have been a security measure banning assembly. Restrictions on rabbis and the study of Torah may reflect attempts to control the activities of potentially troublesome leadership groups. Since the rabbis were only one small, developing group in Jewish society, it is likely that other kinds of leaders were also jailed or executed.

Caves uses by rebels during the Bar Kosiba War.

Anthony J. Saldarini.

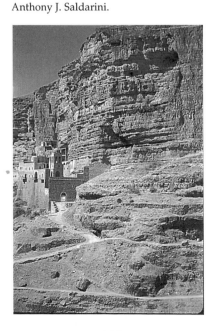

BAR KOSIBA, THE MESSIAH

R ABBINIC TRADITION records that the famous second-century sage Rabbi Akiba supported Bar Kosiba, the popular messianic expectation associated with him, and the rebellion. Since the texts concerning Akiba's support for Bar Kosiba are very brief and have been edited by a later tradition which disapproved of Bar Kosiba, little can be deduced from them concerning the events of 132–5. The least edited passage is found in J. Taanit 4:8 (68d).

1. Rabbi Simeon ben Yohai taught, "My teacher Akiba used to expound, `There shall step forth a star out of Jacob' (Num.

24:17). Thus Koziba steps forth out of Jacob."
2. When Rabbi Akiba beheld Bar Koziba, he exclaimed, "This is the king Messiah."
3. Rabbi Johanan ben Torta retorted, "Akiba, grass will grow between your cheeks and still he will not have come."

Paragraphs 1 and 3 are in Hebrew and represent the original dispute over the status of Bar Kosiba. Paragraph 2 is in Aramaic and is probably a later addition. Note that the text contains the later rabbinic pejorative nickname for Bar Kosiba: Koziba (lie). This text and a few others suggest that Akiba had a lively belief in the coming of earthly freedom for Israel through a leader appointed by God.

The failure of the messiah Bar Kosiba and the devastation of Judea had several long-term consequences. First, though no contemporary historical sources speak of the place of Jewish Christians in these events, later Christian historians recount that Bar Kosiba's messianic claim alienated him from Jewish Christians, who would not support another messiah, and that their rejection of Bar Kosiba at a time of war led to their oppression and the further alienation of the two communities. Clusters of Christian communities grew in Syria, along the coast of the Mediterranean, and in Galilee. Second, the cultural and religious center of Palestinian Judaism shifted from Judea to Galilee. The emerging rabbinic leaders (see the next section) migrated to Galilee and there began to produce the Mishnah, Talmud, and midrashic commentaries, which reshaped Jewish life over the next several centuries. Third, Jews in Palestine and the Diaspora never again engaged in large-scale military resistance to the empire. Though no formal decision was made, three costly defeats at the hands of the Romans and continued Roman vigilance led the people and their leaders to channel their efforts into strengthening their inner community life as a mode of resisting the dominant Greco-Roman, and later Christian, culture.

B. THE EMERGENCE OF RABBINIC POWER

Soon after the destruction of the governing class and the temple in Jerusalem a new group of scholars, fervently devoted to the Jewish way of life, emerged. They were addressed by the traditional title rabbi and referred to themselves as sages. Though later rabbinic documents picture them as immediately taking over the leadership of Judaism, careful analysis of rabbinic literature and other historical sources shows that they only gradually developed their program for Judaism, propagated it within the Jewish community, and then finally, several centuries later, gained full authority over Jewish life.

Between the wars these scholars were found in many Judean towns and had their center in Jamnia (Yavneh) on the coastal plain. They were led by Johanan ben Zakkai and then by Gamaliel II, probably the grandson of the Gamaliel mentioned in the New Testament (Acts 5:34, 22:3). The Mishnah and Talmuds recount the activities of this founding group only sporadically and episodically, often retrojecting the later roles and status of Palestinian and Babylonian rabbis into the first and second centuries. Allowing for this uncertainty, we may reasonably infer that the sages who gathered at Jamnia were educated Jews who wished to live a committed and strict form of Judaism. Their teachings and customs were strongly influenced by the prewar Pharisaic way of life, with its stress on maintaining for themselves the ritual purity proper to priests in the temple, tithing food according to biblical law and later custom, and strictly observing Sabbaths and festivals. In addition, they emphasized close study of the Torah and the development of detailed interpretations to guide Jewish life. Their insistence on learning as well as practice connects them with the prewar scribal class which had maintained and taught Jewish traditions. The presence of priests among their number and the concentration on ritual

"RABBI" AND "SAGE"

IN RABBINIC LITERATURE, THE teachers cited are referred to as "sages" (*hakhamim*, literally, "wise ones"). The title by which they are addressed is "Rabbi," a title that has endured within the Jewish community. "Rabbi" means literally "my great one" and was a first-century honorific connected with positions of prestige and authority that was in common use in the first century (like "Sir" in English). In the Old Testament a "Rab" was a high officer (2 Kings 18:17). According to the testimony of the New Testament, "Rabbi" was used for an honored person, master, or teacher. The Matthean community rejected the use of this traditional Jewish honorific title, especially in its new usage in emerging rabbinic Judaism (Matt. 23:7–8). In the Mishnah (ca. 200) and Tosefta (third century), "Rab" is used for the master of a slave, for a judge, and especially for the teacher or master of students. It became the common title for rabbinic teachers, who often had both scholastic and official roles in the community.

purity and temple matters in the Mishnah suggest that priestly traditions were also incorporated into their view of Judaism.

Though the sources give little reliable information about the original group of rabbis, they seem to have forged priestly and sectarian traditions into a new amalgam that would allow Jews to commit themselves anew to Jewish life without the biblically mandated sacrificial worship, the ancient, central symbols of the temple and Jerusalem, and the guidance of the priests. Though they began with no power or following among the people, their new core symbol, Torah, and their central focus – study – led to a process of reflection, articulation, and activity that allowed Judaism to adapt to radically changed circumstances and ultimately won the allegiance of the whole Jewish community in Palestine and the Diaspora.

The leader of this school of sages was probably not recognized by Rome as the representative of Judaism until the third or fourth century, nor were the sages' rules and rulings accepted by the community at large until then. The sages met in a council which resembled the council or court (*bet din*) of the temple (see p. 388), but it had no authority beyond the voluntary group which submitted to it. The so-called Council of Jamnia, in which the canon of scripture and many Jewish laws were allegedly fixed and promulgated, is an inaccurate modern construct based on a combination of disparate passages in rabbinic literature. Though these sages did not formally legislate for Israel, their learning probably won them a following among Jews seeking to celebrate Jewish festivals and keep laws without the temple or the guidance of the priests.

The Bar Kosiba War destroyed the sages' initial achievements and led to the flight or death of many in the movement. Soon after the war, however, many survivors migrated to Galilee, living first in small towns around the perimeter of Galilee and only later settling in the larger cities, such as Sepphoris and Tiberias. Frequent changes in the place named as their center attest to the difficulties and dislocation they faced. Initially, since they were landless and without wealth, influence, or patronage, they worked as artisans and laborers. Slowly they rebuilt or developed their influence and gained status and prestige in Galilean society so that by the end of the second century, their leader, Rabbi Judah the Prince, was wealthy enough to support some scholars, influential enough to take part in the social and political life of Galilee, and powerful enough to enforce his will on his followers. Although he bore the title of prince, he was most probably simply the head of the rabbinic school and not an official recognized by Rome. However, the Mishnah, the body of idealized laws which he organized, appeals to the interests of the small landowners, the learned class of sages, and the hereditary priests, all of whom formed the fabric of Galilean upper-class society. Judah the Prince was building a coalition of informed Jewish community leaders who could give a new and enduring shape and energy to Jewish life.

Even in 200 C.E. Judah the Prince and his fellow rabbis still had not supplanted the traditional community leadership in Galilee. The absence of any detailed regulations concerning the synagogue indicate that communal prayer was still directed by the village leaders. Synagogue inscriptions from Palestine and the Diaspora during the Roman period mention a number of synagogue offices, such as president, leader, and scribe, but they do not use the title rabbi. Synagogue architecture and art do not follow the prescriptions found in rabbinic literature but correspond to the cultural mileu in which they were created. The sectarian emphasis on purity in the Mishnah and its highly theoretical laws concerning the now destroyed temple suggest that Judah the Prince and his circle did not yet have responsibility for civil matters or for the official interpretation of religious law for the community at large.

In the third through fifth centuries the Palestinian Talmud, Christian literature, and Roman law testify to the eventual power achieved by the rabbis and their "prince" or patriarch. The prevalence of case law and practical community matters in the Talmud witnesses to the growing community involvement of the rabbis as judges and officials. Origen (mid–third century) called the Jewish prince an ethnarch and said that he had the trappings and power of a king. Finally, in the late fourth century the Jewish patriarch was recognized in the Theodotianic Code of Roman law as the official representative of Judaism, a privilege he soon lost (ca. 425–9). Though the patriarch was no longer recognized by the empire by the mid–fifth century and the rabbinic way of life was increasingly oppressed by the Christian emperors and their church, this way of life and the sages who taught it continued to take hold in Diaspora Jewish communities. At the same time (the third through sixth centuries) the Babylonian Jewish community, which replaced Palestine as the most important center of Judaism, produced its own Talmud, which became authoritative for much of world Jewry.

C. LITERARY RESPONSES TO THE WARS AND DESTRUCTION OF THE TEMPLE

Jewish literary responses to the destruction of Jerusalem and the losses in the wars varied greatly. The Jewish historian Flavius Josephus wrote an account of the first war and an account of earlier Jewish history in the Greco-Roman mode to gain recognition for Judaism and to encourage Jewish cooperation with the empire. Several authors in Palestine wrote apocalypses that attributed the loss of Jerusalem to Jewish sin and the evil of the gentiles and that sought its restoration through divine intervention and a renewed commitment of Jews to God and his law. Diaspora Jews used the traditional medium of political protest, the oracle, to predict devastation for the Roman Empire and justice for Israel. The emerging rabbinic movement ignored political and military disasters in its writings and laid the foundation for an inwardly stable Jewish community, established on a reconstituted and reinterpreted model of the biblical community.

TORAH

TORAH (HEBREW FOR "instruction and teaching") is used in the Bible for divine instruction given to Israel and the instruction of Israel's teachers explaining the divine will to the people. This instruction included moral and cultic laws, prophetic guidance, and popular wisdom. In rabbinic Judaism the word "Torah" was used in several senses. (1) In its most restricted meaning it refers to the Pentateuch. (2) It is also used to refer to the whole Bible. (3) In a more comprehensive sense, it refers to the "oral Torah," that is, the teachings set down in the Mishnah, Tosefta, Talmuds, and other rabbinic literature in the period from the second to the sixth centuries C.E. (4) Torah in its most comprehensive sense refers to the whole Jewish tradition, written and oral, text and commentary. (5) Torah is divine revelation and all that is derived from that revelation. In this sense, Torah is the central symbol of rabbinic Judaism and includes the whole relationship of Israel with God. Fidelity to Torah includes both study and practice of Torah and is coextensive with knowledge of, love for, and obedience to God.

1.　Josephus

The Jewish historian Josephus wrote two Greek histories: *History of the Jewish War,* which appeared first in Aramaic for Jews in the eastern empire and was later translated into Greek, and a comprehensive review of earlier Jewish history called the *Antiquities of the Jews.* Josephus was a high-ranking priest of the Hasmonean House (the former rulers) born in 37/8 C.E. He had been well educated and had visited Rome before the war. When the first war with Rome began, he was placed in charge of the forces defending Galilee. When the Romans took Galilee, Josephus surrendered to them and became an ally of the Roman general Vespasian, who eventually became emperor, and of his son Titus, who commanded the siege and destruction of Jerusalem. After the war he was taken to Rome and supported by Vespasian and Titus in his writing projects. His accounts are biased toward justifying his own actions and toward discouraging resistance to the Romans.

Josephus's histories provide much of our information concerning Judaism in the Greco-Roman period. The *Jewish War* provides geographic and background information, a brief sketch of Jewish history leading up to the war, and an integrated narrative of the major events and figures of the war. The first half of the *Antiquities* retells biblical history, and the second half covers the Greco-Roman period up to the revolt. Josephus addressed his Greco-Roman audience using a familiar literary genre, the history, in order to show that Judaism was ancient and respectable and to defend Jewish rights established in previous imperial decrees. The *Antiquities* both informs the gentiles about Judaism and glorifies Jewish laws, institutions, and outstanding men. Josephus's account of the war gives an emotional description of Jewish sufferings, to overcome resentment and gain sympathy for the Jews after the war. Josephus advocated a return to the status quo, in which Jews should take their places as loyal citizens in a diverse and cosmopolitan society. Probably many survivors of the war, especially from the upper classes, agreed with him. The original Aramaic edition of the *Jewish War* was addressed to Jews in the East in order to discourage further revolt. The Greek edition brought the same message to many Greek-speaking Jews throughout the empire. Josephus's initiative failed, however; a few years after his death Diaspora Jews in the East fought bloody battles with the government, and two decades after that, Palestine once again rose in revolt.

Josephus interprets all history, both the destruction of Jerusalem and the ascendancy of the Roman Empire, as the work of divine providence. History is a record of divine providence rewarding good and punishing evil. Josephus substitutes destiny, fate, and providence for the biblical categories of God and covenant in order to make Jewish history and thought comprehensible to his Greco-Roman audience. Outstanding individuals, singular events, and miracles are all cited as testimony to divine providence. For example, Herod's unhappy end follows from his disloyalty to Jewish tradition, and various empires rose and dominated Israel with divine acquiescence because of Israel's sin. Finally, "because God deemed the temple to be no longer a clean place for him, [he] brought the Romans upon us and purification by fire upon the city" (*Antiquities* 20.166).

2. Apocalyptic Literature

Three Jewish apocalypses – 4 Ezra, 2 Baruch, and the Apocalypse of Abraham – have survived from the late first and early second centuries. They, along with the Book of Revelation, show how both Judaism and Christianity adapted this traditional genre to meet the new challenges posed by the Roman Empire and the loss of the temple. All share a strong sense of loss at the destruction of the temple, a quest for the reasons leading to the disaster, and a confidence in ultimate justice at the end of the world. All claim to communicate a special heavenly revelation which offers guidance to God's people as they reconstitute their lives.

4 Ezra

The Book of 4 Ezra was written after the destruction of the second temple (70 C.E.), but, like many other works, it uses the destruction of the first temple by the Babylonians in 587/B.C.E. (see Part I) as a paradigm for understanding the destruction of the second. In the narrative Ezra, the faithful scribe who presided over the reform of early second temple Judaism (see pp. 148–152) in the fifth century, is pictured as receiving revelation in Babylon thirty years after the destruction of the first temple (in the sixth century B.C.E.). Since the chronology is clearly unhistorical, the author signals to his reader that he is really speaking about the destruction of the second temple. The state of Judaism without the temple is conveyed in Ezra's lament:

> Our sanctuary has been laid waste, our altar thrown down, our temple destroyed; our harp has been laid low, our song has been silenced, and our rejoicing has been ended; the light of our lampstand has been put out, the ark of our covenant has been plundered, our holy things have been polluted, and the name by which we are called has been profaned; our free men have suffered abuse, our priests have been burned to death, our Levites have gone into captivity; our virgins have been defiled, and our wives ravished; our righteous men have been carried off, our little ones have been cast out, our young men have been enslaved, and our strong men made powerless. And, what is more than all, the seal of Zion – for she has now lost the seal of her glory and has been given over into the hands of those that hate us. (4 Ezra 10:21–3)

Faced with the loss of political independence, the dissolution of social order, great loss of life, and the destruction of the religious center, Ezra receives seven symbolic visions, which move him, and anyone who accepts his message in this book, from discouragement and lack of confidence in God's justice to consolation and acceptance of God's plan for history.

In the first three visions Ezra engages in dialogue with his angelic interpreter, complaining about the prosperity of the sinful gentiles and

EZRA LITERATURE

EZRA, A PRIEST AND scribe, appears in the biblical book of Ezra as a postexilic community leader and reformer. Because of his role in authoritatively teaching Torah to the community, his name was used by later writers. The names for the books attributed to him in the Septuagint (LXX – Greek translation), Vulgate (Latin translation), and English translation of the Apocrypha are confusing.

1. The Hebrew Book of Ezra is called 2 Esdras in the LXX and 1 Esdras in the Vulgate.

2. The Hebrew Book of Nehemiah is called 3 Esdras in the LXX and 2 Esdras in the Vulgate.

3. The English apocryphal 1 Esdras is called by the same name in the LXX, but 3 Esdras in the Vulgate.

4. The English apocalyptic work 4 Ezra, which is not found in the LXX, is called 2 Esdras in the English Apocrypha and 4 Esdras in the Vulgate.

5. A later apocryphal work, not printed in Bibles, is sometimes designated 5 Esdras.

For those who distinguish the Christian frame (chaps. 1–2 and 15–16) added to the core of 4 Ezra, the following designations are sometimes used:

1. Ezra for the biblical Ezra–Nehemiah.

2. Ezra for chaps. 1–2 of 4 Ezra.

3. Ezra for the LXX 1 Esdras.

4. Ezra for chaps. 3–14 of 4 Ezra.

5. Ezra for chaps. 15–16 of 4 Ezra.

the punishment of Israel despite its adherence to the law. Like Job, Ezra is told that he does not understand God's work in the universe; but unlike Job, at the end of the third vision he is told of the messianic kingdom, the judgment of the wicked, and the punishments of various classes of sinners.

The transition from despair to hope takes place in the fourth vision (4 Ezra 9:26–10:59). With general questions of theodicy taken care of in the first three visions, Ezra sees in the fourth vision a woman mourning the death of her only son on his wedding night. Ezra becomes angry with her because Jerusalem's loss is so much greater and encourages her to be brave and to acknowledge the justice of God's decree: "Keep your sorrow to yourself, and bear bravely the troubles that have come upon you. For if you acknowledge the decree of God to be just, you will receive your son back in due time" (10:15–16). The woman is transformed into a renewed Jerusalem, and Ezra realizes that he has just answered his own questions and consoled himself. The final three visions establish the ground for his hope and show him communicating it to the people.

In the final vision (chap. 14) Israel is reestablished as a nation faithful to God's law. All through 4 Ezra Israel's fault has been rejection of God's law (3:22; 4:23; 7:20; 24, 79, 81; 9:33–4), and Ezra has been granted his visions because of his knowledge and faithfulness to the law (13:54–5). In the final vision Ezra is explicitly compared to Moses and dictates the contents of the twenty-four books of scripture, which have been burned, plus seventy other books that will guide the newly constituted, apocalyptic community while it endures until the end. Ezra the scribe represents both the biblical wisdom and apocalyptic traditions. His special revelation in this book and in the seventy hidden books is for the wise among the people (4 Ezra 12:38; 14:13, 26, 46; see Dan. 11:33), who seem to be identical with the survivors, whom he addressed after the fifth vision (12:40) and in the middle of the seventh (14:27).

The author and his community do not expect to defeat Rome militarily and rebuild Jerusalem. The vision of Jerusalem reestablished is that of a heavenly city, far from human habitation (4 Ezra 10:54) and no mention is made of new priests, temple, or cult. Rather, apocalyptic revelation, which is linked with the law, will be the basis of the community until its vindication by the Messiah. Fidelity to the law, newly understood and accepted, is common to 4 Ezra, 2 Baruch, the emerging rabbinic movement, and, in a different sense, to the Gospel of Matthew.

2 Baruch

The Book of 2 Baruch has a number of materials in common with 4 Ezra and likewise dates from after the destruction of the second temple. In the narrative, Baruch, who was historically a scribe associated with Jeremiah and the destruction of the first temple (Jer. 32, 36, 43, 45), receives revelation from God, as Ezra did, and then encourages and instructs the people. Each of the seven sections begins with a prayer or lament, recounts a dialogue with God, and concludes with an address to the people. The audience addressed by Baruch gradually widens until in the concluding letter all Jewry is addressed. The people are gradually consoled and understand how Judaism is to be lived according to the law after the destruction of the temple.

Anxiety about the ultimate triumph of divine justice is assuaged by several accounts and visions that periodize history and assure the destruction of the wicked. The trials of this world are relativized by stressing the world's corruptibility in contrast with the incorruptibility of the heavenly world (2 Bar. 21). Even the loss of the temple, vividly described in the first chapters of 2 Baruch, is explained as hastening the end (2 Bar. 20:2) and as no real loss in the light of the incorruptible heavenly temple. Baruch, speaking as though he were writing after the destruction of the first temple, also predicts (*ex eventu*) the destruction of the second temple (2 Bar. 32:1–7). The loss of both temples and the sufferings of Israel during these two crises are lessened in importance by reference to the chaos that will usher in the new age and the establishment of a perfect, incorruptible temple.

As in 4 Ezra, but more insistently here, law and wisdom become the center of Judaism. The high priests, temple, and other institutions are gone, mired in the sins of the past, and the author proposes a renewed Israel. No institutional framework is proposed but the new agenda is clear. Those who love and keep the law will be part of the incorruptible world to come:

> When you endure and persevere in his fear and do not forget his law, the time again will take a turn for the better for you. . . . For everything will pass away which is corruptible, and everything that dies will go away, and all present time will be forgotten, and there will be no remembrance of the present time, which is polluted by evils. . . . These are they who prepared for themselves treasures of wisdom. And stores of insight are found with them. And they have not withdrawn from mercy and they have preserved the truth of the law. For the coming world will be given to these, but the habitation of the many others will be the fire. (2 Bar. 44:7–15)

Though no specific interpretation of the law is articulated, fidelity to Judaism is demanded as a condition for ultimate vindication by God, and apostasy is condemned. The author and his group, with their intense commitment to the law, are alluded to as leaders whom the people should follow: "Prepare your heart so that you obey the law, and be subject to those who are wise and understanding with fear" (2 Bar. 46:5).

In 2 Baruch the way in which Israel is to remain faithful is more clearly articulated than in other apocalypses. Since the temple and its leaders are gone, the author places the law at the center of Judaism, just as the emerging rabbis did in their nonapocalyptic scheme for restoring Judaism. When the people complain at the end that they are without leadership and guidance, Baruch's last words to them (immediately before his concluding letter to the Jews in Babylon) establish the law as Judaism's central symbol:

> Shepherds and lamps and fountains came from the law, and when we go away, the law will abide. If you, therefore, look upon the law and are intent

upon wisdom, then the lamp will not be wanting and the shepherd will not give way and the fountain will not dry up. (2 Bar. 78:15–16)

Guidance and sustenance will be provided by the law. Even without the temple, priesthood, and nation, according to this author, Israel has in the law all it needs to survive until the coming of God and the incorruptible world which never changes.

The Apocalypse of Abraham

The Apocalypse of Abraham, like 4 Ezra and 2 Baruch, was probably written around 100 C.E., after the destruction of the second temple in 70 C.E. Though it shares some themes and the apocalyptic genre with them, it lacks their emphasis on the Torah and theodicy. The author sets the disastrous loss of the temple in the context of the broad sweep of history. God's covenantal promise to Abraham in Genesis 15 is rewritten so that Abraham not only hears the divine voice but is taken on a heavenly journey, protected and guided by an angelic mediator. Abraham receives a vision of world history in which the origin and choice of evil are firmly attributed to human responsibility (Apoc. Abr. 23–4) and the loss of the temple is caused by corrupt temple worship and priests (Apoc. Abr. 24). Even in these evil circumstances the people of Israel (represented by Abraham, their ancestor) are not abandoned. In the vision of the universe Jews and gentiles are sharply distinguished right from the beginning (contrary to 4 Ezra), and the gentiles' future judgment and punishment are graphically described (Apoc. Abr. 29–31). The solution to evil is the vindication of faithful Israelites and the reinstitution of a pure worship of God.

The author of the Apocalypse of Abraham put much more emphasis on the temple and its administrators than did the authors of 2 Baruch and 4 Ezra, who distanced themselves from this destroyed institution. The indictment of idolatry in the first, nonapocalyptic part of the Apocalypse of Abraham (chaps. 1–8) and of the temple worship in the second part point to an anonymous author and group who had opposed the temple leadership before 70 C.E. but now hoped for the defeat of Rome and the reinstitution of Israel through divine power. The confidence that such an unlikely reversal would take place is based upon visions that use language found in the later Jewish Merkavah mysticism (merkavah means chariot and refers to the vision of God's chariot in Ezek. 1 and 10). The author does not dwell on the injustice inherent in the victory of the heathen but understands even the loss of the temple as one small part of world history. The coming of God's chosen one (Apoc. Abr. 29–30) and the final judgment of all evil will right all wrongs.

The Bar Kosiba War (132–5 C.E.) manifests the dominant Palestinian response to the loss of the temple and to oppression by Rome: violent revolt. These apocalyptic writings, which look to divine intervention and an ideal kingdom of God rather than a reinstitution of Israel as a worldly power, were a more subtle response to disaster. Though the Apocalypse of Abraham may envision a new temple, the overall tone of these works is otherworldly. The worldly messianism traditionally associated with Bar Kosiba did not derive from these circles, or from the emerging rabbinic movement (which provided another, ultimately successful response to the loss of the temple) but from the political mood of Jewish society between the wars.

3. The Diaspora: The Sibylline Oracles

The flood of Jewish literature from the Diaspora, so characteristic of the hellenistic period, was gradually choked off in the Roman period. The Jewish community in Alexandria experienced vicious anti-semitic persecution in the middle of the first century C.E. and was decimated in the uprising during Trajan's rule (115–17 C.E.). It seems never to have regained its earlier vitality and creativity. The uprising of eastern Jewish communities against Roman rule in 115–17 caused great loss of life and disruption throughout the old hellenistic world. Inscriptional evidence from many places in the empire shows that Jewish communities were numerous during the first few centuries. However, mistakes in some inscriptions show that not all communities were highly literate; the lack of literary remains suggest the same (with the exception of the Palestinian and Babylonian communities).

The oppression within the Roman Empire spawned one of the traditional modes of political protest, the oracle (see pp. 342–344). The Fourth Sibylline Oracle is an oracle from the hellenistic period that was revised in the late first century C.E., perhaps in Syria, to reflect Judaism's confrontation with Rome. The Fifth Sibylline Oracle comes from Egypt between 80 and 130 C.E., perhaps after the defeat of Diaspora Jews in the uprising of 115–17. Both carry on the eastern Mediterranean tradition of anti-imperial political protest through oracles and the Jewish apocalyptic tradition of expecting divine intervention and judgment of the wicked. The names of the authors of these oracles are not known.

The Fourth Sibylline Oracle

The Fourth Sibylline Oracle has at its heart the division of history into four kingdoms, a periodization found in many Jewish and non-Jewish documents in the hellenistic period (see Daniel; and pp. 271–272, 277–280, above). Rome was added to the four kingdoms to bring the oracle up to date (4 Sib. Or. 102–51). References to the destruction of the temple (4 Sib. Or. 116), the eruption of Vesuvius (130–5), and the legend of Nero's imminent return (138–9) all point to a late-first-century C.E. date. The apocalyptic punishments of the kingdoms include the destruction of evil, a conflagration, resurrection, and judgment (173–92).

The Fourth Sibylline Oracle, like the other Sibylline Oracles, rejects idolatry, violence, injustice, and sexual offenses (4 Sib. Or. 1–48). In contrast to the Third and Fifth Sibylline Oracles, it also rejects all temples and animal sacrifices (4 Sib. Or. 5–12, 27–30), including presumably not only idolatry but even the Jewish temple and sacrifices. The Fourth Sibylline Oracle expresses no interest in the Jewish temple or hope for its rebuilding. Finally, the Fourth Sibylline Oracle supports the kind of baptism of repentance found in the New Testament and commonly practiced in Syria and Palestine in the first and second centuries:

> Ah, wretched mortals, change these things, and do not lead the great God to all sorts of anger, but abandon daggers and groanings, murders and outrages, and wash your whole bodies in perennial rivers. Stretch out your hands to heaven and ask forgiveness for your previous deeds and make propitiation for bitter impiety with words of praise; God will grant repentance and will not destroy. He will stop his wrath again if you all practice honorable piety in your hearts. (162–70)

This simple response to the loss of the temple and the dominance of Rome attributes Israel's ills to sin and counsels repentance and baptism as a preparation for divine intervention. Its atmosphere is reminiscent of the Gospel of Mark and may indicate a common Syrian provenance in the latter half of the first century.

The Fifth Sibylline Oracle

The Fifth Sibylline Oracle, in contrast with the earlier Third Sibylline Oracle, manifests great alienation from the gentile government of Egypt. Whereas the author of the Third Sibylline Oracle hoped for an ideal Egyptian king as savior (see p. 343), the author of the Fifth looks for a heavenly savior (5 Sib. Or. 414–19) and an eschatological Jerusalem and temple (249–55, 420–7) to provide a refuge for Jews against the hostile government and powers which rule the world. Nero is excoriated as a symbol of evil power (137–54), and the demise of Babylon and Italy is mediated by a star (possibly a metaphor for the Messiah) which comes from heaven (155–61). The strongest invective is reserved for Rome (162–78) and Egypt (179–99). Jews are promised freedom from gentile domination and security with God forever:

> No longer will the unclean foot of Greeks revel around your land, but they will have a mind in their breasts that conforms to your laws. But glorious children will honor you exceedingly, and they will attend table with devout music, all sorts of sacrifices, and with prayers honoring God. Such righteous men as endured toils will receive greater, pleasant things in exchange for a little distress. But the wicked, who dispatched lawless utterance against heaven, will desist from speaking against each other and will hide themselves until the world is changed. (264–73)

In the aftermath of the defeats by Rome the Jewish writer of the Fifth Sibylline Oracle can only envision a radical reordering of the world by divine intervention and the destruction or subordination of the gentiles to Israel.

4.   Emerging Rabbinic Judaism

Though both 4 Ezra and 2 Baruch promoted a renewed commitment to the covenant as found in Torah, the interest in a zealous understanding of Torah reached its height among a group whose members referred to themselves as sages ("wise ones") and who were addressed by the title rabbi. Their literature – the Mishnah, Tosefta, Talmuds, and midrashim – strangely omits almost all mention of the loss of the temple, the political oppression by Rome, and competition from other Jewish groups and emerging Christianity. Though the sages affirmed the resurrection of the dead and judgment of good and evil, these apocalyptic themes remained firmly in the background. The earliest rabbinic source, the Mishnah, consists almost entirely of detailed discussions of laws affecting everyday life and the (now destroyed) temple. Though the Mishnah and its attendant literature date from about 200–600 C.E. (outside the chronological scope of this book), a quick review of this literature will show the direction in which post-biblical Judaism developed.

Mishnah

The Mishnah is a collection of sixty-three tractates, arranged in six orders: agricultural tithes, public feasts, marriage (especially economic arrangements), torts, sacrifices at the temple, and ritual purity. Some of the tractates repeat biblical law; for example, the tractates on sacrifices. Others elaborate new complexes of rules that go far beyond biblical law; for example, many tractates on purity are much more elaborate and detailed than the biblical laws. The laws have been so thoroughly edited into a coherent structure with stereotyped rhetorical patterns that attempts to use source and form-critical analyses (see Part III) to isolate earlier and later strata have been largely unsuccessful. It is likely that the rabbis built on earlier customs and interpretations of the laws, but in the end they were largely governed by their

---

THE MISHNAH

THE WORDING OF THE Mishnah is very concise and elliptical. It presumes that the reader already knows the biblical and mishnaic laws applicable to the problem brought up, as well as the realities of ancient Jewish life. It then specifies certain difficult or unclear cases. For example, the Mishnah tractate *Betzah*, concerned with activities on festival days, begins as follows. (Words in parentheses and brackets have been added by the translator.)

> An egg which is laid on a
>   festival day,
>   the House of Shammai say,
>   "It may be eaten [on that
>   day]."
> And the House of Hillel say,

"It may not be eaten."
> The House of Shammai say,
>   "[A minimum of] leaven in
>   the volume of an olive's
>   bulk, and [a minimum of]
>   what is leavened in the vol-
>   ume of a date's bulk [are
>   prohibited on Passover
>   (Exod. 13:7)]."
> And the House of Hillel say,
>   "This and that are
>   [prohibited in the volume of]
>   an olive's bulk."

The Mishnah leaves numerous presuppositions unstated in order to concentrate on two very precise problems. The first concerns what may be eaten on a festival on which work is forbidden, as it is on a Sabbath. Thus, knowledge of Sabbath law is assumed, specifically, that food which is to be eaten must be set aside ahead

of time. Is an egg laid by a chicken (presumably one marked for consumption at the feast) part of the chicken or a new item not thus set aside? The second problem concerns Passover law (hinted at by the translator's reference to Exodus). One must know that both leaven and leavened products are to be destroyed before Passover. The question is how big must a piece be in order to come under the ban. The measures used are an olive and a date (which is considered to be bigger). With these preliminaries clear, Mishnah concisely catalogues alternative positions on these problems but does not give the reasoning behind them. One is expected to know the reasons or learn them from oral discussion.

TANNAIM AND AMORAIM

THE RABBINIC DESIGNATION for sages during the Mishnaic period (up to 200–20) is "Tannaim." *Tanna* (pl. *tannaim*) means "teacher" and comes from the Aramaic word meaning "repeat," and thus "repeat and teach a tradition." (The Hebrew "Mishnah" comes from the parallel word root.) Tannaitic literature is the Mishnah, Tosefta, and the tannaitic or halakic midrashim, which quote Tannaim almost exclusively.

'*Amora* (pl. '*amoraim*) means "speaker." Rabbinic literature designates the sages who succeeded the Tannaim and are cited in the Palestinian and Babylonian Talmuds as Amoraim. Their literature consists of the two Talmuds and several midrashim.

own sense of what was implied or encouraged by scripture, the logic of the subjects covered there, and their own contemporary interests. The Mishnah contains no narrative and so ignores the greater part of the Bible. It assumes that its authors and audience are committed to living a Jewish way of life and so does not refer consistently to covenant, God's love, the nation, or any of the other great themes that fill the Bible. The legal discussions assume both an intimate knowledge of biblical law and familiarity with rabbinic concerns and methods. Discussions often begin in midargument without any explanation of the point at issue or the context from which it arose.

The Mishnah is not a public law code, because it treats only a selection of subjects, gives many possible interpretations rather than a definitive statement of law, and has no sanctions for infractions of most laws. It is clearly an instrument to be studied in detail by learned scholars who have received a thorough grounding in the Bible and other aspects of Jewish life and thought. But why study the topics in Mishnah? Half of the Mishnaic laws concern the temple, priests, purity, tithes, and rituals and so were inapplicable after the destruction of the temple. The authors of the Mishnah created an ideal Judaism that preserved in words much of the historical, political, biblical Israel that had been lost. The affirmation of the sanctity of God, the temple, and people countered the loss and despair of the destruction, muted enthusiastic political and apocalyptic responses, turned the attention of the Jewish spirit toward God's world, and in a subtle way scorned and rejected the Roman world by ignoring it as irrelevant.

The Mishnah (Hebrew "to repeat," "to study"), codified about 200 C.E., stands at the center of the development of rabbinic Judaism. An analysis of the development of legal traditions in the Mishnah suggests that in the first two centuries laws concerning ritual purity, tithing, Sabbath observance, and other relatively private matters dominated the Pharisaic and then the rabbinic agenda. These matters are typical of a sect or sectlike group that differentiates itself from society at large, establishes its identity by special beliefs and practices, and claims to be the true heir to the tradition. As the Qumran group had done before, the rabbinic group learned to live without the temple and to find God's presence within itself, especially in the activity of study and zealous adherence to biblical law as understood by the movement. In rejecting the normal way of Jewish living, the rabbis had something in common with the apocalyptic groups that also rejected Israel's established behavior as sinful or inadequate and looked to another and better Jewish world. The rabbis and apocalyptists differed in what they expected and when they expected it, but both saw the necessity for something new.

Though the rabbinic movement began among a small group of zealous and learned Jews who studied and observed the law in a particular way, the traditions they developed appealed to several lower sectors of the Jewish leadership that had survived the war against Rome. The emphasis on purity and tithing reflected the influence of the prewar Pharisees, who had sought to reform Jewish customs. The learned tradition of study and interpretation linked the movement with the scribes, the small group of literate officials, educators, and religious functionaries whose antecedents stretched back to great antiquity. The interest in the temple and its laws brought into the rabbinic movement some of the lower orders of priests who survived when the chief priests were killed in Jerusalem.

After the devastation of Judea in the Bar Kosiba War, the core of the rabbinic group migrated to Galilee and over two generations established political, social, and economic links with the landed aristocracy there. As the movement began to have an impact on society, it developed stories of its origins and heroes. The scope of its legal interests expanded to include civil law and marriage contracts, both of which were matters of interest to the small landholders, who formed the backbone of Galilean society. These larger societal interests continued to grow in the Palestinian Talmud, which is filled with case law, testifying to the growing influence of the rabbis as local judges and officials and of the patriarch as one of the national leaders. At the same time the older interest in purity laws and temple sacrifices waned.

Tosefta

The rest of rabbinic literature can be defined in relation to the Mishnah. The Tosefta (Aramaic "addition") is a collection of materials arranged in sixty-three tractates parallel to those of the Mishnah. The laws, traditions, and stories expand or comment on the laws in the Mishnah; present other traditions parallel to or contradictory to the Mishnah; and gather stories and scriptural interpretations relevant to the themes of the Mishnah. The materials in the Tosefta resemble those found in the Talmud and probably date from the third or fourth century.

The Palestinian and Babylonian Talmuds

The publication of the Mishnah and its acceptance as authoritative within the rabbinic movement immediately stimulated the growth of commentaries in Palestine and Babylon, the two great centers of Jewish life in the third through seventh centuries. The Palestinian and Babylonian Talmuds comment upon the Mishnah sentence by sentence. The commentary, called the Gemara (Aramaic "to learn"), consists of an enormous variety of materials, including atomistic analyses of the words and sentences of the Mishnah, comparisons of one section of the Mishnah with another, traditions related to the Mishnah, interpretations of scripture, stories about rabbis and other figures, and long digressions on a variety of topics. The bulk of the Gemara is written in Aramaic, but many traditions are recorded in Hebrew. The Palestinian Talmud covers the first four orders of the Mishnah – agriculture, feasts, marriage law, and torts – and omits the sacrificial and purity laws, which were no longer relevant. The Babylonian Talmud omits the agricultural laws, which pertained only to farmers in the land of Israel, as well as the purity laws, but meditated on laws concerning the far-away and now destroyed temple and its sacrifices, as well as feasts, marriage law, and torts.

Neither Talmud simply repeated the Mishnah, though each was

HALAKAH AND HAGGADAH

HALAKAH AND HAGGADAH are very general, imprecise rabbinic Hebrew terms used to refer respectively to (1) legal and (2) nonlegal material. Whole works are sometimes characterized as one or the other, though most rabbinic literature contains legal and nonlegal interpretations of scripture, teachings, and stories closely interrelated.

"Halakah" comes from the Hebrew word "to go, follow" and means a "going, walking." It is used for religiously sanctioned law, whether found in the Bible or developed by rabbinic or other authorities on the basis of the Bible. Disputes over halakah and the grounds for establishing new halakah abound in rabbinic and later Jewish thought and are crucial concerns for observant Jews up to the present.

"Haggadah" (or "Aggadah" in the Palestinian Talmud) comes from the Hebrew word "to tell, testify, announce" and means a "telling, communication, evidence." It is used for the telling or preaching of homiletical interpretations and stories in rabbinic literature and generally for anything not defined as halakah.

HALAKIC MIDRASH

THE MIDRASHIM ON SELECT legal portions of Exodus, Leviticus, Numbers, and Deuteronomy are referred to as halakic because they contain extensive discussions of Jewish law. However, they contain much haggadic material as well. They are thought to be early because they quote only Tannaim, but they were probably compiled and expanded during the Talmudic period. One example will show something of the nature of halakic midrash.

The *Mekilta* of Rabbi Ishmael, a commentary on the Book of Exodus, begins with Exodus 12, where discussion of Passover law begins. Exod. 12:5 says that a lamb or kid "of the first year" must be sacrificed. The sages inquire what "first year" means.

"Of the first year." From this I know only that it must be a lamb born during the current calendar year. How about a lamb during the entire first year of its life? Rabbi Ishmael used to say: it can be determined by using the method of argument from the lesser to the greater. If for the more important burnt offering (Lev. 12:6) an animal during the entire first year of its life is as fit as one born during the current calendar year, is it not but logical to conclude that for the less important Passover sacrifice an animal during the entire first year of its life should be as fit as one born during the current calendar year?

Note that the interpreter uses both another scriptural law and reason to solve his problem. The attention to detail and the rigorous inquiry into exactly what scripture means are typical of midrash.

built around it and quoted it constantly. The Talmuds atomized the Mishnah into sentences and words and subjected each unit to exhaustive analysis and recontextualization in their own systems of thought. The elegant construction of the authors of the Mishnah was dismantled and put to work in the changing world of the Talmudic period (third through sixth centuries). For example, the Palestinian Talmud turned its attention to issues of behavior, authority, and community leadership and sought to use both the Mishnah and scripture to prove its case. The role and position of the rabbi as well as more concrete and practical community norms emerged in a way not found in the Mishnah. Likewise, the Babylonian Talmud, reflecting circumstances very different from Palestine, developed its own unique characteristics.

When the power of Palestinian Judaism was destroyed in the fifth century C.E. by the emerging, Christian Byzantine Empire, the most vigorous remaining center of Judaism, Babylon, became the dominant force in Jewish life throughout the world. Over the next few centuries the Babylonian Talmud was edited and expanded much more thoroughly than the Palestinian Talmud. The prestige and influence of Babylonian scholars led to the Babylonian Talmud's acceptance as the most authoritative collection of teachings in Judaism next to the Bible itself, and its rules became the rules governing Jewish communities from Mesopotamia to Europe down to modern times.

Midrashim

Midrash (Hebrew "to search," "inquire," "interpret") is the type of biblical interpretation found in the Talmuds and in collections of exegeses edited during the Talmudic period and after. Midrashic interpretation has much in common with New Testament and patristic biblical interpretation. It pays close attention to the meanings of individual words and grammatical forms. It also relates words, verses, and ideas in the Bible with one another to resolve apparent contradictions

Printed Talmud page.

Anthony J. Saldarini.

and develop a coherent worldview. Finally, many midrashim seek to find a rhetorical basis for Mishnaic laws or connect Mishnaic teachings to the Bible. For the midrashim, neither context nor the obvious sense of a passage is usually determinative of meaning because biblical verses are conceived of as having many layers of meaning. When juxtaposed with other verses and understood in the light of the prevailing concerns of the authors, biblical verses took on new and contemporary meanings.

A brief passage from a midrash on Deuteronomy will illustrate the nature of midrashim. The verse is part of Deut. 1:3, "Moses spoke to the children of Israel according to all which the Lord commanded him for them." The midrashic author asks what exactly Moses communicated to Israel. At stake is the whole of rabbinic teaching, which claims Mosaic authority, and specifically midrashic interpretation.

> Did Moses prophesy only "these words" (Deut. 1:1)? Where [in scripture do we learn that he prophesied] the commandments in the Torah, [interpretations based on] a fortiori arguments, verbal analogy, [arguments from] the general and particular, and from the essentials and details? (Sifre Deut. 2, end)

The author interprets that which God has commanded to include not just Moses' last instruction to Israel in Deuteronomy but all the divine commandments contained in the Pentateuch. The divine origin of these laws is expressed by the use of the verb "prophesy," which involves divine inspiration. But not only the explicit commands found in scripture are included in Moses teachings; all the interpretations developed in rabbinic literature using various kinds of exegetical arguments are integral parts of divine revelation.

The halakic midrashim (see sidebar) on Exodus through Deuteronomy interpret verse by verse many, but not all, sections of these books. Many comments are simple explanations of the plain meaning of words and sentences. Longer exegetical passages dialectically assess all the possible meaning of a word or verse and seek to relate all postbiblical interpretations, customs, and Mishnaic laws to scripture. Often the powers of human interpretive reason are shown to be inadequate for reaching a certain interpretation, and thus reason is subordinated to scripture. Other midrashim, like *Leviticus Rabbah*, consist of homilies, each on a central theme which is developed using numerous scriptural verses. *Genesis Rabbah* combines aspects of commentary and homily. All midrashic works organize their materials to promote a worldview in which Israel's relationship with God is fostered and preserved through the understanding of and fidelity to Israel's biblical traditions.

Abot

The Mishnah tractate *Abot* (The Fathers), which is also called *Pirke Abot* (The Chapters of the Fathers), is a collection of sayings attributed to tannaitic sages. Its core probably comes from the second century and its final form from the third. It is the only Mishnah tractate not completely devoted to the statement and interpretation of

TYPES OF RABBINIC MIDRASH

RABBINIC MIDRASHIC collections are often imprecisely defined by their contents as halakic or haggadic. However, all midrashim contain both kinds of material. Midrashim are better classified by their literary form.

Exegetical midrashim generally comment briefly on passages of scripture, verse by verse. The so-called halakic midrashim on Exodus–Deuteronomy are of this type. The *expositional midrashim* contain brief, verse-by-verse commentary but also enlarge upon many verses, sometimes in long digressions which are sermons or mini-commentaries in themselves. The interpretations of Genesis and Lamentations in the *Midrash Rabbah* are of this type. The *homiletical midrashim* are literary sermons which begin with an introduction (proem). The proem artfully connects numerous verses with one another in order to introduce the subject of the day's reading by concluding with the first verse of the reading from the Pentateuch. Sometimes several proems are grouped together before the commentary on the reading for the day. The interpretation of the reading usually takes off from the first verse or first few verses and digresses into a web of related topics. *Leviticus Rabbah*, *Pesikta de Rav Kahana*, and *Pesikta Rabbati* are of this type. The last two cover reading from major feasts. The later midrashic collections called *Tanhuma* or *Yelammedenu* begin with proems which discuss a halakah. Many other midrashic collections, based on earlier ones, were made right through the Middle Ages.

laws and may have been added to the Mishnah to provide a rationale for the rabbinic way of life. Its thematic focus on love of Torah, study, and proper communal relations shows that it expounds the ideology and aspirations of the rabbinic group who created the Misnah. The teachings of the sages are similar to wisdom sayings in the Bible and seek both to establish the sages' authority as a continuous and coherent group of teachers and to sketch their understanding of how Jewish life should be lived. The scholastic emphasis on Torah and study fits the origins of the group as a learned school of sages seeking to develop a way of life and influence the direction of Jewish society during the second and third centuries C.E.

In the first chapter the chief sages of each generation are arranged in a chain of tradition that resembles the lists of the heads of Greek philosophical schools. The list of sages begins with Moses receiving Torah (meaning both the Bible and the rabbinic interpretations of biblical law) and passing it on to Joshua, the elders, the prophets, the men of the Great Assembly (a legendary body of leaders who are said to have spanned the indeterminate period between the end of prophecy and Simon the Just, high priest at the beginning of the second century B.C.E.), Simon the Just, and then a sequence of sages extending into the third century C.E. By linking themselves with biblical leaders and teachers, the sages implicitly claimed to be the authoritative heirs of the priests and prophets of the Bible (as did Ben Sira before them). When the sages adopted Torah rather than the lost temple as their central symbol and chief concern, they created a different way of life for Jews adapted to the postdestruction era, taking care to root their authority and their teaching in the Bible and God's revelation at Sinai.

The symbols, attitudes, advice, and values espoused by *Abot* became the heart of Judaism in the Talmudic period and have endured for centuries. As the rabbinic mode of understanding and living Judaism came to dominate the Jewish community and as Christianity developed an increasingly distinctive theology to account for its rapid growth among the gentiles, the gap between the closely related Jewish and Christian communities of the first century gradually widened, and the two branches of the biblical tradition grew in different directions.

BIBLIOGRAPHICAL ESSAY

The second temple period in Judaism extended from the return of some of the Jewish exiles from Babylon to Jerusalem in 438 B.C.E. to the destruction of the rebuilt temple by the Romans in 70 C.E. During this time, first the Persians, then the Greeks (332 B.C.E. on), and finally the Romans (63 B.C.E. on) ruled the Near East. Historical, political, religious, and cultural changes were many and permanent. What had been the religion of the Israelites in Israel and Judea developed into what we call Judaism, originally the way of life and thought of those living in the Persian province of Judea.

The second temple period was formerly neglected by Jewish and Christian scholars. Christians devalued this form of Judaism as "late," legalistic, and decadent. In the interests of emphasizing the importance and distinctiveness of Jesus' teaching, the Judaism of his time was treated as effete and ready for replacement. Jewish scholars also neglected this period, moving quickly from the biblical books to the canon of rabbinic literature, which began with the Mishnah (ca. 200 C.E.).

In the last century and a half manuscript discoveries and scholarly editions and translations have made available dozens of Jewish writings from the second temple and early rabbinic (up to 200 C.E.) periods. In the past thirty years numerous books and articles, both scholarly and popular, have illuminated this period and shown its critical importance for the development of both Judaism and Christianity. In an earlier generation, the mature forms of orthodox Judaism and Christianity were projected back into the first century C.E. (and earlier in the case of Judaism). But Jews in the Greek and Roman periods lived varied ways of life and had diverse viewpoints on social, religious, and political matters. Jesus of Nazareth and the early Christians were part of this creative Jewish ferment, as were the early rabbis. The early Christian group gradually separated from the Jewish community and assumed an independent way of life and thought; the rabbis worked for several centuries to gain control of the Jewish community.

Christian treatments of Judaism have improved since the Second World War. Anti-Semitic tendencies in theology have been curbed in the aftermath of the Holocaust. Yet problems remain. Motivated by a desire to understand Jesus and his times, the origin of Christianity within Judaism, and the many ideas, beliefs, attitudes, practices, and texts taken into Christianity from Judaism, Christians have a tendency to make Judaism come out in a way that supports or at least does not contradict their perceptions and experiences of Christian life and thought. They also tend to focus on the parts of Judaism most important to Christianity and not develop a coherent and adequate interpretation of Judaism as a whole. Christians still tend to compare Christianity with Judaism to Judaism's disadvantage and without adequate respect for Judaism as a living religion with a continuous, sophisticated tradition and successful way of life. Most Christians seem compelled to see Jesus as unique or "different" in his life, teachings, or purposes. Thus, Christianity is "special," and its identity and value are protected. But these claims tend to clash at a practical level with the Jewishness of Jesus and the early Palestinian church. The historical and theological consequences of Jesus' and the early church's Jewishness are often not drawn out but treated as an inert past fact. Finally, most Christian scholars lose interest in Judaism by the mid–second century. Thus, implicitly Christianity is seen as more important than Judaism, or as now separate and independent of Judaism and developing on its own. In fact, Christians still struggle with their theological relationship to Judaism.

The books recommended here provide accessible and up-to-date accounts of early Judaism and Christianity. A large number of books survey Judaism and Christianity in the Greco-Roman period, combining history, literature, and religious thought and institutions. Many are organized from a Christian point of view, seeking to show the context in which Jesus worked and how Christianity originated. For an older overview of the period with a selection of the literature joined by brief commentary, see D. S. Russell, *The Jews from Alexander to Herod* (Cambridge: Cambridge University Press, 1967). Russell's more recent brief survey of the period and its literature, *From Early Judaism to Early Church* (Philadelphia: Fortress, 1986), discusses some major topics but suffers from lack of contact with the most recent research. Sean Freyne's *The World of the New Testament* (Collegeville: Liturgical Press, 1980) is a brief, well-written description of Judaism, the Greco-Roman world, and the emergence of Christianity as a Jewish sect and covers the essential people, events, and institutions of the period. A more scholarly study by Freyne focuses on Galilee, *Galilee from Alexander the Great to Hadrian, 323 B.C.E. to 135 C.E.: A Study of Second Temple Judaism* (Wilmington: Glazier, 1980), and another focuses on Jesus and the New Testament, *Galilee, Jesus, and the Gospels* (Philadelphia: Fortress, 1988). A slightly longer and more detailed introduction to the Jewish and Christian context can be found in A.R.C. Leaney, *Cambridge Commentaries on Writings of the Jewish and Christian World, 200 B.C. to A.D. 200*, vol. 6, *The Jewish and Christian World, 200 B.C. to A.D. 200* (Cambridge: Cambridge University Press, 1984). More than half the book is given to history and the rest to brief descriptions of the literature of Judaism and Christianity. An index makes this volume a good small reference work. Earlier volumes in this series cover Jews in the hellenistic world, the Qumran community, Greco-Roman literature on Jews and Christians, and so on.

Frederick J. Murphy's *The Religious World of Jesus* (Nashville: Abingdon, 1991) is a simply conceived, readable, and well-executed textbook. It presumes an antecedent interest in Jesus and draws the reader into the world of first-century Judaism in Israel. It attempts to correct Christian cultural biases against Judaism and to present Judaism as a historically coherent and developing religious tradition. The major historical events and literary products of the second temple period are fairly and comprehensively presented. A selection of original texts are quoted, and special attention is given to topics that are relevant to Jesus and of natural interest to Christians, up to about 100 C.E.

Gabrielle Boccaccini, *Middle Judaism: Jewish Thought, 300 B.C.E.–200 C.E.* (Minneapolis: Fortress, 1991), has attempted to redefine the relationship of Christianity to Judaism and to use methods from the history of philosophy and history of thought to understand the dynamics of Judaism. His book is a preparatory study for a history of Jewish thought, not an organic reconstruction. Boccaccini has an unusual typology of Judaisms. He limits ancient Judaism to the sixth to fourth centuries B.C.E. and assigns the third century B.C.E. through the second century C.E. to "Middle Judaism," a period that encompasses several types of Judaism, including Pharisaism, early Christianity, Essenism, apocalyptic, and others. Out of Middle Judaism came four new types of Judaism: Rabbinism, Karaism, Falashas, and Christianity. The striking innovation in this typology is that Christianity should continue to be understood as a type of Judaism to the present day. Though few have agreed that Christianity should still be understood as a "Judaism," Boccaccini has grappled with the relationship binding Judaism and Christianity and has avoided treating it negatively.

E.P. Sanders, in *Judaism: Practice and Belief, 63 B.C.E.–66 C.E.* (Philadelphia: Trinity International, 1992), attempts to describe in concrete detail Judaism as it was actually lived and experienced in the first centuries B.C.E. and C.E. He also debates with a variety of scholars, including earlier ones who used their sources uncritically and contemporaries with whom he disagrees. Thus his book is wordy and complex. However, all the critical problems of this period are raised in some form. His earlier works, *Paul and Palestinian Judaism: A Comparison of Patterns of Religion* (Philadelphia: Fortress, 1977) and *Jesus and Judaism* (Philadelphia: Fortress, 1985), show how a renewed and accurate picture of Judaism changes one's apprehension of Jesus and the New Testament.

James D. Newsome's *Greeks, Romans, Jews: Currents of Culture and Belief in the New Testament World* (Philadelphia: Trinity, 1992) is a textbook written for Christians interested in Judaism as a background for the New Testament. The bulk of his material is drawn from the Bible and Jewish literature. Approaching the materials historically, literarily, and theologically, he stresses appreciation of religious content and experience. Lots of data, with an attractive selection of illustrative quotations, fill the page and initiate the student into Judaism. Clear parallels between New Testament and Jewish works appear in boxes. Regrettably, stereotypes and outdated views abound. Though not all Pharisees are bad according to Newsome, many are wooden and sterile in comparison with the alleged freedom of Jesus (portrayed as a good modern individualist, if not an American). On the synagogue and many other subjects, the most current scholarship is ignored or, if noted, is slighted. Later rabbinic sources are used inappropriately as sources to reconstruct first-century history. The third-century C.E. rabbinic idea of the centrality of Torah is retrojected into the Persian period five centuries earlier.

James D. G. Dunn, in *The Parting of the Ways between Christianity and Judaism and Their Significance for the Character of Christianity* (Philadelphia: Trinity, 1991), wishes to analyze the implications of the Jewish origins of Christianity and especially how it parted from Judaism and what is the basis for its separate identity. He is reacting against Harnack and Bultmann's earlier concept of a universal Jesus drained of Jewishness, and his book is theologically oriented. He builds his picture of Judaism on four pillars, around which he organizes his book: monotheism, an elect covenant people, Torah, and temple/land. When Christians questioned and redefined these pillars in the mid–second century, the ways parted. Dunn uses Judaism fairly to produce a coherent picture of Christian development.

Three excellent accounts of second temple and early rabbinic Judaism (including early Christianity as a form of Judaism) have been written by American Jewish scholars. The first, Shaye J. D. Cohen,

From the Maccabees to the Mishnah (Philadelphia: Westminster, 1987), treats the period topically, covering its history, common practices and beliefs, Jewish institutions, various Jewish groups and sects, the scriptural canon, and the emergence of rabbinic Judaism, which eventually produced a new canon. He stresses a rigorous and critical analysis of historical and literary evidence and concentrates on cultural and religious developments and processes affecting Judaism, such as hellenization, the "democratization" of religion in the second temple period, and the endurance of Judaism in new social circumstances. Lawrence H. Schiffman, *From Text to Tradition: A History of Second Temple and Rabbinic Judaism* (Hoboken: Ktav, 1991), writing from an orthodox perspective, moves through the centuries of Jewish history from the Persians to the Talmud, stressing the continuities in historical experience, literary development, and religious thought. His is the only introduction to give a full treatment of rabbinic literature, including the Mishnah, Tosefta, Talmuds, midrashim, etc. For him the diversity of Judaism flowed together into the unified, normative tradition found in the Talmud and represented by the rabbinic sages. Thus he values the Pharisees and rabbinic Judaism and treats other forms of Judaism during this period as background for rabbinic literature. Alan F. Segal's *Rebecca's Children: Judaism and Christianity in the Roman World* (Cambridge: Harvard University Press, 1986) is a reflective narrative rather than a textbook and concentrates on the major intellectual and historical movements and trends of the period and devotes considerable space to his main theme, a comparison of Judaism and Christianity until they definitively separated and went their own ways. True to modern ecumenism and American pluralism, he stresses the complementarity and positive relationships between Christianity and Judaism, despite their differences. This is perhaps the easiest book to read through. Finally, Geza Vermes has capped a lifetime of study with *The Religion of Jesus the Jew* (Minneapolis: Fortress, 1993), a series of readable chapters with refreshing insights into Jesus in the context of first-century Judaism.

Three recent scholarly surveys of Judaism function as reference works and starting points for study. Lester Grabbe, in *Judaism from Cyrus to Hadrian*, vol. 1, *The Persian and Greek Periods* (Minneapolis: Fortress, 1991), and vol. 2, *The Roman Period* (Minneapolis: Fortress, 1992), combines comprehensive reviews of ancient and modern literature, balanced discussion of historical problems, and clear historical syntheses for each period of the Persian, Greek, and Roman Empires up until the defeat of Bar Kosiba in 135 C.E. His bibliographies and summaries are a good starting point for most topics. A much more detailed and expensive four-volume reference work is Emil Schürer, G. Vermes, et al., *The History of the Jewish People in the Age of Jesus Christ, 175 B.C.–A.D. 135* (Edinburgh: Clark, 1973–87). This is a thorough revision of a famous late-nineteenth-century handbook that was quite influential and anti-Semitic in its treatment of the Jewish religion and thought. It contains a wealth of information in its dense footnotes, reviews all the historical problems, summarizes all the Jewish literature of the period, and is well indexed. A more readable but still extensive and detailed account of first-century Judaism can be found in the two volumes of S. Safrai et al., *The Jewish People in the First Century* (Philadelphia: Fortress, 1974–6). Chapters by major scholars treat historical, social, economic, religious, and cultural topics. A number of chapters uncritically use later rabbinic literature to reconstruct first-century Judaism, but a wealth of material is gathered in readable form.

A few special topics are worthy of comment. A major influence on Judaism in this period came from Greek or hellenistic culture, so much so that all Judaism may be said to have been hellenized to some extent even as it protected its integrity. Martin Hengel's *Judaism and Hellenism*, 2 vols. (Philadelphia: Fortress, 1974), traces the early stages of this encounter. A briefer and more recent account of his position can be found in his *Jews, Greeks, and Barbarians* (Philadelphia: Fortress, 1980). The complex relationships and conflicts with hellenism during the Maccabean War are lucidly and briefly described in Daniel J. Harrington, *The Maccabean Revolt* (Wilmington: Glazier, 1988). The religious and political ferment of the first century is captured in Richard Horsley and John S. Hanson, *Bandits, Prophets, and Messiahs: Popular Movements at the Time of Jesus* (Minneapolis: Winston, 1985). The rise of many popular leaders helps put Jesus in context and shows how the Great War against Rome began in 66 C.E. For the social roles of various Jewish groups in the first century and the structure of Palestinian society, see Anthony J. Saldarini, *Pharisees, Scribes, and Sadducees in Palestinian Society: A Sociological Analysis* (Wilmington: Glazier, 1988). The flourishing of women's studies has begun to illuminate the place and roles of women in antiquity. Ross S. Kraemer, in *Her Share of Blessings: Women's Religions among Pagans, Jews, and Christians in the Greco-Roman World* (New York: Oxford University Press, 1992), has ferreted out numerous testimonies to women's practice of religion and the positive and negative political and cultural consequences it had for their lives. Finally, a number of studies and books have grappled with the delicate question of anti-Jewish and anti-Semitic attitudes in the New Testament and early Christian literature. Three recent and excellent collections are Alan T. Davies, ed., *Anti-Semitism and the Foundations of Christianity* (New York: Paulist, 1979); Craig A. Evans and Donald A. Hagner, eds., *Anti-Semitism and Early Christianity: Issues of Polemic and Faith* (Minneapolis: Fortress, 1993); Peter Richardson and S. Wilson, eds., *Anti-Judaism in Early Christianity*, vol. 1, *Paul and the Gospels*; vol. 2, *Separation and Polemic*; Studies in Christianity and Judaism 1–2 (Waterloo, Ontario: Wilfred Laurier Press, 1986).

Reading the actual Jewish writings is the most satisfying way of understanding the second temple period. Most of the literature can be found in three collections: James H. Charlesworth, ed., *The Old Testament Pseudepigrapha*, 2 vols. (Garden City, N.Y.: Doubleday, 1983–5); H. D. F. Sparks, *The Apocryphal Old Testament* (Oxford: Clarendon, 1985); Geza Vermes, *The Dead Sea Scrolls in English*, 3d ed. (London: Penguin, 1987). Introductions to these works and their context are George W. E. Nickelsburg, *Jewish Literature between the Bible and the Mishnah* (Philadelphia: Fortress, 1981); Michael Stone, ed., *Jewish Writings of the second temple Period* (Philadelphia: Fortress, 1984); Craig

Evans, *Non-canonical Writings and New Testament Interpretation* (Peabody, Mass.: Hendrickson, 1992); G. Vermes, *The Dead Sea Scrolls: Qumran in Perspective* (Cleveland: Collins World, 1977); and two books by John J. Collins, *The Apocalyptic Imagination: An Introduction to the Jewish Matrix of Christianity* (New York: Crossroad, 1984), and *Between Athens and Jerusalem: Jewish Identity in the hellenistic Diaspora* (New York: Crossroad, 1983). Each of these books summarizes the literature covered and puts it in historical, literary, and religious context.

Jacob Neusner has written a number of books on rabbinic Judaism and its relationship with Christianity. The most accessible are, *Foundations of Judaism* (Philadelphia: Fortress, 1989); *From Testament to Torah: An Introduction to Judaism in Its Formative Age* (1988); *Midrash in Context; Messiah in Context; and Torah: From Scroll to Symbol in Formation Judaism* (Philadelphia: Fortress, 1983–5). For a technical reference book on the complex world of the Talmud and other rabbinic texts, see H. L. Strack and G. Stemberger, *Introduction to the Talmud and Midrash* (Edinburgh: Clark, 1991). It contains comprehensive bibliographies of texts and translations. Neusner has provided readable introductions to the major categories of rabbinic literature in *The Mishnah: An Introduction* (Northvale, N. J.: Aaronson, 1989); *Invitation to Midrash* (New York: Harper, 1989); and *Invitation to Talmud* (New York: Harper, 1973). These invitations give ample examples of the original texts with explanations.

Plate 1. Saint Catherine's Monastery at Mount Sinai. In the fourth century C.E. a church was built in this valley as a shrine of the burning bush. The mountain towering above it was identified as Mount Sinai, and by the sixth century a monastery was built there which has continued to operate to the present day. Among its treasures were superb manuscripts of the Greek Old and New Testaments which were purchased and taken to Russia by Constantine Tischendorf in the mid-nineteenth century and later were purchased by the British Museum. (H. C. Kee.)

Plate 2. The Nile Valley. The Nile River is more than 4,000 miles in length and its basin covers more than 1,000,000 square miles. The water and soil that it brings down from the inland of equatorial Africa provide the essentials for the fertility of the lower valley, which stretches for more than 950 miles from the second cataract of the river down to the delta at the Mediterranean. In Egypt, two major centers of political power and cultural development arose along the Nile: Thebes was located below (north of) the first cataract, and Memphis was just upstream from the delta (near modern Cairo). In Hellenistic times, Alexandria, at the mouth of the Nile, was the capital and a center of world culture. (H. C. Kee.)

Plate 3. Pyramids of Giza, Egypt. Built during the period known by historians as the Old Kingdom (2700–2500 B.C.E.), the pyramids were intended as mausoleums for the kings of Egypt. The Great Pyramid, which was built by Khufu, covers thirteen acres and consists of more than two million limestone blocks, each of which weighs about two and one-half tons. Originally the pyramid was 480 feet in height and is reported by the Greek historian Herodotus to have taken 100,000 workers thirty years to complete. (H. C. Kee.)

Plate 4. Temple at Thebes, Egypt. In the Twentieth Dynasty of the Egyptian New Kingdom (1570–1090 B.C.E.), Rameses III came to power. He faced threats to Egyptian control of territory to the north and east of Egypt. Among others, his enemies were the Sea Peoples (Peleste), who are known in the biblical accounts as the Philistines. On the west bank of the Nile at Thebes he built a great temple for the god Amun. On its walls are inscribed lists of his military accomplishments . (H. C. Kee.)

Plate 5. The Jordan Valley. The sources of the Jordan are at the southern border of Syria, especially from the slopes of Mount Hermon, which is 9,100 feet high and showered with rain and snow. By the time the Jordan River reaches Lake Huleh, it is only 230 feet above sea level, and it continues to drop in the valley through which it flows until it is 695 feet below sea level at the Sea of Galilee; when it reaches the Dead Sea, it is 1,290 feet below the level of the Mediterranean. The geological depression of the valley continues through the Wadi el-Araba until it reaches the Gulf of Aqaba, which is an arm of the Red Sea. (H. C. Kee.)

Plate 6. These spring waters join the Jordan River near the traditional site of John the Baptist's preaching (Matt. 3:1-6). The oasis formed by this spring led to the establishment here of Jericho, the earliest city yet uncovered in Palestine. (Biblical Archaeology Slides, no. 11.)

Plate 7. The earliest fortification structure in the world, thus far discovered, is this circular stone tower built about 7000 B.C.E. at Jericho. The tower was later connected to a massive stone wall which encompassed a city of about ten acres during the seventh millennium B.C.E. (pre-pottery Neolithic Age). (Biblical Archaeology Slides, no. 66.)

Plate 8. This ox-pulled plow is not much different from those first used in Canaan at the beginning of the Iron Age. The iron plowpoint may have been introduced in the twelfth century B.C.E. by the Philistines, who, according to 1 Sam. 13:19 ff., maintained a monopoly for a time over iron-smithing technology. (Biblical Archaeology Slides, no. 16.)

Plate 9. This reaper is harvesting with a curved hand-sickle. Biblical law (Deut. 24:19) allowed widows, orphans, and strangers to follow the reapers to gather any straw stalks missed in the bundling, as described in the story of Ruth (Ruth 2). (Biblical Archaeology Slides, no. 18.)

Plate 10. Several characteristic shapes and decorations of Iron I (twelfth to eleventh centuries B.C.E.) pottery are shown here. The wide bowl from Gezer in the center background displays a stylized palm tree on its inside, a variation of a decoration that had been used earlier and then abandoned. The two small storejars at the side are traditional in shape, but their smaller size and decoration imitate Egyptian glass vials of the period. All the vessels reflect the transition in the cultural climate of Canaan, where Israelites and other new groups were establishing themselves in the region but had not completely displaced the indigenous Canaanite population. (Biblical Archaeology Slides, no. 127.)

11. Paneas (Banias, Caesarea Philippi). Paneas is a grotto at the source of the Jordan River, about twenty-five miles north of the Sea of Galilee and southwest of Mt. Hermon. The name comes from the half-human, half-animal Greek god Pan, who loved woodlands and cool streams. The Emperor Augustus made Herod the Great ruler of the region of Paneas in 20 B.C.E., and Herod built a temple dedicated to Augustus there. Philip, the son of Herod, next ruled Paneas (4 B.C.E.—33/34 C.E.) as part of his tetrarchy and built a city in honor of Augustus named Caesarea (called Caesarea Philippi, to distinguish it from other cities with the same name). (Anthony J. Saldarini.)

Plate 12. The Agora in Athens. The agora was originally an open space in the middle of a Greek city where the citizens met to socialize and transact business. In classical and hellenistic Greece agoras included a variety of public buildings and colonnades where political, judicial, social and commercial activities took place. An agora often included fountains, trees, altars and statues. (Anthony J. Saldarini.)

Plate 13. The Colosseum in Rome. The emperors Vespasian (69–79) and his son Titus (79–81) built this amphitheater at the end of the Forum valley, next to Esquiline Hill. It was about one-third mile around, and its facade was three stories high, supported by Greek columns. It was used for entertainment, including combat between gladiators and between wild animals and humans. Over the centuries its marble and stone were removed for other building projects. (Anthony J. Saldarini.)

Plate 14. Sepphoris, looking to the north-northwest. Sepphoris, on a hill in central lower Galilee, was a major city and commercial center and at various times a regional capital. After destruction by Roman forces in 4 B.C.E. it was rebuilt by Herod Antipas. Sepphoris overlooks the rich agricultural land of the valley, which runs from the Mediterranean Sea to the Sea of Galilee. (Anthony J. Saldarini.)

Plate 15. The Sea of Galilee. The Sea of Galilee, known by several names including Lake Chinnereth and Lake Gennesaret, is about 40 miles long and 8 miles wide. The Jordan river enters it to the north and flows out from the southern end to the Dead Sea. The area was settled in prehistoric times due to the fish in the lake and the fertile land around it. (Anthony J. Saldarini.)

Plate 16. David's Tower in Jerusalem. The fortified citadel near the present Jaffa gate on the western side of the walled city of Jerusalem contains underneath it the remains of a Davidic wall, the second-century B.C.E. Hasmonean walls and towers and the first-century B.C.E. Herodian walls and towers. This tower, traditionally known as David's Tower, is probably the site of Hippicus, one of three towers built by Herod the Great. (Anthony J. Saldarini.)

Plate 17. Synagogue at Masada, the Zealot fortress. Herod the Great's lavish fortress with two palaces, baths and storerooms on the inaccessible plateau of Masada includes a building next to the northwest wall which was probably used in its second phase as a synagogue by the Zealots during the war with Rome (66–70 C.E.). It was about 49 by 36 feet. On three inner walls it had four tiers of benches, and it included a room in one corner. In two pits in that room scrolls of Deuteronomy and Ezekiel have been found. In the earlier Herodian period, before architectural modifications, some say the building was a stable, others a synagogue. (Anthony J. Saldarini.)

Plate 18. Reconstruction of the Jerusalem Temple. Based on the descriptions of the Temple built by Herod in Jerusalem in Josephus's writings (*Antiquities* 15, *Jewish War* 5, *Against Apion* 1) and the rabbinic tractate *Middoth*, a detailed reconstruction of the sacred complex has been built in Jerusalem. Excavations along the standing walls surrounding the Temple enclosure have helped to clarify details of the building, including the elaborate stairways which gave access to the temple from the south. Visible here are the sacred precincts: the Holy Place, accessible to the priests, and the Holy of Holies, which only the High Priest could enter. (H. C. Kee.)

Facing page, top: Plate 19. Triumphal Arch of Titus, Rome. Still standing in the center of ancient Rome is the arch honoring Titus following his death (81 C.E.), on which a bas-relief pictures the Roman soldiers carrying in triumphal procession the treasures taken from the Temple in Jerusalem following Titus's defeat of the Jewish insurrectionists there in 67–70. Visible are the seven-branched lampstand, the sacred trumpets, and other sacred items. (H. C. Kee.)

Facing page, bottom: Plate 20. Harbor of Thessalonica. The Romans made this city the capital of the province of Macedonia in northern Greece. Its location on the major Roman road across the Balkan peninsula, the Via Egnatia, and its role as a seaport made it a prosperous city. Various Greek and Roman gods and goddesses were worshiped there – including Asklepios, Serapis, Isis, Zeus, and Demeter – but especially honored were the Cabiri, deities who fostered fertility and protected sailors at sea. The Thessalonians also honored the Roman emperor as divine during his lifetime. (H. C. Kee.)

Plate 21. Temple of Apollo at Corinth. These columns remain from the temple built in the sixth century B.C.E. in honor of Apollo, who earlier was the god of herdsmen and later was identified as the sun god. The temple is on a low hill overlooking the central marketplace of the city. In the background is Acrocorinth, which towers 1,500 feet above the city and was the location of a temple of Aphrodite, the goddess of love. (H. C. Kee.)

Plate 22. The Judean hills. The hill country of Judea is the southeastern part of the land of Judah, bounded on the south by the Negev (a desert south of the Dead Sea), on the east by the barren mountains which drop off sharply into the Dead Sea, and on the west by the low hills (Stephelah) which overlook the coastal plain. The hill country terminates in the north at the longitude of the northern end of the Dead Sea. The highest point of these hills is 3,500 feet at Hebron. North and east of Jerusalem bare mountains drop off precipitously into the Jordan Valley. Overlooking this wilderness of Judea from the east side of Jerusalem is the Mount of Olives. (H. C. Kee.)

Plate 23. Samaria. The city of Samaria was the capital of the northern kingdom of Israel from the ninth century until 721 B.C.E., when the region fell to the Assyrians (1 Kings 17:1-6). Major roads passed through the valley below the hill on which the city was built, and it continued as capital of the district through the Persian, Hellenistic, and Roman periods. Herod the Great rebuilt the city in a grand style and renamed it Sebaste (the Greek equivalent of "Augustus") in honor of the emperor who had put him in power. (H. C. Kee.)

Plate 24. The Parthenon, Athens. The Acropolis, a steep and rocky hill more than 500 feet high, stands in the center of Athens. The Parthenon was built on its summit in about 438 B.C.E. in honor of Athena, a goddess worshipped in this region before the Greeks came. She was earlier involved with warfare but in the classical Greek period became the patroness of arts, handcrafts, and wisdom. The Parthenon contained a great gold and ivory statue of the goddess fashioned by Phidias. Elsewhere on the Acropolis she was honored as the goddess of victory. Christians converted her temple into a church, and when the Turks took control of Greece, the temple was made into a mosque. (H. C. Kee.)

Plate 25. Center for the mystery cult at Samothrace. Twin fertility gods were worshiped on the small Aegean island of Samothrace even before the time of the Greeks. Initiation into their cult was thought to ensure the favor of the gods in this life and participation in the future life. Rulers from various realms in the eastern Mediterranean, including the parents of Alexander the Great, made contributions to build and maintain the structures there. (H. C. Kee.)

Plate 26. Tell er-Ras, on Mount Gerizim. Emperor Hadrian built on the site of the Samaritan temple one to honor Zeus, which is pictured on a coin of the period. Archeologists have discovered traces of the stair which led from the temple at the top of the mountain to the eastern entrance of the new city below (Neapolis, now called Nablus). (Joint Shechem Expedition.)

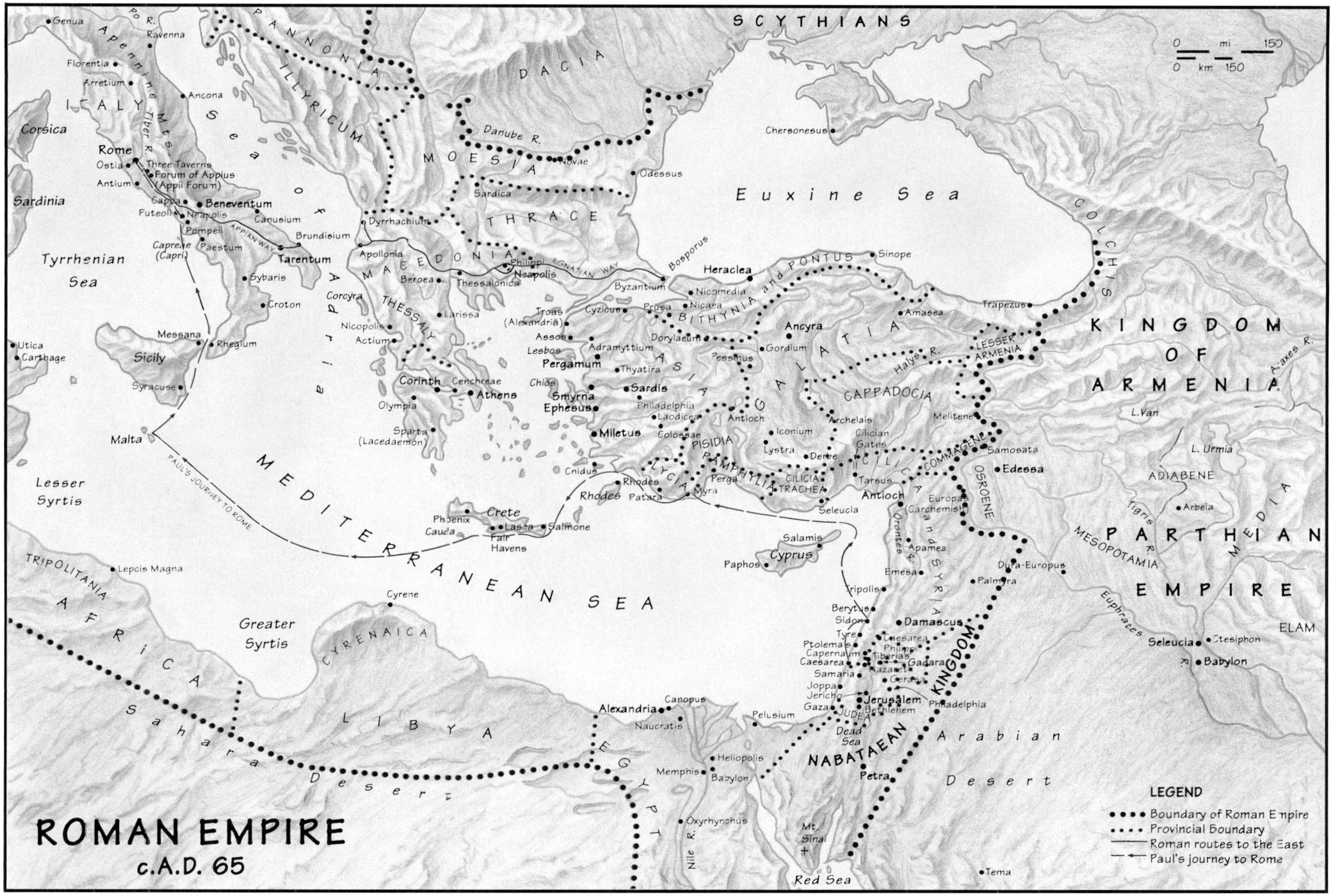

Plate 27. The Roman Empire, circa 65 C.E.

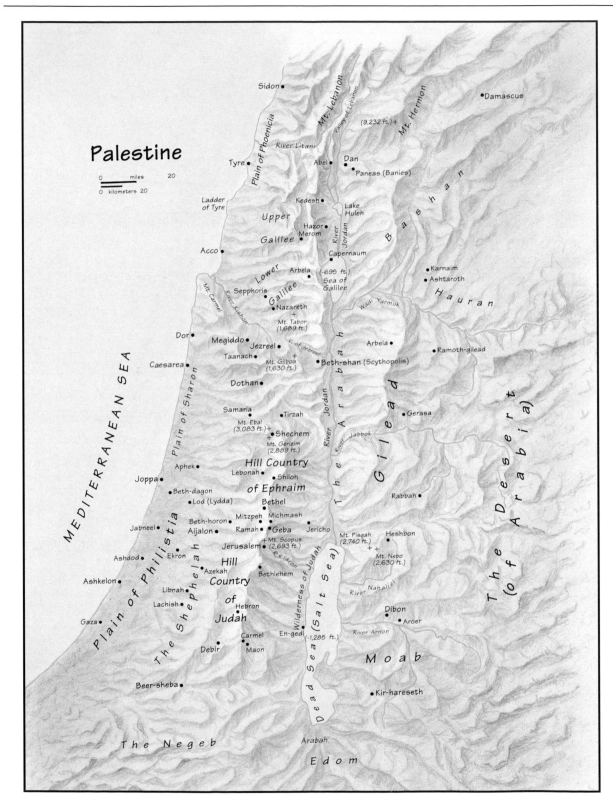

Plate 28. Palestine.

THE FORMATION OF THE CHRISTIAN COMMUNITY

Howard Clark Kee

I.   JESUS AND THE NEW COVENANT PEOPLE

A.   JESUS AND THE JUDAISM OF HIS TIME

Jesus shared with his Jewish contemporaries the conviction that what God had done for and disclosed to his covenant people in the past had continuing relevance for the ongoing life of his people in the present. He also shared with many of his fellow Jews the belief that the traditions embodied in their scriptures were to be interpreted and appropriated in new ways, given the changed circumstances in which Jews lived under Roman dominance. In the tradition of the prophet Jeremiah, the Jews awaited God's renewal of the covenant (Jer. 31:31–4). The basic question for them at this time was, What is the essence of belonging to God's people? We have already seen in the sections on postexilic Judaism how varied the answers were to that question. It is important for the reader of those writings which came to be called – significantly – the New Covenant (a more accurate translation than "New Testament") to see specifically how Jesus differed from his contemporaries in understanding and reclaiming their covenantal tradition.

For the priestly establishment, the central factor in the maintenance of Israel's special relationship with its God was to carry out faithfully the cultic system that centered on the temple in Jerusalem (Colorplate 18). Since the temple was believed to be the place where God was present among his people, the building and its prescribed rites were to be honored fully as a way of ensuring the continuity of Israel's place as God's special people. The daily and other periodic sacrifices had to be performed properly. And faithful Jews from the land of Palestine, as well as from Jewish colonies scattered throughout the Roman world and the Middle East, were required to take part in the sacrifices annually and to make contributions toward the support of the temple and its priesthood.

After Herod the Great rebuilt the temple in such a grandiose manner, it became a popular attraction for non-Jews, with the result that

Jewish pilgrims and gentile tourists made a major contribution to the economy of Jerusalem and Judea. The priestly rites were performed on a rotating basis by members of the priestly families, some of whom lived at a distance from Jerusalem. The economic and social impact of the priestly caste was considerable. Throughout the land of Palestine, the Roman authorities not only sanctioned the carrying out of the sacred ceremonies in the temple but worked through the priestly leaders to maintain social and political control over the subject peoples of Palestine. As early as the first century B.C.E., a candidate for the role of high priest had sought and gained confirmation of his role from the Roman Senate. The mutually beneficial relationship between the Roman authorities and the priestly families continued after the Romans took over Palestine in 63 B.C.E. until the Jewish revolt of 67–70 C.E. (see pp. 355–358).

Jesus, on the other hand, is portrayed in the Gospel tradition as challenging priestly control of the temple and of the worship there (Mark 13). He expelled from the temple those whose function was necessary to making the acceptable temple offerings: the money changers, who exchanged various foreign moneys for the coinage accepted in the temple, and the vendors of the sacrificial animals. Further, he predicted the temple's destruction, with no suggestion that it would be rebuilt. He emphasized that God intended it to be a place of prayer "for all nations" (Isa. 56:7). When Jesus said this, he was standing in the Court of the Gentiles, which was the only part of the temple into which non-Jews were allowed entry. For Jesus to emphasize gentile access could only have been regarded as a threat to the sanctity of the temple as the place where a ritually pure Israel met its God. The priests could scarcely overlook the challenge that Jesus' utterances represented, since they implied that the temple was not necessary as the point

Fallen stones from the Jerusalem temple. By clearing the areas adjacent to the western and southern walls of the temple complex, the enormous size of the stones cut and positioned to form the supporting wall for the temple complex are visible. Also evident are the effects of the Roman attack on Jerusalem and its temple in 66–70 C.E., where the fall of the massive stones can be observed.

H.C. Kee.

Kidron Valley. In the rainy season a brook flowed through the Kidron Valley, located east of Old Jerusalem between the temple mount and the Mount of Olives. It flowed southeast and emptied into the Dead Sea near the site of the Dead Sea community of Qumran. The present valley is filled with rocks and the rubbish of the ages, which reduce the flow of water, but in the days of the monarchy of Israel the spring of Gihon flowed into the valley until it was diverted to form the Pool of Siloam. Near Jerusalem the valley was the location of shrines to other gods, as well as the place of burial of honored and humble dead.

Matson Photo Service.

of connection between God and his people, and that access to Israel's God should be open to non-Jews.

The importance of purity and temple worship in the Judaism of this period has been further confirmed by the discovery among the Dead Sea Scrolls of one known as the Temple Scroll. The Qumran community, which produced this document in the first century B.C.E., was persuaded that the priesthood in charge of the temple was unworthy and that the ritual carried out there was not acceptable to the God of Israel. They were awaiting God's time, when their community leaders would be placed in charge of the temple, which would be rebuilt and purified, as the Temple Scroll detailed. Not only is no portion of this new temple designated as the Court of the Gentiles, but there is a long list of Jews whose personal impurities disqualify them from entering the sacred courts. This list matches in detail the designation in the gospel stories of the kinds of persons whom Jesus – in sharp contrast to the Dead Sea group – befriended and welcomed into the fellowship of his followers: lepers, women with menstrual flow, those who have had contact with the dead, those who deal with evil spirits, children. In the Temple Scroll, non-Israelites are given no place in Israel's approach to God, and even proselytes must wait until the fourth generation before they may enter the middle court of the temple. Women can go no farther than the outer court. Any who violate the purity code are to be executed. Anyone who is considered to be a traitor to Israel or who makes a place for himself among gentiles is to be crucified, though care is to be taken that he is buried on the day of his death, so that the holy land will not be polluted by the exposure of his corpse.

The other Dead Sea Scrolls show in detail how this group of Jews (referred to in some Jewish writings as Essenes) were led by the founder of their movement to believe that it was no longer possible to obey God and preserve the purity of his people so long as they lived in Jerusalem. Contact with impure people and subjection to what they regarded as a corrupt set of religious leaders required them to withdraw to the desert, just as Israel had done in ancient times in preparation for its new existence in the Promised Land. The community saw itself as chosen by God to return to Jerusalem in the near future, to restore the temple worship, and to purify the city and God's people. Meanwhile, their common life in and around the community center overlooking the Dead Sea required them to purify themselves regularly through baptism and to meet regularly for a common meal, which anticipated the great banquet that would take place when God restored them and sent among them the two messiahs (one priestly and one royal). Members were strictly obligated to conform to their heightened rules of purity, under penalty of temporary or even permanent exclusion from the new covenant people.

Some interpreters of the Dead Sea Scrolls have sought to link Jesus with this group, either directly or by positing John the Baptist's membership in the sect. Jesus appears in the gospel tradition as one who shares with the Dead Sea group the expectation of covenant renewal, including celebrating that future event in a meal of bread and wine. But as noted above, the qualifications he sets out for participation in the community preparing for this future event are the opposite of the Dead Sea group's standards: he welcomes the outcasts, the sinners, women, and children and freely contacts the lepers, the dead, gentiles, and the demon-possessed. As we have seen, the future of God's people, as he proclaimed it, had no place for the temple. Purity is seen by him in terms of love of God and neighbor – which includes any human being in need. The revolutionary import of this attitude on the part of Jesus would have been threatening to both the priestly establishment and the Dead Sea community, but the fact that he claimed the support of the God of Israel and of the scriptures for his position confronted his Jewish contemporaries with a crucial question: Is this man from God or from Satan, God's adversary?

During the first century C.E. the Pharisaic movement was changing from an informal, spontaneous movement to a powerful, organized group supported by the Romans after 70 C.E. Like the Dead Sea community, the Pharisees were primarily concerned with the personal purity of the members. Pharisaism's major emphases were on dietary and social modes of maintaining what its constituents saw as a special relationship to God. Adherents gathered for prayer, study of the scriptures, and table fellowship. They saw these gatherings as the equivalent of God's presence in the temple and therefore adapted for their meetings and members the ritual requirements and practices that were laid down in the law of Moses for the temple and its priesthood. Although daily obligations might bring the Pharisees into associations with the impure of this world, their special identity was celebrated and reinforced in their informal fellowship meetings. For them, as with the priests and the Essenes of Qumran, Jesus was a challenge and a threat.

Masada. This steep and rocky mountain, to the southwest of and overlooking the Dead Sea, was used by the Hasmonean Jewish rulers in the early first century B.C.E. as a luxurious place of retreat and pleasure. Four palaces and multiple bathhouses and pools were built on its flat top, as well as cisterns to capture rainwater. Herod greatly expanded the buildings and multiplied the cisterns and bathing facilities. Special facilities were built for the royal guard based there. At the time of the second Jewish revolt (132–5 C.E.), it was a major base for the Jewish revolutionaries. Beginning in 1950, extensive correspondence between Bar Kochba (or Kosiba), the leader of the revolt, and his aides in the revolution was found in caves in canyons running down to the Dead Sea north of Masada. These provide detailed information about the course and strategies of the revolt, although no sources have survived to provide an overall picture of this unsuccessful uprising against the Romans.

H.C. Kee.

Although, as we shall see, the intensity of the antagonism between the Jesus movement and the Pharisees may have been heightened in the post-70 period when the Pharisees (with Roman support) were moving into positions of power among the Jews, Jesus' insistence that God welcomed the penitent and the ritually or ethnically excluded seekers after divine grace was flatly contradictory to the Pharisees' qualifications for membership in God's people.

Another option open to Jews of this period was that of the nationalists: to define Israel in territorial and political terms. Israel would be truly the people of God when it was an autonomous state, with the divinely designated agent (king or priest or both) as its visible ruler. That conviction had given rise to the Maccabean revolt and was given an ironic kind of fulfillment by the Romans when they established Herod as king of the Jews, even though his father was a non-Jewish noble and his mode of life seems to have been uninhibited by Jewish law. From the gospel tradition, it is clear that Jesus refused to take up this option of seizing power or assuming authority in the political sense. In his response to the request of James and John that he grant them special places of honor beside him when he sat on the throne of glory in the coming kingdom of God (Mark 10:35–45), he had to inform them that to follow him was a way of suffering and death before God's rule would be fully established. When he was seized by the authorities and brought to trial, he refused to exercise power to defend himself or to lay claim to a political role. The gospels portray him as dying with the scornful identity of "King of the Jews," which he surely was not in the sense that the Romans or the Jewish nationalists would have understood that title.

Other Jews of the period were persuaded that God's self-disclosure through the law and the prophets gave them special insight into his nature and purpose for them and for the world, but they saw many

APOCALYPTIC

THE TERM COMES FROM THE Greek word *apokalypsis,* which means "disclosure" or "revelation," and is used by scholars to refer to a type of literature produced by a religious community in which their worldview is expressed. As a literary style, apocalyptic claims to be a revelation by God of his purpose for his special people and for the future of the creation. It uses visions, oracles, symbols, and cryptic language to convey its message, since the import of such writing is intended only for the inner group. Typical of apocalyptic are symbolic descriptions of the cosmic conflict that will precede the coming of the end of the age and the establishment of God's rule in the world.

The worldview implicit in apocalyptic assumes that the present age is dominated by the powers of evil, but that God is already at work to accomplish his purpose in the created order and especially for his people. The community of God's people are now called upon to accept suffering and even martyrdom during the present period of cosmic struggle, but they are given assurance that they will be vindicated and will enjoy new life in the age to come.

points of contact and affinity between the scriptural tradition and the learning of the wider world. The figure of Wisdom, as we have seen (pp. 246–249). was the personification of God's revelation to his people. And for those Jews who had lived and been educated under the influence of hellenistic philosophy, there was a basic harmony between revealed (Jewish) and rational (gentile) wisdom. There is no indication that this sort of issue was significant for Jesus, but it surely was for those who in the later first century saw in him the instrument of disclosure of God's purpose. The practice among many Jewish intellectuals of interpreting their tradition along allegorical or symbolic lines established the precedent for appropriating the Jesus tradition in similar ways.

One aspect of Judaism that Jesus clearly shared with his contemporaries was the belief similar to that expressed in Daniel and the Dead Sea Scrolls, as well as in other Jewish writings of the postexilic period, that God would for the present allow his faithful people to be dominated by the powers of evil (both political and superhuman or demonic), but that he would soon act through his chosen agent to defeat his enemies, vindicate the faithful, and establish his rule in the world. The insight as to the divine plan and the identity of the faithful was reserved for the latter. Non-members of the group could not grasp this truth, which was conveyed to the insiders by divine revelation (hence, the development of apocalyptic literature) and expressed in cryptic or symbolic language. We can see in the biblical tradition that this outlook causes problems, especially when the fulfillment of the hopes of the group does not occur on schedule. For example, the promise of Israel's renewal in the space of seventy years expressed by Jeremiah (Jer. 25:11, 29:10) is revised by Daniel to seventy "weeks" of years, or 490 years (Dan. 9:1–27). In the Gospel tradition, and in other parts of the Christian scriptures, there is evidence that with the passage of time the expectation of an imminent end of the age had to be dealt with, and a variety of solutions were offered.

The issues that were posed for Jesus and the early Christians as a result of his Jewish birth and upbringing, therefore, included the following:

Who are the people of the covenant?

How is membership gained and maintained?

What attitude are members to assume toward nonmembers and to the cultural and social patterns in which the latter live, learn, and approach their god(s)?

Who is the agent or what is the agency through which God will achieve his purpose for the creation as a whole and for his people in particular?

How is the Jesus movement to be propagated, and who are its potential members?

What are the style and structure of leadership for the movement?

B. HOW THE JESUS TRADITION WAS PRESERVED

However desirable it might be to have available records of Jesus' words and deeds that were made during his lifetime, we must acknowledge that we have none. There are no detailed reports about him from non-Christian sources, and the oldest of the gospels, Mark, dates from no earlier than the late sixties and was written probably about the time of the Jewish revolt of 66–70. Paul's extant letters, which were written in the decade between 50 and 60, include the oldest surviving references to Jesus, but as we shall see, he mentions only a few of the sayings and activities of Jesus, as noted below. Later Jewish and Roman sources make only passing references to Jesus, which, however, do confirm some of the details in the Gospel accounts.

The primary sources for our knowledge of Jesus, therefore, are the gospels: the Books of Matthew, Mark, Luke, and John. But as the title "gospel" (good news), implies, and as the opening word of Mark makes explicit, they are not objective reports but propaganda. That is, they want to convince the reader of the truth of what they describe, as Luke makes explicit: "That you may know the truth concerning the things of which you have been informed" (Lk 1:4). The authorship and the precise date of these writings cannot be determined. Since each of the gospels was written at a different time and under different circumstances, there are significant differences among them in detail. The first three, as they appear in the Christian scriptures, have traditionally been called Matthew, Mark, and Luke. They share a basic narrative core and include considerable common material. As noted in detail below, Matthew and Luke include distinctive material not found in either Mark or John, presumably drawing on a sayings source known by scholars as Q. Each of the four gospels varies in detail in the use of some material which they have in common with others; and each gospel places in a unique framework the whole of the tradition that is included. Each of these writings was very early associated with the name of a disciple of Jesus or with someone closely connected with one of the apostles. The first and fourth gospels (as they are placed in the New Testament) give no internal indication of authorship but have been associated from the early days of the church's life with two disciples of Jesus: Matthew and John. Analogously, the second and third gospels have been accepted as the work of companions of the apostles: Mark, who is associated with Peter (1 Pet. 5:13), and Luke, who is mentioned as a coworker in letters attributed to Paul (Philem. 24; 2 Tim. 4:11). The characteristic points of view of each of the gospels is explored below.

The fact that other, later Christian writings include sayings attributed to Jesus that resemble those in the gospels, but for which there is no exact equivalent, confirms the theory that the gospel tradition circulated orally before it was produced in written form. It appears that both stories about Jesus and reports of his teachings were handed down in oral form from the beginning of the Jesus movement. Clear evidence of this may be found in Paul, who reflects Jesus' teaching that the primary commandment is to love one's neighbor (Gal. 5:14; cf.

IS MARK OUR OLDEST GOSPEL?

SINCE MARK IS THE SHORTest of the three synoptic gospels, it has sometimes been assumed that it is an abbreviation of Matthew. Careful comparison among the synoptic Gospels (Matthew, Mark, and Luke) shows, however, that both Matthew and Luke presuppose the contents and the order of Mark, though each of the other writers modifies Mark in order to fulfill his own special aims. For example, Matthew and Luke are completely independent of each other in their accounts of Jesus' birth and of the events following his burial; yet in narrative sequence, they closely resemble each other from the point where Mark begins (Jesus' baptism) to where his account ends (at the empty tomb). Passages in Mark that the church later found difficult are either omitted or basically modified. An example is Mark's note that Jesus was *unable* to do many miracles because of the people's unbelief (Mark 6:5). Luke completely rewrites and relocates (Luke 4:16–30) this comment, and both he and Matthew eliminate the mention of Jesus's inability (Matt. 13:58). The most plausible explanation for the relationship among the synoptic gospels is that Mark is the original, with Matthew and Luke drawing on Mark and a second common source (Q) but developing the details of structure and content independently.

HISTORICAL REFERENCES TO JESUS

JOSEPHUS, THE JEWISH historian who wrote *Antiquities of the Jews* in the latter part of the first century C.E., mentions both Jesus and his brother James. They are included in his accounts of nationalists and other trouble-makers of that century. Although the present text of *Antiquities* (18.63) seems to have been altered by Christian copyists to make Josephus bear testimony to Jesus' resurrection and messi-ahship, it almost certainly includ-ed reference to his extraordinary powers, his crucifixion under Pontius Pilate, and the claim of his followers that God had raised him from the dead. The rabbinic sources, which date from much later, never refer to Jesus by name but imply the illegitimacy of his birth and denounce the heretical nature of his teachings.

The Roman historian Suetonius, in his *Lives of the Twelve Caesars*, mentions that during the reign of Claudius (41–54 C.E.), there was a distur-bance among the Jews in Rome instigated by someone named "Chrestos," a common name that he supplied instead of the unfa-miliar "Christos." It is virtually certain that the tensions in the Jewish community at Rome were the result of the arrival there of preachers of Jesus, whom they called "Christos." This would mean that within two decades of Jesus' death, the Christian mes-sage had spread to the capital of the empire. Tacitus in his *Annals* (15.44) reports that when Nero set fire to Rome, he placed the blame on a group called Christians, whose founder had been put to death by the procura-tor Pontius Pilate during the reign of Tiberius (14–37 C.E.). In one of his *Letters*, Pliny wrote to the emperor Trajan (98–117 C.E.) for advice in handling the religious sect of Christians, which was spreading very rapidly in the province he governed (Bithynia, in northeastern Asia Minor).

These sources confirm some of the basic information about Jesus that comes from the Gospels and do not directly contradict any of it, but neither do they supplement what we read in the early Christian writings.

Mark 12:28–34, where Deut. 6:4 and Lev. 19:18 are linked). Paul also has an equivalent version of Jesus' words at the Last Supper (1 Cor. 11:23–6; cf. Mark 14:22–5).

NARRATIVE IN Q

THE STORY OF JESUS' healing of the centurion's slave is the one complete example of a narrative in the Q tradition. Like the rest of Q, it is not in Mark but is shared by Matthew and Luke. Some parts of the Q tradition imply a narrative setting, as in the responses of Jesus to the questioners from John the Baptist (Luke 7:18–35) and to the Jewish leaders who asked him to perform a miracle in order to confirm that God was with him (Luke 11:29–32). Thus the Q tradition does not represent Jesus as mere-ly one who utters sayings but as one who is engaged in public actions and social relationships.

C. THE Q SOURCE

Detailed analysis of the first three gospels, including the schol-arly practice of placing them in parallel columns for close scrutiny, leads to the conclusion that one of the earlier sources behind the gospels as we know them was a collection consisting primarily of say-ings of Jesus. This source was used by the writers of Matthew and Luke. There is nearly universal agreement among scholars that both Matthew and Luke used Mark as the basic document for the structur-ing of their gospels. Although the sayings source must be reconstruct-ed on a hypothetical basis by separating out from Matthew and Luke the common tradition they share that does not derive from Mark, inde-pendent analysis of the gospels has led to clear consensus about this source – not only that it existed but also regarding the details of its con-tents. Much of the early work done on this was by German scholars, with the result that the source came to be known by the first letter of the German word for "source," *Quelle*; hence, Q. Further, it appears that Luke has preserved the Q source in a form that is closer to the original, and that he has even approximated its original order. Accordingly, in what follows we offer the scriptural references to the Q tradition based on Luke:

3:7–9, 16b–17	The eschatological preaching of John the Baptist
4:2b–12	Jesus' struggle with Satan
6:20–3	Beatitudes: God's blessing of the poor, the hungry, and the hated
6:27–36	Promised reward for love and forgiveness
6:37–42	Rewards of faithful discipleship
6:43–6	Parables of moral productivity
6:47–9	Discipleship must survive testing: the parable of the houses with and without foundation
7:2–3, 6–10	Healing of the centurion's son
7:18–23	Jesus responds to John the Baptist's question
7:24–35	The place of John the Baptist in God's plan
9:57–8 (62?)	Leaving behind home and family
10:2–12	Jesus commissions his disciples to extend his work
10:13–15	Doom pronounced on the unrepentant cities
10:16	The disciples share in Jesus' rejection
10:21–2	God's gift of wisdom to his own people
10:23–4	Beatitude: those to whom wisdom is granted
11:2–4	Prayer that God's rule will come on earth
11:9–13	God answers the prayers of his own people
11:14–20	Jesus' defeat of the demons as a sign of the coming of God's rule
11:24–6	The return of the unclean spirit
11:29–32	The sign of Jonah and the one greater than Jonah: Jesus as prophet and wise man
11:33–6	Parables of light and darkness
11:39–40, 42–3	Woes to the Pharisees
11:46–8, 52	Woes to the lawyers
11:49–51	Wisdom predicts the martyrdom of prophets and apostles
12:2–3	What is hidden will be revealed
12:4–5	Do not fear martyrdom
12:6–7	Parable of God's care for his own
12:8–10	Confirmation of those who confess/deny the Son of Man
12:11–12	God's support of the persecuted
12:22–31	Freedom from anxiety about earthly needs
12:33–4	Freedom from possessions
12:39–40	Parable of preparedness: the returning householder
12:42–6	Parable of the faithful steward
12:51–3	Jesus as the agent of crises
12:54–6	Signs of the impending end of the age
12:57–9	Parable of preparedness for judgment
13:20–1	Parable of the leaven
13:24	Difficulty in entering the kingdom
13:25–9	Parable of exclusion from the kingdom
13:34–5	The rejection of the prophet and the vindication of God's agent
14:16–23	Parable of the banquet at the end of the age

CENTURION

THE ROMAN ARMY consisted of large units, called legions, of approximately 5,000 soldiers each. These were divided into cohorts of 480 each, supplemented by smaller cavalry units. The cohorts were divided into 6 "centuries," composed of 80 soldiers each, rather than 100 as the name implies. The centurions commanded the centuries and were more professional than the senior officers, who were from the upper ranks of society and served mostly for short periods of time. The centurions who were especially effective in training and organizing soldiers would be transferred to more prestigious legions. For security and efficiency reasons, soldiers were not usually stationed in the territories where they had originated. In the lifetime of Jesus, four of these legions were on permanent assignment in Syria–Palestine.

SON OF MAN

THIS IS A LITERAL TRANSLA-tion of the Hebrew (*ben 'adam*) and Aramaic (*bar nasha*) phrases used by the biblical writers to underscore human limitations, as contrasted to the sovereignty of God. Major examples of this usage are in Psalm 8, where the splendor of God's creation is contrasted with human frailty (8:3–4), and in Ezekiel, where the prophet falls down in awe before the vision of the divine majesty and when he is instructed to call to account rebellious Israel (Ezek. 1:28 passim). The term is also used to indicate one who is assigned to carry out God's purpose. In Daniel, the figure who represents the faithful remnant of God's people and to whom is given the responsibility of ruling the earth in God's behalf is described as "one like a son of man" (Dan. 7:13); this figure is then identified as a group: "the saints of the Most High" (7:18, 22). In the Similitudes of Enoch (see pp. 401–404), "Son of Man" is the title of the divine agent through whom the powers of evil are overcome and the rule of God is established. Assuming that this was written in the first part of the first century, the term would have been known in Jesus' time. Jesus seems to have applied it to himself in this latter sense, that is, signifying that he was God's agent. (See sidebar p. 278.)

14:26–7	Jesus shatters domestic ties and summons his followers to take up the cross
15:4–7	The joyous shepherd
16:13	The inescapable choice between masters
16:16	The proclamation of the end of the age
16:17	Confidence in God's promise
17:3–4	Forgiveness within the community
17:5–6	Faith within the community
17:23–7	Sudden judgment on all who are in the world
19:12–13, 15–26	Parable of the returning nobleman; the rewards to the faithful servants
22:28–30	The promise to the faithful of a share in God's rule

These passages from Luke (with parallels in Matthew), when viewed apart from the context and connotations that Luke provides in his gospel, give a remarkably full and consistent picture of Jesus, the enterprise in which he is engaged, the responsibilities that he places on the inner core of his followers, and his expectations for them and for his people when God brings the present age to an end and establishes his rule in the world. In this tradition he refers to himself at times in the first person, but often by the indirect term son of man. Since this designation is used in the biblical tradition to refer to both an individual (as in Ezekiel and 1 Enoch) and a faithful community (as in Daniel), it was a highly suitable expression for the role of Jesus and that of his core of followers in preparing for the coming of the kingdom of God.

Some scholars, observing the link between Jesus and wisdom in Q and the emphasis on instruction in the Q material, have concluded that here Jesus is being portrayed as the embodiment of wisdom in the Jewish sense of timeless, universal knowledge of God and the world. If this were the correct assessment of the Q tradition, Jesus would be pictured as a teacher of universal, eternal truths. These scholars acknowledge that within the Q material are apocalyptic features, but they dismiss those elements as later intrusions into the basic picture of Jesus as a kind of philosophical rabbi. Careful analysis of the Q material, however, shows that it is pervaded by an eschatological outlook. Even Q's original form of the Beatitudes, for example, contrasts the present state of God's people with the future blessedness that will come with the new age and does not generalize about the human condition as a whole. The elements of conflict that are typical of the apocalyptic worldview pervade Q: both the conflicts that the elect experience in the final stages of the present cosmic struggle and the battle between the powers of evil and God's agents.

The Q material listed above can be grouped under four headings that focus on Jesus' place in God's purpose and the solemn responsibilities that his followers and his hearers have as God moves to fulfill his plan for his creation. Here are the Q materials grouped thematically:

1. Discipleship: Its Privileges and Trials

| 6:20–49 | The blessedness and obligations of discipleship |

9:57–62	Break with home and family for the sake of the kingdom of God
10:2–16	Participation in proclaiming the kingdom in word and act
10:21–3	God's special revelation of his purpose
11:2–13	God's promise to sustain his people and grant them a role in his kingdom
12:51–3	Jesus the divider of households
14:16–23	Those included and those excluded from the Messianic Banquet
14:26–7	Discipleship shatters ordinary human relations
16:13	The demands of discipleship
17:3–6	Forgiveness and faith: essentials for the life of the new community

2. Repentance or Judgment

11:33–6	Warning about light and darkness
11:39–48, 52	Woes against the religious leaders of Judaism
12:54–9	Prepare for impending judgment
13:23–9	Exclusion from a share in God's new reign
17:23–30, 33, 35, 37	Judgment will be inescapable
19:12–13, 15–26	Reward for the faithful; punishment for the lazy; the importance of perseverance

3. The Prophet as God's Messenger

3:7–9, 16–17	John the Baptist as forerunner of Jesus and as prophet of doom
11:49–51	The fate of the prophet and his emissaries
12:2–3	The promise of the revelation of God's purpose
12:4–10, 11–12, 42–6	God's care for and vindication of his messengers
13:34–5	Jerusalem's rejection and martyrdom of the prophets
16:16–17	John the Baptist as boundary of the old age; God's word is sure

4. Jesus as Revealer and Agent of God's Rule

4:2b–12	Jesus' successful struggle with the Devil
7:18–35	Jesus as agent of liberation: greater than John
10:24	Jesus as Son, agent of revelation
11:14–22	Jesus as agent of God's kingdom
13:20–1	The leaven of God's rule now at work
15:4–7	God's joy at reconciliation with a sinner
22:28–30	God grants a share in his kingdom to those for whom it has been covenanted and who have endured the struggles of its coming

Analysis of the Q material as grouped in the topical arrangement above results in a clear picture of Jesus, of his understanding of God's purpose, and of his followers and their prospects and responsibilities. The material is not neatly divided into different categories of subject matter, but rather, the four major themes emerge in various parts of Q as it has been reconstructed. The analysis that follows here seeks to show how these themes are blended in the Q material.

One of the themes in the Q tradition is the definition of the community of Jesus' followers – in his lifetime, in what was for them the near future, and in anticipation of the new age that God was about to establish. They are portrayed as those who in the present age are deprived and scorned: they are the poor, the hungry, the sorrowing, the hated, the excluded, the reviled (Luke 6:20–2). They are promised a reversal of their condition "in that day" – that is, the day when God's purpose is achieved through the son of man. Their reward is already stored up in heaven in anticipation of the day of their deliverance and vindication. Meanwhile, however, they are to love the very ones who oppose them, to pray for their abusers, to respond generously to those who do them injustices, and to do so in confidence that God will reward their gracious actions in the new day that is coming (Luke 6:27–36). For the withholding of judgment upon others and for extending forgiveness to others, they will be amply rewarded by God in the future (6:37–42). Since their lives are founded on the grace of God, they will be able to withstand the difficulties and storms that await them in the future (6:43–9).

They must be prepared, however, for radical conflict with their families and must be ready to give up traditional obligations toward the family because of the higher demand of proclaiming the coming of God's kingdom in the near future (Luke 9:57–62). Their commitment to the work of the kingdom will cause violent disruptions in their family life (12:51–3). What is called for in the cause of discipleship is described as hatred toward one's own family and even the willingness to abandon one's own life, as Jesus did in his fidelity to what he believed was God's will for him (14:26–7). There can be no wavering as to where one's ultimate obligations and values are based: followers must be devoted to God and his work in the world (16:13).

Jesus' followers are to carry forward the work he launched: they must heal the sick and announce the coming of God's rule. To carry out this activity they must move from town to town, indifferent to any system of support, relying only on the generosity of their hearers, but ready to move on if their message is rejected. Their responsibilities are discharged when they proclaim in word and act the good news of what God is doing through Jesus. God will bring judgment in his own way on those who refuse to heed the message (Luke 10:2–16). The members of the community of Jesus rejoice in the special wisdom about God's purpose that has been disclosed to them through Jesus (10:21–3).

Participation in this new community is open to those who are in need and know it, rather than primarily or exclusively to those who are in the Israelite tradition, many of whom are too preoccupied with routine affairs to respond to the invitation to take part in the new fellowship that God is establishing through Jesus. Those who do respond are precisely the ones who were excluded by Jewish ritual requirements from coming into God's presence in the temple or in the gatherings of his people. The parable of the banquet ends with the report of the complete outsiders who are brought into the new fellowship (Luke 14:16–24). An essential feature of the relationship they share within the community is an attitude of abundant forgiveness (17:3–4). And their confidence in God is to exceed all ordinary human expectations (17:5–6).

A solemn note that is sounded repeatedly in the Q tradition is God's judgment on the human race, and especially on those who claim to be his people. All humanity will be faced with a pair of alternatives: repentance or judgment. Even now, however, there is a sharp distinction between those who hear God's message through Jesus and respond with faith and those who ignore or reject it. Two sayings about light and darkness have been blended in Luke 11:33–6 to make this point: those in the light (i.e., through the knowledge of God which Jesus has brought) have no part in the realm of darkness but have been transformed by the light. Their responsibility now is to see that the light is spread abroad to others. Changing the image to that of predicting the weather by interpreting the signs, such as clouds on the horizon, Jesus is reported as warning those who are indifferent toward his message to be alert to the indications that God is about to do something new in establishing his rule on earth (12:54–6).

Important in the Q source is the need for the faithful to remain so during the interval before the time when God's judgment will fall. A solemn warning is uttered by Jesus (Luke 17:23–30, 33, 35–7) that the end of the age, which will be dramatically demonstrated by the coming of the son of man, cannot be predicted but occurs in God's time like lightning flashing across the sky. Those preoccupied with routine affairs will suffer divine judgment as did all but Noah and his extended family in the time of the Flood, and as did the wicked inhabitants of Sodom. The majority will not know what has happened until they see the vultures circling about the corpses of those who have been slain in the divine judgment that brings the age to a close. In contrast to the indifferent masses, the followers of Jesus are called to be willing to surrender their lives – both figuratively and literally, in martyrdom – in order that they might gain the life of the age to come. This theme of proper stewardship of one's resources in the interim before the end of the age is dramatically illustrated in the parable of the absent ruler, who returns unexpectedly and calls to account those to whom he had assigned certain responsibilities. Some had used their resources effectively, while others had done nothing with them. All receive what is appropriate for their behavior, whether reward or punishment (Luke 19:12–13, 15–26).

The predictions of judgment fall most severely on the religious leaders, whom Jesus depicts as concerned primarily with ritual purity and pious ostentation rather than with moral purity. They are more interested in enforcing conformity to their interpretation of the Jewish law than they are in easing human suffering. Most serious of all is Jesus' charge that the religious leaders are like those who in earlier days rejected both the message God sent to his people through the prophets and the prophets as well. As a result, Jesus is reported as representing the entire biblical narrative as the story of the murder of God's messengers, from Abel in the Book of Genesis to Zechariah in 2 Chronicles (Luke 11:39–48). When God finally gathers his true people in the new age, many of those who had the opportunity to know and hear Jesus will be excluded, while the faithful remnant will join the men and women of faith from the days of Abraham down through the period of the prophets, sharing the fellowship of God's people.

The new community that Jesus is pictured in Q as calling into being is sharply different from those gathered around other prophetic figures of his time, as is apparent in the contrast with John the Baptist. John denounces his contemporaries for counting on their descent from Abraham rather than on their superior moral qualities and their penitence in light of God's impending judgment on his people (Luke 3:7–9, 16–17). Yet Jesus describes John as one whose role is only preparatory for the coming of God's kingdom (7:24–30). John's life was one of abstinence and strictness; Jesus' way of life is one of joy, freedom, and, above all, inclusiveness toward those excluded by way of life or occupation from participation in the community of the covenant people (7:31–5).

Jesus' own role as depicted in Q includes his being engaged in conflict with the powers of evil from the outset of his public career, as in the testing experiences in the desert of Judea, in which he resists the proposals of the Tempter by an exercise of trust in God alone (Luke 4:2–12). In his public activity, the evil powers and the forces that limit or warp human life are already being overcome (7:18–23). With the insight that his disciplines have received through him, they can already discern this new reality (10:23–4). Indeed, through his exorcisms, in which he defeats the prince of demons, Jesus makes the kingdom of God a present reality (11:14–22). Its powers are already at work in the midst of his contemporaries (13:20–1). The message of God's reconciliation with sinners is not merely Jesus' own idea but is represented by him as essential to the nature of God himself, who takes the initiative to restore the lost sheep to the flock – which is his people (15:1–4). It is those who are characterized by trust, by sharing in God's work of reconciliation, and by fidelity to Jesus in the midst of his sufferings and theirs who are promised a share in the feast that will launch the new age (22:28–30).

Thus the Q tradition offers reports of Jesus' words, acts, and parables, which together represent an essential strand of the early Christian understanding of Jesus, of his relationship to God and God's purpose for the creation, and of his portrayal of the responsibilities and destiny of his followers. The authors of Luke and Matthew have incorporated this tradition in their gospels, each in his own way and with distinctive emphases, as we shall note. But there was one early Christian writer, however, who developed his own representation of Jesus and did so independently of the Q tradition. Not content to offer a loose collection of sayings and narrative material, he organized his sources into a consecutive account, which traces the career of Jesus from the period of his entry into public life until the scene of his instructing his perplexed followers after his death. This literary undertaking is what we know as the Gospel of Mark.

D.   MARK: OUR OLDEST GOSPEL

The oldest known theory about the origin of Mark comes from Papias (of Hierapolis in Asia Minor) around the year 130 C.E. He claims, in a passage quoted in the *Ecclesiastical History* of Eusebius, that someone named Mark had been an interpreter of Peter and that he wrote down what Peter recalled that Jesus said or did, since he was not himself one of the original followers of Jesus. It is possible that this is the Mark mentioned several times in Acts (12:12, 35; 13:5; 15:37) and occasionally in letters by or attributed to Paul (Col. 4:10, 2 Tim. 4:11, Philem. 24). This Mark could have been a member of a family of one of Jesus' followers and hence might have had direct access to early traditions about Jesus through his kinsman who was one of the original disciples. But the writing that now bears his name seems to have been compiled from oral and written sources which consisted of small units of tradition from several sources. It does not have the strict narrative sequence one might expect from a report of a firsthand observer (such as Peter) of Jesus' public life. Obviously the baptism of Jesus must have come early, and the confrontation with the authorities in Jerusalem came at the end of Jesus' career, but otherwise there is little if any sure indication of chronological order in the Gospel of Mark. It does not read like a biography but seems to have been written with the

EUSEBIUS

BORN ABOUT 260 C.E., Eusebius became bishop of Caesarea (on the coast of Palestine) after 315, when Emperor Constantine's edict brought to an end the imperial persecution of Christians launched by Diocletian (303–13). Eusebius was directly and deeply involved in the ensuing internal theological disputes within the church concerning the relation of Jesus to God: Was Jesus co-eternal with God? In order to establish specific norms for the beliefs of Christians, Constantine convened a council of the church at Nicaea in 325. The so-called Nicene Creed, which was produced by this conference, was the first widely agreed upon creed of the church, which now had the weight of imperial authority behind it. Eusebius seems to have played a crucial role at that council as adviser to the emperor on these abstruse theological questions about the true nature of Jesus Christ.

There was an excellent library of Christian writings in Caesarea, and Eusebius drew on these in his own extensive writing program, which ranged from responses to intellectual attacks on Jesus (in *Against Hierocles*), through an elaborate effort to correlate the chronological schemes in use in the ancient world, to two elaborate defenses of the faith: *The Demonstration of the Gospel* and *The Preparation for the Gospel*. Among the competing calendrical systems in use in the ancient world, the one promoted by Eusebius placed the birth of Christ as the turning point in history and set the pattern for subsequent chronological schemes in the Western world. In his *Preparation for the Gospel* Eusebius sought to show how God had prepared the world historically and intellectually for the advent of Christ and the Christian faith. His *Ecclesiastical History* is of profound importance, not only for his reconstruction of the origins and growth of the church down to his time, but also because he quoted at length from ancient sources – pagan and Christian – which are otherwise lost. His work is a landmark in the process of the church's transition from its status as a sect under attack by the empire to the official religion of the emperor.

DECAPOLIS

THE TERM MEANS "TEN cities" and refers to a loose federation of ten centers of Greco-Roman culture located from southern Syria (Damascus) to central Nabatea, east of the Jordan River (Philadelphia, which is now Amman, capital of Jordan). Mentioned in the New Testament are Gerasa, where Jesus is reported to have healed a demoniac living in a tomb (Mark 5:1–20), and Gadara, where Matthew locates this exorcism performed by Jesus (Matt. 8:28–34). Scythopolis was the only city of the Decapolis located west of the Jordan in the region of Galilee. Pella, which was named for the birthplace of Alexander the Great, is said by Eusebius the historian to have been the place of refuge to which the Christians fled after the fall of Jerusalem to the Romans in 70 C.E. The significance of these cities for biblical history and literature is that, as elaborate centers with their pagan temples, theaters, gymnasia, and other Greek institutions, they demonstrate the extent to which Jews and early Christians were surrounded by hellenistic culture.

broad features of Jesus' career and teaching in mind, culminating in the account of his death and the promise of meeting him raised from the dead.

The sources that were used by the author were clearly Greek, since quotations from the scriptures are based on Greek, not Hebrew, originals. The language is rather crude Greek, with occasional hints that the writer knew or spoke a Semitic tongue as well as simple Greek. Some terms are derived from Latin as well. It appears, therefore, that Mark was written in a fairly cosmopolitan place, where Greek was the major common language, where there was some exposure to Roman culture, and where the underlying culture was Semitic speaking. A likely candidate would be somewhere in Syria, where all these factors would have been present. The importance for Mark of Jesus' challenges to the Jewish leaders – priests, Sadducees, and Pharisees – suggests that it was written not far from Palestine, where these groups and issues were of major significance. The special attention paid in Mark's narrative to Tyre and Sidon and to the cities of the Decapolis, chief of which was Damascus, the largest of this loose confederation of hellenistic-style cities and a leading city of Syria, tends to confirm this theory.

The time when the Gospel of Mark was written is also uncertain. Its concern with the threatened coming of armies to seize Jerusalem and destroy its temple suggests that it dates from the years after the Jewish nationalists began their revolt against the Romans but before the temple was destroyed: that is, between 66 and 70 C.E.

The most extensive passage in Mark that treats a unified theme is Mark 13, often referred to as "the Markan apocalypse." It portrays the end of the age, the sufferings of the faithful, and the destruction of the temple. The links between this part of Mark and the Book of Daniel reinforce the picture of this final discourse of Jesus in Mark as apocalyptic. It is essential to note that what characterizes apocalyptic is far more than a literary style in which a visionary describes the end of the present order. As is evident from our consideration of the Q tradition, apocalyptic involves (1) a way of understanding history, (2) a belief about how knowledge of God's purpose is communicated to human beings, and (3) a set of assumptions about the community that is the recipient of this knowledge, including their immediate prospects of struggle and suffering and their long-range confidence in divine vindication. In this view of the world, history is the story of the conflict with the forces of evil, which for the time being have seized control of the human situation, subjecting both political powers and individuals to demonic control. God has disclosed to the faithful that they will have to endure suffering, even martyrdom, for some time to come, but that through his chosen agent, the hostile forces will be overcome and the divine rule established. In that new situation, the faithful will share in the rule of God and will be fully vindicated in the triumph over evil. This knowledge cannot be inferred from the course of events or arrived at by human wisdom but is given in veiled form only to the elect community. It is this outlook on God, the world, and the community of faith that pervades the Gospel of Mark.

Although Mark contains reports of the career of Jesus, it is not a

Pella, city of the Decapolis. Evidence for occupation of the mound of Pella goes back to prehistoric times. Pella began to achieve some status and wealth in the late hellenistic period, when it was named for the birthplace of Alexander the Great. Destroyed by the Jewish nationalists for its failure to observe Jewish laws, under the Romans it joined the hellenistic federation of cities called the Decapolis, of which Damascus was chief, and developed many of the features of Greco-Roman culture: a temple, odeum, and baths. The Christians are reported to have fled there after 66 C.E., when the Romans began attacking Jerusalem and the Jewish nationalists based there.

H.C. Kee.

biography, as we have noted. Rather, it resembles a type of document known from the study of other literatures and from traditions studied by anthropologists in non-Western cultures. This form of literature is known as a *foundation document*. It is written as a basic source of instruction for a community. A typical foundation document includes an account of the circumstances under which a community got its start, and especially how its founding figure launched the group. By anecdote and precept, the community learns what its guidelines are to be, what its aims are, and what destiny it may expect. Two closely related examples of foundation documents from the Jewish world are the Rule of the Community and the Covenant of Damascus, both prepared at Qumran for the guidance of the Dead Sea community (see pp. 347–355). Although the details of Mark differ widely from those of these sectarian writings, the basic strategy of Mark is similar to that of these Dead Sea Scrolls.

1.   Major Themes in the Gospel of Mark

The New Things God Is Accomplishing through Jesus

The special role that Jesus has in preparing for the coming of God's rule in the world is announced by John the Baptist (Mark 1:7–8) and confirmed to Jesus by the voice from heaven at his baptism (1:11). His authority is evident from the outset in his teaching (1:21, 27), in his healings and exorcisms (1:23–6), and in his pronouncement of the forgiveness of sins (2:1–12).

That the authority of Jesus involves radical reinterpretation of the older Jewish traditions is also explicit from the beginning of Mark.

SYNAGOGUE

THE GREEK VERB *SYNAGO,* for which *synagoge* is the noun equivalent, means to bring people together in the sense of gathering a group in order to achieve a meeting of minds. The meaning is similar to the Greek word *ekklesia,* which comes from the verb meaning "to call together" or "to call out [a group]." The former term was used by Jews in Palestine and elsewhere for their community gatherings for discussion and interpretation of their scriptures and for table fellowship. This pattern of "gatherings" seems to have begun in Palestine under the auspices of the Pharisees in the second century B.C.E. and to have taken place in private homes or, where necessary for space reasons, in public halls. By the end of the first century C.E., following the destruction of the temple and the disappearance of the priesthood, the synagogue had begun to evolve into what was to become the major instrument for the preservation and fostering of Jewish life. With the support of the Roman authorities, the synagogue began to take on increasingly institutional and authoritative forms, developing leadership roles and establishing prescribed modes of instruction. In the later second and third centuries, distinctive architectural forms for synagogue buildings began to appear. From the New Testament (Acts 16:11–16) and from inscriptional evidence from several sites around the Mediterranean, we can infer that the gathering place for Jews was earlier known as *proseuche,* meaning literally "a place of prayer" (see p. 395). Only later did the term for the gathering (*synagoge*) come to be used for the special and distinctive buildings in which the meetings took place.

John acknowledges the contrast between his role and that of Jesus (Mark 1:7–8). The difference between them is directly asserted by Jesus in his first public statement in Mark, in which he declares the nearness of God's kingdom and the necessity for his contemporaries to change their minds about God and his procedures in the world (1:14–15). Jesus claims that in his exorcisms, God's chief adversary, Beelzebub, or Satan, is already suffering defeat (3:23–27).

Mark is pervaded by quotations from and allusions to the Jewish scriptures (often based on an ancient Greek version!). Hence the read-

Gerasa, city of the Decapolis. Located thirty miles southeast of the Sea of Galilee, Gerasa in the first and second centuries C.E. became one of the most impressive of the cities of the Decapolis, with colonnaded streets, temples, theaters, and a fine forum. The triumphal arch on the southern edge of the city was dedicated to Emperor Hadrian, so some of the architectural remains can be dated to the second century C.E. The distance of Gerasa from the Sea of Galilee calls into question locating "in the region of the Gerasenes" the Gospel story of Jesus expelling the demons into a herd of swine (Mark 5:1).
H.C. Kee.

er is led to assume the fulfillment of the purpose of Israel's God through Jesus and to expect lines of continuity with Jewish tradition. Continuity is also indicated by Jesus' actions, as when he chooses a gathering of Jews studying the scriptures (called a "synagogue") as the setting for launching his preaching and healing activity (Mark 1:39). Yet many of his actions indicate a sharp break with the past on issues explicitly raised in the Jewish scriptures or in subsequent Jewish tradition. For example, the specific objects of his concern and healing activity are precisely those kinds of persons who would be excluded or dismissed to the periphery by the purity standards of the Qumran community (Temple Scroll 45–9): the deaf, the blind, the lame, those with a bloody flux, and those in occupations that compromised their ethnic loyalty and their ritual purity, such as the tax collectors. Indeed, Jesus included one such – Levi, who collected taxes for the Romans – among his inner circle of disciples (Mark 2:13–17).

Mark frequently includes as a detail of his accounts of healing a note that the subject was in some way unclean or that Jesus' act of healing involved a violation of purity laws, such as contact with an ailing person or a corpse. Sometimes the subjects are pagans or those living in pagan territory. The first healing story concerns a leper (Mark 1:40–5), whose disease made him ritually impure (Lev. 13–14). When friends lower a paralytic through the roof of a house where Jesus is (Mark 2:1–12), Jesus does not first heal him but deals with a question of prime importance for Jews of this period: what sinful human act is responsible for this man's ailment? After transcending that issue by pronouncing the forgiveness of the man's sins, Jesus proceeds to cure his disability. In another healing story Jesus is described as violating the sabbath law against work by his act of healing a man with a withered hand (Mark 3:1–6, 10–11). Later his healing activity takes him outside Jewish territory and brings him in direct contact with the dead, unclean persons, and those possessed by unclean spirits (5:1–20, 21–43; 6:56; 7:24–30, 31–7). On his return to Galilee and on his way to Jerusalem, he becomes involved with other unclean persons on the fringe of the Jewish community (9:14–29, 10:46–52). Clearly, the purity traditions of Israel are irrelevant to Jesus' work in preparing for the coming of God's rule in the world.

Issues of purity and the sabbath are dealt with explicitly in other parts of Mark, as when Jesus defends his disciples' action in helping themselves to grain as they move through the fields, thereby performing work on the sabbath (Mark 2:23–8). There is an extended account of Jesus' confrontation with the Pharisees in which he asserts that the essence of purity is not ritual observance but inner moral condition and right relationship with one's neighbor (7:1–23). The boundaries of the people of God are no longer to be drawn by the criteria of observance of ritual law.

Jesus also challenges Jewish convictions and institutions through the positions he adopts toward the temple and toward the nature and destiny of historic Israel. By riding into Jerusalem on a donkey, Jesus was implicitly laying claim to Israel's kingly role, since this act was in fulfillment of the prophecy of Zechariah 9 about the coming of the king

TAX COLLECTOR

ROMAN POLICY FOR collecting revenues was to arrange contracts with local citizens for gathering tolls and taxes. Candidates bid for the post on the basis of what they expected to collect each year, and the job went to the highest bidder. Subject to tax were both local sales and transit of goods from one province to another. Those who gathered the tax money were under obligation to pay to Rome only the amount for which they had contracted and were free to keep anything additional that they collected. Since they had contact with unclean substances and ritually unclean people in the course of their work, the tax collectors were considered by pious Jews to be off-limits socially and traitors to their own people, since the money they collected from local sources went to maintain the alien, pagan power of Rome. Jesus' initiative in associating with tax collectors to the extent of including one among his inner core of followers was abhorrent to Jews of traditional piety and evoked hostility toward him from the religious leaders (Matt. 9:11, 11:19; Luke 15:1, 19:1–10).

of Zion (Mark 11:1–10). Yet after accepting the acclaim of the crowds, Jesus took no steps toward achieving Jewish independence from Rome, as one would expect of a claimant to the role of king, but withdrew instead to the fellowship of his own intimate circle of followers outside the city (Mark 11:11). Later, the solemn covenant meal he ate with the disciples implicitly redefined the Passover celebration of Israel's tradition, replacing the death of the lamb with Jesus' own impending death and interpreting this event as a sacrifice that would ratify the new covenant and therefore a necessary step toward the coming of God's rule (14:12–21). Similarly, his aggressive actions in the temple are not a move toward preserving the uniqueness of Israel's access to God in this holy place but a call for its being open to all nations (11:15–19). According to Mark, God supports Jesus' claim to be the agent of covenant renewal in the symbolic detail which Mark includes (15:38): at the moment of Jesus' death, the temple veil, which separated off the holy place (into which only the high priest was permitted to go), is said to have been torn from the top down (i.e., by God). Now, all humanity has the possibility of access to Israel's God.

In addition to declaring new bases for participation in the covenant people and for access to the God of Israel, Jesus is pictured in Mark as defining in a distinctive way his role as God's agent to establish his kingdom. We have already noted (p. 362) that in Judaism in this period there was no single, uniform understanding of the agent or agents through whom God's purpose was to be achieved. When the term "Messiah" was used, it did not have a commonly agreed upon meaning, nor were the qualifications or even the role(s) of the messianic figure(s) uniformly perceived throughout Judaism in this period. For some, the messianic role was that of a king, whose task was to reestablish an independent Jewish state. A term used in this connection is "Son of God." For others the messianic role was a priestly function, which would result in the purification of God's people and the establishment of the true and proper worship of Israel's God. In the Dead Sea Scrolls, both these roles are depicted, with primacy going to the priestly messiah. Curiously, in Ps. 110 a royal figure is depicted who is referred to as "lord" and described as ruler but is then identified as an eternal priest. But other titles and roles were represented as well in this period, ranging from the prophet of the end time (again, as awaited at Qumran, where Deut. 18:15–22 was understood to refer to the founder of that group) to a celestial, triumphant figure who would defeat the powers of evil and vindicate true Israel (as in the Similitudes of Enoch). Although the actual term "servant" is not applied to Jesus in Mark, the function of serving is linked with his role as son of man in 10:45. As in the case of "Son of God," the designation "servant" is used in the Jewish scriptures (Isa. 42–53) with reference to both the faithful Israelites and the agent divinely ordained to achieve God's will for his people. For these latter functions – prophet, servant, son of man – the term "Messiah" is not used in the Jewish scriptures. In Mark both the narratives about Jesus and the sayings attributed to him draw on a wide range of these terms and traditions in depicting the God-assigned role that he is seen as fulfilling.

SON OF GOD

IN THE JEWISH SCRIPTURES, the phrase "Son of God" is used in at least two different senses: (1) as a corporate image for the historic people of Israel, especially in relation to God's action in bringing them out of slavery in Egypt and into the Promised Land. The basic text on this is Hos. 11:1, where God is quoted as having "called my son" out of Egypt. (2) The phrase also appears in Ps. 2:7, where God addresses David as "my son" and declares, "Today I have begotten you." Further, David is specifically called God's "anointed" (i.e., Messiah). Similar father/son imagery is used in Ps. 89:20–37 to depict the relationship of the Davidic royal line to God, although there David is actually addressed as "servant." These terms are linked in 2 Sam. 7:4–17, where God begets the royal line and David is called God's servant. The term "Son of God" implies a unique relationship and a central role that is to be fulfilled in the working out of God's purpose for his people rather than expressing some form of supernatural origin or the divinization of a human being. The link between "Son of God" and servant underscores the obedient role that this person is to fulfill in accomplishing God's work.

The lack of a common understanding of messiahship is evident in Mark when Peter acclaims Jesus as Messiah (8:29) but rejects Jesus' announcement that in fulfillment of that role, he must experience rejection, suffering, and death (8:31–3). That expectation is repeated in 9:30–1, with increasing detail about what Jesus' experience will be. Not only is his suffering envisioned, however, but also his vindication by God. This is specifically promised in 9:1, where his followers are told that they will live to see the triumph of God's purpose. It is also foreshadowed in the experience of Jesus and the inner core of his followers in the so-called transfiguration scene (9:2–13). This brief narrative recalls Daniel 10, where the seer withdraws and is granted a vision of the divine, which alters his own appearance and which is followed by assurances that he will be sustained through the stressful experiences that lie ahead. The story is akin to the Jewish phenomenon known as Merkavah mysticism, in which the faithful are granted a transforming vision of God in preparation for a time of testing which is to follow. In this scene the glistening appearance of Jesus and the divine voice affirming his special relationship to God clearly stand in the Merkavah tradition. This is wholly appropriate, as Jesus begins at this point in the Markan account to foretell his own sufferings and death – as a part of God's purpose through him.

The Responses to Jesus

Mark also portrays dramatically the range of responses that Jesus elicits from his contemporaries. These include the responses of the crowds that hear and see him, his marvelous acts, and other signs of divine approval. Very different reactions to him are the initial doubts and resistance from his family and followers, and the opposition to him from the religious and political leaders.

The account of Jesus' public activity, which Mark reports as taking place during the first day of his ministry (Mark 1:14–34), comes to a close with throngs surrounding him, including "all" who were sick or demon-possessed and the entire population of the towns and cities of Galilee, including Capernaum (1:21). As Jesus' activity of preaching and healing continued, his reputation spread so that before he could enter a town, the crowds would flock to him in the open country or beside the Sea of Galilee (1:45; 2:13; 3:9; 4:1; 5:21; 6:45, 53–6). The crowds throng around his home, where he is engaged in healings and exorcisms (2:4, 3:20), and in other places where he performs healings (5:24, 7:33, 9:14, 10:46). The crowds are also present when he utters his teachings about purity (7:14), when he tells his followers about the cost of discipleship (i.e., suffering and possibly martyrdom; 8:34), and when he makes his claim that the ultimate Son of David is superior to David (i.e., Jesus is David's lord; 12:37). His activity in the temple is also witnessed by the crowds (11:18, 12:41).

Of special significance are the two stories of miraculous feeding in Mark 6 and 8, in which the presence of a crowd is an important feature (6:34, 8:1). These stories are told in language which points to the past of the biblical tradition and to the future of the community. The feeding of the hungry throngs recalls the biblical stories of God's provid-

MERKAVAH MYSTICISM

MERKAVAH MEANS "chariot" in Hebrew. In ancient Israel, the throne of God was sometimes portrayed as a chariot, as in Ezek. 1:15–21. Those chosen of God for a special role in communicating the divine will to God's people are described as being taken up into the divine presence, as was the case with Isaiah (Isa. 6:1–9). According to this tradition, one who was in God's presence reflected divine glory, as Moses did when he met God on Mount Sinai (Exod. 33–4). Daniel's appearance was changed when he had the vision of God (Dan. 10:8). Paul reports having been taken up into the presence of God when he was told heavenly secrets that he dare not divulge and was given assurance that God's strength would sustain him through the time of persecution and sufferings that he faced (2 Cor. 12). (See p. 354.)

Sea of Galilee. Since the Sea of Galilee is shaped like a harp, it was known as the Sea of Chinnereth, which in Hebrew means "harp." It is referred to in the New Testament as "the Sea of Galilee" (Matt. 4:18, Mark 1:16) and also as "the Lake of Gennesaret" (Luke 5:1), "the lake" (Luke 5:2), and simply "the sea" (John 6:16–25). It lies in the great geological fault that extends from the Jordan Valley, through the Dead Sea and the Red Sea, into Africa. Its surface is about 700 feet below sea level, and it is surrounded by hills of more than 1,200 feet in elevation. Running along its western shore was a major commercial highway connecting Syria and Mesopotamia with the Palestinian coast and Egypt. In spite of the frequent storms to which the lake is subject, it provided a major source of income for fishers, who operated from the towns along its western shore, including Capernaum, where Jesus took up residence (Matt. 4:13).

H.C. Kee.

ing food for Israel in the desert of Sinai. It was that event which demonstrated the unity of God's people, as well as God's providential care for them. The future dimension of the Gospel stories is apparent in the specific terms used by Jesus as the bread is prepared for distribution to the people: "he took, he blessed/gave thanks, he broke, he gave . . ." There is no mistaking the correspondence between these terms and those used in eucharistic accounts given by Mark (14:23–4) and Paul (1 Cor. 11:23–5). The symbolic meaning of these stories is evident: both accounts anticipate the establishment of a new covenant people, the membership of which will be open to all who come to Jesus seeking insight and renewal of life. The fact that one of these stories is described as taking place in predominantly Jewish territory (Mark 6) and the other in a gentile district (Mark 8) underscores that neither social, ethnic, nor ritual factors is a prerequisite for participation in God's people.

In the latter parts of Mark, there are indications of what the wider response to Jesus will be after his death and resurrection. The scene in 14:3–9, in which Jesus is sitting at table in the home of a leper and allows an unknown woman to anoint him – both of which circumstances would have violated his ritual purity – anticipates the openness that was to characterize the early church, and especially the Markan community. There is also a double prediction that the new people of God will include men and women from all over the earth (13:10, 27). That leading figures in both the Jewish and the gentile worlds will be among them is symbolized by the response to Jesus of the centurion (15:39) and Joseph of Arimathea (15:42–6).

An ironic note concerning the crowd is struck in the latter part of Mark (14:43, 15:8–11), where we read that the crowd joins the religious leaders in seizing Jesus and in the successful effort to persuade Pilate to have Jesus put to death. Thus the "crowd" has potential for both faith and unfaith.

That the response to Jesus was mixed but nonetheless was astonishingly productive of results is demonstrated in the parables of Mark 4. There we read of the variety of soils in which the seed (Jesus' good news) is sown, with varied but ultimately very fruitful results (4:1–9). The point that the seed is sown everywhere underscores the fact that there are no ethnic or religious preconditions as to who is an appropriate hearer of the gospel. The impressive response to Jesus' proclamation is implied in the parables of the seed growing by itself (4:26–9) and of the mustard seed (4:30–2). This same point is made in Mark's reporting of Jesus' healing activity primarily among those who were social-ly marginal or ritually excluded from the circles of Israelite piety in this period.

Another mode of response to Jesus in Mark is the evidence of divine approval. Our first clue is the voice from God on the occasion of Jesus' baptism, which acclaims him as "my beloved son" and expresses plea-sure in him (1:11). His departure to the desert is under the power of the Spirit of God, and during his time of trial angels minister to him (1:12). The divine empowering by which he carries on his activities is evident in the cosmic control by which he calms the storm (4:35–41) and in his walking on the water (6:45–52). The paradoxical aspect of his miracles is that he performs them to meet human need but refuses to do so when requested to offer a sign to corroborate his claim to have been sent and empowered by God (8:11–12).

His sense of special relationship to God is disclosed in his prayer in the Garden of Gethsemane (Mark 14:32–43) and in his claim that he is the Son of God and that he expects divine vindication as son of man in the presence of God (14:62, quoting a mixture of Dan. 7:13 and Ps. 110:1). The overt evidences of God's support of these claims appear in the tearing of the temple veil (15:38), in the darkness that falls at the time of his death (15:33), and in the opening of his tomb (16:4–6).

The third kind of response to Jesus that Mark describes is that of his family and the inner core of his followers, the disciples. Ambivalence is characteristic of these people in Mark. The first evidence of this inability to understand who Jesus is and how he fits into God's plan appears in Mark 3:19–20, where Jesus has gone to his home in Capernaum (Mark 2:1) (not his family residence in Nazareth; Mark 1:9)

Gethsemane. On the western slope of the Mount of Olives, across the Kidron Valley from the Jerusalem temple mount, was an area called in Aramaic *geth-semani*, which means "oil vat." The olive groves in this area were destroyed by Titus and the Roman troops during the Jewish revolt of 66–70, so the exact site cannot be deter-mined. Churches honoring Jesus' struggle in Gethsemane as he faced death (Mark 14:32–42) have been erect-ed in the vicinity since the fourth cen-tury.

H.C. Kee.

and certain persons come to take him out of public view because he is crazy. Who they are is disclosed in 3:31: his mother and his brothers (and possibly his sisters). The reaction of Jesus to this misguided, though well-meaning act on the part of his family is to redefine the family: those who are united with him in commitment to doing the will of God (3:34–5). Since the family was the primary ground of personal identity and obligation in Jewish society, as in nearly every other culture, Jesus' teaching here is as socially radical as his stance against ritual purity was radical for religious identity.

The inability of Jesus' disciples to grasp his understanding of the role God had assigned to him – with its emphasis on suffering and death – led them to dream up various kinds of power roles for themselves, which elicited from Jesus stern rebukes (Mark 8:32–3, 9:32–7, 10:35–40). His warnings that his disciples would deny, betray, and abandon him were challenged but were proved to be accurate, as the stories about Judas (14:17–21, 43–6) and about Peter's denial and consorting with the enemy (14:26–31, 54, 66–72) demonstrate. At the moment of his seizure in Gethsemane by the agents of the religious authorities, all the disciples were asleep (14:37–42). The details of the young man and then all the disciples fleeing when Jesus was arrested (14:50–51) show that they had not grasped or been willing to accept his basic understanding of his role as the suffering son of man. Only a group of women, who in Jewish tradition of the time were not given a significant place in the life of the religious community, remain faithful at the cross and the tomb (15:40–1, 47; 16:1–8). Yet even they are unprepared to accept as true the report of Jesus' having been raised from the dead.

The fourth kind of response to Jesus in Mark's account is that of the religious and political leaders. From the outset, Jesus' authority in interpreting the purpose of God for his people is contrasted with that of the scribes. The scribes, the Pharisees, and, in one instance, the disciples of John the Baptist are puzzled by Jesus' authority (Mark 1:22) and question the basis of his ability to control the demons (2:6–10). They are shocked by his eating with tax collectors and sinners (2:13–17) and by the failure of his disciples to fast (2:18–22). Pharisees and leaders of the synagogue challenge his condoning of the violation by his disciples of the sabbath law against work (2:24, 3:1–6). Later Jesus is offered a series of test questions by the Pharisees and other religious leaders on such subjects as when divorce is permissible (10:1–12), what the source of his authority is (11:27–33), whether Jews should pay tribute to Caesar (12:13–17), whether resurrection has a basis in scripture (12:18–27), and which is the chief of the divine commandments (12:28–34). With the exception of the last question, his answers range from the controversial to the radical and intensify the opposition of the religious leadership toward him. In response, he warns his disciples against the prideful religious ostentation of the scribes.

Yet Jesus is pictured by Mark as participating in much of the religious tradition of Israel in his day: taking part in the voluntary gatherings known as the synagogue (Mark 1:39), recommending that a

SCRIBE

THE HEBREW AND GREEK terms for "scribe" carry the same connotations as does the English word "writer." The function of scribes included keeping military records (Judg. 5:14) and fulfilling administrative roles in finance and government (2 Kings 22, Jer. 36:10). By the time of Israel's return from exile, however, when the law code was the dominant factor in reorganizing the nation, "scribe" became the designation of those skilled in the interpretation of the law of Moses, as Ezra 7 and Wisdom of Ben Sira 38–9 attest. This role in the first century C.E. seems to have involved both administrative and interpretive functions, which earned scribes a place of power in local affairs. It seems that only after 70 C.E., with the destruction of the temple and the establishment of more direct political control by the Romans, did the scribes become primarily religious functionaries, devoted to debate over and interpretation of the Mosaic law.

cured leper fulfill the law (Lev. 13:49, 14:22) by showing himself to the priest, and visiting the temple in Jerusalem (11:11). At least one leading figure in a synagogue came seeking Jesus' help to restore his ailing daughter (5:22–36). Nonetheless, his challenge to Jewish traditions was so severe that to plan for his destruction the Pharisees joined with the Jewish group that backed Herod Antipas (3:6). The worshipers in the synagogue are offended by Jesus' claims and actions (6:1–6). The report of the interest in Jesus expressed by Herod Antipas, who links him with John the Baptist and the prophets (6:14–16), which is followed by the gruesome account of John's cruel execution, serves to notify the reader that Jesus will suffer a comparable fate through the combined actions of Jewish and secular leadership.

At the midpoint of Mark, Jesus begins to announce explicitly his own fate: suffering, death, and resurrection (8:31, 9:31, 10:33), including his being turned over to the gentiles. The conspiracy of the religious leaders to be rid of him is confirmed in 11:18, following his cleansing of the temple. The hostility is intensified when Jesus predicts the temple's destruction (13:1–4) and does so by an appeal (13:14) to the precedent described in Dan. 9:27 and 12:11 of the desecration of the sanctuary under Antiochus Epiphanes in the event which triggered the Maccabean revolt. At the same time, Jesus warns his followers that they should expect persecution in the Jewish synagogues (13:9). The issues that divided the Jesus movement from the emergent synagogue-based Judaism of the later first century are sharply drawn in Mark.

The closing chapters of Mark (14–16) describe the combination of forces which led to the crucifixion of Jesus. The coalition of leading priests and scribes mentioned earlier in Mark is now seen going into action to arrest him "by stealth" and kill him. The stealth is an effort to avoid any popular uprising of support for Jesus. It is to this group that Judas went, according to 14:10–11. The role that Judas played in the plot was apparently to lead the guards to where Jesus was, outside the city and in the dark of night. Once that objective was achieved (14:43–6), Jesus was taken before the council (in Greek, *synedrion*, which is transliterated into Hebrew as "Sanhedrin"), which by Roman law was qualified to make decisions affecting local problems, including a solution by executing an offender against local customs. The membership included three power groups: the chief priests, the elders, and the scribes. When the guards came to seize Jesus, he asked if they had come to seize him as a militant nationalist (often misleadingly translated as "robber"). That was, indeed, the case they wanted to make against him, in order to shift responsibility for him to the Roman authorities.

The climax of the hearing before the council came when the high priest asked Jesus if he was the Messiah, the Son of God (14:62), with obvious reference to the king of Israel in the Davidic tradition. Jesus affirms that he is the Messiah but goes on to link his role with the coming vindication by God at the end of the age, in the apocalyptic tradition of Dan. 7:13 (Mark 14:62). His point gets through to his examiners, who mockingly demand of him that he begin to prophesy (14:65). The council's decision to turn him over to Pilate (15:1) and his subsequent

SYNEDRION, SANHEDRIN

IN THE HELLENISTIC PERIOD, and subsequently in the Roman Empire, the Greek term *synedrion* was used for local councils given responsibility for establishing and enforcing regional policy on a range of issues. Under Roman rule, councils of local religious, economic, and social leaders were brought together to order and stabilize the society and were given power to adjudicate purely local issues. The evidence from the gospels and from Josephus indicates that in Palestine in the first century c.e. the membership of the council included priests, elders (honored because of their wealth or prestige), and scribes. The scribes would interpret local law and ensure that it was administered properly. In later centuries, the designation for these councils was transliterated into Hebrew and Aramaic as "Sanhedrin," and the function became the defining and adjudication of religious issues based on the traditions for interpretation of the law of Moses.

INSURRECTIONIST

IN MARK 15:27 AND MATT. 27:38, we read that Jesus was crucified along with two others, who are described in most English translations as "thieves" or "robbers." The Greek term, *lestes,* can carry that meaning. A careful analysis of the socioeconomic conditions of Palestine in the first century, however, indicates that the wealth of the land had become concentrated in the hands of a small elite, which included those who were connected with the temple (the chief source of revenue in the land) and those who served in the administrative group established by the family of the Herods with the support of the Roman governors. Much of the land was tilled by tenant farmers, whose absentee owners could expel them if they failed to produce what the owners regarded as adequate revenue. Deprived of legitimate income and residence, they had to resort to robbery in order to survive, taking money and marketable objects from travelers passing through their district. Although Jesus did not condone theft, he identified with deprived and unjustly treated people in his mission to preach "good news to the poor" (Luke 4:18). Some scholars have suggested that those crucified with Jesus were revolutionaries attempting to overthrow Roman rule. But the earliest clear evidence of such a political revolt against Roman rule is from the second half of the first century, just prior to the Jewish revolt of 66–70 C.E. Jesus befriended the poor and forgave those who violated the law but did not side with or promote political revolution.

Garden Tomb. Although there is no way to determine where the body of Jesus was laid, the site (now known as the Church of the Holy Sepulchre) identified by the church in the time of Constantine is presently within the walled Old City of Jerusalem. The city wall in the time of Jesus, however, probably ran north and east of this church, which would have put the site outside the city. But in the nineteenth century a rocky hill outside the present city wall was identified as Calvary, and a nearby rock-hewn tomb was designated as the burial place of Jesus. Gordon Converse.

interrogation by Pilate were to determine whether he claimed to be the king of the Jews – understood in the political sense. The unclarity of this issue is depicted by Mark as the reason for Pilate's reluctance to execute Jesus. The accusations by the religious leaders continue (15:3) and are supported by the crowd (15:11–14) as well as by the soldiers, who in mockery treat him as a royal figure, with crown (of thorns) and kingly robe (14:16–32). The charge is made explicit in the inscription placed on the cross, "The King of the Jews" (15:26), and is echoed once more by the religious leaders (15:31–2a) and by the real revolutionaries who are being crucified with him (15:32b). This mockery continues down to the moment of his death. He is hastily buried in a tomb outside the city (16:8).

The Mystery of the Kingdom of God

In keeping with the apocalyptic tradition that characterizes Mark, Jesus' understanding of what God is doing and will accomplish in the future is disclosed only to the circle of his followers (4:11–12, 33–4). For those outside that group, everything that Jesus says and does is an enigma (literally, "a parable," but the underlying semitic term means "riddle"). This pattern of public statements and private explanations is confirmed in 8:14–21, where the meaning of the (eucharistic) loaves is reserved for the insiders.

The restriction to the inner circle of his followers of full understanding of who Jesus is and what God is doing through him includes his repeated orders to those whom he healed and even to the demons that he expelled not to spread abroad the news of what he has done (Mark 1:34, 3:12, 5:43, 7:33, 36; 8:26). An exception to this call for secrecy occurs when the demoniac from Gerasa is told to report to his friends "how much the Lord has done for you," and he does so in the gentile territory in which he lives (5:19–20). The time will come, following Jesus' death and resurrection, when the good news about him and the new community will be disseminated. This will include the mission to the gentiles, which the disciples are to take up after his resurrection, in preparation for the end of the age (13:10). The coming of the new age is sure, as the parable of the fig tree implies (13:28–9), and will occur during the generation of Jesus disciples (13:30), but the exact time is a secret known only to God (13:32–7).

The theme of the hidden nature of the divine purpose is implied in the strange ending of Mark (16:8), where the women who have seen the empty tomb say nothing to anyone but are filled with astonishment, fear, and trembling. Those reactions, however, are precisely the ones attributed to Daniel (Dan. 10:7–12) after God has granted him visions of the end time and of the throne of God. The very terms used here by Mark are those found in one of the ancient Greek versions of Daniel at this point. The framework in which Mark portrays Jesus and the revelation of God and his purpose that came through him is that of apocalyptic.

The Responsibilities of the Markan Community

From the beginning Jesus charges his followers with carrying forward his work: preaching the good news, healing the sick, expelling the demons (Mark 3:13–19). They are to call people out of the mass of humanity into the fellowship of God's people, just as they have caught fish in their nets (1:16–19). Relying on the authority that Jesus gave them to accomplish these goals, and on the hospitality of the towns they visit for their daily sustenance, they are sent forth by Jesus (6:6–13).

At the same time, they are to be prepared for violent opposition, persecution, even martyrdom, because of their association with Jesus (Mark 8:35–8, 9:38–41, 10:35–45). As God's new people, they face the prospect of conflicts, from the personal to the international level (13:5–8), and hostility from both religious and political powers (13:9–11). They are promised that God will sustain them through these times of suffering, and they are called upon to persevere until the end of the age (13:12), especially in light of the appearance among them of false messiahs and false prophets (13:21–3). The whole of humanity will undergo turmoil of unprecedented intensity (13:17–20), and there will be cosmic disturbances as well (13:24–5). The culmination of all this will be Jesus appearance as the triumphant agent of God to establish God's rule on the earth – the son of man (13:26) – and the consequent assembling from all over the world of the new covenant people (13:27).

Meanwhile, the community has guidelines by which to regulate the lives of its members on a range of subjects: divorce and remarriage (Mark 10:1–11), the place of children in the group (10:13–16), and the attitude toward wealth (10:13–16) and toward the pagan state (12:13–17). Guidelines about such theological issues as the resurrection (12:18–27), which is the chief commandment (12:28–34), and the relationship of Jesus to traditional expectation of a royal Messiah (12:35–7) are all sketched. The virtues that are to characterize the community include true obedience to God's will rather than pious evasion (7:9–13), true purity (7:17–23), true generosity (12:41–4), and – above all – unrelenting personal discipline (9:42–50). Clearly, Mark is written to serve as the foundation document for his community, building on the example, the precepts, and the promises of Jesus.

II. PAUL: THE JESUS MOVEMENT LAUNCHED IN THE ROMAN WORLD

Historically, Paul was the most important figure in spreading to the wider Roman world the movement that began with Jesus and came to be known as Christianity. He is also important literarily, since no fewer than thirteen of the Christian scriptures were written by him or are attributed to him. In the Book of Acts Paul is the central figure, although as we shall see (pp. 529–537), there are some points of difference between what he reports or implies in his letters and what is told about him in Acts. On the other hand, Acts does preserve valuable information about Paul's career and the strategy of the apostles in spreading the Christian message to the wider Roman world.

In reconstructing and analyzing the career of Paul and the subsequent spread of Christianity across the Roman Empire, it is important to have in mind the chronology of the successive emperors from the time of Jesus' birth to the emperor under whom the Jews suffered defeat in the second revolt (Bar Kosiba War):

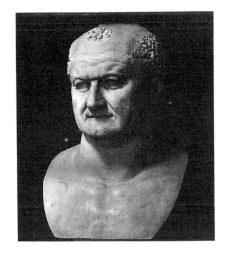

Augustus	30 B.C.E.–14 C.E.	Vitellius	69
Tiberius	14–37	Vespasian	69–79
Gaius (Caligula)	37–41	Titus	79–81
Claudius	41–54	Domitian	81–96
Nero	54–68	Nerva	96–8
Galba	68	Trajan	98–117
Otho	69	Hadrian	117–38

A. THE CULTURAL AND GEOGRAPHICAL SPHERE OF PAUL'S CAREER

Paul's letters reveal him to have much in common with other Jews of the Diaspora during the first part of the first century C.E. In general his thought remains faithful to the biblical heritage. Yet in many details, his writings show substantial influence from the hellenistic culture that permeated the eastern Mediterranean world in his day. Fortunately, Paul includes in his letters some details of his own background in Judaism, as well as of his conversion experience. In Phil. 3:5–6 he describes his Jewish heritage, which he represents as based on his historic and linguistic roots – born of the people Israel, the tribe of Benjamin, and Hebrew-speaking parents – as well as his fidelity to Jewish practices, evidenced by his parents having circumcised him on the eighth day and by his own commitment to the Jewish law. The approach to the law with which he identified was that of the Pharisees: that is, the commitment to maintain the ritual boundaries, transferred from the temple cultus to personal life, that mark off the people of God as pure and obedient. It is wholly in keeping with this outlook that his arguments in two of his major letters, Galatians and Romans, deal with the definition of the covenant people.

The scene of Paul's conversion is Damascus, the largest of the cities of the Decapolis and the oldest city in Syria. Although he does not say whether he was residing in Damascus, he reports that he tried to destroy the church there (Gal. 1:13–17). Clearly he regarded the church as a basic threat to what he, as a Pharisee, was persuaded was the purity of God's people. To an outsider, the "church" and the "synagogue" in Damascus – or anywhere else – would have looked very similar: both were voluntary, unstructured gatherings of people who believed that the tradition of Israel, as set forth in the scriptures, was coming to fulfillment among them. To understand and to enter into the purpose of God for his people, both groups met regularly for study of scripture, prayer, and above all for table fellowship, in which they celebrated their common life as God's chosen people. The basic difference was

Emperor Vespasian. Following the murder of Nero in 68 and a succession of ineffective emperors (Galba, Otho, and Vitellius) in a single year, Vespasian was declared emperor by the army, part of which he was leading in the successful effort to put down the Jewish revolt of 66–70. Leaving Titus in charge of the troops, he returned to Rome and began to rebuild the city and its financial and administrative structure. He authorized construction of the Colosseum, completed by Titus, where so many Christians were to die. H.C. Kee.

CLAUDIUS

AFTER THE EMPEROR Gaius Caligula was assassinated in 41 C.E., Claudius assumed power as the fourth of the Roman emperors. Suetonius, in his *Lives of the Twelve Caesars* (25.4), reports that a disturbance among the Jews in Rome reached such an intensity that Claudius decided to expel them all from the city, probably in 49. The instigator of this struggle is said to have been Chrestos – which is probably an incorrect reference to Christos, whose gospel would have reached Rome about this time, with resultant divisions within the Jewish community there. This incident is also referred to in Acts 18:3 and resulted in the move of some Jews who had converted to Christianity to places like Corinth, as was the case with Priscilla and Aquila (1 Cor. 16:19, Rom. 16:3).

that, as a result of the activity of Jesus, the "church" set aside ritual and cultic requirements for membership and welcomed marginal Jews and even gentiles into its common life. This is why Paul was persuaded that loyalty to the tradition required him to take the initiative in destroying the church.

It is paradoxical that someone with this set of values would become convinced that God had called him to take the initiative in carrying the Christian message to the gentiles. In Acts we are given more details of Paul's conversion experience, but in his letters Paul tells us only that "God was pleased to reveal his Son in me" (or "to me"; Gal. 1:16). Elsewhere he notes simply that, like the other apostles, he has "seen Jesus our Lord," risen from the dead (1 Cor. 9:1, 15:7). What was important for Paul were not the circumstances or details of his vision of the risen Christ but the fact that his vision occurred, that it corresponded to the experience of those who had followed Jesus during his lifetime, and that it resulted in his special divine commissioning as the primary apostle to the gentiles. Following this vision, he withdrew to "Arabia," by which he could mean the territory east of the Jordan or east of Syria, and then he returned to Damascus (Gal. 1:17). Only after three years did he confer with Peter (Cephas) and James (Jesus' brother) in Jerusalem, and they acknowledged that he and they were preaching a common faith, and "glorified God" that their former enemy had become a co-worker (Gal. 1:18–24). Paul describes his activities following his initial visit with James in Jerusalem as having taken place in the "regions of Syria and Cilicia," and he specifies that he was unknown to the churches in Judea, which was the district where Jerusalem was located.

When did his conversion and early Christian activity occur? From the few chronological details that Paul offers in his letters (three years until the first visit to Jerusalem; fourteen years until the next) we can infer that he had spent seventeen years of evangelistic activity in Syria and southern Asia Minor by the time he launched his wider work in Asia, Greece, and to the west. The fact that when he reached Greece there were already Christians there who had been driven from Rome by the decree of Claudius provides a highly probable date: about 50 C.E. This means that Paul must have been converted at least seventeen years earlier – that is, in the early thirties. This would have been within a year or two of Jesus' crucifixion, which requires us to assume that there was a church in Damascus at that early date which was large enough and ethnically inclusive enough to attract the hostile attention of the dedicated Pharisee Paul. This conclusion supports the Gospel report that the message of Jesus reached the cities of the Decapolis during his lifetime (Mark 5:20, 7:31).

Like Jesus, Paul was persuaded that not all who considered themselves to be God's people really were, but that God had disclosed to the elect his purpose for the new covenant community. In short, Paul's outlook was thoroughly apocalyptic: he regarded Jesus as the agent through whom God had disclosed his plan and through whom it would be accomplished. His death on the cross and his resurrection were the ground of Paul's assurance that, through the faithful suffering of his people, God would sustain and ultimately vindicate them. This program of redemption was already in process and would soon come to conclusion. What was new about this outlook for both Jesus and Paul is that there were no ritual or ethnic prerequisites to participation in this new people of God. Paul saw the death of Jesus as the divine sacrifice through which the purification of God's people was being accomplished. We shall see how these details are developed in Paul's letters.

Although Paul's primary concern is Jesus' redefining of the covenant people, the hellenistic influence on him is apparent in both the literary structure of his writing and aspects of the contents. When Paul describes what the Spirit produces in the moral life of the believer (Gal. 5:22), he begins with qualities that are based in the biblical tradition: love, joy, peace. But then he quickly shifts to terms which come out of Stoic ethics: patience, kindness, goodness, faithfulness, gentleness, self-control. The argument of the Letter to the Romans builds on the assumption that, just as Jews have the law of Moses given to them by God, so the gentiles have the law within (or what Stoics would call the law of nature), which provides them with the norms by which they should live. Although he then goes on to show that both Jews and gentiles disobey the law they have received, his assumption about the law of nature is pure Stoicism. Far from finding any conflict between his convictions as a devout Jew and the insights he has gained from pagan culture, Paul draws on both to make his arguments. Similarly, Paul's style in his letters shows affinity with Jewish modes of interpretation of scripture, while at the same time he also utilizes the rhetorical style of his Greco-Roman contemporaries. For instance, he poses questions that would be raised by his opponents and then goes on to answer them – a method of argument characteristic of hellenistic culture.

The fact that Paul had this cultural mix in his background and outlook contributed in major ways to his effectiveness in reaching out to the wider gentile world. As is evident from his letters, he was articulate – even eloquent – in Greek. Although he does not detail his missionary strategy, as Acts does for him, we can infer from his letters both where he carried on his work and the degree of effectiveness he had in bringing together Christian communities that bridged ethnic, cultural, economic, and social distinctions. References in his letters link him to the district known as Galatia in central Asia Minor, as well as to Ephesus, one of the chief cities of the eastern Aegean area dominated by Greek culture and the center of the worship of Artemis, the fertility goddess. Once he crossed to mainland Greece we hear of his connections and activities in Philippi and Thessalonica in the northern district of Macedonia, as well as in Athens (1 Thess. 3:1) and especially Corinth, in the southern district known as Achaia. He mentions in writing to the Romans that his missionary activity has taken him as far west as Illyricum, on the west coast of what is now Bosnia and Croatia, and that he intended to complete the evangelization of the northern half of the Mediterranean world by going beyond Rome to Spain (Rom. 15:24, 28).

It is in his Letter to the Romans that Paul gives the most complete

Emperor Claudius. The fourth emperor of Rome ruled from 41 to 54 C.E. Following the assassination of Gaius Caligula, Claudius was virtually forced into the imperial office, and his reign was hampered by constant conflicts with the Senate, which debated restoring the Republic. Although he is reported by Josephus (*Antiquities* 19.290) as having made a decree granting Jews the right to carry out their religious practices, he later expelled some or all the Jews from Rome, as noted by Suetonius (*Life of Claudius* 25.4) and by the author of Acts (18:2). His rule was plagued by the schemes of his four wives, of his children, and of freedmen who exploited their relationship with him for their own advantage.

James Stewart.

The fertility goddess, Artemis. Known in classical Greek times as the daughter of Zeus and Leto and the twin sister of Apollo, Artemis served several roles: she was a huntress and the goddess of the moon and of birth. The Romans saw her as identical with Diana, who punished the wicked but could sustain and renew the lives of the faithful. Her statue depicts her as surrounded by bullous appendages, which may be breasts or bull testicles. In Asia Minor Artemis became identified with a local mother goddess who had been worshiped for centuries at a huge temple in Ephesus, which was 180 feet wide and 360 feet long, with more than one hundred 50-foot-high columns. With the pyramids of Egypt and the hanging gardens of Babylon, it was one of the most admired structures in the ancient world. The public uprising against Paul in Ephesus (Acts 19) was instigated by the silversmiths, whose business in making and selling miniatures of the temple or of Artemis declined because so many Ephesians became followers of the Christ whom Paul preached.

James Walters.

and systematic statement of his understanding of Christ and of the new community of faith. Although tradition has long linked the launching of Christianity in Rome with Peter, we have no firm literary or historical evidence for that claim. But the fact that for some years there had been a church there and that some of its members had been driven out under Claudius (Acts 18:1–2) shows that its founding was very early. The high mobility of some of the early Christians is apparent in that Priscilla and Aquila, whom Paul met first in Corinth and who later opened their house as the meeting place of the church in Ephesus (1 Cor. 16:19), had returned to Rome by the time he wrote his letter to that church (Rom. 16:3). Paul wants to visit his friends and the community of faith there, and apparently did so.

Ancient tradition reports that both Peter and Paul were martyred in Rome in the time of Nero (54–68 C.E.). Some scholars have suggested that Paul, after reaching Rome, went on to Spain or that he returned to the eastern Mediterranean, but these are merely conjectures. All we can be certain about is that he did return to Jerusalem with the offering he had taken up among the gentile churches of Greece and Asia Minor, as he explained in Rom. 15:25–9. According to Acts 21–8, he was awaiting trial in Rome, having been sent there by the Roman authorities in Jerusalem, in order for the allegations of his having performed acts against the peace of the empire to be weighed by the emperor himself, based on Paul's own appeal (Acts 25:10–12). He last appears in Acts under house arrest, pending the hearing before Caesar (28:30).

B.   PAUL'S MISSIONARY STRATEGY

An important social feature of life in the Roman world was the existence and apparent popularity of voluntary groups, based on shared occupational, religious, or other interests. Many of these gatherings consisted of devotees of a god or goddess, such as Isis, Asklepios (the god of health and healing), or Dionysus (the god of wine). Some of these groups indulged in ecstatic group experiences, while others fostered personal devotion and dedication of one's life to the deity. The increasing mobility of the population, brought about by military conflicts as well as the need for relocation on economic grounds, gave many people a sense of a break with their own heritage. For such, the development of a local shrine to a familiar deity helped them regain a sense of purpose and identity. In a port city like Ostia (down the Tiber from Rome), for example, vestiges have been found of altars and shrines of divinities from many parts of the empire. Among Jews, the voluntary gatherings (the synagogue) provided a comparable structure in which their roots with the past and their identity as members of the covenant people could be regained or reinforced.

Not surprisingly, Paul's strategy in launching his mission in a new city seems to have been to go first to the synagogue, where he could offer his Christian interpretation of the Jewish scriptures, and especially of the prophetic writings. Gentiles who were on the fringes of the synagogue would be natural candidates for Paul's inclusive redefini-

Vatican, Piazza of Saint Peter. Although the main part of Rome lay east of the Tiber, Nero (54–68) finished a circular sports arena begun by Caligula west of the river in the section known as the Vatican. Since excavation fifty years ago of Constantine's basilica built there in honor of Saint Peter in the midst of pagan graves and sarcophagi, the tradition that Peter was executed there has become more plausible. A church tradition lists fourteen of the leaders of the church in Rome – including Peter – who are said to have been buried in a chamber beneath the Vatican. A report by Caius from about 200 C.E. says that Paul was martyred farther west, on the main road to Ostia (quoted in Eusebius, *Ecclesiastical History* 2.25).

H.C. Kee.

Emperor Nero. A son of Emperor Claudius by his fourth wife, Nero reigned from 54 to 68 C.E. He murdered his mother and his wife Octavia so he could marry another woman, Poppea, and then murdered her as well. Early in his reign he was influenced by the philosophical counselor Seneca, but his moderation soon gave way to cruelty and a sensuous way of life. He launched a campaign to have himself honored as divine during his lifetime and spent huge sums of money to entertain the masses and to rebuild the city of Rome after a disastrous fire, which he blamed on the Christians. Finally, he left Rome and took his own life, but the legend arose that he would return.

H.C. Kee.

tion of the covenant, and other non-Jews who admired the monotheism and lofty ethics of Judaism would find in Paul's recasting of the people of God new possibilities for their own adherence and participation. When new groups formed, they chose as their self-designation a Greek term, *ekklesia*, which means "called out," or "called together": they were called together from Jewish or pagan backgrounds to be the new covenant people. This strategy had an appeal that spanned the whole socioeconomic spectrum of urban Roman society. In 1 Corinthians, for example, Paul indicates that most of the members of the church there were poor and socially undistinguished (1:26). Yet as his greetings from the church at Corinth to the church at Rome show, the membership also included such a central figure in urban life as the city treasurer of Corinth (Rom. 16:23). Some members in Corinth and Ephesus had houses large enough to serve as gathering places for the entire Christian community (1 Cor. 16:19, Rom. 16:23).

The membership seems to have grown in large increments by the conversion of entire households, presumably including children and

Asklepios, god of healing. Earlier identified as a human who had been taught medicine, Asklepios was later seen as the son of Apollo and as the god of healing, whose presence was visible in sacred serpents clustered at his shrines. Major shrines honoring him were at Pergamum, on the island of Cos, where a school of medicine developed in his name, and at Epidaurus on the coast of Argolis, southwest of Corinth. His cult was later brought to Rome; the Latinized form of his name is Aesculapius. Those seeking healing slept in a grotto where they awaited a visit from the god. Found by archeologists at his shrine at Epidaurus were signed testimonies to the god's healing power and descriptions of the process of cure.

College of Physicians, Philadelphia.

EKKLESIA, ECCLESIA

IN GREEK CULTURE, THE term *ekklesia* means an assembly of persons convened for political or entertainment purposes. Among Greek-speaking Jews, it came to mean the gathering of the covenant community in any place for purposes of information, instruction, or worship, as in Deut. 31:30, 1 Sam. 17:47, and 1 Kings 8:14. The early Christian community took over this term as a group designation, as is apparent in 1 Cor. 11:18; 14:4, 19, 28, 35. It is usually translated "church." There is direct evidence that originally the "assembly" took place in private homes (Rom. 16:5, 1 Cor. 16:19, Philem. 2, Col. 4:15). In Acts (14:23) and in the letters of Paul (1 Cor. 16:1) rules are laid down to be observed in each of the individual "assemblies." The assemblies of Christians throughout certain metropolitan areas or districts are referred to collectively as "the churches of . . ." (Gal. 1:2, 22; 2 Cor. 8:1). Occasionally, Paul uses the term in a comprehensive way to refer to the whole body of God's new people (as in 1 Cor. 10:32, 12:28; Phil. 3:6; and probably Gal. 1:13). Even when he addresses the "church of God," he sometimes adds "which is at," followed by the name of the city or province (2 Cor. 1:1, 1 Thess. 2:14). The blend of local assembly with comprehensive membership of God's people is explicit in 1 Cor. 1:2, where the letter is addressed to "the church of God which is at Corinth" but also to "all those who in every place call on the name of the Lord."

In the later writings attributed to Paul, *ekklesia* has come to mean the whole body of Christians, as in Eph. 1:22. Accordingly, the church is described in structural, organizational terms in Eph. 2:19–22, where the metaphors used are those of hierarchy, foundation, and temple. Similarly universal in implication is the most familiar reference to *ekklesia* in the gospel tradition, Matt. 16:16: "On this rock I will build my church." The generalized force of the term "church" is highlighted by the description of the totality of Palestinian Christians in the period after Pentecost as "the church throughout all Judea and Galilee and Samaria" (Acts 8:31). What began as a designation for a local fellowship of Christians had become by the end of the first century a title for the body of believers across the Roman world.

slaves (1 Cor. 1:16). The problem of a community in which both slave and master are members is addressed in Paul's Letter to Philemon. The need to foster some sense of unity and commonality among such a socially and economically diverse group of people is a pervasive theme in Paul's letters, especially those to the Corinthians. His favorite term in addressing the members is "saints," which means, basically, "set aside for" or "dedicated to" [God].

Paul's own letters, unlike those later written in his name, are not concerned with defining offices in the church but with describing the range of functions appropriate for the life of the community. He does mention deacons and deaconesses (Phil. 1:1, 1 Cor. 16:1, 1 Thess. 3:2), but the term seems to mean "those who serve [the other members]" rather than those appointed to some formal role. In a later letter he does once use the term *episkopos* (Phil. 1:1), which is elsewhere often translated "bishop" and which thus may indicate the emergence of some hierarchy of official functions, as is emphatically the case in the later letters written in Paul's name (1 and 2 Tim., Titus) and in Acts. His primary concern, however, is with the community as a whole – the *ekklesia* – which is identified as the people of the new covenant in all of Paul's letters, but most fully in Galatians and Romans. Instead of defining offices, Paul takes care to indicate the range of roles and functions that members of the community fulfill for the benefit of the entire membership (1 Cor. 12). These include the utterance of wisdom and prophecy, the performance of healing or other miracles, addressing the community in ecstatic speech ("tongues"), and the interpretation of what is thus uttered. All these activities are made possible by the work of the Spirit of God among the members. The community as a whole is the place where God dwells among his people by the Spirit.

The community is to see itself in three tenses: its past, which is founded in God's act of love, sending Jesus as the sacrifice that ratifies the new covenant and thereby brings his new people into right relationship with God; its present, in which God is active among his people by the Spirit, calling new members into the fellowship through the reconciling work of the apostles and the other Christian preachers, and in the sharing of bread and wine, which reminds them of the past and points to the prospect of fulfillment in the future; its future, in which God's purpose will be achieved, all his people will be brought into the fellowship, the powers of evil will be defeated, and God will be fully

BISHOP

THE ENGLISH WORD DERIVES from the Greek term *episkopos*, which means "overseer." In Phil. 1:1 Paul extends greetings to the leaders of the church in Philippi, whom he designates as "bishops and deacons." The distinction in roles seems to be between those who serve the group (deacons) and those who oversee and safeguard the common life of the community (bishops). The post-Pauline writing 1 Timothy contains an impressive list of qualifications for those who aspire to the major leadership in the community: "the office of bishop" (3:1–7). Titus 1:7–9 also states the requirements, including fidelity to "sound doctrine" in preaching. A pastoral role for the elders as sketched in Acts 20:28 (overseers of the flock; shepherds of the church of God) is assigned by the Holy Spirit. In Acts 1:20, the replacing of Judas among the Twelve Apostles is justified by appeal to Ps. 109:8, and the Greek term in Acts for the "position" or "office" is *episkope*. Clearly, in the New Testament the terminology for church leadership roles is fluid. In 1 Clement 42:2–4 and 44:1–2, however, the *episkopos* is an authoritative office, and due process must be observed in replacing the bishop when he dies. Yet even in 1 Clement, the bishop is also spoken of as elder (*presbyteros*), indicating that categorical distinctions are not yet made.

SAINTS

THE TWO HEBREW WORDS often translated as "saints" have different connotations. One expresses faithful commitment to others with whom one has a covenant relationship (as in Gen. 21:22–4, 24:27–49), including God's fidelity to his covenant people (Exod. 20:2–6, 34:6–7; Jer. 33:11). The other term means set apart for God, in service and obedience, as when the priests approach the presence of the Lord (Exod. 19:22–3) or when David and his associates are sanctified in preparation for his anointing as king (1 Sam. 16:1–6). The faithful community who remain obedient to God in spite of pressures and threats from the pagan ruler are called "the holy ones (saints) of the Most High" (Dan. 7:22, 27).

In the New Testament the Greek equivalent term for "saints" is a favorite designation for the people of God. Paul addresses his readers as such in his letters (Rom. 1:7, 1 Cor. 1:2, Phil. 1:1), and it is a frequently used term for the church as a whole, as when Christ intercedes with God for his people (Rom. 8:27) or when several churches (Phil. 4:21–2) or all the churches are addressed (1 Cor. 14:33). The future destiny of God's people involves the prospect of martyrdom (Rev. 13:7, 16:6) and oppression of the "saints" (Rev. 20:9), although they will have a say in the final judgment of the world according to Paul (1 Cor. 6:2). The major connotation of "saint" is the special role and relationship of the new people to God.

TIMOTHY IS IMPORTANT IN the New Testament, both as companion and coworker with Paul and as symbolic figure for the generation of leadership in the church following the death of the apostles. In Paul's earlier letters, Timothy participated with Paul and Silvanus in the work of the gospel (1 Thess. 1:1, 2 Cor. 1:1). He was sent by Paul back to Thessalonica to see how the church was faring under the persecution they were experiencing (1 Thess. 3:1–5) and brought back a hopeful report (3:6–13). 1 Cor. 16:10–11 indicates Paul's expectation of sending Timothy to the church in Corinth, when he pleads for acceptance of his emissary. Other details are found in Acts, some of which are difficult to reconcile with Paul's letters, including Paul's agreement to have Timothy circumcised (Acts 16:1–3). Acts 17:13–16, however, offers more details of Timothy's return to Thessalonica in Paul's behalf.

The two Letters to Timothy are clearly from a period in the life of the church decades after the time of Paul and reflect formal developments in terms of doctrine, leadership, and church administration. See sidebar on Assigned Roles in the Churches according to Colossians and the Pastorals (p. 494).

sovereign over his people and the whole creation. Paul's letters make it clear that his work is the announcing of God's act in Jesus to set things right and to reconcile the world to himself (2 Cor. 5:9).

In spite of the assumption that is sometimes made that Paul was the first Christian messenger to preach the gospel to gentiles, there were precedents for his mission to the gentiles. This can be concluded from the fact that Paul was determined to destroy the church in Damascus. What troubled him was not merely that a rival group had emerged claiming to be heirs of the covenant promises. What enraged Paul as a Pharisee was that those who claimed to be the true heirs of God's promises to his covenant people included in their membership gentiles and ritually impure persons. Yet as a result of his vision at Damascus he had become convinced that God had called him to preach to precisely such people: the gentiles and those marginal to Judaism. We must conclude, therefore, that the gentile mission implied in the gospels had already begun in cities like Damascus. Acts describes the outreach of the apostles to gentiles and those on the fringe of Judaism as taking place before Paul's conversion, which is not unlikely, even though Acts may have a special reason for having this precedent set before Paul comes on the scene: to show that the basic policy of gentile inclusion was reached by the Jerusalem-based apostles. We have already noted the evidence for Christian activity in Rome before Paul reached Corinth. The fact that Acts notes the Spirit's resistance to Paul's going into the northern parts of Asia Minor (Acts 16:6–7) may indicate that others had already begun to preach about Jesus there – possibly Peter, as 1 Peter suggests (1:1). Paul, however, takes the lead in bringing the good news about Jesus to the gentiles and does so by agreement with the leaders of the church in Jerusalem, which remains more closely oriented to Jewish tradition (Gal. 2:1–10).

C. PAUL'S LETTERS: CONTEXT, INTENT, AND CONTENT

It seems likely that Paul wrote many more letters to the churches that he had founded or where he was active than those that have been preserved. The letters included in the New Testament date from the period beginning almost twenty years after his conversion and extend to a time shortly before his imprisonment in Rome. Only one is addressed to an individual (Philemon).

1. First and Second Thessalonians

Probably the earliest of the preserved letters are the two to the Thessalonian church. The Christians of Thessalonica, the capital of Macedonia, seem to have been converted mostly from paganism rather than from Judaism (1 Thess. 1:9). They were subjected to severe hostility from their fellow citizens and were praised by Paul for their fidelity in spite of persecution (1 Thess. 1:6–8, 2:13–15). After he left their city, Paul was concerned about how they would survive the opposition and so sent his younger companion, Timothy, to observe them and report to him. The news was good, and the letter is one of praise and encouragement for their perseverance (1 Thess. 3:6–9). He urges them to continue to live in a way that is pleasing to God, to be faithful in marital relationships, and to maintain the respect of outsiders by their high moral standards (4:1–12).

Paul advises the Thessalonian community on two closely related matters. The members are to live each day in consciousness that the appearance of Christ in triumph (*parousia*) is to take place in the near future (1 Thess. 4:9–12), even though the exact time cannot be predicted (5:1–11). Meanwhile, however, they are to take care to maintain their moral purity as God's people. Hence there is recurrent use of such terms as "holiness" and "saints," which indicate the importance of their achieving and exemplifying the life of obedience to which God has called them.

2 Thessalonians was apparently written shortly after the first letter. It assures the members of the community that the end of the age is near, but that there are certain divinely determined events which must precede the end. These events – following the apocalyptic tradition – include the effort on the part of the powers of evil to seize control and to mislead God's people (2 Thess. 2:1–11). But through Jesus, God will defeat the agents of evil and will vindicate his people (1:5–12). Accordingly, as in 1 Thessalonians, Paul exhorts the Thessalonians to fulfill their role as God's holy people by continuing in faithfulness and obedience (2:13–15, 3:1–13).

In both these letters there is evidence of the emergence of a struggle

PROBABLE CHRONOLOGY OF LIFE OF PAUL

Born	10 C.E.
Converted	33–5
Three years in Arabia	34–8
Initial visit with apostles in Jerusalem	37/8
Active in Antioch and Syria	38–47
Active in south Galatia	47–9
In Corinth during rule of Gallio	50–1
Council in Jerusalem	50–1
Active in Ephesus	52–4
Writes letters to Galatians, 1 Corinthians, Philemon, Philippians	53–5
In Corinth	55–6
Writes Letter to the Romans	56–8
Arrested in Jerusalem and imprisoned in Caesarea	60
Imprisoned and executed in Rome	62–3

PAROUSIA

THIS IS THE TERM USED IN the gospels and letters of the New Testament for the appearing of Christ in triumph at the end of the present age. Although it is usually translated as "coming" (Matt. 24:3, 1 Cor. 15:23, 1 Thess. 2:19, James 5:7), its basic meaning is "presence," "being there," or, in the case of a monarch, "public appearance." The *parousia* of Jesus Christ was understood to be God's public manifestation of him as the triumphant agent of defeat of the evil powers and vindication of his faithful community. The earlier New Testament writings expect this to take place within the lifetime of the first generation of his followers (Mark 9:1, 1 Thess. 4:15). In what is probably the latest New Testament book, 2 Peter, there is discussion of those who scoff at the promise of the *parousia* and a reminder that God does not calculate time as humans do: "With the Lord one day is like a thousand years, and a thousand years are like one day" (3:3–8).

AUTHENTICITY OF 2 THESSALONIANS

SINCE PAUL'S FIRST LETTER to the Thessalonians claims that the coming of Christ in triumph is soon to occur, the fact that in 2 Thessalonians there is an indication of events which must take place before Christ's return has led some scholars to deny that this second letter is by Paul. But in fact, Jewish apocalyptic writings of this period frequently manifest these dual characteristics, combining expectation of an imminent end with indications of events which will precede the end. Since 2 Thess. 2:4 assumes that the temple is still standing, and since it recalls the threat of the emperor Caligula to erect a statue of himself there (in 41 C.E.), the letter appears to be from the time of Paul, and its similarity in overall style and outlook confirms its authenticity.

GALATIANS

GALATIA WAS A REGION IN north central Asia Minor where the dominant inhabitants were Gauls, a Celtic tribe. The Romans gave the name Galatia to a province which included this district and territory to the south. Scholars have debated without firm conclusions whether Paul's missionary activities were concentrated on the Gauls to the north or included the ethnically more mixed region to the south, as implied by Acts 16 and 18. In either case, Jews would have been a minority in this part of Asia Minor.

for power among those who aspire to leadership roles in the Thessalonian church (1 Thess. 4:9–10). Paul perceives his letters as instruments of authority (1 Thess. 5:27, 2 Thess. 3:14–17) and reminds his readers of their obligation to respect and obey those who have been given positions of responsibility within the community (1 Thess. 5:11). In view of the expectation of a speedy end of the age, there is no necessity for an ongoing organization, but the structures of authority that exist in the interim should be respected.

2.   Galatians

The Letter to the Galatians seems to have been written in great haste. The result is that it lacks the organized structure of 1 Corinthians, as well as the formal introductory and concluding features which characterize Paul's other letters. In passing, he gives the most important chronological clues that we have concerning the span of time his mission activity lasted: three years after his conversion until his first visit with the Jerusalem apostles; and fourteen more years until his second consultation with them (Gal. 1:18–24).

Paul's point in mentioning these details is to strengthen his basic claim that his conversion, his apostolic mission among the gentiles, and the gifts of the Spirit that were evident through him were wholly from God and were not mediated through the Jerusalem-based apostles or their aides. It is highly significant that he uses the same term, *apokalypsis,* to describe his original vision of the risen Christ (Gal. 1:16), his having been commissioned with the gospel for the nations (Gal. 1:12), and his decision to check in with the apostolic leaders in Jerusalem (Gal. 1:24). He sought confirmation from them, but they were not the source of his conversion, his commissioning, or his ministry to the gentiles.

The central issue for Paul in Galatians was the question about ethnic and ritual requirements for participation in the new people of God. It was this issue that made his own conversion so radical and so dramatic. As he states (1:13–14), he had excelled as a Pharisee in his devotion to the traditions of that movement within Judaism, which was primarily concerned with defining the people of God based on criteria which arose when the Pharisees transferred the ritual purity requirements from the temple and its priesthood to the voluntary gatherings of the pious in their homes or public halls for worship and table fellowship. This resulted in a huge increase of ritual criteria for membership in God's covenant people. Paul's conversion brought about a reversal of this position, so that he set aside even the basic practice of circumcision as a requirement for covenant membership (1:6–11). The sole requirement that Paul established for entrance into the new community was that one should see in Jesus God's agent whose sacrifice was the ground for forgiveness of sins and whose resurrection was the guarantee of God's triumph over death and the powers of evil. The original nucleus of Palestinian followers of Jesus, having themselves been circumcised, were inclined to think of circumcision as a ritual requirement universally binding on all male converts, as indeed it was on gentiles who converted to Judaism. Not only did Paul reject this principle, but his position was confirmed and endorsed by the Jerusalem church leaders when he conferred with them (2:1–10). Further, Peter had accepted this policy when he first visited the Christian community in Antioch. But under pressure from Judean Christians, he had withdrawn from table fellowship with the uncircumcised gentile Christians (2:11–13). The example set by Christians like Peter, who came from a Jewish heritage, and the impact of the study of the Law and the Prophets within the new community combined to raise the question for the Galatian Christians whether members who joined out of gentile religion and culture must obey the Jewish law. Paul's letter to the Galatians presents a forceful case for his position on the issue, historically and biographically, but he takes care to ground his law-free principle on biblical precedent and principle.

The Galatians' own experience of the Spirit of God as members of the new community should have shown them that the gifts of God are not earned by human achievements but are solely the outpouring of divine grace. Apparently Christians had visited or perhaps joined the Galatian community who still felt bound to obey at least a minimum of Jewish ritual requirements. Paul must make the point that even in the biblical tradition of the origins of God's covenant people, the requirement for participation was trust in God, not ritual performance. The prime biblical example of this for Paul is the story (3:6–18) of Abraham's becoming the father of the covenant people, even though up to that moment in his life, he had been incapable on his own of having a child by Sarah, his wife. Abraham's son Isaac, the father of Jacob and the ancestor of those for whom the twelve tribes of Israel are named, was given to his parents by God. Further, the gift of the son was the means of fulfillment of a blessing for all the nations (Gen. 12:3), not merely for Israel. Participation in the people of God can be perceived in two different ways: through obedience to the law, under threat of a curse for failure to conform (Deut. 27:26); or through the gift of God's grace, received by trusting in God and resulting in those who trust being placed by God in right relationship to himself (Hab. 2:4). On the basis of the vicarious death of Jesus (Lev. 18:5), all the promises to Abraham of covenantal participation are open to those who, through their faith, show themselves to be Abraham's true offspring (Gen. 12:7).

The law of Moses, which Paul the Pharisee regarded as normative, he now sees to be a late, temporary instrument to keep God's people in line morally until God's ultimate solution of the human problem could be disclosed through Jesus (3:17). Paul uses two images to depict this temporary function of the law: that of a child-trainer (*paidagogos*), whose services are not needed when maturity is attained (4:1–11); and that of a slave, who eventually is granted freedom (4:12–20). The true relationship with God and his people is characterized by love and trust (4:21–5).

These relationships are experienced through freedom in the Spirit of God. To insist on circumcision or legal conformity would be to abandon one's freedom (5:2–12). Yet this freedom does not mean (in the

LOVE COMMAND

JESUS' REPLY TO THE QUEStion of the Jewish scribes about which is the most important ("first") of God's commandments to his people is a combination of two texts from the law of Moses: the command to love God with all one's capabilities ("heart . . . soul . . . mind") from Deut. 6:5 and the call to love one's neighbor as oneself from Lev. 19:18. Luke links with this command the parable of the Good Samaritan, which defines concretely who one's neighbor is: one who is in need, regardless of what ethnic origin or physical condition. The only direct parallel in Paul's letters to the moral teachings of Jesus concerns love of one's neighbor (Rom. 13:8–10).

contemporary cliché) "to do your own thing": instead, it carries with it responsibility toward all other members of the new community, taking into account their different backgrounds and sensibilities (5:13–15). As Jesus did in the gospel tradition (Mark 12:31, Matt. 22:39, Luke 10:27), Paul quotes from Lev. 19:18 the commandment to love one's neighbor as oneself (Gal. 5:14, Rom. 13:9). The powerful new factor that transforms the lives of the people of faith is the Spirit. So long as they live out of their own weak and fallible human resources, they will be characterized by religious, moral, social, and personal failings (5:20–1). But when they live by the power of the Spirit of God, they will display the virtues enjoined by both the Jewish and the hellenistic traditions (5:22). Such a life of obedience through the power of the Spirit will be characterized by fulfillment of the moral demands of both the Jewish law and the natural law; Paul characterizes this new way of life in the phrase "Against such there is no law" (5:23). The Spirit at work in the members will result in a community life that is characterized by mutual responsibility to the erring and the weak (6:1–5), sharing insights with others (6:6), and dedication of time and energy for the work of God and the welfare of the community (6:7–10).

Underscoring the personal nature of this appeal to the Galatians, Paul added to the letter which he had just dictated a final paragraph written in his own hand (6:11–17) and concluded with a formal, liturgical farewell (6:18).

3.   First and Second Corinthians

Commercially and strategically, Corinth was the most important city in Greece in the first century. Located on the narrow neck of land that joins the Peloponnesus to the mainland, it was central for overland commerce in Greece and for movement of people and cargo by sea, since ships regularly stopped at one of the two ports (one east and one west) of the city and had their cargo transported over the peninsula to the other side for reshipment. The city had been destroyed in 146 B.C.E., and when it was rebuilt by the Romans about a century later, it was populated by people from various lands and cultures in the eastern Mediterranean. Although Greek was its official and commercial language, it had a mixed population. The Isthmian Games and other major sports events in the vicinity brought thousands of visitors, as did such religious sites as the shrines of the healing god, Asklepios, located in Corinth and in nearby Epidaurus. By the time of Paul, the once famous Corinthian shrine of Aphrodite, the goddess of love, was probably being restored. Corinth was a lively, cosmopolitan city, though it lacked the rich intellectual traditions of Athens. Presumably, the original core of converts to Christianity there were Jewish, as is suggested by the fact that two of the leaders, Aquila and Priscilla, had come from Rome when Claudius's decree had expelled the Jews after the disturbance arose among them with the arrival of the Christian message about Jesus and the resultant divisions within the Jewish community. The Christians of Jewish background in Corinth were soon joined by gentiles, who came to dominate the membership of the church there.

From the two letters to the Corinthians included in the New Testament we can infer that Paul had an ongoing correspondence with this Christian community made up of predominantly gentile members. At both the personal and the conceptual levels, Paul's relationship with the Corinthian Christians was full of problems. These letters provide the modern reader with insight into the nature of the early Christian communities that began to appear in major cities of the Roman world two decades after the death of Jesus.

First Corinthians, after an introductory section (chaps. 1–4) in which Paul discusses his apostolic role in relation to that of other apostles and Christian leaders, turns to a kind of checklist of problems in the Corinthian church that have been reported to him: gross immorality condoned by the members (chap. 5); internal disputes (6:1–8); moral laxness and involvement with immoral persons (6:9–19); questions of sex and marriage (chap. 7); participation in idol worship or eating food that had been offered to idols (chap. 8); problems connected with the celebration of the Eucharist (11:17–34) and with the exercise of charismatic gifts, such as prophecy and ecstatic speech (chaps. 12, 14); and understanding the resurrection and the end of the age (Ch 15). Interspersed are personal appeals concerning Paul's freedom to marry or to remain single, to ask for support or to work to support himself (chap. 9), and a solemn warning about disobedience, based on Israel's judgment by God in the wilderness of Sinai (chap. 10). The letter concludes with instructions about the Corinthians' contribution to the offering that is being taken up among the gentile churches for the benefit of the church in Jerusalem (chap. 16).

Second Corinthians, by contrast, is not written in a topical style and is most probably (in its present form) a composite of two or more original documents. Second Corinthians 1–9 was probably a letter in which Paul seeks to challenge the growing impact on the church in Corinth of a group of rivals to his apostolic authority and style. Second Corinthians 10–13 is a response to a group that scorns Paul for regarding his trials, sufferings, and imprisonment as evidence of God's support for his apostolic role. These letters are the last in a series that can be inferred to have included an earlier letter (mentioned in 1 Cor. 5:9), 1 Corinthians as we have it, and a "tearful letter" alluded to in 2 Cor. 2:3–4, 9; 7:8, 12. Some scholars think that 2 Cor. 6:14–7:1, which seems to interrupt the flow of thought between the verses that precede and follow it, may be a fragment of yet another letter of Paul to the Corinthians.

The treatment of the theological issues at Corinth is always intermingled with social and cultural tensions, between Jews and gentiles, and between Paul and his critics. There is evidence throughout these letters of the dual influences on Paul: his Jewish heritage and the hellenistic environment in which he was reared and trained.

Central in the Corinthian correspondence is the role of Paul as apostle and founder of the church there. That role was under steady attack

PAUL'S CORRESPONDENCE WITH THE CORINTHIANS

ALTHOUGH THERE ARE only two letters to the Corinthians in the New Testament, it is clear from these writings that Paul wrote other letters to the Corinthian Christians, and that the members of the church there wrote to Paul as well. The following sequence may be inferred from the preserved correspondence:

A letter to Paul from the Corinthian Christians (1 Cor. 7:1)

A letter from Paul, which the Corinthians seem not to have heeded (1 Cor. 5:9)

1 Corinthians, which includes Paul's responses to the question raised by the Corinthians' letter to him

An anguished letter from Paul, which caused pain among the Corinthians (2 Cor. 2:4)

2 Corinthians, in which Paul seeks to restore a relationship of mutual understanding with the Corinthians

In addition, there is the possibility that 2 Cor. 6:14–7:1 is part of yet another letter: the anguished letter mentioned in 2 Cor. 6:4. This has been proposed because this passage in 2 Corinthians seems to break the flow of the letter from 6:13 to 7:2. A plausible explanation, however, is the theory that Paul was interrupted as he was dictating what we know as 2 Corinthians and therefore did not follow neatly his original line of argument.

from unnamed detractors of various types. Some scoffed at what they considered to be his lack of rhetorical and intellectual sophistication (1 Cor. 1:17, 21–5), to which he replied that wisdom is a gift of God, not a human attainment. He notes in passing that the Corinthian Christians themselves were not an impressive group in terms of education, wealth, or noble birth (1 Cor. 1:26–31). The members there did include, however, one of the prominent leaders of the city, Erastus, the city treasurer or commissioner of public works (Rom. 16:23, written from Corinth), as well as people of sufficient means as to be able to hold the gatherings of the entire church in their own homes. To his detractors Paul responds with accounts of his own divine call, including visions of the risen Christ (1 Cor. 15:5–10) and of the throne of God (2 Cor. 12:1–10). He recalls the miracles and other apostolic signs performed by him in their midst (2 Cor. 12:12).

He also indicates that he has authority from God and is willing to assert it when necessary in settling moral issues or internal disputes, to the point of expelling an unworthy member (1 Cor. 5:3–5; 2 Cor. 10). On specific issues he makes binding pronouncements (1 Cor. 7:12, 25, 37–40), supplementing those that had come down through the Jesus tradition. He regards these regulations as commonly agreed to by all the churches (1 Cor. 11:16). His authority is also represented by his aides, such as Timothy, who is arranging for the collection (1 Cor. 16:10–11), and those he has left in positions of responsibility, such as Stephanas (1 Cor. 16:15–16).

Paul's major concern expressed in the letters is for the church to understand and experience its identity and unity as the new covenant people of God. This is to be achieved in spite of the tendency of the members to identify with one of the leaders ("I belong to Apollos," "I belong to Cephas"; 1 Cor. 1:10–17) or to exploit for self-gratification or ostentation the particular spiritual gift (*charisma*) that God may have granted them for the benefit of the community as a whole (1 Cor. 12–14). The dominant quality and dynamic of their common life is love, which Paul describes in 1 Corinthians 13. That relationship goes beyond feeling and is to be expressed concretely for the benefit of Christians elsewhere in the form of the collection for the church in Jerusalem (1 Cor. 16; 2 Cor. 8–9). It is also a major factor in the shaping of outsiders' attitudes toward the church (1 Cor. 11:27–9). The motivating power that is creating this new people is the Spirit of God, which is manifest for the common good (1 Cor. 12:3–7). The elaborate image of this new entity is the human body, with its diversity of members and its commonality of function and destiny (1 Cor. 12:14–26). It represents a new creation, not merely an amelioration of the old (2 Cor. 5:17–20).

Although Paul uses religious terms derived from the Jewish biblical tradition in describing this new community, such as "saints" and "holy" (1 Cor. 1:2, 8; 6:11; 7:14; 2 Cor. 1:1), he goes on to show that the formation of the new covenant people involves radical redrawing of both Jewish and other socio-cultural distinctions: non-Jewish membership (1 Cor. 12:2), cultic requirements set aside (1 Cor. 7:19), and social gaps transcended (1 Cor. 7:22–3). Only in the future will the purpose

GAMALIEL

THE NAME GAMALIEL appears in Num. 1:5–10 as one of the leaders of the tribe of Joseph, descended from Manasseh, who is to assist Moses in conducting a census of Israel. According to Acts, Gamaliel is also the name of a Pharisee who warns the Jewish council in Jerusalem against taking harsh action to destroy the movement launched through the apostles (Acts 5:17–40). Presumably this is the same man whom Paul identifies as having been his teacher in Jerusalem (Acts 22:3). Although no biographical information has been preserved, rabbinic sources list him as one of the patriarchal figures in the rabbinic movement. Another Gamaliel in the late first and early second century is credited by later rabbinic sources with having had an important role in the transition of Judaism from temple-centered to law-centered religious life and thought.

of God for his people be fully disclosed (1 Cor. 15:12–58). Although Paul throughout quotes scripture or refers to scriptural precedents to show the continuity between what God promised earlier and what has now occurred through Jesus, he also makes a radical break with the Jewish norms for covenantal identity. This is most clear in his dismissing of circumcision as of no significance (1 Cor. 7:19), although it was the crucial rite for Jewish covenantal participation (Gen. 17:1–17, 34:13–25; Exod. 12:44–8; Lev. 12:3; Josh. 5:2–8). It seems likely, therefore, that in 2 Cor. 6:14–7:1 Paul is discussing moral responsibility within the Christian community and the need to preserve moral purity among its members. It is not that he has abandoned his basic point of view throughout his letters: that trust in God's reconciling work in Jesus Christ is the primary basis for human acceptability to God. Rather, he is reaffirming his earlier statements that, once one is within the community, it is essential to observe and maintain moral purity by avoiding marital or other intimate associations with those who are not members of the community. But as noted earlier, this passage does not fit its present context in 2 Corinthians and may originally have been part of one of the other letters of Paul.

Paul's advice for the Corinthian community rests in part on tradition, in both faith and practice, but is modified on the basis of insights which he believes he has been given by God. The gospel message, and especially the assurance of the resurrection of Jesus, are part of the tradition which Paul himself received (1 Cor. 15:1–11). The practice of the Eucharist is also patterned after a tradition traced back to the Last Supper (1 Cor 10:14–22, 11:23–6). But the ground of his apostolic call was personal: his having seen Jesus after God had raised him from the dead. This was, however, recognized and confirmed by the other apostles. On some issues, Paul quotes a Jesus saying handed down in the tradition, but on others he offers his own opinion (1 Cor. 7:2, 5). Paul's views on these matters carry authority as a "command of the Lord" (1 Cor. 14:37–8).

For Paul, the functioning of the Christian community is not egalitarian: there is a clear hierarchy and a range of leadership roles that are to be recognized by members of the church. These functions are not assigned in terms of titles of office (bishop, deacon) but are listed by rank in 1 Cor. 12:27–30: apostles, prophets, teachers, workers of miracles, healers, helpers, administrators, those with the gift of ecstatic speech, and interpreters. Each of these has value as a contribution to the life of the community as a whole, and none is to be used for personal power or gratification. The welfare of the whole is the prime concern for those who serve in each of these roles.

Paul's language throughout the Corinthian correspondence shows the deep influence of the hellenistic intellectual environment in which he was evidently educated. This is the case whether or not one takes as historically reliable the report in Acts 22:3 that Paul studied under Gamaliel, the famous Jewish interpreter of the law. The educated among the populace in Syrian cities – whether Jew or gentile – were strongly influenced by Stoic philosophy, with its appeal to the universal human capacity (conscience) to know the law of nature that was

CONSCIENCE

IN STOIC PHILOSOPHY AND among those influenced by Stoicism, conscience was the innate human capacity to be aware of the natural law – and especially the moral law – inherent in the universe. Morality was the product of the human will and its decision to recognize these moral standards and to live by them. Paul, influenced as he was by Stoicism, describes the moral condition of gentiles who, though they have the inner possibility of living in accord with natural law ("what the law requires is written on their hearts"), do not obey it and therefore stand condemned on moral grounds (Rom. 1:18–31).

inherent in all the universe. The Stoics called for people to persevere in conformity to this law, in spite of suffering, and in confidence that in the future they would be called to account for their way of life and rewarded for their conformity to the divine law. This point of view had been readily assimilated to the Jewish understanding of the law of Moses, as the extensive writings of Philo of Alexandria and such books as 4 Maccabees demonstrate. It is not surprising, therefore, that Paul often refers to conscience (a term for which there is no equivalent in Semitic language or thought) and appeals to his readers to exemplify fidelity, self-control, and discipline (1 Cor. 7:9, 8:7–10, 9:25–7, 10:29; 2 Cor. 1:12). In his references to the future Day of Judgment (2 Cor 5:10), Paul unites elements of this Stoic tradition with the basically apocalyptic outlook that he takes over and modifies from his Jewish heritage, since Stoicism taught that human beings would in the future be held accountable to God for their deeds in this life. Similarly, when Paul is enumerating the Christian virtues, some of his terms are drawn from the Bible and others from Stoicism (2 Cor. 6:4–5). Yet the prime examples to which he points are the experiences of the old covenant people (1 Cor. 10), which are to serve as warnings to the new covenant people that obedience, holiness, and endurance are essential for the maintenance of status, now and in the age to come. But unlike the old covenant moral responsibilities, these new qualities are made possible through the death and resurrection of Christ and through the power of the indwelling Spirit of God.

4.   Romans

The Letter to the Romans is unique among Paul's surviving writings in that it was written by Paul to a church he had not founded and had never visited. It was known to him earlier through his associations with Priscilla and Aquila, first in Corinth and later in Ephesus. Now, however, these two coworkers with Paul had returned to Rome, where they had been apparently part of the original core of believers (Rom. 16:3). Although we have no direct evidence about the founding of the Christian community there, it appears from the fact that its members were expelled by the decree of Claudius against the Jews there that most of the original converts were Jewish. This would help to explain why Paul takes such an extensive section of the letter to deal with the question of God's future purpose for his historical people Israel (Rom. 9–11).

The identity of the original apostle who took the gospel to Rome is unknown, although tradition has long identified Peter as the one who carried out that mission. Paul gives no hint of this in his letter to the Romans, but the very fact that he does not regard it as a place where his own brand of pioneer evangelism can be carried out shows that someone else had been there long before his planned journey and had established a church in the capital of the empire. His apostolic role of preaching the good news about Jesus as the Christ where the message had not been heard before had already taken him around the entire northeastern quadrant of the Mediterranean world: from Jerusalem to

Claudian aqueduct and the Appian Way, Rome. Among the major public works carried out by Claudius during his reign as emperor (41–54 C.E.) were two great aqueducts and a new harbor at Ostia, the port of Rome. The Appian Way, described by the first-century C.E. historian Statius as "the queen of the long roads," stretched southward 350 miles from Rome to the major port of Brundisium. The arches of the Claudian aqueduct that runs beside the Appian Way as it nears Rome are more than 110 feet in height. The Forum of Appius, where Roman Christians came to meet Paul (Acts 28:15), was 43 miles south of Rome.

Gordon Converse.

Illyricum, which included parts of Asia Minor, Greece, and other lands as far west as the shores of the Adriatic (Rom 15:18–19, 23). Now he planned to pass through Rome to the next region where his primary missionary work could be carried out: Spain (15:24). This seems to imply that not only Rome and Italy but perhaps also southern Gaul had heard the gospel, although that area does not certainly come into the history of Christianity until well on in the second century. In any case, Paul hopes to see the Roman Christians as he passes through their city. But first he must take to the leaders of the Jerusalem church the collection he has arranged to gather from the gentile churches of Asia Minor and Greece (15:24–9).

From the opening lines of this letter to the Romans, Paul seeks to make clear that the gospel is in accord with the Jewish scriptures and that God has from the beginning of human history had a special place in his purpose for ancient Israel as the covenant people (Rom. 1:2). He repeats a liturgical formula concerning the human and divine sonship of Jesus (1:1–4), which some scholars think was in use in Rome and is quoted here by Paul to help establish rapport with this Christian community largely unknown to him. That effort is surely evident in the personal remarks in 1:8–15, where he draws attention to mutual concerns and the hopes for enriched common understanding. The fact that he refers to them as being "among the rest of the gentiles" (1:13) indicates that the church is now predominantly gentile, but that there are tensions in the relationships between pagan and Jewish converts to the Christian faith (1:16).

The goals of introducing himself and easing tensions within the Roman community are both addressed by his focus on what is usually translated "the righteousness of God" or "justification." The concept must be understood against its semitic background, in which its primary reference is to the work of God whereby he sets his people in the right relationship to himself. Paul emphasizes that this divine goal is achieved by God's own gracious action, not by human merit or moral achievement (Rom. 1:17). The only appropriate human response is to rely upon or trust ("believe" is an inadequate translation) in what God has done through Jesus. He then proceeds to show that this is the way to right relationship with God for both Jews, who were given the law of Moses and the prophetic insights, and gentiles, who lacked both.

The gentiles should have been able to infer from the order and splendor of the universe the nature of the God who created it. But instead, they turned to worship images of created things, animal or human (1:18–23). The consequence of the human refusal to acknowledge God is the disordering of all human relationships. The sinful and corrupt condition of the human race is the result of its refusal to honor God, not the cause of its estrangement. Because the basic pattern of relationship with the Creator has been warped by human acts and attitudes, all human relationships are likewise misshapen (1:24–32). Drawing on the traditions of the Stoics, Paul declares that the conscience of all human beings makes them aware of what their moral responsibilities are, and he reminds them of the future day when God will call them to account for their behavior in life (2:1–16). Jews assume that they have a special relationship to God because they were given the law of God through Moses, but even if that were the basis of their status as God's covenant people, they in fact "dishonor God by breaking the law" (2:17–29). The ground of human relationship to God is an inward commitment of trust, not outward conformity to a set of rules or to such religious ritual as circumcision.

It is true that those who stand in the Jewish tradition have a potential advantage over the gentiles, in that the former have received the oracles of God and therefore have a special insight into his purpose for his people. Yet many Israelites have not been faithful to God. Does this show that God's plan has failed? No, it demonstrates that right relationship with God is not attained by human performance, not even by those specially favored with the gift of the law of Moses and the words of the prophets (3:1–8). The result is that all humanity, whether gentiles informed by conscience or Jews instructed by the scriptures, stand condemned before God on the basis of their failure to meet their moral and religious obligations. All that law does, whether natural law or Mosaic law, is provoke disobedience and remind humans of their failings (3:9–20). But through Jesus, God has provided a remedy: it is God's way of setting his people in right relationship to himself on the sole ground of their trust in what he has done (3:21–6). It is a mode of dealing with the human condition that excludes human pride, that shows God's demands to be just, and provides a new basis – trust – by which human beings can gain their proper standing before God (3:27–31).

This divine program is not an innovation: it goes back to Abraham, whose role as the father of the covenant people rested solely on his trust in God's promise, and to David, who saw that God forgave rather than holding humans responsible for their moral failures. But the new covenant community will include "many nations" – people who did not know and could not have conformed to the Mosaic ritual or moral commandments. The proof that God has accomplished this through Jesus is seen in his having raised Jesus from the dead (4:1–25).

In describing the moral consequences of this relationship to God by faith, Paul notes that the full realization of God's purpose for humanity – to share the glory of God (Gen. 1:26, Ps. 8:3–5) – lies in the future. The difficulties and sufferings that his people undergo in the present age are purifying and preparatory for the final goal of sharing the glory of God (5:1–10). Paul develops an elaborate series of contrasts between the two modes of human existence: in Adam, according to which human disobedience forfeited the right to share the glory of God and led to estrangement and death; and in Christ, through whom God's people are reconciled and enabled to become obedient (5:12–21). The rite of baptism is a symbolic instrument of participation in the death and resurrection of Jesus, which both demands and empowers God's people to live a life of faithful obedience and service (6:1–23).

Paul perceives sin to be a subtle, pervasive agent that perverts the law and its reminders of human obligations, impelling men and women to disobey its demands. Apart from Jesus, humans would live lives of hopeless ambivalence, aware of the consequences of sin, yet unable to avoid committing it (7:1–25). Christians have a new place in which they can live and enjoy the benefits of God's provision for them: "in Christ" (8:1). Not only is Jesus the agent through whom new life is made available to the people of faith; he is also the prime model of that mode of life. He came in human form and yet triumphed over the powers of evil by his life of total obedience to the will and purpose of God. For those who live by the Spirit, which is the enabling, transforming force at work within this new community, the moral demands of the law are indeed met. To live out of one's own human resources (usually translated "according to the flesh") is to preclude a life of obedience to God. To live by the power of the Spirit is to experience true life and peace – and this new life will know no end (8:2–11).

This life will not be free of suffering, however. The creation itself will continue to undergo strife and struggle, just as a woman in childbirth endures pain in order that new life may be born. The members of the new people live in hope, therefore, that God, who triumphed over evil and death in raising Jesus from the dead, will attain the final and full deliverance of his people and of the whole creation from the power of sin and death. Jesus is the prototype for God's new people; all will be conformed by God to his image. Nothing on earth and no force in the superhuman realm will be able to thwart the achievement of God's purpose for his new covenant people (8:12–38).

Both logically and autobiographically, Paul feels obligated to explain for himself and for his Roman readers the connection between the promises God made through Jesus to his new people and those he made historically to Israel. Three chapters of his letter (Rom. 9–11) are devoted to wrestling with this issue. He begins by spelling out in detail what the privileged position of historic Israel is: God has given the Israelites a special relationship as "son"; in the sanctuary in their midst has been the radiant cloud of the divine glory; they were given the covenantal relationship, the law, the proper service (or worship) of God, the divine promises; God worked on their behalf through the patriarchs and promised to send the Messiah(s) as agent(s) to accomplish his purpose (9:1–5). For all this, Paul can only praise God. Yet why has not the right relationship of this people to God been maintained? From the outset of Israel's history, it was clear that genetic or ethnic links with the patriarchs did not guarantee participation in the life of the covenant, since not all the descendants of Israel are within the community of faith. The ground of human relationship to God is his choice, not human effort or attainment (Exod. 33:19). The offspring of Isaac are in one case the object of love (Jacob) and in the other case the object of hate (Esau; Gen. 25:23, Mal. 1:2–3).

Yet God, in his sovereignty, uses the wicked to accomplish his objectives (Rom. 9:17–30). Paul cites examples from the Old Testament. Pharaoh's hostility toward Israel in Egypt resulted in events that proclaimed the name and power of Israel's God throughout the nations of the world (Exod. 9:16). Some hearts are unresponsive to the word of God because he has hardened them (Exod. 4:21; 7:3; 9:12; 14:4, 7). God's sovereignty will be evident in that not all historic Israel will be included in the ultimate covenant people, yet many who are "not my people" will be included (Isa. 10:22–3; Gen. 22:17; 2 Kings 19:4; Hos. 1:10, 2:23). The members of the new community will be gathered from among all the nations (Isa. 11:10–16).

Why does Israel fail to understand and accept the message about what God is doing through Jesus to reconstitute his people (Rom. 9:30–3)? The answer lies in their involvement with their own method of obtaining a right relationship with God through their conformity to the law of Moses, and thus they have tripped up on the rock which God had set down as the foundation of the renewal of the covenant: Jesus Christ (Rom 10:1–4). They have not been enlightened, as Paul has been, about how God is achieving his purpose. Christ has shown the impossibility that the law can be the ground for human achievement of right relationship with God. It is easy to understand how Israel would have taken this mistaken route to God: it has been perceived by Jews as laid down in the law of Moses (Lev. 18:5) and as confirmed in the later Jewish writings (Neh. 9:29–31), including the prophets, such as Ezekiel (Ezek. 20:11–26), who describes Israel's exile as the consequence of its failure to obey the law, especially with regard to Sabbath and the sacrifices.

Over against this, Paul sets forth (Rom. 10:6–10) the true ground of human relationship with God: trust in what God has done through Jesus to set his people right. Nothing more needs to be done to achieve this: the word that Paul preaches about Jesus' death and resurrection is already at hand, to be heard, believed, and publicly confessed. That message is already spreading throughout the earth for all to hear and, for all who are willing, Jew or gentile, to trust in as the ground of human relationship to God. The quotations from the scriptures in 10:18–20 serve to make Paul's point that this is not an innovation but has always been foundational to God's purpose.

This inclusive definition of the covenant people does not mean that historic Israel no longer has a place in God's purpose, as passages like 1 Sam. 12:22, Jer. 31:37, and Jer. 33:24–6 make clear (Rom. 11:1–2). But as Elijah recognized, only a remnant of Israel will ultimately share in the ongoing life of God's people (Ps. 94:14, 1 Kings 19:10, 2 Kings 19:4, Isa. 11:11). This remnant has been chosen by the grace of God, not as a reward for its achievements (Rom. 11:3–6). Even the hostile attitude that Israel has taken toward Jesus is a part of the divine plan, whereby the hardening of Israel's heart (Isa. 29:10, Deut. 29:4, Ps. 69:22–3) has resulted in the gospel being preached among the gentiles (Rom. 11:7–12). Using a play on words in Greek, Paul notes that Israel's gross mistake (*paraptoma*) in rejecting Jesus will result ultimately in Israel's full participation (*pleroma*) in the life of the covenant people. He uses two analogies to show the long-range effect of what God has begun to do in reconstituting his people. (1) Dough, part of which is offered as a firstfruit, eventually transforms the whole of the lump. (2) Developing the image of vine (or tree) and branches, which pervades the prophetic writings and the Psalms (Ps. 80; Isa. 5:1–7, 11:1; Jer. 5:10, 11:16, 17:5–8; Ezek. 15, 17, 19, 31; Dan. 4; Joel 1; Zech. 3, 4, 6), Paul sees Israel as the natural branches of God's people, who have now been replaced by the gentile believers, who are the branches grafted into the original vine (Rom. 11:17–24). To this extended metaphor he adds the warning that the gentile Christians must be faithful in this relationship, or like historic Israel, they may be cut off as well. The result of these divine actions is that, in the time of the end, "all Israel will be saved" (Rom. 11:26), by which he means that the elect and faithful, from among both Jews and gentiles, will be brought to the fulfillment of God's plan through and for them as his covenant people. This section of the letter ends, appropriately, with an ascription of praise to the sovereign God and an acknowledgment of the inability of the human mind to grasp these divine ways (11:33–6).

In the remainder of the letter, Paul addresses more practical matters, such as the need for mutual concern and purity of life on the part of the members of the new community, and the appropriate attitudes toward outsiders, including one's enemies and the Roman government. This concluding section of the letter begins with imagery drawn from the worship traditions of Israel, though what constitutes the transformed worship of God in the new covenant era (12:1) is their presentation of their whole selves as a living sacrifice. Their values and norms are not to derive from those of the evil age in which they live but from the transformation of attitude and expectation that enables them to perceive and to fulfill God's will for his new people (12:2). The result of this will be their seeing themselves modestly as instruments of God rather than as proud achievers. They will recognize that the capacities they enjoy are not for fostering their own self-esteem but for the shared welfare of the whole community (12:3–8). These responsibilities range from mutual love to sharing goods with those in need (12:9–13). They are also required to show grace and forgiveness toward those outside the community, including their enemies. Here the influence of the Jesus tradition is evident (12:14–21).

Paul is persuaded that the pagan Roman state is not a threat to the young church, but as the instrument of maintenance of social order it is to be honored and Christians are to pay the required taxes to support it (Rom. 13:1–7). Up to this point in his career, Roman authority made possible Paul's safe travel and the sure delivery of messages, and protected him against attack by his opponents. In Paul's letter to the Philippians and in Acts, Paul is seized and imprisoned by civil authorities as a disturber of the peace, but the Roman powers do not charge him with political subversion, exhibit hostility, or prohibit him from carrying on his work. Even when he is sent from Palestine to Rome for a hearing before Caesar, the regional Roman authorities can find nothing subversive or contrary to Roman law in his activities (Acts 26:32). If the tradition that he was martyred under Nero is correct, then some formal political charge must have been brought against him, which could have led him to a changed perspective on Rome by the end of his life. But in his letters, his conviction that the present age and world order were soon to come to an end prevented him from mounting any politically subversive movement, as this passage shows.

Most of the rest of the letter is taken up with spelling out in detail what it means for members of the community to accept responsibility for others within the group, in spite of basic differences in insight and conviction. Thus, those who have brought into their lives as Christians beliefs about food that is unclean are to be respected by those who do not share their views (14:1–23). The basic rule is to seek to please one another, so that there can be mutual support, peace, and harmony among the membership (15:1–6).

Before turning to his personal notes about his travel plans and the long list of greetings that he conveys from the Christians in Corinth to those he hopes soon to see in Rome (Rom. 15:14–16:23), he underscores the authority of the mission to the gentiles in which he is engaged by quotations from several scriptures (Pss. 18:49, 117:1; Deut. 32:43; Isa. 11:10) that anticipate the inclusion of the gentiles in the covenant people (Rom. 15:7–13). The final paragraph of the letter emphasizes that the work of preaching Christ is the outworking of the divine mystery, which is now being made known to all the nations in order to lead them to faith and thus into the fellowship of the new people of God (16:25–7).

5.   Philemon and Philippians

We do not know where these letters were written although both were written from prison. They may have been written from the same prison, but Paul mentions that he was often incarcerated (2 Cor. 6:5, 11:23). One possibility is Ephesus, which would have been easily accessible to both Colossae in Asia Minor and to Philippi in mainland Greece. Scholarly proposals for the place of Paul's imprisonment from which he wrote these letters include Caesarea in Palestine, where he was in Roman custody for an extended period (Acts 23:23–27:2). Other scholars have assumed that Paul was writing from a prison in Rome, since he mentions the Praetorian Guard, which was an imperial unit. But elements of this guard were found wherever major Roman officials

---

PHILIPPI

THE CITY OF PHILIPPI WAS founded and named for himself by Philip II of Macedonia (ruled from 359 to 336 B.C.E.), the father of Alexander the Great. The site was chosen because of its proximity to gold and silver mines on the northwest coast of the Aegean Sea. The city became important as a major Roman military and commercial location near the eastern end of the highway, Via Egnatia, that served as a main route across northern Greece from the Aegean to the Adriatic. The deities worshiped there included major Roman gods and others whose cults developed in the region. Acts 16:11–15 mentions a "place of prayer" outside the city. These were gathering places for Jews and proselytes who met for social and religious purposes in the period before the institutional and architectural development of the synagogue.

were stationed, and thus Ephesus and Caesarea would both have had such units.

More important than the specific place of origin for these letters from prison is the fact that the Christian mission had now come into direct conflict with the Roman imperial power, and this was a harbinger of the conflict that was to come in succeeding centuries. Paul is not sure whether he will be released from prison, and thus enabled to return to his mission, or whether he will be executed. But he is prepared for either (Phil. 1:19–26).

The shortest of Paul's surviving letters, Philemon, is the one purely personal communication from him that has been preserved. Paul is writing from prison to Philemon about Onesimus, who is a slave – now converted to Christianity – and who is mentioned in Col. 4:9 as a member of the church in Colossae. Philemon is praised for his love for his fellow members of God's people (Philem. 4–7) and is urged to accept his former slave as a brother in the community of faith. If Onesimus owes anything to his former owner, Paul himself will repay it (Philem. 8–20). Here we have dramatic evidence of the way in which the relationships within the new people of God transformed the social and economic patterns of the day.

The immediate occasion for writing to the Philippians is to thank them for the contribution that they have once more made to Paul's support (1:3–11). His being in prison has given him opportunity to preach to the members of the imperial guard (1:12). The opposition that resulted in his imprisonment did not end his mission activity but instead provided him further opportunities to preach his version of the Christian message (1:15–18). This difficulty provides the occasion for him to remind his readers of the importance of total commitment to

Philippi: the Via Egnatia. Founded by Philip II of Macedon, father of Alexander the Great, this city became important in Roman times because of its location on the Via Egnatia, the Roman highway which joined ports on the Aegean Sea with those on the Adriatic, thereby serving as a vital military and commercial link between Rome and its eastern provinces. Worshiped there were the local Greek deities, as well as those imported from Rome (Jupiter and Mars), Egypt, and Asia Minor (Cybele, the mother goddess).

H. C. Kee.

the gospel, even when it leads to suffering or death (1:19–20). He then goes on to repeat or rephrase an early Christian hymn that depicts Jesus as the prototype of complete obedience to God, which leads beyond death to divine vindication (2:5–8). This is the pattern according to which God will vindicate the faithful, and Jesus' example will lead them on until the universal proclamation of the gospel has been accomplished (2:9–11).

Meanwhile, however, Paul must advise the Philippians about the guidelines for individual and corporate life within the community, in the confidence that God is at work among them (2:12–13). They are to beware of those who want to enforce circumcision, as though it were a badge of merit (3:2–3). Paul has plenty to boast about if he thought any of it was important – including his origins, training, and Pharisaic zeal – but he dismisses these things as worthless dung or refuse (3:4–8). The sole ground of his relationship with God is trust in what God has done on behalf of his new people; Paul places no value on legal conformity or moral achievement as such (3:9). He wants to follow the example of Jesus through obedience to divine vindication (3:10–11). He sees his life as a process of growth toward maturity, which will culminate in the call to meet the triumphant, returning Christ (3:12–15).

Further, the community must purge itself of those false teachers who consider Christian freedom to be a license for total self-indulgence (3:17–19). Instead, Christians are to regard themselves as members of God's perfect society (*politeuma*), a term Paul borrows from the Stoic tradition of a humanity obedient to natural law, but which Paul perceives to be the new community in process of transformation by God until corporately it conforms to the image of the risen Christ (3:20–1). In the interim, the members are encouraged to promote mutual understanding and to live lives free from anxiety and filled with joy and peace (4:1–7). The body of the letter closes with a repeated expression of thanks for the financial support that the Philippians have provided for Paul (4:6–20).

The concluding greetings are extended from the entire body of "saints" (wherever Paul may have been at the time), including "those of Caesar's household." This would fit the circumstances in Rome, but it could also refer to members of the imperial establishment assigned to Ephesus, or wherever Paul was imprisoned, who had become members of the new covenant people. This detail gives the modern reader an indication of the astonishing speed with which the gospel found its way from a fringe group in rural Palestine to a movement with an impact on the upper levels of Roman society.

D.   TOWARD ORGANIZATION AND ORTHODOXY: THE LATER PAULINE TRADITIONS

Among the Christian scriptures, five writings identify Paul as their author but (for reasons we shall sketch) seem to have come from a somewhat later period and to have been written by persons who saw themselves to be carrying forward the traditions linked with Paul. These documents are

Colossians
Ephesians
1 Timothy
2 Timothy
Titus

The first two of these writings stand closer to Paul in style and approach to the needs of the churches, but all of them evidence significant shifts toward formalization of faith and church organization compared to the letters surely written by Paul. As noted throughout our analysis of the biblical writings, the practice of writing in the name of an earlier prophet or leader of the community was not seen as dishonest but as a way of honoring the work of the former leader.

The factors that contributed to this move toward consolidation within the churches founded by Paul are typical of the social forces in any group movement. At first, the leadership of the churches was *charismatic,* as sociologists have labeled the spontaneous, self- (or divinely) appointed leaders who launch movements like the church's mission to the gentiles. This resulted in different styles and strategies for carrying out various missions, as the letters of Paul attest. With the passing of the original apostolic generation, however, it was necessary to lend authority to their successors in leadership roles to ensure the stability of the churches the pioneer apostles had formed. This need was intensified by the fact that the movement was beginning to come to the attention of the Roman authorities. Organization and assignment of specific responsibilities were required if the church was to survive.

Paul was willing to tolerate certain differences in the understanding of what Christians should believe and practice: for him the most important thing was to convert Jews and gentiles to trust in Jesus as God's Messiah, in view of the shortness of the time before the coming of the new age. But as his generation passed, it became increasingly clear that the churches must prepare for possibly a long period of expectation of the end and therefore must consolidate their beliefs and practices. It was inevitable that the earlier contrast between this age and the next would be gradually replaced by a contrast between the realm of time and that of eternity, following the familiar distinction in Greek philosophy. We shall see that in these later Pauline writings there is a significant shift away from expectation of a speedy end in the direction of portraying Jesus as the agent of the eternal world in the present life of humanity. Faith, like the leadership of the Christian communities, will no longer be spontaneous but increasingly formal and unified.

1.   Colossians: Jesus as Cosmic Redeemer

The Christians in Colossae, a small city near Ephesus in Asia Minor, are addressed in this letter, which follows the general pattern of Paul's letters: identification of the writer and the recipients, prayers and thanksgiving for the church there (1:1–14), statements about the

ASSIGNED ROLES IN THE CHURCHES ACCORDING TO COLOSSIANS AND THE PASTORALS

Within the household:

Wives (Col. 3:18)
Husbands (Col. 3:19)
Children (Col. 3:20)
Fathers (Col. 3:21)
Slaves (Col. 3:22–5)
Masters (Col. 4:1)

Within the leadership of the churches:

Bishops (1 Tim. 3:1–7)
Deacons (1 Tim 3:8–13); these instructions may include women who are deacons (1 Tim. 3:11, Rom. 16:1)
Elders (1 Tim. 5:17–20)

It is possible that the widows described in 1 Tim. 5:3–16 are not simply women members of the church who have lost their husbands, but women who have special roles now that they no longer have obligations toward a husband and children. They would resemble the women who in more modern times were members of religious orders.

role of Christ in God's plan (1:15–23), expression of the writer's concerns for them (1:24–2:15); advice and exhortations (2:16–4:5); personal greetings from the writer's companions and to specific members of the church at Colossae (4:7–17), with a final personal greeting (4:18).

This letter displays important differences from the letters of Paul in the vocabulary used for depicting Jesus as God's redemptive agent, in the writer's view of the present state of the church, in his use of hellenistic terminology for portraying Christ, and in the tactics he employs for guiding behavior in the church. Certain philosophical distinctions are made that have no parallel in the letters of Paul, such as the contrast between "shadow" and "substance," which sounds Platonic. Terms that appear in Paul's letters, such as "truth," "faith," and "knowledge," are all given intellectual connotations that are not found in Paul and that do not depict the basis of the personal relationship to God in the same way as these terms do when used by Paul: through dependence, trust, and personal knowledge. In contrast to Paul's scorning of human wisdom, as in 1 Corinthians 1, the writer contrasts human wisdom and divine wisdom in principle but then uses technical philosophical terminology and speaks of Christ as the one in whom are hidden all the treasures of wisdom and knowledge (Col. 2:3) – presumably constituting a synthesis of secular and sacred wisdom. He seeks to place the Christian faith in competition with human philosophy – a term never used by Paul (Col. 2:8). It seems clear that by the time Colossians was written, Christian faith, with its claim to offer divine wisdom, was having to engage in debate with human intellectual systems.

In contrast to Paul, who links statements about what God has already done through Jesus with the hope of his still-to-come defeat of the powers of evil (1 Cor. 15, 1 Thess. 4), the writer of Colossians here describes Christ as having already achieved victory over the worldly powers and the forces of evil (2:15). The effect of this shift is to remove the problem of the nonfulfillment of the hope of Christ's return in triumph. Instead of depicting the people of God as meeting Christ when he returns to earth in victory at the end of the age (1 Thess. 4:17, 1 Cor. 15), the writer of Colossians expects Christians to appear with Christ enthroned in heaven (3:4). In Paul's letters, he uses the image of the body to illustrate the twin factors of differentiation of role and mutual dependence among the members of the church (1 Cor. 12–14). In Colossians, however, the emphasis falls on Christ as the head of the body, the church, as well as master of all powers, earthly and heavenly (2:10, 19).

Life within the church as described in Colossians is significantly different from what one sees in Paul's letters. Instead of focusing on roles within the community – such as prophecy, performing miracles, speaking in ecstatic language, and teaching (1 Cor. 12:27–31) – the writer makes social distinctions in terms of husbands and wives and of masters and slaves within the community (Col. 3:18–4:1). This contrasts sharply with Paul's declaration in Gal. 3:28 that in Christ neither sexual nor social distinctions have any meaning. It appears that church membership has developed in terms of households rather than indi-

GNOSIS

GNOSIS, ONE OF THE GREEK words for "knowledge," came to be used in the second century C.E. to refer to a mode of religious thought that claimed to have exclusive information about the origin and destiny of the universe and its inhabitants. It taught that the material world was the work of evil powers, which had operated in defiance of the god of light, who was the true and beneficent sovereign of the universe. Human beings were caught in material existence, and were therefore helpless to escape until the agent of divine knowledge came into the material world to explain and to demonstrate liberation from the material world. Some of the followers of this movement (which came to be known as Gnosticism) thought that they could display their ability to rise above the material world by living in a strictly ascetic manner, while others took the route of unbridled self-indulgence as a way of showing that the material world was of no significance.

Knowledge of this movement in its various forms was limited until modern times by the fact that the only sources of information about the Gnostics were the attacks on Gnosticism in the writings of the defenders of orthodox faith in the church from the second to fourth centuries C.E. But in 1954 an entire library of Gnostic documents was found at Nag Hammadi in Upper Egypt. Written in thirteen volumes on papyrus (a writing material made from reeds), some of which are not complete, the documents are in Coptic, a form of late Egyptian used by Christians in Egypt and written in Greek characters. They include gospels (Gospel of Thomas; Gospel of Truth); acts (Acts of Peter and the Twelve Apostles); apocalypses (of Paul, of Peter, of Adam, and two of James); and dialogues (the Sophia of Jesus Christ; the Dialogue of the Savior). These documents provide primary evidence of Gnosticism.

Although scholarly opinion is divided, it seems probable that the Gnostic type of dualistic speculation about the cosmos and human destiny may have had antecedents in Jewish wisdom speculation in the early Roman period but was adapted and developed by some Christians in the second century. The latter identified Jesus as the agent of divine knowledge whose followers could escape from the material world and regain union with the truly divine. It is likely the beginning of this movement that is under attack in passages from later New Testament writings such as 1 Tim. 6:20, where false teachers and their false claims to knowledge are denounced. The Gnostic documents expand and modify the Jesus tradition in order to make him fit the role of agent of secret knowledge and liberator from the material world.

---

vidual conversions, and the traditional hierarchical roles of the household are merely transferred to and confirmed in the Christian community.

One of the major concerns throughout this letter is what the author regards as the perversion of Christianity through two kinds of false teaching: speculation about the nature of Christ; and the attempt to force Christians to adopt an ascetic mode of life, with strict requirements about diet and observance of holy days (2:16–23). Instead of denouncing this as a return to being enslaved to the law, as Paul does in Romans and Galatians, the author of Colossians urges his readers to divert their attention from earthly to heavenly matters (3:1–4) and to put on a new nature (3:5–10). This interest in otherworldliness, which the writer is calling for, will come to full realization in the second century in the movement known as Gnosticism, which the mainstream of the church will combat.

Although in Paul's letters there are frequent references in the personal notes to his associates, in Colossians there is a sense of authority delegated by Paul to these coworkers, who are to serve as guides and to develop the life of the church (4:7–17). Once again, this development points to, and helps achieve, the transition between the first generation, when the apostles claimed their authority on the basis of their having seen Jesus risen from the dead (1 Cor. 9:1), and the period after their passing. Significantly, there is mention here of Mark and Luke (Col. 4:10, 14), whose authority was to be attached to the gospels which now came to bear their names. Also, the authority of Paul's letters is evident in the mention in Col. 4:16 of another (otherwise unknown) letter from him, which is to be read in the church, along with other authoritative letters sent to other churches. Clearly, we have the beginning of a formal collection and transmission of the Pauline letters – which serves to show how important it was that this letter was written in the name of Paul.

2.   Ephesians

It is significant that the oldest existing copies of this letter do not include the name of a particular church to which it was addressed. Only later copies mention "to the Ephesians" (1:1). That the document now known as "Ephesians" was indeed sent to a group of churches, rather than to a specific congregation, is apparent from the fact that the letter – unlike Paul's letters that we have examined above – does not address the issues of a specific situation. Instead, the structure of the letter is twofold: an extended introduction, with an elaborate form of prayer (announced in 1:15–16; referred to in 3:1 and again in 3:14) that culminates in the blessing of God (3:20–1); the concluding exhortations, instructions (with only the briefest personal note in 6:21–2), and closing prayers that end the letter (4:1–6:24). A middle section dealing with specific problems and concerns, such as we find in Paul's letters, is simply not there in Ephesians. It seems clear, therefore, that this letter was intended to be circulated widely among various churches, with the aim of promoting unity among them in faith and practice.

The writer does develop Pauline themes. Jesus is referred to as Lord, as he is with great frequency in Paul's letters. At times the word for Lord, *kyrios,* could refer to Jesus or to God, just as is the case with Paul. Only once, however, is Jesus spoken of as "son" in Ephesians (4:13), although that is also an important term in the letters of Paul. The Spirit is referred to as the guarantee of the fulfillment of God's promises (Eph. 1:13; 2 Cor. 1:22). What is more significant, however, is the distinctive meaning that this letter gives to terms found in Paul. The term "heavenly" is used by Paul in contrast with things that are of earthly origin (1 Cor. 15:40, 48). But Ephesians uses the word in the plural to refer to the sphere of eternity, where Christ is and where his followers have already entered (Eph. 1:20, 2:6). This is part of a shift in Ephesians which reduces the expectation of a future fulfillment to an insignificant feature, emphasizing instead the cosmic, *timeless* transformation of the human situation that God has accomplished in Christ. The new reality is not the age to come, awaited in the near future, as in Paul. It is the cosmic change that has already taken place (2:5–6, 11–13; 4:10). This new reality is also internalized: Christ dwells in the hearts of the faithful (3:17), and they have the possibility of being "filled with all the fullness of God" (3:19). The term *pleroma* (fullness) is used by Paul to refer to the divinely determined time of the birth of Jesus (Gal. 4:4), but in Eph. 4:13, as in Col. 2:9 and John 1:16, it seems to mean the fullness of the divine nature, which Jesus possesses and which he shares with his people.

The goal of God's redemptive program through Jesus, according to Ephesians, is to create a new and transformed humanity (Eph. 2:13–18). That idea is implicit in Paul's statements in Romans about the contrast between being in Adam and in Christ (Rom. 5:12–21), but here the emphasis is on the participation in the divine nature (Eph. 4:24). An important feature in Ephesians is the unity of this new humanity which God has established in Christ. The old split between Jew and gentile, which had practical implications in Paul's time, is now pictured as no longer significant, because through Christ, God has created "one new humanity" (2:11–19).

Then the image shifts from the creation of a new society of God's people to the building of a new sanctuary in which God is present (Eph. 2:20–2). In this new structured society, Christ is the foundation (as he is for Paul: 1 Cor. 3:10), but the apostles and prophets are the building material from which the temple of God has been constructed, and where God dwells in the Spirit. There is now a hierarchy of roles in the church: apostles, prophets, evangelists, pastors, teachers (4:11). These are not the charismatic gifts that Paul describes in 1 Corinthians 12, but ecclesiastical functions essential for the development of the church in its institutional forms.

The goal of this leadership pattern is to enable the church to "attain to the unity of the faith." This is explained to mean fullness of knowledge, maturity of Christian living, and, above all, orthodox doctrines. These qualities alone will make possible the proper growth in faith within the community (4:13–16).

The members of the church are to seek to exhibit the very nature of God (Eph. 5:1), with purity of life and thought, avoiding associations with any who might corrupt their morals or their doctrine (5:3–13). The sanctity of the life of the community is to be evident not only in its moral performance but also in its common life of devotion to God in worship (5:19–20). Probably Eph. 5:14 is a portion of an early Christian hymn, based on Isa. 60:1. The concrete expression of the unity of the faithful is to be seen in their willingness to be subject to one another (5:21).

There follows a list of social roles and responsibilities within the community, as in Colossians. Rules are given for wives and husbands, children, slaves, and masters (5:22–6:9). The final exhortation describes the cosmic conflict in which the people of God are now engaged against the hosts of evil (6:10–20). This may well point to the beginning of general hostility toward the Christian movement in the later first or early second century, as it began to penetrate the upper levels of Roman society and to arouse suspicions concerning its social and political implications. Appropriately, the author identifies himself as "an ambassador in chains," which was very likely the actual fate of Paul. Presumably by the time Ephesians was written, the final conflict of Paul with the Roman authorities and his execution – which would not have been anticipated in view of his positive attitude toward what he regarded as a benign political power – had become a paradigm of the subsequent church–state struggle and the threat of martyrdom that is reflected here and in later writings of the New Testament, such as 1 Peter and Revelation.

3. First and Second Timothy and Titus: The Pastorals

With the exception of the brief letter to Philemon, the letters of Paul are all addressed to churches rather than to individuals. The Pastorals, however, are written to individuals: Timothy and Titus. Both the addressees are mentioned elsewhere in the New Testament writings as associates of Paul in his missionary work: Timothy in Acts 16:1 and Titus in Gal. 2:1–3. More important than the difference in the address of these writings, however, is the divergence in vocabulary and attitude between these documents, commonly known as the Pastorals, and the letters of Paul. So different are the vocabulary and the circumstances of the life of the church in these letters from those in the writings of Paul that the modern reader can be certain that these are written in the name of Paul but not by him. They are extremely important for our knowledge of the development and change within the Christian movement, however, since they document basic shifts in the inner life of the church and in its relationship to the wider Greco-Roman culture. Although the exact date of their writing cannot be determined, it is likely that they were written about the year 100 C.E. The continuity of the Pastorals with the Pauline tradition is also evident however, since they not only mention Paul and his associates but also include some of the characteristic themes of Paul's letters: grace toward sinners, Jesus' coming into the world to save them, and his death as a ransom (1 Tim. 1:12–16, 2:6).

The vocabulary of the Pastorals demonstrates the changes that had taken place in the Christian community since the time of Paul. For example, instead of using the term "faith" as a description of the relationship of trust that God expects from humans, the Pastorals speak of "*the* faith," by which the writer means the correct doctrines that are to characterize the Christian religion. There is a "pattern of sound words" (2 Tim. 1:13) or of "sound doctrine" (Titus 2:10) that the leadership of the church is to entrust to those who will teach it faithfully and accurately (2 Tim. 2:2–7). Significantly, this body of correct beliefs is referred to as "our religion" (1 Tim. 3:16), a phrase never found in the letters of Paul but widely used among the religions with which Christianity was in competition as it spread throughout the Mediterranean world. It is not surprising that the author of these pastoral letters substitutes terms that were in common religious use in his era, but which Paul does not employ, such as "epiphany" (divine disclosure) and *palingenesia* (born again). Respectively, these words replace Paul's terms for the coming of Christ at the end of the age and believers' admission by faith into the new covenant community.

Related to these changes in terminology and perspective is the shift to a more abstract representation of Jesus as God's agent for the re-

EPIPHANY

DERIVED FROM A GREEK word that means "to show oneself" or "to manifest one's presence," "epiphany" is a term for the appearance or self-disclosure of a divinity to human beings. It may take the form of a vision or of a divine action, such as a healing. Although in one New Testament text the word is linked with the *parousia* (which refers to Jesus' appearing in triumph at the end of the age), it is found in non-biblical texts that describe mystical experiences in which a divinity is revealed to humans. These revelations are private and personal and are timeless in nature. The preference for this term (instead of *parousia*) as a way of describing the awaited revelation of Jesus as the triumphant Christ fits well with the outlook of the later Christian scriptures, in which interest in the continuing personal revelation of Christ replaces the hope of his imminent public coming as victor over the powers of evil.

demption of his people. When the author speaks of "God our Savior," as he does in 1 Tim. 2:3, he seems to be referring to what Paul would have called "the Father." But in Titus 2:11–13, "God and Savior" is identified as Jesus Christ. The role of Jesus in salvation is called mediator and ransom (1 Tim. 2:5), but there is no direct reference to suffering, crucifixion, or death. Similarly, in 2 Tim. 1:9–10, the purpose of God is said to have been manifested through the appearing (epiphany) of Christ Jesus, who abolished death and brought immortality to light. Once again there is no allusion to the historical events of Jesus birth, suffering, and death, such as we find in Paul's letters. Titus 2:13–14 is similar to these two descriptions of Jesus role as redeemer, but *epiphany* is used in this text for what Paul would call the *parousia,* or the coming of Jesus in triumph at the end of the present age.

The truth of the Christian religion is set out in contrast with false teaching, different doctrines, myths, speculations, and vain discussions proclaimed by those who have "swerved from the truth" (1 Tim. 1:3–7). The gross immorality of their adherents demonstrates that they are not following "sound doctrine" (1 Tim. 1:8–11). The greed, conceit, envy, wrangling, arrogance, gluttony, and deceit with which they go about their religious endeavors match the corruption and wild irresponsibility of their teachings (1 Tim. 6:3–10, 2 Tim. 3:1–9, Titus 1:10–16). Christians are to avoid involvement in these "stupid controversies, . . . dissensions and quarrels, which are unprofitable and futile" (Titus 3:9–11). It is evident from these passages that some claiming adherence to the Christian faith are promoting elaborate mythical speculations, some of them based on Jewish tradition. The author denounces these notions as "godless chatter and contradictions" and disputes the claim of those who peddle these ideas that they have access to true "knowledge" (*gnosis*).

The proper pattern of life is expressed in a term that was common to religions in the Greco-Roman period: *eusebeia,* which means "proper behavior" or "piety." The life of true piety is to be characterized by a pure heart, a good conscience, and sincere faith (1 Tim. 1:5, 2 Tim. 1:3–5). This way of life is handed down from one generation to the next (2 Tim. 1:5). It will manifest itself in gentleness, courtesy toward others, freedom from quarreling, and avoidance of slavery to passions and pleasures (Titus 3:1–3). Just as household vessels in the Jewish tradition were to be kept ritually pure, so members of the church are to exhibit purity of heart and act. The pious include wealthy men and women (1 Tim. 6:17–19) as well as slaves (1 Tim. 6:1–2, Titus 2:9). All are to exhibit this peaceable, gentle, respectable style of life. Their obedience to the Roman civil authorities, combined with the peace and quiet of their lives, will help to enhance the reputation of Christians as respectable citizens (1 Tim. 2:2).

Considerable attention is given in these books to outlining the leadership roles within the community. Specifically mentioned are the offices of bishop and deacon (1 Tim. 3:1–13, Titus 1:5–9). What is called for is gentleness, efficiency of management, and a good reputation among outsiders. There are also assignments of roles to those identified as *presbyters* (male and female) and to widows. The Greek term *presbyteros* could refer simply to older members of the community, but it is at times used to identify certain persons who have leadership functions (1 Tim. 5:17). For example, it was the presbyters as a group who were to bestow the gift of prophetic utterance by laying their hands on the head of the candidate, who would then have this capability (1 Tim. 4:14). Obviously, the community now has the equivalent of modern processes of ecclesiastical ordination by an official body. The extended discussion of the place of widows in the community (1 Tim. 5:3–16) implies that the community will take care of destitute, solitary older widows, but it encourages the younger widows to remarry. Yet the use of what seems to be a technical term, "enroll" (5:9), may indicate that some widows were assigned roles of service within the community, like that of sisters or nuns in the medieval and modern churches.

According to the writer of the Pastorals, the primary responsibility of the church leaders is instruction. Although the roles of apostle and preacher are mentioned (1 Tim. 2:7), the chief function of the writer, who assumes the place of Paul, is that of teacher of the gentiles. Timothy is portrayed here as the prime example of someone who has been reared in such a process of instruction (2 Tim. 3:14–15). It is wholly appropriate, therefore, that the author's instruction to Timothy, which begins as advice about preaching, shifts into counsel and warning about his role as a teacher (2 Tim. 4:1–4). Titus is given similar advice about teaching sound doctrine (Titus 2:1–9), where what is important is not only the content of his instruction but his own mode of life as exemplifying the sound teaching. To characterize the lifestyle that he sees as fitting for Christians, the author uses throughout these letters terms never found in Paul but related to Greek philosophical concepts, such as *sophrosune*, which implies rationality, decency, orderliness. This approach to instruction in the church fits perfectly with what we have already observed about the stress upon and definition of piety.

The letters conclude with some personal remarks and greetings, as do the letters of Paul (2 Tim. 3:10–13, 4:6–13, 19–21; Titus 1:5–9, 3:12–13). In the course of these, reference is made to "Paul's" (the author's) imprisonment and possible martyrdom, and there is mention of several of the associates of Paul known from Acts and from his letters. These are probably included to lend a sense of continuity between the historical Paul and the later developed tradition, as we have it embodied in these letters. Further links with earlier New Testament tradition appear in 2 Tim. 4:11, where Mark and Luke are mentioned. Clearly, the farther the community moves from its origins in the first generation of Jesus' followers, the more important it is to affirm the continuity of the tradition. That continuity is dramatically demonstrated in the observation that Timothy, following in the tradition of his mother and his grandmother, is now a third-generation member of the Christian faith (2 Tim. 1:5).

III. CHRISTIANITY RESPONDS TO FORMATIVE JUDAISM

In the period following the destruction of the temple and the termination by the Roman Empire of even the semblance of local autonomy for Jews in Palestine, Judaism underwent basic changes that were to have enduring effects on Judaism down to the present day. With the fall of Jerusalem in 70 C.E., at least three groups within Judaism seem to have disappeared: (1) the nationalists, who promoted the unsuccessful revolt (although they were to resurface in the second century); (2) the priesthood and the aristocratic families that dominated Palestine politically through their collaboration with Rome and were presumably linked with the Sadducees; (3) the Dead Sea sect, whose community center was ruined by the Roman armies as they passed through that area. The Romans turned to the Pharisees as the one surviving group who had the possibility of establishing a Jewish identity that would be nonpolitical. The evidence for this development is late and largely inferential, but the pattern seems clear: the Pharisaic movement, with its transfer of ritual purity from the temple to the voluntary gatherings in homes and public halls, was ideally suited to provide Jews with an ongoing structure of social and religious identity following the destruction of their priestly and political leadership.

Although the details are unclear, the leaders of the Pharisees are reported in later tradition to have had an extended series of meetings at Yavneh (Jamnia was its Greek name) on the seacoast, not far from modern Tel Aviv. Whatever historical evidence may lie behind this tradition about a council at Jamnia, beginning about 90 C.E. the basic patterns for Jewish piety began to be formulated and the decisions were made about which of the sacred Jewish writings were to be authoritative. The center for this formative movement shifted to Galilee in the second century C.E., perhaps after the failure of the second Jewish revolt against the Romans in 132–5 and the subsequent rebuilding of Jerusalem as a pagan capital, named Aelia Capitolina. Meanwhile, a comparable development began among the Jews who had remained in Babylon instead of returning to Palestine from the Babylonian exile. This process of rethinking and adapting the scriptures and the way of life prescribed there for Jews as the people of God continued for the next five centuries, reaching its climax in the creation of the Mishnah and the Talmuds and the development of patterns for instruction and worship that gave structure and direction for the emergence of the synagogue in its institutional forms. (See Part Two, pp. 288–434.) This formative process of Judaism seems to have been in frequent contact and competition with the emer-gent Christian church. Concrete evidence for this development of competing claims of Jews and Christians about the nature of, and requirements for, identity as God's covenant people is embodied in the Gospel of Matthew.

At the same time, there continued to develop within Judaism certain responses to the tensions that Jews throughout the Greco-Roman world had long felt between their traditions and the alien culture within which they lived. In strongly hellenized centers, such as Alexandria

MISHNAH AND TALMUD

By 200 C.E. THE RABBIS HAD developed an elaborate series of interpretations of Jewish law, some of them based on the scriptures and others deriving from more recent developments in Jewish life in the period following the destruction of the Jerusalem temple in 70 C.E. Rabbi Judah the Prince organized these legal materials into sixty-three tractates, which were grouped under six headings: tithes on agricultural produce, feasts, women and marriage, violations of the rights of others, sacrifice at the temple, and ritual purity. This collection of interpretive material was known as the Mishnah. Obviously the regulations about the long-destroyed temple were purely theoretical, but since so much of the Mosaic law dealt with the temple cultus, it had to be treated in any comprehensive discussion of the legal tradition.

The Talmud was a later development of legal interpretation. Two concurrent projects were launched, one in Palestine and one in Babylonia, where many Jews had continued to live after others had begun to return from the exile in Babylon in the sixth century B.C.E. These collections consist of detailed commentaries, together with comparisons between the various parts of the Mishnah and the written Law of Moses. Although most of the Talmud was written in Aramaic, parts of it that claim to date from the second century C.E. or earlier are in Hebrew. The Palestinian Talmud (fifth century C.E.) consists of discussion of the first four themes of the Mishnah, and the Babylonian Talmud (sixth century C.E.) offers interpretations concerning feasts, women, rights violations, and sacrifices. Since the Mishnah and Talmud are centuries more recent than the New Testament, and since they picture a Judaism with structures and concepts for which there is no evidence in the first century C.E., only a small segment of the material from the Mishnah and Talmud is appropriate as a basis for comparison between Jewish and early Christian interpretation of the laws set out in scripture.

and Antioch, Jewish thinkers developed ways of synthesizing their biblical tradition with the best of pagan philosophical thought, especially the Platonic view of the structure of reality and the Stoic view of moral responsibility. The Christians were attracted to this synthetic approach, as we have seen in the letters of Paul, and as is even more clearly evident in the Letter of James and the Letter to the Hebrews. On the other hand, some Jews continued to hold the apocalyptic view that the world political power (whether the hellenistic monarchs or Rome) was an agency of Satan. They believed God would soon intervene in human history, destroying the powers of evil and vindicating the faithful remnant of his people. The writings known as 2 Esdras and the Book of Enoch (see pp. 335–339), which are not in the Hebrew canon of scripture, incorporate this outlook, as do such New Testament writings as Jude, 2 Peter, and Revelation. We begin our analysis of Christian responses to Judaism in the first century C.E. with a survey of the Gospel of Matthew.

A.   THE GOSPEL OF MATTHEW

This Gospel is anonymous, like the others. When the church in the second century sought to lend authority to its Gospels, it assigned each of them to an apostle or an associate of an apostle. About 130, Papias attributed this Gospel to Matthew (who seems also to have been known as Levi; cf. Matt. 9:9 and Mark 2:13) and claimed that he

Early manuscript of the Gospel of Matthew. This manuscript, which dates from the third century, is written on papyrus, a writing material made from a type of reed that grew abundantly in the Nile Delta. Cut into thin strips and pressed together, papyrus was readily available and surprisingly durable in the dry climate of Egypt. Containing parts of the first chapter of Matthew, this is one of the oldest surviving copies of that book.

University of Pennsylvania.

wrote it in Hebrew. But its author used the Greek Gospel of Mark as a source, and the many scriptural quotations are from the Greek translation rather than directly from the Hebrew Bible. Although we cannot determine who the author was, careful analysis shows us what his concerns were and on what basis he modified and expanded the Gospel tradition. The issues that are central for him reflect the developments described above that were taking place in Judaism around the years 95–100. Those concerns can be grouped under three themes: how God has reconstituted his covenant people; the correct ways to interpret the law and the prophets; and how Jesus is the agent of God to establish his rule over the earth. This Gospel emphasizes both the continuities between Jesus and the biblical tradition and the radically new dimensions of covenantal identity and obligation that God has introduced through Jesus. For convenience we refer to the author and his Gospel as Matthew.

1. The Structure and Method of Matthew's Gospel

More than any of the other Gospels, Matthew seems to have been consciously structured. An introductory section sets forth the origins of Jesus and his links with Jewish tradition (chaps. 1–3). A climactic concluding section describes Jesus' historic fate and divine destiny (chaps. 27–8). In between there are five main sections, each of which begins with a narrative account of Jesus' words and works and ends with a cluster of his teachings, unified in each case by style and content and ending in the stylized phrase "When Jesus had finished . . ." These phrases appear at 7:28, 11:1, 13:53, 19:1, and 26:1. The resulting structure is as follows:

Chaps. 1–2   The divine origins of Jesus

Chaps. 3–25   The words and works of Jesus in preparation for the new covenant community:

Narrative	Discourse
Chaps. 3–4	Chaps. 5–7 (Sermon on the Mount)
Chaps. 8–9	Chap. 10 (commissioning of the Twelve Disciples)
Chaps. 11–12	Chap. 13 (parables of the kingdom)
Chaps. 14–17	Chap. 18 (rules of the community)
Chaps. 19–22	Chaps. 24–5 (apocalyptic instruction)

Chaps. 26–8   The divine destiny of Jesus and his followers

The fivefold structure of the middle section recalls the five books of Moses. This inference is confirmed by the explicit contrast between Jesus' rules for his people and those given by Moses in the first discourse (Matt. 5:21, 27, 31, 33, 38, 43). Just as Moses went up on the mountain to give instruction to God's people (Deut. 8:1–2), so Jesus repeatedly in Matthew ascends a mountain to inform God's new people and to manifest his divine authority (Matt. 4:8; 5:1; 14:23; 15:29, 39; 17:1; 28:19–20). In Jesus' sketch of his people's responsibility to God in this gospel there is a distinctive emphasis on true righteousness, in contrast to that of the Pharisaic tradition (3:15; 5:6, 10, 20; 6:1, 33). That theme is most fully developed in a discourse section that does not fit the pattern sketched above in our outline and that may have been added to an earlier form of the gospel as the hostility between Matthew's community and the Pharisees intensified (Matt. 23).

The divine purpose at work through Jesus is apparent in the opening section of the gospel, where Jesus' geneaology is traced back to Abraham (the progenitor of the covenant people) through David (Israel's king and model for the future rule of God) and through the historical period of Israel's judgment, the exile (Matt. 1:2, 6, 12). The claim that Israel's history developed in a sequence of epochs covering fourteen generations in each stage (1:17) is presented as further evidence of a divine scheme. As in Dan. 2:2, the divine purpose is disclosed to the characters in the drama through dreams – not only to

Mary and Joseph and the wise men (1:20; 2:12, 13, 19, 22) but, in the concluding section, to Pilate's wife as well (27:19). A second mode of communication of God's purpose for his people takes the form of the private explanations that Jesus offers to his followers about his teachings.

Confirmation that God's plan is being achieved through Jesus is offered to the faithful by Matthew's pervasive allusions to, or quotations from, the Jewish scriptures. There is a formula of fulfillment in which each event is portrayed as having taken place "in order to fulfill what was spoken . . ." (or similar phraseology) in Matt. 2:15, 17–18, 23; 4:14–16; 8:17; 12:17–21; 13:14–15, 35; 24:4–5; 27:9–10. At times Matthew

Nazareth. High in the hills near Sepphoris, the seat of government in Galilee in the first century C.E., is Nazareth. Crossing the more level land below were the major highways north and south, east and west, connecting with Damascus in the north, the cities along the Sea of Galilee and farther east, the seaports to the west, and Jericho and Jerusalem to the south. Although Sepphoris is not mentioned in the New Testament, it would have served as the economic and occupational center for the outlying village of Nazareth.

Matson Photo Service.

shapes the quotation to fit his aim, as in his claim that the scriptures predicted Jesus' living in Nazareth, whereas the Hebrew Bible never mentions Nazareth but has two non-local terms: *nezer*, which refers to a special consecration to God (Num. 6:2–21, Lev. 21:12), and *netzer*, which means "shoot" (Isa. 11:1, 53:2). Elsewhere Matthew shapes the events he reports in order to make them fit his understanding of scripture, as when he describes Jesus riding into Jerusalem on two animals, since two are mentioned in scripture (Matt. 21:7, Zech. 9:9). The aim is clear, and the method matches that of Jewish interpreters in that period: the interpreter of scripture is interested in what it means in his own situation, not what it meant in the time of the writer.

2. The New Law for the New People of God (Matt. 4–7)

Building on both the Markan narrative and features from the Q source, Matthew portrays Jesus as the authoritative Son of God, whose identity is publicly affirmed at his baptism (Matt. 3:17). The gentile participation in God's people is shown to have scriptural precedent in the days of Elijah and Elisha (4:13–16). According to Matt. 4:23–5, Jesus' reputation as healer is depicted as having spread at the outset of his ministry throughout the whole of Galilee, Judea (Colorplate 22), and the hellenistic cities east of the Jordan (the Decapolis). Yet the first instructions are addressed, not to the crowds that flocked to him to see and experience his healings, but to his disciples as the original core of the new people of God (5:1). Instead of the direct, immediate address of the Q tradition ("Blessed are you poor"; Luke 6:20), Matthew reports Jesus as uttering generalized and spiritualized teachings: "Blessed are the poor in spirit . . ." (5:3). For Matthew the emphasis also shifts from the expectation of future fulfillment ("Blessed are you who hunger now: you shall be satisfied"; Luke 6:21) to the promise of entering now into a share in the blessings of God's rule. As a result, we have the picture of a community hoping for future fulfillment but prepared for an extended period in its present mode of existence.

Meanwhile, the community is given a series of interpretations of the biblical code of law on subjects that continued to be important for Jews but that are now redefined for the members of the new community. Matthew contrasts the norms of Pharisaic piety with those that are to be binding on the Christian community in an array of subjects: basic relations with others, sexual behavior and divorce, oaths, nonretaliation, love of enemies, almsgiving, prayer, fasting, possessions, anxiety, judging others (5:21). Jesus is portrayed by Matthew as approaching these moral issues, not in terms of what is legally required or permissible, but in terms of what is the responsible way of relating to God and one's fellow human beings. This constitutes for Matthew the true righteousness, which fulfills the intention of God for his people through the law and the prophets (5:17–20).

3. Preparing the Disciples for Their Mission (Matt. 8–10)

Building on the Markan tradition about the sending out of the twelve disciples (Mark 3:13–19, 6:1–11), Matthew has used the Q source, as well as adding his own distinctive material, to give an extended picture of Jesus commissioning his followers to carry forward his mission. In Matthew 8–9 there is a mixture of private instruction for the disciples and demonstration that those who by the standards of Pharisaic piety are outsiders have access to the healing and forgiving power of God through Jesus. The transition passage (Matt. 7:28–9) announces that, in contrast to the Pharisaic scribes, who had to quote authorities to back up their interpretations of the law, Jesus *had* authority. This authority is evidenced dramatically in his stilling the storm, on which occasion his followers address him as "Lord" (*kurios*), which already as early as the time of Paul had become a confessional title for Jesus (Phil. 2:9–10). Yet he also is seen as having taken on the authoritative role of teacher, since his critics object to his setting aside the ritual food laws in order to eat with outsiders (Matt. 9:11).

The exclusive sphere in which the disciples are to carry out their mission is "the lost sheep of the house of Israel" (Matt. 10:6). This phrase does not mean that all historic Israel is lost, but that there is a place among God's people for those Jews who are beyond the bounds of the Pharisaic standards for religious acceptability. It is these people, as we have already seen, who are portrayed in Matthew as the special objects of Jesus' concern. The advice to the messengers is that they are to carry forward the work which Jesus had begun: heal the sick, raise the dead, cleanse the lepers, cast out demons (10:8). They are to go out dependent solely on the hospitality that is offered them in the cities and villages they visit in the course of their mission. The destiny of the inhabitants of each place will depend on their response to Jesus' messengers (10:9–15, 40–2). The disciples are to be prepared for opposition, suffering, martyrdom, and violent hostility, even from the members of their own families (10:16–39).

4. Defining the New Community (Matt. 11–13)

The next narrative section depicts Jesus engaged in this healing activity, encountering opposition from the Pharisees as he opens his fellowship to gentiles. His inclusiveness is defended by a quotation from scripture (Matt. 12:18–21 = Isa. 42:1–4) and by an appeal to examples of gentile faith in the time of Jonah and Solomon (Matt. 12:38–42). Drawing on a tradition from Mark (Mark 3:31–5), Matthew quotes Jesus as redefining membership in the family of God in such a way as to eliminate all ethnic or ritual requirements (Matt. 12:46–50).

Even though Jesus is pictured as presenting his parables to the "great crowds" (13:2), it is only to the inner circle of his followers that he gives the essential interpretations of them (13:10–17). In addition to the basic point of the Markan parables about the mixed but ultimately astounding results of the proclamation of the gospel, Matthew adds parables that make a different point: that the new community which is in process of formation will include among its members both those who are worthy and those who are not. These are the good and bad seed (13:24–30), the weeds and the wheat (13:36–43), as the private explanation makes clear (13:47–50). The point is that the Christian community will include both suitable and unfit members, but the process of sorting them out is God's business at the end of the age.

5. Guidelines for the New Community (Matt. 14–18)

After the characteristic transition passage ("when Jesus had finished . . ."; 13:53), Matthew presents additional examples of how the gospel will reach outsiders (14:1–15:39) and the ensuing conflict with the Jewish religious leaders (16:1–4). These are followed by Peter's confession of Jesus as the Messiah, which is expanded significantly from the Markan source (Mark 8:27–33; Matt. 16:13–23). Peter's messianic identification of Jesus includes the phrase "the Son of the living God" (16:16) and elicits from Jesus an indication of the source of this belief. But it then goes on to speak of Peter (or perhaps his confession) as the rock on which the church will be built, and to promise that this new community will prevail in spite of opposition from the evil powers. And further, Peter will be given the crucial authority to include or exclude those who seek to join this new people (16:18–19). Peter's insight is confirmed within the week (17:1) by the experience at the transfiguration of Jesus and the heavenly testimony to him as God's Son (17:5). Unlike Mark (9:6), there is no comment in Matthew that the disciples did not understand the significance of these events.

Meanwhile, there is to be no hostility toward the Roman state. Christians are to meet the demands of the state, whether for assistance in providing transportation (5:41) or in paying the tax to the Roman state that had been collected for support of the Jerusalem temple but that now supported the shrine to Jupiter built in its place (17:24–7). God will provide what is necessary to meet these human obligations. Paying taxes to Caesar is confirmed later in Matt. 22:15–22 as well.

The discourse passage that brings to a close this section of Matthew includes detailed instructions for the members of the new community: the image of childlikeness (18:1–4); the need to nurture the members (18:5–6); the avoidance of temptation (18:7–9); the necessity of restoring members who stray (18:10–14); and the informal (18:15–16) and formal (18:17–20) procedures for settling disputes within the church. The section ends with advice (18:21–3) and a parable (18:23–35) about the importance of forgiveness for the health of the community.

It is highly significant that only in Matthew is the church alluded to as such. The new community is referred to in Matthew and the other gospels by metaphors, such as "flock" (Matt. 26:31, Luke 12:32, John 10:16). But Matthew alone quotes Jesus as referring to the new community as "church," with indications of its growth and structure ("on this rock I will build my church" (Matt. 16:18) and of the decision-making process that will go on in this new institution (Matt. 18:15–18). These passages show that this gospel is meant to serve as a guidebook for the church as it develops institutional form and function, enabling it to understand its origins and its ongoing responsibilities.

6. Vindication for Jesus and the New Community; Judgment on the Old Covenant People (Matt. 19–25)

Related concerns occupy the next section, following the transition in Matt. 19:1: attitudes toward sex and marriage, including divorce and remarriage as well as abstinence from sexual life (19:1–12). Attitudes toward children (19:13–15) and wealth (19:16–30) appear once more. A parable unique to Matthew (20:1–16) deals with the church's problem with seeming inequality of responsibility and reward among members by declaring flatly that God's sovereign decisions are not subject to human review. The disciples are shielded by Matthew from seeming to vie for positions of power in the new age (as they do in Mark 10:35–41) by having the mother of the sons of Zebedee make the request for places of special honor for them (Matt. 20:20–8). As he does in Matt. 8:28–34 and 9:27–31, Matthew increases the miraculous feature of Jesus' activity by reporting that he healed not one but two blind men as he passed through Jericho (20:29–34; cf. Mark 10:46–52).

The issues about Jesus' claim to be king are much more explicit in Matthew than in Mark, as is the prediction of God's judgment on historic Israel. The formula quotation ("this took place to fulfill what was spoken by the prophet") from Zech. 9:9 and Isa. 62:11 in Matt. 21:4–5 is followed by the direct identification of Jesus as king (21:9) and as the prophet (21:11) – presumably the one expected at the end of the age (Deut. 18:15–18), who, like Moses, performs signs and wonders (Deut. 34:10–12). Matthew returns to the issue of the source of Jesus' authority in cleansing the temple (21:12–13), in healing the blind and the lame (21:14–17), and in cursing the fig tree (i.e., historic Israel; 21:18–22). The basic question here is, Who authorizes and empowers Jesus to carry out his work: God or some evil power? A corollary question is, Who are the true heirs of God's promises to his covenant people?

These issues become explicit in the interchange reported in Matt. 21:23–7. Its implications for reconstituting God's people are evident in a series of parables, including the parable of the two sons, where the climax comes in the prediction that tax collectors and harlots will enter the kingdom (21:28–32), and the parable of the vineyard workers, where the point is explicit that the kingdom will be taken from its traditional heirs and given to a new nation, that is, the church (21:43). Matthew offers a different version of the Q-source parable of the guests invited to a feast (Matt. 22:1–14, Luke 14:16–24), in which Israel is depicted as rejecting and killing God's messengers, with the result that the king (God) destroys their city (Jerusalem) and now invites all manner of people to enjoy the feast. Yet when the feast takes place, those who are not properly attired (i.e., clothed in true righteousness) will be expelled and brought under judgment.

Beginning at Matt. 22:23 and extending through chapter 23, we find a series of controversies between Jesus and the Jewish interpreters of scripture on such subjects as resurrection (22:23–33), the priority among the commandments (22:34–40), and the identity of the Messiah (22:41–5). In these Matthew largely follows Mark. But from 23:1–36 we have a series of bitter attacks on the Pharisees, in which they are denounced as religious show-offs (23:1–12), as more zealous in making converts to Judaism than in living in true obedience to God (23:13–15), and as evading the clear import of the law by subtle tactics (23:16–28). The climax of the section comes in the charge that the Jewish people have always rejected and even put to death the messengers of God, from the beginning (Genesis) to the end (2 Chronicles) of their scriptures (Matt. 23:29–36). God is about to judge them for their refusal to hear his messengers, including Jesus, who is seen by Matthew as the fulfillment of the messianic hope expressed in Ps. 118:26 (quoted in Matt. 23:39).

The details of these impending judgments are spelled out in Matthew's extended version of the Markan apocalyptic discourse (Matt. 24–5), which (as in Mark 13) is spoken on the Mount of Olives overlooking Jerusalem. Only here do we find predictions of the difficulties within the community caused by the emergence of false prophets and of hatred, lawlessness, and indifference among the members of the group (24:9–14). Similarly, Matthew adds to the Q-source parable about the servants who misbehave when their master delays his return (Luke 12:42–6) the prediction of the weeping and gnashing of teeth that the unfaithful will experience in the Day of Judgment (24:45–51). In addition to the Markan tradition about the certainty that the end of the age is near (Mark 13:28–32, Matt. 24:32–6), Matthew has

Mount of Olives. East of Jerusalem, the Mount of Olives stretches for nearly a mile north and south. This ridge is part of the main range of mountains running through central and southern Judea. From the crest of the ridge is a superb westward view across the Kidron Valley to the central part of Jerusalem. To the east can be seen the deep cleft in which the Jordan flows as it empties into the Dead Sea. Towns located on the southern end of the Mount of Olives are Bethphage and Bethany, which are linked in the Gospels with Jesus and his followers (Mark 11:1; Luke 19:21; John 11:1, 18). H.C. Kee.

TALENTS AND MINAS (POUNDS)

TWO DIFFERENT KINDS OF coins are mentioned in the two versions of the parable in Matt. 25:14–30 and Luke 19:12–27. According to Luke, the money given to the slaves by the nobleman was a *mina*, which was equal to 100 drachmas (in Greek coinage) or about $20 in American money, which has been estimated at three months' wages for a laborer. The *talent* in Matthew's account was worth more than $1,000 in Greek coinage, so that the responsibility placed on the slaves in this version is far heavier.

---

the distinctive parable of the ten maidens (25:1–13), with its point about the need for being prepared for the bridegroom's delayed return, and the parable of the talents (adapted from Q; Luke 19:12–27), which shows that responsible stewardship is necessary when the master at last (25:19) returns and calls his servants to account (25:14–30). The discourse ends with the pageantlike depiction of the judgment at the end of the age, when the nations of the world are accepted or condemned by one criterion: how they responded to the messengers ("the little ones") whom Jesus had sent to work and witness among them. In accepting or rejecting these representatives of Christ they had accepted or rejected him (25:31–46).

7.   The Destiny of Jesus and God's New People (Matt. 26–8)

The final transitional phrase (26:1) brings the reader to Matthew's account of Jesus' experience of human rejection and divine vindication (chaps. 26–8). The basic pattern of the narrative is that of Mark 14–16, but there are significant supplements and changes in detail, many of which reflect the tensions between the church and Judaism. In 26:2, 53–6, there is a direct prediction of Jesus' death and of his impending vindication by God, in accord with the scripture (possibly Ps. 91:11 or the vision of Elijah in 2 Kings 6:17). Judas' gruesome death and the payment he received for his betrayal are seen by Matthew to fulfill the scripture (Matt. 27:3–10; cf. Zech. 11:12–13, Jer. 32:7). The judgment on Judas, the earthquake that occurs at the moment of Jesus' death (27:51–3), and the descent of the angel and the earthquake at the tomb of Jesus (28:2) are for Matthew signs of God's direct involvement in the career of Jesus and the outworking of the divine purpose through him. Pilate's washing his hands in public (27:24–6), combined with the Jewish acceptance of responsibility for the death of Jesus, shifts the blame from Rome to the Jews. The report of the disciples' having stolen the body of Jesus is also attributed to the Jewish leaders (28:11–15).

Matthew has basically altered the Markan story of the empty tomb (Mark 16:1–8) and has provided details of the promised appearances of Jesus to his followers. The supernatural features are heightened by Matthew, and the instructions for the disciples are more explicit than in Mark. Both these features reflect the growing sense in the church of the importance of divine confirmation of the claims made concerning Jesus as the Messiah and divine agent of renewal of God's people. The women who go to prepare the body of Jesus experience an earthquake, and the message they hear about Jesus' having been raised from the dead is not from a "young man" as in Mark but from an angel who comes down to them from heaven (28:2–8). This is confirmed by an appearance of Jesus to the women on their way back to the city from the tomb (28:9–10) and then by his meeting the disciples (significantly, on a mountain) in Galilee (28:16–20). In this post-resurrection encounter between Jesus and the disciples, the emphasis is on two themes: (1) the authority with which Jesus sends forth his disciples and (2) their obligation to carry out a worldwide program of instruction in the commandments that Jesus has given them. The members of this new community of disciples from all nations are united by the rite of baptism, by the trinitarian confession with which that rite is performed, and by the members' obedience to Jesus' commands. The combination of community definition over against emergent rabbinic Judaism, of regulations for members' behavior and for the internal processes of the organization, and of prescriptions for liturgical practice provide clear evidence that the Gospel of Matthew was intended to serve as a constitution for the emerging institution: the church.

B. THE LETTER TO THE HEBREWS: REINTERPRETING THE JEWISH HERITAGE IN TERMS DERIVING FROM HELLENISTIC CULTURE

In the last century B.C.E. and the first century C.E., there were Jews who sought to make connections between the philosophical and literary traditions of the hellenistic culture and the Jewish tradition. The Book of 4 Maccabees, with its retelling of the struggle of the Jews for freedom from the Seleucids (see pp. 404–405), pictures these events as exercises in the Stoic virtues of courage and perseverance. The Jewish philosopher and interpreter of scripture Philo of Alexandria describes the experiences of the patriarchs and the establishing of the central cult of ancient Israel in allegorical terms, using Platonic ideas of God and assuming compatibility between knowledge of God as set forth in scripture and as gained through human achievement in Greek philosophy. It is not surprising, therefore, that the Christians of the later first century should take their cue from this intellectual precedent

PHILO OF ALEXANDRIA

PHILO, A WEALTHY AND learned Jew of Alexandria, lived from 30 B.C.E. until 40 C.E. His energies were devoted to interpreting the five books of Moses (Genesis through Deuteronomy) in such a way as to show by allegorical method the basic compatibility of Greek philosophy and biblical understanding. The migration of Abraham from Ur of the Chaldees to Hebron in what became the land of Israel, for example, he interpreted as an allegory of the seeking soul who moves from the realm of shadowy perceptions of reality to direct encounter with an illumination by the light of God. This corresponds to the Platonic vision of the flight of the soul from the physical world, subject to decay and misperceptions, through the world of the forms (or ideas), where the fundamental principles of the universe are discerned, to the direct vision of the divine. Philo believed that Plato had these insights into truth and the proper mode of apprehending it because he had access to the writings of Moses. Philo's method of interpreting scripture and his striving to correlate philosophical wisdom and the truth contained in the scriptures set the pattern followed chiefly by Christian scholars in Alexandria in the second and third centuries C.E.

in Judaism and conceive their own heritage as a synthesis of biblical tradition and hellenistic philosophy. A prime example of this development within early Christianity is the Letter to the Hebrews.

Although this document has often been called "Paul's Letter to the Hebrews," it is almost certainly not a letter and was not written by Paul, nor was it addressed primarily to Hebrews. It is, however, a highly important work that helped recast the Christian tradition along lines that made possible its communication to the intellectually trained minds of the Roman world. The Letter to the Hebrews builds throughout on the Jewish biblical tradition and contrasts what God has done and is doing through Christ for his new people with the experiences recounted in the Jewish Bible. Because from the beginning of the church all Christians used the biblical tradition, this line of argument was probably not directed especially toward Jews or even Jewish Christians but served to provide a framework for appreciating that tradition while showing that in Christ, God has transcended the old covenant and transformed his covenant people.

The fact that this is not a letter is apparent from the absence of the conventions of letter writing (identification of the writer and the recipients, personal greetings), except for a brief note at the end (13:22–5). Throughout the writing there are references to speaking and hearing (2:5; 5:11; 6:9; 9:5; 10:25, 32; 12:4), and in 13:22 the author describes what he has presented as a "word of exhortation." It is possible, therefore, that what we have in this "letter" is a transcription of a formal speech, to which the personal greetings were later appended. The writing probably achieved its present form in the late first or early second century.

The strategy of the work is that of Greco-Roman oratory, in which the speaker alternates between providing information or insights to his hearers and exhorting them to change their way of life. The first example of this tactic is evident when we compare the affirmations of 1:1–14 with the exhortations of 2:1–4. The basis of the moral appeal is a mixture of lessons from the past activity of God in the world and among his people and reminders of the new network of relationships that God has created among his new covenant people. This method of reinterpretation of the biblical tradition closely resembles what other Jewish writers of the hellenistic–Roman period were doing – most notably Philo of Alexandria, who employed basic insights from Platonic and Stoic philosophy to reinterpret the law of Moses and the experiences of the patriarchs of Israel. Similarly, the author of the Wisdom of Solomon (see pp. 406–407) retells the story of creation and the history of Israel by the use of philosophical categories adapted from the hellenistic culture. Basic to the argument of Hebrews is the language commonly used by philosophically oriented writers of the period – for example, *hypodeigma,* "pattern" (4:11, 8:5, 9:23); and *hypostasis,* "substance" (1:3, 3:14, 11:11).

The basic claim of Hebrews is that the historical experiences and the laws that God has given to Israel offer valuable but imperfect copies of the ideal modes and principles by which he is working to accomplish through Jesus Christ his purpose for his people and the whole of the creation. The philosophy of Plato contrasted the earthly, temporary, imperfect copies of objects, ideas, and experiences with their heavenly, eternal models or ideals. Employing this same view of reality, the author contrasts the imperfect copies of the instruments and procedures for approaching God and gaining right relationship with him as perceived in historical Israel with the eternal mode of access to and acceptance by God as revealed and accomplished through Jesus. The full disclosure of the timeless model of the sanctuary is yet to occur, but true faith is able to see in Jesus the heavenly reality. The author has combined basic aspects of the Platonic contrast between the eternal realm of the ideal and the transitory nature of human existence with the Jewish concept of eschatology, which contrasts the divine disclosure of purpose in the past and the future achievement of that purpose. Without abandoning the fundamentally historical orientation of the biblical writers, the author has been able to incorporate this perspective on the purpose of God for his people into a philosophically sophisticated framework. The later intellectual leaders of the church, such as Origen of Alexandria (186–253 C.E.) and Augustine of Hippo (354–430 C.E.), developed in their own way this method of combining biblical insights and philosophical understanding.

The argument of the work proceeds by alternating between setting forth information and insights and exhorting the hearers (or readers) to accept their appropriate responsibilities. The information in each case concerns Jesus and God's special role for him in the renewal of the creation and the establishment of the new covenant people. The first claim made concerning Jesus is that as Son of God, he is superior to the angels (Heb. 1:2–2:18). As Son of God, he is worshiped by the angels (1:4–5); they are servants of God, but Jesus is God's anointed Son, the agent of creation and redemption of the world. They pass away; he remains forever (1:6–11). Yet for a little while, Jesus was made lower than the angels, in order for him to identify fully with human beings in suffering and death; now he has been crowned with glory and honor (2:5–9; cf. Ps. 8:4–6). He is the leader, the prototype of the people of God, and through him the unity and the sanctity of his people will be accomplished (2:5–11). In the midst of this new community (ekklesia) Jesus proclaims the name of God (2:12; cf. Ps. 22:12). It is important to note that the psalms are quoted here from the Greek version, which in the passage quoted in Heb. 2:7 differs widely from the Hebrew original ("you have made them a little lower than God"), but in Heb. 2:12 follows closely the Hebrew original of Ps. 22:23.

Before continuing with his demonstration of Jesus' superiority to other factors and persons in the biblical tradition, the author turns to exhortation: how are the new people of God to act in this new situation? The answer, given in various ways, is that they are to hold fast what they have received, the message first spoken by Jesus and his way of life, which have now been confirmed by those who heard him (Heb. 2:1–3). Thereby they can avoid the punishment that befell the disobedient angels.

The second aspect of Jesus' superiority is his role as high priest, which occupies the whole central section of the work: Heb. 3:1–6,

MELCHIZEDEK

MELCHIZEDEK IS IDENTIFIED in Gen. 14:17–20 as king of Salem (Jerusalem) and priest of "God Most High" when Abraham was dwelling in Hebron (Gen. 13:18). Melchizedek's blessing of Abraham is understood in Ps. 110:4 as the model for the dual role of the kings of Israel as monarch and priest. They rule as God's chosen agents and they serve as the intermediary between God and his people. The passage from Ps. 110 is quoted in Heb. 5:20, where the promise of an eternal priesthood is interpreted in the Platonic mode: the lack of mention of ancestors or descendants of Melchizedek is understood to mean that he is from the realm of eternity (Heb. 7:3). This eternal priesthood is the model for the royal priesthood of Jesus (Heb. 7:11–28).

4:14–5:10, 7:1–10:17. Interspersed throughout this section are exhortations and warnings to the people. Moses foresaw that God would build a house; Christ is the Son given authority over the "house," which is the new covenant people (3:1–6). With full understanding of human frailty, Jesus has already entered the presence of God on behalf of his people (4:14–16). He has no need to offer sacrifice for himself or to seek appointment as priest, since he was appointed by God and will serve in this role forever, as both king and high priest, like Melchizedek (Ps. 110:4), in total obedience to the will of God.

The inadequacy of the Levitical priesthood is evident in that they had to repeat their offerings continually, which could never bring their people to holiness and perfection. Jesus' self-offering is the perfect sacrifice, once and for all (Heb. 7:15–28). And it was presented in the *true* tent; that is, in the ideal, or archetypal, dwelling place of God in heaven rather than in the earthly tent, which is an imperfect copy of that eternal reality of God's presence (8:1–2, 9:11–28). It purifies, not the externals, but the *conscience* – a concept that the author has taken over from Stoicism, as we have seen that Paul did in explaining how those who never knew the law of Moses are aware, through the law of nature, of what human behavior should be. This is the new reality of which Jeremiah spoke in his prophecy of the new covenant (Heb. 8:3–13, Jer. 31:31–4). Jesus' perfect sacrifice has ratified the new covenant; his appearance at the end of the age will attest the completion of his covenantal work in the presence of God (9:1–28). Once more the author presents contrasts between the inadequate old covenant (10:1–4) and the perfect, true covenant that has been established through the death and exaltation of Jesus (10:5–14).

Under the new covenant a whole series of new resources are open to God's new people, as well as some solemn warnings (10:19–39):

10:20	A new way to God
10:22	The conscience made clean
10:23	The hope of ultimate deliverance from sin
10:24	The new commandment: love one another
10:25	The ongoing practice of the community meeting, for mutual encouragement in light of the coming Day of the Lord
10:26–31	The necessity to avoid the fate of the apostates, who failed to repent
10:32–9	The necessity to persevere in the face of mistreatment, confident in the words of warning and promise from the prophet Habakkuk (2:3–4)

Faith, therefore, is not only confidence in the unseen realm of the ideal, heavenly reality; it is also enduring trust as the ground of daily living.

Chapter 11 of Hebrews lists the great figures of the biblical tradition of Israel who are paradigms of faith, including Noah, Abraham, Jacob, Joseph, Moses, and the Israelites at Jericho. The summary statement about the faith of the people in the biblical narratives appears in Heb. 11:32–8, where the confidence in God that characterized his people and their leaders was sustained, not only in times of triumph, but in periods of severe testing through which they passed. In the face of threats and painful trials, they sometimes experienced deliverance, but at other times martyrdom. But whether confronted by joy or suffering, they all displayed confidence in God and his promises. That trust remained even though the ultimate promise was not fulfilled for them, since God had a future agent by whom his purpose for his people was to be achieved: Jesus, the primary agent and guarantor of faith (12:1–2). God has already vindicated him, by seating him at his right hand in glory.

It is this Jesus who is to be the model for the people of God (Heb. 12:3). But there are warnings about incurring divine judgment if there is rebellion or disobedience in response to the disciplinary trials that the people are called to endure prior to their final deliverance (12:3–29). Further, there is a series of moral injunctions that the people are to obey (13:1–22):

13:1–3	Mutual love and concern
13:4	Integrity in marriage
13:5	Avoidance of greed
13:7	Remembrance and emulation of the faith of former leaders
13:9	Avoidance of unnecessary rules, such as food laws
13:10–13	Preparedness to accept rejection and scorn
13:15–16	Making the appropriate offerings of praise to God and generosity to others
13:17	Obedience to leaders, who are accountable to God
13:18	Praying for the author (= "us")
13:19	Praying for his speedy return to the hearers or readers of his message
13:20	Heeding his message of encouragement

Interspersed through these exhortations are reminders of the basis for what the author regards as true faith: the eternal, unchangeable Jesus Christ (13:8) and the promise of the "city" that is to come (13:14). In conclusion, there is the solemn prayer, in developed liturgical form. The ultimate source of action in all this is God, who is working to achieve true peace in the creation. The agent whose self-sacrifice ratified the new covenant is Jesus, whom God attested by raising him from the dead. God is now at work among his people, enabling them to do what is pleasing to him, and again the agent of this saving activity is Jesus Christ, who is to be glorified forever (13:20–1).

The work as we have it concludes with personal greetings to the members of the community and to their leaders, with special mention of Timothy, who has just been released from prison, and with special greetings from "those from Italy," which may mean that the writer is in Italy or that a group of Italian expatriates are sending greetings back to the recipients of this message.

Whatever the date and specific circumstances of this letter, the church is confronted with the prospect of suffering persecution and expects to undergo trials similar to those experienced by the faithful in historic Israel. At the same time, the church is facing intellectual challenges concerning what it proclaims as the truth. These challenges arise from Jewish thinkers, who are developing interpretations of

THE CITY

THROUGHOUT THE HISTORY of the ancient Middle East, cities rose and fell as symbols and centers of political and military power, for which divine authority was claimed. As a nomadic people, the early Israelites had no significant role in urban life until David and Solomon established Jerusalem as the royal capital of Israel, with its temple as the earthly dwelling place of Yahweh. In the hellenistic period the Greek concept of *polis* (city) became a major factor in the shaping of human existence. Each city dominated its region and was characterized by a diversity of roles and institutions essential for the common life: food supply, crafts, marketplace, municipal authorities (including a council of leading citizens), public entertainment in theaters, and central places of worship. Impressive colonnades, temples, towers, and gates gave the city the image of wealth, power, and stability. Greek and Roman philosophers, most notably Plato (in the *Republic*) and Aristotle, regarded the city in its stability and diversity as a symbol and model for human existence, with the hope for achievement of enduring beauty and justice. The early Christians utilized this model of the city in diverse ways: the author of Revelation developed his vision of the ultimate hope for God's people in terms of a city conceived in apocalyptic terms; the author of Hebrews projects a model involving the philosophical distinction between temporal and eternal, with the city of God as image for the fulfillment of God's purpose.

scripture as confirmation of the move toward consolidation of what was to become rabbinic Judaism, but also from Greco-Roman intellectuals, who were probably scornful of the Christian claim concerning possession of the truth about the nature and purpose of God. In response to this configuration of issues, the author's prescription for the needs of the readers/hearers is faith: focus on the unchanging, eternal realities of the sacrifice of Christ, the true sanctuary, where Jesus is with God, and the true covenant people, who are thereby brought into existence as the new "house of God." This will enable them to challenge their conceptual critics and to remain firm while enduring hardship, hostility, even martyrdom. By persevering they can be sure of sharing one day in the life of the eternal city of God (Heb. 11:13–16).

C. JUDE AND 2 PETER: THE CONTINUING INFLUENCE OF JEWISH APOCALYPTIC

1. Jude

Among the characteristic features of Jewish apocalyptic literature are (1) a sense of urgency about warning the true and faithful group concerning the error and corruption that are rampant in the larger religious community, (2) advice to the faithful as to how they are to endure until the end of the age comes, and (3) reassurance of God's continuing support. All these elements are present in the little letter of Jude.

The authority of this late-first-century writer is reinforced by his being linked with James – presumably the brother of Jesus who presided over the Jerusalem church in the time of Paul (Gal. 1:19). This seems to be evidence that in some parts of the church, hereditary links with Jesus were important for leadership roles – in contrast to Paul's view, for whom the single requirement was to have been commissioned by the risen Jesus (1 Cor. 9:1).

The main body of the letter consists of a series of warnings about those who have abandoned the true faith and a string of vivid characterizations of these apostates. Analogies are pointed out between various groups in the biblical history who forfeited their place as God's people: the first generation of Israelites who escaped from Egypt in the Exodus but whose disobedience led to their death in the desert (Jude 5); the angels who exploited their powers and fell from favor with God (Jude 6); the inhabitants of Sodom and Gomorrah, whose indulgence in immorality and sexual perversion brought down destruction on the people and their land (Jude 7). Like these horrible examples of self-indulgence and disobedience, those who have now fallen away from the faith have defiled themselves, dishonored God and the angels, and taken authority to themselves in a way that not even the archangels would dare to do (Jude 8–10). They follow the example of the self-willed and rejected of Israel's past – Cain, Balaam, and Korah (Gen. 4:3, Num. 22–4; Num. 16) – and they will share similar destruction at the hand of God. The assurance that God will render to them the punishment they deserve is given through a quotation from the Book of Enoch (see pp. 335–338), which deplores the irreligion of these people. They are described as "grumblers, malcontents, passion-driven, loud-mouthed boasters, flattering people to gain advantage" (Jude 14–16). The fact that Enoch is quoted as scripture reminds us that this book was highly regarded in Jewish circles of the first century, as the discovery of quantities of fragments of the Enoch literature among the Dead Sea Scrolls attests. Its use here in Jude also indicates that the decisions as to which of the Jewish writings were to be considered authoritative by Jews – and by Christians – had not yet been firmly reached.

The author notes that there should be no surprise that the ranks of God's people have been infiltrated by the unworthy and disobedient: the apostles had given warning of this (Jude 17–19). This appeal to apostolic authority is an indication that Jude has been written a generation after the apostles have passed, when the church needed to ground its authority in the past. Meanwhile, the leaders of the church are to build up the true members in the true faith, urging them to pray in the Spirit, to manifest the love of God, and to await the ultimate manifestation of God's mercy and the entrance into eternal life that will bring to a close the present age (Jude 21). The best that can be hoped for is that some of the waverers on the border between the faithful and the apostates may be kept from the fires of destruction. Yet even as the true believers act with a mix of fear and mercy, they need to despise the corruption that the borderline cases have been carrying with them (Jude 22). The letter ends with a beautiful liturgical ascription of glory to God, who through Jesus Christ is able to preserve his people from disobedience and apostasy (Jude 24–5).

2.   Second Peter

One of the most remarkable features of 2 Peter is that it paraphrases or quotes thirteen verses from Jude (cf. Jude 4–16 with 2 Pet. 2:1–18). The author, writing in the name of Peter, shares the basic apocalyptic outlook of Jude but has modified Jude in significant details. He deals directly with the problem of the delay in the fulfillment of the expectation expressed by Paul and others of the first generation of Christians that Jesus would quickly return to gather his people and establish on earth God's rule. His description of the defecting from Christian faith and practice goes far beyond the sketch in Jude, so that those who formerly "escaped the defilements of the world through the knowledge of our Lord and Savior Jesus Christ" end up in a worse condition than before their conversion (2 Pet. 2:20). Clearly, defection from the faith is a major problem for the author of 2 Peter.

In several basic ways, however, the author of 2 Peter differs significantly from the outlook of the first-generation apostles. First, he deals with the delay in the triumphant return of Christ to earth by telling his readers that God has a different way of calculating time than humans do (2 Pet. 3:8) and supports the point by quoting Ps. 90:4 in such a way as to claim that humans simply cannot calculate the divine timetable. Second, depicting those events when God subdues the wicked and renews the creation, he uses terms derived from hellenistic culture, such as the reference to the pits of gloom where the fallen angels are incarcerated by a form of Tartarus (2:4), a technical term in hellenistic mythology for the realm of the dead. Similarly, when he describes the destiny of the faithful, he uses terms from the mystical tradition of hellenistic religion, such as *eusebeia* (1:3, 6; 3:1; a term for piety never used by Paul or in the gospel tradition). What constitutes true piety is spelled out in a passage in which a string of virtues are linked together in a style familiar in hellenistic moral treatises. In 1:16, the technical term *epoptes* (eyewitness) is used, which is a central element in hellenistic mystical religion. It claims to offer divine illumination to the initiates or devotees of a god. In 1:19, the mythical image of the morning star is employed to point to the fulfillment of prophetic expectations.

Along more intellectual lines, faith – which has been central for both Paul and the Gospel tradition – is increasingly replaced by knowledge. *Knowing* the truth is an essential feature throughout this writing: 1:2, 3, 8; 2:20–1; 3:18. Using language and concepts that have counterparts in hellenistic philosophy (such as that of Epictetus, 46–120 C.E., a contemporary of the author of 2 Peter), the author deals with such questions as, Why does God allow the suffering of the righteous to continue? And how and when will God call to account the wicked, as the Stoics were asking? In the Jewish tradition, Philo of Alexandria deals repeatedly with the issue of theodicy. The issue of the justice of God in dealing with humans is touched on elsewhere in the New Testament in passages such as the address on the Areopagus in Athens (see p. 534) attributed to Paul in Acts 17: "God has fixed a day on which he will judge the world in righteousness" (17:31). But on the whole, throughout the New Testament, God's freedom in dealing with evil and with justice for human beings is simply assumed. Second Peter, however, treats the theme extensively in his short letter. This confirms the impression that the writer and his readers are from a cultural setting significantly different from that of the readers of the Pauline letters and the gospels.

Further evidence from 2 Peter for changes within the church arises from references to and attitudes toward the authority and interpretation of the Christian scriptures. In 1:17, there is an extended excerpt from the gospel tradition describing the scene of the transfiguration of Jesus, at which Peter was present. It would seem that the Gospels are known and appealed to as evidence. There is a reference in 3:1 to an earlier letter of Peter, which implies that letters by (or in the name of) the apostles are known and are accepted as in some sense authoritative. With regard to the letters of Paul, 3:15–16 refers to them as "scripture," ranking them along with "the other scriptures," thereby attributing authority for the church to some of the writings that later were brought together to form the New Testament. The difficulties in interpreting Paul's letters are acknowledged, and the distortions of their meaning are noted, although there is no indication in 2 Peter of

THEODICY

ONE OF THE CONCEPTUAL problems in any religious system is that of justifying the actions of God or the gods which bring suffering or harm to humans. Such a defense is called theodicy. The effort to discern a reason and a greater good than the obvious human pain takes a variety of forms in religious systems of thought. For early Christians, the suffering and death of Jesus and the persecution and martyrdom suffered by his followers called for a theological explanation that would enable the members of the community to see these seemingly sad events in the context of a universal divine plan for the benefit of the creation and of God's people.

the specific problems that had arisen in interpreting them. Even though the acceptable interpretive process is not detailed, the author declares that there are to be no private interpretations of scripture: all instruction is to be given within the context of the church by its authorized leaders. This serves as a solemn warning not to heed the "false teachers" who deny "the Master who bought them" and thereby bring upon themselves eternal destruction.

Clearly, the issues of correct doctrine and authorized interpretation of the scriptures are interrelated at this stage in the life of the church and are of paramount concern. The availability and wide use among the churches of the range of writings with their diverse perspectives that came to constitute the New Testament required the development of overarching credal and theological formulations that would demonstrate conceptual unity in spite of the evident diversity among the documents. Some leaders tried to solve the problem of diversity by choosing a smaller group of writings and establishing them as normative. A major example of this was Marcion (see p. 568), the second-century Gnostic who rejected the Old Testament and reduced the New Testament to his own expurgated versions of Luke, Acts, and the letters of Paul. The church as a whole rejected this kind of solution, however. The final warning and exhortation of 2 Peter are to avoid being "carried away with error" and to seek to "grow in grace *and knowledge*" (3:18). The church has entered a stage – probably in the early second century – where the norms of right doctrine and right behavior are the central issues.

IV. CHRISTIANITY RESPONDS TO ROMAN CULTURE AND IMPERIAL POLICY

A. LUKE–ACTS, PROPAGANDA FOR WORLD MISSION: THE CHURCH'S INTERNAL AND EXTERNAL RELATIONS

The Gospel of Luke and the Book of Acts, now separated in the Christian canon of scripture by the Gospel of John, were written as part of a two-volume work, which begins with the divine preparation for the birth of Jesus and ends with the launching of the worldwide mission of the church. The similar opening lines of each and the reference in Acts 1:1 back to "the earlier book" imply a common author. The similarity in editorial style and overall point of view confirms this conclusion, which is taken for granted by scholars across the spectrum from conservative to the most radical.

From the second century to the present, the author has been identified as the Luke who is mentioned as a co-worker of Paul in Philemon 23 and 2 Tim. 4:11 and described as a "beloved physician" in Col. 4:14. Some scholars have inferred from the occasional shifts in the narrative of Acts from "they" to "we" (cf., e.g., Acts 16:1 with 16:11; 20:1 with 20:5) that the author was a companion of Paul on part of his journeys around the Mediterranean Sea. But the change from third person to first person plural is found often in historical writings of that epoch.

LUKE AS HISTORIAN

SINCE THE LATER NINETEENTH century, scholars have continued to debate the degree to which Luke's accounts of Jesus and the apostles (especially Paul) are historically reliable. Careful studies in the earlier part of the present century, such as H.J. Cadbury's *The Making of Luke–Acts*, have shown the extent to which Luke used the historical–literary methods of his time, and the impressive amount of historically reliable detail that he includes, especially in Acts. It must be noted, however, that both ancient and modern historians are not interested merely in reporting facts, but in placing what was said and done by the historical figures in a larger framework of meaning. Luke makes clear to his reader

(continued on p. 520)

(continued from p. 519)

what that historical framework is when he contrasts in Luke 16:16 the earlier epoch of "the Law and the prophets" that ended with John the Baptist with the new era inaugurated by Jesus, which will culminate in the evangelization of the world (Acts 1:8) and the triumphant return of Christ (Acts 1:11).

In setting out his story of Jesus and the work of the apostles in preparation for the completion of God's purpose for the world, Luke uses a popular literary style of the early second century C.E. and subsequent centuries, known by classical scholars as "the hellenistic romance." The title is misleading, however, since the romance is not a love story or merely entertaining narrative (although some of them do have erotic passages), but rather an engaging tale, filled with human interest details, describing a life of devotion to a divinity, with vivid accounts of the resulting trials and rewards. Examples of this genre include Xenophon's *Ephesiaca* and Apuleius' *Metamorphoses*, both of which depict lives of devotees of the Egyptian goddess Isis and their resulting transformation. Luke has employed features of this narrative style in the interest of setting out his historical view of what God has done through Jesus and the apostles to accomplish the renewal of his people and the establishment of his rule in the world.

More likely, the author, as he tells us in Luke 1:1–2, was not an eyewitness of the events he reports but based his account on reports he had heard or read from those who were. For convenience, we refer to him as Luke, but as is the case with the other gospels, the identity of the author is simply unknown, and probably has been from the earliest years of the document's existence.

The author is remarkably skilled as a writer. This is apparent in his ability to modify his style in ways that are appropriate to the material he is presenting. In the opening section of the Gospel (Luke 1–3), his writing sounds "like the Bible" – that is, he effectively mimics the style of the Septuagint (which was, of course, the version of the Bible that he was using) and thus gives the reader a sense of continuity between the characters from biblical history and the events he is recounting. Some of these connections are implicit, such as the parallels between the divine gift of a son, John, to the childless couple Zechariah and Elizabeth (1:5–25, 57–80) and the story of the birth of Samuel in 1 Samuel 1. The exultant hymns which celebrate these miraculous births are similar (cf. 1 Sam. 2 and Luke 1:67–79). Other connections are explicit, such as the angelic voice that links the birth of Jesus to the divine assurance to David that he will have an enduring royal line (2:10). The care with which the ritual requirements are fulfilled for both the boys and the testimony of the pious men and women around the temple strengthen this sense of continuity within the history of God's covenant people, from the old to the new. Luke's depiction of the new community's outreach to the humble and to outsiders is anticipated in the coming of the shepherds at Jesus' birth (Luke 2:8–20).

Although the author has used Mark and Q as his basic sources, he adapts them to his own purposes, rearranging the sequence and adjusting the details. In his editorial additions he shows familiarity with literary conventions of his time, such as the dating of events by reference to several concurrent rulers (Luke 3:1–2) and the composing of extended speeches by leading characters in his story. In the overall narrative of Acts, where we learn how the gospel moved from Jerusalem to Rome, the style resembles that of a popular literary genre of the second century C.E. and later, known as the romance (sidebar p. 519). But Luke's commitment to the basic principle of the biblical tradition, whereby God accomplishes his purpose in the world through human beings in the circumstances of historical existence, requires him to picture Jesus (in the Gospel of Luke) and the apostles (in Acts) involved in the context and process of human history. His work displays, therefore, the methods and features of Greco-Roman historical writers. He has remarkably accurate knowledge of details of urban life in the eastern Mediterranean, such as the distinctive titles of the civic leaders in Thessalonica (Acts 17:6) and the names of the various rulers and authorities in Palestine in this period. At some major points, however, there are tensions between his account of Paul's career and the apostle's own biographical notes in his letters. For example, Luke reports that Paul's consultation with the leaders of the Jerusalem church resulted in his agreeing that even gentile Christians were to observe some minimal Jewish dietary laws ("abstain from

Shepherds' fields near Bethlehem. In Luke's account of the events that occurred in connection with the birth of Jesus, shepherds tending flocks in fields near Bethlehem visit the new-born child (Luke 2:8–20). The terrain in this picture is typical of the open land surrounding Bethlehem in modern times.

H.C. Kee.

things strangled and from blood"; Acts 15:20; cf. Lev. 3:17, 17:10–14). Paul, however, declares that no ritual or dietary requirements were placed on gentile Christians by an agreement reached with James and the other leading apostles (Gal. 2:7–10). It appears that Luke's account reflects one of the developments in the later situation of the church, such as we have seen in Matthew and the later Pauline tradition, as it moved toward rules for regulating the life of its membership. Luke is not concerned for detached, objective reporting but for showing the importance of this tradition for Christian readers in his own time – probably the early second century.

The major objective of Luke in both volumes of his work (Luke and Acts) is to show that from the beginning, the covenant people of God have had the divinely intended potential to become a universally inclusive community. He acknowledges that not all will be persuaded by God's message through Jesus, but everyone has the possibility of responding in faith to this gospel. For example, when Simeon blesses the child Jesus in the temple (Luke 2:28–32), he declares that Jesus' coming is intended as "a light to reveal your will to the gentiles, and to bring glory to your people Israel." Similarly, in the extended quotation from Isaiah at Jesus' baptism, we read, "All humanity will see God's salvation" (cf. Mark 1:3). That aim is apparent in the special material that Luke has included, as well as in his modification of sayings and narratives taken over from his gospel sources. Before examining some of this special or modified material in detail, it is essential to see how Luke has structured his account of God's work in the world, and especially his perception of the unfolding of the career of Jesus.

The direct connection between the ascension of Jesus (which is reported only by Luke) and the coming of the Spirit to launch the world mission of the church is explicitly stated in Acts 2:33 and 3:20–1. His people will not see him until he returns, following his having been taken up to God (Acts 1:11). But God's presence with his people in the extended interim of Jesus' absence from them will be powerfully evident through the work of the Spirit, which will enable them to carry out their mission "to the ends of the earth" (Acts 1:6–8).

This divine plan for world evangelism is set forth by the author of Luke–Acts as taking place in three historical epochs:

1. The history of Israel from ancient times until the ministry of John the Baptist.
2. The coming of Jesus, his ministry and message, death and resurrection.
3. The ascension of Jesus and the commissioning of the apostles for their mission to the world.

The Gospel of Luke describes the end of the first epoch and the whole of the second epoch. Acts recounts the launching of the third epoch.

After Jesus' commissioning by the Spirit at his baptism (Luke 3:21–2) and his time of testing (4:1–15), he begins his public ministry in the midst of his own townspeople in Nazareth, choosing as the basis of his address a passage from Isa. 61:1–2. His interpretation of this text makes clear the first phase of his activity: to invite "the poor" to share in the blessings of God's people – that is, those who are considered impure or unworthy or outside the boundaries of the covenant. His illustrations from the Jewish Bible of this divine outreach are the story of the Syrian widow from Sidon, whose child was healed by Elijah (Luke 4:26; 1 Kings 17:1–16), and the report that the only leper who was cured by Elisha was a Syrian (Luke 4:27; 2 Kings 5:1–14).

It is the Spirit of God upon Jesus that commissions him to carry out this work of healing and renewal on the margins of Israel. The preaching and healing activity in which Jesus engages for the next four chapters reaches out to precisely this kind of person, as Luke 6:17–19 makes clear. Jesus pronounces the blessedness of "the poor" in his (Q) version of the Beatitudes (6:20) (see p. 452). The term "poor" does not mean simply the economically deprived but includes those who by the standards of Jewish piety were excluded from participation in the life and benefits of God's people by reason of their physical condition, ritual impurity, or occupation. Jesus' love of "the poor" is explicit in his response to the questioners sent to him by John the Baptist, which is framed in Luke by stories of the healing of the slave of a centurion (7:1–10), the cure of a widow's son (7:11–17), and the acceptance of and justification for direct contact with a sinful woman (7:36–50). Jesus calls attention to his reaching out to the socially and ritually rejected people and then accepts the characterization of himself as "a friend of tax collectors and sinners" (7:22–3, 34).

In order to extend his work among Jews and those on the periphery of Judaism, Jesus sends out the twelve apostles, the number symbolizing the twelve tribes of Israel. The spectacular results of their work are described in symbolic form in Luke 5:1–11, where the Markan story of Jesus' calling fishermen to be his disciples (Mark 1:16–20) is expanded into a miracle story of the astounding catch of fish, which is the result of direct obedience to the command of Jesus.

In Luke 10:1, however, a new stage in the outreach to the wider world is depicted: Jesus sends out seventy people to spread his message about sharing in the life of God's people. The number seventy represented for Jews of that day the number of the nations of the world. That the transition to the wider field of mission is in view is made evident by 9:51–3, where the prospect of Jesus' rejection by his fellow Jews is asserted and the confrontation with the authorities in Jerusalem is implied. Many of the stories and sayings found in Mark and Matthew are in Luke as well, but at several points Luke emphasizes the element of Jesus' outreach beyond Judaism. Examples of this are the story of the Good Samaritan (10:29–37), which commends the generosity and human concern shown by a member of a group despised by the Jews; and the sign of Jonah (11:29–32), which reminds the hearer or reader that Jonah's preaching and Solomon's wisdom were heeded by non-Israelites. The Lukan form of the parables makes the same point: that the intention of God is to reach out to the outsider, especially in the parables Jesus tells in response to the charge of the religious leaders that he is having fellowship with impure people (15:1): the joyous shepherd, who rejoices at the restoration to the flock of a lost sheep (15:2–7); the joyous housewife, who rejoices at the recovery of a lost coin (15:8–10); and the joyous father, who rejoices at the recovery of a runaway son and rebukes the unforgiving older brother (15:11–32). Preceding this triad of parables is one with a similar point: the parable of the supper guests (14:12–24), where the original invitees are too preoccupied with their own affairs to accept the invitation, which finally goes out to, and is accepted by, the society's outcasts. The same basic point is made in such uniquely Lukan stories as the rich man and Lazarus (16:19–31) and Jesus' visit to the home of Zacchaeus, the tax collector in Jericho (19:1–10), which ends with the assertion that the purpose of Jesus' having come into the world is "to seek and save the lost." This leads to the third stage of Luke's account of Jesus' career: the encounter with the authorities – civil and religious – in Jerusalem, which occupies the rest of the Gospel until the transitional chapter (Luke 24), which prepares for the launching of the world mission in Acts.

The rejection of Jesus is anticipated in the concluding words of Luke's version of the parable of the pounds (Luke 19:11–27). Unlike Matthew's version (Matt. 25:14–20), where the issue is investing the wealth of an absentee owner, for Luke the major factors are the granting of royal power to a nobleman (19:12, 27) and the refusal of the people to accept him as king. The point for Luke is Israel's rejection of Jesus as God's agent to establish his kingdom on earth. His rejection by the Jewish leadership is foretold in the Lukan version of what follows. When the disciples acclaim Jesus as he descends the Mount of Olives on his way to the temple, their words echo the song of the angels at his birth (19:38, 2:14; cf. Ps. 118:25–6). When his acceptance of this acclamation is challenged by the Pharisees, he predicts the destruction of Jerusalem, including details of the methods the Romans will use to besiege the city and starve its inhabitants (see pp. 410–414). Unlike Matthew, Luke follows closely Mark's account of Jesus in the temple and the series of subsequent controversies with the Jewish religious

EUCHARIST

DERIVED FROM THE GREEK word for "give thanks" (*eucharisteo*), "eucharist" is used in the New Testament for thanksgiving to God for his benefits (1 Cor. 14:18; 2 Cor. 4:15, 9:11; Col. 4:2) but also is an important feature of the Lord's Supper in both the Gospel tradition (Mark 14:22–4, Matt. 26:26–8, Luke 22:19–20) and in the letters of Paul (1 Cor. 11:23–6). The Eucharist is a solemn recalling of Jesus' death, symbolized by the broken loaf and the wine poured out, but it is also a grateful celebration in the present of the significance of that sacrificial death, as well as an anticipation of the time when God's rule will be universal (Matt. 26:29, Mark 14:25, Luke 22:17, 1 Cor. 11:26).

leaders, culminating in the apocalyptic discourse, to which Luke adds only a brief additional warning about the unpredictability of the return of Christ (21:34–6). Luke does omit the Markan account of the cursing of the fig tree, but the themes of judgment and reformation of the covenant people have been affirmed by Luke in other ways. As a transition to the story of Jesus' arrest and execution, he notes that Jesus continued to teach in the temple and that "all the people" came to hear him. The testimony to Jews continues in spite of the impending official rejection of him.

The Lukan account of the Last Supper differs in both order and content from Mark in so many ways that scholars have proposed that Luke had access to an independent tradition for this section of his Gospel. Luke's version emphasizes that Jesus' final meal with the disciples includes the prediction of the future fulfillment of God's purpose for his people. This is highlighted by placing at the outset the reference to the establishment of the kingdom of God (22:15–16) – that is, the new age in which God's rule is established on the earth – and the appearance here (from the Q source; cf. Matt. 19:28) of the reward the disciples will receive for their fidelity to Jesus in his time of testing (22:28–30). But Luke's language also includes the use of the Greek verb *dietheto*, which is linked with the noun *diatheke*, which means "covenant." Thus the force of this statement is to promise that the twelve disciples will have a central role when God fulfills his purpose for the new covenant people of Israel. Meanwhile, the eucharistic meal is an anticipation and a reminder of what God is yet to do for his people.

During the time of transition from the present situation to the coming age of peace, they are to expect conflict and hostility. Luke 22:35–8 seems to be a temporary, emergency setting aside of Jesus' earlier instructions (9:3, 10:4) about traveling unencumbered, dependent solely on local hospitality. Now Jesus wants to be sure that no secret assassination prevents the public confrontation and display that are to place his impending death in the context that God intended.

The hearing before Pilate begins with the explicit charge by the coalition of Jewish leaders that Jesus is "perverting our nation," forbidding the payment of taxes to Rome, and claiming to be the messianic king (Luke 23:2). Pilate states directly that he finds Jesus guilty of no crime (23:4). Then Pilate sends Jesus to Herod Antipas (see pp. 395–397), within whose jurisdiction Jesus lived and had been carrying out his work of preaching and healing (23:6–16). Herod and his soldiers treat Jesus mockingly as a king, but he does not find Jesus guilty of the accusations the authorities have brought against him. This motif is of great importance for Luke in the Book of Acts: Jesus and his followers were repeatedly brought before the civil authorities, who were unable to find him or the apostles guilty of acts against the state.

On the way to the crucifixion in Luke's account (23:26–32), Jesus turns to tell the women who are following him with lamentations that their sorrow should be for themselves and for their offspring, who will suffer when divine judgment falls on the city. This special attention to women is characteristic of the whole of Luke's Gospel. Women are prominent in the infancy stories, as we have noted, and among those who herald the birth of Jesus is a prophetess, Anna (2:36–8). Women are frequently among the beneficiaries of Jesus' acts of grace and healing – more so than in the other gospels. Examples are the healing of the widow's son (7:11–17); the expanded version of the woman with the ointment (7:36–50); the women who provide financial support for Jesus (8:1–3); the story of Mary and Martha's response to Jesus (10:38–42); the blessedness of Jesus' mother (11:27–8); and the healing of the woman with the infirmity (13:10–17). We shall see that in Acts women also have a significant role, which conflicts with the wholly subservient place of women in the Jewish tradition of that period.

The inclusiveness of the community of faith is indicated in other distinctively Lukan material: Jesus' compassion for the Samaritans, in spite of their initial rejection of his message (9:51–6); the healing of the man with dropsy (14:1–6); the healing of the ten non-Jewish lepers (17:11–19); and the story of the Pharisee and the tax collector (18:9–14). Other themes include the necessity for persistence in prayer (11:5–8, 18:1–8); the folly of trusting in material possessions to guarantee one's well-being (12:13–21, 16:14–15); the need to fulfill one's responsibilities in the service of God (17:7–10); and the certainty that God will call all humanity to account for their deeds (12:47–8, 13:1–9). Then there are specific assurances that God is already at work through Jesus to accomplish his plan for his people (13:31–3) and that the powers of the new age are already present and active in the words and works of Jesus (17:20–1).

Details of the story of the crucifixion of Jesus and the discovery of the empty tomb are unique to Luke as well. Instead of the cry of abandonment (Mark 15:34), Jesus commits himself to the Father (Luke 23:46); the women who witness his death and who hear the word of the angel at the empty tomb are specifically said to have been with Jesus in Galilee (23:49, 55; 24:10). Unlike Mark, where the disciples are instructed to return to Galilee, and Matthew, where they do so, in Luke all the appearances of the risen Lord take place in the vicinity of Jerusalem. Jesus' death and resurrection are shown to be in fulfillment of scripture (24:13–27), but it is in the breaking of bread (told in language that uses the technical eucharistic terms "took, blessed, broke, gave") that he was "made known to them" (24:28–35). The disciples' resources for understanding and interpreting to others the significance of Jesus are the scriptures, the experience of the risen Lord, and the shared meal (24:36–47). This message is to go out to all nations, once his followers have been endued with power from God – an event that is to occur in Jerusalem (24:48–53).

Acts pictures three major stages in the development of the church's transitions from a primarily Jewish to a gentile outreach, and of its encounter with the imperial power of Rome. Acts 1–8 depicts the empowering of the apostles and the constitution of the new community; Acts 9:1–21:26 describes Paul as the primary agent of outreach to the gentile world; and Acts 21:27–28:31 presents Paul as the prototype for Christian confrontation with Roman authority.

APOSTLE

DERIVED FROM THE GREEK word *apostolos*, which means "one who is sent out," the term "apostle" was used by first-century Christians to designate the inner circle of the first followers of Jesus. Lists of the apostles appear in Mark 3:16–19, Matt. 10:2–4, and Luke 6:13–16; there are always twelve in number (like the tribes of Israel), although there are variations in the names included. Two New Testament passages suggest qualifications for the role of apostle: Acts 1:21–6 specifies having been an eyewitness of Jesus' activity from baptism until his resurrection; in 1 Cor. 9:1 Paul mentions having "seen Jesus our Lord" after he was raised from the dead, just as the other apostles did (1 Cor. 15:7–9). Paul refers to himself as an apostle regularly at the opening of his letters (Rom. 1:1, 1 Cor. 1:1, 2 Cor. 1:1, Gal. 1:1) but sees his special role as emissary of Christ (apostle) to the Gentiles (Rom. 11:13, Gal. 1:16–17). Although connections with the apostles were important for second-century leaders and writers as confirming authority and correctness of doctrine, the title "apostle" was no longer used for church officials.

Following Jesus' ascension into the presence of God (Acts 1:1–11), the new people of God – who have witnessed Jesus' life and work, death and resurrection – receive the outpouring of the Spirit (Acts 1:8) to enable them to fulfill their new mission. Significantly, this testimony is to begin in Jerusalem, which was seen as the dwelling place of God among his people in the old covenant, and which was so central in the career of Jesus. In preparation for that event, a twelfth member of the apostolic circle is chosen to replace the traitor, Judas. By lot, Matthias is chosen (1:12–26), and the circle of apostles is complete.

The outpouring of the Spirit takes place on a Jewish holiday commemorating the promise of a new beginning for God's people: Pentecost. The experience of wind and fire recall Elijah's experience when God spoke to him on Mount Sinai (1 Kings 19:11–12), commissioning him to challenge the leadership of Israel. In Acts 2:9–11, all the apostles were gathered in a house when the wind and fire came from heaven, and they all began to speak in other languages, which were immediately understood by the throng of Jews and the devout – presumably, gentiles – who had come to Jerusalem from all over the known world of the time. Peter's explanation of this astounding event is based on allusions to and quotations from the Jewish scriptures (Acts 2:17–21 = Joel 2:28–32), as is his linking of this public event with the death and resurrection of Jesus (Acts 2:25–8 = Ps. 16:8–11; Acts 2:34 = Ps. 110:1). About three thousand were persuaded by this event and its meaning, submitted to the public rite of baptism, and joined the community, into which they were integrated through the instruction and fellowship led by the apostles (2:41–2).

The apostles' ability to perform miracles was evidence of God's support for these claims about the significance of Jesus and the divine origin of the Spirit. Those who joined the movement gave their support tangibly in the resources they pooled for the benefit of the group (2:43–7). Peter's healing of the lame man in the temple by appealing to "the name of Jesus of Nazareth" (3:6) explicitly connects the work of the apostles with the work of Jesus. This healing is followed by another sermon preached by Peter (3:11–26). Its thematic structure is similar to most of the sermons attributed to the apostles throughout Acts:

1. Jesus stands at the culmination of the line that runs from Abraham (covenant people) through Moses (the law), David (the promise of renewal of God's rule), and the prophets.
2. What Jesus did was approved by God, as is evident from the great deeds he performed through the power of the Spirit.
3. The Jewish leaders put Jesus to death, or arranged for his death, without realizing what they were doing, and thereby fulfilled prophecy.
4. Gentiles should be aware that God is also concerned for them and has promised through the prophets their inclusion in God's people.
5. God has vindicated Jesus by raising him from the dead; he is now exalted at God's right hand.
6. All humanity, Jews and gentiles, are called to repent and to receive God's deliverance in the name of Jesus, whom God has designated to be the final judge of the human race.

Not all these themes are present in every sermon in Acts, but these are the recurrent motifs.

The religious authorities attempt to silence the apostles but cannot intimidate them (Acts 4:1–4). At the hearing before the local council Peter delivers yet another speech (4:8–12), in which he makes the claim that "in all the world there is no one else whom God has given who can save us." In spite of further warnings, the apostles continue to tell about Jesus, with growing numbers of followers (4:4, "about 5,000") and mounting conviction and commitment on the part of the members of the community (4:13–37). Already, however, there are those who are not totally committed, as is evident when Ananias and Sapphira are struck dead for their failure to give all that they had to the community (5:1–9). As the group grew in numbers (5:12–16), the official opposition mounted (5:17–39) – even though an occasional cautionary voice was raised, such as that of Gamaliel, a leading Pharisee (5:34–9), who suggested that God might be behind this new movement.

Barnabas, a Levite who appears to have been a respected member of the law-abiding Jewish community in Jerusalem, is persuaded by the message of the apostles about Jesus and the completely shared life of the new community and makes a public commitment to it of himself and his tangible resources. His subsequent role was to be a witness of the propriety of the outreach of the messengers of the gospel to the wider world, and a faithful aide of Paul in his transition to the mission to the gentiles, with the result that he too became a victim of Jewish-instigated persecution of the Christians (Acts 13:44–51).

PENTECOST

ORIGINALLY AN AGRICULtural festival at the time of harvest (Exod. 23:16), and earlier known as the Feast of Weeks (Exod. 34:22), Pentecost was the occasion required by the law of Israel for thanking God for the grain just harvested. It was to take place fifty days (seven weeks plus one day) after the Feast of Passover (Lev. 23:15–16). ("Pentecost" is derived from the Greek word for "fifty.") In the hellenistic period, it came to be associated with the covenant between God and Noah, which some Jews regarded as po-tentially inclusive of all human beings. It is this dimension of meaning that lies behind the Acts 2:1–42 account of the outpouring of the Spirit on the Day of Pentecost. The result of this coming of the Spirit was the symbolic hearing of the gospel by human representatives of peoples from all over the known world of that time.

BAPTISM

DERIVED FROM THE GREEK word baptizo, which means "to bathe or submerge," this term was used occasionally in the Septuagint for acts of purification, as in 2 Kings 5:14, where the Aramean army officer washes himself in the Jordan and is cured of leprosy. The Dead Sea community had tubs in which ceremonial acts of purification were performed. John's baptism involved a call to confession and repentance addressed to the people of Israel but including tax collectors and soldiers on the periphery of Judaism (Luke 3:10–14). Jesus accepted baptism from John as a public sign of the need for the basic renewal of God's covenant people (Luke 7:18–23). The first divine witness concerning Jesus' special place in God's purpose comes at the moment of his baptism (Mark 1:9–11).

In the New Testament baptism is a ritual symbol for the renewal of God's people, of which God's provision of food and water for Israel during the Exodus from Egypt ("baptized into Moses"; 1 Cor. 10:1–5) was a prototype. It is also a symbol for the Christian's identification with Christ in death to the old life and resurrection to the new life of faith (Rom. 6:1–4). Baptism became the normal rite by which members publicly indicated their identification with the new covenant community (Acts 2:38, 41; 8:36–8; 16:15, 33; 19:5; 22:16; 1 Cor. 1:13–15; Gal. 3:27).

EPISTLE OF BARNABAS

THIS WRITING IS ATTRIBUTED to Barnabas, the co-worker of Paul mentioned frequently in Acts and also in the letters of Paul (1 Cor. 9:6, Gal. 2:1–13, Col. 4:10). The document refers to the temple in Jerusalem as lying in ruins, which would imply that it was written after 70 C.E., when that catastrophe took place, but before 135 C.E., when Emperor Hadrian ordered that a shrine of Jupiter be built on the site of the Jewish temple. The Epistle uses the allegorical method of scripture interpretation, which suggests that it may have originated in Alexandria, where that method was widely used by Jewish and early Christian scholars. Yet there are also features of apocalyptic thought and style in expressing the author's expectations about the imminent end of the present age. Apocalyptic shows up in a variety of settings, and thus the presence of this characteristic offers no clue as to the work's place of origin.

The apostles continue their associations with the temple, even while carrying on meetings in homes, as the Pharisees were doing in this period. Their work became so demanding that they had to look to others for assistance in the administration of funds for the group. Chosen for this task were Greek-speaking Jews, which signals to the reader the move the group was to take toward inclusion of the gentiles. The names of all seven chosen for this role are Greek (Acts 6:1–6). One of the seven, Stephen, is accused by the Jewish leaders of subverting the temple and the law of Moses in the name of Jesus of Nazareth (6:8–15). His defense traces the founding of the covenant with Abraham, its renewal through Jacob and his twelve sons, the giving of the law through Moses, the movement of the portable shrine of God's presence from Egypt to Canaan, and its replacement by the temple in the time of Solomon (7:1–47). But Stephen declares that God does not dwell in houses built by human hands, and he quotes scripture to make his point (Acts 6:48–50 = Isa. 66:1–2). With that revolutionary statement, he turns to a denunciation of the leaders for their rejection of God's Messiah (7:51–3). Understandably, they put him to death by stoning, even while he is claiming to see Jesus at God's right hand (7:54–60). From this point on, the work of the apostles increasingly moves across the boundaries of the Jewish people out toward the wider Roman, gentile world.

In spite of the beginning of severe persecution of the church (Acts 8:2–3), the inclusive movement continued with successful preaching among the Samaritans, the conversion of a magician named Simon (8:4–25), and Philip's providential encounter in the desert with an Ethiopian eunuch (an official of the queen) who had visited the temple in Jerusalem and was puzzled by the Jewish scriptural reference to someone who would be killed like a slaughtered lamb (8:26–40; cf. Isa. 53:7–8). The persecution was launched by a leader of those Jews who were enraged by the apostles' inviting impure and non-Israelite peo-

STONING

THE LEGAL TRADITIONS OF Israel authorized execution by stoning for a range of offenses, including the worship of gods other than Yahweh (Deut. 13:6–10, 17:2–7), participation in child sacrifice to the Canaanite god Molech (Lev. 20:2–5), breaking the Sabbath law (Num. 15:32–6), and in certain cases of adultery (Deut. 22:20–1). Even certain forms of disobedience of a son to his father were to be punished by stoning the guilty son. The procedure is not described in

the Bible, but it usually took place outside the city (Lev. 24:14; Deut. 17:5, 22; 1 Kings 21:13) and was a corporate act by multiple members of the community, rather than the task of a single executioner. It is likely that more was involved than throwing fist-sized rocks from a dozen yards away, as some Bible illustrators have pictured this action. The stones were probably large and heavy, so that the guilty one was simultaneously crushed to death and hidden from sight under the mound of rocks that were hurled at and heaped on

the culprit. Jesus' reference to his own impending death in terms of his body being "broken" for his followers (Mark 14:22) may mean that he expected to be executed by stoning rather than by the Roman mode of crucifixion. This interpretation is confirmed by Jesus' perceiving the hostility that was mounting against him as leading to mass action against him which would result in his being denounced as "a glutton and a drunkard" and then experiencing the group execution ordered in Deut. 21:18–21.

SAMARITANS

THE CITY OF SAMARIA WAS the luxurious capital of the northern kingdom of Israel from the ninth to the late eighth century B.C.E., as the prophet Amos attests in his description of its aristocrats (Amos 6:4–6) and as the excavation there of such luxury items as ivory-inlaid furniture confirms. In 721 B.C.E., the Assyrians invaded the territory and carried off the inhabitants into captivity in their land. By the hellenistic period, Samaria was rebuilt with public buildings and temples typical of Greek-style cult-ure. Herod the Great developed it in grand style and renamed it for the Roman emperor: Sebastia, the Greek equivalent of "Augustus." To the east of the city of Samaria was Shechem, which had been the first location of the shrine of Yahweh when Israel entered the land (Josh. 24). In the hellenistic and Roman periods, those who wanted to recover the traditions of Moses built a temple on nearby Mount Gerizim and produced an edition of the Pentateuch that they claimed was the authentic version of the scriptures of Israel, in contrast to the expanded and edited version of the Law of Moses produced during and following the return of the Jews from exile in Babylon. These northern people, calling themselves Samaritans, asserted that the priesthood which carried out the cultus in their temple was legitimate, in contrast to the unholy priesthood and practices of the Jerusalem temple. So fierce was the hostility of other Jews toward the Samaritans that they avoided even journeying through that district lest there be some inadvertent contact with these Samaritan people, whom they regarded as perverters of the legal and priestly traditions of Israel.

ple to enter the covenant community – by someone named Saul, later to be known as Paul (8:1–3) – but the movement continued. This is manifest in the preaching activity of Philip along the hellenized coast from Azotus to Caesarea (8:40).

The transition to the second major part of Acts begins with the account of Saul's conversion. As persecutor of the new community, Saul has a vision of the crucified Jesus, is struck blind, is healed, is baptized, and begins to preach Jesus as the Son of God (9:1–20). After escaping a plot to assassinate him and after checking in with the Jerusalem apostles, Paul moved back to Tarsus. The Acts narrative marks the transition by a summary statement of the growth and strength of the church in "Judea, Galilee, and Samaria" (9:31).

The second major phase of the Acts account opens with Peter's shift of evangelistic operations to the coastal cities of Lydda, Joppa, and Caesarea, which were dominated by hellenistic culture and served as centers for the Roman military control of Palestine. After the apostles achieved spectacular success in healing a lame man and restoring to life a faithful and generous Christian widow (9:32–43), Cornelius (a Roman military officer who was attracted to the God of the Jews) was told by an angel to contact Peter. A vision also came to Peter – and was repeated twice – instructing him to overcome his ritual and ethnic prejudices against gentiles. The messengers from Cornelius arrived with an invitation to Peter and his associates to spend the night with him – which would result in their violating Jewish purity laws. Then he accepted the invitation to visit this Roman officer. The result of Peter's explaining the good news to these gentiles was that Cornelius and his associates believed, were given the gift of the Spirit, and were baptized. Peter also learned a basic lesson: "that God treats everyone on the same basis," so that "everyone that trusts in Jesus will receive forgiveness of sins" (10:1–48). These events were reported to the

TARSUS

THE CITY OF TARSUS WAS located at a strategic place for commerce, with access to the central regions of Asia Minor through the Cilician Gates to the north and to Syria and the East through the narrow passes between the Mediterranean Sea and the Amanus Mountains in the extreme southeastern section of Asia Minor. Tarsus was inhabited as early as 5000 B.C.E. and under the Romans had become a major center for commerce and learning. Zeno and other philosophers in the Stoic tradition had lived and taught there. Although Paul does not mention the city in his letters, referring instead to Antioch-on-the-Orontes (in Syria) as his earlier place of residence (Gal. 2:11), he reportedly identifies himself with Tarsus in Acts 9:11 and 21:39. The influence of Stoicism on Paul is readily understandable if he grew up and was educated in Tarsus, which in the early Roman period rivaled Alexandria as a center of hellenistic learning.

Mediterranean coast near Ashdod. References to Ashdod in ancient texts go back to the fourteenth century, and in the Bible to the time of Joshua (Josh. 11:21–2). The city was a major Philistine center, and it was there that the ark of the covenant was carried in the time of Samuel (1 Sam. 4–6). The city prospered and expanded in the Persian and hellenistic periods but became much smaller when taken over by Herod and was destroyed when the Romans put down the Jewish revolt of 66–70. The main coastal road runs east of the city. Two and a half miles west of the city was a port at the mouth of the Lachish River, which remained hellenistic in its culture, while Jews and Samaritans resided in the inland city.

H.C. Kee.

Jerusalem apostles, whose prejudices were overcome, and who concluded, "God has also given the gentiles the opportunity to repent and live" (11:1–18).

Once the precedent has been set for preaching to gentiles and for their full inclusion in the community, the challenge to extend the geographical scope of the gospel to predominantly gentile territories leads the Jerusalem apostles to commission Paul to take the initiative in this second phase of the church's work (11:19–30, 13:1–3). Persecutions continue (12:1–5), but God acts to set free his messengers (12:6–18) and to punish those rulers who oppose his purpose (12:20–4). The details vary, but the pattern is consistent: Paul and his associates in the gentile mission seize the opportunity in each place as it presents itself:

CAESAREA

TWO CITIES OF THIS NAME are important for early Christianity: Caesarea Philippi and Caesarea Maritima. The former, which is located in northern Palestine near one of the sources of the Jordan River, was the site of a pagan shrine named for the god Pan and was called Paneas. Philip, one of the sons of Herod the Great, rebuilt the city along hellenistic lines in the early decades of the first century c.e. It was here, according to Mark 8:27, that Jesus first discussed with his disciples the link between his messiahship and his impending death and resurrection.

The other Caesarea, with the added designation of Maritima, was located on the Mediterranean coast north of Jaffa. Herod the Great built it on the site of a tiny port city and greatly improved its harbor. Its elaborate buildings and extensive port facilities made it well suited to serve as the capital of Palestine during the Roman period, and the Roman governors and troops had their primary base there. The Christian gospel was preached early in this city, according to Acts 8:40 and 10:1–11, and it was the point of departure and arrival for several of Paul's journeys (Acts 9:30, 18:22, 21:8, 27:1–2), as well as the setting for his imprisonment and initial judicial hearings by the Roman authorities (Acts 23–6).

Harbor of Caesarea Maritima. On the shore of the Mediterranean midway between Joppa and Ptolemaïs, Caesarea Maritima was originally a small town called Strabo's Tower. Emperor Augustus added this area to the kingdom assigned to Herod the Great, who renamed it Caesarea in his honor. It served as the official seat of Roman power in Palestine for more than half a millennium. The Roman troops declared Vespasian emperor there after his success in crushing the Jewish revolt of 66–70. The city had all the typical features of a Greco-Roman center: temple, hippodrome, theater, aqueduct, sewers, and palaces for the Roman authorities.

H.C. Kee.

(*below*) Anatolian plateau. The central part of what is now Turkey is a vast plateau, where archeological evidence shows occupation back to Paleolithic times and a rich mixture of cultural influences. After Alexander drove out the Persians from this land, Greek culture became dominant, followed by the Romans, who built characteristic Roman cities at such places as Ephesus, Sardis, Pergamon (Pergamum), and Antioch-in-Pisidia. The journeys of Paul as reported in Acts took him through this territory, and in seven of the cities there are located the seven churches which were the recipients of the letters in Revelation 1–3.

H.C. Kee.

On Cyprus, they confront a magician and strike him blind, which leads to the conversion of the governor (13:4–12).

In Antioch-in-Pisidia, they preach in the synagogue, at first with spectacular results (13:13–43) and then with mounting resentment from the synagogue leaders because of the inclusion of the gentiles (13:44–52).

In Iconium, the same responses are evoked from Jews and gentiles (14:1–7).

In Lystra and Derbe, the gentiles are so dazzled by the apostles' ability to heal a lame man that they acclaim them gods, to which Paul and Barnabas respond by preaching the gospel. Opposition from the Jews continues to follow them (14:8–20).

From there Paul and his colleagues complete their circuit of cities in Asia Minor and return to Antioch in Syria, where they report on the results of their mission (14:21–7). Word of their work was brought by hostile reporters to the leaders of the church in Jerusalem, and a council is convened to settle the issue of the status of gentiles within the church, as Paul recalls in his letter to the Galatians. As we noted, the results of the conference as told in Acts differ significantly from Paul's report (Gal. 2:1–10), according to which there were no ritual or legal obligations for gentiles to become members of God's new people. Here, however, the agreement is that gentiles are to abstain from eating food made ritually unclean by being offered to idols, from sexual immorality, and from eating any animal that had been strangled or any meat containing blood. All these are forbidden in the Jewish law (Exod. 34:15–17; Lev. 18:6–23, 17:10–13) and are here in Acts represented as binding on gentile Christians. It is not at all likely that Paul would have agreed to such ritual obligations for gentiles. More likely is the theory that, as gentile Christians became increasingly steeped in

Antioch-on-the-Orontes in Syria. Located on a plain between the Lebanon Mountains and the Orontes River, near where it empties into the Mediterranean, Antioch was from its founding in about 300 B.C.E. the capital of the Seleucid kingdom and, after 64 B.C.E., of the Roman province of Syria. From the early days of Antioch, many Jews lived there. The city was important commercially, with fertile lands nearby and a major seaport, Seleucia, a short distance away. It was also a center of Greco-Roman intellectual and cultural life.

Matson Photo Service.

Harbor of Troas. Taking its name from the nearby ancient city of Troy, Troas was an important port city on the northwestern coast of Asia Minor since it was the major access point for the Romans to the northern provinces there. The district was designated by the Romans as a Roman colony, and the Roman historian and geographer Strabo refers to it as "one of the renowned cities." Paul departed from Troas for the mainland of Europe (Acts 16:8–10) and passed through there again on the way to his final visit to Jerusalem (Acts 20:5–12).

Gordon Converse.

PURPLE DYE

A RARE AND COSTLY DYE shading from red to purple was produced from a fluid secreted by a shellfish (*Murex*) that flourishes on the coast of Syria and Palestine. Only royalty and others of great wealth could afford it. Second Chronicles 2 reports the negotiations of King Solomon with the king of Tyre to obtain the services of a craftsman who could produce this purple dye for him. The sacred tent described in Exodus was to be decorated abundantly with purple (Exod. 35–6, 38), as were the garments of the priests (Exod. 39:1–3). In the gospel tradition, purple is the sign of wealth (Luke 16:19), as well as of royalty. Jesus, in mockery of his claim to be king, is robed in purple (Mark 15:17–20; John 19:2–5). The evil monarch of the end time is pictured in Revelation 17 and 18 as a harlot clothed in purple. The fact that purple dye was such a luxury item suggests that Lydia, whose business was selling it and who was Paul's first convert in Europe (according to Acts 16), was a woman of considerable means.

---

the Jewish scriptures, they were willing to adopt certain ritual norms for differentiating themselves from non-Christians.

Paul and Barnabas, following some disagreements about their associates, part ways (15:36–41), with Paul revisiting the cities of Asia Minor en route to the mainland of Europe (16:1–10). There his first convert is a businesswoman named Lydia, in Philippi, the capital of Macedonia, named in honor of the father of Alexander the Great. The purple dye in which Lydia dealt was a luxury item in the Roman world, which implies that she was a woman of considerable means. The Acts account (16:11–15) implies that she was the owner of a sizable house and presided over a household that included servants: these were baptized and joined the community along with Lydia. The activities of Paul were centered at the Jewish "place of prayer" (16:13, 16), which was a common designation of the gathering places of Jews in predominantly gentile towns and cities. The exorcism of an evil spirit from a slave-girl prophetess resulted in Paul and his companion, Silas, being imprisoned, but the outcome was their miraculous release from their bonds, the conversion of the jailer and his household, and the liberation of Paul and Silas by the Roman authorities (16:16–40). The author wants to show that Christianity is not a politically subversive movement and that its claims are credible, as various Roman officials (such as the centurion in Caesarea and this jailer and the local magistrates) had recognized from the outset of the apostles' mission to the Greco-Roman world.

In Thessalonica and in Berea, Paul and Silas have remarkable results from their preaching about Jesus as the anointed of God, but Jewish opposition tries to discredit them as anti-Roman (17:1–15). In Athens,

PLACE OF PRAYER

THE GREEK TERM *proseuche* is used for places where Jews gathered, not only for prayer, but also for community assemblies of a more general nature. The group that gathered there referred to itself as a *synagoge*, which means "gathering" or "assembly." Only much later did this latter term come to be used for the buildings where the group met. Archeological analysis of ancient synagogue buildings, the oldest of which date from the second century C.E., shows that originally they were mostly private homes where the members assembled. As the groups grew in size and self-confidence, they would incorporate adjacent court-yards into their meeting places. Eventually they began to construct distinctive buildings for their religious meetings, later adding facilities for more formal instruction as well. The oldest firmly dated Jewish meeting place that has been excavated is in Delos and was originally a private house (second century B.C.E.), but it was later altered to serve as an assembly hall. The largest such structure adapted to function as a Jewish place of worship is a vast public hall excavated at Sardis in Asia Minor (third century C.E.). The destruction of the Jerusalem temple in 70 C.E. and the failure of the second revolt in 135 C.E. led Jews in Palestine and else-where to begin to construct spe-cial buildings as places of worship and instruction. Prior to this, these "places of prayer" served local and traveling Jews as places of study where they could meet with others of similar convictions.

AREOPAGUS

A SMALL ROCKY HILL WEST of the Acropolis (the central hill where the Parthenon is located) in Athens was named the Hill of Ares (the Greek god of war), or the Areopagus. A council met on this hill that earlier gave advice to the Athenian kings and later gave rulings on certain local social and moral issues. It is before this group that Paul is given a hear-ing, according to Acts 17. From among its members he was able to make one convert. This account gives evidence of Luke's detailed knowledge of Greek cities, as well as of the Greek poets, whom he here reports Paul as quoting in his own defense.

however, following some discussions in the synagogues, Paul is invit-ed by the civic authorities responsible for the moral life of the city – the council of the Areopagus – to explain to them his teaching (17:16–31). His message to the Athenian intellectual leaders takes a very different approach from the themes used by him and the apostles in the other sermons in Acts. Here, he begins by affirming certain aspects of uni-versal natural law as taught by Stoic philosophers of the time and by noting the basic unity of the human race under the Creator. He even quotes Greek poets to make his point. But when he claims that God will judge the world by the resurrected Jesus – rather than by Stoic nat-ural law – his hearers think he has lost his mind. Only a handful of men and women are persuaded by his message.

In Corinth and Ephesus – two of the leading cities of the Greek world – Paul's strategy is to begin his work in the synagogues, until the Jewish opposition mounts (18:1–28, 19:1–10). In addition, in both cities he was brought before the civil authorities (18:12–16, 19:21–41). In this series of accounts several details give us important information about the spread of Christianity. A couple of tent makers, named Priscilla and Aquila, had Paul live and work with them in Corinth, where they had fled from Rome when Emperor Claudius had expelled the Jews, who were in turmoil as a result of the coming among them of Christian messengers. This couple had already been converted when Paul met them; later they moved to Ephesus, where they also had lead-ership roles in the young church, which met in their home there (1 Cor. 16:19). Gallio, the Roman governor in Corinth, refused to accept the charges brought against Paul by the Jews. After a return visit to Syria and Caesarea, Paul went to Ephesus, where he met Apollos, a convert from Judaism and a native of Alexandria, who was apparently skilled in the Jewish wisdom tradition and in the style of biblical interpreta-tion best known from Philo of Alexandria (see pp. 407–408). Paul gave him further instruction about Jesus, and consequently Apollos was

Athens, Stoa of Attalos. The public marketplace and gathering place in Athens, the *agora,* was lined with colonnaded structures in which took place informal social encounters, business transactions, and addresses to the public who chose to listen. The columns, called by the Greeks *stoa,* provided the name for the followers of the Greek philosopher Zeno. They chose to address and challenge listeners in these public places rather than in the more formal lecture halls where the followers of other philosophers gathered for instruction and discussion. On the eastern side of the *agora* stood a large colonnade which has been reconstructed as here pictured.

American School of Classical Studies, Athens.

effective in both Ephesus and Corinth in persuading Jews about Jesus as God's Messiah (Acts 18:24–8).

The healings and exorcisms performed among the Christians in Ephesus attracted vast public attention but also opposition from those who made their living as priests and attendants in the world-renowned temple of Artemis located in this city. The result was a riot, and Paul departed for Macedonia (19:1–20:1). His announced intention was to return to Jerusalem before sailing west to Rome (19:21–2). On his journey to Jerusalem, he met with the elders from the church at Ephesus and told them that they would not see him again: a clear indication of his impending martyrdom (20:13–38). In Jerusalem he is seized by the religious and political authorities. In reporting these events, the author of Acts recounts Paul's description of his life, including a defense of himself as not guilty of violating religious or civil regulations – a judgment that is confirmed by all the authorities who heard his defense (22–6). In his final hearings at Caesarea, the official seat of Roman rule in Palestine, he appeals to Caesar, which was his right as a Roman citizen, and is sent off to Rome as a prisoner (27:1). The voyage is interrupted by a shipwreck, from which the crew and passengers are saved (27:13–44). The narrative style is typical of the romances of the second century (sidebar p. 519), which have influenced the author's mode of telling this story. After another sign of divine deliverance – a deadly snake bites Paul but he is unharmed (28:1–6) – and other indications of God's favor upon Paul (28:7–10), he lands at Puteoli (near Naples). When he reaches Rome, he is placed under house arrest. This enables him to be visited by Jewish leaders, whom he tries to convince through his interpretation of the law and the prophets that Jesus was God's Messiah (28:16–23). Some are persuaded, but others he consigns to the people spoken of by Isaiah who lack understanding of God and his purpose (Isa. 6:9–10 = Acts

The theater at Ephesus. Settled by Greeks in the tenth century B.C.E., Ephesus was a major city on the western coast of Asia Minor and home of the renowned temple of Artemis, the fertility goddess. The theater there seated 24,000 and may have been the setting for Paul's fight "with beasts at Ephesus" mentioned in 1 Cor. 15:32 or where Paul's coworkers were dragged to confront the people (Acts 19:21–41). James Walters.

Ephesus, aerial view.

Appian Way. The Appian Way linked Rome with the port of Brundisium and is probably the route by which Paul went north from Puteoli (Acts 28:13) and entered Rome.

Gordon Converse.

28:26–7). The message has been sent to the gentiles, and they will give heed. The story ends with Paul carrying forward his work of preaching and teaching, even though the earlier narrative has already informed the reader of Paul's impending death in the service of the gospel.

Thus Acts serves as a major document for the early church, in that its style provides a contact with the literate gentile world, and its content serves both as a justification for the claim that the church is the new covenant people and as a rebuttal to those who see in the Christian gospel either a threat to the political status quo or a perversion of the Jewish scriptures. Since the emphasis is on the worldwide mission to be performed by the apostles and their successors, the issue of when the new age will come is of secondary importance. Of primary importance is carrying out the commission to spread the news about Jesus to the ends of the earth, as was articulated when the Spirit was poured out at Pentecost. Greco-Roman writers in the second century C.E. told stories of divine visions and intervention of the deities in behalf of humans devoted to them or searching for them. Prime examples of this type of literature are the *Metamorphoses* of Apuleius, which details a young man's search for the goddess Isis, and the *Sacred Discourses* of Aristides, whose devotion to the god Asklepios led to transforming mystical experiences. Such popular literary styles were employed in the second and subsequent centuries by Christian writers in order to surround what they saw as significant for the life of the church with an aura of the miraculous as a sign of contact with God. We shall examine some of this material later.

B. THE GOSPEL OF JOHN: MYSTICAL PARTICIPATION IN THE DIVINE LIFE

Two major cultural factors are evident in the reworking of the gospel tradition in the Gospel of John. The first derives from the wisdom tradition of the hellenistic age, especially as wisdom was perceived in Judaism. The second is apparent in the keen interest among both Jews and gentiles of the first century C.E. in forms of religion that offered the possibility of direct experience of God, especially through visions or the hearing of sacred messages. With the growing sense of the vast difference between God and human beings ("As high as the heavens are above the earth, so high are my ways and thoughts above yours"; Isa. 55:8) and the awesomeness of God's presence (Ezek. 1), there was a yearning for some instrument or agent by which mere humans could have contact with the sovereign, holy God. For some, this mediating agency was found in Wisdom, viewed as the first of God's creations (Prov. 8) and as the channel through which knowledge of God comes to human beings (Sir. 1). Others hoped for a direct vision of God, on the model of the experience of Moses, Ezekiel, and Daniel, whose very appearance was altered as a consequence of their having seen God. In the gentile world of this time, there was a similar striving for some religious experience that would bring together the hallowed traditions of divine wisdom with a direct and immediate experience of the deities.

One of the most effective forms of these aspirations developed in this period around the goddess Isis. In older Egyptian tradition she had a role as the one who restored to life her husband, Osiris, whose death at the hands of his enemy and return from the dead symbolized the annual cycle of fertility caused by the rise and fall of the Nile. By hellenistic times Isis had taken over the role of goddess of wisdom and was believed to appear to those seeking her help or insights, with the result that the lives of her devotees were renewed and fulfilled by sharing in the divine life. In his portrayal of Jesus, the author of the Gospel of John combines these factors of human participation in the divine life and understanding of the divine purpose.

1. The Prologue to John's Gospel

The prologue to the Gospel of John (1:1–16) speaks of the Word, or Logos, of God as the instrument of creation and of divine self-disclosure (1:1, 10, 18). In a way that recalls the roles of Wisdom, but at the same time is significantly different, the Word enables human beings to become members of God's own people (1:12–13). This admission to the new community of faith differs completely from natural birth into a merely human family. Indeed, the Word's own people did not receive him (1:11). This unique Son of God is the source of the light of the knowledge of God (1:4) and of the radiance of God's glory (in contrast to the temple, where God's glory once shone) and is the channel of God's grace and truth (1:14, 16, 18). The requirement for becoming God's child is to trust God's Son (1:12). It was John the Baptist who

LOGOS

TWO TRADITIONS, EACH from a separate culture, merge in the meaning of *logos* in the Gospel of John. (1) In Greek philosophy, this term was used with reference to the rational process seen as characterizing the universe and its ongoing functions. Humans, by perceiving this *logos*, can gain understanding of the inherent order that pervades all reality. The term, which may have taken on these connotations with Heraclitus, the sixth-century B.C.E. philosopher who sought to discern order in the universal processes, was employed by the Stoics in connection with their similar concept of the law of nature, which dominates all that is. (2) The other tradition is the biblical understanding of creation through the *word* of God, which in the Septuagint is translated as *logos*. In the Jewish wisdom tradition, the instrument through which God called the world into being and rules it is "wisdom" – in Greek *sophia*. This role of wisdom is described in such passages as Prov. 8:22–31 and Wisdom of Solomon 9:1–2. For Philo of Alexandria, the *logos* was both the means by which God communicated his purpose to his people – the Word of God – and the agent by which the world was created and sustained. Further, this understanding of divinely ordered reason in the universe was fully compatible with the insights of the philosophers of that period.

In the prologue to the Gospel of John, however, another crucial dimension is added to the *logos*: the creative, reasoned purpose of God has been disclosed in a human form: "The word became flesh" and dwelt among human beings, so that they can come to discern the divine purpose and to see themselves as God's children (John 1:1–18).

prepared for Jesus' coming (1:6–9, 19–27), who denied that he was himself the Light, but who acclaimed Jesus of Nazareth as the Lamb of God, who takes away the world's sin (1:29), and as the Spirit-anointed Son of God (1:32–4). At the outset of his public career, Jesus begins to rally around him the core of his followers, who acclaim him as Lamb of God, Son of God, and King of Israel (1:36, 41, 49). He responds by promising them that they will see his ultimate vindication by God's angels as son of man (1:51). Paradoxically, John's Gospel pictures Jesus as fully human ("son of Joseph"; 1:45) but also as sharing the very nature of God (1:18, 8:58, 17:21).

Although we do not know who wrote this anonymous work, the frequent references to "the disciple whom Jesus loved" (13:23–5; 19:26–7; 20:2–8; 21:7, 20) and the fact that such a person seems to be identifying himself as the one who recorded this Jesus material led many in the early church to the conclusion that the gospel was written by John, the son of Zebedee (Mark 1:19), although he is never mentioned by name in the gospel. The reference in 21:22 to the possibility that this disciple might live until Jesus returned to earth led some to suppose that he was writing at a greatly advanced age, perhaps late in the first century. But these are no more than ancient guesses. What is clear is that the writer is not literarily dependent on the other gospels and that he is more interested in symbolic meaning than in historical narrative. Indeed, he delights in using words with double meaning and intended his readers to grasp both meanings rather than choose between them. For example:

"be born again" – "be born from above" (3:3–7)
"living water" – "running water" (4:13–15)
"born of wind" – "born of the Spirit" (3:8)
"lifted up" = exalted or crucified (3:14, 8:28, 12:32)

JOHN

JOHN, AN ABBREVIATED form of the Semitic Johanan, was a common name in the centuries before Jesus. In the New Testament, those with this name include John the Baptist (John 1:19–34); John, the father of Simon Peter (John 1:42); John, from the family of the high priest (Acts 4:6); John Mark (Acts 16:37); John, the son of Zebedee (Mark 1:10); and John, the author of the Book of Revelation (Rev. 1:4–10). The authorship of the fourth gospel has traditionally been assigned to John the disciple, who was with Jesus at the transfiguration (Mark 9:2) and during the struggle of Jesus in the Garden of Gethsemane (Mark 14:33). John and his brother James were called by Paul "pillars" in the Jerusalem church (Gal. 2:6–10). It was this John who very early was identified as the unnamed "beloved disciple" mentioned repeatedly in John and assumed to be the author.

The language of this gospel is disarmingly simple Greek. But the symbolic strategy of the author, with the focus on timeless meaning rather than merely reports of what happened, and the fact that in many narrative and teaching details this gospel differs widely from the other gospels, suggest that it was written by someone who later became a follower of Jesus, not an eyewitness. In sharp contrast to the Gospel of John, the Revelation of John is written in thoroughly apocalyptic style, and its major interest is never touched on in the Gospel of John: the political and cosmic conflict between the Roman Empire and the people of God, which is soon to culminate in the final battle between God and the powers of evil. The confrontation which is shaping up between the church and the empire, with their incompatible claims to the divinity of Christ and of the emperor, is the distinctive focus of the author of Revelation.

As is evident throughout the material included in this gospel, the strategy of the writer is evocative rather than primarily informational. In addition to the unique account of Jesus' arrest, execution, and post-resurrection appearances (18:1–24), the author focuses his gospel on two quite different kinds of material: the narratives of Jesus' miraculous acts, or "signs," and the extended discourses uttered by Jesus according to John, most of which include the characteristic expression "I am . . ."

2. The Signs of Jesus

Throughout his gospel John highlights the *signs* of Jesus, commenting near the conclusion on their meaning (John 20:31), even mentioning them by number at certain points (2:11, 4:54). Like the English word "sign," the Greek term assumes that a sign points beyond itself to some larger reality. For John the miracles of Jesus are important not only as acts of mercy and healing but as indicators of Jesus' special relationship to God and of God's unique purpose at work through him. John tells the reader that he has chosen to report this selection of Jesus' signs to evoke trust that Jesus is the Messiah, the Son of God, and that those who thereby trust in him attain new life among God's new people (20:30–1). From the outset, Jesus' signs disclosed his glory and confirmed his disciples' faith in him (2:11).

The first of the signs is Jesus' changing water into wine, which he did after the wine supply was exhausted at a wedding feast to which he and his followers had been invited. The symbolic dimensions of the story include the fact that it was a wedding (which is a common Jewish symbol for God's completion of his purpose for his people; Hos. 3), that the receptacles for the new wine are the jars containing water for ritual purification, and that the best has been kept until the last (2:1–10). Although it is not included among John's numbered list of the signs, Jesus' cleansing of the temple (which occurs at the end of his career in the other gospels) is interpreted here in signlike fashion (2:19–22) as pointing to his resurrection and the establishment of "his body," the Christian community, where God now dwells. Similarly, the story of Jesus' debate with Nicodemus symbolizes the contrast between Pharisaic and early Christian understanding of how one becomes part of God's people (i.e., not by ethnic descent but by the new birth through faith) and by a new understanding of the Jewish scriptures as pointing to their ultimate fulfillment in such events as the lifting up of Jesus on the cross as the remedy for human sin (3:1–17). The discussion between Jesus and the Samaritan woman (4:1–41) demonstrates God's welcome to such complete outsiders from pious Israel as this sinful Samaritan woman. And it leads to the dismissal of the question as to whether God dwells in the temple in Samaria or the one in Jerusalem, turning instead to the proclamation that the true worship of God is not in some sacred earthly place but in the Spirit.

The next sign (by John's listing) is Jesus' healing of the son of a governmental official (4:43–54), which points once again to access by outsiders to the healing power of God through Jesus. The healing of the lame man at the pool (5:1–18) takes place in violation of the Sabbath law and reaches its climax in the explicit claim by Jesus to be the Son of God – both of which factors are sufficient to convince the religious authorities to seek to have him put to death. The feeding of the five thousand and the associated account of Jesus walking on the water (6:1–21) are the only miracle stories reported by both John and the other gospels (Mark 6:30–52, Matt. 14:13–33, Luke 9:10–17). The feeding of the throng recalls the miraculous supply of food to Israel in the desert (Exod. 16), but its wording ("he took, he gave thanks, he broke, he gave") points to the Christian eucharistic meal. The walking on the water likewise recalls God's control of the waters of chaos in the creation story (Gen. 1:1–10) and the miraculous passage of the liberated people of Israel across the sea from Egypt to Sinai (Exod. 14). But it also points to the Christian experience of being buried and raised to new life in the baptismal waters (John 3:5, Rom. 6:2–4).

The story of Jesus healing the man born blind (John 9) is pictured as an unprecedented event (9:32) and implicitly as the fulfillment of prophecy about the new age (Isa. 35:5). The immediate issues are two: Jesus' violation of the Sabbath and the official decision among the Jewish leaders that those who confess Jesus to be the Messiah are to be expelled from the synagogue (9:22). The concluding paragraph of the chapter (9:35–41) makes clear that what is at stake is not merely physical ability to see but spiritual insight as to who Jesus really is. The last in the series of signs is the story of Lazarus being raised from the dead by Jesus (11:1–44). Lazarus's sisters believe in theory in the final resurrection of the dead but are not prepared for Jesus the Messiah to demonstrate in person the triumphant power over death. As in the case of the healing of the lame man on the Sabbath, Jesus' act consolidates the opposition that seeks to destroy him (11:45–57). The authori-

"I AM"

THE SPECIAL NAME OF THE God of Israel used in the Hebrew Bible, *yhwh*, was considered so holy that it should not even be pronounced. Down to the present day, most pious Jews when reading the scriptures substitute a general designation for God, *'adonai* (Lord), instead of giving the Hebrew word in the text (which is spelled without vowels) what was probably its original pronunciation, Yahweh. In the Greek translation of the Bible, the Septuagint, this name of God is often rendered as *ego eimi*, which means "I am" or "it is I." This practice is derived from the incident in Exod. 3:13–14 in which Moses asks how he is to identify to his people who this God is who has commissioned him to lead them out of slavery into the land of promise. God replies that his name is "I Am Who I Am." Since the hallowing of the name of God by abstaining from pronouncing it is very ancient, Jesus' practice according to the Gospel of John of referring to himself as "I am" would have been understood by ancient Jews as an audacious, even sacrilegious claim to identity with God.

ties plot to seize him when he comes to Jerusalem to take part in the Passover ceremonies, which are seen by John as symbolic of the death of Jesus, the Lamb of God, who takes away the world's sin.

3. The "I Am" Sayings of Jesus

In John's account of Jesus walking on the water (6:20), his response to the terror of the disciples is to address them with the words, "It is I" – in Greek, *ego eimi*. This is an emphatic form of the ordinary first-person singular of the verb "to be": "I am." It is also the exact phrase found in Exod. 3:13–14, where in response to Moses' inquiry as to who is sending him to lead Israel out of Egyptian slavery, God gives his name (in the Greek version) as *"ego eimi."* The "I am" declarations of Jesus in John's Gospel concern not only Jesus' relationship to God but also the response to him on the part of his new people.

The first of these sayings occurs in John 6, following the story of the miraculous feeding, when Jesus announces, "I am the bread of life" (6:35). There is a vital distinction to be made between bread (even miraculously supplied bread), which can merely sustain life on ordinary terms (such as Moses provided for Israel in the desert), and "the bread of life." All who partake of the true bread from heaven (6:32–5) will share in eternal life. These constitute the true people of God, who are called into new life by Jesus, who has come down from heaven, as the manna did in the days of Moses. Those who share in his flesh and blood will live forever. "Flesh and blood" symbolize both his true humanity and the eucharistic elements by which his people are united and nurtured (6:53–8).

In the following chapter (John 7), Jesus goes up to Jerusalem for the Feast of Tabernacles (or Booths), which had acquired three associations for Jews: a recollection of the years in the wilderness when God was with his people en route to the land of promise; the occasion for the dedication of the temple of Solomon, where God was believed to dwell among his people; and the time prior to the giving of the law of Moses (Exod. 19–20) when God revealed himself to Moses by name (I am; Exod. 3:14). Jesus' words and actions link these factors, in that he appears in the temple, is teaching, and is challenging the legalistic basis for membership in God's people and even the claim of those who worship God in the temple that they know God or the one he has sent among them (John 7:28–9). The symbol of Moses' having provided water for thirsty Israel in the desert (Exod. 17:6) is built upon by Jesus when he claims that he provides the Spirit, which renews and sustains human life as God intended it to be (7:37–9). Even though the phrase "I am" is not used, the claim of Jesus is that his teaching is from God (7:17) and that he comes from God (7:28) and is going to be with God (7:33–6).

The second "I am" saying is preceded in some ancient copies of John by the story of the woman caught in adultery (8:1–11). But it is very likely that the original version of John went directly from 7:52 to what we know as 8:12–30, where Jesus claims oneness with the God whose name is "I am" (8:24, 28, 58). In the process of these declarations, Jesus claims to have existed before Abraham, the founder of the

LIFE

IN THE NEW TESTAMENT there are three common words for "life." (1) *Bios* refers to the basic functions of ordinary human life: its duration, its means of subsistence, and its patterns of conduct. Examples include Mark 12:44 and Luke 15:12, 30. (2) *Psyche* means the breath of life, as in Luke 12:20 and Acts 20:10. In Mark 10:45 Jesus speaks of giving up one's life (*psyche*) for the benefit of others. Similar uses of this term occur in Phil. 2:30 and John 15:13. In some contexts, this word implies the quality of life in its potential for love of God or love of fellow humans (1 Thess. 2:8, Matt. 22:37, Eph. 6:6). In Greek philosophical usage *psyche* is the soul, an eternal dimension of human existence which transcends death. It is possible that the word carries these connotations in such passages as Mark 8:35, Matt. 10:39, and 1 Pet. 1:9, 22, but it is more likely that here also the issue is, What are you going to do with the life that is at your disposal? God will fulfill, reward, or judge individuals according to the way in which that responsibility is discharged. (3) *Zoe* is occasionally used with the same connotations as *bios* for ongoing physical existence (Luke 16:25, 1 Cor. 15:19, Heb. 7:3), but more often it appears contrasted with life under ordinary conditions of human limitations and despair. *Zoe* refers to the transformed life that will be available in the age to come through trust in Christ. Sometimes it is identified with Christ himself, as in John 6:35, 11:25, and 14:6. More often it concerns the life of the believer, either now (Rom. 6:14, 2 Cor. 2:16, 1 John 5:12) or in the future (Mark 10:30; Gal. 6:8; 1 Tim. 6:19; Rev. 2:7, 22:1–2).

covenant people, was born, and denounces as unfit for membership in God's people all who fail to see in him the true Son of God, who truly honors God and conveys God's truth to those who are ready to receive it. The third "I am" saying builds on the scriptural images of God as shepherd and of Israel as God's flock (Ps. 23, 80:1; 1 Kings 22:17; Isa. 14:30; Mic. 7:14). Expanding the image, Jesus claims to be both the door of access to the true flock (10:7) and the good shepherd (10:11, 14–15), who is willing to die for the sheep. His giving up his life will result in God's raising him from the dead (10:17–18). The response of his hearers is mixed: some see him as crazy (10:20), while others are persuaded that only God could give anyone the capacities that Jesus possessed (10:40).

In the course of actions and statements connected with his raising Lazarus from the dead, Jesus declares that he not only makes possible resurrection but also *is* "the resurrection and the life" (John 11:25–6). Jesus' power to renew life is not automatic: it must be responded to by trust in him as God's agent for human transformation. The religious authorities recognize that these astounding claims cannot be merely ignored: many people are believing them, and the developing movement has implications for the future of the covenant community. Accordingly, the priestly and Pharisaic leaders form a coalition – in spite of their own differences – in order to be rid of Jesus and to preserve what they see as the integrity of Israel (11:45–57). The reactions of the people are varied: Mary, the sister of Lazarus, shows that she understands Jesus' destiny by anointing him for his death (12:1–8); the crowds turn out for his entry into the city in fulfillment of the prophecies about Israel's future king (Ps. 118:25–6, Zech. 9:9). But significantly, some Greeks (i.e., gentiles) come seeking Jesus, which leads him to declare that the way is now open for all of humanity to respond to him and his message (12:20–2). At this point Jesus begins to speak directly

THE STORY OF THE ADULTEROUS WOMAN

THIS MOVING STORY OF Jesus' compassion toward a sinful woman, which appears in many late manuscripts of the Gospel of John (7:53–8:11), is not found in the oldest manuscripts. In some manuscripts it is found following Luke 21:24 or 21:38. Very likely it is not part of the original Gospel of John, although it fits well with this section of that gospel, where Jesus is engaged in disputes with the Jewish religious leaders.

THE ABODE OF THE DEAD

IN THE JEWISH TRADITION, *she'ol* was the place below the surface of the earth to which the dead departed from this life. It was as though the grave provided access to this dark and inescapable place. The important possibility for life was in what one made of earthly life, especially in having offspring, rather than looking for life beyond the grave. Children were produced so that one's heritage might be continued beyond death. The grave and *she'ol* were regarded with despair in much of the Jewish wisdom tradition (Job 17:1, Eccles. 9:10, Prov. 30:16). Although *she'ol* is in some texts regarded as the special destiny of the wicked (Prov. 5:5, Ps. 9:17), the faithful are confident that God will be with them, even in *she'ol*. In other later texts, however, there is an expectation and hope of renewal and restoration of the righteous dead (Ps. 16:10; quoted in Acts 2:27, 31, in connection with the resurrection of Jesus). At times resurrection seems to refer to the restoration of the whole faithful community, as in Ezekiel 37. But in Isa. 26:19 and Dan. 12:2, it is the faithful individual members of God's people who are given personal assurance that their fidelity to God will be rewarded when they are raised up from among the dead.

This hope was given concrete expression in the early Christian assurance that God raised Jesus from the dead and that his people will share in the resurrection of the faithful and in the age to come (1 Cor. 15). In passages like John 11:25–6, however, the benefits of the resurrection life are seen as already being enjoyed by God's people in the present age. In hellenistic tradition there was a belief that the human soul would be released from the body at death and might ascend to the realm of the eternal and divine. That notion was taken up by some Jewish thinkers in the hellenistic period, as Wisdom of Solomon 3:1–4 attests. But when Paul describes the state of the faithful in the new age, it is not in terms of a disembodied soul but as a transformed human body – the spiritual body (1 Cor. 15:35–49). Similarly, in Rev. 20:11–22:5, the righteous find their ultimate joy and fulfillment – not as souls ascending to heaven – but in the new order, the new city, and the new temple, which come down out of heaven to a renewed earth (Rev. 21:10).

---

of his impending death (12:23–32). Yet most of the people cannot grasp his message or the significance of his death. In rejecting him and his word, they reject the life of the age to come (12:35–50).

Chapters 13–17 of John mingle promises and instructions for the new community with additional "I am" declarations by Jesus. Before analyzing the advice to the community, we will consider two other "I am" statements as they bear on the role of Jesus and the response of the covenant people. In 14:1–14 Jesus announces that he is going away to the dwelling place of the Father in order to prepare a place for his followers. His disciples do not know the way to reach God. Jesus announces that he is *the* way to God, the embodiment of the truth about God, as well as the life that God intends for human beings to enjoy (14:6). It is through seeing him that men and women can see God; through remaining faithful within the community that his followers can do God's work and grasp God's truth. While Jesus is gone from them, preparing for them to enter and remain in God's presence, he has provided the Spirit, who will teach them God's will and fill them with God's peace (14:15–31). Modifying the biblical image of Israel as God's vineyard (Isa. 5:1–7), Jesus pictures himself as the true vine (15:1–7), with God as the gardener who cares for and prunes the branches (i.e., Jesus' followers) and enables them to produce the appropriate fruit (i.e., the deeds of love and mercy). Those who adopt this way of life will experience hatred from the world, which rejected and crucified Jesus (15:18–16:4). But by the Holy Spirit, God will guide them, enable them to persevere, and reveal to them the truth about God and his purpose in the world (16:5–23). In spite of the seeming defeat represented by the impending death of Jesus, his crucifixion and resurrection are God's triumph over the world and its hostile powers (16:25–33).

Jesus' farewell messages conclude with a series of self-declarations: eternal life means to know God and Jesus, whom God has sent (17:3); Jesus and the Father are one (17:11); his people share in this divine unity (17:21); that unity is to be expressed in and to the world (17:23); love is the bond that binds together God, Jesus, and the people of the covenant (17:26). Running through these farewell discourses are guidelines and promises. The sole commandment that Jesus gives is for the members of the community to love one another (13:34; 15:12–13). Such forgiving, accepting love is to be expressed symbolically in the washing of one another's feet (13:14). The most important public witness that the members of the community bear is their love for one another (13:35). The Spirit is the divinely provided instrument for guiding them into the wider reaches of knowledge of God (16:12–14). Its presence and power will give assurance of God's ultimate victory over the world and its evil forces (16:33). Meanwhile, the experience of unity among the faithful enables them to be sustained in their reliance upon God (17:9–12) and bears testimony to their essential unity as God's new people (17:20). Thus, throughout the Gospel, the symbolic actions and declarations of Jesus point to God's purpose: to experience the unity in love and trust that is to characterize the people he has called into being through Jesus.

Unlike the letters of Paul or the Gospel of Matthew, John's Gospel sets forth no guiding principles for the life of the church other than the commandment to love one another (13:34–5). There is not even a command to love one's neighbor, as in the other gospels. Clearly, the primary concern in John is for mutual love within the community, symbolized by the washing of one another's feet (13:12–15). Issues such as the appropriate attitude toward the Roman government are not addressed in John. The prime focus is on the common life within the group.

4.   The Death and Resurrection of Jesus

Although the overall structure and content of John's story of Jesus' arrest, trial, and execution resemble the pattern found in the other gospels, a number of significant details are unique to John. When the large number of soldiers come to seize Jesus (John 18:5–9), and he identifies himself with the words "I am," they fall to the ground before him, obviously (for the believing reader, but unknowingly for the soldiers) overwhelmed in the presence of God. The preservation of the eleven from arrest or trial is seen as fulfillment of Jesus' prediction about their being kept by God's power (John 6:39, 10:28, 17:15). His own impending death is pictured metaphorically as his drinking the cup that God has prepared for him (18:11) and theologically as taking place in behalf of all his people (18:13–14).

CAPITAL PUNISHMENT

JOHN 18:31 QUOTES THE Jewish authorities as declaring that they could not put anyone to death, but prior to the fall of Jerusalem in 70 C.E., the Jewish council (*synedrion*) did have the right to execute those Jews who violated Jewish law, although they needed the prior approval of the Roman authorities to do so. On the other hand, those whose misdeeds were seen as threats to the public order had to be turned over to the Roman authorities for judgment and appropriate action. A decision by the Jewish council leading to the death of the offender is described in Acts 5:27–40. Further, early rabbinic sources report executions carried out by authority of the Jewish council according to their laws.

From this point on, references are made to the special relationship to Jesus and his mother reserved for "the beloved disciple," whose name is not given but who is reported to have a special connection with the high priest, which makes possible his admission to the court-yard where the hearing is to occur (18:15–18). Jesus commends his mother to the care of this disciple, who remains as a witness of the cru-cifixion (19:25–7); he is the first witness of the empty tomb (20:1–10) and is said to have the possibility of remaining until Jesus' triumphal return (21:20–4). As we have noted above, it is the special role assigned to this disciple throughout this gospel that led to its being assigned to John, who, according to the common testimony of the gospels, was from the outset part of the inner circle of Jesus' followers.

The account of Jesus' confrontation with the religious authorities is reported in a distinctive way in the Gospel of John. When Jesus declares before the high priest that his testimony to God and his pur-pose have been wholly public, rather than a hidden plot, he is struck for his audacity in challenging the high priest (18:19–24). Although the religious leaders will not enter Pilate's courtyard lest they defile them-selves for the Passover, which begins at sundown (18:28), they urge that Jesus be executed as a threat to Roman imperial rule on the ground that they had no right to perform capital punishment. Later they continue to press the point that Jesus is a threat to Roman rule and that the only sovereign they acknowledge is Caesar (19:15).

In contrast to the accounts of Jesus' death in the other gospels, John reports no agony or struggle on the cross but only a word to the beloved disciple concerning the new relationships within the commu-nity ("Here is your mother"). His cry of thirst results in his being offered wine, which John notes is in fulfillment of scripture (Ps. 69:21). At this point the symbolic meaning of his life and death is complete for the disclosure of God's purpose to and for his people, and Jesus says simply, "It is finished," and dies.

In conformity to Jewish law prohibiting exposure of a corpse on the Sabbath (a regulation mentioned in the Qumran Temple Scroll) orders are given to ensure the death of Jesus and the others. Even though Jesus is already dead, his side is pierced, thus fulfilling both the law against the breaking of the bones of a sacrificial victim at Passover (Exod. 12:46, Num. 9:12) as well as the prediction of the wounded side (Zech. 12:10). Two details found only in John's account of the burial of Jesus are the note that Joseph of Arimathea was a secret disciple of Jesus (19:38) and that Nicodemus, who had come to Jesus at night (John 3), assisted in the preparation of his body for entombment. Clearly, these two individuals represent for John that segment of Judaism that was to recognize Jesus as God's Messiah. That the burial was *in a garden* is perhaps a backward look to the Garden of Eden, where humans are pictured in scripture as first assigned responsibility by God (Gen. 2), and a forward look to the restoration of God's new covenant people in the future garden of abundance as depicted by the prophet Jeremiah (Jer. 31).

Mary Magdalene figures prominently as a witness to the risen Lord (John 20:1–2, 11–18). It is the disciples who are slow to understand what has happened (20:3–10, 24–9). When they see Jesus' pierced hands, they are certain that he is the one who had been crucified, now risen from the dead. The risen Christ, like the "word become flesh" in the prologue of John, is present in fully human form and is not merely a spirit or an apparition. He commissions the disciples to "cast the net" (21:6) and to "feed my sheep" (21:15–17) – that is, to accept responsibility for drawing new members into the fellowship and for nurturing the members of the community. Jesus' final words to Peter are interpreted by John to be a prediction that this disciple who recently denied him will one day follow Jesus to a martyr's death at the hands of the civil authorities.

The question as to whether or not some of his followers will live until his return is left open (21:20–3). There are no clues about organization or distribution of authority within the community.

C. THE LETTERS OF JOHN: TOWARD UNITY OF FAITH AND AUTHORITY

There is a basic analogy between the changes that are apparent as one moves from the Gospel to the letters of John and from the genuine letters of Paul to the later writings in his name. The spontaneous, loosely organized group bound together by mutual love that is reflected in the Gospel of John seems not to have been able to survive on those terms. In the letters of John it is in process of developing into a social structure which includes clear definition of qualifications for admission to the group and for maintenance of good standing. And further, there are now established agents with authority to enforce conformity on matters of doctrine and practice within the community.

The urgency of these changes was heightened by intellectual developments in the wider Roman world and by forms of speculation that were developing within Judaism. Among pagan philosophers, the thought of Plato was recast along lines now known as Neo-Platonism (see p. 548), which saw as the goal of existence the union of the human spirit with the divine spirit. It disdained the physical universe as transitory and subject to decay while affirming the eternal nature of pure spirit. Among Jewish speculative thinkers, wisdom was defined as the divinely provided instrument by which individuals could be liberated from their involvement in the material world (which had come to be regarded by some as inherently evil) and ascend into the presence of God.

Among certain Christian groups, therefore, there arose by the first half of the second century C.E. a style of religious thinking that claimed that the created world was made by an evil divinity and that the human body was a tomb from which the human spirit was to be freed. The body of Jesus was depicted as a kind of costume behind which the real Jesus was concealed, and which he could set aside at will. Among some people of this persuasion, moral behavior was a matter of indifference because it involved the worthless, illusory mode of bodily existence. The only worthy goal of life was to rise above the material world, including life in the material body. These conceptual trends

PETER IN ROME

ALTHOUGH THERE IS NO evidence directly linked to the event, it is highly probable that Peter was martyred in Rome ca. 65–7 C.E., when Nero made the Christians the scapegoats for the burning of Rome, which he had himself initiated. The clear implication of John 21:15–18 is that Peter is to die a martyr's death. 1 Clement 5:1–6:1 confirms and consolidates this tradition. Modern excavation of the ruins of the ancient structure beneath the present Saint Peter's Church in Rome gave no evidence of a burial, but if his body was torn apart by wild animals in the arena one would not expect to find his remains. The evidence is substantive for the flourishing in Rome of a tradition linked with Peter, of which 1 Peter is a prime example. Written from Rome, for which "Babylon" is the cryptic designation as the center of power threatening God's people, 1 Peter demonstrates that Rome has become a major center for the life of the church and that its clientele include those at an impressively high cultural level, as the language and style of this letter demonstrate. The production of an abundance of material attributed to Peter in the subsequent four or five centuries (Acts of Peter and Paul; Passion of Peter and Paul; Letter of Peter to Philip; Acts of Peter; Apocalypse of Peter) shows how important he became for that segment of the church that wanted to exalt him as the chief among the apostles and as the major figure in the church at Rome.

NEO-PLATONISM

ALTHOUGH WHAT historians designated as Neo-Platonism did not develop into an elaborate system until the time of Plotinus (early third century C.E.), important anticipations of this philosophical system can be found in the writings of the Jewish philosopher and biblical interpreter Philo of Alexandria in the first century C.E., and of Plutarch and Numenius of Apamea in the second century C.E. Central to this developing philosophical view are (1) the defining of a system of hierarchical principles by which the universe is ordered and sustained; (2) the identification of a supreme principle, which is transcendent and designated as "the One," or the Mind, in which all the Platonic ideas or forms are located; (3) the necessity of the mind or soul to escape from the body in order to ascend for contemplation and understanding of the One; (4) the understanding that evil is an inherent feature of the material world. The influence of this system on Gnosticism and on the increasingly otherworldly outlook of some later Christian writings is obvious.

within Christianity became known as Gnosticism (see p. 495) and produced an extensive literature. These notions were in direct contradiction to the biblical beliefs in the goodness of God's creation and in God's call to his people for purity of life in this age and the age to come.

The three letters attributed to John give evidence of how the Johannine community in and for which the writings were produced was trying to come to terms with the twin problems of order within the group and the appeal of incipient Gnosticism. The letters are anonymous, although the writer refers to himself at the beginning of 2 and 3 John as "the Elder." But since the style and point of view most nearly resemble those of the Gospel of John, they have been from earliest times linked with that – also anonymous – Gospel. Contemporary scholarship agrees in linking these writings and assigning them to what is called for convenience "the Johannine community."

The issue of the true humanity of the earthly Jesus is asserted at the outset in 1 John 1:1–2 in the declaration that he was seen *and touched* by his followers. This is affirmed in response to those influenced by the Neo-Platonists or by the movement that would become Gnosticism in the later second century who wanted to regard Jesus as a divine being who merely masqueraded as a human in order to convey his sublime truths. Those who held that Jesus merely seemed to have a physical body were denounced by the major thinkers of the early church as *docetists*, from the Greek word for "seem." This letter, like the Gospel of John, insists on the full and true humanity of Jesus as the one through whom God's renewal of humanity was disclosed and through whom it is being accomplished. Purity of life is affirmed, but it may be obtained only through the death of Jesus and the cleansing that his blood effects. How essential it is for Christians to live moral lives is developed by calling attention to the need for confession (1:8) and for the forgiveness provided through the death of Christ. The life of full obedience makes possible the perfection of human existence through the love of God (2:1–6), which calls to mind the single commandment from the Gospel: to love one another (2:7–11). Parents and children are given instructions, as they are in the later Pauline tradition (Col. 3:18–23; 1 Tim. 5). To love this corrupt and cruel world system is incompatible with love of the Father (2:15–17). These themes are repeated throughout the letter (4:7–19), where God's very nature is said to be love.

Meanwhile, there are enemies within the church: not some satanic figure of past or future, but those who deny that Jesus is the Christ (2:18–29). The resources to combat this evil are readily available: the Spirit within the community (2:27) and the hope of Jesus' coming again, when his people will be made like him (2:28–3:3). Now his people must maintain their purity, living in love rather than sin, in spite of the hatred that God's people always have experienced and continue to experience (3:11–15). True love manifests itself in actions, not merely in words (3:16–24), and is dependent upon God, not on one's inner feelings. The guideline for testing the faith and action of others is their stance on the question of the true humanity of Jesus (4:1–6). It is the

Spirit that conveys to God's people the love and the conviction of God's support. The themes of love of God, obedience to God's commands, life in union with God, and victory over the world are repeated in 1 John 5. There are warnings about false gods (5:21), about sins so gross that they are not forgiven (5:16–18), and about the power of the Evil One in this world (5:19). In addition to continuing reference to the Spirit, there is also a hint of ritual practice in the mention (5:7) of water and blood (baptism and the eucharistic cup?). There are not only final warnings concerning continuing in sin (5:18) and the worship of false gods (5:21) but also assurance of true understanding about and vital union with God (5:20).

Second John is addressed to a particular church under the title of "the Lady" (in Greek, *kuria*, which is the feminine equivalent of the basic Christian title for Jesus, *kurios*, "Lord"). In this letter there is even greater emphasis on knowing the truth and on living by obedience to God's love commandment. There is also strong condemnation of those who deny that Jesus truly became human. Both false teaching and false teachers are to be avoided, and the latter are not even to be offered the hospitality of the community (8–10). The Elder closes with a statement of his intention of visiting the members.

Third John conveys the delight of the Elder on hearing the report of the community's fidelity to the truth in faith and practice, and of the members' extension of hospitality to the teachers of the truth who have visited them. At the same time, he denounces one Diotrophes, who has questioned and threatens to displace the authority of the Elder. Clearly, we have the emergence within an early Christian community of ecclesiastical disciplinary action. These doctrinal and structural regulations stand in sharp contrast to the atmosphere of mutuality and the simplicity of belief and standards of behavior apparent in the Gospel of John.

D. THE LETTER OF JAMES: PURE AND PEACEABLE WISDOM

The writer of this message identifies himself as "James," although it is not certain which early Christian leader he was. Clearly, he was not a former Galilean fisherman (Mark 1:19–20), since it is highly unlikely that someone from that background would write such smooth Greek, with such effective use of Greco-Roman rhetorical style and the technical terminology of hellenistic philosophy. Further, we should expect a disciple of Jesus to evidence more interest in the Jesus tradition than is apparent in this writing, which mentions the name of Jesus only twice (1:1, 2:1) and never quotes his teachings. There are no references to the cross or the resurrection of Jesus, to baptism or the eucharist. Although the love commandment is quoted, it is given in its Jewish form (James 2:8 = Lev. 19:18). There are also brief references to Jewish law against adultery and murder (James 2:11; cf. Exod. 20:13–14, Deut. 5:17–18). But references to the law depict it as universal law, binding on all humanity, and describe it in language akin to that of Stoic natural law. The way of life that is laid out for the reader

DOCETISM

DERIVED FROM THE GREEK word *dokeo*, meaning "seem," the term "docetism" has been used by modern scholars for the belief of certain early Christian thinkers that Jesus did not have a physical body or ordinary human limitations. Influenced by Greco-Roman stories about deities who masqueraded as humans, appearing and then vanishing into the heavens, the docetic Christians portrayed Jesus' suffering and death as described in the gospel tradition as a kind of stunt to deceive his opponents. For example, in the later apocryphal Gospel of Peter, Jesus does not die on the cross but leaves his body there and ascends to heaven (5:19). Later, a voice from heaven asks a question, and an answer comes from the cross, even though the body of Jesus has been removed (10:41–2).

JAMES

JAMES IS THE ENGLISH equivalent of the Hebrew name Yacov, or Jacob. It has obviously been a common name among Jews in every era, including the first century C.E. There are at least five men with this name mentioned in the New Testament:

James, the son of Zebedee, brother of John, disciple of Jesus (Mark 1:19–20, 3:17)

James, the son of Alphaeus, disciple of Jesus (Mark 3:18, Acts 1:13)

James, the brother of Jesus, initially hostile to Jesus' message and activity (Mark 3:21, 31–5); later a witness to the risen Jesus (1 Cor. 15:7) and major leader in the Jerusalem church (Gal. 2:1–12)

James, the father of Jesus' disciple Judas (Luke 6:16)

James, the author of the New Testament writing that bears his name (James 1:1)

Efforts to link this epistle with any of the other four who bear this name are unpersuasive. As the analysis of this book shows, it was written by a later, intellectually sophisticated Christian who was at home in the vocabulary and literary styles of the wider Roman world.

is also identified as the word (*logos*) of truth (1:18) and is depicted as wisdom that comes "from above." It is peaceable, gentle, open to reason, full of mercy and good fruits, and free of uncertainty or insincerity (3:17). The author perceives a close correspondence between this wisdom and the Stoic notion of universal reason, which communicates to receptive human beings the rational law that pervades and orders the universe.

James's presentation of his case for this wisdom is offered in the literary and rhetorical style that is known from Cynic and Stoic philosophers of the first centuries C.E., such as Seneca and Epictetus. Many of the details of James, such as the emphasis on divine accountability and judgment of human behavior, have close corresponding features in the writings of Seneca, a major Roman philosopher. The communication style of posing questions and then offering answers is a feature of the Stoic diatribe. In James, at least one example of this style appears in every chapter: 1:26, 2:18, 3:13, 4:13, 5:13. Similarly, many of the metaphors used in this popular philosophical style of that era are found in James: seeing oneself in a mirror (1:23); reining in the tongue compared with guiding a ship with a rudder (3:3–12); the divine nurturing of growth in human beings (5:7–8). Where references to other New Testament material occur, such as the familiar prayer "lead us not into temptation" (Matt. 6:13) and Paul's teaching about being made right with God by faith apart from works (Gal. 2:16), James seems to take an opposing position (cf. James 1:13, 2:14–26). The goal of the Christian life for James is the attainment of wisdom, which makes possible peace and perseverance in obedience to God. We become his children through the word of truth, James declares (1:18).

Much of the letter is occupied with practical ethics:

Be aware that wealth is transitory (1:9–11)
Avoid anger and unworthy conduct (1:19)
Put God's wisdom into practice (1:20–5, 3:13–18)
Refuse to give preference to the rich (2:1–6)
Avoid conflicts over possessions (4:1–6)
Avoid judging others and boasting (4:11–16)
Beware of riches (5:1–6)
Pray when difficulties come (5:13)
Pray for and anoint the ill (5:14–15)
Confess one's faults and pray for each other (5:16–18) (examples of effective prayer are those of Elijah, Abraham, and Rahab the harlot; Josh. 2:1, 6:17)
Bring the wanderers back to the truth (5:19–20)

Counsel of a more strictly religious nature includes resisting the Devil (4:7), purifying the self (4:17), and expecting the coming of Christ, who will appear as judge (5:7–9). Using a word for religion (*threskeia*) that appears once in Acts (26:5, where it is used by a Roman official describing the conflict between the apostles and the Jews) and once in Colossians (2:18, where it refers to the forbidden practice of worshiping angels), James describes the Christian faith as "pure and genuine *religion*" (1:26–7), thereby placing it in the larger framework of religions in general. He also incorporates into his letter concepts that are peculiar to pagan philosophy, such as the speculative notion of the transmigration of souls (3:6) and the contrast between the heavenly bodies, which cast changing shadows, and "the Father of Lights," who does not change (1:17). At one point (4:5) he claims to be quoting scripture, but there is no such text in any known canonical or other document – which suggests that he is employing a wide range of traditions and literature in the shaping of wisdom in which he is engaged. He sees himself primarily as a teacher (3:1), and his major task as fostering wisdom among Christians, so that they may live consistent and virtuous lives. His grounding in the earlier Christian tradition is perhaps most clearly evident in his reference to "our Lord Jesus Christ, the Lord of glory" (2:2).

E.   FIRST PETER: A COMMUNITY FOR PEACE, HOLINESS – AND SURVIVAL

This letter is written in the name of Peter and is linked with the names of companions of the apostles (Mark and Silas; 1 Pet. 5:12–13; cf. 2 Cor. 1:19; 1 Thess. 1:1–2; Col. 4:10; Acts 12:12; 13:13; etc.), but many features of the writing show that it comes from a time after the age of the apostles, probably in the last decade of the first century C.E. Its smooth, literate Greek, its use of technical terms from hellenistic philosophy and mythology, and its quotations from the Greek version of the Bible indicate that it was not written or dictated by a former Galilean fisherman named Simon Peter. The circumstances of the community and the document's absorption of hellenistic culture suggest that it originated some decades after the death of the apostles. It is possible that Peter did in fact carry on evangelism in the provinces along the southern coast of the Black Sea, where the Christians live to whom this letter is addressed. This would account for Paul's reported decision not to go into this territory (Acts 16:6–7), which would have been based on his conviction that he should evangelize only those areas where no one had done so before (Rom. 15:20). If this inference is correct, then perhaps Peter or some of his associates had already preached the gospel and established Christian communities in these southern Black Sea coastal districts. The issue that had caused conflict between Peter and Paul – how binding the Jewish law was on Christians (Gal. 2) – is wholly absent from 1 Peter, however. For 1 Peter the church appears to be the successor of Israel, is referred to as "exiles" and "the dispersion" (1:1), and considers non-Christians to be "gentiles" (2:12). In this part of the world, the heated issues between Jews and Christians seem to have no significance.

A paramount issue for this community was the prospect of their "suffering as Christians" (4:16). From Roman sources, we may infer that the imperial policy toward the growing church was first explicitly formulated in the early second century in precisely this region when the newly arrived local governor, Pliny, wrote Emperor Trajan asking how to cope with the surge of Christianity in these provinces. The issue was not new, but although there had been local persecutions of

Christians as early as the reign of Nero (ruled 54–68), the movement had been too small to require official action. But by the beginning of the second century it could no longer be ignored. Punishment was to be given to those who, in response to official inquiry, identified themselves as Christians (Pliny, *Letters* 10.96; Trajan's response, 10.97). The pattern was set for direct confrontation between Roman authority and Christian confession of faith, and the issue was the refusal of Christians to participate in ceremonies honoring the emperor as divine. The writer of 1 Peter shares the apocalyptic point of view (1:5): the end of the age will come quite soon; meanwhile, Christians should expect to suffer (1:6, 5:9–10); they must persevere, awaiting God's vindication of them (4:7); meanwhile, they are not to oppose the state (2:13–14, 5:4). During this interim they are to live as holy pilgrims, in anticipation of the transition to the new age (1:1, 2:11).

The cultural background of the writer reflects both hellenistic and Jewish features. He speaks of rebirth (1 Pet. 1:3), as do the mystery religions, and calls for his readers to prepare to offer a formal, logical defense (in Greek, *apologia*) for their convictions (3:15). The imagery he employs elsewhere, however, includes Jewish speculation about divine messengers exhorting the evil spirits and the souls of the dead (3:18–4:6), as well as the more familiar notion of the Devil as seeking to subvert God's people (5:8–9). Out of this spectrum of cultural features, the author has fashioned a coherent view of the church and its perilous place in the Roman world toward the end of the first century.

The major image of the church is that of a living structure (1 Pet. 2:5–9). Its base is the conviction that God raised Jesus from the dead (1:3), that Jesus died as the sacrificial lamb (1:20), and that God has disclosed his purpose to his people through his Word (1:25). They are the living stones in this structure (2:5). The author employs a skillful variant of the image of the rock: Christ is for outsiders the stone of stumbling (1 Pet. 2:7, Ps. 118:22, Isa. 8:14–15), but for those inside the community, he is the rock of their existence. The members as a whole – not certain assigned clergy – are the priests that offer the appropriate sacrifices to God. The community is called "a royal priesthood," which indicates that the royal and national aspirations of Israel are transformed and find fulfillment in the leadership and sacrificial roles which the church members carry out (2:9–10). Their lives are to manifest the holiness that God enjoined on his people of old (1 Pet. 1:16, Lev. 11:44–5). They are to bear witness to their faith before the gentiles (2:12, 3:17), and they are not to retaliate when attacked or accused (2:21, 3:15). Prepared for suffering (4:12–16), they await God's ultimate vindication (5:10).

Meanwhile, they are bound together by their union with Christ and the unity in the Spirit (1 Pet. 3:18). The leaders of the group are given the title of "elder" (5:1–15). Each of them is to be concerned for the welfare of the whole, and each will be rewarded appropriately when the Chief Shepherd appears (5:4). The only one to whom the title *episkopos* (bishop, or guardian) is assigned in this letter is Christ (2:25). Even though this title is not to be given to any leader in this community, there are ranks and levels of responsibility within the organization

DIVINE HONORS TO THE ROMAN EMPEROR

ON HIS ACCESSION TO THE office of emperor in 30 B.C.E., Octavian accepted the designation of himself as "Augustus," and the senate affirmed the divinity of his deceased predecessor Julius. The pattern was set from the beginning of the empire for the deification of and the offering of appropriate divine honors to the dead emperors. Gaius Caligula (37–41 C.E.) and Nero (54–68 C.E.), however, sought to promote the notion of their divinity while they were alive and ruling. But it was Domitian (81–96 C.E.) who actually demanded that he be addressed as lord and god (*dominus et deus*). Nearly all the subjects of the empire were willing to take part in the rites of the imperial cult, because it was regarded as essential to the maintenance of the stability of the empire and the continuing favor of the gods. Jews, however, were excused from participation in these rites, and until the Jewish revolt against the Romans in 66–70 C.E., Jews throughout the empire were permitted to pay an annual tax for the support of the Jerusalem temple and its priestly establishment. So long as Christians were regarded by Roman officials as a sect of the Jews, the issue of their taking part in the divine honors to the emperor seems not to have arisen. Both Jesus (Mark 12:13–17) and Paul (Rom. 13:1–7) taught that their followers should meet the legitimate demands of the Roman state, although the question of divine honors is not raised and was probably not yet a problem.

Even when Nero tried to place the blame on the Christians for the fires in Rome, the question of the imperial cult was not raised. But it may lie behind the puzzling fragmentary evidence that Domitian executed some of his imperial staff on the charge of lapsing into "Jewish customs" and "atheism," which may have been an indirect reference to the discovery of Christian converts within the imperial establishment. The fact that Flavius Clemens and Flavia Domitilla were put to death on this charge by Domitian (Dio Cassius, *Roman History* 67.14) and that the name of the latter is linked with one of the catacombs in Rome where Christians were buried seems to support this inference about persecution of Christians under Domitian. As the correspondence between Trajan and Pliny (in his *Letters* 10.94) indicates, by the early second century, Christians were expected to take part in divine honors, and failure to do so was criminal.

(3:1–7), along lines similar to those that developed in the Pauline communities after Paul's death (1 Tim., 2 Tim., Titus). A particular problem is the ostentation of the wealthy and their ignoring of the poor (3:3–5). Baptism is described as the agent of human salvation – just as Noah's ark saved him and his family from the Flood (3:20–1). Yet its effects are not automatic, since the transformation of the believer is linked with personal purification and "a good conscience." The ultimate ground of its effectiveness is the resurrection of Jesus Christ and his exaltation at God's right hand (3:22). It is the death and resurrection of Jesus which provide the essence of the call to share in this new community (2:4), just as it is his example that provides the paradigm for the life of its members. The letter synthesizes Jewish biblical tradition and Jesus tradition and incorporates conceptual and organizational structures from the Roman culture.

F.   THE REVELATION OF JOHN: THE COMMUNITY IN CONFLICT WITH THE STATE

The problem of the proper Christian attitude toward the Roman state, which under Emperor Trajan (98–117 C.E.) moved toward autocracy, intensified in direct proportion to the incumbent emperor's demand to receive divine honors from his subjects. Around the turn of the second century that problem was addressed in direct and radical form by John, the author of Revelation (see p. 000 on the authorship of Revelation). He was convinced that the only solution to the situation of the church in the world, including the mounting imperial opposition, was the appearance or disclosure (in Greek, *apokalypsis*; Rev. 19:11–16) on earth of Jesus Christ.

In developing his dramatic sketch of the way in which God will defeat the powers of evil, will call to account the disobedient human race, and will vindicate his own people, the author of Revelation draws on the imagery of older biblical apocalyptic writings: the fantastic portraits of the world empires (Dan. 7), the majesty of God's dwelling place (Ezek. 43), and the symbolic use of numbers as indicators of God's having predetermined the events of human history (Dan. 12:11–12; cf. Rev. 12:6, 13:3). The overall view is that the universe is approaching the end of the agelong conflict between God and the Adversary (i.e., Satan, or the Devil). The dominant political power of the world, Rome, is the instrument of Satan, who seeks to force the faithful to abandon God and serve him. The community addressed is a small segment of humanity, scorned and dismissed as worthless by the major religious and political powers. To this brave band of the faithful God has given special insight as to his purposes for the world. Their most severe treatment at the hands of the evil powers lies in the near future and will serve as a time of divine testing of their ability to endure. Beyond this impending period of unparalleled difficulties lies their vindication by God through Jesus Christ.

The literary approach of the author differs in some ways from that of the Jewish apocalyptic writers in that the author identifies himself and is apparently well known to his readers. In the older apocalypses the author adopts a pseudonym – usually of someone from a much earlier era, such as the time of Moses (Testament of Moses), the age of

Colosseum, Rome. Some years after the death of Paul, the emperors Vespasian (69–79) and Titus (79–81) erected this enormous elliptical stone structure. In it many Christians died as martyrs, torn to pieces by wild animals or shot with arrows, as was Saint Sebastian during the great persecution of Christians by Diocletian (284–305).
H.C. Kee.

the patriarchs (Enoch), or the time of Israel's exile in Babylon (Daniel). The Book of Revelation is addressed to Christians living in the writer's own time and speaks to their immediate situation: the churches of Asia Minor threatened by pressure from the empire to conform to requirements that all subjects of Rome perform ceremonies honoring the emperor as divine. Therefore, the focus is wholly contemporary. The book is not to be sealed (Rev. 22:10; cf. Dan 12:4) but is to be read by the community (1:3) until the end of the age comes. The symbolic use of the number 7 pervades the book:

Seven churches are addressed (2:1–3:22)
Seven seals are on the scroll containing God's plan (6:1–8:1)
Seven trumpets announce the divine plan (8:2–9:21, 11:14–19)
Seven bowls of God's wrath will be poured out on the wicked (15:1–16:21)

Although the specific details of the triumphs and failures of the seven churches cannot be recovered by modern interpreters, the central concern is very likely the one enunciated in 2:13, where Pergamum is described as "where Satan dwells." This is probably a reference to the great altar of Zeus there, which was the major center in the eastern Mediterranean world of the divine cult of the Roman emperors. As we have noted, Asia Minor yields the earliest documentation for the conflict between church and state over this issue. The characteristics of each of the seven churches seem to span the whole range of conditions and responses of churches everywhere in this period. In each case (except the Laodicean church) the faithful remnant is described and differentiated from the wider professing group, which will renounce the faith when the pressure is applied by the state:

| Ephesus (2:2) | Patience, fidelity, suffering; need to renew love |
| Smyrna (2:9) | Encouragement to accept suffering; warning against those who claim to be God's people ("Jews") and against the imperial cult |

Altar of Zeus at Pergamum. After the regional monarch Attalus (241–197 B.C.E.) allied himself with the Romans as they were extending their power over Greece and Asia Minor, his chief city, Pergamum, became a center of major political, cultural, and intellectual significance. Two of its chief attractions were the shrine of Asklepios, the god of healing, and the Altar of Zeus, built by Eumenes II (197–159), which became a central focus for divine honors to the Roman emperor – hence the reference in Rev. 2:13 to this city as "where Satan's throne is" and "where Satan dwells."

H.C. Kee.

Pergamum (2:13)	Most have remained faithful, but some have participated in idolatry and prostitution
Thyatira (2:20)	Also patience, fidelity, suffering; but they tolerate a false prophetess (1 Kings 16:31)
Sardis (3:4)	Only a few remain pure; the rest have lost their place or have died
Philadelphia (3:9)	Have endured and are faithful; promised a place in God's temple
Laodicea (3:17–18)	Utterly self-satisfied; wholly disqualified from sharing in God's new age

The letter section ends with a series of final warnings to the churches (3:20–1).

The main section of Revelation opens and closes with visions of the throne of God, on which is seated in triumphant majesty the Lord of creation and Savior of the faithful community. The first such vision (4:1–11) recalls the visions of Ezekiel and Daniel and emphasizes in symbolic language the brilliance, power, and purity of the divine presence. The cry of adoration is led by a group of twenty-four elders – that is, twice the number of the twelve tribes of Israel (4:10).

Unlike the earlier biblical visions of the throne of God, also present in this celestial scene is the Agent of God, through whom the redemptive purpose for the creation is achieved: the one who is both Lion and Lamb (5:4, 6). To him is given the scroll, which is the embodiment of the divine purpose for the creation and for God's people. He alone is worthy "to take the scroll and open its seals" (5:3–14). This means that he alone is qualified to know God's plans for the future of the world and to be God's agent in carrying them to fruition. Universal honor is given him (5:9). His people combine the two traditional Jewish messianic functions: they are a "kingdom of priests" (5:10).

As the details of the redemptive scenario unfold in the successive series of sevens (seals, bowls, trumpets), periodic interludes in the literary flow offer reassurance to the faithful in the midst of these cosmic and social disturbances:

7:1–17   depicts the faithful community, first in symbolic form as the twelve tribes of Israel multiplied by 12 × 1,000 (= 144,000), and then as an innumerable throng from every nation on earth.

10:1–11:14   gives a symbolic picture of the angels making available the divine plan in the form of a scroll to be eaten (10:9–10). The measuring of the temple in Jerusalem symbolizes its destruction (11:1–2). The two witnesses represent the final opportunity for humanity to hear and respond to the gospel before the end of the age comes. This is to occur three and one-half years after they begin their testimony, which will end in their martyrdom at the hand of the satanic agent (11:4–10) and their resurrection, which signals the final outpouring of divine judgment (11:1–13).

14:12–13   is a brief encouragement to those who face martyrdom. They will obtain rest and their works on behalf of the gospel will endure forever.

15:2–8 depicts the heavenly temple in the time just before the final judgments of God are poured out on the world. In contrast with the disasters that are to follow, John here describes the joy and the serenity shared by those whose trust is in God.

Five of the seven seals, whose sequential opening represents the unfolding of the divine plan, symbolize the fearful catastrophes that are to come upon the disobedient human race and the diabolically controlled world:

Absolute political control (6:2)
Slaughter (6:3–4)
Famine (6:5–6)
Widespread death (6:7–8)
Cosmic destruction (6:12–17)

The sixth seal, however, symbolizes the fidelity of the martyrs, who remain true in the face of death (6:9–11). The seventh seal (8:1–5) serves as a transition to the next series of seven, the trumpets, which introduce:

Scorching of the earth (8:7)
Destruction in the sea (8:8–9)
Pollution of the springs and rivers (8:10–11)
Dimming of the sun, moon, and stars (8:12)
Stinging by locusts (demons) of those not sealed by God (9:1–11)
Destruction of one-third of the human race by 200,000 horrendous horses (9:13–19)
Final defeat of the evil powers (11:15)

In spite of these fearful judgments that befall the earth and its inhabitants, the majority of the human race continues to worship idols and demons and to participate in murder and magic (9:20). Following the seventh trumpet, however, elders (whose number again represents twice that of the ancient tribes of Israel: 12 × 2 = 24) join in the worship of God, in the celebration of the fulfillment of his promises, and in the opening of access to the heavenly sanctuary where God dwells (11:16–19).

Two contrasting visions follow: the woman and the child (12:1–6), representing God's people and the Messiah; the war in heaven between the angels, led by Michael, and the demonic forces, led by "the dragon" (Satan), which seek to destroy the woman and her child (12:13–18). Assurance is given of the triumph of God over these enemies through the Messiah (12:10–12). Similarly, Revelation 13 describes a vision of two Beasts: the first claims divine honors (= the emperor) and the second is his chief publicity and enforcement agent, who requires all to honor the first Beast as divine. The first Beast's symbolic number, 666, probably derives from the name of Emperor Domitian (81–96 C.E.): the numerical equivalents of the letters of his name add up to that number. Domitian was the first to insist that he be addressed as *dominus et deus* (Lord and God). In contrast to these symbols of idolatry in the Roman culture is the portrait of the Lamb of God and his people, who number, symbolically, twelve times the sacred

MICHAEL

THE ANGEL MICHAEL, whose name means "Who is like God?" had a special role as messenger and agent in the fulfillment of God's purpose for his people in Jewish apocalyptic writings, beginning with Daniel (10:13, 21; 12:1) and continuing in many of the Jewish apocalypses and testaments, including the Books of Enoch, the Sibylline Oracles, the Testaments of Moses and Solomon, and the War Scroll from Qumran. In the Christian scriptures, his name appears in two apocalyptic contexts, Jude 9 and Rev. 12:7, which say he is waging war against the dragon (Satan).

tribal number 12 multiplied by 1,000 (= 144,000; Rev. 14:1–11). The angels of God summon this throng to honor God alone (14:6–7) and to refuse to worship the Beast while announcing the fall of "Babylon" (Rome), which is the captor and oppressor of the new Israel as ancient Babylon was of Israel in the days of the exile.

From Rev. 14:14 to 19:4 there is a string of images of the unleashing of divine wrath on the wicked earth and its inhabitants. The angelic harvest symbolizes God's calling humanity to account (14:14–20) and is followed by the pouring out of the bowls of God's judgment (15:5–16:20). The effects of these resemble the effects of the seven trumpets on the whole, but the new feature is the emphasis on the destruction of "the great city" (16:19) – that is, Rome, the symbol and center of the evil, idolatrous, diabolical empire, and the embodiment of human schemes that corrupt or combat God's purpose for human life in the created order. The theme is expanded in 17:1–5, where the city is called a prostitute; in 17:9, where its seven hills are mentioned; and in 17:18, where its dominance over all the kings of the earth is noted. Its successive emperors are symbolized as "horns," whom ironically God will use to bring about the destruction of the city and finally their own defeat (17:12–16). Wicked as the city is, a voice from heaven utters a dirge in which both the wickedness and the impressiveness of the city are marked (18:1–24). Only God's people rejoice at Rome's ruin (18:20, 19:4).

The final group of visions represent the new age and God's new order. The wedding feast of the Lamb builds on and modifies the older biblical image of Israel as the wife of Yahweh to indicate the fulfillment of God's plan for his new people (19:5–10). The rider on the white horse (19:11–21) pictures the Messiah (Word of God) as triumphing over God's enemies, destroying the Beast and the False Prophet and inviting the world's birds of prey to come and gorge themselves on the dead bodies. Before the ultimate conclusion of God's triumph and renewal, there is an intermediate period during which the faithful share in the Rule and during which Satan and his agents are chained (20:1–6), although this is followed by a period during which the powers of evil exercise control prior to their final defeat and eternal destruction (20:7–15). The wicked, and even death itself, are consumed in an eternal fire. The sequence reaches its grand climax in a series of new things:

New Heaven and New Earth (21:1)

New City of God (21:2–21), for which 12 is the key symbol: 12 gates = 12 tribes, each consisting of a single pearl; 12 foundation stones = 12 apostles

New Presence of God (21:21), for which no temple is needed, since God and the Lamb are present always and forever; all the faithful may enter their presence, and no impurity or deceit are allowed in their presence

New Tree of Life (22:2), which bears fruit 12 times a year

New Light of the World (22:5) and thus no more day and night

All these transformations are linked with the coming of Jesus in triumph at the end of the present age (22:6–7, 12–13, 16–17, 20). In preparation for these glorious events, the faithful are called to worship God alone (22:8–9), to strive for purity (22:10–11), and to denounce those whose actions exclude them from God's people: perverts, magicians, the immoral, idolaters, and those who lie by word and deed (22:14–15). The book ends with a warning against adding to or subtracting from the prophetic words of John (22:18–19). Like the heavenly scroll in which are recorded the predetermined acts of God to defeat the powers of evil and redeem his people (5:1–14), so this revelation of God's purpose for his people is to stand unaltered, awaiting its fulfillment.

V. CONCEPTUAL AND ORGANIZATIONAL DIVERSITY IN THE CHURCH

A. REVISIONS OF THE TRADITIONS ABOUT JESUS AND THE APOSTLES

The effort to establish a single, uniform scheme of doctrine for all the churches was not accomplished until the time of Constantine in the early fourth century. But by the beginning of the second century there was such a range of understandings of Jesus and of interpretations of the New Testament writings that those who called themselves Christians were affirming widely different ideas about faith and practice. The various reactions are evident in the writings of the church leaders in various parts of the Roman world. In some cases these writings took the form of critical writings, which sought to combat what was widely regarded by the church as error. In other instances, writers undertook to supplement the basic New Testament texts with new, expanded accounts of the stories of Jesus and the apostles. Some of these latter writings were quickly accepted as authoritative in segments of the early church, equaling or surpassing the authority of the documents that came to be included in the official canon of the New Testament (see pp. 568–573).

What follows is a description of some representative examples of such writings, especially those produced by a group known as Gnostics and those that have come to be known by modern scholars as the New Testament Apocrypha. Recently, some scholars have argued that among the writings classified by the mainstream of the church as "apocryphal" are works that are older and more authentic than some included in the canon. What is more likely, however, is that these documents were written in the period that begins with the writing of the later books of the New Testament; that is, in the early decades of the second century. We shall examine first two gospel-type writings preserved by the Gnostics that consist entirely of sayings attributed to Jesus. Then we shall analyze several apocryphal narratives. Some are gospels and others are accounts of the activities of the apostles.

CONSTANTINE

BORN IN 274 C.E., SON OF the emperor Constantius, Constantine was in the vicinity of York in England when his father died after having subdued the Caledonians in the year 306. Five others competed for power in the empire, including Galerius, who had shared with Constantius the title of Augustus. Internal conflicts among the competitors, in addition to the intelligence and leadership skills of Constantine and his support of the Christians (who had been outlawed and persecuted by Diocletian), led to his eventual attainment of supreme power in the empire. His decision to side with the Christians was encouraged by a vision he reported having seen in which he was urged to take the sign of the cross as his imperial standard, with the promise that he would thereby conquer his enemies. By 323 he was the sole ruler, and he transferred the seat of power to Byzantium, which was renamed Constantinople. His edicts outlawed idolatry, restored the property of Christians, and reorganized the empire in such a way as to foster the church and its institutions. His friend Eusebius, a native of Palestine, served Constantine as adviser on churchly and doctrinal matters, including presiding at the very important Council of Nicaea in 325, which made important decisions about terminology for describing the nature of Christ and his relationship with God.

NEW TESTAMENT APOC-
RYPHA

MANY TEXTS WERE PRO-
duced by various Christian
groups from the second to the
ninth centuries that supplement,
and in some cases contradict,
what is found in the writings recognized as the New Testament.
These works seem to have been
a popular literature, produced for
the most part by pious imagination rather than by scholarly
research. But they do provide
insights into what many
Christians were interested in: How
did God confirm the claims of
Jesus and the apostles that God
was at work through them? How
should Christians deal with their
opponents? How should they face
the prospect of martyrdom? What
are the proper attitudes toward
wealth and sex?

The writings can be grouped
according to literary type: (1)
gospels, including stories of Jesus'
birth and childhood; (2) acts of
various apostles; (3) correspondence between Jesus or Paul and
their followers or with prominent
public figures; and (4) apocalypses, including secret revelatory
letters. This material has been
supplemented by the discovery in
the middle of the present century
of a library from a Gnostic community in second-century Egypt
(see p. 495).

1. The Gnostic Gospels

The Gospel of Thomas and the Gospel of Truth are among the
writings found in the middle of the present century among the ruins
of an ancient library in Upper Egypt at a place called today Nag
Hammadi (see p. 495). The first of these includes 114 sayings of Jesus
(by modern count), many of which are close approximations of passages in the canonical Gospels. On the basis of quotations from the
Gospel of Thomas found in other early Christian documents, it is probably to be dated to the middle of the second century. The Gospel of
Truth, on the other hand, contains only a few references to material
found in the four canonical gospels and in each case interprets it in a
metaphorical fashion.

The Gospel of Thomas

Many images and parables familiar from the New Testament
gospels appear in Thomas as well. Examples include the parable of the
sower and the seed (9); the parable of the mustard seed (20); city on a
hill (32); the kingdom compared with a seed (57); the parables of the
feast (64), the pearl (76), the tenant farmers (65); the persecuted and
hated are blessed (68); harvest is great / laborers are few (73); and foxes
have holes (86). Many sayings are unique to Thomas in form and content. Many other sayings are outwardly similar to those in the canonical gospels but differ significantly in meaning. For example, the need
to become as a child in order to enter the kingdom is not a call for simple trusting acceptance, as in Mark (10:15), but a demand to lose one's
sexual identity (Thomas 22, 37). This is an important feature of the
overall emphasis in Thomas on achieving *unity*, which is variously
described as being solitary (75) or as two becoming one (11, 16, 61, 75,
106). This means that the divided nature of human existence (body and
soul, or flesh and spirit) is overcome and transcended as one enters a
new realm of spiritual unity. This is a basic concept of Gnosticism,
which regards the material world, including bodily existence, as inherently evil. Through the disclosure of divine knowledge that God provides through Jesus the ultimate individual unity is attained. Anyone
who gains this status is free of human limitations and liberated from
the body, which Thomas regards as a corpse (15, 60, 71, 80, 111).

These insights are gained only through the divine knowledge that
God has provided, which includes true knowledge of the self (3, 5, 6,
13, 17, 18). Divine knowledge exists as inner light (24, 70) and is
already within the elect individuals, waiting to be recognized (61, 62,
70). It is through Jesus that this divine awareness comes (77, 108): he
enables men and women to overcome their sexual separateness and
thus to achieve divine androgyny (114). Those who receive this new
knowledge will be free from the body and its enticements (27, 28, 56,
87) and will become detached observers of the passing world (42). No
redemptive significance is attached to the death of Jesus in this gospel,
which is mentioned as only an instance of spirit triumphing over the
body. There are no references to the sacraments and no mention of
covenant or community responsibilities, either within the group or

toward outsiders or toward the state. Issues concerning community identity and relationships were central for both Judaism and Christianity in the period following the return of Israel from exile until the early second century C.E. Their total absence from the Gospel of Thomas shows why this document has properly been regarded as beyond the limits of the tradition, and why it has been considered by the mainstream of the church as an inappropriate adaptation of the gospel tradition.

The Gospel of Truth

The Gospel of Truth, which is referred to by Irenaeus in about 185 C.E. in his work *Against Heresies* (3.11–12), was also found in the Gnostic library at Nag Hammadi. It is an extended discourse in which the themes of inner divine knowledge and freedom from the body and earthly involvements set out in the Gospel of Thomas are developed more fully. The references to the original gospel material found in the New Testament are even fewer than in Thomas, and purely metaphorical: Jesus is said to have been nailed to a tree "because Error was angry at him" (18.20, 20.25); from that situation symbolizing a threat from evil (the cross) Jesus published the edict of the Father, which consisted of letters written by the Unity (23.15). The primary role of Jesus throughout the text is to enlighten those in conceptual darkness, thereby making visible the Invisible Father.

The goal of human existence is to know one's origin and destiny (22), the latter of which is the attainment of unity by self-purification through knowledge (25). The parable of the lost sheep is a metaphor for achieving the completeness (*pleroma*) of being. The Son is the Name of the Father (38) and came from the depths of the Father to explain him and to disclose secret things (40). None of the issues, aims, or values of the original tradition – the renewal of the created order, the transformation of the covenant people, God's offer of reconciliation to an estranged, disobedient humanity – are evident in this Gnostic document which claims to offer the secret clues to understanding Jesus and his role as renewer of the covenant.

2. Apocryphal Gospels and Acts

The Gospel of Peter is in part a composite of the canonical Gospels and in part an expansion of them along lines which further two of the writer's major concerns: (1) the conviction that everything which happened to Jesus in connection with his death and resurrection was in fulfillment of scripture; (2) the determination to put the blame primarily on the Jews for the death of Jesus. This Gospel has survived only as a Passion story, in which Jesus' arrest, trial, crucifixion, suffering, and death are depicted. Whether it once included accounts of Jesus' earlier activities and teachings cannot be determined. The writer depends in general on Mark, but many of the details are adapted from Matthew and John. The minor role of Herod in the trial and crucifixion of Jesus as described by Luke (Luke 23:6-12) has been considerably expanded in the Gospel of Peter, and the author has confused Herod

IRENAEUS

APPOINTED BISHOP OF Lyons in what is now France in 178 C.E., Irenaeus (130–ca. 203) in the succeeding years produced writings which provided an approach to reasoned Christian understanding of the faith, as well as a thoughtful basis for rejecting such offshoots of the faith as Gnosticism. His basic view was that the human race had been in process of maturation since creation, so that Adam was the prototype of immature, erring humanity, while Christ was both teacher and exemplar of mature human existence. In the future, that divine plan for humanity would be achieved in the new age which the coming of Jesus had made possible. Irenaeus shared with Marcion (see p. 568) the conviction that one must designate an authoritative list of biblical writings, but unlike Marcion, he chose and gave reasons for choosing the four Gospels, the Acts, the epistles, and Revelation that make up the New Testament as the basis for God's ongoing disclosure of his cosmic purpose. He ruled out both the allegedly secret supplements on which the Gnostics were basing their teachings and the other apocryphal works that were being presented with claims of authority. Irenaeus's work stands as a model of reason and as a coherent theological scheme that considered divine revelation to be a reasoned process.

the Great, who was king of Judea at the time of Jesus' birth, with Herod Antipas, who was governor of Galilee during Jesus' ministry (Luke 3:1) and would therefore have had no authority in Jerusalem over judicial matters. Yet this Gospel reports Herod as having direct responsibility for Jesus' crucifixion. It also describes the Jews as coming in large numbers to wait at his tomb on the Sabbath, which would have been unthinkable in terms of first-century Jewish piety. The author is obviously writing at a time and in a culture in which first-century Palestinian Jewish practices are not accurately known.

The Protoevangelium of James sets out, as the title suggests, to give the primary account of the birth and childhood of Jesus. It includes details of the miraculous circumstances of the virgin birth of Mary, of Mary's part in the preparation of the veil of the temple that was torn at the moment of Jesus' death, and of the immaculate conception of Jesus – that is, without human sexual activity. Both Joseph (who had no intercourse with Mary) and Mary (who had no extramarital sex) are vindicated by a magical act, in which they are given to drink "the water of conviction" and are unharmed by it. The work is a combination and expansion of the infancy stories in both Luke and Matthew and was written at a time when the church was concerned to defend the purity of Mary and the miraculous nature of the birth of Jesus.

The Infancy Gospel of Thomas seeks to enhance the canonical Gospels' portrait of Jesus as a miracle worker. Building on oral traditions and pious imagination, it pictures Jesus as putting down his opponents, performing healings, and helping his family, to the point of correcting some of his father's carpentry errors. At the same time, he displays supernatural knowledge, as in his allegorical interpretation of the alphabet.

Similarly, the apocryphal Acts embody imaginative developments of traditions concerning the apostles, modeled on those in the canonical Acts of the Apostles, especially in connection with divine affirmation of them in public scenes and in the presence of religious and political authorities. These writings range in date from the Acts of Peter and the Acts of Paul, which were written in the latter half of the second century, to the Acts of John, which seems to come from the fourth century. Gnostic influence is evident in the Acts of Thomas and the Acts of Andrew. A dominant concern in the older of these apocryphal Acts is abstinence from sex, as in the case of two young women in the Acts of Peter who are kept by Peter in a state of impaired health to prevent them from being sexually exploited.

In the Acts of Peter, Peter's preaching and healing activity in Rome, following the departure of Paul for missionary activity in Spain, consists mainly of spectacular public performance of miracles. Some of these involve only Peter and his listeners, as when he makes a tuna fish swim after it has been removed from a display in a fishmonger's shop. Others are more showy events in which Peter's miracles not only outdo those of the legendary magician Simon (Acts 13:6–8) but also bring the latter under divine judgment.

A major section of the Acts of Paul consists of a travel narrative, modeled after the hellenistic romances (see sidebar, p. 519) that were so popular in the second and third centuries C.E., in which the devotees of a divinity wander about the Mediterranean world, with opportunities to bear witness to their religious convictions in public gatherings and in the presence of religious and political authorities. In the hellenistic romances there are dramatic displays of divine deliverance, as well as direct communications from the deity which confirm the travelers' convictions and commitments about the purpose and power of the deity. This is precisely what happens to Paul and his female companion, Thecla, as they carry forward their journey for Christ. It can be inferred from the writer's use of this literary medium in the Acts of Paul that the Christian movement has made its way into the wider reading public of Roman society, offering its own equivalent of the popular religious romances of that epoch.

The Acts of John are taken up with more speculative features of the Jesus tradition and transform certain aspects of it so as to heighten the divine supernatural aspects of Jesus. The cross is not so much the symbol of death or of atoning suffering but the focus of the divine light, or the intersection of divine disclosure and human response. It is equated with the Logos (cf. the Word in John 1), by which God communicates with human beings. In the Acts of John, when John describes his experience with Jesus during his lifetime and after the resurrection, he indicates that Jesus' appearance and even the tangibility of his body varied considerably.

Yet like the other apocryphal acts, the Acts of John includes delightful stories of miracles, such as one about the bedbugs that had been keeping John awake at an inn but that cooperatively withdrew to enable him to get a good night's sleep. Other miracles include the destruction of the temple of the pagan goddess Artemis, and the divine judgment in the form of a deadly snakebite on someone who first comes to the true faith and then defects from it.

These writings alternate between the motivations of enticement and solemn warnings. At the same time, they show by the example of the apostles that fidelity to the will and purpose of God may lead to martyrdom. These documents are dealing with the internal and external pressures – social, moral, doctrinal, and political – under which the church was living in the larger Roman society in the centuries prior to its establishment as the religion of the emperor in the time of Constantine (325 C.E.). There were pressures to distance Christianity from Judaism and to accommodate it to other religious and philosophical options. Some schools of Christian thought denied the value of the material world (as in Gnosticism and in some forms of Neo-Platonism) and sought direct participation in the life of God, and some called for a complete break with the Old Testament and Jewish tradition. The main body of the developing church had to identify these alternative forms of Christian tradition and to challenge and reject them while affirming its own beliefs and practices.

VI. CHRISTIANITY SEEKS TO UNIFY FAITH AND PRACTICE

A. THE APOSTOLIC FATHERS

By the end of the first century, Christianity had taken root in widely scattered areas and in diverse cultures, stretching from western Europe to Iran and across the Mediterranean coast of Africa. It was under pressure from a variety of sources: Roman political authorities, intellectual challenges from Greek and Roman philosophy, competition from various popular religions, and the diversity of beliefs and modes of organization that had developed within Christianity itself. In such circumstances, how was the Christian movement to survive as a unified entity?

In their efforts to bring order and unity to Christianity, the primary strategy of perceptive thinkers and leaders in the church in this situation was to focus on three areas: conformity to proper norms of behavior, acceptance of authoritative leadership, and adherence to true doctrine and proper performance of the rites of the church. Indications of the development of these issues and of strategies for dealing with them are evident in the later New Testament writings, but they became more urgent, more explicit, and more nearly central in the early-second-century writings of a group of church leaders designated by modern scholars as the Apostolic Fathers. These men were in some sense the successors of the apostles, who had been the original leaders of the Christian movement. Appeal is frequently made in the works of the Apostolic Fathers to the earlier documents that came to be known in the Christian setting as the Old and New Testaments. There was no effort on the part of ancient scholars (as there has been none by modern scholars) to have the writings of the Apostolic Fathers included in the canon of the New Testament. Indeed, the basic question as to which of the books in the biblical tradition were to be considered authoritative (i.e., canonical) was not yet resolved or even directly addressed in the early second century.

1. Standards for Ethics and Worship

A late-first-century document, probably known as the Two Ways, was incorporated into two early-second-century writings: the Teaching of the Twelve Apostles (known as Didache) and the Epistle of Barnabas. In both of these works, a primary concern is the behavior of the members of the early Christian community. They have a choice between the Way of Life and the Way of Death – a theme that appears in Matt. 7:13–14 and is akin to Jesus' identification of himself as "the Way" to the Father in John 14:4–6. In the Didache, the instruction begins with quotations and paraphrases of Jesus' words about the first commandment: to love God and neighbor (Didache 1). But it then expands on the moral obligations of both members (Didache 2) and those under instruction for membership (Didache 3). Among the things to be avoided are love potions, magic, omens, enchantment,

DIDACHE

A COPY OF THE DIDACHE (which means "teaching") was recovered in the later nineteenth century from a monastery in Constantinople. The text preserves a version of a document called the Two Ways, which was apparently a widely used late-first-century manual of discipline for the church. The tradition of the Two Ways is found in a more primitive form in the Epistle of Barnabas (see p. 528). The material from the Epistle in Didache 1:1–6:2 has been reworked in light of the mounting tensions between Christianity and emergent rabbinic Judaism – a development that began to gain momentum in the late first and early second centuries. The place of origin of both the original document and of this adaptation of it is impossible to determine. The Didache reflects a simple organizational structure of the church, with no clear indication as to whether a single bishop presided over the churches of a city or a region.

astrology – all of which were flourishing among the upper classes of Roman society in this period. These practices were included among the works that lead to divine punishment by death (Didache 5). The same basic pattern is repeated in the Epistle of Barnabas.

The Didache also offers detailed advice along liturgical lines: how baptism, prayers, fasting, and the Eucharist are to be performed within the life of the community (Didache 7–10). The church's program of instruction is of major importance, as is evident from the counsel to accept orthodox teachers and prophets, who teach the truth, even though no details are offered here as to what constitutes truth or orthodoxy (Didache 11). The members are to accept as well as to offer hospitality and are to provide financial support for these apparently itinerant prophets who offer instruction to the communities. Although their roles are not sharply defined, the leaders of the church are also mentioned: apostles, bishops, and deacons (Didache 11, 15). The deacons appear to serve as prophets and teachers. The work ends with solemn warnings about being prepared for the end of the age, which will be preceded by corruption within the church and by oppression from without. The members are called to persevere, in expectation of the resurrection of the dead and vindication by the returning Christ (Didache 16). The final exhortations of Barnabas similarly call for faithful obedience in view of the coming Day of Judgment and deliverance (Barnabas 21).

In other Christian writings of this period, the basis of the moral appeal is not only the words of Jesus as preserved in the New Testament tradition but also the philosophical insights of the time, especially from Stoicism. In 1 Clement, for example, there is an appeal for unity within the communities based on the letters of Paul and various parts of the Old Testament, especially the Psalms. Yet when the virtues are specified, the list includes such Stoic terms as "piety," "self-control," and "sobriety." Similarly, in the Letter to the Ephesians (10, 14–17) by Ignatius, the early-second-century bishop of Antioch in Syria, the virtues extolled are also expressed in Stoic terminology, although the larger framework of Christian moral responsibility includes quotations from the sayings of Jesus and warnings of the coming judgment. In a highly allegorical writing, the Shepherd of Hermas, one of the visions described is of seven women who represent

CLEMENT OF ROME AND 1 CLEMENT

CLEMENT WAS THE THIRD bishop of Rome according to Eusebius's *Ecclesiastical History* (1.4.10) and thus would have been the second one to succeed Peter in that office. His term lasted from 92 (in the reign of Emperor Domitian) until 101 (in the reign of Emperor Trajan). Later tradition claims that he was consecrated for the office by Peter and that he is the Clement mentioned by Paul in Phil. 4:3. His surviving writing came to be known as 1 Clement, to distinguish it from 2 Clement, an anonymous sermon attributed to Clement but different from 1 Clement in style and perspective. It probably was written in Alexandria in the later second century.

IGNATIUS

IGNATIUS WAS BISHOP OF Antioch in Syria during the reign of Trajan – probably 110–17. He saw himself as the central authority for the church in this important city and wrote in that capacity to churches and individuals in Rome and cities in Asia Minor, of which his letters to the churches of Ephesus, Magnesia, Trallia, Rome, Philadelphia, and Smyrna, as well as his Letter to Polycarp, have been preserved. His primary concern was to preserve the church by unifying both organizational structure and doctrine. Taken to Rome by imperial authority, he was martyred there by being thrown to wild beasts in the amphitheater.

SHEPHERD OF HERMAS

ATTRIBUTED TO THE brother of Pius, who was bishop of Rome from 139 to 154 C.E., this writing is a mix of prophetic, apocalyptic, and allegorical styles. It is in three sections: Visions (communications from heaven), Mandates (requirements for members), and Parables (images and lessons drawn from them concerning present values and future hopes). One major concern is how to deal with church members who have lapsed into sin after baptism. On the question of whether or not such persons could be restored and renewed in the community, Hermas emphasized grace and forgiveness.

PHOENIX

The phoenix is a bird in Greek mythology that was sacred to the sun, famed for splendid plumage and a musical voice, and mentioned by writers from the fifth century B.C.E. on. The bird, which was always male, was said to live for a long time – from 500 to 13,000 years – and then to burn itself alive in its nest of twigs. From the ashes emerged its successor, which when it could fly, transported the remains of its predecessor to the temple of the sun at Heliopolis in Egypt. Serious discussions of the country of origin of the phoenix appear in such works as the *Natural History* by Pliny (23–79 C.E.).

PLUTARCH

Plutarch was a philosopher and prolific writer who lived from 46 to 120 C.E. Born in central Greece at Chaeronea, he studied philosophy at Athens and then lived for an extended period in Rome, where he lectured on philosophy and, according to later tradition, tutored the emperor Hadrian. He is best known for his *Parallel Lives*, in which he presents comparative biographical studies of twenty-three figures from Roman history and twenty-three from Greek tradition. Plutarch also wrote speculative and metaphysical essays.

the seven virtues, which include the traditional biblical ones of faith and love but also philosophical abstractions: simplicity, intellectual knowledge, purity, reverence, and godliness. This appropriation of terms from the contemporary philosophical traditions is evident to a limited degree in the letters of Paul (especially Phil. 4:8–9, Gal. 5:22–3) but has been considerably developed in these later Christian writings. First Clement (25) goes so far as to claim that the Greek myth of the phoenix was a sign of the Christian belief in the resurrection. The myth was not denounced; it was transformed by this Christian writer.

An important feature of Greco-Roman culture that Christian writers of the second century adapted for their own purposes was the allegorical interpretation of older literature. There are allegorical passages in the Old and New Testaments, of which Isa. 5:1–7 and its correlative passage in Matthew (21:33–46) are obvious examples. But the transformation of narratives into abstract and even philosophical concepts flourished in the early centuries C.E., as is shown by the writings of the Jewish scholar Philo of Alexandria and such Greco-Roman writers as Livy and Plutarch. It is through allegory that Barnabas explains the symbolic meaning of the sacrificial system and the food laws of ancient Israel (Barnabas 7–70). For example, he writes that permission in the law of Moses for Israelites to eat the meat of certain animals that chew the cud (Deut. 14:6) refers to the virtue of meditating on the word of God. The parables section (9) of the Shepherd of Hermas contains an elaborate allegory of twelve mountains, which represent the twelve tribes of the earth. Some are blessed; some are cursed for rejecting the message of God. The accepted include innocent babies, suffering believers, church leaders and those who contribute to their support, the simple, the guileless, and the blessed. The rejected tribes range from apostates and blasphemers to misbehaving deacons and rich believers, preoccupied with their own affairs. In the visions section of this same document, the church is pictured first as a great lady and then as a tower, into which some stones fit, some are reworked, and some are rejected (Visions 2 and 3). The allegorical details give the modern reader a vivid picture of the social situation of the church in the second century, including the problems of diversity of membership as well as the ways in which features of the contemporary culture were appropriated by the church for its own purposes.

2.   Leadership in the Churches

In 1 Clement and Ignatius we have especially clear evidence of the growing necessity to enforce acceptance of the church leadership by the members. The picture that emerges is one of bishops presiding over churches, some of which are in the major city of the region, and others are in smaller cities or rural areas. Chapters 41–3 of 1 Clement make the case that the pattern of having God's people ruled by bishops, with the aid of deacons, is foretold in the Old Testament and goes back to Moses. Military organization, in which soldiers obey their generals, is commended (37). In Ignatius's Letter to the Magnesians (5) he declares that the bishop presides in the place of God, and presbyters

have the same role as the council of the apostles. That deacons are commissioned to perform services for the community is affirmed in this letter (7), as well as in that to the Trallians (2), where subjection to the bishop is compared to submission to Jesus Christ. The people of God are defined in Ignatius's Letter to the Philadelphians as those who stand with or submit to the bishop (3). The bishop, together with the one eucharist and the one altar, represents the unity of the church (4). Similar appeals to submit to the bishop appear in his letters to the Smyrnaeans (8–9) and to Polycarp (6).

3. Basis for Proper Beliefs

In these second-century Christian writings the principle of doctrinal truth is affirmed, but not much specification is given of what those doctrines are. One of the latest of the writings included among the Apostolic Fathers is 2 Clement, in which "the truth" of Christianity is described as "knowledge." Such terms show that faith is not primarily trust in God and what he is doing for his people through Jesus, as is the case in the gospels and Paul, but that the emphasis is on the content of faith, which is now perceived as conceptual in nature, so that authentic faith means sound doctrine. In the later New Testament books and in the so-called apostolic period (late first century), the writers were content to call for sound doctrine without defining what it included. But from the middle of the second century on, such intellectual leaders of the church as Irenaeus and Clement of Alexandria devoted their energies to the definition of true doctrine in detail.

Similarly, the writings from the first half of the second century assume the truth and the authority of a body of sacred scriptures which are in some sense normative for the Christian church, even though they do not state the principles by which scriptural authority is to be established or specify which books compose the Old and New Testaments and are therefore to be considered as scripture. In Acts 20:35, for example, Paul is reported as basing his appeal to the Ephesian elders for generosity on an otherwise unknown saying of Jesus. In 2 Pet. 3:1–16 the author's call for purity and patience is grounded in "the scriptures," which include the letters of Paul. The authority of these writings is simply assumed. Similarly, Ignatius in his Letter to the Ephesians (19) refers to the mystery of the nativity as God's way of overcoming magic and death, although he does not quote the gospel traditions that report this event. First Clement appeals to precedent from the Old Testament and the letters of Paul in his effort to overcome schisms that are dividing the churches (45–56). The images of the tower and the stones developed by the Shepherd of Hermas (vision 3 and parable 9) presuppose such biblical passages as Mark 12:10, Matt. 21:43, as well as Ps. 118:22–3, which is being quoted in the gospels, yet no explicit reference to a gospel or Old Testament passage is given.

Direct quotations from the gospels occur in some documents of this period, however. Didache 1 quotes phrases from Matt. 7:12, Luke 6:31–3, Matt. 5:44–7, and later (9) from Matt. 7:6. Similarly, Polycarp

2 CLEMENT

ALTHOUGH THIS DOCUMENT is written in the outward form of a letter, it is actually a discourse intended to be read aloud to congregations. It was probably composed in Alexandria after 150 C.E., or perhaps somewhat later in Rome. The emphasis in 2 Clement is on the full deity of Christ, as well as on the claim that human flesh (and not merely the human spirit) will take part in the life of the age to come. There is warning of future judgment and an appeal to live by the power of the Spirit, thus overcoming the temptations that beset God's people.

POLYCARP

BISHOP OF SMYRNA IN ASIA Minor, Polycarp lived from about 69 to 155 C.E. He is mentioned by Irenaeus, bishop and scholar from Gaul (130–ca. 203) and was addressed by Ignatius in a letter that has been preserved. Polycarp's major concerns were to uphold what he saw as true doctrine and to oppose heresy, which was infiltrating the church. As a guarantee of the truth of his views of faith and practice, he appealed to associations he claimed to have had with the apostles. His leadership was so effective and so many pagans converted to Christianity through his efforts that he was attacked by Roman authorities, who considered him to be undermining the traditional religious roots of the Roman order.

MARCION

IN THE MID–SECOND CENTURY C.E., Marcion became the leader of a group in Rome that made a radical distinction between the God of Jesus Christ and the God proclaimed in the Law and Prophets of the Hebrew scriptures. They also rejected many of the New Testament writings, limiting their canon of scripture to an edited edition of Luke–Acts and the letters of Paul. They were ascetic in mode of life, frowned upon marriage, and did not eat certain kinds of food. Marcion's ideas are best known through a refutation of them by Irenaeus (130–ca. 203 C.E.) in his treatise *Against Heresies.*

repeats words from Matt. 7 and Luke 6 that are part of their respective versions of Jesus' Sermon on the Mount / Plain. Through direct quotation and especially by allusion to the narrative and instructional content, the existence and the authority of the New Testament writings are simply assumed and used by these writers, who do not specify their sources or provide authoritative lists of the writings. The ambivalence of the church in this period toward the Jewish scriptures is evident in that they are appealed to repeatedly for precedent or authorization – by direct reference or allegorical interpretation – and yet a writer like Ignatius in the Letter to the Magnesians makes a strong point that Christians are not to adopt Jewish doctrines or laws; are to observe, not the Sabbath, but the Lord's Day; and are to liberate Christianity from Judaism. Complicating this definitional process was the concurrent move within Judaism to set the limits of its recognized scriptures and to draw a sharp line between themselves as the true people of God and the Christian church. That the Christians had not yet drawn up a universally accepted list of their own is apparent in the fact that 2 Clement 12 quotes as authoritative the Gospel of Thomas, which the church was soon to reject. On the other hand, around the middle of the second century Marcion was asserting that Christians should reject all the Jewish scriptures and all of the New Testament except the letters of Paul and an expurgated (i.e., de-Judaized) version of Luke–Acts. Marcion's radical proposal seems to have stimulated the leaders of the church to define formally what they understood to be the scriptural authority for Christians. That process of deciding which writings were to be regarded as normative or canonical was of major importance for the subsequent development of the life and thought of the church.

B. THE BIBLE ASSUMES A NORMATIVE FUNCTION

1. Stages in the Selection of the Biblical Books

By the beginning of the common era there was a partial consensus among Jews as to which books in the biblical tradition were to be considered authoritative. Central were the five books attributed to Moses: Genesis, Exodus, Leviticus, Numbers, and Deuteronomy. Known as Torah, these books provided the basic guidelines for Jewish self-understanding as covenant people and for their life as God's people and the basic stories of their origins. The historical books of Samuel and Kings – supplemented by Ezra and Nehemiah – were likewise commonly agreed upon as central to an understanding of Jewish origins and for community self-definition. Similarly, there was common agreement about the importance and authority of a core of prophetic books and about some of the poetic writings. But as the accompanying list shows, there was disagreement about some of the poetic and prophetic documents.

The most conservative list came to be incorporated in the Hebrew Bible, which was also to be regarded as normative a millennium and a half later by Protestant Christians, who adopted the translations of these Hebrew writings as their Old Testament. A longer list, which

THE OLD TESTAMENT APOCRYPHA AND PSEUDEPIGRAPHA

THE FOLLOWING BOOKS ARE included in the Septuagint and the Roman Catholic canon of the Old Testament but not in the Hebrew Bible or the Protestant canon. These writings are known as the Old Testament Apocrypha. They include additions to the books in the Hebrew canon and writings similar to the Hebrew scriptures but extant only in Greek. They can be classified as (1) historical, (2) prophetic (or apocalyptic), (3) wisdom, and (4) writings, but the historical and writings books contain prayers and exhortations which cause them to resemble the other two types.

1 and 2 Esdras (1)
Tobit (4)
Judith (4)
Additions to Esther (also called the Rest of Esther) (4)
Wisdom of Solomon (3)
Wisdom of Ben Sira (or Sirach) (also called Ecclesiasticus) (3)
Baruch (2)
Epistle of Jeremy (or Jeremiah) (2)
Additions to Daniel: Prayer of Azariah; Song of the Three Jews; Susanna; Bel and the Dragon (2)
Prayer of Manasseh (4)
1 Maccabees (1)
2 Maccabees (1)

Other similar writings, called Old Testament Pseudepigrapha, were never included in the canon by the great majority of Jews or Christians. These writings include apocalypses and testaments. Typical are the following:

Apocalypse of Enoch
Sibylline Oracles
Fourth Book of Ezra
Apocalypse of Baruch
Testaments of the Twelve Patriarchs
Testament of Moses
Testament of Solomon
Letter of Aristeas
Jubilees
Joseph and Aseneth
3 and 4 Maccabees
Psalms of Solomon
Prayer of Joseph
Odes of Solomon
Ezekiel the Tragedian
Artapanus

included late narrative and poetic works, was incorporated by Greek-speaking Jews into the Greek translation that came to be known as the Septuagint (see pp. 293–294). Made for the use of Jews living in various lands across the Greco-Roman world whose basic language was Greek (which had become the common language of the eastern Mediterranean world through the hellenizing efforts of Alexander's successors in the fourth and third centuries B.C.E.), the Greek version was adopted by the early Christians as their Bible and is the basis for most of the quotations from and allusions to scripture in the New Testament. When Latin replaced Greek as the common language of the Mediterranean world in the second and third centuries C.E., Latin translations of the Bible included variants and additions to the traditional Jewish scriptures. These Latin versions have provided the canon for Roman Catholics down to the present day. But how and why were the authoritative lists of books drawn up and how did they come to be incorporated in the standard versions?

With the destruction of the Jerusalem temple in 70 C.E. and the crushing of the Jewish nationalist movement by 135, the significant and enduring option was what became rabbinic Judaism, which began taking shape around the end of the first century C.E. For this movement, the scriptural tradition replaced the temple as the major focus of the life of the religious community. It was essential, therefore, not only to set the limits of what members of the community were to consider as sacred scripture but also to differentiate this movement from another that was at the same time claiming to have the true and authorita-

tive interpretation of these scriptures: the early Christians. The Jews reportedly formulated their official list at Yavneh on the Mediterranean coast of Palestine in the last decade of the first century C.E., although no documentary evidence confirms this tradition. An extended consultation appears to have resulted in the production of the standard text of the Hebrew Bible, which has been normative ever since.

For the early Christians this issue of an authoritative scriptural basis for their identity as covenant people was more complicated. They chose the longer list of Jewish scriptures (the Septuagint) as their canon (from a Greek word meaning "rule" or "guideline"). But they had also been producing writings of their own, which soon came to be regarded as in some sense authoritative as well.

2. Supplementing the Biblical Writings

The Jewish community from the late first century C.E. onward began to develop material that could serve to interpret the biblical texts and to apply them to the life of the Jewish community in circumstances quite different from those in which they had been produced. The outcome of this process was the Mishnah and the Talmud (see pp. 428–434), which continue to the present day to serve as the normative approach to the interpretation and application of the Jewish scriptures. In the same period, the Christians were having to come to terms with the Jewish scriptures that they had taken over and claimed to have the keys to interpret properly, but they also had produced their own writings depicting the origins and destiny of their movement: the gospels and Acts. Writings such as the letters of Paul, which had originated in or were sent to various centers of early Christianity, were understandably highly regarded in the places where they first appeared, but then they also began to be circulated from region to region and came to be accepted as interesting, important, and even authoritative throughout the Christian communities worldwide. Yet well into the second century, some Christians, like Papias of Hierapolis in Phrygia (western Asia Minor), preferred the oral reports transmitted through those who had heard the disciples of Jesus as having greater authority than the written accounts. The question could not be avoided as to which of these writings, diverse in origin and content, were to be regarded as authoritative for the churches of different cultural orientations spread across the Mediterranean world and the Middle East.

3. Establishing the Christian Biblical Canon

By the middle of the second century, the leaders of the church known as the Apostolic Fathers recognized the importance of having accounts of Jesus and the apostles which were available and accepted as authoritative throughout the churches across the civilized world. In a conscious or unconscious attempt to lend authority to these writings, the accounts of the life and teachings of Jesus, although preserved in anonymous documents known as the gospels, came to be associated

with disciples of Jesus (Matthew and John) or with associates of the disciples or apostles (Mark, said to be Peter's companion, and Luke, associated with the apostle Paul). The place of origin of the gospels cannot now be determined, but Matthew became the central document in Rome; John was linked with Ephesus; Mark, with Alexandria. In Acts Luke demonstrates close knowledge of Asia Minor and Greece, but this gospel writer and historian may have come from any city in Syria, Asia Minor, Greece, or Italy. The apostolic link was crucial to the authority of writings: later documents were written in the name of an apostle (such as the later letters attributed to Paul) and anonymous writings were attributed to an apostle (as Hebrews was assigned to Paul). Since there were no official copies of these writings – either Jewish or Christian – it was inevitable that they would be modified by those who copied or used them. Additions and adaptations were made, such as harmonizing differences in the gospel accounts of Jesus. A painstaking and brilliantly successful effort to unify the gospel accounts of Jesus' words and works was undertaken by Tatian, who harmonized the four gospels into a consecutive account that included most of what was in each of them. It was called the Diatessaron (Through the Four [Gospels]) and helped to set the pattern for other gospel harmonies and for the weaving together of the narratives and sayings of Jesus from all the gospels. Furthermore, insertions from one gospel to another were made in copying the documents, and passages were added in some copies of a gospel, such as the story of the adulterous woman in John 8 (see p. 542).

As their respective communities were taking shape in the early centuries of the Common Era, both Jews and Christians were struggling with the issue of which writings concerning the origins of Judaism were to be regarded as authoritative, including historical, prophetic, and wisdom books. For example, some wanted to add to the traditional Hebrew canon of scripture such later writings as the Wisdom of Solomon, the Wisdom of Ben Sira, the later books attributed to Ezra (Esdras), and the various Books of Maccabees. The decision by some Jews to limit the authoritative scriptures to those of Hebrew origin was probably reached by the end of the first century C.E. (see list on p. 294), but the Christians had not yet drawn up a definitive list of their scriptures by the middle of the second century. Two kinds of pressures made it unavoidably necessary that such decisions be made. One factor was the pronouncement by Marcion, who came to Rome from Pontus on the Black Sea, that the contradictions between the Old Testament and the Christian scriptures were to be seen as evidence that the God of the Jews and the creator of the material world was an inferior being, whereas the sovereign and just Lord was the God whose messenger Jesus was. Accordingly, by the middle of the second century, Marcion had rejected the Old Testament and purged the gospels and apostolic letters of all features based on the Old Testament, thereby creating what he regarded as the proper canon of Christian scriptures. The second factor was the production in this period of gospels and Books of Acts by Gnostics and others that claimed to supplement, to interpret, or even to correct what was in the more

TATIAN

IN THE SECOND CENTURY C.E. Tatian, who was widely regarded as a distinguished interpreter of Greek philosophy, was converted to Christianity by Justin Martyr (died in 164 C.E.). He became an effective intellectual champion of Christianity, offering a challenge to the concepts of Greek philosophy in his treatise *Against the Greeks.* Later he became the leader of a rigidly ascetic Christian sect, which substituted water for wine in the Eucharist. His most enduring contribution, albeit highly controversial, was his synthesis of the four gospels into a single sequential account of the career of Jesus: the Diatessaron (Through the Four [Gospels]).

CLEMENT OF ALEXANDRIA

CHRISTIAN INTELLECTUAL who flourished in Alexandria between 192 and 217. In addition to his extensive knowledge of Greek philosophy, he studied Hebrew with a Jewish scholar (probably Pantaenus), who introduced him to Stoic thought as well. Clement drew on Platonism for his theory of the universe and on the Stoics for details of his ethical concepts. His major writings were (1) *Stromata*, a collection of insights on a range of religious and philosophical issues; (2) *Protrepticon*, in which he sought to persuade pagans of the truth of Christianity; (3) *Paedagogus*, a book of instruction for new Christians; (4) *Can a Rich Man be Saved?* a tract warning about the moral danger of wealth. Another writing, the *Hypotyposes* is now lost, but it was denounced by early critics as incompatible with the scriptures.

widely accepted Christian writings. Around 170 an ecstatic visionary named Montanus from Phrygia in western Asia Minor claimed to have had a revelation about the detailed fulfillment of the Revelation of John concerning the coming of the end of the age. His claims spread westward, and many were convinced by his predictions, which expected the consummation to occur in his native territory. The leaders and scholars of the churches had to make decisions about which of the proliferating Christian claims and writings were to be considered normative for Christians as a whole.

Since there was no central agency to make such decisions, steps toward drawing up an authoritative list were made by various regional leaders of the church. Justin, a Christian philosopher who found his way from his native Palestine to Rome, where he was martyred in about 167, noted in his *Apology* (1.67–3) that preaching and instruction in the churches were based not only on "the writings of the prophets," by which he seems to have meant the Jewish scriptures, but also on "the memoirs of the apostles," by which he referred to what came to be known as the writings of the New Testament. Since he quotes from Matt. 16:4 as a "memoir," it is clear that the gospels were being used as scripture in the churches by the middle of the second century. A more explicit claim was offered by Irenaeus, bishop of Lyons in the second half of the second century, in his *Against Heresies* (3.11.8): there are four gospels because of the way the universe is structured, with its four winds and four points of the compass. In the course of his writings, Irenaeus indicates his admiration also for the letters of Paul, for 1 Peter, 1 John, and the Revelation of John. He includes as authoritative the Wisdom of Solomon and the Shepherd of Hermas, both of which would have attracted him by their philosophical orientation and method. Not named by him are 2 and 3 John and 2 Peter.

By the early third century, Clement of Alexandria was more specific about which writings were to be considered authoritative by Christians: the four gospels, the letters of Paul (among which he included Hebrews), and what he called the "catholic letters" (from the Greek phrase *kath holos*, "according to the whole"), since they were addressed to a general audience rather than to a specific community. These included James, 1, 2, and 3 John, 1 and 2 Peter, and Jude. But he also listed among the authoritative writings 1 Clement, Wisdom of Solomon, Wisdom of Ben Sira, the Letter of Barnabas, and the Apocalypse of Peter.

In the later third century, the term "canonical" began to be used, thereby implying that the inherent authority of a document is given official status. For example, Origen of Alexandria, one of the leading biblical scholars of the early church, includes in his canonical list the four gospels, fourteen letters of Paul (although he thinks Hebrews is not really by Paul), 1 Peter, 1 John, and Revelation; he omits 2 and 3 John, 2 Peter, Jude, and James. Of uncertain date (second to fourth century) is an anonymous canonical list discovered by a librarian named Muratori in Milan in the later nineteenth century and hence known as the Muratorian Canon. The first part of the list is lost but must have included Matthew and Mark, since it takes up with Luke and John. It goes on to Acts, thirteen letters of Paul (excluding Hebrews), Jude, 1 and 2 John, Revelation – but also the Wisdom of Solomon and the Apocalypse of Peter. The Shepherd of Hermas is said to be worthy of being read to the church but is not to be considered authoritative.

In the early fourth century, Eusebius, whose *Ecclesiastical History* is our most important source of information about early Christianity apart from the New Testament, gives the same basic canonical list as Origen. It is only in the second half of the fourth century, in an episcopal letter sent by Athanasius, bishop of Alexandria, that we find a list of canonical writings identical with what is now called the New Testament. Although Athanasius reports the list of disputed works mentioned by other writers and notes that these may be profitable reading for Christians, he is clear that they are not to be considered part of the canon.

4. Criteria For Canonicity

The judgments offered about the authoritative status of these early Christian writings were not based ultimately on scholarly decisions or ecclesiastical decrees but derived instead from the functions these writings had been serving over the centuries in the communities for whom they were produced. The gospels and the letters had initially been written to help the communities understand who Jesus was and how he had disclosed what was to be their place in the purpose of God. These writings enabled the early Christians to discern the origins of their movement and provided guidelines for the ongoing life of the group. The decisions about canonicity rested on three factors: (1) what had proved useful in the Christian communities; (2) what could be traced back to the earliest times of the church; and (3) what could be shown to have been written by an apostle or an apostolic associate. Eusebius noted that one could determine the authenticity of documents that claimed to come from the apostles by style and vocabulary (*Eccl. Hist.* 3.25.6–7). This powerful interest in affirming links with the past of the tradition is evident not only in the church at that time but also in the wider Roman society, where strong and effective literary and cultural enterprises were seeking to regain access to the life and thought of classical Greece and Rome.

The primary considerations in assembling the canon, therefore, were the needs, the experience, and the corporate judgments of the early Christian communities. The decisions did not derive from objective criteria offered by detached observers. In the process of deciding what writings would constitute the Bible, both Jewish and Christian decision makers demonstrated the conviction held by the biblical writers themselves: that God addresses his people, calling them to account and disclosing his purpose for and through them, and that this takes place in the living context of social and cultural crisis and change.

SYRIAC

SYRIAC IS A DIALECT OF Aramaic, the Semitic language spoken by Middle Eastern Jews in the hellenistic and Roman periods. Unlike Aramaic, which uses the same alphabet as Hebrew, Syriac has a more flowing script and was widely used in Syria and Mesopotamia until Arabic became the dominant semitic language after the thirteenth century. Ancient versions of the Jewish biblical writings have been preserved in Syriac manuscripts and must be taken into account in establishing the original version of the Hebrew text of the Bible.

C. ANCIENT COPIES AND ANCIENT AND MODERN TRANSLATIONS

Until the invention of printing in the fifteenth century, all copies of documents were handmade and thus subject to all sorts of copyist errors. No two ancient copies of biblical texts agree in every detail, although an effort was made by Jewish scholars over a period of centuries to determine an official text and to provide the Hebrew (which was originally written only in consonants) with the appropriate vowels for easier reading by nonscholars. Scholarly opinion varies as to the date when this normative text was established, but the oldest copy available is from the ninth century C.E. Since the eighteenth century, scholars have worked to reconstruct what they consider to be the original of the Hebrew text and have done so through detailed comparison of this text with the translations of the Jewish Bible, especially those in Greek, Latin, and Syriac, taking into account scribal errors and fragments of various portions of the Jewish Bible that have been found in Egypt and Palestine.

Similar efforts to reconstruct the original text of the New Testament writings began about three hundred years ago, when scholars noted the differences among the established texts of the New Testament in use among churches which had this material in Greek, Syriac, Latin, Armenian, Ethiopic, Georgian, and other languages into which it had been translated in the early centuries. The text of the Greek New Testament that was accepted as normative was analyzed through comparison with ancient copies that were discovered or seriously studied in the sixteenth century and subsequently. The standard edition of the Greek text, or Received Text as it was called, was shown to contain tens of thousands of errors or questionable readings, some of them deriving from simple, obvious mistakes by the copyists, and many from the effort to harmonize passages in the Gospels with each other or to incorporate within the text later theological ideas or liturgical practices (such as the ending to the Lord's Prayer in Matt. 6:13).

The process of analyzing these divergences with the aim of reconstructing something closer to the original text was launched in the nineteenth century and continues down to the present day. In 1831 serious efforts to reconstruct the Greek text of the New Testament began with the work of Karl Lachmann, who recognized that the so-called *Textus Receptus* (Received Text) was late and composite and that a few older manuscripts from the eastern Mediterranean more likely preserved something closer to the original. A major step in this analytical process was made when C. Tischendorf in the middle of the nineteenth century discovered a fourth-century manuscript in the library of Saint Catherine's Monastery on Mount Sinai in Egypt. He developed a method of listing and classifying the alternative readings from various manuscripts and on this basis decided which of the variants was more likely to be the original. After his death, this approach was carried forward by two British scholars, B. F. Westcott and F. J. A. Hort, who analyzed by this method both Codex Sinaiticus and Codex Vaticanus, as well as other ancient copies of the New Testament in various languages (especially Syriac) and quotations from the New Testament in the writings of the early church fathers. As a result, the method of classification and evaluation of the textual variants was better informed, and the results more nearly persuasive.

This work is still being carried on by an international group of scholars. The resultant text of the Greek New Testament has established a wide consensus. Leading this program are Kurt Aland and Barbara Aland of Muenster/Westphalia in Germany. A comparable international text-critical project on the Hebrew Bible is now in process, with a base at the University of Fribourg in Switzerland, under the direction of Dominique Barthélemy.

As we have observed, some of the oldest manuscripts of the Bible that we have are of ancient translations, such as the Septuagint or the Latin and Syriac versions of the New Testament. The sixteenth and seventeenth centuries saw the rise and spread of the practice of making available the Bible in contemporary languages. That policy has continued to the present day, with a current surge of activity worldwide to make the Bible available in local languages. At present, translations of all or portions of the Bible exist in more than 2,000 languages, and work on translations into more than 600 new languages is currently in process. Clearly, the significance of the Bible has transcended the cultural and linguistic worlds in which it originated. Yet study of its worlds and of the social and linguistic contexts out of which it came are essential for understanding it today.

D.   HOW TO INTERPRET THE BIBLE

We have sought to show that to understand the Bible, made up as it is of a variety of types of literature produced in a range of cultural settings and over a period of more than a millennium, it is essential to give close attention to the social and cultural aspects of the historical circumstances in which these documents were produced. One must also take into account that the various writers' perceptions on such basic questions as the nature and activity of God, individual and social morality, and human knowledge of the divine are expressed in terms of the perspectives of the diverse historical settings in which each of them lived, and thus vary considerably over the course of centuries.

As a result of these changing circumstances and viewpoints, the same incidents or issues are described by various writers in significantly different ways. For example, in 2 Sam. 24:1–2, David's decision to determine the number of his subjects (which was regarded as a secret known only by God) by taking a census is said to have been the result of the Lord's anger with the people. But in 1 Chron. 21:1, which was written after the Persians liberated Israel from captivity in Babylon and hence when Jewish thinking was under the influence of Persian dualistic thinking (God and his Adversary), the motivator behind David's sinful census taking is said to have been Satan. In the New Testament, Paul, the converted Pharisee and onetime champion of strict conformity to the law of Moses as the ground of acceptability with God, came to the radical conclusion that human beings can gain right relationship with God, not through "works of the law," but only by trust in Christ as God's agent to set things right with his people (Rom. 3:19–26). A generation later, the author of the letter of James was so strongly influenced by the Stoic concept of natural law as universally binding on humanity, as well as by commandments in the Jewish scriptures, which the Christians had adopted as the core of their scriptures, that he insisted that "faith without works is dead" (James 2:14–26).

To understand and to deal with the range of points of view and modes of communication represented in the Bible, one must be aware of these basic cultural and historical differences reflected in the Bible. The primary aim of this *Companion to the Bible* is to provide information and insight so that those who read and study the Bible may be more aware of and better informed about the dynamic process of historical change in which these outstanding Jewish and Christian writings were produced.

BIBLIOGRAPHICAL ESSAY

I.   JESUS AND THE NEW COVENANT PEOPLE

On the history of Judaism in the Greco-Roman period and the diversity of social and religious forms it took in this period, see the Bibliographical Essay for Part II. A good summary of the developments within Judaism in the Greco-Roman period is William Scott Green and J. Andrew Overman, "Judaism (Greco-Roman Period)," in *Anchor Bible Dictionary* (New York: Doubleday, 1992), 3:1037–54. An appraisal of the current approaches to the study of the New Testament from literary, historical, and theological perspectives is offered by N. T. Wright in vol. 1 of his *The New Testament and the People of God* (London: SPCK, 1993), which includes a comprehensive bibliography on the issues under discussion. A more complete overview of the changing methods and historical approaches to the study of Jesus is offered in S. C. Neill and N. T. Wright, *The Interpretation of the New Testament, 1861–1986* (Oxford: Oxford University Press, 1988). For a very perceptive analysis of the issues involved in the historical study of Jesus, see A. E. Harvey, *Jesus and the Constraints of History*, Bampton Lectures (London: Duckworth, 1982).

In *Jesus in History*, 3d ed. (Fort Worth: Harcourt Brace, 1995), I offer a sketch of the rise of the questions about historical knowledge of Jesus and an analysis of the evidence from the gospels and other ancient sources. For a study of John the Baptist as the organizer of a protest movement against the priestly establishment and as the prophetic voice of renewal of the people of God, see the essay on John by Paul Hollenbach in the *Anchor Bible Dictionary* (New York: Doubleday, 1992), 3:887–99. In this same volume are two perceptive essays on Jesus: (1) Ben F. Meyer sets out the historical methods and results for reconstructing the figure of Jesus that come from critical analysis of the gospels and the letters of Paul, with a comprehensive bibliography (pp. 773–96); (2) N. T. Wright gives a useful survey of the ways in which the question of historical knowledge of Jesus has been addressed in scholarly circles from the eighteenth century to the present (pp. 796–802), including recent efforts to picture him as a mouthpiece for popular wisdom. A sympathetic survey of recent scholarly efforts to portray Jesus as noneschatological is offered by Marcus Borg in *Jesus in Contemporary Scholarship* (Valley Forge, Pa.: Trinity Press International, 1994).

The Q source behind the Gospels of Matthew and Luke is reconstructed in my *Jesus in History;* and a concordance of the content of the Q source was prepared by Richard A. Edwards, *A Concordance to Q* (Missoula, Mont.: Scholars Press, 1975). A recent detailed analysis of the contents of Q is David R. Catchpole, *A Quest for Q* (Edinburgh: T. & T. Clark, 1993). The hypothesis that Q originally was a collection of wisdom sayings of Jesus to which other elements were added is presented in John Kloppenburg, *The Formation of Q* (Philadelphia: Fortress Press, 1987). An older but useful analysis of Mark is D. E. Nineham, *The Gospel of St. Mark,* Pelican New Testament Commentaries (London: Pelican, 1968). Sociological approaches to Mark are offered in Herman Waetjen, *A Re-ordering of Power: A Socio-political Reading of Mark's Gospel* (Minneapolis: Fortress Press, 1989); J. D. Kingsbury, *Conflict in Mark: Jesus, Authorities, Disciples* (Minneapolis: Fortress Press, 1989); and my *Community of the New Age: Studies in Mark's Gospel* (Philadelphia: Westminster; London: SCM Press, 1977). A study of the Gospel tradition in terms of the historical background of the Jewish revolutionary movements during the first century is Richard A. Horsley, *Jesus and the Spiral of Violence* (San Francisco: HarperCollins, 1987).

Studies of Jesus' titles and beliefs in Jesus as the Christ include James D. G. Dunn, *Christology in the Making* (London: SCM Press, 1980); Ben Witheringon III, *The Christology of Jesus* (Minneapolis: Fortress Press, 1990); and Reginald H. Fuller and Pheme Perkins, *Who Is This Christ? Gospel Christology and Contemporary Faith* (Philadelphia: Fortress Press, 1983). An analysis of the Gospel of Mark and a survey of theories that have been advanced for its interpretation are set out in my *Jesus in History.* A survey of the models for the covenant community found in the literature of postexilic Judaism and of early Christianity is offered in my *Who Are the People of God? Early Christian Models of Community* (New Haven: Yale University Press, 1995).

II. PAUL: THE JESUS MOVEMENT LAUNCHED IN THE ROMAN WORLD

The classic survey of Pauline studies is by Albert Schweitzer, *Paul and His Interpreters: A Critical History,* trans. W. Montgomery (London, 1912; New York: Macmillan, 1951). An important analysis of Paul that helped to recover understanding of the apocalyptic aspects of his thought is J. C. Beker, *Paul the Apostle: The Triumph of God in Life and Thought* (Philadelphia: Westminster, 1980). A fine study of the chronology of Paul's life is Robert Jewett, *A Chronology of Paul's Life*

(Philadelphia: Fortress Press, 1979). Information about the authenticity of letters attributed to Paul and the circumstances of their origin is provided by W. G. Kümmel, *Introduction to the New Testament,* trans. H. C. Kee (London: SCM Press, 1975). More elementary introductions to the Pauline letters are offered in Marion L. Soards, *The Apostle Paul: An Introduction to His Writings and Teachings* (New York: Paulist Press, 1987), and in my *Understanding Jesus Today* (Englewood Cliffs, N.J.: Prentice-Hall, 1993). Important studies of aspects of Paul's thought are Ernst Käsemann, *Perspectives on Paul* (London: SCM Press, 1971); Victor P. Furnish, *Theology and Ethics in Paul* (Nashville: Abingdon, 1968); and Richard B. Hays, *Echoes of Scripture in the Letters of Paul* (New Haven: Yale University Press, 1989).

A good survey of interpretive questions relating to Paul's Letter to the Romans was edited by K. P. Donfried, *The Romans Debate,* rev. ed. (Minneapolis: Fortress Press, 1991). Substantive commentaries on the letters of Paul include W. F. Orr and J. A. Walther, *First Corinthians,* Anchor Bible (New York: Doubleday, 1976); V. P. Furnish, *Second Corinthians,* Anchor Bible (New York: Doubleday, 1984); and Frank J. Matera, *Galatians,* Sacra Pagina (Collegeville, Minn: Liturgical Press, 1992). An important study of letter writing in the time of Paul is Stanley K. Stower, *Letter Writing in Greco-Roman Antiquity* (Philadelphia: Westminster, 1986).

III. CHRISTIANITY RESPONDS TO FORMATIVE JUDAISM.

The term "formative Judaism" was coined by Jacob Neusner as a counter to the phrase "normative Judaism" employed by George Foot Moore in his widely influential study *Judaism in the First Centuries of the Christian Era,* 3 vols. (Cambridge: Harvard University Press, 1927–30), where Moore constructed a picture of Jewish rabbinical orthodoxy built on the Mishnah and the Talmud – which were produced only in the period from the second to the sixth centuries C.E. Neusner's insightful approach has shown that Judaism in the postexilic and post-Maccabean period was in a complex process of formulation and self-definition. He produced a series of volumes under the title *Method and Meaning in Ancient Judaism,* Brown Judaic Studies (Atlanta: Scholars Press, 1979–81), and another series, *Formative Judaism: Religious, Historical, and Literary Studies,* Brown Judaic Studies (Atlanta: Scholars Press, 1983–5). He has also edited more than thirty-five volumes of translation and analysis: *The Talmud of Babylonia* (Atlanta: Scholars Press, 1994–) and *The Talmud of the Land of Israel* (Chicago: University of Chicago Press, 1988–).

Using this historical reconstruction of Judaism in the time of Jesus, advances have been made in understanding how these developments related to the origins of Christianity. Two important works considering this factor as central to the writing of the Gospel of Matthew are J. Andrew Overman, *Matthew's Gospel and Formative Judaism: The Social World of the Matthean Community* (Minneapolis: Fortress Press, 1990), and Anthony J. Saldarini, *Matthew's Christian–Jewish Community*

(Chicago: University of Chicago Press, 1994). An older approach to Matthew is that of W. D. Davies, *The Setting of the Sermon on the Mount* (Cambridge: Cambridge University Press, 1964). An important shift in method is represented by the analyses of the adaptation of the gospel tradition evident in Matthew by G. Bornkamm, G. Barth, and H. J. Held, in *Tradition and Interpretation in Matthew's Gospel* (London: SCM Press, 1963). This basic method is adopted by Georg Strecker in an analysis which assumes that Matthew pictures Jesus as calling for obedience to his understanding of Torah, in *The Sermon on the Mount: An Exegetical Commentary*, trans. O. C. Dean (Edinburgh: T. & T. Clark, 1988). E. P. Sanders continues to picture Jesus as basically a law-abiding Jew, in *Jewish Law from Jesus to the Mishnah* (London: SCM Press; Philadelphia: Trinity Press International, 1990), and rejects Neusner's major thesis about the nature of Pharisaism and the origins of the Mishnah, and instead pictures Jesus as engaged in Mishnaic-type debate. But more convincing insights into Matthew are offered by those who take into account the dynamic changes that were developing within Judaism in the first century – as recognized by Neusner, Overman, and Saldarini.

Raymond E. Brown has prepared illuminating analyses of the birth narratives in Matthew and Luke in his *The Birth of the Messiah: A Commentary on the Birth Narratives in Matthew and Luke* (New York: Doubleday, 1977). A fine comprehensive study of Matthew is offered by Graham N. Stanton in *A Gospel for a New People: Studies in Matthew* (Edinburgh: T. & T. Clark, 1992).

The finest recent commentary on Hebrews is that of Harold W. Attridge, Hermeneia Series (Philadelphia: Fortress Press, 1989), which includes a comprehensive analysis of the text, its cultural background, and the scholarly literature on this unusual early Christian writing. Briefer and less technical commentaries are those of Donald G. Hagner (San Francisco: Harper, 1983; repr., Peabody, Mass.: Hendrickson, 1990) and of R. M. Wilson, New Century Bible Commentary (Basingstroke: Marshall Morgan & Scott; Grand Rapids: Eerdmans, 1985). Wilson takes into account the influence of middle Platonism, which leads to a modification of the earlier eschatological expectation of a new age by including a contrast between the temporal and the eternal spheres. John Dunnill's study *Covenant and Sacrifice in the Letter to the Hebrews* (Cambridge: Cambridge University Press, 1992) employs a structuralist method of interpretation which seeks to find the meaning inherent in the text as distinct from the conscious aim of the author.

Recent analyses of the Letters of Jude and 2 Peter, with good bibliographies, are those in the Anchor Bible by Richard Bauckham (vol. 3) and John H. Elliott (vol. 5) respectively. Bauckham notes the pervasive influence of apocalyptic on Jude and describes its distinctive mode of interpretation of scripture. As Elliott shows, 2 Peter mingles features of Jewish apocalyptic and hellenistic philosophy, as well as alluding to the letters of Paul as scripture and showing direct dependence on the Letter of Jude.

IV. CHRISTIANITY RESPONDS TO ROMAN CULTURE AND IMPERIAL POLICY.

A. Luke–Acts

Current studies of Luke and Acts continue to be influenced by the monumental five volumes in the series *The Beginnings of Christianity*, pt. 1, launched by F. J. Foakes-Jackson and Kirsopp Lake but brought to completion by H. J. Cadbury (London: Macmillan, 1920–33). The most enduring volumes are vol. 4 (a commentary on Acts) and vol. 5 (a collection of critical essays). Cadbury also wrote a review of older critical studies of Acts in *The Book of Acts in History* (London: A. & C. Black, 1955). A more recent useful survey of critical studies of Acts is by W. Ward Gasque, *A History of the Criticism of the Acts of the Apostles*, rev. ed. (Peabody, Mass.: Hendrickson, 1989). Charles H. Talbert was a central figure in fresh analysis of Acts through the Society of Biblical Literature seminar that he led, published as *Perspectives on Acts* (Edinburgh: T. & T. Clark, 1978) and in *Luke–Acts: New Perspectives* (New York: Crossroad, 1983). Literary studies of Luke and Acts include Robert C. Tannehill, *The Narrative Unity of Luke–Acts* (Philadelphia: Fortress Press, 1986); the Luke–Acts section of David E. Aune, *The New Testament in Its Literary Environment* (Philadelphia: Westminster, 1987), pp. 77–157; Colin J. Hemer, *The Book of Acts in the Setting of hellenistic History*, ed. C. H. Gempf (Tübingen: Mohr, 1989; and a collection of essays on Acts, M. C. Parsons and J. B. Tyson, eds., *Cadbury, Knox, and Talbert: American Contributions to the Study of Acts* (Atlanta: Scholars Press, 1992).

Important among studies of historical and sociological issues for the understanding of Acts are Wayne Meeks, *The First Urban Christians: The Social World of the Apostle Paul* (New Haven: Yale University Press, 1983); and Gerd Lüdemann, *Early Christians According to the Traditions in Luke–Acts* (London: SCM Press, 1989). Four volumes in the Society for New Testament Study Monograph Series of importance for the study of Acts are P. F. Esler, *Community and Gospel in Luke–Acts* (Cambridge: Cambridge University Press, 1987); John C. Lentz Jr., *Luke's Portrait of Paul* (Cambridge: Cambridge University Press, 1993); W. A. Strange, *The Problem of the Text of Acts* (Cambridge: Cambridge University Press, 1992); and Paul Trebilco, *Jewish Communities in Asia Minor* (Cambridge: Cambridge University Press, 1991). A series of volumes of essays on Acts has been edited at Tyndale House in Cambridge by Bruce Winter: vol. 1, *The Book of Acts in Its Ancient Literary Setting* (Carlisle: Paternoster; Grand Rapids: Eerdmans, 1993); vol. 2, *The Book of Acts in Its Graeco-Roman Setting*; vol. 3, *The Book of Acts and Paul in Roman Custody* (Grand Rapids: Eerdmans, 1994). A forthcoming volume in this series is *The Book of Acts in Its Palestinian Setting*.

Excellent commentaries on Luke include Joseph A. Fitzmyer's two-volume contribution to the Anchor Bible (New York: Doubleday, 1981–5); and Luke T. Johnson's contribution to Sacra Pagina (Collegeville, Minn.: Liturgical Press, 1991). Other important commentaries on Acts are Ernst Haenchen, *Acts of the Apostles* (London: Blackwell, 1971), and Luke T. Johnson, *Acts of the Apostles*, Sacra Pagina (Collegeville, Minn.: Liturgical Press, 1992). A more traditional approach is offered by I. Howard Marshall, *Acts of the Apostles*, Tyndale New Testament Commentaries (Leicester: Intervarsity Press, 1980).

B.   The Gospel and Letters of John

Two of the major perspectives dominating study of the Gospel of John for decades were the historical approach of C. H. Dodd, in his *Historical Tradition in the Fourth Gospel* (Cambridge: Cambridge University Press, 1963), and the existentialist interpretation of it by Rudolf Bultmann, *The Gospel of John* (1950; Oxford: Blackwell, 1971). Literary analytical theory was employed for the study of John by Robert Fortna in his *The Gospel of Signs: A Reconstruction of the Narrative Sources Underlying the Fourth Gospel* (Cambridge: Cambridge University Press, 1970), and more recently in his *The Fourth Gospel and Its Predecessor* (Edinburgh: T. & T. Clark, 1988). Alan Culpepper used an analogous approach in *Anatomy of the Fourth Gospel: A Study in Literary Design* (Philadelphia: Fortress Press, 1983). D. Moody Smith's earlier contribution in this field, *Composition and Order of the Fourth Gospel: Bultmann's Literary Theory* (New Haven: Yale University Press, 1965), was followed by his *Johannine Christianity: Essays on Its Setting, Sources, and Theology* (Columbia: University of South Carolina Press, 1984) and *John among the Gospels: The Relationship in Twentieth Century Research* (Minneapolis: Fortress Press, 1992).

A masterful two-volume commentary on John was written by Raymond E. Brown for the Anchor Bible (Garden City: Doubleday, 1970). Less technical are those of Barnabas Lindars for the New Century Bible (London: Oliphant, 1972); Pheme Perkins, *Gospel according to John: A Theological Commentary* (Chicago: Franciscan Herald Press, 1978); Robert Kysar for the Augsburg Commentary on the New Testament (Minneapolis: Augsburg, 1986); and Gerard S. Sloyan for the Interpretation Commentary (Atlanta: John Knox Press, 1988).

The Letters of John have been analyzed as sources for theological and community development in the early church by Raymond E. Brown, *The Community of the Beloved Disciple* (New York: Paulist Press, 1979), and by Urban C. van Wahlde, *The Johannine Commandment: 1st John and the Struggle for the Johannine Tradition* (London: A. & C. Clark, 1973). Commentaries on the Letters of John include Raymond E. Brown in the Anchor Bible (New York: Doubleday, 1982); Judith Lieu, *The Second and Third Epistles of John* (Edinburgh: T. & T. Clark, 1986); D. Moody Smith, *First, Second, and Third John*, Interpretation Commentary (Louisville: John Knox Press, 1991); Robert Kysar, *First, Second, and Third John* (Minneapolis: Augsburg, 1986); and J. L. Houlden for Black's Commentary (London: A. & C. Black, 1973).

C.   The Letter of James

The Letter of James, as well as the Letters of Peter and Jude, received a learned but traditional analysis by Bo Reicke in his commentary for the Anchor Bible, *The Epistles of James, Peter, and Jude* (New York: Doubleday, 1964). A superb study of James, taking into account the influence of Stoic philosophy, is that of Sophie Laws, *The Epistle of James,* Black's Commentary (London: A. & C. Black, 1980).

D.   1 Peter

John H. Elliott's work *A Home for the Homeless: A Sociological Exegesis of 1 Peter, Its Situation and Strategy* (Philadelphia: Fortress Press, 1981) is equally important for its analysis of this writing and as a prime example of sociologically based exegesis of the text. F. W. Beare wrote a substantive study of the Greek text of 1 Peter, *The First Epistle of Peter,* (Oxford: Blackwell, 3d ed. 1970). Another useful commentary on 1 Peter is that of Ernest Best, *First Peter,* New Century Bible (London: Oliphant, 1971).

E.   Revelation of John

On the history and strategy of apocalyptic, see the bibliographical essay for the Introduction above. Recent commentaries on Revelation are those of Gerhard A. Krodel, Augsburg Commentary on the N.T.: Acts (Minneapolis: Augsburg/Fortress, 1989); M. E. Boring, *Revelation,* Interpretation (Louisville: Westminster, 1989); and Wilfrid J. Harrington, *Revelation,* Sacra Pagina (Collegeville, Minn.: Liturgical Press, 1993).

V.   CONCEPTUAL AND ORGANIZATIONAL DIVERSITY IN THE CHURCH

The expansions and revisions of the canonical traditions about Jesus and the apostles flourished in the second and subsequent centuries. The entire body of extant works of this type was brought together by E. Hennecke and W. Schneemelcher in two volumes which have been translated, edited, and expanded by R. M. Wilson in *New Testament Apocrypha,* 2 vols., rev. ed. (Cambridge: J. Clarke; Louisville, Ky.: Westminster, 1991–2).

Some scholars have advanced the theory that these so-called apocryphal gospels actually include texts and traditions that are older and more reliable than those in the canonical New Testament writings. For example, Helmut Koester claims in *Ancient Christian Gospels: Their History and Development* (Philadelphia: Trinity Press International, 1990) that the Gospel of Thomas is the oldest of the Gospels and that an earlier version of the Q source than the one used by Matthew and Luke did not include references to judgment, to apocalyptic expectations, or to the conflict between the followers of Jesus and those of John the Baptist (pp. 162–71). John D. Crossan, in *Four Other Gospels:*

Shadows on the Contours of the Canon (San Francisco: Harper & Row, 1985), likewise claims that the Gospel of Thomas and the Secret Gospel of Mark are older than the canonical Gospels and that the Gospel of Peter is based on a narrative account of the Passion of Jesus which is older than that used in the canonical Gospels. (The Secret Gospel of Mark was published by Morton Smith in *The Secret Gospel of Mark: The Discovery and Interpretation of the Secret Gospel according to Mark* [New York: Harper & Row, 1973]. Smith claimed to have found a very late copy of this document on a sheet pasted inside the cover of an old book in a Palestinian monastery.) These opinions are purely circular arguments, since the investigators have found material which they prefer to what is in the canonical Gospels and, in support of their preferences, attribute this material to more ancient sources. No ancient evidence confirms these theories, but the theories have been welcomed and widely publicized in the popular press.

VI.   CHRISTIANITY SEEKS TO UNIFY FAITH AND PRACTICE

The Greek text and a translation of the writings of the Apostolic Fathers are in the two volumes by Kirsopp Lake in the Loeb Classical Library (London: Heinemann; Cambridge: Harvard University Press, 1925–6). Translation and commentary of this material are also available in a series of volumes edited by Robert M. Grant, *The Apostolic Fathers:* vol. 1. *Introduction,* by R. M. Grant (New York and London: Nelson, 1964); vol. 2: *First and Second Clement,* by R. M. Grant and Holt R. Graham (New York and London: Nelson, 1965); vol. 3: *Barnabas and Didache,* by Robert A. Kraft (New York and London: Nelson, 1965); vol. 4: *Ignatius of Antioch,* by R. M. Grant (London and Camden, N.J.: Nelson, 1966); vol. 5: *Polycarp, Martyrdom of Polycarp, Fragments of Papias,* by Willam R. Schoedel (London and Camden, N.J.: Nelson, 1967); vol. 6: *Hermas,* by Graydon F. Snyder (London and Camden, N.J.: Nelson, 1968).

An older, standard, and still useful study of the development of the canon is that of Hans F. von Campenhausen, *The Formation of the Christian Bible* (Philadelphia: Fortress Press, 1972). More recent analyses of the canon of scripture and the processes by which it developed include James Barr, *Holy Scripture: Canon, Authority, and Criticism* (Oxford: Clarendon Press, 1983), and James A. Sanders, *Canon and Community: A Guide to Canonical Criticism* (Philadelphia: Fortress, Press 1984).

Studies focusing on the canon of the New Testament include David G. Meade, *Pseudonymity and Canon: An Investigation into the Relationship of Authorship and Authority in Jewish and Early Christian Tradition* (Grand Rapids, Mich.: Eerdmans, 1986), and Bruce M. Metzger, *The Canon of the New Testament: Its Origin, Development, and Significance* (Oxford: Clarendon Press, 1987).

INDEX OF
BIBLICAL REFERENCES

b = boxed material

NEW TESTAMENT APOCRYPHA/PSEUDEPIGRAPHA

Apostolic Fathers

GENERAL INDEX

b = boxed material